MCSA All-in-One De... Reference For Dummies®

BESTSELLING BOOK SERIES

For Dummies: Bestselling Book Series for Beginners

MCSA All-in-One Desk Reference For Dummies®

Cheat Sheet

Objective	Book Element
Configuring, Managing, Securing, and Troubleshooting Active Directory Organizational Units and Group Policy	Chapter 5
Create, manage, and troubleshoot User and Group objects in Active Directory	Chapter 5
Manage object and container permissions	Chapter 5
Diagnose Active Directory replication problems	Chapter 5
Deploy software using Group Policy	Chapter 5
Troubleshoot end-user Group Policy	Chapter 5
Implement and manage security policies by using Group Policy	Chapter 5
Configuring, Securing, and Troubleshooting Remote Access	Chapter 6
Configure and troubleshoot remote access and virtual private network (VPN) connections	Chapter 6
Troubleshoot a remote access policy	Chapter 6
Implement Terminal Services for remote access	Chapter 6
Configure and troubleshoot Network Address Translation (NAT) and Internet Connection Sharing	Chapter 6
The Network+ Exam	**Book IV**
Media and Topologies	Chapter 2
Recognize the following logical or physical network topologies given a schematic diagram or description	Chapter 2
Specify the main features of 802.2 (LLC), 802.3 (Ethernet), 802.5 (token ring), 802.11b (wireless) and FDDI networking technologies	Chapter 2
Specify the characteristics of 802.3 (Ethernet) standards	Chapter 2
Recognize media connectors and/or describe their uses	Chapter 2
Choose the appropriate media type and connectors to add a client to an existing network	Chapter 2
Identify the purpose, features, and functions of common network components	Chapter 2
Protocols and Standards	Chapter 3
Given an example, identify a MAC address	Chapter 5
Identify the seven layers of the OSI model and their functions	Chapter 5
Differentiate between network protocols in terms of routing, addressing schemes, interoperability, and naming conventions	Chapter 5
Identify the OSI layers at which network components operate	Chapter 5
Define the purpose, function, and/or use of TCP/IP protocols	Chapter 5
Identify and define the function of TCP/UDP ports	Chapter 5
Identify the purpose of network services	Chapter 5
Identify IP addresses (Ipv4, Ipv6) and their default subnet masks	Chapter 5
Identify the purpose of subnetting and default gateways	Chapter 5
Identify the differences between public versus private networks	Chapter 5
Identify the basic characteristics of WAN technologies	Chapter 4
Define the function of remote-access protocols and services	Chapter 4
Identify security protocols and describe their purpose and function	Chapter 6
Network Implementation	Chapters 5 and 6
Identify the basic capabilities of server operating systems	Chapter 6
Identify the basic capabilities of client workstations	Chapter 6
Identify the main characteristics of VLANs	Chapter 6
Identify the main characteristics of network attached storage	Chapter 6
Identify the purpose and characteristics of fault tolerance	Chapter 6
Identify the purpose and characteristics of disaster recovery	Chapter 6
Given a remote-connectivity scenario, configure the connection	Chapter 6
Identify the purpose, benefits, and characteristics of a firewall	Chapter 6
Identify the purpose, benefits, and characteristics of using a proxy	Chapter 5

For Dummies: Bestselling Book Series for Beginners

MCSA
ALL-IN-ONE DESK REFERENCE
FOR
DUMMIES®

by Ron Gilster, A+, Network+, and
Server+ certified
and Curt Simmons, MCSA, MCSE, CTT

Wiley Publishing, Inc.

MCSA All-in-One Desk Reference For Dummies®

Published by
Wiley Publishing, Inc.
909 Third Avenue
New York, NY 10022
www.wiley.com

Copyright © 2003 by Wiley Publishing, Inc., Indianapolis, Indiana

Published by Wiley Publishing, Inc., Indianapolis, Indiana

Published simultaneously in Canada

For general information on our other products and services or to obtain technical support, please contact our Customer Care Department within the U.S. at 800-762-2974, outside the U.S. at 317-572-3993, or fax 317-572-4002.

Wiley also publishes its books in a variety of electronic formats. Some content that appears in print may not be available in electronic books.

Library of Congress Control Number: 2002110246

ISBN: 0-7654-1671-X

Manufactured in the United States of America

10 9 8 7 6 5 4 3 2 1

1B/QS/RQ/QS/IN

Wiley Publishing, Inc. is a trademark of Wiley Publishing, Inc.

About the Author

Ron Gilster (Network+, Server+, A+, i-Net+, CCNA, MBA, and AAGG) has been operating, programming, and repairing computers for more than 30 years, and networking them for more than 13 years. Ron has extensive experience in training, teaching, and consulting in computer-related areas, having spent more than 15 years as a college-level instructor in A+, CCNA, MCSE, MOUS, and computer programming programs. His experience includes mainframes, minicomputers, and virtually every type of personal computer and operating system in use. In addition to a wide range of positions that have included systems programming supervisor, customer service manager, data processing manager, management information systems director, and executive positions in major corporations, Ron has served as a management consultant with both an international accounting firm and his own consulting firm.

He is the author of *A+ Certification For Dummies, Network+ Certification For Dummies, Server+ Certification For Dummies, i-Net+ Certification For Dummies, CCNA For Dummies, Cisco Networking For Dummies,* and *CCDA For Dummies,* plus several books on computer and information literacy and programming, including the upcoming *PC Repair Bench Book.*

Curt Simmons, MCSE, MCSA, CTT is a technology author and trainer based in Dallas, Texas. Curt is the author of more than twenty high-level computing books, including *MCSE Windows 2000 Server For Dummies* and *Active Directory Bible*, both published by Wiley Publishing. When he is not writing new books and learning about new software, Curt spends his time with his wife and daughters, and constantly works on his 100-year-old Victorian home. Visit Curt on the Internet at `http://curtsimmons.hypermart.net` or send him an e-mail at `curt_simmons@hotmail.com`.

Dedication

To Lynda, whose encouragement and support has been very important to me.

— Ron Gilster

Acknowledgments

Thanks to the wonderful folks at Wiley who helped get this book published, especially Melody Layne, Linda Morris, and Rebekah Mancilla. I would also like to thank Trevor Kay for the excellent technical editing job he provided.

Special thanks to Margot Maley Hutchison and the fine folks at Waterside Productions for sharing my often convoluted vision and making this book possible.

— Ron Gilster

Thanks to Linda Morris, Melody Layne, Charles Hare, as well as Margot Maley Hutchison at Waterside.

— Curt Simmons

Publisher's Acknowledgments

We're proud of this book; please send us your comments through our online registration form located at www.dummies.com/register/.

Some of the people who helped bring this book to market include the following:

Acquisitions, Editorial, and Media Development

Project Editor: Linda Morris

Acquisitions Editor: Melody Layne

Copy Editors: Rebekah Mancilla, Jerelind Charles

Technical Editors: Charles Hare, Trevor Kay

Editorial Manager: Kevin Kirschner

Media Develpment Specialists: Megan Decraene, Kit Malone

Media Development Supervisor: Richard Graves

Editorial Assistant: Amanda Foxworth

Production

Project Coordinator: Jennifer Bingham

Layout and Graphics: Beth Brooks, Joyce Haughey, LeAndra Johnson, Barry Offringa, Jacque Schneider, Jeremey Unger, Erin Zeltner

Proofreaders: Melissa D. Buddendeck, Charles Spencer

Indexer: Sharon Hilgenberg

Special Help: Teresa Artman, Barry Childs-Helton, Nicole A. Sholly

---

Publishing and Editorial for Technology Dummies

Richard Swadley, Vice President and Executive Group Publisher

Mary C. Corder, Editorial Director

Andy Cummings, Vice President and Publisher

Publishing for Consumer Dummies

Diane Graves Steele, Vice President and Publisher

Joyce Pepple, Acquisitions Director

Composition Services

Gerry Fahey, Vice President of Production Services

Debbie Stailey, Director of Composition Services

Table of Contents

Introduction

Welcome to the world of Windows 2000 and the Microsoft Certified Systems Administrator exam track! If you have bought this book, you are most likely taking the certification plunge so you can become one of "The few, the proud, the MCSAs." The MCSA certification gives you a competitive edge in the marketplace because it proves your knowledge of Windows 2000 and Microsoft networking, along with related Network+ and Server+ skills.

We don't mind telling you up-front that obtaining the MCSA is no picnic. If you want to pass the exams, you should plan on many hours of study and practice. The exams are designed to test your theoretical and hands-on knowledge of Windows 2000 Professional, Windows 2000 Server, Windows 2000 networking, and your Network+ and Server+ knowledge. This book can help you master all of these, but you will have to study and get some hands-on practice to get the skills you need for the exam. The MCSA exams can be complicated, but this book tells you what you need to know — and don't need to know — for the exam.

About This Book

This book is a complete resource for mastering the MCSA exams 70-210, 70-215, 70-218, and the CompTIA exams N10-002 (Network+) and SK0-001 (Server+). When we wrote this book, we kept our attention focused on the exam objectives — after all, the test questions are developed from the objectives. Everything in this book focuses on preparing you for the exams.

As you study this book, you need to keep in mind what is exactly on the test. The first chapter in each book explains the exam objectives to you and shows you how that exam fits into the MCSA certification track. Every book and every chapter is focused specifically on the exam objectives. With this approach, you can rest assured that you are studying information you are likely to see on the exam.

To help you pass the exams, every chapter contains the following elements to keep your studies focused:

✦ A concise listing of exam objectives covered in the chapter.

✦ To-the-point, easy-to-read text so you can digest the exam content quickly and easily.

✦ Lab exercises that focus on configuration topics you are likely to see on the exam.

✦ A Prep Test at the end of every chapter so you can make certain you master the chapter's content.

✦ Tables and bulleted lists of important information you need to memorize for the exam.

In addition to all of these chapter tools, we also provide a full-length practice exam for each book. These Practice Exams can be found as PDF files on the CD-ROM that accompanies this book. The Practice Exams are designed to test you on the exam objectives you have studied in each book. In addition to all of this, the CD-ROM contains hundreds of practice questions using the Dummies test engine. The CD-ROM also contains demonstrations and sample software products for your review as well.

How This Book Is Organized

This book is divided into books that explore each exam. This design keeps your studies focused exactly on the exam objectives. In other words, you can be certain you are not wasting your time studying information that is not on the exam. The following sections tell you what you can expect to find in each book.

Book I: Installing, Configuring, and Administering Microsoft Windows 2000 Professional: Exam 70-210

Book I explores the exam objectives for Exam 70-210, Installing, Configuring, and Administering Microsoft Windows 2000 Professional. In this book, you'll learn about Windows 2000 Professional in light of the exam objectives, and you'll explore the features and functions Windows 2000 Professional brings to the Windows network.

Book II: Installing, Configuring, and Administering Microsoft Windows 2000 Server: Exam 70-215

Windows 2000 Server is a complex server operating system, and Exam 70-215 tests your knowledge of installing, configuring, and administering

Windows 2000 Server. You'll explore the exam objectives in this book, and you'll have the opportunity to learn about the server features you are most likely to see on the Windows 2000 Server exam.

Book III: Managing a Microsoft Windows 2000 Network Environment: Exam 70-218

Exam 70-218, Managing a Microsoft Windows 2000 Network Environment, was specifically developed for the MCSA track, and this exam tests your knowledge of general networking concepts, but specifically the use of Windows 2000 Professional and Windows 2000 Server in a Microsoft network environment. The exam objectives explore the tasks and issues you are likely to run across when you manage a Windows 2000 network, and this book covers all of these issues.

Book IV: The Network+ Exam

An alternative path to your MCSA certification allows you to receive credit for passing the Network+ exam. The Network+ exam (N10-002) is the result of an industry-wide analysis of a networking technician's storehouse of skills and knowledge after 18 to 24 months of on-the-job experience. The final test, published in January 2002, reflects the culmination of more than five years of skill set and test development by the IT Skills Project task force.

This book presents the information you can expect to find on the Network+ exam. It covers the four topic areas of the exam: media and topologies, protocols and standards, network implementation, and network support.

Book V: The Server+ Exam

The Server+ exam can be used to satisfy your MCSA requirements. Passing the Server+ exam not only satisfies part of your MCSA requirements, it also certifies to the world that you are a server and networking professional who possesses the knowledge required to perform a full range of server-related technical activities. The Server+ certification was developed by a team of subject-matter experts from around the world and is a global certification that has been endorsed by such companies as 3Com, Adaptec, IBM, Intel, Hewlett Packard, Microsoft, and StorageTek.

This part of the book provides information on the subject matter included on the Server+ exam in its seven topic areas: installation, configuration, upgrading, proactive maintenance, environment, troubleshooting, and disaster recovery.

Conventions Used in This Book

This book is designed to be user-friendly. We want to you to get the necessary exam content in the easiest manner. We hope this book makes your journey through your MCSA studies much easier. To help you, watch for these features:

✦ The lab exercises are straightforward and quick. We don't say things like, "Click the Start Menu, then point to Programs, then point again to Administrative tools, and then navigate to DNS..." Instead, we use a command arrow to simply say Click Start ➪Programs ➪ Administrative Tools➪ DNS. This feature makes the labs much easier to read and follow.

✦ Another convention used is `monotype font`. When you see this font, you know you are looking at a URL you can access for more information about a particular subject.

✦ Tables and bullet lists are used to help you learn information quickly and easily. When you see information in a table or bullet list, you need to memorize it!

✦ Finally, the Practice Exams (located on the CD-ROM accompanying this book) and Prep Tests contain questions designed to mimic the kinds of questions you might see on the exam. Pay attention to them and study the questions carefully!

Icons Used in This Book

To help you with your studies, we use several icons, each of which appears in the margins next to key paragraphs. The icons help you pinpoint information that warrants close attention as you study. The following icons are used in this book.

The Tip icon points out some handy piece of information for getting the most out your studies and an important piece of information you should keep in mind for the exam.

The Remember icon helps you target information that's worth remembering for the exam.

The Warning icon points out some potential problem or pitfall you may encounter. Keep this information in mind for the exam.

When you see the Instant Answer icon, you know the text provides you with information that can help you respond correctly to a test question.

 This icon points out information that can keep you and the server safe from nasty, unexpected electrical shocks.

Best of Luck ....

Undertaking the MCSA testing requirements may seem like a daunting task. However, we believe this book is an excellent starting point. Remember as you go through the testing sequence that you really do know this stuff. A bit of luck can't hurt, so we wish you the best of luck and we would like to be the first to congratulate you on your success.

Book I

Installing, Configuring, and Administering Microsoft Windows 2000 Professional: Exam 70-210

The 5th Wave   By Rich Tennant

OF THE MANY INSTALLATION SCENARIOS, THE MOST DIFFICULT IS INSTALLING WINDOWS 2000 PROFESSIONAL ON A PENTIUM 133Mhz IN A HERD OF RESTLESS CAPE BUFFALOS

RICHTENNANT

Contents at a Glance

Chapter 1: About Exam 70-210

In This Chapter

✔ What you should already know

✔ What objectives are covered

✔ What you can expect

Exam 70-210, Installing, Configuring, and Administering Microsoft Windows 2000 Professional tests your knowledge of Windows 2000 Professional and its operations in a Microsoft network. That's a mouthful for certain. The exam has a rather broad scope in that you are expected to know a thing or two about Windows 2000 Professional as a desktop operating system and are also expected to understand how to configure and administer Windows 2000 Professional in a Microsoft network. This includes how Windows 2000 Professional operates with other clients as well as Windows 2000 Server.

With all that said, are you ready to tackle exam 70-210? That all depends on you. We wish we could give you a magic pill that would make Exam 70-210 easier to swallow, but the exam is designed to test your current knowledge of Windows 2000 Professional, as well as your background knowledge of Microsoft operating systems and networking.

What You Should Already Know

Before you begin studying this book for Exam 70-210, we assume you bring a few prerequisites to the certification table. If you are deficient in any of these following areas, you should stop studying for this exam and learn some background information from other books devoted to these topics:

✦ **Windows 2000 Professional:** You should already be working with Windows 2000 Professional in a hands-on manner. In other words, before you begin studying for this exam, do you consider yourself a "power user" of Windows 2000 Professional? If not, you should spend some time working with the operating system first and perhaps studying a higher-end user book about the operating system.

✦ **Networking:** This book assumes that you have some networking experience and are currently working with Windows 2000 Professional in a networking environment. If you have no networking experience, you need to study up on networking first and try to get some hands-on experience. You may find this book difficult to understand without any prior networking knowledge.

✦ **Windows 2000 Server:** Believe it or not, the Windows 2000 Professional exam may ask you questions that involve Windows 2000 Server, because Windows 2000 Server is used to manage Windows 2000 Professional. The exam objectives may not even denote server usage, but you need to have good hands-on practice with Windows 2000 Server for this exam as well. Again, you may need to study a general Windows 2000 Server book.

✦ **Experience:** Like all Microsoft exams, you should have 1-3 years of experience working with Windows 2000 Professional in a Microsoft network. This book can help you review the exam objectives, but it cannot replace hands-on practice and experience.

What Exam Objectives Are Covered

The Windows 2000 Professional exam objectives are readily available on the Microsoft Web site and are also included here for your convenience. This book strictly adheres to the exam objectives and covers the test material you are most likely to see concerning the exam objectives. On the exam, you can expect to see the following issues:

✦ **Installing Windows 2000 Professional**

✦ Perform an attended installation of Windows 2000 Professional.

✦ Perform an unattended installation of Windows 2000 Professional.

- Install Windows 2000 Professional by using Windows 2000 Server Remote Installation Services (RIS).

- Install Windows 2000 Professional by using the System Preparation Tool.

- Create unattended answer files by using Setup Manager to automate the installation of Windows 2000 Professional.

✦ Upgrade from a previous version of Windows to Windows 2000 Professional.

- Apply update packs to installed software applications.

- Prepare a computer to meet upgrade requirements.

✦ Deploy service packs.

✦ Troubleshoot failed installations.

✦ **Implementing and Conducting Administration of Resources**

✦ Monitor, manage, and troubleshoot access to files and folders.

  • Configure, manage, and troubleshoot file compression.

  • Control access to files and folders by using permissions.

  • Optimize access to files and folders.

✦ Manage and troubleshoot access to shared folders.

  • Create and remove shared folders.

  • Control access to shared folders by using permissions.

  • Manage and troubleshoot Web server resources.

✦ Connect to local and network print devices.

  • Manage printers and print jobs.

  • Control access to printers by using permissions.

  • Connect to an Internet printer.

  • Connect to a local print device.

✦ Configure and manage file systems.

  • Convert from one file system to another file system.

  • Configure file systems by using NTFS, FAT32, or FAT.

✦ **Implementing, Managing, and Troubleshooting Hardware Devices and Drivers**

✦ Implement, manage, and troubleshoot disk devices.

  • Install, configure, and manage DVD and CD-ROM devices.

  • Monitor and configure disks.

  • Monitor, configure, and troubleshoot volumes.

  • Monitor and configure removable media, such as tape devices.

✦ Implement, manage, and troubleshoot display devices.

  • Configure multiple-display support.

  • Install, configure, and troubleshoot a video adapter.

✦ Implement, manage, and troubleshoot mobile computer hardware.

  • Configure Advanced Power Management (APM).

  • Configure and manage card services.

✦ Implement, manage, and troubleshoot input and output (I/O) devices.

- Monitor, configure, and troubleshoot I/O devices, such as printers, scanners, multimedia devices, mouse, keyboard, and Smart Card reader.

- Monitor, configure, and troubleshoot multimedia hardware, such as cameras.

- Install, configure, and manage modems.

- Install, configure, and manage Infrared Data Association (IrDA) devices.

- Install, configure, and manage wireless devices.

- Install, configure, and manage USB devices.

✦ Update drivers.

✦ Monitor and configure multiple processing units.

✦ Install, configure, and troubleshoot network adapters.

✦ **Monitoring and Optimizing System Performance and Reliability**

✦ Manage and troubleshoot driver signing.

✦ Configure, manage, and troubleshoot Task Scheduler.

✦ Manage and troubleshoot the use and synchronization of offline files.

✦ Optimize and troubleshoot performance of the Windows 2000 Professional desktop.

- Optimize and troubleshoot memory performance.

- Optimize and troubleshoot processor utilization.

- Optimize and troubleshoot disk performance.

- Optimize and troubleshoot network performance.

- Optimize and troubleshoot application performance.

✦ Manage hardware profiles.

✦ Recover system state data and user data.

- Recover system state data and user data by using Windows Backup.

- Troubleshoot system restoration by using safe mode.

- Recover system state data and user data by using the Recovery Console.

✦ **Configuring and Troubleshooting the Desktop Environment**

✦ Configure and manage user profiles.

✦ Configure support for multiple languages or multiple locations.

   • Enable multiple-language support.

   • Configure multiple-language support for users.

   • Configure local settings.

   • Configure Windows 2000 Professional for multiple locations.

✦ Manage applications by using Windows Installer packages.

✦ Configure and troubleshoot desktop settings.

✦ Configure and troubleshoot fax support.

✦ Configure and troubleshoot accessibility services.

✦ **Implementing, Managing, and Troubleshooting Network Protocols and Services**

✦ Configure and troubleshoot the TCP/IP protocol.

✦ Connect to computers by using dial-up networking.

   • Connect to computers by using a virtual private network (VPN) connection.

   • Create a dial-up connection to connect to a remote access server.

   • Connect to the Internet by using dial-up networking.

   • Configure and troubleshoot Internet Connection Sharing.

✦ Connect to shared resources on a Microsoft network.

✦ **Implementing, Monitoring, and Troubleshooting Security**

✦ Encrypt data on a hard disk by using Encrypting File System (EFS).

✦ Implement, configure, manage, and troubleshoot local security policy.

✦ Implement, configure, manage, and troubleshoot local user accounts.

   • Implement, configure, manage, and troubleshoot auditing.

   • Implement, configure, manage, and troubleshoot account settings.

   • Implement, configure, manage, and troubleshoot account policy.

   • Create and manage local users and groups.

   • Implement, configure, manage, and troubleshoot user rights.

✦ **Implementing, Configuring, Managing, and Troubleshooting Local User Authentication**

   • Configure and troubleshoot local user accounts.

   • Configure and troubleshoot domain user accounts.

✦ Implement, configure, manage, and troubleshoot a security configuration.

What You Can Expect

Now that you reviewed the exam objectives, what can you expect when you sit in front of the computer on exam day? As you study this book and prepare for the exam, keep the following points in mind:

✦ You can expect to see all of the exam objectives covered, however, some will be stressed more than others. In fact, some objectives may appear more indirectly in questions supporting other objectives.

✦ You can expect the exam questions to be complicated. Microsoft exams love to ask questions in a convoluted way and make them more difficult to read than necessary. The Windows 2000 Professional exam is no exception.

✦ You can expect the Windows 2000 Professional exam questions to intersect with each other, giving you combination questions, and you may even see issues that seem to come from the Windows 2000 Server exam. Because Microsoft expects your knowledge to be global and not product-specific, expect some questions that seem to cross over with the Windows 2000 Server exam.

✦ You'll always see the Windows 2000 Professional exam questions presented in light of networking. The exam does not test your knowledge of operating system basics and usage, but rather administration from a networking point of view.

The only way to be successful on the Windows 2000 Professional exam is to combine your existing knowledge and experience with the principles explored in this book! Then, practice, practice, practice before taking the exam!

Chapter 2: Installing Windows 2000 Professional

Exam Objectives

✔ Performing an attended installation of Windows 2000 Professional

✔ Performing an unattended installation of Windows 2000 Professional

✔ Upgrading from a previous version of Windows to Windows 2000 Professional

✔ Deploying service packs

✔ Troubleshooting failed installations

The Windows 2000 Professional exam expects you to know a thing or two about installing Windows 2000 Professional, and rightly so. After all, as an IT professional, operating system installations will be a common task, and you should know how to solve problems that come your way and plan installations that can be carried out in a timely manner.

In this chapter, you'll read about attended and unattended installations of Windows 2000 Professional. Because our main goal here is to prepare for the Windows 2000 Professional exam, we limit our discussion to the exam issues that you are most likely to run across. Let us also mention that your hands-on practice with installation is vitally important for the exam, so study this chapter, roll up your sleeves, and get to work! In this chapter, you find out about

✦ Installing from a CD or the network

✦ Installing using automated methods

✦ Upgrading to Windows 2000

✦ Solving problems

Taking a Look at the Hardware Requirements for Windows 2000

Windows 2000 is a powerful operating system that requires powerful computer hardware. Check your computer's documentation to see if your computer meets the minimum requirements listed here:

✦ Processor: 133 MHz Pentium or equivalent.

✦ RAM: At least 64MB of Random Access Memory.

✦ Hard drive: 2GB with at least 650MB free.

✦ Standard monitor, keyboard, mouse, and CD-ROM drive.

The two biggies are your processor and RAM. Your system processor handles all Windows 2000 and application processes, and the RAM affects how fast applications can run. 133 MHz processor and 64MB of RAM are barebones minimums, so you really need more if you want a system that runs well. Windows 2000 Professional supports up to two processors per computer.

You may need drivers for other devices, such as modems. If you are using any older hardware, such as older CD-ROMs, modems, and so forth, you can also refer to the Hardware Compatibility List (HCL). You can find the HCL in the Support folder on your installation CD-ROM, or you can access it on the Internet at www.microsoft.com/hcl. The HCL is a long list of every device that is compatible with Windows 2000. Check the list to see if your device is on it. If your hardware isn't listed, this does not mean it will not work with Windows 2000, but it is a red flag. You can also check out the hardware man-ufacturer's Web site to see if it has information about compatibility with Windows 2000.

A final note about hardware: If you are using a compressed hard drive, such as one compressed with DriveSpace or DoubleSpace, you need to uncom-press it before beginning Windows 2000 installation.

Performing an Attended Installation of Windows 2000 Professional

An *attended installation* simply means that the installation is not automated: you "attend" to it. With Windows 2000 Professional, there are two methods for performing an attended installation:

✦ From an installation CD-ROM

✦ From a network share

The next few sections describe these two methods.

Installing Windows 2000 Professional from CD-ROM

To install Windows 2000 Professional from CD-ROM, you simply insert the CD-ROM into the CD-ROM drive and begin the installation by following the steps in Lab 2-2. If the computer does not support booting from a CD-ROM drive, you'll need to create setup boot disks.

The easiest way to make the floppy disks is to take your trusty Windows 2000 Professional CD-ROM to a computer that has an operating system, and then follow the steps in Lab 2-1.

Lab 2-1   Creating Windows 2000 Setup Boot Disks

1. **Insert the CD-ROM into the CD-ROM drive. A dialog box then appears, informing you that an older operating system is on the computer and asks you if you want to upgrade. Click No.**

   If you are using a computer that already has Windows 2000 installed, you will not see this message. After you click No, you see the Windows 2000 Professional CD screen.

2. **Click Browse This CD.**

   The CD opens, and you see the various folders that hold your installation files.

3. **Double-click the BOOTDISK folder.**

4. **In the Boot Disk folder, double-click the icon for MAKEBT32.**

   An MS-DOS window appears. The text on your screen indicates that you need four high-density floppy disks to create the boot disks. The computer asks you to specify the drive to copy the image to.

5. **Enter the drive letter of your floppy drive, which is A, and then press the Enter key.**

   Now you are ready to begin creating the disks.

6. **Label a floppy disk and then insert it into the floppy drive.**

   Just write "boot disk" on the first one. The first disk will be the Windows 2000 Boot Disk.

7. **Press any key on the keyboard to start the file copy.**

   The system begins creating the disks. This process takes a few minutes.

8. **When the computer prompts you, remove the disk and insert another; you repeat this three times. Remember to label the disks as you go (1, 2, 3).**

After you have created your four installation disks, follow these steps to boot your computer from these disks:

1. **Make sure the computer in which you are installing Windows 2000 is turned off.**

2. **Insert the Windows 2000 Boot Disk (the first disk you created) into the floppy disk drive, and then turn on your computer. When the computer begins to boot, insert your Windows 2000 Professional CD into your CD-ROM drive.**

While the computer is reading the boot disk, you see a blue screen that says "Windows 2000 Setup."

3. **When the computer tells you to insert Disk # 2, press Enter. You repeat this step for each of the four installation disks.**

As soon as the computer has all the data from the floppy disks, it can then begin to set up your computer and access your CD-ROM. Data from the floppy disks enables the Setup program to interact with your computer's components (such as your CD-ROM drive).

After your computer has booted from the installation disks, you're ready to begin installation. To install from CD-ROM, just boot from the CD-ROM drive. After files are copied, the GUI interface appears. Lab 2-2 outlines the setup procedure.

Lab 2-2   Performing an Attended Installation of Windows 2000 Professional

1. **On the Welcome screen, read the End User License Agreement (EULA), click the I Accept This Agreement radio button, and then click Next to continue.**

   The EULA tells you the copyright license you have with your new software. You must accept the agreement for installation to continue. If you do not accept the agreement, installation stops.

   Next, you see a Product Key window.

2. **Find your CD-ROM case and locate the 25-character key. Type the key into the boxes exactly as it appears on the CD-ROM case and then click the Next button.**

   The key is usually on the back of the case on a yellow sticker.

   After you click Next, the Windows Compatibility window appears. This window asks if you want to connect to the Microsoft Web site to read information about compatibility with your computer's hardware.

3. **If you want to connect to the Microsoft Web site, click the Click Here link. If you don't want to go to the site, simply click Next.**

   If you click the Click Here link, your Web browser opens and launches an Internet connection. Click Next to continue the installation.

After you click Next, Setup examines your computer system and provides you with an Upgrade Packs window. Upgrade Packs are provided by software manufacturers so that certain software applications will work under Windows 2000.

4. **Click the Next button.**

5. **Now, you need to make a choice about your file system. Select the option to upgrade your computer to NTFS and then click Next.**

   Windows 2000 recommends that you use the NTFS file system. NTFS provides you with advanced security features, and it conserves room on your hard disk. The only exception is if you want to use another operating system on your computer (called "dual-booting"). This option does not damage any of your programs or files. If you are not sure about using NTFS, simply click No. You can always convert to NTFS later.

   At this time, Setup has gathered all the information it needs from you. Setup examines your computer and then creates an upgrade report for you to review. It may take several minutes for Setup to examine your computer and create the report.

   The report tells you if there are hardware devices, such as modems, or any software, such as programs, that may not work with Windows 2000. If the report tells you that some of your hardware or software may be incompatible, you need to either print the report or save it in case you need it later.

6. **Print or save the upgrade report at this time, if necessary, and then click the Next button.**

   If you have a printer attached to your computer that was configured to work under the old operating system, you can print the report by clicking the Print button.

   If you want to save the file, click the Save As button. This action opens another window that allows you to choose the location on your computer to save it. By default, the system saves the file as a text (.txt) file in My Computer. After installation is complete, you can open the file, reread it, and even print it later if you want.

7. **Setup is now ready to install Windows 2000 on your computer. Click Next to start the installation.**

   The upgrade normally takes between 45 to 90 minutes and your computer will reboot four times. Setup will take care of the reboots on its own. This is a good time to raid the refrigerator or watch TV.

The following steps tell you what happens as your computer installs Windows 2000 Professional:

1. Setup copies the files it needs to install Windows 2000 from the CD to your computer, and then your computer automatically reboots.

2. Setup continues by inspecting your computer and loading files it needs to install Windows 2000. Then, Setup inspects your hard disk and converts it to NTFS, if you chose this option. Other actions include creating a list of files needed and copying those files to installation folders. Again, you don't have to do anything while all of this is going on.

3. Your computer reboots and you see a Windows 2000 Professional background. Installation continues, and you see a Please Wait message for some time.

4. Windows 2000 begins the device installation part of Setup. Windows 2000 detects and attempts to install all of the devices attached to your computer, such as your keyboard, mouse, modem, scanner, and so on. This part of Setup takes a while, but you don't have to do anything here. Your computer screen may flicker several times during this process; this is normal, so don't be alarmed.

5. If your computer has a network adapter card, which is a piece of hardware that allows your computer to connect to a network, Windows 2000 configures your card so that you can connect to the network. After this, Setup installs various Windows 2000 components, saves the settings, and then removes any temporary files Setup used during the installation. After these chores are finished, Windows reboots.

6. Now, after the long wait, Windows 2000 needs some input from you. A Password Creation window appears. This window tells you the accounts that were created. Typically, you see your name (taken from the old operating system) and an administrator account. Two dialog boxes appear where you can create a new password and confirm the new password. You need this to log on to the system. Enter your desired password, and then click Next.

7. After Setup completes and reboots, you can enter your username and password and log on to the system. Windows 2000 completes the installation cycle and you are now ready to begin using Windows 2000.

Installing Windows 2000 Professional over a network

Aside from using the installation CD-ROM to install Windows 2000 Professional, you can also install Windows 2000 Professional by connecting to a network share. In this case, a network administrator copies all of the data from the Windows 2000 Professional CD-ROM and places that data in a shared folder. Users are instructed about the share path and name. After you connect to share, all you have to do is launch the setup.exe icon. From that point, installation begins and you see the same series of steps presented in the preceding section.

Performing an Unattended Installation of Windows 2000 Professional

By using an unattended installation, you can roll out Windows 2000 to multiple computers without having to physically sit at those computers and answer Setup questions. To prepare for an unattended installation, you have to complete two basic tasks:

✦ Create a distribution folder

✦ Review Setup switches

A *distribution folder* is a network share that holds the Setup files. With this network share, you can perform unattended installations to the computers on your network.

You can create the network share on any computer on your network. Simply create a folder called i386 and then copy the contents of the Windows 2000 installation CD-ROM to the shared folder. Depending on your needs, you may also choose to create a OEM subfolder within the i386 folder. You can use the OEM subfolder to store any additional subfolders needed to satisfy the Microsoft OEM requirements and your own installation needs.

In addition to creating the distribution folder that holds the Setup files, you should review the Setup switches that are available for both WINNT.EXE and WINNT32.EXE.

Here's the syntax for WINNT.EXE:

```
WINNT [/s[:sourcepath]] [/t[:tempdrive]
 [/u[:answer file]] [/udf:id[,UDF_file]]
 [/r:folder] [/r[x]:folder] [/e:command] [/a]
```

The brackets identify optional switches, and the italics highlight information that you need to supply — for example, pathnames and filenames. You don't type the brackets when you enter the WINNT command.

Table 2-1 explains the WINNT Setup switches. You need to memorize this information for the exam.

Table 2-1	WINNT.EXE Setup Parameters
Parameter	*What It Does*
/s[:*sourcepath*]	Specifies the source location of the Windows 2000 files. The location must be a full path of the form x:[*path*] or *servershare*[*path*].
/t[:*tempdrive*]	Directs Setup to place temporary files on the specified drive and to install Windows 2000 on that drive. If you do not specify a location, Setup attempts to locate a drive for you.
/u[:answer file]	Performs an unattended Setup by using an answer file (requires /s). The answer file provides answers to some or all of the prompts that the end user normally responds to during Setup.
/udf:id[,UDF_file]	Indicates an identifier (id) that Setup uses to specify how a Uniqueness Database File (UDF) modifies an answer file (see /u).The /udf parameter overrides values in the answer file, and the identifier determines which values in the UDF file are used. If no UDF_file is specified, Setup prompts you to insert a disk that contains the $Unique$.udb file.
/r[:*folder*]	Specifies an optional folder to be installed. The folder remains after Setup finishes.
/rx[:*folder*]	Specifies an optional folder to be copied. The folder is deleted after Setup finishes.
/e	Specifies a command to be executed at the end of GUI-mode Setup.
/a	Enables accessibility options.

You also need to know the WINNT32 Setup switches for the exam. Here's the syntax for WINNT32.EXE:

```
WINNT32 [/S:sourcepath] [/tempdrive: drive_letter] [/unattend
    [num] [:answer_file]] [/copydir:folder_name] [/copysource:
    folder_name] [/cmd: command_line] [/debug [level] [: file-
    name]] [/udf: id [, UDF_file]] [/syspart: drive_letter]
```

Table 2-2 explains the WINNT32 Setup switches.

Table 2-2	WINNT32.EXE Setup Parameters
Parameter	*What It Does*
/S: *sourcepath*	Specifies the location of the Windows 2000 files.
/tempdrive: *drive_letter*	Tells Setup to place temporary files on a specified drive and to install Windows 2000 on that drive.
/unattend[*num*][:*answer_file*]	Installs Windows 2000 in unattended mode by using the answer file.
/copydir: *folder_name*	Creates an additional folder within the folder that contains the Windows 2000 files.

Parameter	What It Does
/copysource: *folder_name*	Creates a temporary folder in the folder that contains the Windows 2000 files.
/cmd: *command_line*	Tells Setup to carry out a specific command before setup is complete.
/debug*[level][:filename]*	Creates a debug log at the level specified.
/udf:*id[,UDF_file]*	Indicates an identifier (id) that Setup uses to specify how a Uniqueness Database File (UDF) modifies an answer file.
/syspart: *drive_letter*	Enables you to copy Setup startup files to a hard drive, mark the drive as active, and then install the drive in another computer. You must use the /tempdrive parameter with /syspart.
/checkupgradeonly	Checks your computer for upgrade compatibility with Windows 2000. For Windows 95 or Windows 98 upgrades, Setup creates a report named Upgrade.txt in the Windows installation folder. For Windows NT 3.51 or 4.0 upgrades, it saves the report to the Winnt32.log in the installation folder.
/cmdcons	Adds to the operating system selection screen a Recovery Console option for repairing a failed installation. It is only used post-Setup.
/m:*folder_name*	Specifies that Setup copies replacement files from an alternate location. Instructs Setup to look in the alternate location first and if files are present, use them instead of the files from the default location.
/makelocalsource	Instructs Setup to copy all installation source files to your local hard disk. Use /makelocalsource when installing from a CD to provide installation files when the CD is not available later in the installation.
/noreboot	Instructs Setup to not restart the computer after the file copy phase of winnt32 is completed so that you can execute another command.

Creating an Answer File

During an attended installation, you interact with the Setup program by manually entering answers to the questions that Setup asks about your installation. In this way, you tailor the installation to meet your needs. For an unattended installation, however, you supply an *answer file* that Setup uses to get the answers to its questions.

To prepare for an unattended installation, you first create a distribution folder and review the command-line syntax for WINNT.EXE and WINNT32.EXE. (See the preceding section in this chapter.) Then, you create an answer file. The default name for the answer file is Unattended.txt, but you can use any desired name, as long as you point to the correct name when you enter the command to start the setup process. This feature enables you to create multiple answer files for different Windows 2000 installations.

You can create an answer file in either of two ways: manually or by using Setup Manager, which you find on the Windows 2000 CD-ROM. Because using Setup Manager is the preferred method (and the one you need to know for the exam), this section focuses only on Setup Manager.

You use Setup Manager to start the Windows 2000 installation and create an answer file for an unattended installation. Launch Setupmgr.exe on the installation CD-ROM or from the Windows 2000 Resource Kit.

Setup Manager presents you with a wizard that helps you create an answer file or edit an existing one. Lab 2-3 walks you through the steps for using Setup Manager. You need to know the options presented for the exam, so use this lab to practice creating answer files on your server.

Lab 2-3   Creating an Answer File

1. **Launch Setup Manager from the Windows 2000 CD-ROM or from the Resource Kit.**

2. **On the Welcome screen, click Next.**

3. **Click the Create a New Answer File radio button and then click Next.**

   The Product to Install dialog box appears.

4. **Select Windows 2000 Professional and click Next.**

   The User Interaction Level dialog box appears.

5. **Select the level of user interaction desired, as shown in Figure 2-1. For a complete unattended setup, select Fully Automated. Click Next.**

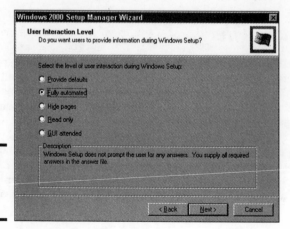

Figure 2-1:
Choose an
interaction
level.

6. **Accept the license agreement by clicking the check box and clicking Next.**

7. **Type your name and organization and click Next.**

8. **Enter the CD Key for the computers that you want to set up and then click Next.**

   You need a separate license for each copy of Windows that you install.

9. **Select either Per Server or Per Seat for the licensing mode and then click Next.**

   Per Server licensing requires a separate CAL for each concurrent connection to the server and per seat licensing requires a separate CAL for each client computer that accesses a Windows 2000 Server.

10. **Enter the desired names of the destination computer(s) and click Next.**

    You can also choose to automatically generate computer names based on your organization's name by selecting the check box at the bottom of the dialog box.

11. **Enter and confirm the administrator password and then click Next.**

    You can also specify for the system to automatically log on with the administrator password when the system first boots.

    The Display Settings dialog box appears.

12. **Use the drop-down lists to select colors, screen area, and refresh frequency or click Custom to select additional display setting options. Click Next.**

    The Network Settings dialog box opens.

13. **Select one of the following options and then click Next:**

    Typical Settings: This option installs TCP/IP, enables DHCP, and installs Client for Microsoft Networks.

    Custom: With this option, you select the desired networking components to install.

    The Join a Domain dialog box appears.

14. **Enter either the domain or workgroup the server should join. To join a domain, enter the name of the domain and provide a user account that has permission to join a computer to a domain (such as an administrator's username and password). Click Next.**

15. **Select the appropriate time zone and click Next.**

16. **If necessary, configure additional settings. Click Next.**

    Additional settings include such information as telephony and regional settings.

    The Distribution Folder dialog box appears.

17. **Specify whether Setup should create or modify a distribution folder if the unattended installation will be performed from a CD-ROM. Then click Next.**

18. **Enter a name and path for your answer file and click Next.**

    The default name is Unattended.txt.

19. **Click Finish.**

After you create the answer file, you can view it and even manually edit it by using Notepad. After you create the answer file, you can run Setup so that it uses the answer file. Review the list of parameters to determine how you would like to run Setup. Typically, you provide the Winnt parameters that point to the location of the setup files and the answer file. The following example shows how to run Setup from a CD-ROM and point to a desired answer file:

```
Winnt /S:drive_letter\I386 /U:drive_letter\unattended.txt
```

Using Other Setup Methods

In addition to attended and unattended installation of Windows 2000 Server, the exam also expects you to understand two other major Setup options. The following sections explore what you need to know about these additional setup methods.

Using Sysprep

You can use the Sysprep utility to duplicate a disk and install the image on another computer. For example, you can install a Windows 2000 Server, configure it as desired, and install additional software. Then, you use Sysprep to create an image of the server's hard disk that you can copy to another server. You use the Sysprep utility along with a Sysprep.inf file that serves as the answer file for cloning. You find Sysprep on the Deployment.cab file on your installation CD-ROM.

You don't need to know a lot about Sysprep for the exam, but you may run across a question where you want to use Sysprep to install images on a computer without using a Security Identifier (SID). You can perform this action by using the *nosidgen* switch with Sysprep.

Using Syspart

Syspart is like Sysprep, but you use it when the master computer on which you create the image has different hardware from the computer to which you are copying the image. Essentially, this method greatly speeds up installation by removing the file-copy portion of Setup (because it is already contained on the image). Like Sysprep, Syspart is available on the Deployment.cab file on your installation CD-ROM.

Upgrading from a Previous Version of Windows to Windows 2000 Professional

You can upgrade from a previous version of Windows to Windows 2000 Professional. Before upgrading, however, it is always important to take a close look at the current computer. Make sure the computer has enough RAM and processing power to handle Windows 2000 Professional (see "Taking a Look at the Hardware Requirements for Windows 2000" section, earlier in this chapter). Also, make sure that you have updated drivers for hardware on hand, and realize that some applications or games installed may not work well with Windows 2000.

Keep in mind you have two choices when installing an operating system: either as an upgrade to an older system or as a new operating system on a computer that does not already have one. If you want to upgrade to Windows 2000, you can upgrade directly to Windows 2000 from Windows 98 or 95, Windows Me, Windows NT 4.0 Workstation, or 3.51 Workstation. You cannot directly upgrade from any other version. For example, let's say you have a Windows 3.1 operating system. In order to upgrade to Windows 2000 Professional, you must first upgrade at least to Windows 95. Of course, you can install a clean copy of the operating system, but you will lose all data and settings from your 3.1 version, and you better check out the hardware, too. In a system that's old, odds are pretty good your hardware will not be able to handle Windows 2000. You cannot upgrade to Windows 2000 Professional from any server product, such as Windows NT 4.0 Server.

In order to run an upgrade, simply insert the Windows 2000 Professional installation CD into the CD-ROM drive. A window appears, asking if you want to upgrade to the newer version of Windows, as shown in Figure 2-2. After that, the setup routine is essentially same as a clean install, but your files and settings are preserved.

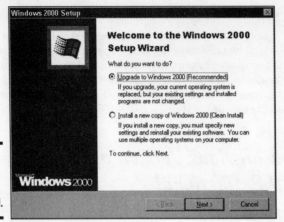

Figure 2-2:
Choose to
upgrade or
clean install.

Deploying Service Packs

From time to time, Microsoft releases service packs for operating systems. Service packs contain updates and bug fixes, and other items, such as security patches. You can download the service pack from www.Microsoft.com and install the download, or you can purchase the service pack on CD and install the service pack that way.

For the exam, the only detail you really need to know about service packs is integrating them with distribution images. Let's say you are installing 1,000 Windows 2000 Professional computers. Rather than running the installation, and then running the service pack installation, you can do them both at the same time through a process called *slipstreaming*.

To deploy the service pack with a distribution image, run Update.exe with the /slip switch. This will overwrite the necessary files in the distribution image so that the service pack and the distribution image are deployed together.

Troubleshooting Failed Installations

For the most part, Windows 2000 Professional is easy to install and trouble-free. If you have checked the computer hardware or are performing an upgrade over a supported operating system, you are not likely to experience many problems.

However, like all things in life, problems can occur. The following bullet list points out some common problems you are most likely to see on the exam:

✦ **Installation stops:** If the installation stops, a hardware conflict has most likely occurred. Wait for 10-15 minutes. If installation does not continue, restart the computer. Installation should pick up where it has left off. If installation will not continue, you need to stop and compare the hardware installed on the computer with the supported Windows 2000 hardware.

✦ **A domain controller cannot be located:** If you receive an error message that Windows 2000 Professional cannot find a domain controller, make sure you have entered the correct domain name and that a DNS Server is available on the network. If you still have problems, simply choose to join a workgroup so that installation can complete. You can then join the domain at a later time.

✦ **A hardware problem occurs:** A common cause of installation problems is hardware. If a hardware problem occurs, try to continue with setup and ignore the problem. You may have to configure some hardware after installation is complete, but at least you can finish the setup routine.

If you do experience problems during setup, some setup logs are created that you can review. The logs are found in the directory to which Windows 2000 is being installed. The following logs are created and available for review:

✦ **Setupact.log:** Contains details about the files copied during setup.

✦ **Setuperr.log:** Contains details about any errors that occurred during setup.

✦ **Setupapi.log:** Contains details about the device drivers copied during setup.

✦ **Setuplog.text:** Also contains details about device drivers copied during setup.

Prep Test

1 **What is the minimum amount of RAM required to install Windows 2000 Professional?**

A ○ 32MB

B ○ 64MB

C ○ 128MB

D ○ 256MB

2 **Before installing Windows 2000 Professional, what should be checked for hardware compatibility information?**

A ○ HCL

B ○ LHC

C ○ Run the Hardware wizard

D ○ View the hardware test log

3 **You want to use WINNT32 to install Windows 2000 Professional, but you want Setup to copy all files to your local hard disk. What Setup switch allows this option?**

A ○ /cmdcons

B ○ /nosidgen

C ○ /makelocalsource

D ○ /copylocalfiles

4 **What is the default answer filename used in Windows 2000 Professional?**

A ○ Answer.txt

B ○ Unattended.txt

C ○ Provide.txt

D ○ Submit.txt

5 **What two ways can you create an answer file? (Choose all that apply.)**

A ❑ Manually

B ❑ Setupansw.exe

C ❑ Setuprsrs.exe

D ❑ Setupmgr.exe

6 You need to install Windows 2000 Professional on a number of computers by using Sysprep. You do not want to use a Security Identifier. What switch can you use?

A ○ /noid

B ○ /nosidgen

C ○ /nosid

D ○ /nosidID

7 Which image-creation method should you use when computers have different hardware?

A ○ Sysprep

B ○ Syspart

C ○ Winnt

D ○ None of the above

8 Which operating system cannot be directly upgraded to Windows 2000 Professional?

A ○ Windows 3.1

B ○ Windows 95

C ○ Windows Me

D ○ Windows NT 4.0 Workstation

9. You need to combine a service pack with a distribution folder in order to install 400 Windows 2000 computers. What switch do you need to use with Update.exe?

A ○ /run

B ○ /combine

C ○ /slip

D ○ /flat

10 You are installing Windows 2000 Professional and you want to view a log file of setup errors. What log file should you view?

A ○ Setupact.log

B ○ Setuperr.log

C ○ Setupapi.log

D ○ Setuplog.txt

Installing Windows 2000 Professional

Answers

1 **B.** Windows 2000 Professional requires 64MB of RAM. *Review "Installing Windows 2000 Professional from CD-ROM."*

2 **A.** Check the HCL for hardware compatibility. *Read "Taking a Look at Hardware Requirements for Windows 2000."*

3 **C.** Use the /makelocalsource WINNT32 switch to copy the installation files to the local drive. *Review "Performing an unattended installation of Windows 2000 Professional."*

4 **B.** Unattended.txt is the default answer file name, but you change it as desired for use with Winnt and Winnt32. *See "Creating an Answer File."*

5 **A and D.** You can manually create answer files using a text editor, and you can use the Setupmgr.exe to create answer files. *Study "Creating an Answer File."*

6 **B.** Use the /nosidgen switch to stop Sysprep from assigning a SID. *Study "Using Sysprep."*

7 **B.** Syspart is used if you find different hardware on the client computers. *Study "Using Syspart."*

8 **A.** You cannot directly upgrade Windows 3.1 to Windows 2000. *Study "Upgrading from a Previous Version of Windows to Windows 2000 Professional."*

9 **C.** The /slip switch is used to deploy a service pack with a distribution folder or image of Windows 2000. *See "Deploying Service Packs."*

10 **B.** View the Setupact.log file to see a listing of errors that occurred during setup. *Study "Troubleshooting Failed Installations."*

Chapter 3: Implementing and Conducting Administration of Resources

Exam Objectives

✔ Monitoring, managing, and troubleshooting access to files and folders

✔ Managing and troubleshooting access to shared folders

✔ Connecting to local and network print devices

✔ Configuring and managing File Systems

The primary reason for networking is the sharing of information and resources. On any network — whether it's a Windows 2000 domain or a simple home network — sharing information and resources is often the driving factor behind networking. Windows 2000 Professional gives you an operating system that's optimized for network functionality, and the management and administration of resources is certainly a big part of that networking picture.

In this chapter, you'll read about the management and administration of resources from an exam point of view. We assume that you have worked or are currently working in a Windows domain environment in which Windows 2000 Professional is used to share resources on the network. As you can imagine, the topics explored in this chapter can be quite lengthy, but we limit our discussion to the issues that you are most likely to see on the exam. In this chapter, you'll find out about

✦ Managing shared folders and access to shared folders

✦ Connecting to local and network print devices

✦ Managing file systems

Monitoring, Managing, and Troubleshooting Access to Files and Folders

File and folder access issues are one of those exam objectives that Microsoft loves to throw at you. After all, the topic is broad and can cover many different kinds of issues. In other words, this one is designed to test your hands-on knowledge of Windows 2000 Professional. As such, we assume that you are working with Windows 2000 Professional and that you have some hands-on experience from which you can draw. The following sections explore the issues concerning file and folder management that you are most likely to see on the exam.

File compression

Compression enables you to reduce the amount of space that files are taking up on your computer's hard drive. Using NTFS compression supported in Windows 2000 Professional, you can easily save space while using compressed files seamlessly. That's good news because Windows 2000 Professional handles all of the compression and decompression tasks — you simply use the files as you like.

NTFS compression is the only compression scheme that will work on Windows 2000 Professional computers. In fact, you can't even use DriveSpace, which is a compression program developed for Windows 95. NTFS compression, though, is all you really need — it is easy to use and it compresses files by about 50 percent.

To enable file compression on a particular file, follow the steps in Lab 3-1.

Compression is only available on NTFS drives.

Lab 3-1	Compressing a File

1. **Right-click the desired file and click Properties.**

2. **In the Properties dialog box, select the General tab and click the Advanced button at the bottom of the tab. If no Advanced button is present, the drive needs to be converted to NTFS.**

3. **On the Advanced Attributes dialog box that appears, click the Compress contents to save disk space check box and click OK, as shown in Figure 3-1.**

   The file is now compressed. You can uncompress the file at any time by simply clearing this check box.

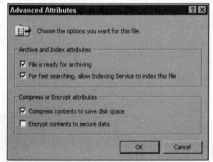

Figure 3-1:
You can
compress a
file from the
Advanced
Attributes
tab.

Windows 2000 compression and encryption can't be used together. You can encrypt a file or folder or compress a file or folder, but not both at the same time.

Aside from compressing individual files and folders using the Advanced Attributes dialog box, you can also compress an entire drive. This feature enables you to simply compress all items on the drive at one time in order to save space, rather than compressing individual files and folders. To compress an entire drive, open My Computer and right-click the drive that you want to compress. Click Properties. On the General tab, shown in Figure 3-2, click the Compress Drive to Save Disk Space check box and click OK.

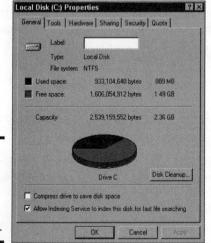

Figure 3-2:
You can
compress
an entire
drive on the
General tab.

Aside from these two methods for compressing files, folders, and drives, you can also use a command line tool called compact.exe. Using compact.exe, you can compress, decompress, and manage compressed files easily. You should get familiar with this tool for the exam, and check out Table 3-1 for the common switches you can use. If you use Compact without any parameters, it shows the status of the files in the current directory.

```
Compact [/c] [/u] [/s] [/f] [/I] [/a] [/q] file/foldername
```

Table 3-1	Compact.exe Command Line Switches
Switch	*Explanation*
/c	Compresses the selected files.
/u	Uncompresses the selected files.
/s	Performs the operation on all data in the folder.
/f	Forces compression on selected files.
/I	Continues compression after errors have occurred.
/a	Displays files with hidden or system attributes.
/q	Reports on the essential information.
file/foldername	Determines the file and or folder you are working with.

You can compress an entire drive, but keep in mind that any encrypted files aren't compressed, and your Pagefile.sys file isn't compressed either.

Finally, you should keep a few compression rules in mind for the exam, concerning compressed files that are moved and/or copied:

✦ Files that are copied inherit the attributes of the folder that they are copied to. In other words, copied files don't remain compressed unless they are recompressed in a folder that is currently compressed. So, copied files don't retain their compression settings.

✦ If you move a compressed file or folder to a new partition, it is the same as a copy operation — the compression is lost.

✦ If you move a file or folder to a new location on the same partition, the compression is retained.

If you want to keep track of which files and folders are compressed, you can have them appear in an alternate color. In Control Panel, open Folder Options, click the View tab, and check the Display Compressed Files and Folders with Alternate Color check box.

Control access to files and folders using permissions

You manage file and folder access on NTFS drives by using NTFS permissions. On FAT32 drives, folder permissions can be applied, but for extended file permissions and controls, you should always share files and folders on NTFS drives.

Book I
Chapter 3

Implementing and
Conducting
Administration
of Resources

Windows 2000 Professional provides all of the features of NTFS security, including file permissions that can become a huge, ridiculously complex monster if you aren't careful. The adage "Strive for simplicity" certainly applies regarding file and folder permissions. Complicated permissions cause a lot of problems and headaches for network administrators.

However, Windows 2000 Professional gives you all the flexibility that you need to create permissions that are right for your organization. NTFS permissions apply both locally (users logging directly onto your machine) and over the network (users accessing shared data over a network connection). Either way, you can control access to files and folders both locally and over the network by using permissions. The following sections give you the skinny on file and folder permissions, and you need to make sure that you have all of these tables memorized for the exam!

File permissions

File permissions consist of full control, read and execute, modify, read, and write. Each permission contains a logical grouping of what is known as "special" permissions. Table 3-2 lists the special permissions that are contained in each file permission.

Table 3-2	File Special Permissions
Permission	*Special permissions*
Read	Users can list folders, read data, read extended attributes, read attributes, read permissions, and synchronize.
Write	Users can create folders and append data, create files and write data, write attributes, write extended attributes, read permissions, and synchronize.
Read & Execute	Users can traverse folder and execute files, and perform all of the read permissions.
Modify	Users can delete items and perform all permissions of read and write.
Full Control	Users can delete subfolders and files and take ownership, and perform all other permissions of read, write, read and execute, and modify.

Folder permissions

Folder permissions work in the same way as file permissions, but you see an additional option that enables you to give users the right to browse through a folder's contents. The permissions of Read, Write, Read and Execute, Modify and Full Control still apply, but you also have a List Folder Contents option, which gives users the special permissions of Traverse Folder, Execute File, List Folder, Read Data, Read Attributes, and Read Extended Attributes. Users with this permission can also read permissions and synchronize.

Permissions rules

Suppose that you assign a user Read, Write, and Modify — what is the actual user's permission?

You must remember two simple rules when using NTFS permissions:

+ NTFS permissions are cumulative. In other words, if you assign a user Read and Write permission, the user has all of the special permissions for both Read and Write.

+ All permissions are cumulative, except for the Deny permission, which overrides other permissions. Suppose that you assign a user Write permission, but you deny all others. Guess what? The user has no permission at all. Because you allowed Write permission but denied other permissions such as Modify and Full Control, which contain all of the Write special permissions, the user has no access.

As you are sifting through tricky permissions exam questions, remember to apply these basic rules, and then sort out the question. You'll find that permissions questions aren't that difficult if you keep these basics in mind at all times.

Inheritance

Windows 2000 computers use a very helpful feature known as permissions inheritance. Suppose that you have a folder with several subfolders. You place permissions on the parent folder. Rather than having to assign permissions to each individual folder as well, the permissions are automatically inherited by the subfolders because of the parent (darn those genetics!).

However, suppose that you also have a parent folder with certain permissions that you don't want inherited by the other subfolders (because you have assigned them their own permissions). What can you do? No problem — you can block the inheritance. On the desired subfolders, simply right-click the folder and click Properties. You'll see a Security tab. At the bottom of the tab, clear the Allow Inheritable Permissions from Parent to Propagate to This Object check box and click OK.

Setting permissions

To set permissions on a file or folder, simply follow these steps:

1. Right-click the file or folder and click Properties.

2. On the Security tab, select the group or click the Add button to locate the particular group or user for whom you want to configure permissions. In the Permissions window, select the desired permissions that you want to apply, as shown in Figure 3-3.

Book I
Chapter 3

Implementing and
Conducting
Administration
of Resources

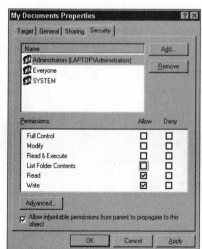

Figure 3-3:
Security tab.

3. Click OK to save the permissions.

4. If you have certain special permissions that you want to assign, or if you want to override the basic special permissions that are included in the standard permissions, click the Advanced button.

This opens the Access Control Settings dialog box for the file or folder, as shown in Figure 3-4.

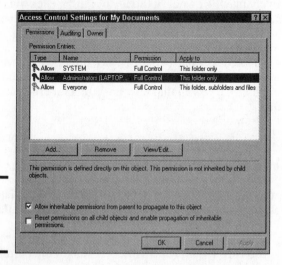

Figure 3-4:
Access
Control
Settings.

5. Select a user or group that you want to edit and click the View/Edit button. This opens the Permission Entry dialog box for the share. As Figure 3-5 shows, you can edit the special permissions, giving you a finer level of control over the permission for the file or folder. Make any desired edits and click OK.

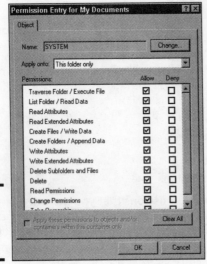

Figure 3-5: Permission Entry dialog box.

6. If you want to change the owner of the file or folder, click the Owner tab in the Access Control Settings dialog box. Select a new owner and click OK.

Keep in mind that the Access Control Settings are provided to give you a very fine level of control in situations where that fine level of control is needed. On a normal basis, you should only need to apply the standard NTFS permissions.

Optimize access to files and folders

Optimization is one of those test areas that Microsoft loves to throw at you. Again, optimization tests your real world knowledge of file and folder access and problem permissions. No single trick or tool exists to optimize access to files and folders, but you should keep these general ideas in mind for the exam:

✦ **NTFS permissions are cumulative:** The total sum of the permissions is the user's effective permission. Remember to keep permissions as simple as possible. Complicated permissions where you have edited the

**Book I
Chapter 3**

Implementing and
Conducting
Administration
of Resources

Access Control Settings often cause more problems than they solve. In scenario questions that you may see on the exam, remember that deny permission overrides all other permissions, and simplicity is your best option.

✦ **By default, inheritance is in effect for subfolders:** You can override this behavior by clearing the inheritance option on the Security tab of the folder or file's properties.

✦ **Anyone with full control can delete files and directories.**

✦ **Users who belong to multiple groups may have difficulties with permissions:** For example, Sue is a member of the marketing group that has full control permission over a file, but Sue is also a member of the accounting group that has no access. What permission does Sue have? None — the deny access overrides all other permissions.

Manage and Troubleshoot Access to Shared Folders

Shared folders are generally easy to manage and troubleshoot because you are only likely to see a limited amount of problems. We suggest that you get some hands-on practice, though, and read the following sections for a quick review.

Create and remove shared folders

You can easily share a folder and remove that folder from shared status quickly and easily by following the steps in Lab 3-2.

Lab 3-2   Sharing a Folder

1. **Right-click the folder that you want to share and click Properties.**

2. **Click the Sharing tab.**

3. **Choose the Share This Folder radio button and give the folder a share name.**

   You can choose to limit the number of users who are allowed to connect to the folder if you like, but the default setting is unlimited, as shown in Figure 3-6.

   You can also consider caching settings that determine how users can cache the folder and documents over the network.

4. **If you click the Caching button, you see the Caching Settings dialog box, where you can configure manual caching for documents or automatic caching. Make any desired selections and click OK.**

5. **Click OK again to share the folder.**

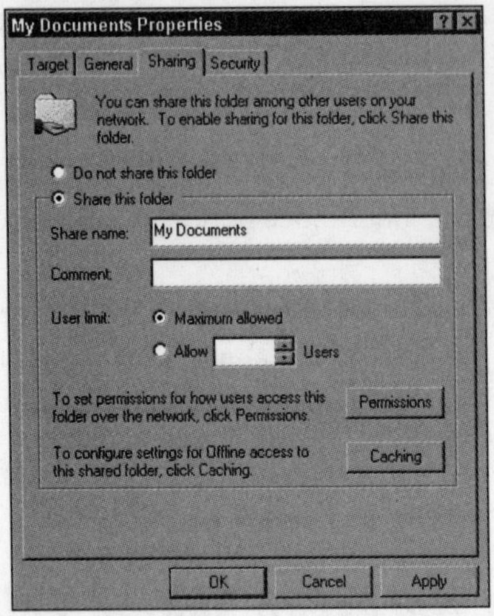

Figure 3-6:
Sharing tab.

After you share the folder, a hand appears under the icon noting that it is shared. You can easily stop sharing a folder at any time by accessing the Sharing tab again and deselecting the Share This Folder radio button so that the folder is no longer shared.

Control access to shared folders using permissions

Permissions for shared folders work like NTFS permissions, and you can apply NTFS permissions to users and groups on a shared folder. However, you can also apply folder permissions, consisting of full control, change, and read. By default, the Everyone group has full control (which includes basically everyone), so you'll want to change the Everyone permission as necessary for your share and the needs of your environment. Aside from these folder permissions, you can use the Security tab to assign NTFS permissions, assuming that the folder is stored on an NTFS drive. See the "Control access to files and folders using permissions" section earlier in this chapter for more information about NTFS permissions.

You can manage shared folders and the share and NTFS permissions for those folders more easily from the Computer Management console, as shown in Figure 3-7. Open Administrative Tools in Control Panel and double-click Computer Management. Expand shared folders in the left console pane. You can examine the shares, sessions, and all currently open files. Right-click a folder to stop sharing it or to access its properties to manage permissions.

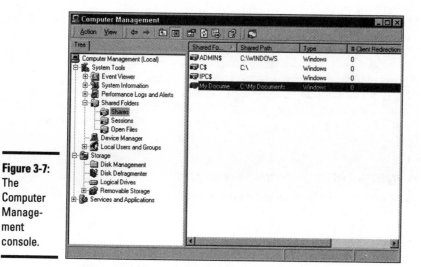

Book I
Chapter 3

Implementing and
Conducting
Administration
of Resources

Figure 3-7:
The
Computer
Manage-
ment
console.

Manage and troubleshoot Web server resources

You can run Internet Information Services (IIS) on Windows XP Professional in order to share folders on an intranet site. However, the primary use of IIS is on Windows 2000 Server. For the Windows 2000 Professional exam, you need to know the basics of using IIS as a Web server and how to share and manage folders or directories. However, you are unlikely to see many questions on the use of IIS. In the interest of avoiding repetition, you can get familiar with IIS and managing Web server resources in Book II, Chapter 3.

Connect to Local and Network Print Devices

Shared printers are commonly used in Microsoft networks. In fact, in a Windows domain, you may have multiple printers to which you can connect and use. Fortunately, Windows 2000 Professional makes accessing and connecting to local and network print devices easy. In the following sections, you can take a look at the exam issues that you are likely to encounter, and once again, you should get some hands-on practice as well.

Connect to a local print device

You can easily install a new printer on Windows 2000 Professional. In most cases, you simply attach the printer to the correct port (such as LPT or USB) and run the manufacturer's setup software in order to install the printer. Make sure that the printer supports Windows 2000 Professional and make sure that you have the most up-to-date drivers. Visit the printer manufacturer's Web site to learn more.

If you are having problems setting up the printer, you can use the Add Printer Wizard, found in Start⇨Settings⇨Printers. Under normal circumstances, however, you shouldn't need to use the wizard. If you are having problems installing a printer, check the printer device's documentation for help and support.

Manage printers and print jobs

After you install a local printer, you can manage the printer through the printer's icon in the Printers folder. By accessing the printer's properties pages, you can control the ports used for the printer and even when the printer is available for use.

Most of the settings that you'll find on the printer's properties pages are self-explanatory. However, a few settings on the Advanced tab, as shown in Figure 3-8, make great exam fodder:

✦ **Priority:** The printer software is simply that — software that runs the print device. However, what do you do if you need to restrict the printer so that one group has priority use over other groups? The answer — create two printers for the same print device and give the preferred group a priority of 1 and the other groups a lower priority, such as 50. The group with a priority of 1 will always get serviced first when multiple print jobs are submitted.

✦ **Spool Settings:** By default, the print spool is used, which holds the print job on the hard disk while printing is occurring. This returns control of the application to you. If you see a question about a printer that locks up the application until the printing is complete, the spool setting is the culprit.

✦ **New drivers:** These are developed and released from time to time. If a newer driver is created for your printer, use the Advanced tab to update it easily.

During your day-to-day routine, you can manage print documents by using the print queue. The print queue, shown in Figure 3-9, gives you a simple window listing the documents that are waiting to print, their status, owner, and when they were submitted. As the administrator, you can stop documents from printing and delete them from the print queue by simply selecting the document and clicking the Document menu to pause or cancel. If you want to pause all documents or cancel all printing, select the desired option on the Printer menu.

**Book I
Chapter 3**

**Implementing and
Conducting
Administration
of Resources**

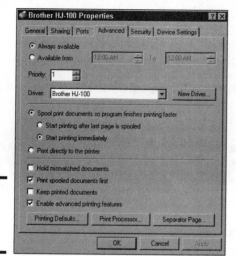

Figure 3-8:
Advanced
printer
properties.

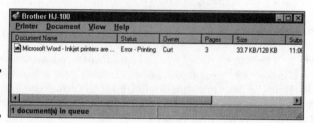

Figure 3-9:
Print queue.

Control access to printers by using permissions

Like any shared resource, you can control which users can access what
printers and what permissions those users have when they are connected.

The three printer permissions are as follows:

+ **Print:** This permission allows a user to print to the printer.

+ **Manage Printers:** This permission allows the user to access the
printer's properties and make changes to the printer configuration.

+ **Manage Documents:** This permission allows the user to open the print
queue and manage printer documents.

Most all users simply have the print permission, and only a few administrators have the right to manage printers and manage documents. Aside from
the permissions options, you assign permissions by using the standard
Security tab that you'll find by right-clicking the printer icon in the Printers
Folder and clicking Properties.

The exam is most likely to test your knowledge of printer permissions by giving you a scenario and asking what permission to assign. You may also see scenarios in which two different groups need to use a certain printer, but one group should only use the printer at certain hours, blah, blah, blah. Most of these scenario problems can be solved by creating more than one printer for a single print device. You create the printers, and then assign permissions and configurations as needed — this meets your differing group requirements.

You'll see more questions about printing and running a print server on the Windows 2000 Server exam. However, the printer software is exactly the same on both Windows 2000 Server and Windows 2000 Professional, so if you want to find out more details about printing, turn to Book II, Chapter 3.

Connect to a network printer

Aside from local printing, you can also use the Add Printer Wizard to connect to a local printer on your network. This process is easy, and if you have the permissions necessary to use the printer, the drivers for the printer are automatically downloaded to your computer from the print server and you're ready to go.

To connect to a network printer, use the Add Printer Wizard and choose to connect to a network printer. In the Locate Your Printer window, shown in Figure 3-10, type the printer name or click Next to browse for the network printer. After you have selected the network printer that you want to use, click Finish and the printer is installed. You can now print to the network printer.

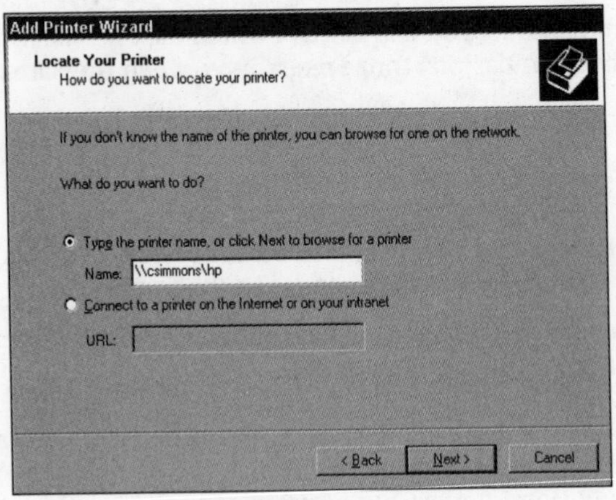

Figure 3-10: Connect to a network printer.

> **Add Printer Wizard**
>
> **Locate Your Printer**
> How do you want to locate your printer?
>
> If you don't know the name of the printer, you can browse for one on the network.
>
> What do you want to do?
>
> ○ Type the printer name, or click Next to browse for a printer
>   Name: \\csimmons\hp
>
> ○ Connect to a printer on the Internet or on your intranet
>   URL:
>
>   < Back   Next >   Cancel

Book I
Chapter 3

Implementing and
Conducting
Administration
of Resources

If you aren't sure what printer you want to connect to, you can search the Active Directory for a printer that you want to use. Also, when you share a printer from a Windows 2000 Professional computer, that printer is automatically stored in the Active Directory so that users can search for and locate it. If you don't want to store the shared printer in the Active Directory, just clear the List in Directory check box on the Sharing tab.

Connect to an Internet printer

Windows 2000 Professional can connect to an Internet printer or a printer on an intranet. For example, suppose that your company consists of two offices — one in Tampa and one in New York. You work at the New York office, but you want to print a document for a colleague at the Tampa office. Can you do it? Yes, if a printer in the office has been configured for Internet printing, you can easily connect to the printer by using Internet Explorer or an HTTP address.

Once again, simply use the Add Printer Wizard and choose to connect to a printer on the Internet or your intranet. Internet printers are accessed via the http://*printservername*/Printers/*printername* format. If you don't know the name of the printer, just type http://*printservername*/Printers.

You can only access an Internet printer from Internet Explorer 4.0 (or later version). If you are having problems connecting to an Internet printer, you'll need to verify that you have Internet or intranet connectivity and that the print server is online.

Configure and Manage File Systems

Configuring and managing file systems sounds like a complicated objective. In truth, you only need to know two things about file systems: which file systems are supported under Windows 2000 Professional and how to change from one file system to another. Beyond that, file systems take care of themselves, with the exception of fragmentation from time to time.

File systems supported

Windows 2000 Professional supports FAT, FAT32, and NTFS. However, you will find the best security and management benefits with the NTFS file system. In fact, Windows 2000 Professional was developed with NTFS in mind.

So why would you want to use FAT at all? For two possible reasons: First, if your computer is using a hard drive under 4GB, you will see better use of space using FAT32. However, the odds are quite good that any hard drives that you are currently using well exceed 4GB. The second reason is down-level compatibility with an older operating system, such as Windows 9x or Me. Windows 9x and Me operating systems can't read NTFS, so if you are dual-booting with one of these, you may want to leave your computer partitions formatted with FAT32 so that your downlevel operating system can read all of the data.

Aside from these, there are no other real benefits of using FAT or FAT32 over NTFS. Keep that in mind for the exam.

Converting from one file system to another

If the drives on your computer are currently formatted with FAT32, you can easily convert those drives to NTFS by using a convert utility. Conversion is easy and poses no threat to any of your data.

To convert to NTFS, follow the steps in Lab 3-3.

Lab 3-3   Converting to NTFS

1. **Click Start⇨Run and then type** CMD **and click OK.**

2. **In the command window, type** convert *driveletter*: /FS:NTFS **where driveletter is the letter of the drive you want to convert.**

   As Figure 3-11 shows, we converted the C drive to NTFS.

3. **Press Enter to start the conversion. Depending on the size of the drive, conversion takes several minutes.**

Figure 3-11:
Convert
command.

In the event that you need to convert a drive from NTFS to FAT, the process becomes more complicated. In fact, you can't convert at all. If you need to change a drive from NTFS to FAT, you must back up all of your data and reformat the drive by using Computer Management or a disk-formatting utility. There is no direct way to convert an NTFS drive to FAT, and after you convert a FAT drive to NTFS, you can't go back without reformatting.

Prep Test

1 Which Windows 2000 feature isn't compatible with file compression?

A ○ Encryption

B ○ Dynamic Disks

C ○ Volumes

D ○ Disk Quotas

2 You are currently managing a group of folders that are compressed. You run the compact /u command on one of the folders. What effect does this command have?

A ○ None

B ○ Compresses the folder

C ○ Uncompresses the folder

D ○ Changes the permissions

3 You move a compressed folder to another location on a different partition. What effect does the move have on compression?

A ○ The folder remains compressed.

B ○ The folder is uncompressed.

C ○ The folder is uncompressed and inherits the target location's settings.

D ○ You can't move a compressed folder to another partition.

4 Which NTFS permission can perform all of the actions of read and write, but also delete items, but not take ownership?

A ○ Full control

B ○ Modify

C ○ Read and execute

D ○ No permission allows this.

5 Which statement is true concerning NTFS permissions?

A ○ NTFS permissions are cumulative.

B ○ Deny doesn't override full control.

C ○ A user can't be assigned both read and write.

D ○ Modify contains all of the permissions of full control.

6 **Which of the following isn't a folder permission?**

A ○ Full Control

B ○ Write

C ○ Change

D ○ Read

7 **A user document has been sent to a shared printer. The document contains 87 pages and is clogging up the print queue. What menu in the print queue do you need to use to delete this print job only?**

A ○ Document

B ○ Printer

C ○ File

D ○ Cancel

8 **A user complains that a local printer attached to his Windows 2000 Professional computer seems to lock up during printing. After printing has completed, the computer returns to normal. What is the problem?**

A ○ The driver

B ○ Spool settings

C ○ RAM

D ○ CPU cycles

9 **You need to use Internet Explorer to connect to an Internet printer. The print server's name is PRNTSRV, but you don't know the printer's name. What address should you use?**

A ○ *PRNTSRV*\?

B ○ *PRNTSRV*\Printers

C ○ http://*prntsrv*/print/printing

D ○ http://*prntsrv*/printers

10 **Which of the following statements is true concerning file systems?**

A ○ Windows 2000 only supports NTFS.

B ○ You can convert an FAT drive to NTFS.

C ○ You can convert an NTFS drive to FAT.

D ○ Only FAT32 is supported under Windows 2000.

Answers

1 **A.** Windows 2000 compression and encryption can't be used at the same time on the same file or folder. *Review "File Compression."*

2 **C.** The compact /u switch uncompresses the target folder. *Read "File Compression."*

3 **C.** When you move a folder to a different partition, it is uncompressed. After it is moved, it inherits the target folder's properties, so it may be compressed again if the parent folder is compressed and is configured to compress all subfolders. *Review "File Compression."*

4 **B.** The Modify permission can perform all of the actions of Read and Write, but can also delete items. *See "File permissions."*

5 **A.** NTFS permissions are cumulative with the exception of Deny, which overrides all other permissions. *Study "Permissions rules."*

6 **B.** Write isn't a folder permission. *Study "Control access to shared folders using permissions."*

7 **A.** Use the Document menu to manage individual documents. Use the Printer menu to manage all print jobs at the same time. *Study "Manage printers and print jobs."*

8 **B.** The settings are configured to print directly to the printer instead of using the spool. This will lock up the application until printing is complete. *Study "Manage printers and print jobs."*

9 **D.** If you don't know the name of the printer, just use the /printers option to see a listing. If you are still having problems, just look under http://prntsrv. *See "Connect to an Internet printer."*

10 **B.** You can't directly convert an NTFS drive to FAT without reformatting. *Study "Converting from one file system to another."*

Chapter 4: Implementing and Managing Hardware Devices and Drivers

Exam Objectives

✔ Implementing, managing, and troubleshooting disk devices

✔ Implementing, managing, and troubleshooting display devices

✔ Implementing, managing, and troubleshooting mobile computer hardware

✔ Configuring and managing modems

✔ Implementing, managing, and troubleshooting input and output (I/O) devices

✔ Monitoring and configuring multiple processing units

✔ Installing, configuring, and troubleshooting network adapters

Computer hardware can be a real pain. After all, the hardware has to be installed correctly, you must have a driver that works with Windows 2000, and the hardware must play nicely with other devices on Windows 2000. The good news is that hardware has come a long way in the past few years, and Windows 2000 easily works with most hardware devices, if a Windows 2000 supported driver is used.

In this chapter, you find out about hardware management on Windows 2000. The exam expects you to know how to install, configure, and troubleshoot hardware devices, so in this chapter, we delve into the topics and issues you are most likely to see on the exam:

✦ Managing disk devices and display configuration

✦ Using and troubleshooting mobile computer hardware and I/O devices

✦ Managing drivers

✦ Using multiple processing units and configuring network adapter cards

Implementing, Managing, and Troubleshooting Disk Devices

Disk devices in Windows 2000 fall into two basic categories: removable disks and fixed disks. Windows 2000 supports *removable* disks, such as CD-ROM drives, floppy drives, and Zip drives (among others) as well as *fixed* disks, such as the computer's internal hard drive. For the exam, you need to know a few aspects about both removable and fixed disks, and the next two sections explore these exam objectives.

Installing, configuring, and managing DVD and CD-ROM drives

DVD and CD-ROM drives are rather easy to install and use. You can install internal DVD/CD-ROM drives on Windows 2000 Professional, or you can install external models that attach to common ports, such as USB. Regardless of your choice, you should always do the following:

✦ Check the Hardware Compatibility List (HCL) at www.microsoft.com/hcl to see whether the device that you want to install is compatible with Windows 2000.

✦ Make sure that you have an up-to-date driver that works with Windows 2000. Your best bet is to visit the manufacturer's Web site and see about updates to drivers.

DVD and CD-ROM drives are installed like any other device; attach the device to your system, and Windows 2000 can automatically detect it. If you are having problems with a particular device, use the Add/Remove Hardware Wizard in Control Panel and make sure that you have the device driver ready when it is needed.

After the DVD or CD-ROM device is installed, you then use it as you normally would. However, if you need to disable the device or uninstall it, use Device Manager. Follow these steps:

1. **Access System properties in Control Panel.**

2. **On the Hardware tab, click the Device Manager button.**

   The Device Manager opens.

3. **Expand DVD/CD-ROM drives and right-click the CD/DVD-ROM drive that you want to view.**

   You can Disable or Uninstall the device from this location, and you can access the device's properties page.

One exam item appears on the Properties tab, shown in Figure 4-1. You have the option to Enable digital CD audio for the CD-ROM device. If you are having problems with digital audio playback, clear this check box so that the system can read the data as analog.

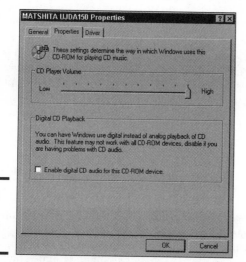

Figure 4-1:
The
Properties
tab.

Monitoring and configuring removable media

Removable media, along with CD and DVD-ROM drives, also includes such items as tape drives, Zip disks, Jaz drives, and other removable media. The key point to remember is that you can use Device Manager to manage these devices as well, along with any additional management software that may have shipped with the drives. Beyond that, you can also find removable media devices in My Computer, where you can access removable disks, store data on them, and delete data as well.

Though generally beyond the scope of the exam, you should also check out Removable Storage in Computer Management (found in Administrative Tools in Control Panel). The Removable Storage console can help you manage removable media and help catalog data.

Monitoring and configuring disks

A new feature of Windows 2000 disk management involves the distinction between *basic* and *dynamic* disks:

✦ **Basic disk:** A basic disk consists of partitions and logical drives. If you upgrade from Windows NT 4.0, your disk configuration remains intact, and it is a basic disk. With a basic disk, you can manage the partitions and the logical drives, and you can create additional partitions. However, you cannot create any new volume sets, stripe sets, and so on.

✦ **Dynamic disk:** Windows 2000 manages a dynamic disk that contains dynamic volumes, which are simply volumes that you create with the Disk Management console.

Dynamic disks do not contain partitions or logical drives; they contain volumes. With this design, disks are no longer limited to a certain number of partitions, and they can contain multiple volumes. This design gives you greater flexibility for disk management, without the restrictions imposed by previous versions of Windows. Also, you can make changes to your disk configuration on a dynamic disk without having to reboot your computer.

Previous disk management solutions and fault-tolerant solutions are still available on dynamic disks, but the names have changed. (More terminology!) You need to know the differences, so take the time to memorize the following terms:

✦ **Spanned volume:** A spanned volume, formerly called a volume set, is a collection of volume (formerly partition) "pieces" that the system treats as one volume. By using spanned volumes, you can make constructive use of small portions of disk space, but spanned volumes have no inherent fault tolerance. *Fault tolerance* means that the system is able to tolerate a disk failure because the data on the failed disk can be recovered.

✦ **Striped volume:** A striped volume, formerly called a striped set, stores data on two or more physical disks. Striped volumes allocate data evenly (in stripes) across the disks in the striped volume, so you must have the same amount of storage space on each disk. Striped volumes are an excellent storage solution and provide excellent read performance, but they offer no fault tolerance. If one disk in the stripe volume fails, you lose all data on the entire striped volume.

✦ **Mirrored volume:** Mirrored volumes, formerly called mirror sets, represent a fault-tolerant solution that duplicates data on two physical disks. One disk is the primary disk, while the other disk is the mirror (or a copy of the primary disk). If one disk fails, you can reconstruct data by using the mirror. In fact, in Windows 2000, if one of the disks fails, your system continues to operate as though nothing has happened by using the mirror. You can replace the failed disk and re-create the mirror for continued fault tolerance. Mirrored volumes are effective fault-tolerance solutions but have a high cost in terms of megabytes (50 percent). In other words, if you want to mirror a 2GB disk, you must have another 2GB disk available. This configuration requires twice as much disk space as you would normally use without the mirror. So, in terms of disk megabyte expense, you are only getting to use half of your total storage space.

In order to manage your disks in Windows 2000, you need to upgrade each disk from basic to dynamic. You can perform this action by right-clicking the disk (not the partitions) in the Disk Management console and then choosing Upgrade to Dynamic Disk. You need to reboot your computer for the upgrade to take effect.

After you upgrade to dynamic disk, you cannot boot previous versions of Windows on the dynamic disk because these operating systems cannot access dynamic volumes. So, dynamic disks are a Windows 2000-only solution, but you should implement them as soon as possible to take advantage of the features that dynamic disks offer.

When you upgrade a basic disk to a dynamic disk, you must have 1MB of unformatted free space at the end of the disk, which Windows uses for administrative purposes. To maintain previous volume sets, striped sets, and so on, from a basic disk, you must upgrade all the basic disks to dynamic disks. Also, keep in mind that you cannot upgrade removable media to dynamic disks.

Understanding online and offline disks

In addition to the distinction between basic and dynamic disks, Windows 2000 introduces two more disk-related terms: online and offline. The Disk Management console displays this status for each disk. *Online* means the disk is up and running. In contrast, an *offline* disk has errors and is not available.

You can access the properties of either an online or offline disk by right-clicking the disk in Disk Management and clicking Properties. From the Properties dialog box for an offline disk, you can use the disk tools to attempt to repair the disk. Alternatively, you can attempt to repair the offline disk by right-clicking it and then choosing Reactivate Disk.

Understanding disk status

The Disk Management console provides several pieces of information about each disk volume, such as layout, type, file system, status, capacity, and free space. For the exam, you need to know about disk status and the possible status indicators that can occur.

You need to memorize these status indicators for the exam:

✦ **Healthy:** The volume is accessible and has no problems.

✦ **Healthy (At Risk):** The volume is accessible, but I/O errors have been detected. The underlying disk, which is the physical disk on which the volume is located, is displayed as Online (Errors). Usually, you can solve this problem by reactivating the disk (right-click the disk and choose Reactivate Disk).

✦ **Initializing:** The volume is being initialized and will display as Healthy after initialization is complete. This status does not require any action.

✦ **Resynching:** The system is resynchronizing mirrored volumes. After Windows 2000 completes the resynchronization, the status is displayed as Healthy, and no action is necessary from you.

✦ **Regenerating:** Data on RAID-5 volumes is being regenerated from the parity bit. This process occurs after a disk failure and disk replacement by an administrator. No action is required.

✦ **Failed Redundancy:** The underlying disk is offline on fault-tolerant disks. In this case, you no longer have any fault tolerance on either mirrored or RAID-5 volumes. You need to reactivate or repair the disk to avoid potential data loss if one of the disks fails.

✦ **Failed Redundancy (At Risk):** This status is the same as Failed Redundancy, but the status of the underlying disk is Online (Errors). Reactivate the disk so that it returns to Online status.

✦ **Failed:** The system cannot start the volume automatically, and you need to repair the volume.

Creating volumes

You can easily create new volumes on your dynamic disks in Windows 2000 in the Disk Management console. Simply right-click the free space where you want to create a new volume and then choose Create Volume. This action launches the Create Volume Wizard.

You can create any volume, spanned volume, or striped volume (assuming you have the number of drives required) by using the Create Volume Wizard. Mirrored and RAID-5 volumes are only supported on Windows 2000 Server.

The Create Volume Wizard is rather straightforward and easy to use, but the exam does expect you to understand how the wizard works. Review Lab 4-1, which creates a simple volume, to make certain that you understand how the wizard works.

Lab 4-1   Creating a Simple Volume

1. **In the Disk Management console, right-click the area of free space where you want to create the volume and then choose Create Volume.**

2. **Click Next on the Create Volume Welcome screen.**

3. **Select Simple Volume from the list of options and click Next.**

   If you want to create a different kind of volume, select the desired type and click Next.

4. **Select the desired disk and click Add. You can also adjust the MB size for the volume, if desired (see Figure 4-2). Click Next.**

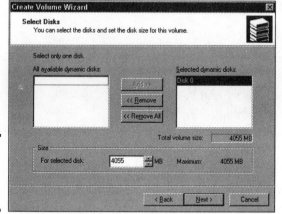

Figure 4-2:
Select the
disk and
volume size.

5. **Select a drive letter for the volume or choose to mount (or direct) the volume to an empty folder. You can also choose not to assign a drive letter or drive path at this time. Make your selection and click Next.**

   See the section "Using Mounted Volumes," later in this chapter, for more information about mounted volumes.

6. **Indicate whether you want to format the volume. If you choose to format it now, select a file system, an allocation unit size, and a volume label. You can also choose to perform a quick format and enable file and folder compression, if desired.**

   The data compression option enables the Disk Management console to compress data on the volume so that more storage space is available.

7. **Click Finish to complete the wizard.**

   The system creates the volume and formats it (if specified).

Checking Out Common Management Tasks

After you configure your volumes in the desired manner, disk management requires very little time on your part. Your basic tasks include occasional management and troubleshooting.

You can manage your disk volumes through the Disk Management console. By right-clicking a dynamic disk or disk volume, you can perform several tasks. These tasks may vary depending on the type of disk or volume, but you should understand the following basic management actions, which you need to remember for the exam:

+ **Open/Explore:** Enables you to open the disk or volume and view its contents.

+ **Extend Volume:** You can dynamically extend a disk volume to incorporate more space from free disk space. You can only extend volumes with other NTFS volumes — not FAT or FAT32.

+ **Change Drive Letter and Path:** You can dynamically change a volume's drive letter and path by entering the desired change.

+ **Reactivate Volume/Disk:** Use the Reactivate feature to correct Online (Error) status readings.

+ **Delete Volume:** Removes the volume from your computer.

+ **Properties:** In the Properties dialog boxes for disks and volumes, you can see general information about the disk and its hardware, and you can access disk tools, such as Error Checking and Disk Defragmenter.

Using Mounted Volumes

By using mounted volumes in Windows 2000, you can easily replace drive letters so that a disk volume appears as a folder. In other words, by mounting a drive to a folder, you can give the drive a friendly name and you do not run out of available drive letters. To create the mounted volume, you create an empty folder with a desired name and then mount the desired volume to the folder by using Disk Management.

To create a mounted volume, follow the steps in Lab 4-2.

Lab 4-2   Creating a Mounted Volume

1. **Right-click the volume that you want to mount and choose Change Drive Letter and Path from the pop-up menu.**

   The Change Drive Letter and Path dialog box opens.

2. **Click Add.**

   The Add New Drive Letter or Path dialog box opens, as shown in Figure 4-3.

3. **Select the Mount in this NTFS Folder option, enter the path to the shared folder, and click OK.**

   You can also click Browse and then navigate to the shared folder.

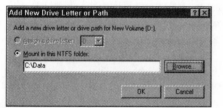

Figure 4-3:
Enter the
name of the
NTFS folder.

After you mount the volume to the NTFS folder, the folder appears as a drive on your system, as shown in Figure 4-4.

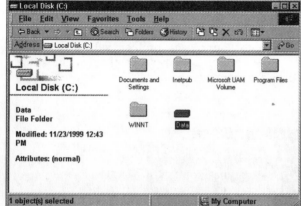

Figure 4-4:
The
mounted
volume now
appears as
a drive on
your system.

Implementing, Managing, and Troubleshooting Display Devices

Display devices refer to the display adapter card that the computer uses to display data on the computer's monitor. For the most part, managing and solving display problems is not terribly complicated, and most display problems typically come back to either a corrupted driver or a driver that is not compatible with Windows 2000.

Installing, configuring, and troubleshooting a video adapter

You install video adapters, or video cards, on Windows 2000 by inserting the video card and rebooting your system. Windows 2000 can automatically detect the new hardware and install it for you. If Windows has trouble installing the new video card, you can use the Add/Remove Hardware Wizard.

Doing your homework before installing video cards and making sure that they are compatible with Windows 2000 is important. Check the HCL for details. Also make sure that you have the most up-to-date Windows 2000 driver when you install.

If installation should fail, or your reboot fails, boot into Windows 2000 by using the Safe Mode VGA mode option. This uses a basic video driver with the card and allows you to change the driver or remove the card from the system.

Also, you can configure colors and screen size for the card by accessing the Settings tab of the Display Properties dialog box, shown in Figure 4-5. The troubleshoot option you see here can help you solve any problems you might be having, and the Advanced options give you additional settings you can try that may be able to solve specific problems.

In most cases, though, your biggest problem will be incompatible drivers. If you install a video card on Windows 2000 that is compatible with the system and uses a current, compatible driver, you are unlikely to experience problems.

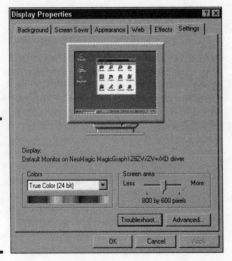

Figure 4-5:
Configure settings for the video card in the Display Properties dialog box.

You should get some hands-on practice with installing video cards and configuring them. Practice makes perfect, and the exam is no exception!

Configuring multiple display support

First introduced in Windows 98, multiple display support allows you to use more than one monitor with a single Windows 2000 computer. Why, you might ask? Multiple monitors can be useful to people who work with more than one application at the same time or who work with graphics programs. The two monitors can display the same image split onto both monitors, or it can display separate applications. One video card is considered the primary monitor while the second is considered the secondary monitor.

You have a few basic rules to keep in mind when you are using multiple monitors:

✦ The maximum number of monitors that can be used is ten.

✦ You must use drivers compatible with Windows 2000 for all monitors.

✦ Only PCI or AGP video cards are supported.

✦ If one video adapter is built onto the motherboard, that video adapter must serve as the VGA device.

After you install the secondary video card so that you have at least two video cards and monitors, you can now set up the multiple monitor configuration. Lab 4-3 shows you how.

Lab 4-3   Configuring Multiple Monitors

1. **Access Display properties in Control Panel.**

2. **Click the Settings tab.**

   All the display adapters are listed.

3. **Select the monitor number for the primary display device and select the adapter for the monitor. Adjust the color scheme as desired.**

4. **Select the monitor for the second display device and select the adapter for this monitor as well.**

5. **Select the Extend my Windows Desktop to This Monitor check box.**

6. **Configure the color scheme as desired.**

7. **Click OK to save your settings and close the dialog box.**

Configuring and Managing Modems

You don't have to worry about a lot of modem questions on the exam (if any), so we won't delve into a lengthy discussion of modems and modem management. In the past, modem installation and configuration could be really difficult. Today, however, with Plug and Play technology, modems work just like any other hardware device that you want to install. You simply insert or connect the modem and Windows automatically detects it. You should use the most updated modem driver for the best result.

Concerning modem configuration, the main issue you are likely to come across on the exam is a disconnect from the Internet. If you access modem properties, you see that you can configure a modem timeout value where the modem disconnects you from the Internet automatically if you are not using the modem for a period of time. It is also important to note that individual dial-up connections can also be configured with a disconnect value.

Implementing, Managing, and Troubleshooting Mobile Computer Hardware

In many networking environments, laptop computers have virtually replaced desktop computers, and why not? After all, today's laptops are just as powerful but more versatile than similar desktop models. Also laptop computers give users flexibility so that they can work from the office, at home, or on the road.

Because of the popularity of laptops, the exam expects you to be proficient in laptop hardware. The good news is that laptop hardware works the same way in terms of installation and configuration. Laptop computers today generally support the Advanced Configuration and Power Interface (ACPI) or Advanced Power Management (APM) so that hardware components that are not in use or not needed can be powered down without affecting the rest of the system.

Laptop computers allow hot-pluggable devices, which means you can insert a PCMCIA card or USB device without powering down the system. You can use these card services with a number of different PCMCIA devices, such as modems, network connections, digital cameras, and such. However, keep in mind that card services consume battery power, so when they are not in use, such as in a mobile scenario, use a hardware profile to disable them.

For the exam, you should keep in mind two important issues concerning mobile computer hardware:

✦ **Power Options should be configured to conserve energy:** You can use standard schemes but you can also use stand-by and hibernation:

- Stand-by uses a low power mode, but keeps enough power flowing to the system to preserve the data in RAM.

- Hibernation writes data that is in RAM to the hard disk and completely shuts down the system. When the computer is restarted, the data is read back into RAM so that the computer appears as it did when left unattended.

Exam questions are likely to give you a situation where a user is using a laptop computer. The situation will ask you about certain power settings that should be used to help the user. Just keep the stand-by and hibernation features in mind and you can answer the questions. Also, keep in mind that you can enable these features on the Power Options tabs by simply selecting the desired check boxes.

✦ **The best way to manage hardware and battery consumption on a laptop computer is to use different hardware profiles:** You can learn more about hardware profiles in Book I, Chapter 5.

Implementing, Managing, and Troubleshooting Input/Output (I/O) Devices

Input/Output devices refer to any group of devices that allows you to enter information into the computer system or receive some output. Printers, mice, keyboards, scanners, cameras, and many other devices all fall into this category.

Because Windows 2000 is a Plug and Play system, installing and configuring I/O devices is typically not difficult. If you are using hardware that is compatible with Windows 2000 and up-to-date drivers, you are not likely to experience a lot of problems. So, what does the exam want you to know? This kind of objective is used to primarily test your real-world knowledge of Windows 2000 hardware installation and configuration. The questions you might see are typically not difficult, but they are designed to find out whether you have ever put your hands on a Windows 2000 computer.

Questions typically revolve around installation and driver problems, or getting the device to behave in a way that you want. Device Manager is your key tool for managing hardware and seeing whether any conflicts or problems exist. The following sections point out what you are likely to run across on the exam. The issue of I/O devices is a lengthy topic, but we only mention the issues you are most likely to see. Use the following sections as a study guide and as a hands-on practice guide.

Printers

Printers can be installed automatically on Windows 2000, and you can also use the manufacturer's installation CD. Make sure that you have a supported printer and driver before attempting to use the device on Windows 2000. If you are having problems with installation, make sure that the printer is connected correctly to the LPT, USB, or infrared port. Other than that, installation problems almost always revolve around the driver.

Scanners

Scanners are supported under Windows 2000 and are attached to USB, SCSI, or parallel ports. Make sure that the scanner is compatible with Windows 2000 and that you have the correct driver. Use the Scanners and Cameras applet in Control Panel to install and configure a scanner.

Keyboards

Windows 2000 supports wireless keyboards, USB keyboards, or PS/2 keyboards. You can access the Keyboard properties in Control Panel for configuration options. The keyboard configuration options you find are self-explanatory, but you should review them for the exam.

Mice

Wireless, USB, and PS/2 mice are supported in Windows 2000. Like the keyboard, you find a Mouse icon in Control Panel that allows you to adjust the mouse behavior. Spend some time working with the mouse properties features before you take the exam. Pay special attention to pointer options and track wheel speed.

IrDA and wireless devices

IrDA, or infrared devices, communicate wirelessly through an infrared port on your computer, if your computer is equipped with an IrDA port. IrDA support must be enabled in the computer's BIOS, and many desktop systems do not support IrDA devices in order to free up IRQs for other purposes. However, you will find that many laptop computers support the feature for wireless printing and communication with PDAs. You're not likely to run into complicated IrDA questions on the exam, but you'll see the feature appear in scenario-based questions.

USB devices

The Universal Serial Port (USB) brings a lot of functionality to the Windows 2000 table, and if you peruse the local computer store, you'll discover that USB seems to be the most popular kind of device. And why not — you plug the device into the USB port, Windows 2000 installs it, and you're ready to go.

On the exam, you are not likely to run into many (if any) direct USB questions. However, one issue can appear. USB devices connect to either self-powered hubs or bus-powered hubs. Bus-powered hubs use the computer's power to run. If you connect too many devices to the bus-powered hub, they may stop working because there is not enough power to run them. If you see questions about connecting an external disk drive to a bus-powered USB hub, the problem is going to be the power — you need a self-powered hub.

Multimedia hardware

Multimedia hardware, such as digital cameras, are not different from any other device. Make sure that the device is compatible with Windows 2000 and make sure that you have the appropriate drivers. Follow the manufacturer's setup instructions and refer to the manufacturer's Web site for help.

Updating Drivers

A *driver* is software that enables the operating system to control a particular hardware device. You can think of a driver as the bridge between the operating system and the hardware. Typically, the company that makes the hardware device also manufactures the driver, which you get on a floppy disk or CD-ROM when you purchase the hardware.

The Windows 2000 operating system also contains an extensive list of generic drivers. When you install a new piece of hardware, Windows searches for the best driver for the device, including drivers that you provide with a floppy disk or CD-ROM. As we explain in the following sections, you manage drivers through the Driver tab in a device's Properties dialog box.

Each hardware device has a Driver tab in its Properties dialog box. As you can see in Figure 4-6, the Driver tab lists information about the driver and its manufacturer, and you have the options to view driver details, uninstall the driver, or update the driver:

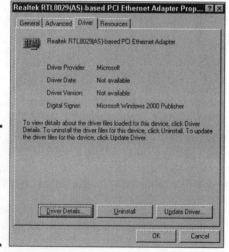

Figure 4-6:
Use the
Driver tab to
uninstall or
update the
device
driver.

✦ **Driver Details:** To view the driver file, provider, file version, and copyright, click Driver Details.

✦ **Uninstall:** If you click Uninstall, a warning message appears, telling you that you are about to remove the device from your system. If you remove the driver and then decide that you want to use the device after all, Windows 2000 must repeat the detection and installation process to install the hardware device.

For the exam, remember that removing a device's driver effectively removes the device from the system. Hardware cannot function with your operating system without an appropriate driver.

✦ **Update Driver:** By clicking Update Driver on the Driver tab, you open the Upgrade Device Driver Wizard. Due to the constant updates and refinements of device drivers, Microsoft provides this handy wizard so that you can update device drivers when updates become available. The wizard prompts you for the location of the new driver, searches for it, and then automatically installs it for the device. This wizard offers an easy way to make driver updates and changes.

Monitoring and Configuring Multiple Processing Units

Windows 2000 Professional supports computers that use up to two processors. Using two processors gives the system and applications more power. Multiple processors are not often used, but in some environments, in which particular Windows 2000 Professional computers need a lot of processing power, multiple processor configurations must be used.

For the exam, remember the following points:

✦ **The two processors must be Intel processors.** You cannot use non-Intel processors such as Alpha, PPC, or MIPS.

✦ **Make sure that both processors are being used to service tasks.** In other words, the computer is utilizing both processors at the same time. This process, called *affinity*, can be configured for tasks by using Task Manager. Click the Processes tab and right-click the desired task to configure affinity.

On the exam, if you see a question about using both processors for a particular task, you know that the affinity setting needs to be configured.

Installing, Configuring, and Troubleshooting Network Adapters

Network adapters work like any other hardware device in Windows 2000, so it is somewhat of a mystery why network adapters are spelled out in the exam objectives. If you need to install a network adapter, make sure that the network adapter is compatible with Windows 2000 and that you have the correct drivers. After you install the network adapter, Windows 2000 can automatically detect and install it on your Windows 2000 system. Like other hardware, if you are having problems with the network adapter, consult the device manager to see whether any conflicts exist. Also, be sure to visit the manufacturer's Web site for any known issues.

Prep Test

1 What should you always check before installing any hardware device?

A ○ LCH

B ○ CHL

C ○ HCL

D ○ Warranty

2 You need to store data across several disks. You need to ensure the best performance. What kind of volume should you use?

A ○ Spanned

B ○ Striped

C ○ Mirrored

D ○ RAID-5

3 You install a new video card in a Windows 2000 computer. On reboot, the boot process fails. What should you do?

A ○ Run the Recovery Console.

B ○ Use the ERD.

C ○ Boot into VGA Mode.

D ○ Rerun the registry.

4 Jill uses a mobile computer. When she is not connected to the network and working on batteries, Jill notices that her battery runs down rather quickly. What does Jill need to do?

A ○ Buy a new battery.

B ○ Create a hardware profile.

C ○ Use hibernation.

D ○ Create an offline folder.

5 You recently added a USB scanner to a bus-powered USB port. When you try to use the scanner, the scanner does not work. What is the most likely cause of the problem?

A ○ The scanner does not work.

B ○ You need a self-powered hub.

C ○ The device needs to connect directly to the computer.

D ○ The scanner needs to be channeled through the SCSI port.

6 What happens when you uninstall a device's driver from the computer?

A ○ The device uses a generic driver.

B ○ The device is disabled.

C ○ The device is uninstalled.

D ○ Nothing.

7 You need to uninstall a device driver. What tool is best to use?

A ○ Device Manager

B ○ Computer Management

C ○ Driver console

D ○ Group Policy

8 How many processors does Windows 2000 Professional support?

A ○ 2

B ○ 4

C ○ 6

D ○ 9

9 On a computer with two processors, you need to make sure that a certain application is using both processors. What do you need to adjust?

A ○ Multitasking

B ○ Affinity

C ○ Grouping

D ○ Thread string

10 Which statement is *not* true concerning network adapter use on Windows 2000?

A ○ Only PCI adapters can be used.

B ○ You must use a correct driver.

C ○ The adapter must be compatible with Windows 2000.

D ○ They should install through Plug and Play.

Answers

1 **C.** Always check the HCL to make sure that any hardware you install is compatible with Windows 2000. *Review "Installing, configuring, and managing DVD and CD-ROM drives."*

2 **B.** Striped volumes provide the best read performance. *Read "Monitoring and configuring disks."*

3 **C.** VGA mode allows you to boot by using a basic driver so that you can remove the new driver or install a different one. *Review "Installing, configuring, and troubleshooting a video adapter."*

4 **B.** The hardware profile disables devices that are using power unnecessarily while Jill is running on batteries. *See "Implementing, Managing, and Troubleshooting Mobile Computer Hardware."*

5 **B.** The bus-powered hub is unable to provide the power needs of the scanner. *Study "USB devices."*

6 **C.** Removing a driver effectively uninstalls the device. *Study "Updating Drivers."*

7 **A.** Use Device Manager to manage drivers and devices. *Review "Installing, configuring, and managing DVD and CD-ROM drives."*

8 **A.** Windows 2000 Professional only supports two processors. *Study "Monitoring and Configuring Multiple Processing Units."*

9 **B.** Adjust the affinity setting by using Task Manager. *See "Monitoring and Configuring Multiple Processing Units."*

10 **A.** Other network adapters can be used, including USB. *Study "Installing, Configuring, and Troubleshooting Network Adapters."*

Chapter 5: Monitoring and Optimizing System Performance and Reliability

---

Exam Objectives

✔ Manage and troubleshoot driver signing

✔ Configure, manage, and troubleshoot the Task Scheduler

✔ Manage and troubleshoot the use and synchronization of offline files

✔ Optimize and troubleshoot performance of the Windows 2000 Professional desktop

✔ Manage hardware profiles

✔ Recover system state data and user data

As an IT professional, the issues of performance, optimization, monitoring, and reliability will be a constant source of thought and time (not to mention all the other things that you'll have to accomplish). The good news is that Windows 2000 Professional makes performance, optimization, monitoring, and reliability issues rather easy to manage and configure — if you know what you need to do.

This chapter covers system performance and reliability as well as monitoring and optimizing the Windows 2000 Professional system. As you might guess, you can find entire books written on these topics alone, but this chapter explores only the issues that you're likely to see on the Windows 2000 Professional exam:

✦ Manage drivers and the Task Scheduler

✦ Use offline files

✦ Optimize the desktop and manage hardware profiles

✦ Back up and recover data

Manage and Troubleshoot Driver Signing

Windows 2000 provides a new feature called driver signing. Simply put, *driver signing* allows the operating system to verify the files that you've installed or are about to install to determine whether Microsoft has certified those files. With driver signing, you can rest assured that you are installing certified drivers that will work with Windows 2000 and not cause you a bunch of problems.

Typically, driver signing is useful when you have installed different hardware devices, such as keyboards and mice, as well as different internal cards. During installation, Windows 2000 scans the driver and determines whether the driver is digitally signed; then you can determine whether you want to ignore the unsigned driver, see a warning about it, or block it from being installed. Note, however, that just because a driver isn't digitally signed doesn't mean that the driver won't work with Windows 2000. It does, however, mean that you should take precautions because the driver hasn't been tested. You should also make sure that the driver you're attempting to install is coming from a reliable source.

To configure how driver signing works on your computer, right-click My Computer and click Properties from the menu that appears. Click the Hardware tab and click the Driver Signing button. This opens the Driver Signing Options dialog box, as shown in Figure 5-1, from where you can choose the level of Ignore, Warn, or Block. Warn is the default setting.

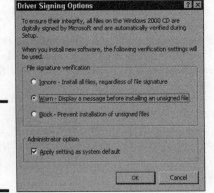

Figure 5-1:
Assign
driver
signing
here.

Also note that you can apply the setting that you choose as the system default. When other users log on to the Windows 2000 Professional computer, the default setting configured by the computer administrator is always applied. This feature allows you to have control over driver signing so that a setting is applied uniformly to all users.

If you want to check the driver files that are currently installed on your computer, you can also run the Signature Verification utility, which you can find in the System Information console, or by just typing **sigverif** at the run line. This simple utility allows you to scan the drivers in your system and check for files that are not signed. You can also create a log file of the results.

Book I
Chapter 5

Monitoring and
Optimizing System
Performance and
Reliability

Configure, Manage, and Troubleshoot the Task Scheduler

Use the Windows 2000 Professional Task Scheduler to schedule mainte-nance tasks that run at specified intervals. In other words, Windows 2000 Professional can help automatically take care of some housecleaning work for you.

The good news is that the Task Scheduler is easy to use. With the exception of a few possible hiccups that we mention in this section, it's generally prob-lem free.

The steps in Lab 5-1 walk you through the process of setting up a scheduled task.

Lab 5-1   Creating a Scheduled Task

1. **Choose Start⇨Settings⇨Control Panel⇨ Scheduled Tasks⇨Add Scheduled Tasks to start the Scheduled Task Wizard.**

2. **Click Next on the opening welcome screen.**

3. **In the task window, as shown in Figure 5-2, choose the application that you want to schedule and click Next.**

   You may need to browse for the application.

Figure 5-2:
Choose a
task to
schedule.

4. **Enter a name for the task and choose how often you want to run the task. Click Next.**

   If you choose a daily, weekly, or monthly schedule, a day/time window appears from which you set when you want the task to run.

5. **Make your selections and click Next.**

6. **Enter your username and password, confirm the password, and then click Next.**

7. **Click Finish.**

   The new task now appears in the Scheduled Tasks folder, which you can access by choosing Start⇨Settings⇨Control Panel⇨Scheduled Tasks.

After you create the scheduled task, you can double-click its icon in the Scheduled Tasks folder and make changes to the task at any time. You can also delete the task by right-clicking it and clicking the Delete option from the menu that appears. Also, you can override the schedule and force the task to run by right-clicking it and clicking Run from the menu that appears.

So what issues concerning the Task Scheduler might the exam throw your way? Remember these important usage and troubleshooting tips:

+ The scheduled task runs regardless of who is logged on to the computer at the moment. If a user is logged on who didn't configure the scheduled task, the task runs in the background.

+ If a task doesn't run, check the schedule and also make sure that the computer's date and time are correct.

+ You can transfer a scheduled task from one computer to another by simply copying the task. However, no security settings are transferred with the task. To manage the security settings after the task has been transferred, right-click the task and click Properties. Click the Security tab and configure security settings as desired.

+ By default, tasks don't run on laptop computers when the computer is running on batteries. However, you can override this behavior by right-clicking the task and clicking Properties. Click the Settings tab; there, clear both the Don't Start the Task if the Computer Is Running on Batteries and the Stop the Task if Battery Mode Begins check boxes.

+ You can also choose to not allow the task to run unless the computer has been idle for a certain period of time. Configure this setting on the Settings tab of the task's Properties dialog box.

Manage and Troubleshoot the Use and Synchronization of Offline Files

Book I
Chapter 5

Monitoring and
Optimizing System
Performance and
Reliability

Suppose that you're working on a document that's stored on a network server. You use a laptop computer, and you must leave the office and travel to a client site. Wouldn't be it be great if you could save that file on your computer and then resynchronize with the server's copy when you're back on the network?

In Windows 2000 Professional, you can do just that by using a feature called *Offline Files*. Offline Files enables you to make editorial changes to a network file when you're not connected to the network. When you reconnect, the file is automatically synchronized with the network copy. The good news (or bad, depending on your perspective) is that you can continue to work on network files, whether you're connected or not.

Offline Files is rather easy to work with after you get it set up. In order to manage Offline Files, you use the Synchronization Manager tool found in Windows 2000 Professional. Note that you can also use this tool to configure Web page offline content. In Lab 5-2, read how to set up your computer for offline file use and how to configure Offline Files.

Lab 5-2   Configuring Offline Files

1. **Make sure that your computer is configured to allow offline files by opening the Control Panel and then opening Folder Options.**

2. **On the Offline Files tab of the Folder Options dialog box, as shown in Figure 5-3, select the Enable Offline Files check box.**

   From this tab, you can enable reminders and automatic synchronization during log off, and you can also determine the maximum amount of disk space that can be used for temporary offline files.

3. **Make any necessary selections and click OK.**

4. **Next, locate the network file or folder that you want to make available offline by right-clicking the file or folder and clicking Make Available Offline from the menu that appears.**

   This opens the Offline Files Wizard.

5. **Click Next on the Welcome screen.**

6. **In the next window, you can choose to automatically synchronize the files when you log on. Leave the Synchronization check box selected and click Next.**

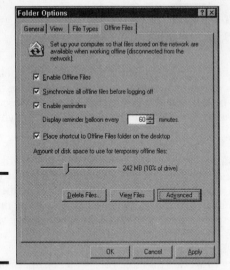

Figure 5-3:
Enable offline file access here.

7. **In the next window, you see that reminders are enabled by default. Leave these enabled if you like (you'll see balloon pop-up reminders from the System Tray), and you can create a shortcut on the desktop to the Offline Files folder. Make your selection and click Finish.**

8. **The Confirm Offline Subfolders dialog box appears, shown in Figure 5-4, where you can choose to make any subfolders available offline as well; make a selection and click OK.**

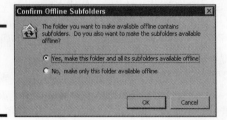

Figure 5-4:
Make sub-folders available offline.

The files are now downloaded and are made available offline. You can see the folder in your Offline Files folder, as shown in Figure 5-5.

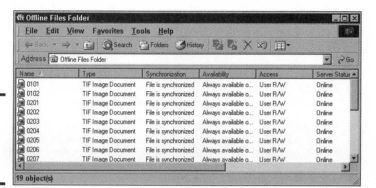

Book I
Chapter 5

Monitoring and
Optimizing System
Performance and
Reliability

Figure 5-5:
Find
available
offline files
here.

On a file server, a Windows 2000 administrator can disable offline access of
folders so that users cannot configure offline access.

After you configure your offline files, you can use the Synchronization tool
to manage synchronization of offline content. You find the Synchronization
Manager by choosing Start⇨Program⇨Accessories⇨Synchronize. See the
Synchronize tool in Figure 5-6.

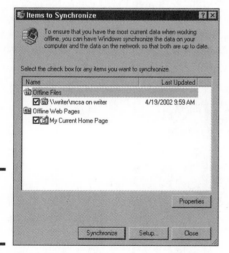

Figure 5-6:
The
Synchroni-
zation tool.

The Synchronization tool is easy to use, so we don't waste your certification
study time wading through the basic options that you'll find here. If you
click the Setup button, though, you can choose how synchronization with
your offline files will occur . . . and even create a schedule.

Offline files are generally easy and problem free to use, but the following are a few issues for troubleshooting purposes that you should keep in mind as you answer questions on the exam:

✦ You can't configure items to synchronize by using the Synchronization Manager. Use this tool to manage synchronization of offline files (or Web pages) that you've already made available offline.

✦ Offline Files is a client-side application; you can make any network-shared files available offline from any computer. In other words, the files don't have to reside on a Windows 2000 Server in order for offline files to work.

✦ If synchronization doesn't seem to work, check the settings and try to use the Synchronization Manager to manually synchronize the file. *Note:* You must be online *and* the computer that holds the master file must be online as well for synchronization to work.

✦ When you're working on a network file, you can determine what offline files should do if you lose network connectivity. This issue seems to be an exam favorite, and the exam may try to confuse you about where to configure the behavior. *Hint:* It's not Synchronization Manager; rather, you return to the Offline Files tab on the Folder Options dialog box. Click the Advanced button. You'll see the Offline Files — Advanced Settings dialog box, as shown in Figure 5-7. You can have the computer notify you and begin working offline when a connection is lost — or never go offline, which will prevent you from working with the file. You can also create an exception list so that your computer acts a certain way with a certain computer by clicking the Add button.

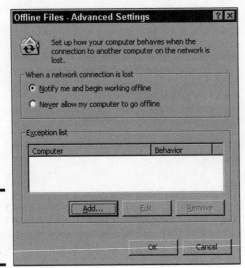

Figure 5-7:
Advanced settings for offline files.

Optimize and Troubleshoot Performance of the Windows 2000 Desktop

Book I
Chapter 5

Monitoring and
Optimizing System
Performance and
Reliability

Desktop performance refers to general performance of Windows 2000 Professional. In other words, this defines how quickly Windows 2000 is able to handle processor requests and how the system generally behaves.

As an IT professional, you're likely to see a lot of complaints and problems concerning performance — some legitimate and some not — but you'll need to be able to troubleshoot a variety of issues. Read about the likely exam issues concerning those potential performance problems in the following sections.

Optimize and troubleshoot memory performance

A simple truth governs all actions that you might take concerning memory performance: No substitute exists for physical RAM. If your Windows 2000 Professional computer is barely limping along, you simply need to add more RAM. If you're running high performance applications, such as video and picture-editing software, you'll probably need more RAM.

Aside from adding more physical RAM to the system, you can also take a couple of actions to make sure that your computer is using the RAM that it has to the best of its ability.

Right-click My Computer and choose Properties from the menu that opens. On the Advanced tab, click the Performance Options button. In the Performance Options dialog box, you should optimize performance for Applications, not Background Services. The Background Services setting is sometimes needed on server platforms, but for a client operating system, Applications optimization is your best choice, as shown in Figure 5-8.

Figure 5-8:
Set per-
formance
options
here.

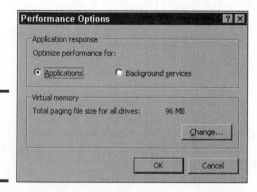

You also take a look at virtual memory settings here as well. Click the Change button and the Virtual Memory window appears, as shown in Figure 5-9. By default, Windows 2000 handles the virtual memory settings automatically, and this is almost always the best choice. The system creates an initial and maximum site of the paging file, based on the size of your computer's hard drive, so that data can overflow from RAM and be written to the hard drive. Note that virtual memory is a helper application for RAM — not a replacement for it. Increasing or decreasing the size of the paging file size is likely to cause you more problems than it solves. So once again, if the computer is low on memory, the only real solution is to add more physical RAM.

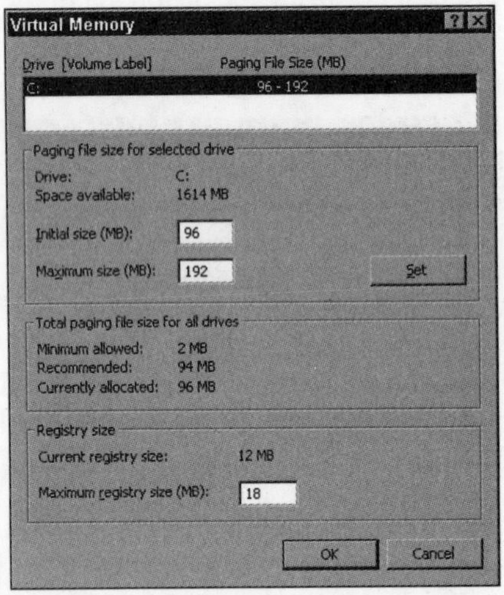

Figure 5-9:
Set virtual
memory
here.

Optimize and troubleshoot processor utilization

The processor handles requests placed on it by the Windows 2000 Professional operating system and all applications that you have running. The more applications that you run, the more you tax the CPU cycles. So how can you really optimize a processor? The only real thing that you can do is either reduce the number of applications that are in use at any single given time or upgrade the hardware to a faster processor. If your processor meets the minimum requirements required by Windows 2000, you'll be able to get by; however, many applications require faster processors to handle the processor cycles that they need.

You can use System Monitor, found in the Performance console, which is found in the Administrative Tools folder in Control Panel, to monitor the performance of the processor. Although offering much information on the use of Performance Monitor is beyond the scope of this book, you should get familiar with it and use it before taking the exam just so that you're familiar with how it works and how it can help you troubleshoot problems.

Book I
Chapter 5

Monitoring and
Optimizing System
Performance and
Reliability

If the system seems to be running slowly, use Performance Monitor to monitor the processor counters. If the processor appears to be utilized over 80 percent of the time, you probably need an upgrade.

Optimize and troubleshoot disk performance

For the most part, hard drives require little to no attention from you. After hard drives are installed and configured how you want, they take care of themselves. However, one problem that can occur with hard drives is fragmentation. As files are written, rewritten, deleted, edited, and moved, pieces of those files are stored in different locations on the hard drive instead of a contiguous format. This process, called *fragmentation*, is a normal part of disk use. However, disks that are heavily fragmented don't perform as well.

What are the signs that a disk is fragmented? If opening, closing, and saving files has become slower and slower over time, the problem is most likely fragmentation. The good news is that Windows 2000 Professional includes a Disk Defragmenter utility that can at least reduce the amount of fragmentation on a hard drive.

You'll find Disk Defragmenter by choosing Start⇨Programs⇨Accessories⇨ System Tools. Use the Disk Defragmenter interface, as shown in Figure 5-10, to analyze a drive to see whether it needs to be defragmented — and then easily defragment that drive if necessary. Depending on the size of the hard drive, defrag may take several hours.

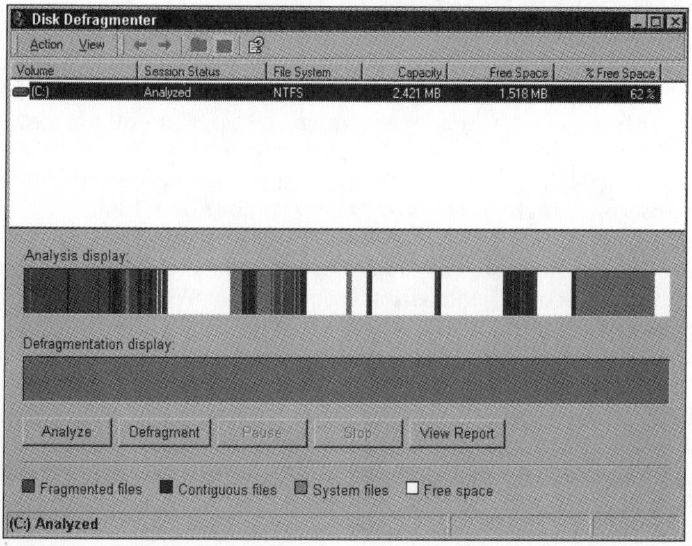

Figure 5-10:
Defrag a
disk from
here.

If Disk Defragmenter keeps stopping before it has completed, you need to close all programs and close the programs in the system tray. Disk Defragmenter needs exclusive disk access to run, so make sure that everything else is closed, including any antivirus programs.

Optimize and troubleshoot application performance

Application performance primarily falls into the same category as memory and processor utilization performance. Any applications that you attempt to run on Windows 2000 Professional should be compatible with Windows 2000 Professional. Although some older programs will work just fine, your best bet is to only use programs that are tested and compatible with Windows 2000.

Besides the compatibility issue, your programs must have enough RAM and processor power available to run the way that they should. There is simply no substitute, so make sure that applications will get what they need before installing them on a particular Windows 2000 Professional computer.

Most all processes and functions on Windows 2000 Professional can be monitored with Performance Monitor, which is the same tool available in Windows 2000 Server. See Book II, Chapter 5 to discover more about using Performance Monitor and possible counters that you might run across on the exam.

Manage Hardware Profiles

Hardware profiles enable you to configure a computer for use in different situations. Consider this example. Suppose that you use a laptop computer that connects to a docking bay when you're in the office. You have several PC cards installed that connect to different peripheral devices. However, when you're traveling and using battery power, you want to make sure that the PC cards don't drain the battery and waste system resources. Situations like this are exactly where hardware profiles are helpful.

Hardware profiles are easy to configure and easy to manage, and you should certainly get some hands-on practice on your Windows 2000 Professional computer.

A computer has one default hardware profile, which basically contains all the hardware currently configured on the system. With this default profile, all the hardware that you've configured works when you boot your computer. The concept of a hardware profile even existing is initially invisible to users because they don't have to interact with it. However, in the case of a mobile computer or even a desktop computer with special needs, you can easily create an additional hardware profile, or even more if needed. After

Book I
Chapter 5

Monitoring and
Optimizing System
Performance and
Reliability

the profile is created, you'll see a boot menu appear each time that you start Windows 2000 Professional so that you can select the profile you want to boot into.

To create a hardware profile, follow the steps in Lab 5-3.

Lab 5-3   Configuring a Hardware Profile

1. Right-click My Computer, choose Properties from the menu that appears, and click the Hardware tab.

2. Click the Hardware Profiles button.

From the Hardware Profiles dialog box that opens, you can see the Original Configuration (default or current) listed under Available Hardware Profiles, as shown in Figure 5-11.

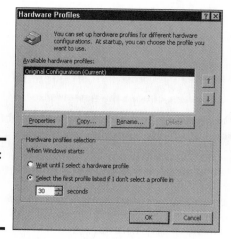

Figure 5-11:
Set
hardware
profiles
here.

3. To create a new profile, click the Copy button.

The Copy dialog box appears in which you can name the copy.

4. Enter a name in the Copy dialog box and then click OK.

5. The new profile now appears with the original profile in the Hardware Profiles dialog box. Click the Properties button.

6. On the General tab that appears for the new Profile Properties window, as shown in Figure 5-12, you can let Windows know whether this is a portable computer and what state the computer is in under this profile. Make any desired selections and click OK.

You're returned to the Hardware Profiles dialog box.

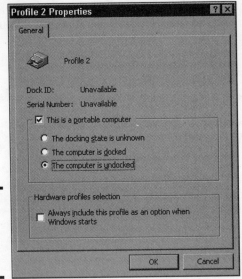

Figure 5-12:
Set new
profile
properties
here.

7. **Click OK on the Hardware Profiles window and restart the computer.**

8. **When the boot menu appears, choose the new profile.**

9. **After the computer boots, open Device Manager and disable any devices that you don't want to use under the profile.**

The next time that you start your computer under this profile, the devices that you chose to disable are automatically disabled.

If you run across exam questions concerning laptop computers and hardware that drains the batteries when disconnected from the network, the answer is to always create an additional hardware profile that disables the devices that aren't used when not connected to the network.

Recover System State Data and User Data

For the exam, understand the difference between System State data and User data. *User data* simply refers to data on your system that is accessed by users. Common examples include documents, files, applications, and so forth. *System State data* is used by your operating system and contains the following, which you need to know for the exam:

✦ Registry

✦ COM+ Class Registration database

✦ System boot files

Windows 2000 domain controllers also contain the Active Directory services database and the SYSVOL directory — member servers don't contain this data because they don't run the Active Directory. Watch out for tricky exam questions concerning the differences in member server and domain controller System State data.

Book I
Chapter 5

Monitoring and
Optimizing System
Performance and
Reliability

Reviewing Backup Concepts

Like Windows NT, Windows 2000 has some different types of backup that you can implement. In fact, both systems support the same backup types, and this section reviews those concepts for you.

We can't define only one correct way to back up data. Your backup plan depends on the needs of your network, the type of data used, and the critical nature of the data. You don't need to back up files on a regular basis if those files rarely change, but you do need an effective backup plan for data that changes daily so that you can recover the most recent version of that data.

Windows 2000 enables you to use various backup media, such as tape drives, Zip drives, CD-ROM drives, and even hard drives on remote computers.

You need to know the different types of backup for the exam, so you should carefully review the following descriptions:

✦ **Normal:** Backs up all files and folders that you select. A normal backup doesn't use markers to determine which files have been backed up, and it doesn't remove existing markers. Each file is marked as having been backed up. A normal backup is the easiest type of backup to restore, but it can be slow depending on the amount of data.

✦ **Copy:** Backs up all selected files and folders but doesn't look at markers and doesn't clear any existing markers.

✦ **Differential:** Backs up only selected files and folders that contain a marker. A differential backup doesn't clear the existing markers.

✦ **Incremental:** Backs up selected files and folders with a marker and then clears the existing marker.

✦ **Daily:** Backs up all selected files and folders that have changed during the day. A daily backup doesn't look at or clear markers but is an effective way to back up files and folders that have changed during the day.

Creating a backup plan is an important part of the planning process. Most network environments use a combination of normal backups and differential or incremental backups. For example, you may use a normal backup on Monday and then perform incremental backups throughout the rest of the week. The key is finding the balance between ease of data recovery and the amount of time required to perform the backup each day.

Using Windows Backup

Windows 2000 offers an easy-to-use Backup tool. You access the Backup tool
by choosing Start⇨Programs⇨Accessories⇨System Tools⇨Backup.

As shown in Figure 5-13, the Backup tool's interface has four tabs. You can
start the Backup Wizard by clicking its button on the Welcome tab, or you
can manually create a backup job by using the other tabs.

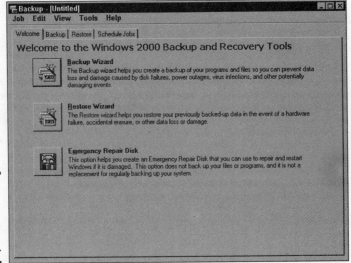

Figure 5-13:
Use the
Backup tool
to configure
backup jobs.

For the exam, you need to know how the Backup Wizard works. You also
need to know how to configure a backup job manually. You can review both
processes in the following sections.

Working with the Backup Wizard

Lab 5-4 walks you through the steps for using the Backup Wizard. You
should practice this lab on your server.

Lab 5-4   Using the Windows Backup Wizard

1. **On the Welcome tab, click the Backup Wizard button.**

2. **Click Next on the Welcome screen that appears.**

3. **In the What to Back Up dialog box that appears, specify whether you
   want to back up everything on the computer, only selected files,
   drives, or network data, or only System State data. After you select
   the appropriate radio button, click Next.**

Book I
Chapter 5

Monitoring and
Optimizing System
Performance and
Reliability

If you choose to back up only selected files, the wizard displays a dialog box so that you can select the files that you want to back up.

4. **If necessary, select the desired files and then click Next.**

5. **Select the backup media that you plan to use by entering the drive path or by clicking the Browse button and then selecting the desired path in the provided dialog box. Click Next.**

6. **In the wizard's completion dialog box, click Advanced to configure additional options.**

7. **In the Type of Backup dialog box (Figure 5-14) that appears, use the drop-down list to select either normal, copy, incremental, differential, or daily backup; you can also select the Backup Migrated Remote Storage Data check box. Click Next.**

Windows 2000 supports *remote storage,* which enables your computer to store data in a remote storage location — for example, a tape drive — if the storage space on your hard drive runs low. If you select the backup remote storage option, Windows Backup reads the data stored in remote storage and backs it up as well.

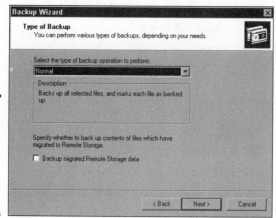

Figure 5-14:
Select the backup type as well as remote storage data backup.

In the How to Back Up dialog box, you have options for verifying data after backup and using hardware compression.

You can specify that the system should verify the backup data for integrity before the backup job completes. This option causes your backup job to take more time, but it does ensure that your backup job was successful. If hardware compression is available on your server, you can use hardware compression to reduce the amount of storage space that a backup job consumes.

You can only restore compressed backups on drives that support compression. If your hardware doesn't support compression, this option will be grayed out.

8. **Select the desired backup options and click Next.**

   In the Media Options dialog box that appears, you can choose to append the backup job to existing media or to replace the data on the backup media with this backup. If you choose to replace the media, you can also specify that only the owner or an administrator can have access to the backup data and to backups appended to the replacement data.

9. **Select the desired media options and click Next.**

10. **In the Backup Label dialog box that appears, provide a backup label and media label, if desired, and then click Next.**

11. **In the When to Backup dialog box that appears, indicate whether you want to run the backup now or later by selecting the appropriate radio button and clicking Next.**

    If you choose later, enter a job name and start date. If you click the Set Schedule button, you can enter an exact start time and other minor options, such as beginning the backup when the computer is idle.

12. **Click Finish to complete the wizard.**

    Depending on the options you chose, the backup job begins immediately or at the scheduled time.

Performing a manual backup

The Backup Wizard is a handy tool to help you configure backup jobs. After you become a pro at creating backup jobs, you may want to perform them manually. This is usually quicker, and you have the same options that the wizard provides.

To manually configure a backup job, access Windows Backup by choosing Start➪Programs➪Accessories➪System Tools➪Backup and then click the Backup tab, as shown in Figure 5-15.

Specify what you want to back up by selecting the appropriate check boxes. You can back up individual files, System State data, or entire drives, as desired. At the bottom of the Backup tab, use the Browse button to select the backup media.

If you want to configure additional options for the backup job, choose Tools➪Options. On the tabs in the resulting Options dialog box, you can select the type of backup, backup log, and other features that you also see when using the Backup Wizard.

Book I
Chapter 5

Monitoring and
Optimizing System
Performance and
Reliability

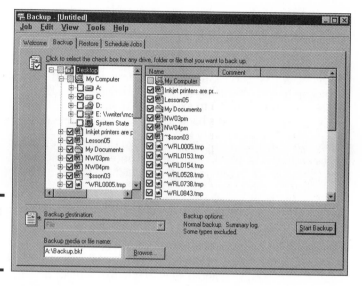

Figure 5-15:
Manually
configure a
backup job.

After you select the desired options, you can click the Start Backup button on the Backup tab, or you can click the Schedule Jobs tab to schedule the job. The Schedule Jobs tab displays a calendar on which you can select the backup dates and times.

Restoring Data

You realize the benefits of backing up data after you experience a system or disk failure. After your system becomes operational again, you can use the Windows Backup tool to restore the data that you previously backed up.

To restore data, you can use the Restore Wizard (accessible from the Welcome tab of the Backup tool), or you can use the Restore tab to manually run the restorable process. The wizard displays only a few dialog boxes that enable you to determine what you want to restore and the location of the backup job. Use the Advanced button to determine where on your hard drive to restore the data and whether the restore operation should replace any of the same existing files on your system. The system then restores the data. You can manually select the same restore all options by using the Restore tab.

Using Safe Mode

All Windows 2000 computers have Safe Mode capabilities (thank goodness!) so that you can attempt to solve problems with your server when it won't start.

Windows 2000 provides the following types of Safe Mode, and you need to know them for the exam:

✦ **Safe Mode:** Starts Windows 2000 by using only basic files and minimal drivers. With this type of Safe Mode, you can start the system so that you can troubleshoot and hopefully resolve the problem. If you still can't start your system by using Safe Mode, you probably need to use the Emergency Repair Disk (ERD) to correct system problems.

✦ **Safe Mode with Networking:** Starts Windows 2000 by using only basic files and drivers, but also provides a network connection so that you can gain access to the network while in Safe Mode.

✦ **Safe Mode with Command Prompt:** Starts Windows 2000 with only basic files and drivers. After you log on, the system displays the command prompt instead of your Windows desktop.

✦ **Enable Boot Logging:** Starts Windows 2000 while logging all the drivers and services that are or are not loaded by the system. The log file is called NTBTLOG.TXT, and it's located in the %WINDIR% directory. By using this feature, you can review the boot log and determine the exact cause of your system problem.

✦ **Enable VGA Mode:** Starts Windows 2000 by using the basic VGA driver. It's not uncommon to have problems after installing a new video card and driver, so this option installs the basic VGA driver. By using this option, you can resolve the VGA driver problem. Windows always uses VGA mode when you start the system in Safe Mode, Safe Mode with Networking, or Safe Mode with Command Prompt.

✦ **Last Known Good Configuration:** Starts Windows 2000 by using the registry information that Windows saved during the last shutdown. (Windows NT also offers this option.) This feature boots the system using the last good configuration that was saved and is only useful when incorrect configuration has caused the problem. Last Known Good Configuration doesn't solve problems with corrupt files or drivers, and any configuration changes made since the last successful startup are lost.

✦ **Debugging Mode:** Starts Windows 2000 while sending debug information to another computer through a serial cable.

Windows 2000 domain controllers also have a Directory Service Restore Mode, which you can use to troubleshoot Active Directory problems or restore the Active Directory database when a failure has occurred. Keep in mind for the exam that this option is available only on domain controllers and not on member servers.

To start your system in Safe Mode, turn on your server and hold down the F8 key. The Safe Mode menu appears, and you can select the type of safe mode that you want to use by pressing the arrow keys.

**Book I
Chapter 5**

Monitoring and
Optimizing System
Performance and
Reliability

Using the Recovery Console

The Recovery Console is command-line console feature of Windows 2000 that enables you to perform powerful administrative tasks on a system that won't start. Use the Recovery Console to start and stop services, read and write data to the local drive(s), format drives, and perform many other tasks. The Recovery Console is particularly useful if you need to replace corrupt system files with new copies from the installation CD-ROM. Only administrators have rights to use the Recovery Console.

You can start the Recovery Console in two ways. First, if you can't start your server, you can launch the Recovery Console from the setup disks or from your installation CD-ROM (if your computer supports booting from a CD-ROM drive). Second, you can install the Recovery Console on your computer so that it's available as a boot menu option.

To install the Recovery Console so that it appears as a boot menu option, follow the steps in Lab 5-5.

Lab 5-5   Installing the Recovery Console

1. **Insert your Windows 2000 installation CD-ROM into the CD-ROM drive.**

2. **At the command prompt, switch to your CD-ROM drive and then type** \i386\winnt32.exe/cmdcons.

   A message appears, telling you about the Recovery Console.

3. **Click Yes to install it as a start-up option.**

   File copy begins, and the console is installed.

When you boot your computer by using the Recovery Console (either by start-up disk, CD-ROM, or as a start-up option), the basic console is displayed. You're prompted to select which Windows 2000 installation you want to log on to (for dual-boot systems). You then provide your administrator password. You can then perform the desired actions, or you can type **Help** to see a list of available actions and proper syntax.

You don't need to know every syntax option for the exam, but you do need to know the basic options and what you can do with them. Table 5-1 describes those options so that you can easily memorize them.

Table 5-1	Recovery Console Tasks
Task	*What It Does*
Disable	Disables system services or device drivers
Enable	Enables system services or device drivers
Exit	Closes the Recovery Console and restarts your computer
Fixboot	Writes a new partition boot sector to the system partition
Fixmbr	Writes a new master boot record to the hard drive
Logon	Logs you on to an installation of Windows 2000
Map	Displays a mapping of drive letters to physical device names
Systemroot	Sets the current directory to the systemroot folder

In addition to the basic console tasks listed in Table 5-1, several Recovery Console commands are available. Table 5-2 describes these commands, which you should memorize for the exam.

Table 5-2	Recovery Console Commands
Command	*What It Does*
Attrib	Changes the attributes of a file or directory
Batch	Executes the commands specified in a text file
ChDir (CD)	Displays the name of the current directory or changes the current directory
Chkdsk	Checks a disk and displays a status report
Cls	Clears the screen
Copy	Copies a single file to another location
Delete (Del)	Deletes one or more files
Dir	Displays a list of files and subdirectories in a directory
Diskpart	Manages partitions on your hard drives
Expand	Extracts a file from a compressed file
Format	Formats a disk
Listsvc	Lists the services and drivers available on the computer
Mkdir (Md)	Creates a directory
Rename (Ren)	Renames a directory
Rmdir (Rd)	Deletes a directory
Set	Displays and sets environment variables

Prep Test

1 Which default driver signing setting is used in Windows 2000?

A ○ Ignore

B ○ Warn

C ○ Block

D ○ Disable

2 You notice that scheduled tasks don't run when your laptop computer is running on batteries. You want to make sure that scheduled tasks continue to run, even in battery mode. What do you need to do?

A ○ Configure the option in the Synchronization Manager.

B ○ Configure the laptop for compatibility mode.

C ○ Change the battery options on the Settings tab of the task's Properties dialog box.

D ○ Change the battery options on the Advanced tab of the task's Properties dialog box.

3 You need to configure a folder for offline use. However, the folder is stored on a Windows XP computer. Which statement is true?

A ○ You can use the folder offline with no additional configuration.

B ○ Offline Files isn't compatible with Windows XP.

C ○ You must run the `WINOFFXP` command.

D ○ Windows XP requires background synchronization.

4 You have an offline file configured, but when the server computer goes offline, the file becomes unavailable. What do you need to do to make the file work when offline?

A ○ Configure the option on the Offline Files tab of the Advanced Settings dialog box.

B ○ Use Synchronization Manager to force the connection.

C ○ Move the file to a Windows 2000 Server.

D ○ Configure the offline file for a persistent connection.

5 Your computer runs out of memory very quickly when two applications are open. You check the memory and realize that the amount of RAM barely meets the minimum requirements for Windows 2000 Professional. What solution will help you?

A ○ Increase virtual memory.

B ○ Decrease virtual memory.

C ○ Run the applications in compatibility mode.

D ○ Install more physical RAM.

6 Which tool can help you identify problems with processor, RAM, application performance, and other problems?

A ○ Network Monitor

B ○ System Monitor

C ○ System Change Tool

D ○ Disk Defragmenter

7 You use a laptop computer that runs on batteries when you're away from the office. When you're at the office, you use several peripherals and PC cards. The PC cards seem to put a drain on your batteries, however, when you're not connected to the network. What is your best solution?

A ○ Purchase better batteries.

B ○ Create a hardware profile.

C ○ Disable the devices when they're not in use.

D ○ Remove the device drivers when they're not in use.

8 Which of the following is not a part of System State data in Windows 2000 Professional?

A ○ COM+ Classes

B ○ Registry

C ○ Active Directory database

D ○ System boot files

9 Which kind of backup backs up the files and clears the existing markers?

A ○ Normal

B ○ Copy

C ○ Differential

D ○ Incremental

10 You've recently installed a new video driver. When you tried to reboot the computer, the boot failed. What do you need to do?

A ○ Boot and use System Restore.

B ○ Boot by using Enable VGA Mode.

C ○ Create a new hardware profile.

D ○ Boot by using Debugging Mode.

Answers

1 **B.** The default driver signing setting is Warn to warn of driver files that aren't digitally signed. *Review "Manage and Troubleshoot Driver Signing."*

2 **C.** You can clear the power management options on this tab so that tasks will run when the computer runs on batteries. *Read "Configure, Manage, and Troubleshoot the Task Scheduler."*

3 **A.** Offline Files is a client-side service, so it doesn't matter what network computer holds the actual file. *Review "Manage and Troubleshoot the Use and Synchronization of Offline Files."*

4 **A.** Use the Advanced Settings dialog box to make sure that you see a warning that the computer is offline and that allows you to continue working on the file. *See "Manage and Troubleshoot the Use and Synchronization of Offline Files."*

5 **D.** The only viable solution in this case is to simply install more physical RAM. *Study "Optimize and troubleshoot memory performance."*

6 **B.** System Monitor allows you to chart Windows 2000 performance items and find problems. *Study "Optimize and troubleshoot processor utilization."*

7 **B.** The hardware profile is your best solution in cases like these so that the laptop works well in both situations. *Study "Manage Hardware Profiles."*

8 **C.** The Active Directory database only resides on Windows 2000 domain controllers. *Study "Recover System State Data and User Data."*

9 **D.** Incremental backups back up the selected files and clear existing markers. *See "Reviewing Backup Concepts."*

10 **B.** This option boots Windows 2000 with a basic VGA driver so that you can remove the card or update the real driver *Study "Using Safe Mode."*

Chapter 6: Configuring and Troubleshooting the Desktop Environment

Exam Objectives

✓ Configuring and managing user profiles

✓ Configuring support for multiple languages or multiple locations

✓ Managing applications by using Windows Installer packages

✓ Configuring and troubleshooting desktop settings

✓ Configuring and troubleshooting fax support

✓ Configuring and troubleshooting accessibility services

The desktop environment refers to a number of Windows 2000 settings and options that makes the desktop helpful to users, including user profiles, multiple languages, desktop settings, and other features. As an IT professional, you need to know a thing or two about supporting the Windows 2000 Professional desktop, and the Windows 2000 Professional exam (Exam 70-210) certainly expects you to know a thing or two as well.

In this chapter, we take a look at desktop configuration issues. You should study this chapter and get some hands-on practice configuring the options explored. As always, we only focus on the issues you are most likely to see on the Windows 2000 Professional exam.

- ✦ Managing user profiles
- ✦ Configuring Windows 2000 Professional for multiple languages
- ✦ Managing desktop settings and Windows Installer packages
- ✦ Configuring desktop settings
- ✦ Configuring fax and accessibility services

Configuring and Managing User Profiles

User profiles allow two or more users to use the same computer, but have individual desktop settings and folders. Let's say that in your environment, two different shifts of workers log on to the same computers. With user profiles, the user can set his or her own wallpaper and other desktop settings that appear each time he or she logs onto the computer. The user can also maintain separate documents and folders.

User profiles are certainly nothing new in Windows operating systems, but they are easier to use and configure in Windows 2000 networks. User profiles are stored in `\Documents and Settings\`*Username*. Inside the folder are additional folders that hold the user's settings, such as Favorites, Cookies, and a folder called Desktop.

When a new user is created, a new *Username* and *Username*`\Desktop` folder is created for him or her. This keeps users' settings and information separate.

It is important to keep in mind that Windows 2000 Group Policy can also impact what users can see on their desktops and what they can do. User profiles work with group policy as necessary, but any Group Policy settings from a Windows site, domain, or organizational unit can always override any user settings.

Because Windows 2000 Professional handles profile creation automatically by creating the necessary folders for each user, you don't have to manually configure anything. However, depending on your network needs, you may choose to invoke some additional settings. Lab 6-1 shows you how to access the Profile properties dialog box for an existing user account.

Lab 6-1   Accessing Profile Properties

1. **Choose Start⇨Settings⇨Control Panel⇨Users and Passwords.**

2. **Click the Advanced tab and then click the Advanced button.**

3. **The Local Users and Groups console appears. Select the Users container, shown in Figure 6-1.**

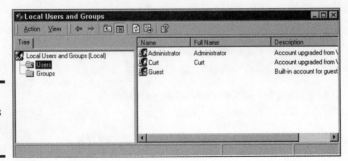

Figure 6-1:
Local Users
and Groups
console.

Book I
Chapter 6

Configuring and
Troubleshooting the
Desktop
Environment

4. **In the right console pane, right-click the desired user account and choose Properties from the context menu that appears.**

   This brings up the Properties dialog box for that user, which contains three tabs: General, Member Of, and Profile.

5. **Click the Profile tab, shown in Figure 6-2.**

   By default, you see no entries on the tab. The default profile is storing information in the user's folder and has no additional configuration.

   In this tab, you can change settings for the Profile path, Logon script, and the Home folder, which we discuss in the next sections.

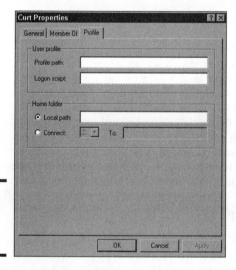

Figure 6-2:
Accessing
a user's
profile.

Profile path

The Profile path tab in the Properties dialog box, shown in Figure 6-2, tells Windows where to look for the user profile. If this dialog box is empty, Windows defaults to the standard location, `system_drive\Documents and Settings\Username`.

However, what if you move the Username folder to a different drive on the computer in order to save disk space on the primary drive? In this case, you would need to change the path to point to this new location. There are a couple of other reasons for changing the profile path, which you should keep in mind for the exam:

✦ You can use the profile to point to a different account. For example, say you normally log on as "user" but you occasionally log on as an administrator. You can configure the administrator profile to point to the "user" account so that you have the same desktop settings, regardless of what account you log on.

✦ Because the Documents and Settings folder holds all user profile folders, you can consider moving the profile folder to a different location or even a different disk for security purposes.

✦ If you log on to two different domains, you'll have a user profile for each domain. You can change this behavior by editing the profile path to point to one profile. This way, your settings are the same regardless of what domain you log on.

Using a roaming profile

You can move the profile path to any location on your computer, as long as you enter a path in the Profile path box. However, you can also store the profile on the network and enter a network address to the path as well. As you may imagine, the ability to store the profile on the network has many implications. This feature, known as a *roaming profile*, allows a user to log on to any network workstation and receive the same profile, rather than just a local machine. To use a roaming profile, simply store the Username folder on a desired server. Pull up the Profile tab on the user's Properties box (see Lab 6-1 earlier in this chapter), enter the Profile Path as \\servername\ sharename\username, and then click OK. The server folder must be shared and permissions configured accordingly so that users can access the roaming user profile. Also, the user must have a local account on each computer he or she wants to log on.

Using logon scripts

Logon scripts are not used as much as they were in the past, but Windows 2000 still allows you to configure a logon script for the user. In the Logon script entry, just enter the name and path to the logon script. When the user logs on, the profile is checked and the script is run.

Using a home folder

When you save a document for the first time, Windows typically defaults to My Documents. However, when you set a home folder, the home folder becomes the new default location to save documents. You can specify a local path to the home folder or use a mapped network drive by clicking the Connect radio button and selecting the drive from the drop-down list box, as you can see in Figure 6-2. However, some applications do not query Windows for the home folder to use, and in this case, you have to manually choose the location that you want the user to save to.

Configuring Support for Multiple Languages and Locations

Book I
Chapter 6

Configuring and
Troubleshooting the
Desktop
Environment

Windows 2000 Professional supports the use of multiple languages as well as locations. By locations, Windows means geographic locations where languages, currency, numbers, and other features vary. At first glance, the option of configuring multiple languages and locations seems very easy. In truth, the actual configuration is easy, but the exam may ask you tricky questions concerning multiple languages and locations. You need to get some hands-on practice configuring these options. You also need to memorize the features.

Enabling multiple language support

Multiple language support allows you two major features. First, you can configure a language and see Windows screens and dialog boxes in that language. Or, you can create documents and send e-mail in a different language. Choosing a "locale" enables you to tell Windows how you want to see Windows components (screens, dialog boxes, and so on). Windows 2000 supports 24 major languages. You can install additional languages by accessing the Language Options feature during Windows 2000 Professional setup.

Configuring multiple language support for users

You can configure locale settings by choosing Start⇨Settings⇨Control Panel⇨Regional Options to open the Regional Options dialog box. Also note that if you are a domain or OU administrator, you can apply locale settings to all desktops through Group Policy as well.

After you open the Regional Options dialog box, you see a General tab that displays the current locale, shown in Figure 6-3. By default, the system is set to English as the locale, but the system supports document reading and writing in a variety of standard other languages. These settings mean that we use United States English, numbers, currency, time, and date information in the system, but we can also type documents in different languages and read documents in a different language as well. Again, the multiple language feature allows you to set a locale, but read and write documents in different languages as needed. To change the locale, just use the drop-down menu and select a different locale. Then, use the numbers, currency, time, and date tabs to make adjustments to these values as needed.

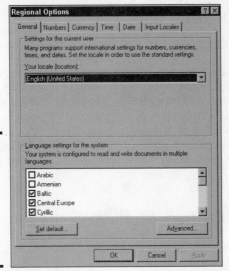

Figure 6-3:
Set a locale
in the
General tab
of the
Regional
Options
dialog box.

Configuring multiple locations

For example, say you work on a laptop computer. You are fluent in both English and French and travel frequently between Paris and New York. You want to be able to quickly and easily change locales between Paris and New York.

As an IT support specialist, you may run into this kind of situation, and you may certainly see it on the exam. The good news is that Windows 2000 can easily support multiple locales and you can toggle between those locales with a hot key. Users do not need to manually change the configuration: They just press the hot key to change over to another language. You need to know how to set up a computer for multiple locations for the exam, and Lab 6-2 walks you through this process.

Lab 6-2   Configuring Multiple Locations

1. **Open Regional Options by choosing Start⇨Settings⇨Control Panel⇨Regional Options.**

2. **Click the Input Locales tab.**

   On the Input Locales tab, you see the current input language in the provided dialog box, shown in Figure 6-4.

Book I
Chapter 6

Configuring and
Troubleshooting the
Desktop
Environment

3. To add another input language, click the Add button.

The Add Input Locale dialog box appears.

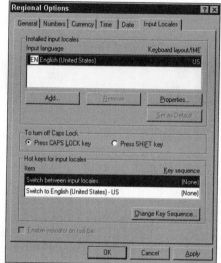

Figure 6-4:
Add another
Input
language in
the Input
Locales tab.

4. In the Add Input Locale dialog box (Figure 6-5), click the drop-down menu, select the input language that you want to add, and click OK.

Now both languages appear on the Input Locales tab.

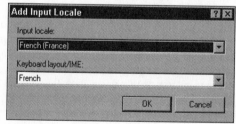

Figure 6-5:
Add another
input locale.

5. Repeat Steps 3 and 4 to add additional input locales.

6. To enable users to toggle between the input locales by pressing a hot key, click the Change Key Sequence button.

7. In the Change Key Sequence dialog box, shown in Figure 6-6, click the Enable Key Sequence check box. Select either the CTRL or Left ALT radio button to select which key users press in combination with a keyboard character to activate the hot key by using the provided check boxes.

8. Click OK again on the Input Locales tab to save your changes.

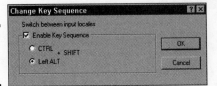

Figure 6-6:
Creating a
hot key.

Managing Applications Using Windows Installer Packages

Windows Installer Packages are one of those exam objectives you are unlikely to see much of on the exam, mainly because the issues surrounding Windows Installer Packages do not make very good exam fodder. We hit the high points and move on because this one won't give you much worry.

Applications can be installed and uninstalled on Windows 2000 by using Windows Installer Packages. The Windows Installer Packages contain all of the EXE and DLL files that are found in an application. The installer's job is to install the package on a computer. Software developers handle the creation of software and often the packaging in Windows Installer packages.

What does all of this have to do with the IT professional? Your job is to deploy and manage applications, and Windows Installer Packages can certainly make that job easier. Using Windows Installer Packages, users can manually install an application by running setup.exe locally or over the network. For the exam, the mention of Windows Installer Packages you are likely to see concerns Group Policy. Using Windows 2000 Server, you can deploy Windows Installer Packages to Windows 2000 Professional desktops by publishing or assigning them in the Group Policy. You can also remove applications automatically by using the same process.

On the Windows 2000 Professional exam, you are not likely to see detailed questions about using Group Policy, but it pops up from time to time. Just remember that in a Windows network, Group Policy on Windows 2000

Server is the preferred method of rolling out and managing software, using Windows Installer Packages.

The Windows 2000 Professional exam tests your knowledge of administering Windows 2000 Professional, which you sometimes do through Windows 2000 Server. If your server knowledge and skills are weak, study Book II (which covers Exam 70-215) as well as Book I before taking the Windows 2000 Professional exam.

Configuring and Troubleshooting Desktop Settings

Desktop settings refer to a collection of settings that comprise what the user sees on the desktop. This refers to Start menu items, wallpaper, taskbar configuration, and a variety of other settings. For the most part, configuring desktop settings is easy, and in this section, we look at desktop settings from an administrative point of view because that is the approach the exam takes. However, you should spend some hands-on time with Windows 2000 Professional and get used to configuring desktop settings on the local computer. The rest of this section focuses on managing those settings.

Group Policy

Group Policy is the major method for managing desktop settings on the local computer or in a Windows network. Group Policy functions at the site, domain, and OU level in the network, but there is also a local Group Policy console found in Windows 2000 Professional. For example, if you are the administrator of the local machine, you can invoke a desktop policy setting on all other users that log on locally. However, you should keep in mind that local group policy is the weakest form of Group Policy. When connected to a Windows domain, any site, domain, or OU policy can override local policy settings.

To access the local Group Policy console, simply type **gpedit.msc** at the run dialog box. In the Group Policy console, shown in Figure 6-7, you can make editorial changes to the user policy and computer policy and enable or disable any number of desktop policies.

Keep in mind that excessive Group Policy settings can be more of a hindrance to users than a help. So configure the policy settings that you need, but don't become Big Brother.

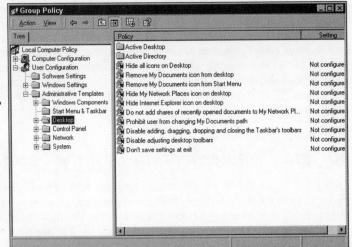

Figure 6-7:
Make
changes to
user and
computer
policy in the
local Group
Policy
console.

Power Options

Aside from using Group Policy to manage local and network desktops, you can also use the Display Properties dialog box to configure the background, screensaver, appearance, and related settings. To bring up this box, right-click an empty area of the desktop and choose Properties. All of these items are self-explanatory, but we touch on Power Options because you are likely to see power issues on the exam.

If you click the Screen Saver tab and then click the Power button, you can see the Power Options Properties dialog box, shown in Figure 6-8. Here are a few items you should keep in mind about Power Options for the exam:

✦ Use the Power Schemes tab to select one of the default schemes. You can change any scheme setting by simply changing the timeout values in the provided drop-down menus. You can also create your own scheme by entering the desired values and then clicking Save As.

✦ If your computer's BIOS supports hibernation, you can use the Hibernate tab to turn on hibernation by clicking the Enable Hibernate Support check box. Hibernation writes memory to the hard disk and shuts down the computer after a specified period of time. When you reboot the computer, the data is read back into memory and the desktop and any applications and files are returned to their pre-hibernation state.

Book I
Chapter 6

Configuring and
Troubleshooting the
Desktop
Environment

✦ You may see questions about power issues and laptop computers. Keep in mind that most computers can be configured to go into stand-by mode when the laptop lid is closed. Hibernation is useful, but if you simply want to conserve power while you are away from the computer for a few minutes, stand-by is the best option because it does not shut down the computer.

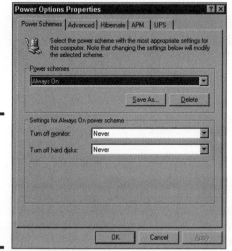

Figure 6-8:
Configure
power
options in
the Power
Options
Properties
dialog box.

Configuring and Troubleshooting Fax Support

Windows 2000 includes a fax monitor and console if you have a fax modem or other fax device installed on the computer. You find a Fax icon in Control Panel, if a fax device is available. Overall, the fax service and capabilities are rather self-explanatory, and you'll probably only see one question (if any) on the exam because fax support is not a major administrative function. So this section gives you the skinny on faxing and the fax service.

If you select Fax from the Control Panel, you'll see the Fax Properties dialog box, shown in Figure 6-9.

The User Information and Cover Pages tabs enable you to configure user information and cover pages that can be used in a fax session. The Status Monitor tab simply gives you information about what form notifications take when a fax is sent or received (a sound plays, for example). On the Advanced Options tab, you can add a fax printer, open fax management help, or you can open the Fax Service Management console, which is an MMC console, shown in Figure 6-10.

Figure 6-9: Configure user information and other options in the Fax Properties dialog box.

Figure 6-10: Access fax devices in the Fax Service Management console.

In the Fax Service Management console, you can access the fax devices and view log files for troubleshooting purposes. One exam item you should note is the sending and receiving of faxes. By default, Windows 2000 Professional configures the fax service to send faxes only, not receive. If you see an exam question about a fax that will not receive faxes, the correct response is to simply open the Fax Service Management console and select Devices in the left pane. In the right pane, select the device, and then choose Action⇨ Receive. The fax will now send and receive faxes. If you want to change either of the send and receive options, select the fax and choose Action⇨ Properties. In the Properties dialog box, shown in Figure 6-11, you can configure the fax for sending, receiving, or both.

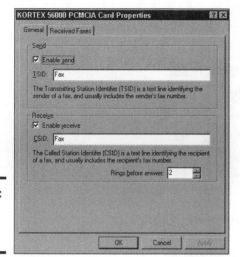

Figure 6-11:
Set fax
properties
here.

Configuring and Troubleshooting
Accessibility Services

Windows 2000 provides a number of accessibility services and features for
users with certain disabilities. For the exam, you need to know what those
accessibility services and features are. Enabling them typically requires
simply clicking a check box and possibly choosing an option, so the configuration of the services is not difficult — you just need to know what feature
might help what user. When you open the Accessibility Options dialog box
(by choosing Start➪Settings➪Control Panel➪Accessibility Options), you see
several tabs that contain different options for these features.

Keyboard

The Keyboard tab, shown in Figure 6-12 contains three features, which you
need to work with and remember for the exam:

✦ **StickyKeys:** StickyKeys enable users to press one key at a time for key
   sequences. For example, instead of having to press CTRL+ALT+DEL, you
   can press CTRL, and then ALT, and then DEL.

✦ **FilterKeys:** FilterKeys ignore brief or repeated keystrokes.

✦ **ToggleKeys:** ToggleKeys play tones when you press Caps Lock, Num
   Lock, and Scroll Lock.

For any of the features, click the Settings button to turn on hot keys that will activate the features and configure other minor options.

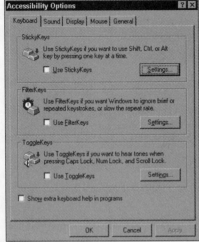

Figure 6-12:
The Keyboard tab enables you to change several accessibility-related options.

Sound

The Sound tab contains two options:

✦ **SoundSentry:** The SoundSentry shows visual warnings when Windows makes a sound in order to help the hearing impaired.

✦ **ShowSounds:** This option displays captions for speech and sounds that programs make.

Display

The Display tab contains a single option that allows you to use high contrast. High contrast settings configure fonts and colors for easy reading. Click the Settings button to adjust the contrast features and configure a shortcut to turn on high contrast.

Mouse

The Mouse tab contains a single option, MouseKeys. MouseKeys enables you to use the keyboard's numeric pad for mouse movements rather than actually using the mouse. Click the Settings button to configure the speed and the hot key for MouseKeys.

Book I
Chapter 6

Configuring and
Troubleshooting the
Desktop
Environment

General

The General tab, shown in Figure 6-13, gives you a few additional setting options that are important to remember. You can set a timeout value for all accessibility services. (By default, all accessibility services turn themselves off after five minutes of inactivity, but you can change this as needed.) You also see an option to provide notifications when the accessibility services are turned on. You can use SerialKey devices, which are specific devices developed to assist those with handicaps, and you can apply the accessibility settings to all logon desktops and all users, if necessary.

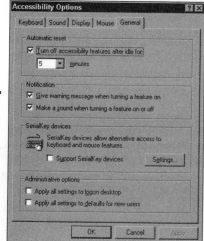

Figure 6-13: Configure a variety of miscellaneous accessibility options on the General tab.

Prep Test

1 John, a user in your network, needs to log on to different Windows 2000 Professional computers throughout the day. John needs the same profile on each Windows 2000 computer. What kind of profile should you configure?

A ○ Standard profile

B ○ Roaming profile

C ○ Encrypted profile

D ○ Home Folder profile

2 What is the default location of user profiles in Windows 2000 Professional?

A ○ *system_drive**Username*

B ○ *system_drive*\Folders*Username*

C ○ *system_drive*\Document and Settings*Username*

D ○ *system_drive*//*Username*

3 Jean, a user in your environment, will be working out of the Paris office for the next six months with her Windows 2000 Professional computer. Jean wants to use French as her default locale in Windows 2000. You open Regional Options in Control Panel. What tab allows you to configure Jean's computer?

A ○ General

B ○ Numbers

C ○ Time

D ○ Input Locales

4 Jean later needs to toggle between the United States locale and the French locale. You want Jean to be able to easily switch between locales without reconfiguring the Regional Options. On what tab can you configure this?

A ○ General

B ○ Numbers

C ○ Currency

D ○ Advanced

5 You need to deploy a Windows Installer Package to 400 users in a domain. What is the best way to accomplish this goal?

A ○ Manual installation

B ○ Group Policy

C ○ Distribution folder

D ○ You cannot deploy to this many computers.

6 Four users access your computer. They each have their own profile. You want to enforce a collection of desktop settings so that all users have the same desktop. How can you do this?

A ○ Edit the profiles into one profile.

B ○ Use local Group Policy.

C ○ Run the DESKCONF.EXE tool.

D ○ You cannot control users' desktops.

7 Pablo travels with a laptop computer. Pablo complains that the battery power does not last long enough, and he would like the computer to automatically shut down during idle times. What feature should you use?

A ○ Power Schemes

B ○ Standby

C ○ Hibernation

D ○ Sleep

8 On a particular Windows 2000 computer, you configured fax support. The computer can send faxes, but does not receive faxes. You need to enable the computer to receive faxes. Where can you configure this?

A ○ Control Panel

B ○ Fax Service Management console

C ○ Modem Properties

D ○ Printer Properties

9 A user in your environment is unable to press multiple keys simultaneously, such as ALT+Print Screen. What can you enable to help the user?

A ○ FilterKeys

B ○ StickyKeys

C ○ ToggleKeys

D ○ ShowSounds

10 A certain user has several accessibility services configured on his computer. However, the user complains that the accessibility services keep turning themselves off after a few minutes of inactivity. You need to configure the user's computer so that the services remain available. Where can you configure this in Accessibility services?

A ○ Keyboard tab

B ○ Sound tab

C ○ Mouse tab

D ○ General tab

Answers

1 **B.** A roaming profile is stored on a server and can be accessed from any computer. *Review "Using a roaming profile."*

2 **C.** The default user profiles are stored in the *system_drive*\Documents and Settings*Username* location, but you can move them and specify a new path if you like. *Read "Configuring and Managing User Profiles."*

3 **A.** The default locale is listed on the General tab. If you want to change the default, use the drop-down menu and select a different locale. *Review "Configuring multiple language support for users."*

4 **D.** Use the Advanced tab to configure multiple locales. *See "Configuring multiple locations."*

5 **B.** You can deploy Windows Installer Packages by using Group Policy. *Study "Managing Applications Using Windows Installer Packages."*

6 **B.** Use local Group Policy to enforce desktop settings on all users. *Study "Group Policy."*

7 **C.** After a specified period of time, hibernation writes RAM data to the hard disk and shuts down. *Study "Power Options."*

8 **B.** You can use the Action menu in the Fax Service Management Console to enable Receive. *Study "Configuring and Troubleshooting Fax Support."*

9 **B.** StickyKeys "stick" when pressed. *See "Keyboard."*

10 **D.** Use the General tab to configure the timeout value. *Study "General."*

Chapter 7: Implementing and Troubleshooting Network Protocols and Services

Exam Objectives

✔ Configure and troubleshoot the TCP/IP protocol

✔ Connect to computers by using dial-up networking

✔ Connect to shared resources on a Microsoft network

*W*indows 2000 Professional contains all the features and functions needed for highly effective networking in a Microsoft network. Naturally, Windows 2000 Professional is designed to work hand-in-hand with Windows 2000 Server.

From an exam point of view, you'll be expected to manage and implement Windows 2000 Professional in a Microsoft network. As such, you need to know the basics of Transmission Control Protocol/Internet Protocol (TCP/IP) configuration, how to connect to a network by using dial-up networking, and how to connect to resources on a Microsoft network. You can review the following topics in this chapter:

✦ Configuring TCP/IP on Windows 2000 Professional

✦ Connecting by using dial-up networking, including using a Virtual Private Network (VPN)

✦ Accessing shared resources

Configure and Troubleshoot the TCP/IP Protocol

You install and configure network protocols for any network interface card (NIC) that you have installed on your Windows 2000 Professional computer. If you have multiple NICs, you can configure different protocols and services for each NIC, depending on how you want to use it for network communication. The process for installing and configuring protocols is rather easy, and the following sections point out what you need to know for the exam.

Installing protocols

You install new protocols for a NIC by accessing the Properties dialog box for that NIC. To access the Properties dialog box for a NIC, right-click My Network Places on your desktop and then choose Properties from the menu that appears. Windows 2000 opens the Network and Dial-up Connections dialog box, which shows the local area network (LAN) connections or NICs installed on your server.

To install and configure protocols for a NIC, right-click its icon and choose Properties from the menu that appears. Windows 2000 opens the Local Area Connection Properties dialog box for that NIC, as shown in Figure 7-1.

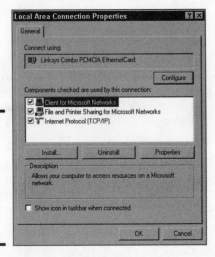

Figure 7-1:
Use the
Local Area
Connection
Properties
dialog box
to install
protocols.

To install a new protocol, follow the steps in Lab 7-1. You should remember how to perform this process for the exam.

Lab 7-1   Installing a Protocol

1. **In the Local Area Connection Properties dialog box of the NIC, click the Install button.**

2. **In the Select Network Component Type dialog box that appears, select Protocol and then click Add.**

   This brings up the Select Network Protocol dialog box.

Book I
Chapter 7

Implementing and
Troubleshooting
Network Protocols
and Services

3. **In the Select Network Protocol dialog box, select the protocol that you want to install by clicking its check box and then click OK.**

   If you want to install a different protocol that doesn't automatically appear, click the Have Disk button. (You must have a disk or CD-ROM containing the protocol in your disk drive to use this option.)

   Windows 2000 installs the protocol on your system. The protocol now appears in the list that's displayed in the Local Area Connection Properties dialog box.

Configuring TCP/IP

To configure a protocol after you install it, select the protocol in the Components Checked Are Used by This Connection area in the Local Area Connection Properties dialog box and then click Properties.

If you select a protocol and the Properties button appears grayed out (unavailable), that protocol has no configurable options, such as in the case of NetBEUI. The Properties dialog box for Internet Protocol (TCP/IP) has a General tab where you can configure the IP address, subnet mask, and default gateway, as well as preferred DNS server IP addresses. You can also configure TCP/IP to obtain its IP address from a Dynamic Host Configuration Protocol (DHCP) server.

The good news is that the Windows 2000 Professional exam doesn't expect you to have in-depth knowledge about TCP/IP. You should, however, know the primary TCP/IP configuration items and when they might need to be configured or changed. Memorize the following list and get some hands-on practice configuring TCP/IP on Windows 2000 Professional.

✦ **IP address:** The IP address of each computer on an IP network must fall within an IP address range determined by network architects. For example, a typical TCP/IP address might be 131.107.2.200. Each computer on the network would have a unique IP address in the same range. A DHCP server can automatically assign network clients an appropriate IP address, or you can manually assign one by entering the desired IP address on the IP addressing Properties page. In networks where no DCHP server is used, you can also use Automatic Private IP Addressing (APIPA, which assigns IP addresses in the 169.254.x.x range). This feature enables a workgroup to use automatic IP addressing.

✦ **Subnet mask:** A *subnet mask* determines the subnet to which the client belongs. Each client must have at least a default subnet mask. A subnet mask hides, or masks, a portion of the IP address so that computers know what portion of the address is the node address and which part is the network address.

✦ **Default gateway:** The *default gateway* is the IP address of the router that leads off the subnet. Clients may be configured with an IP address if one is necessary.

✦ **DNS and WINS servers:** The TCP/IP configuration can also contain the IP addresses of the domain name system (DNS) and Windows Internet Name Service (WINS) servers on the network. This information can also be provided by DHCP.

These items are all configurable on the Internet Protocol (TCP/IP) Properties page, as shown in Figure 7-2. You can manually enter the IP address and the subnet mask, as well as DNS server IP addresses. If you need to configure WINS servers, click the Advanced button and enter the server's IP address.

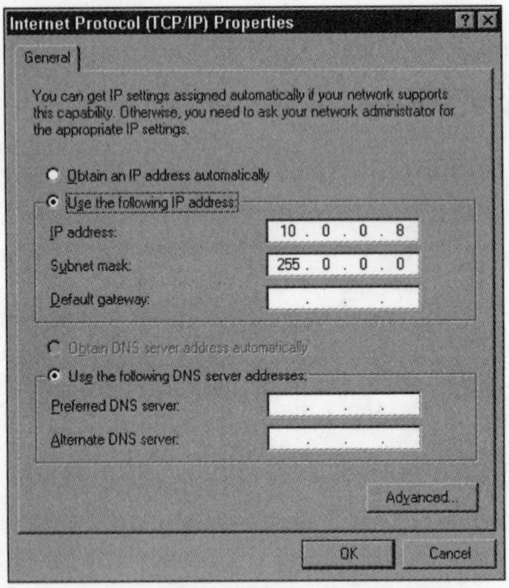

Figure 7-2:
IP
addressing
properties.

Troubleshooting TCP/IP

In order to troubleshoot TCP/IP addressing problems, you can use a few different command line utilities. The exam expects you to be familiar with these command line tools, and the best way that you can prepare is to get some experience using them on Windows 2000 Professional. Experiment with the following tools in order to prepare for the exam:

✦ **Ping:** ping is a utility that allows you to check connectivity with another computer on the network or against your own computer's network interface card. Simply type **ping *ipaddress*** at the command line. You can also ping a host by name or host name (such as www.hungryminds.com).

Book I
Chapter 7

Implementing and
Troubleshooting
Network Protocols
and Services

✦ **Ipconfig:** Ipconfig is a utility that gives you IP addressing information about your computer. Simply type **Ipconfig** at the command line, and if you want to see the available switches, type **Ipconfig /all**.

✦ **Netstat:** Using the Netstat utility displays all connections and protocol statistics for TCP/IP. You can type **netstat** at the command line and see the current connections to your computer and the protocols being used. You can also type **netstat /?** at the command line to see available switches.

✦ **Tracert:** Use this utility to trace the path from one host to another. Type **tracert** *ipaddress* or **tracert** *URL* and see the number of hops and path to the host.

Connect to Computers Using Dial-Up Networking

Remote networking using dial-up connections continues to be of major importance in networking environments today. Many corporate users dial in to remote access servers, not to mention the users who access the Internet through dial-up connections.

The Windows 2000 Professional exam expects you to know how to connect to computers using dial-up networking. On the exam, you can expect several questions concerning dial-up access, so make sure that you study the following sections carefully. Also make sure that you get some hands-on practice before taking the exam.

Dialing in using remote access service

A remote access server (RAS) allows remote network clients to establish a remote connection with a RAS. After the connection is established, the remote client functions just like a locally connected network client. The user can browse the network, use permitted resources, connect to other servers — anything that a locally connected client can do — provided that the RAS client has appropriate permissions. In recent years, RAS access has become more and more important as more and more users work from laptops in different locations.

In order to access a remote access server — or an ISP server for that matter — you have to configure a dial-up connection on Windows 2000 Professional. Dial-up connections require the phone numbers that you need to dial, a username, password, and any additional authentication that might be required by the RAS. Lab 7-2 shows you how to configure a dial-up connection.

Lab 7-2   Configuring a Dial-up Connection

1. **Choose Start⇨Settings⇨Network and Dialup Connections⇨Make New Connection.**

   The welcome screen for the Make Network Connection Wizard appears.

2. **Click Next on the wizard welcome screen.**

   This brings up the Network Connection Type window of the wizard.

3. **In the Network Connection Type window, as shown in Figure 7-3, select the Dial-up to Private Network radio button and then click Next.**

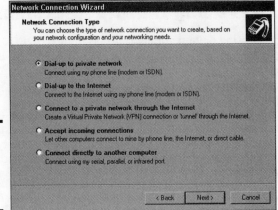

Figure 7-3: Choose the type of network connection.

4. **In the Phone Number to Dial window that appears, enter the phone number that you want to dial and then click Next.**

   You can select the Use Dialing Rules check box here if necessary. Keep in mind that dialing rules must be configured on the modem's properties sheets if you want to use them. Dialing rules tell your computer how to handle long distance numbers and calling cards, as well as area codes.

5. **In the Connection Availability window that appears, either choose to make the connection available to all users who use this local computer, or for yourself only, and then click Next.**

6. **Click Finish.**

   The connection window appears, and you can now connect to the network by providing a username and password.

Book I
Chapter 7

Implementing and
Troubleshooting
Network Protocols
and Services

After you create the connection, the connection now appears as an icon on the Network and Dial-up Connections folder. You can access some important settings from the Properties dialog box that control how the dial-up account works, and you need to be familiar with these options for the exam. Right-click the dial-up connection icon and then click Properties. You'll see the Properties dialog box with its five tabs. The following list points out the major options on the tabs that you need to know for the exam. Keep in mind that you should spend some time configuring dial-up connections and getting some hands-on practice.

✦ **General:** On the General tab, you can configure the modem by clicking the Configure button. You can also adjust the phone number that's dialed when the connection is used. Click the Alternates button to enter additional alternate phone numbers should the primary number be busy.

✦ **Options:** On the Options tab, as shown in Figure 7-4, notice the basic settings that manage connectivity. Also notice the Idle Time before Hanging Up setting. If a value other than Never is selected in this drop-down list, the connection is automatically dropped after so many minutes of inactivity. Change this setting to Never to make sure that the connection doesn't automatically disconnect itself.

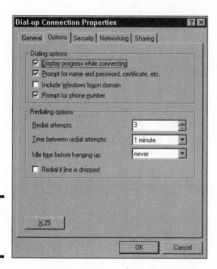

Figure 7-4:
Dial-up
options.

✦ **Security:** On the Security tab, you can configure the security level that's required by the remote access server. The default is to use Typical settings and allow unsecured passwords, but you have a number of options, including encrypted passwords and the selection of desired security protocols.

✦ **Networking:** On the Networking tab, you see the same networking installation window that you see when you open the LAN connection's Properties dialog box. Notice that for a dial-up connection, File and Printer Sharing for Microsoft Networks is automatically disabled. This is a security feature to prevent the use of this service from Internet intruders.

✦ **Sharing:** The Sharing tab allows you to enable Internet Connection Sharing. See "Using Internet Connection Sharing" later in this chapter for details.

Configuring virtual private networks

A *virtual private network* (VPN) is an extension of a local private network that contains links across public networks, such as the Internet. With a VPN, you can establish a link between two computers across a public network and send information as if it were through a private point-to-point link.

To emulate this private link, data is encapsulated in a frame that provides routing information so that the data can travel over the public network to its destination. At the receiving end, the outer frame is removed to reveal that actual data inside. The data in the frame is encrypted for safety as it travels over the private network.

VPNs are effective solutions in many scenarios where one office needs to send data intermittently to another office without maintaining an expensive wide area network (WAN) link. By using the Internet as a transport mechanism, data can be transmitted safely and inexpensively.

You should keep these new features of VPNs in Windows 2000 in mind for the exam:

✦ **Layer Two Tunneling Protocol (L2TP):** Windows 2000 supports both Point to Point Tunneling Protocol (PPTP) and L2TP, which is used with Windows 2000 Internet Protocol Security, IPSec. This combination creates very secure VPNs. Note, however, that L2TP doesn't work with Windows NT 4.0 servers.

✦ **Remote Access policies:** *Remote Access policies* can be used to set connection conditions for VPNs. This feature allows you to enforce different kinds of authentication and security features.

✦ **MS-CHAP V2:** With MS-CHAP V2, VPNs are greatly strengthened in terms of security because you can send encrypted data that requires the use of encryption keys for decoding.

✦ **Extensible Authentication Protocol (EAP):** EAP is supported for VPN connections. EAP allows you to use new authentication methods with RASes and VPNs, specifically Smart Card logon.

Book I
Chapter 7

Implementing and
Troubleshooting
Network Protocols
and Services

✦ **Account Lockout:** Account Lockout after a specified number of failed VPN connection attempts is now supported, but it's disabled by default.

To configure a RAS connection in Windows 2000 Professional, you use the Network Connection Wizard, which you access by choosing Start⇨ Settings⇨Network and Dial-up Connections⇨Make New Connection. Lab 7-3 shows you how to create a VPN connection to another computer.

Lab 7-3   Creating a VPN Connection

1. **In the Network Connection Wizard, click Next to bypass the Welcome screen.**

   This brings up the Network Connection Type window.

2. **On the Network Connection Type window, select the Connect to a Private Network through the Internet radio button and then click Next.**

3. **On the Public Network page, choose the dial-up connection that you want to dial.**

   Keep in mind that a VPN tunnel works on top of an existing dial-up connection, so if no dial-up connection is configured, click Cancel to quit the wizard; then create a basic dial-up connection and restart the wizard.

4. **Enter the host name or IP address of the computer that you're connecting to in the provided dialog box.**

   Remember that the IP address must be the public IP address held by the computer that functions as the remote access server.

5. **Make the connection available for yourself only or for all users and then click Next.**

6. **Click Finish.**

   The VPN connection now appears as an icon in the Network and Dial-Up Connections folder.

Like a dial-up connection, you can access the VPN connection's Properties dialog box to configure dialing and security options.

You can also allow your Windows 2000 Professional computer to act as a VPN server by allowing incoming connections. When you allow incoming connections, the modem is configured to receive a call and authenticate the user. You can allow basic dial-in access or VPN connections as needed.

Lab 7-4 shows you how to create an incoming connection.

Lab 7-4   Creating an Incoming Connection

1. **Choose Start⊅Settings⊅Network and Dial-up Connections⊅Make New Connection to open the Network Connection Wizard and then click Next on the Welcome screen.**

2. **In the Network Connection Type window that appears, select the Accept Incoming Connections radio button and then click Next.**

3. **In the Devices for Incoming Connections page that appears, choose the modem that you want to allow incoming connections and then click Next.**

4. **In the Incoming Virtual Private Connection window that appears, shown in Figure 7-5, select the Allow Virtual Private Connections radio button and then click Next.**

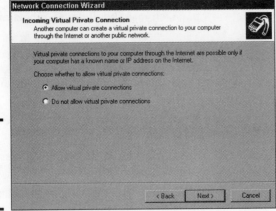

Figure 7-5:
Incoming
virtual
private
connection.

5. **In the Allowed Users window that appears, choose the users who are allowed to connect to this computer using a VPN. If a local user account doesn't exist for the user, click Add to create one. This opens an Add User dialog box, where you can create a new user account. Once you are done, click Next.**

6. **In the Networking Components window, choose the networking components that are allowed and then click Next.**

   Notice that both Client for Microsoft Networks and File and Printer Sharing for Microsoft Networks are allowed.

7. **Click Finish.**

   An icon for the incoming connection now appears in the Network and Dial-up Connections folder.

Book I
Chapter 7

Implementing and
Troubleshooting
Network Protocols
and Services

Using Internet Connection Sharing

Internet Connection Sharing (ICS) allows a single Internet connection to be shared among network clients. ICS is designed for use in a small home or office network where one Internet connection can be configured, and then all network clients can connect to the Internet through the shared connection.

To enable ICS, go to Start⇨Settings⇨Network and Dial-up Connections and right-click the icon of the Internet connection that you want to share access to. Select Properties from the context menu and then click the Sharing tab of the Properties dialog box that appears. Here, you can enable Internet Connection sharing as well as on-demand dialing so that the modem can be dialed when a network client needs to access resources from the Internet. All clients and the ICS host are connected to each other through the LAN, and the host has the connection to the Internet. The client computer requests information over the LAN cabling to the host computer, and then the host computer acts on behalf of the client computer. The host computer is assigned an IP address of 192.168.0.1 and it acts as the DHCP server and as a NAT server for the ICS clients.

Connect to Shared Resources on a Microsoft Network

This objective basically repeats other objectives that you find on the Windows 2000 Professional exam. When Windows 2000 Professional computer resides on a network, you can connect to different resources on that network by using

✦ **UNC Path:** You can access a shared resource by the UNC path convention, such as `\\servername\sharename`. You must, of course, have the proper permission to actually access the resource.

✦ **My Network Places:** You can browse the network and the resources available through My Network Places.

✦ **Internet Explorer:** If resources are found on an intranet, you can use Microsoft Internet Explorer to connect to those resources.

Beyond these three connection options, other features, such as the Add Printer Wizard, can help you connect to network printers. These options are simple and self-explanatory, so like all things on the exam, make sure that you get some hands-on practice.

Prep Test

1 **Which is not a part of the TCP/IP address?**

A ○ IP address

B ○ Frame type

C ○ Subnet mask

D ○ Default gateway

2 **Your network has two subnets. Clients on Subnet A are unable to contact clients on Subnet B. Ping tests show that the hosts are unreachable. However, clients on Subnet B are able to reach clients on Subnet A. What is the most likely cause of the problem?**

A ○ Default gateway

B ○ Subnet mask

C ○ IP address

D ○ No client services installed

3 **What feature allows Windows 2000 Professional clients to self-assign an IP address when a DHCP server isn't available?**

A ○ NWLink

B ○ APIPA

C ○ Subnet

D ○ Default gateway

4 **You're having problems connecting a computer on your network, but you are able to connect to other client computers. What connectivity test should you use to test basic network connectivity with the client?**

A ○ Ping

B ○ Ipconfig

C ○ Tracert

D ○ Netstat

5 **On your Windows 2000 Professional computer, what tool can you use to quickly and easily see all the TCP/IP settings configured and assigned by the DHCP server?**

A ○ Ping

B ○ Ipconfig

C ○ Tracert

D ○ Netstat

6 You need to dial in to a remote access server (RAS) using an existing connection on your computer. However, this RAS requires the use of EAP. Where can you configure this option on the dial-up connection's properties?

A ○ General tab

B ○ Options tab

C ○ Security tab

D ○ Sharing tab

7 Your dial-up connection disconnects after ten minutes of idle time. What Properties dialog box tab can you configure to stop this?

A ○ General tab

B ○ Options tab

C ○ Security tab

D ○ Sharing tab

8 You need to use Windows 2000 Professional to dial in to a Windows NT 4.0 RAS. What protocol should be used?

A ○ PPTP

B ○ L2TP

C ○ IPSec

D ○ EAP

9 On a small LAN, you enable sharing on the internal network adapter, but clients are still unable to access the Internet through the shared connection. What is wrong?

A ○ The clients aren't configured.

B ○ You enabled sharing on the internal connection instead of the external.

C ○ You need to configure permissions.

D ○ The connection isn't established.

10 You need to connect to a share named *doc* found in the Temp folder on the ARC7 computer on your network. What is the correct UNC path to use?

A ○ `\\arc7\temp\doc`

B ○ `\\arc7\doc\temp`

C ○ `\\temp\doc: arc7`

D ○ `\\doc\temp\arc7`

Answers

1 **B.** Frame type refers to NetWare (IPX) connections. *Review "Configuring TCP/IP."*

2 **A.** The clients need a default gateway configured so that they reach the second subnet. *Review "Configure and Troubleshoot the TCP/IP Protocol."*

3 **B.** APIPA is used to auto-assign an IP address. *See "Configuring TCP/IP."*

4 **A.** Use ping to test connectivity against another host. *Study "Troubleshooting TCP/IP."*

5 **B.** Use Ipconfig to easily see all IP addressing information for the local computer. *Study "Troubleshooting TCP/IP."*

6 **C.** EAP is a security protocol, and all security settings are configured on the Security tab. *Study "Dialing in using remote access service."*

7 **B.** Use the Options tab to manage dialing options and controls. *Study "Dialing in using remote access service."*

8 **A.** Windows NT 4.0 only supports PPTP for VPN connections. *Read "Configuring virtual private networks."*

9 **B.** You enabled sharing on the internal connection instead of the external. Share the connection to the Internet, not the internal LAN connection. *Read "Using Internet Connection Sharing."*

10 **A.** The UNC path functions by *servername**share**share*. *See "Connect to Shared Resources on a Microsoft Network."*

Chapter 8: Implementing, Monitoring, and Troubleshooting Security

Exam Objectives

✔ Encrypt data on a hard disk by using Encrypting File System (EFS)

✔ Implement, configure, manage, and troubleshoot local security policy

✔ Implement, configure, manage, and troubleshoot local user accounts

✔ Implement, configure, manage, and troubleshoot local user authentication

✔ Implement, configure, manage, and troubleshoot a security configuration

Security in the corporate environment is an ongoing issue. In fact, over the past couple of years, network security has become more important than ever because threats from corporate electronic theft as well as from the Internet pose more and more security problems for local area and wide area networks (LANs and WANs). Windows 2000 Professional contains a number of tools to help you secure the local computer and also audit what is happening. Note that the exam primarily focuses on local security of Windows 2000 Professional, but in a domain environment, domain security is of paramount importance and is handled by server administrators.

This chapter tackles security issues. Keep in mind that the concept of security could be a book by itself, so this chapter only explores the issues that you're most likely to see on the exam. You should study this chapter and get some hands-on practice configuring these options:

✦ Using EFS

✦ Managing a local security policy as well as all local user accounts

✦ Managing local and domain authentication

✦ Configuring and troubleshooting a security configuration

Encrypt Data on a Hard Disk by Using Encrypting File System (EFS)

Encrypting File System (EFS) is a powerful new security feature in Windows 2000. With Encrypting File System, you can encrypt your files and folders.

EFS only functions on NT File System (NTFS) volumes, so to implement EFS, you should convert any FAT or FAT32 volumes to NTFS.

EFS is invisible to the user. You, as the encrypting agent, specify for a file or folder to be encrypted, but you work with the file or folder just as you normally do. In other words, you don't have to decrypt a file to use it and then re-encrypt it again. You can open and close your files, move them, rename them — any action — without having to be aware of the encryption. However, if intruders attempt to open, move, copy, or rename your file or folder, they receive an access-denied message.

For the exam, you should remember these important points about EFS:

✦ Only files or folders on NTFS volumes can be encrypted.

✦ Compressed files or folders can't be encrypted. You must uncompress the file or folder to encrypt it, and compressed volumes must be uncompressed to encrypt any files or folders on the volume.

✦ Only the user who encrypts the file or folder can open it.

✦ Encrypted files should not be shared.

✦ Encrypted files moved to a FAT or FAT32 volume lose their encryption.

✦ System files can't be encrypted.

✦ Encrypted files aren't protected against deletion. Anyone with delete permission can delete an encrypted file.

✦ Encrypt your Temp folder so that files remain encrypted while they are being edited. This action keeps temporary files created by some programs encrypted while they are in use. It's also a good idea to encrypt the My Documents folder.

✦ You can encrypt or decrypt files and folders stored on a remote computer that's been enabled for remote encryption. However, the data isn't encrypted while it's in transit over the network. (Other protocols, such as IPsec, can provide this feature.)

✦ You can't drag and drop files into an encrypted folder for encryption purposes. If you want to put files into an encrypted folder, use the copy-and-paste method so that the files will be encrypted in the folder.

You can encrypt a file or folder by accessing its Properties dialog box. Right-click the file or folder icon, select Properties from the context menu that appears, and then select the General tab (if it's not selected already). On the General tab, click the Advanced button, which brings up the Advanced Attributes dialog box. Then select the Encrypt Contents to Secure Data check box, as shown in Figure 8-1, and click OK.

Book I
Chapter 8

Implementing,
Monitoring, and
Troubleshooting
Security

Figure 8-1:
Enabling
encryption
on a file or
folder.

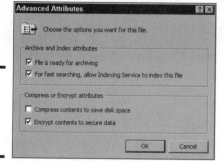

If a file or folder is already encrypted, you can decrypt it by following the same steps and simply clearing the Encrypt Contents check box. Keep in mind that you don't have to encrypt or decrypt your files and folders to work with them — the encryption feature is invisible to you.

When you encrypt a folder, you're asked whether you want all files and sub-folders within the folder to be encrypted. When you encrypt a file, you're asked whether you want to encrypt the folder in which it's stored as well.

You can also encrypt files and folders by using the `cipher` command at the command line. If you type **cipher /?**, you see a list of options.

Data recovery is available for EFS as a part of the security policy for your system. A recovery policy is automatically generated when you encrypt your first file or folder. Should you lose the file encryption certificate and private key, such as in the case of a disk failure, a recovery agent can decrypt the file or folder for you.

By default, an administrator is the default recovery agent when an administrator logs on to the system for the first time. In the case of an employee leaving the company, the administrator can log on to the machine and recover any encrypted data. The recovery agent feature is part of the security policy.

The recovery agent has a special certificate and associated private key that allows data to be recovered by the recovery policy. Recovery can be accomplished by using the Export and Import commands from the Certificates Microsoft Management Console (MMC), which allows you to back up the recovery certificate and associated private key to a secure location. The default recovery policy is configured locally for stand-alone computers. For networked computers, the recovery policy is configured at either the domain, organizational unit, or individual computer level and applies to all Windows 2000 computers within the scope.

You can specify a recovery agent for a local computer by opening the Group Policy MMC snap-in in Local Computer mode. Click the Public Key Policies container; right-click the Encrypted Data Recovery Agents option, and then click Add. This action opens a Recovery Agent Wizard that allows you to specify the user who is the recovery agent for the local computer.

Implement, Configure, Manage, and Troubleshoot Local Security Policy

Security settings determine how the computer implements and enforces various security behavior. Basically, a *policy* is a collection of settings that are applied to a computer that determines what security features are in effect.

In a Windows 2000 network, security policies continue to be an important aspect of your overall security plan, as they were in Windows NT. However, security policies in Windows 2000 are now defined through Group Policy, a powerful feature that allows you to manage the security settings of computers within a domain or organizational unit.

Local policies are local to the computer. They are based on the computer that you are logged in to and the rights that you have on that local computer. Local policies affect a number of security components, such as the enabling or disabling of security settings, digital signing of data, user log-on rights and permissions, and the audit policy.

Account policies apply to the user account and the rules of security behavior for that account.

Finally, system policies are applied to the computer system, based on registry settings in Windows NT 4.0 and made by using the System Policy Editor. In Windows 2000, the System Policy Editor is mainly replaced by Group Policy.

Windows 2000 computers have a local Group Policy object. With this feature, group policy settings can be stored on individual computers, even if they're not in an Active Directory environment. However, the local Group Policy settings can be overwritten by group policy objects on the site, domain, or organizational unit level. Local policies are implemented first, and then site, domain, and OU policies.

Book I
Chapter 8

Implementing,
Monitoring, and
Troubleshooting
Security

Group Policy settings for the local computer can be made by opening the Group Policy snap-in and selecting Local Computer Policy. From this interface, as shown in Figure 8-2, you can configure local settings for the computer for both the computer configuration and the user configuration.

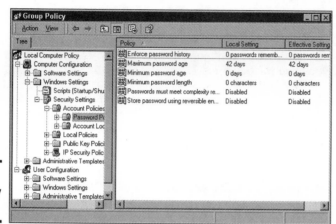

Figure 8-2:
Group Policy
snap-in.

Using Auditing

Auditing is the Windows 2000 Server security feature that monitors security events on your server. By using auditing, you can determine whether intruders or other security breaches are occurring on your server.

You can audit many events on your system, including access to files and folders, management of user and group accounts, and log-on and log-off activity.

The Windows 2000 auditing feature generates an audit trail to help you keep track of the security administration events that occur on the system. This feature is particularly useful because you can see how auditing has occurred. You can also determine whether other administrators with access to your server have changed any auditing of events.

To implement auditing on your server, you complete three major steps:

1. **Determine which categories of events that you want to audit and then turn on auditing for those events.**

2. **Determine the size of the security log that the auditing process will generate, as well as the storage location and file type.**

3. **Modify the security descriptors for certain objects that you plan to audit, such as folders or files, so that you can audit successful or failed access attempts.**

Configuring an audit policy

To start auditing, you configure an audit policy. The policy tells the system what you want to audit.

To configure an audit policy, open an MMC and then add the Group Policy snap-in. Beneath the Local Computer Policy Tree (left pane), expand Computer Configuration, Windows Settings, Security Settings, and Local Policies, and then select Audit Policy, as shown in Figure 8-3.

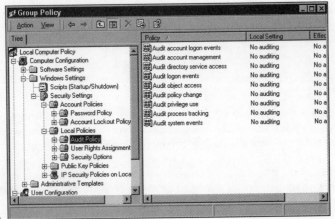

Figure 8-3:
Use the Group Policy snap-in to configure an audit policy.

In the details (right) pane, you can see the different audit policies that you can configure. By default, auditing is turned off for all of them.

To enable auditing, double-click the desired audit policy, which brings up the Local Security Policy Setting dialog box. Click either the Success or Failure check box (or both) to audit the event, based on success or failure, as shown in Figure 8-4.

Book I
Chapter 8

Implementing,
Monitoring, and
Troubleshooting
Security

Figure 8-4:
Set the
Success or
Failure
check box
to enable
auditing.

Continue down the list of policies and enable auditing for each event desired.

Auditing access to files and folders

You can audit access to files and folders on NTFS partitions. Before you configure the file or folder for auditing, you must enable the Audit Object Access event in the Group Policy snap-in (see the previous section).

To configure auditing for a particular file or folder, follow the steps in Lab 8-1.

Lab 8-1   Configuring Auditing for a File or Folder

1. **Right-click the desired file or folder and choose Properties from the context menu.**

2. **In the Properties dialog box that appears, click the Security tab and then click the Advanced button.**

3. **Click the Auditing tab and then click Add.**

4. **Select a user or group account for which you want to audit access to the file or folder and then click OK.**

5. **In the Auditing Entry for My Documents dialog box that appears, shown in Figure 8-5, select the events that you want to audit by selecting the Successful or Failed check boxes, and then click OK.**

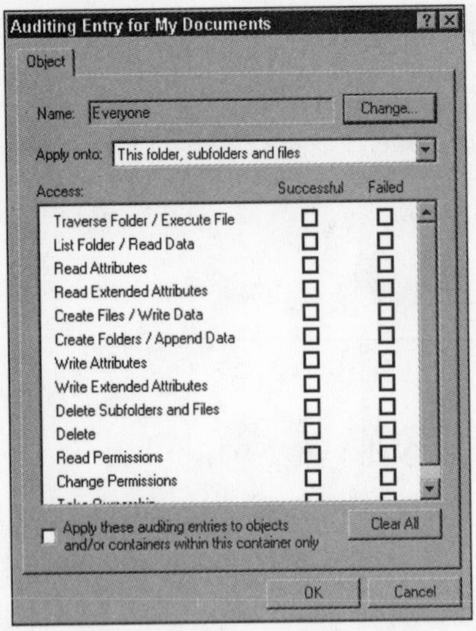

Auditing Entry for My Documents

Object

Name: Everyone   [Change...]

Apply onto: This folder, subfolders and files

Access: Successful Failed

Traverse Folder / Execute File   ☐   ☐
List Folder / Read Data   ☐   ☐
Read Attributes   ☐   ☐
Read Extended Attributes   ☐   ☐
Create Files / Write Data   ☐   ☐
Create Folders / Append Data   ☐   ☐
Write Attributes   ☐   ☐
Write Extended Attributes   ☐   ☐
Delete Subfolders and Files   ☐   ☐
Delete   ☐   ☐
Read Permissions   ☐   ☐
Change Permissions   ☐   ☐
Take Ownership   ☐   ☐

☐ Apply these auditing entries to objects
  and/or containers within this container only   [Clear All]

                              [OK]   [Cancel]

Figure 8-5:
Configure
auditing for
the file or
folder.

The auditing options that you configure appear in the Access Control Settings for My Documents dialog box, as shown in Figure 8-6.

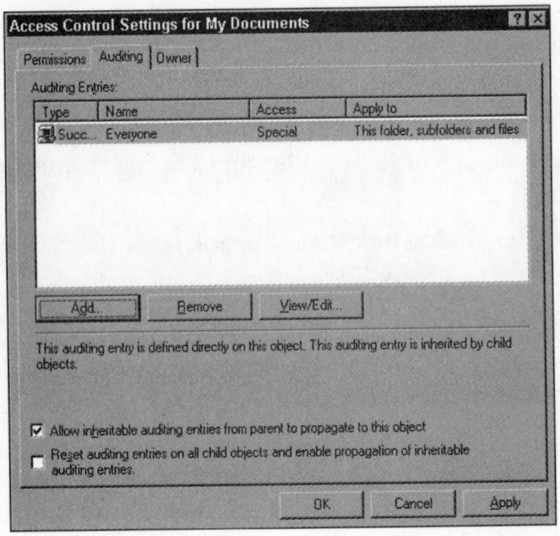

Access Control Settings for My Documents

Permissions Auditing Owner

Auditing Entries:

Type	Name	Access	Apply to
Succ...	Everyone	Special	This folder, subfolders and files

[Add...]   [Remove]   [View/Edit...]

This auditing entry is defined directly on this object. This auditing entry is inherited by child objects.

☑ Allow inheritable auditing entries from parent to propagate to this object

☐ Reset auditing entries on all child objects and enable propagation of inheritable
  auditing entries.

                              [OK]   [Cancel]   [Apply]

Figure 8-6:
Auditing
entries
appear
here.

By selecting a check box at the bottom of the Access Control Settings for My Documents dialog box, you can allow inheritable auditing entries from the parent to propagate to this object, or you can choose to reset auditing entries on all child objects and enable propagation. With these features, both the parent and the child objects can inherit auditing entries. You can disable both or either of these options by clearing the check boxes.

Book I
Chapter 8

Implementing,
Monitoring, and
Troubleshooting
Security

Viewing the Security Log

After you implement auditing, you can view the Security Log by choosing Start➪Programs➪Administrative Tools➪Event Viewer and then clicking Security Log in the left console pane. You see the list of audited events, which you can use to determine whether your system has security problems or issues that you need to address.

The Security Log is limited in size, so you should choose carefully which events you want to audit.

Implement, Configure, Manage, and Troubleshoot Local User Accounts

You configure local accounts on Windows 2000 Professional for users who log on to the local machine. Accounts on domain controllers are stored in the Active Directory.

On a Windows 2000 Professional, you create and manage local accounts by using the Computer Management tool, which is available in Administrative Tools. In the Computer Management (Local) console, expand Local Users and Groups to see the Users and Groups containers. If you click either container, you see a list of users and groups in the details pane, as shown in Figure 8-7. By default, a Windows 2000 server has an administrator account and a guest account, which is disabled by default.

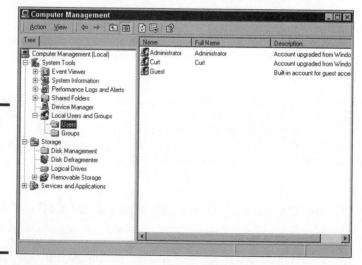

Figure 8-7:
Use Computer Management to configure local user and group accounts.

To create a new user or group account, select the desired container and then choose either Action⇨New User or Action⇨New Group. In the dialog box that's displayed, you can enter the user name and password and also determine the following password-related settings:

+ User must change password at next logon
+ User cannot change password
+ Password never expires
+ Account is disabled

Weak management of passwords translates directly into weak security. Microsoft recommends that all passwords should be at least seven characters long, shouldn't contain a user's name, and should comprise a mixture of upper- and lowercase letters, numbers, and symbols. For example, xjjB34!2 is an appropriate password in Windows 2000.

After you create user accounts, you can add them to groups as desired, and you can configure account properties. Right-click a user account and choose Properties to open the Properties dialog box for that account.

For the exam, you don't need to worry about the specifics of the Properties dialog boxes for user and group accounts. Just remember that you can configure account properties and manage the account's password, group memberships, and profile from these dialog boxes.

In addition to creating accounts and configuring their properties, you can configure the Account Policy for your server.

To configure your Account Policy, open an MMC and add the Group Policy snap-in. Expand Computer Configuration, Windows Settings, and Security Settings, and then select Account Policies. You see the policy entries in the details pane.

Double-click either the Password Policy container, the Account Lockout Policy container, or the Kerberos Policy container, and then double-click the entries to configure the desired policy settings. You can define various policy settings, such as account lockout duration, account lockout threshold, enforce password history, and maximum password age.

Implement, Configure, Manage, and Troubleshoot Local User Authentication

User authentication concerns the actual logon process for the user. In truth, the same issues concerning the management of local users and groups also

**Book I
Chapter 8**

Implementing,
Monitoring, and
Troubleshooting
Security

concern authentication. After all, it's through a user account and password that a user is able to log on to the local system. Keep in mind that logging on to the local system is different from logging on to a domain. Domain logons are handled by a domain controller, but local logons give the user access to the local computer only.

For the exam, all you really need to know about authentication concerns the creation of user accounts. Remember to use passwords that are complex, and use the Local Users and Groups Console to manage local users. Keep in mind that the Local Users and Groups console gives you the option to lock out accounts when they shouldn't be used.

Implement, Configure, Manage, and Troubleshoot a Security Configuration

Windows 2000 Server includes a tool set that you can use to manage your security configuration. You have a Security Configuration and Analysis snap-in and a Security Templates snap-in that you can manually add to an MMC.

You need to know about both of these snap-ins for the exam, and the following sections explain the issues that you're likely to see on the exam.

You use the Security Configuration and Analysis tool to analyze and configure local computer security. The tool uses a security database, which you need to create before you use the tool for the first time. Right-click the Security Configuration and Analysis object and choose Open Database. In the dialog box that appears, click Open. In the resulting dialog box, select the database template to open and then click Open.

After you open a database, you can perform three major tasks. Select the Security Configuration and Analysis object in the console and then click the Action menu. By choosing options in the Action menu, you can perform the following tasks, which you need to remember for the exam:

+ **Analyze Computer Now:** This process analyzes your security configuration and reports issues or potential problems to the database. This feature is an excellent troubleshooting tool.

+ **Configure Computer Now:** This process applies any templates that you have chosen to your computer.

+ **Import Template:** This action enables you to import a security template that you want to apply to your system. After importing a desired template, choose Action⇨Configure Computer Now.

The Security Templates snap-in contains a list of security templates that you can edit to configure your system security as desired. You can also create new templates and import other templates into this snap-in. For each template, you can define account policies, local policies, event logs, restricted groups, system services, the registry, and file system. For each category, you can open the templates and adjust the settings as desired.

Like the Security Configuration and Analysis snap-in, the Security Templates snap-in gives you an all-in-one location where you can implement and configure the desired security settings for your server.

Prep Test

1 Which rule applies to encrypted files?

A ○ Encrypted files must be at least 500 KB in size.

B ○ Encrypted files must be compressed.

C ○ Encrypted files can't be stored on a FAT volume.

D ○ Encrypted files can't be deleted.

2 What command line utility can be used to encrypt or decrypt files?

A ○ Ping

B ○ Crypt

C ○ Cipher

D ○ Sec

3 Local security policies are mainly controlled by what feature in Windows 2000 Professional?

A ○ Group Policy

B ○ System Policy

C ○ IPsec

D ○ Security Configuration

4 You need to audit a particular folder. What do you need to do in Group Policy first?

A ○ Enable Audit Object Access

B ○ Disable Audit Object Access

C ○ Enable Group Object Access

D ○ Disable Group Object Access

5 You have several users who log on to your local computer. You want to assign static passwords that can't be changed. Where can you configure this? (Choose all that apply.)

A ❑ Group Policy

B ❑ Accounts in Control Panel

C ❑ Local Users and Groups container

D ❑ SecEdit

6 **For the best password protection, which statement is true?**

A ○ Passwords should only contain letters.

B ○ Passwords should only contain numbers.

C ○ Passwords should contain letters and numbers.

D ○ Passwords should contain letters, numbers, and symbols.

7 **Local users are authenticated by**

A ○ The local security system

B ○ Policy

C ○ Windows 2000 domain controllers

D ○ SecEdit

8 **You would like to lock an account after three failed logon attempts. Where can you configure this?**

A ○ Local Users and Groups.

B ○ Group Policy.

C ○ IPsec.

D ○ This option isn't available.

9 **You need to import a security template into Windows 2000 Professional. What tool can you use?**

A ○ IPsec

B ○ Security Templates snap-in

C ○ Computer Management

D ○ Local Users console

10 **You want to run a security analysis on your computer. Which tool can you use?**

A ○ Security Templates snap-in

B ○ IPsec

C ○ Security Configuration and Analysis

D ○ Local Users console

Answers

1 **C.** Encrypted files can't be stored on a FAT volume. Encryption only works on NTFS volumes. *Review "Encrypt Data on a Hard Disk by Using Encrypting File System (EFS)."*

2 **C.** Cipher. Use the Cipher command to manage encryption at the command line. *Read "Encrypt Data on a Hard Disk by Using Encrypting File System (EFS)."*

3 **A.** Group Policy. Group Policy is the preferred method for managing local security. *Review "Implement, Configure, Manage, and Troubleshoot Local Security Policy."*

4 **A.** Enable Audit Object Access. Enable this policy in Group Policy so that you can audit access to files and folders. *See "Auditing access to files and folders."*

5 **A** and **C.** Group Policy and the Local Users and Groups container. You can configure accounts with the User Cannot Change Password option to invoke the desired security setting. *Study "Implement, Configure, Manage, and Troubleshoot Local User Accounts."*

6 **D.** Passwords should contain letters, numbers, and symbols. The more complex the password, the more difficult the password is to guess. *Study "Implement, Configure, Manage, and Troubleshoot Local User Accounts."*

7 **A.** The local security system. The local security system handles user authentication when logging on locally. *Study "Implement, Configure, Manage, and Troubleshoot Local User Authentication."*

8 **B.** Group Policy. You can set lockout policies in Group Policy. *Study "Implement, Configure, Manage, and Troubleshoot Local User Authentication."*

9 **B.** Security Templates snap-in. Manage security templates with this snap-in. *See "Implement, Configure, Manage, and Troubleshoot a Security Configuration."*

10 **C.** Security Configuration and Analysis. Use this tool to analyze the security settings on your computer. *Study "Implement, Configure, Manage, and Troubleshoot a Security Configuration."*

Book II

Installing, Configuring, and Administering Microsoft Windows 2000 Server: Exam 70-215

The 5th Wave   By Rich Tennant

"We sort of have our own way of mentally preparing our people to take the MS Windows 2000 Server exam."

Contents at a Glance

Chapter 1: About Exam 70-215

In This Chapter

✓ **The things you should know before you begin studying**

✓ **The objectives for Exam 70-215**

✓ **What to expect on the test**

Exam 70-215, Installing, Configuring, and Administering Microsoft Windows 2000 Server, tests your knowledge of Windows 2000 Server and its operations in a Microsoft network. This exam also tests your knowledge of configuring the server itself, but primarily using the server to provide services to network clients, especially for Windows 2000 Professional. You can expect the exam to test your knowledge of major Windows 2000 networking features and services, including Active Directory, DNS, DHCP, terminal services, Web services, and print services — just to name a few.

With this in mind, are you ready to tackle Exam 70-215? That depends on your current knowledge of networking services and your hands-on experience with Windows 2000 Server.

What You Should Already Know

Before you begin studying this book for Exam 70-215, we assume that you bring a few prerequisites to the certification table. If you are deficient in any of these areas, you should stop studying for this exam and learn some background information from other books devoted to these topics:

✦ **Windows 2000 Professional:** Although you can take the Microsoft exams in any order to achieve your MCSA, we recommend that you pass the Windows 2000 Professional exam before taking the Windows 2000 Server exam. We say this because the Windows 2000 Server exam tests your knowledge of using Windows 2000 Server to provide networking services to clients, namely Windows 2000 Professional. You may find the Server exam easier if you pass the Professional exam first.

✦ **Networking:** This book assumes that you have some networking experience and are currently working with Windows 2000 Server in a networking environment. If you have no networking experience, you need to study networking first and try to get some hands-on experience. You may find this book difficult to understand without any prior networking knowledge.

✦ **Networking Services:** Aside from basic networking skills, you should already be familiar with common networking services and protocols, such as DNS, DHCP, WINS, TCP/IP, as well as other common services.

✦ **Windows 2000 Server:** You should be familiar with the Windows 2000 Server interface and where different services are configured.

✦ **Experience:** Like all Microsoft exams, you should have one to three years of experience working with Windows 2000 Server in a Microsoft network. This book can help you review the exam objectives, but it can't replace hands-on practice and experience.

What Exam Objectives Are Covered

The Windows 2000 Server exam objectives are readily available on Microsoft's Web site, and are also included here for your convenience. This book strictly adheres to the exam objectives and covers the test material that you are most likely to see concerning the exam objectives. On the exam, you can expect to see the following issues:

✦ **Installing Windows 2000 Server**

✦ Perform an attended installation of Windows 2000 Server.

✦ Perform an unattended installation of Windows 2000 Server.

  • Create unattended answer files by using Setup Manager to automate the installation of Windows 2000 Server.

  • Create and configure automated methods for installation of Windows 2000.

✦ Upgrade a server from Microsoft Windows NT 4.0.

✦ Deploy service packs.

✦ Troubleshoot failed installations.

✦ **Installing, Configuring, and Troubleshooting Access to Resources**

✦ Install and configure network services for interoperability.

✦ Monitor, configure, troubleshoot, and control access to printers.

✦ Monitor, configure, troubleshoot, and control access to files, folders, and shared folders.

  • Configure, manage, and troubleshoot a standalone Distributed file system (Dfs).

  • Configure, manage, and troubleshoot a domain-based Distributed file system (Dfs).

- Monitor, configure, troubleshoot, and control local security on files and folders.

- Monitor, configure, troubleshoot, and control access to files and folders in a shared folder.

- Monitor, configure, troubleshoot, and control access to files and folders via Web services.

✦ Monitor, configure, troubleshoot, and control access to Web sites.

✦ **Configuring and Troubleshooting Hardware Devices and Drivers**

✦ Configure hardware devices.

✦ Configure driver signing options.

✦ Update device drivers.

✦ Troubleshoot problems with hardware.

✦ **Managing, Monitoring, and Optimizing System Performance, Reliability, and Availability**

✦ Monitor and optimize usage of system resources.

✦ Manage processes.

- Set priorities and start and stop processes.

✦ Optimize disk performance.

✦ Manage and optimize availability of System State data and user data.

✦ Recover System State data and user data.

- Recover System State data by using Windows Backup.

- Troubleshoot system restoration by starting in safe mode.

- Recover System State data by using the Recovery Console.

✦ **Managing, Configuring, and Troubleshooting Storage Use**

✦ Monitor, configure, and troubleshoot disks and volumes.

✦ Configure data compression.

✦ Monitor and configure disk quotas.

✦ Recover from disk failures.

✦ **Configuring and Troubleshooting Windows 2000 Network Connections**

✦ Install, configure, and troubleshoot shared access.

✦ Install, configure, and troubleshoot a virtual private network (VPN).

✦ Install, configure, and troubleshoot network protocols.

✦ Install and configure network services.

✦ Configure, monitor, and troubleshoot remote access.

    • Configure inbound connections.

    • Create a remote access policy.

    • Configure a remote access profile.

✦ Install, configure, monitor, and troubleshoot Terminal Services.

    • Remotely administer servers by using Terminal Services.

    • Configure Terminal Services for application sharing.

    • Configure applications for use with Terminal Services.

✦ Install, configure, and troubleshoot network adapters and drivers.

✦ **Implementing, Monitoring, and Troubleshooting Security**

✦ Encrypt data on a hard disk by using Encrypting File System (EFS).

✦ Implement, configure, manage, and troubleshoot policies in a Windows 2000 environment.

    • Implement, configure, manage, and troubleshoot Local Policy in a Windows 2000 environment.

    • Implement, configure, manage, and troubleshoot System Policy in a Windows 2000 environment.

✦ Implement, configure, manage, and troubleshoot auditing.

✦ Implement, configure, manage, and troubleshoot local accounts.

✦ Implement, configure, manage, and troubleshoot Account Policy.

✦ Implement, configure, manage, and troubleshoot security by using the Security Configuration Tool Set.

What You Can Expect

After you've reviewed the exam objectives, what can you expect when you sit in front of the computer on exam day? As you study this book and prepare for the exam, keep the following points in mind:

✦ You can expect to see all of the exam objectives covered, but some will be hammered more than others. In fact, some objectives may appear more indirectly in questions supporting other objectives.

✦ You can expect the exam questions to be complicated. Microsoft exams love to present information in a convoluted way and make questions more difficult to read than necessary. The Windows 2000 Server exam is no exception.

✦ You can expect the Windows 2000 Server exam questions to intersect with each other as combination questions, and you may even see issues that seem to come from the Windows 2000 Professional exam. Because Microsoft expects your knowledge to be global and not product-specific, expect some questions that seem to cross over with the Windows 2000 Professional exam.

✦ You'll always see the Windows 2000 Server exam questions presented in light of networking. The exam doesn't test your knowledge of operating system basics and usage, but rather administration from a networking point of view.

The only real way to be successful on the Windows 2000 Server exam is to combine your existing knowledge and experience with the principles explored in this book! Then, practice, practice, practice, before taking the exam!

Book II
Chapter 1

About Exam 70-215

Chapter 2: Installing Windows 2000 Server

Exam Objectives

✔ Upgrading a server from Microsoft Windows NT 4.0

✔ Performing an attended installation of Windows 2000 Server

✔ Deploying service packs

✔ Troubleshooting failed installations

✔ Perform an unattended installation of Windows 2000 Server

*I*f you're like us, you always have a few butterflies in your stomach when you begin a new server installation. Windows 2000 certainly offers an easier, more intuitive installation process than Windows NT Server 4.0, but you still need in-depth knowledge of the steps for installing the server software and troubleshooting problems. You can expect to perform both tasks as an IT professional, and you can also expect exam questions on these topics.

For Exam 70-215, you need to understand everything that happens during a typical installation. To help you prepare for the installation-related questions on the exam, this chapter reviews the following tasks:

✦ Upgrading from Windows NT

✦ Performing an attended installation

✦ Perform an unattended installation

✦ Deploying service packs

✦ Troubleshooting installation problems

Getting Ready for Installation

Thorough, careful planning helps to ensure a successful installation. Although you may be tempted to start the installation right away, you should first perform several planning actions in order to ensure that you have a successful and painless installation.

The following sections tell you about the planning actions you should perform. You need to know these tasks for the exam, and they apply to both a clean (new) installation and an upgrade.

Examining hardware requirements

No matter whether you plan to do an upgrade or a clean installation, make certain that your server meets the Windows 2000 hardware requirements before you ever attempt a Windows 2000 installation.

Table 2-1 lists the installation hardware requirements that Microsoft recommends. Memorize them for the exam. For your work in the real world, however, remember that these are *bare-minimum requirements*. You actually need much better hardware if you expect your server to function in a desired manner. But for the exam, you need to know the minimum requirements published by Microsoft.

Table 2-1	Windows 2000 Minimum Hardware Requirements
Component	*Requirement*
Processor	Pentium 133 MHz processor or higher.
RAM	128MB minimum and 256MB or higher recommended.
Hard Disk	Partitions large enough to support the setup process. (1 GB is usually the minimum, but with the size and low cost of hard drives, your existing hard drive is probably much larger than the minimum.)
Resolution	VGA or higher.
Keyboard	Standard keyboard.
Mouse (optional)	Standard mouse.
CD-ROM	For installation, at least 12X speed or faster.
Network Card	For network installations, a NIC compatible with Windows 2000. (To figure out whether you have Windows 2000-compatible hardware, you can check the Hardware Compatibility List (HCL) at www.microsoft.com/windows2000/compatible.)

Checking hardware compatibility

Before attempting an installation, you need to make certain that your hardware is compatible with Windows 2000.

Fortunately, Windows 2000 is a Plug and Play operating system, so hardware issues don't pose as much of a problem as they did in previous Windows versions. Regardless, you should check out the Hardware Compatibility List (HCL) on your installation CD-ROM or at www.microsoft.com/ windows2000/compatible — better safe than sorry, right? For legacy devices, you need installation disks, which must be Windows 2000-compatible; again, check the HCL. If a device isn't listed in the HCL, this doesn't mean the device won't work with Windows 2000 — it simply means that Microsoft hasn't tested the device. Visit the hardware vendor's Web site to find out more information about compatibility with Windows 2000.

Choosing a file system

Windows 2000 supports File Allocation Table (FAT), File Allocation Table 32 (FAT32), and NT File System (NTFS). Before beginning the installation, determine which file system you want to use on the server. Of course, the file system of choice is NTFS. NTFS in Windows 2000 is an enhanced version that supports the security features of the Kerberos protocol. Without NTFS, you have very limited security on your system. Also, many configuration options require NTFS. FAT and FAT32 are provided for backward compatibility, but you don't need them unless you plan to dual-boot your server with Windows 9*x* (which probably isn't going to happen). In short, use NTFS.

Performing a backup

If you're upgrading to Windows 2000 from a previous version of Windows, you should perform a complete backup in case you run into problems during the installation. By doing a complete backup, you protect all your data and your current operating system.

Also, make certain you uncompress any DriveSpace or DoubleSpace volumes before upgrading to Windows 2000. Do not upgrade to Windows 2000 on a compressed drive unless you compressed the drive with the NTFS compression feature. As in any installation, if you have disk mirroring in effect on your system, disable it before beginning the installation.

Checking your applications

Before installing Windows 2000, make certain that any applications currently installed on your system are compatible with Windows 2000. The readme.doc file on your installation CD-ROM provides a list of compatible applications. Read this file to avoid any surprises with your applications after the installation is complete. Also, check your application versions against the more updated information that may be found on the vendor's Web site concerning incompatibility issues.

Upgrading from Windows NT to Windows 2000

In many networking environments, you will upgrade Windows NT 4.0 servers to Windows 2000 servers rather than perform a clean installation. Upgrading preserves your major settings, keeps your data intact, and enables you to migrate the user and group accounts from Windows NT domain controllers to Windows 2000 and its Active Directory.

If your Windows NT 4.0 Server is a primary or backup domain controller, the Windows 2000 setup process first installs the server software and then automatically launches the Active Directory installation process, which upgrades the server to a Windows 2000 domain controller and migrates your user and group accounts into Active Directory.

For the exam, you'll need to know the following points about upgrading from Windows NT to Windows 2000:

✦ You can upgrade directly from Windows NT 3.51, Windows NT Server 4.0, and Windows NT 4.0 Terminal Server to Windows 2000.

✦ You cannot upgrade directly from Windows NT versions earlier than 3.51. If you have an earlier version of NT, you must first upgrade to at least NT 3.51 before you can upgrade to Windows 2000 Server. You cannot directly upgrade Windows NT Workstation to Windows 2000 Server.

✦ You cannot upgrade Windows 95 and 98 to Windows 2000 Server. If you want to install Windows 2000 Server on a Windows 95 or 98 computer, Setup will delete the older operating system and begin a fresh installation.

Aside from these issues, the upgrade process works the same as a clean installation, and an upgrade involves essentially the same planning steps as a clean installation. For more information about preinstallation planning, see the section "Getting Ready for Installation," earlier in this chapter.

Running Setup

You have a few different options for starting the Windows 2000 setup program.

You need to memorize the following Setup options for the 70-215 exam:

✦ **Starting Setup directly from the CD-ROM:** If you're upgrading from an earlier version to Windows 2000, simply insert the CD-ROM into your CD-ROM drive and click Yes to begin the installation. On a blank machine that supports booting from a CD-ROM, you can also start the installation this way.

✦ **Starting Setup from a network share:** If you're installing Windows 2000 Server from a network share, connect to the share and change to the I386 folder. From a computer running MS-DOS or Windows 3.*x*, run winnt.exe. From a computer running Windows 9*x*, Windows NT 3.51, Windows NT 4.0, or Windows 2000, run winnt32.exe.

+ **Starting Setup on a computer running MS-DOS:** To start Setup on a computer running MS-DOS, insert the installation CD-ROM into the CD-ROM drive. At the command prompt, access your CD-ROM drive letter, change to the I386 folder, and run winnt.exe.

+ **Starting Setup from a floppy disk:** On a blank machine that doesn't support booting from the CD-ROM drive, you need to make a set of installation floppy disks to start the installation. On any computer running any version of Windows, put the Windows 2000 installation CD-ROM in the CD-ROM drive, choose to browse the CD, open the BOOTDISK folder, and then double-click MAKEBOOT. A command window appears. Follow the instructions. You need four blank, formatted floppy disks, which MAKEBOOT numbers 1, 2, 3, and 4, respectively.

Book II
Chapter 2

**Installing
Windows 2000
Server**

Performing an Attended Installation

After you determine how you will start Setup (see the preceding section), you simply need to start the installation process and follow the instructions that appear on-screen.

For the exam, you need to know what occurs during an attended installation. Lab 2-1 walks you through an attended installation. You should already have some hands-on experience installing the server software before taking the exam, so you can use Lab 2-1 as a guide for your practice sessions.

Lab 2-1 Performing an Attended Installation

1. **If you need to start the installation using a setup, insert installation Disk 1 and turn on your computer. If you are booting from a CD-ROM, skip to Step 5.**

    Setup inspects your system's hardware configuration and begins loading necessary setup files.

2. **When prompted, remove Disk 1, insert Disk 2, and press Enter.**

    Setup continues to load necessary setup files and then prompts you to insert Disk 3.

3. **Load the setup files from Disks 3 and 4, as directed by the on-screen prompts.**

    After reading the final disk, Setup asks whether you want to install Windows 2000, repair a Windows 2000 installation, or quit setup.

4. **Press Enter to continue the installation.**

5. **Read the licensing agreement that's displayed and then press F8 to continue.**

6. **Select a partition on your hard disk for the installation and press Enter.**

   Depending on your disk configuration, Setup may need to format your disk or partition.

7. **If Setup needs to format your disk or partition, select either NTFS or FAT and then press Enter.**

   Setup creates a list of files that it needs to copy to your hard disk for installation, and then it automatically begins the file-copy process.

   After Setup completes the file-copy process, your computer automatically reboots.

   Remove any floppy disks from your disk drive before the system reboots.

   After the system reboots, Setup launches a GUI interface and the setup process continues.

8. **Click Next on the Welcome screen.**

   Setup detects and installs hardware devices on your system. This process takes several minutes, and your screen may flicker during the detection.

   After hardware detection, Setup displays a window in which you can customize Regional settings as desired.

9. **In the Customize Windows 2000 window, use the customize buttons to adjust the settings, or click Next to continue.**

   This brings up the Personalize Your Software window.

10. **In this window, enter your name and organization in the text boxes and then click Next.**

    This brings up the Licensing Modes window.

11. **In this window, select either the Per Server radio button or the Per Seat radio button.**

    If you select Per Server, enter the number of concurrent connections; each connection must have its own Client Access License (CAL).

12. **Make your selections and then click Next.**

13. **Enter the desired computer name, enter and confirm the administrator password (limited to 256 characters), and then click Next.**

    The Windows 2000 Setup Components window appears.

14. **In this window, select the components you want to install and click Next.**

    You can also install these components later.

15. **Enter your country, area code, and the number used to access an outside phone line (if applicable) and click Next.**

16. **Adjust the date and time settings so that they're correct for your time zone and click Next.**

    Windows automatically installs network components and then prompts you to choose either Typical settings or Custom settings.

17. **Choose either Typical settings or Customs settings and click Next.**

    If you choose Typical settings, Setup installs network connections for Client for Microsoft Networks, File and Print Sharing for Microsoft networks, and TCP/IP with automatic addressing.

18. **Click the appropriate radio button if your server is a member of a workgroup or domain. If it's a member of a domain, enter the domain name in the Networking dialog box that appears.**

19. **Click Next.**

    Setup builds a file list and continues installing components. This process may take several minutes.

    Setup performs the final tasks of installing Start menu items, registering components, saving settings, and removing temporary setup files.

20. **Click Finish to complete the installation.**

    Windows 2000 automatically reboots when installation is complete.

**Book II
Chapter 2**

**Installing
Windows 2000
Server**

Preparing for Unattended Installations

When you perform an attended installation of Windows 2000 Server, you physically "attend" to the installation of that computer. (We provide the steps for doing so in Lab 2-1.) However, what if you need to install 500 servers? Using the attended method, you'd have to invest a lot of your time!

The good news is that Windows 2000 Server provides you a few different ways to install the software without having to baby-sit the setup routine. The following sections review the unattended methods available to you.

By using an unattended installation, you can roll out Windows 2000 to multiple computers without having to physically sit at those computers and answer setup questions. To prepare for an unattended installation, you have to complete three basic tasks: create an answer file, create a distribution folder, and review setup switches.

A *distribution folder* is a network share that holds the setup files. With this network share, you can perform unattended installations to the computers on your network.

You can create the network share on any computer on your network. Simply create a folder called either i386 or some other friendly name, and then copy the contents of the Windows 2000 installation CD-ROM to the shared folder. Depending on your needs, you may also choose to create a OEM subfolder within the i386 folder. You can use the OEM subfolder to store any additional subfolders needed to satisfy the Microsoft OEM requirements and your own installation needs.

In addition to creating the distribution folder that holds the setup files, you should review the setup switches that are available for both winnt.exe and winnt32.exe.

Following is the syntax for winnt.exe:

```
WINNT [/s[:sourcepath]] [/t[:tempdrive]
 [/u[:answer file]] [/udf:id[,UDF_file]]
 [/r:folder] [/r[x]:folder] [/e:command] [/a]
```

The brackets identify optional switches, and the italics highlight information that you need to supply — for example, path names and filenames. You don't type the brackets when you enter the WINNT command.

Table 2-2 explains the WINNT setup switches. You need to memorize this information for the exam.

Table 2-2	winnt.exe Setup Parameters
Parameter	*What It Does*
/s[:sourcepath]	Specifies the source location of the Windows 2000 files. The location must be a full path of the form x:[path] or \server\share[path].
/t[:tempdrive]	Directs Setup to place temporary files on the specified drive and to install Windows 2000 on that drive. If you don't specify a location, Setup attempts to locate a drive for you.
/u[:answer file]	Performs an unattended Setup using an answer file (requires /s). The answer file provides answers to some or all of the prompts that the end user normally responds to during Setup.
/udf:id[:UDF_file]	Indicates an identifier (id) that Setup uses to specify how a Uniqueness Database File (UDF) modifies an answer file (see /u). The /udf parameter overrides values in the answer file, and the identifier determines which values in the UDF file are used. If no UDF_file is specified, Setup prompts you to insert a disk that contains the $Unique$.udb file.
/r[:folder]	Specifies an optional folder to be installed. The folder remains after Setup finishes.

Parameter	What It Does
/rx[:folder]	Specifies an optional folder to be copied. The folder is deleted after Setup finishes.
/e	Specifies a command to be executed at the end of GUI-mode Setup.
/a	Enables accessibility options.

You also need to know the winnt32 setup switches for the exam. Here's the syntax for winnt32.exe:

```
WINNT32 [/S:sourcepath] [/tempdrive: drive_letter] [/unattend
    [num] [:answer_file]] [/copydir:folder_name] [/copysource:
    folder_name] [/cmd: command_line] [/debug [level]
    [: filename]] [/udf: id [, UDF_file]] [/syspart:
    drive_letter]
```

Table 2-3 explains the winnt32 setup switches.

Table 2-3	winnt32.exe Setup Parameters
Parameter	What It Does
/S: sourcepath	Specifies the location of the Windows 2000 files.
/tempdrive: drive_letter	Tells Setup to place temporary files on a specified drive and to install Windows 2000 on that drive.
/unattend[num][:answer_file]	Installs Windows 2000 in unattended mode using the answer file.
/copydir: folder_name	Creates an additional folder within the folder that contains the Windows 2000 files.
/copysource: folder_name	Creates a temporary folder in the folder that contains the Windows 2000 files.
/cmd: command_line	Tells Setup to carry out a specific command before setup is complete.
/debug[level][:filename]	Creates a debug log at the level specified.
/udf:id[,UDF_file]	Indicates an identifier (id) that Setup uses to specify how a Uniqueness Database File (UDF) modifies an answer file.
/syspart: drive_letter	Enables you to copy Setup startup files to a hard drive, mark the drive as active, and then install the drive in another computer. You must use the /tempdrive parameter with /syspart.

(continued)

Book II
Chapter 2

Installing
Windows 2000
Server

Table 2-3 *(continued)*

Parameter	What It Does
/checkupgradeonly	Checks your computer for upgrade compatibility with Windows 2000. For Windows 95 or Windows 98 upgrades, Setup creates a report named upgrade.txt in the Windows installation folder. For Windows NT 3.51 or 4.0 upgrades, it saves the report to the winnt32.log in the installation folder.
/cmdcons	Adds a Recovery Console option (for repairing a failed installation) to the operating system selection screen. It is only used post-Setup.
/m:folder_name	Specifies that Setup copies replacement files from an alternate location. Instructs Setup to look in the alternate location first and, if files are present, use them instead of the files from the default location.
/makelocalsource	Instructs Setup to copy all installation source files to your local hard disk. Use /makelocal-source when installing from a CD to provide installation files when the CD isn't available later in the installation.
/noreboot	Instructs Setup to not restart the computer after the file copy phase of winnt32 is completed so that you can execute another command.

Creating an Answer File

During an attended installation, you interact with the Setup program by manually entering answers to the questions that Setup asks about your installation. In this way, you tailor the installation to meet your needs. For an unattended installation, however, you supply an *answer file* that Setup uses to get the answers to its questions.

To prepare for an unattended installation, you first create a distribution folder and review the command-line syntax for winnt.exe and winnt32.exe. (See the preceding section in this chapter.) Then, you create an answer file. The default name for the answer file is unattended.txt, but you can use any name you want, as long as you point to the correct name when you enter the command to start the setup process. This feature enables you to create multiple answer files for different Windows 2000 installations.

You can create an answer file in either of two ways: manually or by using Setup Manager, which you find on the Windows 2000 CD-ROM. Because using Setup Manager is the preferred method (and the one you need to know for the exam), this section focuses only on Setup Manager.

You use Setup Manager to start the Windows 2000 installation and create an answer file for an unattended installation. Launch setupmgr.exe on the installation CD-ROM or from the Windows 2000 Resource Kit.

Setup Manager presents you with a wizard that helps you create an answer file or edit an existing one. Lab 2-2 walks you through the steps for using Setup Manager. You need to know the options presented for the exam, so use this lab to practice creating answer files on your server.

Lab 2-2   Creating an Answer File

1. **Launch Setup Manager from the Windows 2000 CD-ROM or from the Resource Kit.**
2. **Click Next on the Welcome screen.**
3. **Click the Create a New Answer File radio button and then click Next.**
4. **In the Product to Install dialog box, select Windows 2000 Server and click Next.**
5. **In the User Interaction Level dialog box, shown in Figure 2-1, select the level of user interaction desired. For a complete unattended setup, select Fully Automated and click Next.**

**Book II
Chapter 2**

Installing
Windows 2000
Server

Figure 2-1:
Select the
level of user
interaction
from this
dialog box.

6. **Accept the license agreement by selecting the check box and clicking Next.**
7. **Type your name and organization and click Next.**
8. **Enter the CD key for the computers you want to set up and then click Next.**

    You need a separate license for each copy of Windows that you install.

9. **Select either Per Server or Per Seat for the licensing mode and then click Next.**

   Per server licensing requires a separate CAL for each concurrent connection to the server, and per seat licensing requires a separate CAL for each client computer that accesses a Windows 2000 Server.

10. **Enter the desired names of the destination computer(s) and click Next.**

    You can also choose to automatically generate computer names based on your organization's name by selecting the check box at the bottom of the dialog box.

11. **Enter and confirm the administrator password and then click Next.**

    You can also specify for the system to automatically log on with the administrator password when the system first boots.

12. **In the Display settings dialog box, use the drop-down lists to select colors, screen area, and refresh frequency, or click Custom to select additional display setting options, and then click Next.**

13. **In the Network Settings dialog box, select either Typical Settings (which installs TCP/IP, enables DHCP, and installs Client for Microsoft Networks) or Custom. If you choose Custom, select the desired networking components to install. Click Next.**

14. **In the Join a Domain dialog box, enter either the domain or workgroup the server should join. To join a domain, enter the name of the domain and provide a user account that has permission to join a computer to a domain (such as an administrator's user name and password). Click Next.**

15. **In the Time Zone dialog box, select the appropriate time zone and click Next.**

16. **If necessary, configure additional settings; click Next to bring up the Distribution Folder dialog box.**

    Additional settings include such information as telephony and regional settings.

    In the Distribution Folder dialog box, you specify whether Setup should create or modify a distribution folder if the unattended installation will be performed from a CD-ROM.

17. **Make your selection and click Next.**

18. **The Name dialog box appears. Enter a name and path for your answer file (the default name is unattended.txt) and click Next.**

19. **Click Finish.**

After you create the answer file, you can view it and even manually edit the file by using Notepad, as shown in Figure 2-2.

Figure 2-2:
You can use
Notepad
to view
and edit
unattended.
txt.

```
unattend - Notepad
File  Edit  Format  Help
;SetupMgrTag
[Unattended]
    UnattendMode=FullUnattended
    OemPreinstall=No

[GuiUnattended]
    AdminPassword=admin
    TimeZone=90

[UserData]
    ProductID=111111-111111-111111-111111-111111
    FullName="Curt Simmons"
    OrgName=Simmons
    ComputerName=SIMM8765

[Display]

[LicenseFilePrintData]
    AutoMode=PerServer
```

After you create the answer file, you can run Setup so that it uses the answer file. Review the list of parameters to determine how you would like to run Setup. Typically, you provide the WINNT parameters that point to the location of the setup files and the answer file. The following example shows how to run Setup from a CD-ROM and point to a desired answer file:

```
Winnt /S:drive_letter\I386 /U:drive_letter\unattended.txt
```

Troubleshooting Failed Installations

Many problems can arise during an installation that can leave you very frustrated. Fortunately, Windows 2000 has a relatively stable setup process.

As a general troubleshooting note, you can find the cause of many setup problems in drivers and hardware that aren't compatible with Windows 2000. Incompatible drivers or hardware can halt Setup during the hardware detection phase. Make sure that you carefully plan your installation and check the HCL before you run Setup. For the details about planning an installation, check out the section "Getting Ready for Installation" earlier in this chapter.

During installation, you may receive STOP errors. A STOP error message identifies a problem that has stopped the installation. For the 70-215 exam, you need to know the most common STOP errors and how to handle them:

✦ **STOP Message IRQL_NOT_LESS_OR_EQUAL:** This STOP message occurs when a device driver is using an improper memory address. If you can start Windows, check the system log for more detailed information, and remove any new hardware and device drivers that may be causing the problem.

+ **STOP Message KMODE_EXCEPTION_NOT_HANDLED:** Kernel mode exceptions, which may result from various events, cause this STOP message. Typically, you can attempt to troubleshoot this problem by ensuring that you have enough disk space for the installation, removing unnecessary or new device drivers, using a standard VGA driver, and making certain that your system BIOS is current. If you can boot Windows, try using the Last Known Good Configuration by pressing the F8 key at startup.

+ **STOP Message FAT_FILE_SYSTEM or NTFS_FILE_SYSTEM:** A heavily fragmented drive, file I/O problems, disk mirroring, or the operation of some antivirus software can all cause this error. Run **CHKDSK /f** to check the hard drive for corruption and then restart the computer. You can also use the Last Known Good Configuration option by pressing the F8 key at startup.

+ **STOP Message DATA_BUS_ERROR:** A parity error in the system memory will give you this error message. Try restarting the computer in Safe Mode. You can also try disabling memory caching in the BIOS.

+ **STOP Message NO_MORE_SYSTEM_PTES:** This error occurs because a driver isn't cleaning up properly. Remove any recently installed software and hardware devices and try running setup again.

+ **STOP Message INACCESSIBLE_BOOT_DEVICE:** This error occurs during the initialization of the I/O system; typically, a boot-sector virus causes it. Run a virus-scan program to check for a boot-sector virus.

About Those Service Packs

The 70-215 exam expects you to know about service packs. From time to time, Microsoft releases service packs in order to update portions of the Windows 2000 operating system and to provide fixes for portions of the operating system that may not be functioning properly. You can purchase service packs on CD-ROM at a minimal cost, or you can download service packs from www.microsoft.com for free.

For the exam, just remember the purpose of service packs and also remember that an effective, timely rollout of service packs to your Windows 2000 servers is an important component of keeping your operating systems updated.

You can deploy service packs in one of three ways, which you should keep in mind for the exam:

+ **CD-ROM:** You can purchase service packs on CD-ROM and manually install them. You can also download the service pack and perform the installation that way.

+ **Network Share:** You can place the service pack on a network share so that network clients can connect to and install the service pack. Just browse to the network share and launch the service pack's .exe file.

+ **Slipstreaming:** You can also deploy service packs during a new installation through a process called slipstreaming. Simply copy all service pack files to the installation distribution folder so that the updates can be installed when the operating system is installed.

Using Other Setup Methods

In addition to attended and unattended installation of Windows 2000 Server, the exam also expects you to understand two other major Setup options: Sysprep and Syspart. The following sections explore what you need to know about these additional setup methods.

Using Sysprep

You can use the Sysprep utility to duplicate a disk and install the image on another computer. For example, you can install a Windows 2000 Server, configure it as desired, and install additional software. Then, you use Sysprep to create an image of the server's hard disk that you can copy to another server. You use the Sysprep utility along with a sysprep.inf file that serves as the answer file for cloning. You find Sysprep on the Deployment.cab file on your installation CD-ROM.

You don't need to know a lot about Sysprep for the exam, but you might run across a question regarding where you want to use Sysprep to install images on a computer without using a Security Identifier (SID). You can perform this action by using the *nosidgen* switch with Sysprep. Also, note that when using Sysprep, the machine that the image is coming from and the one the image is going to must have the same HAL, ACPI, and mass storage controllers.

Using Syspart

Syspart is like Sysprep, but you use it when the master computer on which you create the image has different hardware from the computer to which you're copying the image. Essentially, this method greatly speeds up installation by removing the file-copy portion of Setup (because it is already contained on the image). Like Sysprep, Syspart is available on the Deployment.cab file on your installation CD-ROM.

Prep Test

1 Before attempting a Windows 2000 Server installation, which resource should you check to ensure that your computer's hardware is compatible with Windows 2000?

- **A** ○ readme.doc
- **B** ○ HCL
- **C** ○ LCH
- **D** ○ HLC

2 Which file system supports the new security features provided by the Kerberos protocol?

- **A** ○ FAT
- **B** ○ FAT32
- **C** ○ NTFS
- **D** ○ KER32

3 You need to install Windows 2000 on a computer running MS-DOS. After switching to your CD-ROM drive, what do you need to run?

- **A** ○ WINNT
- **B** ○ WINNT32
- **C** ○ SETUP
- **D** ○ SETUP32

4 When you're upgrading previous versions of Windows to Windows 2000, on which operating systems can you run Winnt32.exe? (Choose all that apply.)

- **A** ❑ Windows NT 4.0
- **B** ❑ Windows 3.1
- **C** ❑ Windows 9x
- **D** ❑ Windows NT 3.51

5 You notice that during a particular portion of Setup, your screen flickers several times. At what Setup stage does this occur?

- **A** ○ File copy
- **B** ○ Networking component installation
- **C** ○ Automatic reboot
- **D** ○ Hardware detection

6 During which phase of setup is the Setup program most likely to lock up?

A ○ Drive format

B ○ Registry configuration

C ○ Hardware detection

D ○ Networking component installation

7 Which tool can you use to resolve disk problems that have generated a FAT_FILE_SYSTEM or NTFS_FILE_SYSTEM error?

A ○ CHKDSK

B ○ Defragmenter

C ○ FDISK

D ○ CLNDSK

8 What operating system updates and fixes are released by Microsoft on a periodic basis?

A ○ Repair pack

B ○ Service pack

C ○ GEN pack

D ○ None of the above

9 You have an answer file named unattended4.txt. You want to use this file to run an unattended setup on a computer by using the installation CD-ROM. The CD-ROM letter is D. Which command-line syntax is correct for this installation?

A ○ Winnt /C:D\I386 /X:D\unattended4.txt

B ○ Winnt /UDF:D\I386 /UDF:D\unattended4.txt

C ○ Winnt /CMD:D\I386 /S:D\unattended4.txt

D ○ Winnt /S:D\I386 /U:D\unattended4.txt

10 You want to create an image of a particular drive that can be copied to other Windows 2000 Servers. However, the other servers have differing hardware. Which tool do you need to use?

A ○ UDF:id

B ○ Sysprep

C ○ Syspart

D ○ Winnt32

Answers

1 **B.** To ensure that your hardware is compatible with Windows 2000, you should check the Hardware Compatibility List (HCL), which is available at `www.microsoft.com/hcl` and on your installation CD-ROM. *Review "Checking hardware compatibility."*

2 **C.** The new NTFS in Windows 2000 supports the advanced security features of the Kerberos protocol, the primary authentication protocol in Windows 2000. *Review "Choosing a file system."*

3 **A.** On a computer running MS-DOS, access the CD-ROM drive at the command prompt and run WINNT to start the installation. *Review "Running Setup."*

4 **A** and **D.** All these systems and Windows 2000 support winnt32.exe. *Review "Running Setup."*

5 **D.** During the hardware detection phase of Setup, your screen may flicker for a few moments. This is a normal part of the installation process. *Review "Performing an Attended Installation."*

6 **C.** Setup is most likely to experience problems during the hardware detection phase. You can reduce the likelihood of this occurring by checking the HCL before beginning Setup to make certain that all your hardware devices are compatible with Windows 2000. *Review "Troubleshooting Failed Installations."*

7 **A.** You can run CHKDSK to attempt to fix a corrupt hard drive that prevents installation to continue. *Review "Troubleshooting Failed Installations."*

8 **B.** Microsoft periodically releases service packs to update the operating system and to resolve problems. *Review "About Those Service Packs."*

9 **D.** This command syntax provides a sourcepath to the installation files (/S:D), and it provides the unattended (/U) portion of setup by pointing to the unattended4.txt file. *Review "Creating an Answer File."*

10 **C.** You can use Syspart to copy drive images to computers that don't have the same hardware. *Review "Using Syspart."*

Chapter 3: Installing and Configuring Access to Resources

Exam Objectives

✔ **Install and configure network services for interoperability**

✔ **Monitor, configure, troubleshoot, and control access to printers**

✔ **Monitor, configure, troubleshoot, and control access to files, folders, and shared folders**

✔ **Monitor, configure, troubleshoot, and control access to Web sites**

A major purpose of server software is to provide access to a variety of network services and features to network clients. That can be a tall order to fill, and Windows 2000 Server provides these features through a number of services that you can configure, monitor, and manage.

For Exam 70-215, you need to know how to install and configure these services on a Windows 2000 server, as well as how to manage its operations. To help you prepare for the DHCP-related questions on the Windows 2000 Server exam, this chapter focuses on the following topics:

✦ Installing and managing DHCP

✦ Installing and managing DNS

✦ Managing shared file and folder access

✦ Monitoring and configuring access to Web sites

Installing and Configuring Network Services for Interoperability

Windows 2000 Server offers a number of services for interoperability in Windows 2000 networks. In this section, we take a look at the basic services, including DHCP and DNS. You should carefully review these subjects for the exam because Windows 2000 member servers are often used to provide these services.

Understanding DHCP

DHCP (Dynamic Host Configuration Protocol) is a server service that dynamically assigns, or *leases,* IP addresses and related IP information to network clients. At first glance, this may not seem like an important task. However, you have to remember that, on a TCP/IP network, each network client must have a unique IP address and an appropriate subnet mask. Without these items, a client can't communicate on the network. For example, if two clients have the same IP address, neither will be able to communicate on the network.

Windows 2000 server can function as a DHCP server and provide IP addressing information to network clients. To learn more about configuring DHCP, see Book III, Chapter 3.

Reviewing DNS Concepts

Windows 2000 offers complete integration with Domain Name System (DNS) — the industry standard for resolving host names to IP addresses. DNS is very extensible. In other words, as your organization grows, your network's DNS-based naming structure, or namespace, can grow accordingly — with virtually no limits.

Because DNS is fully integrated with Windows 2000, a domain, such as www.microsoft.com, can also be the name of a local network. For example, KarenS@tritondev.com is an e-mail address, and it can be a username in a Windows 2000 network. Windows 2000 networking with Active Directory is based on DNS, and all Active Directory names are DNS names. This approach provides a global naming system so that the local network has the same naming structure as the Internet. In short, you can't separate Windows 2000 and DNS.

The 70-215 exam expects you to understand basic DNS concepts and the use of a Windows 2000 member server as a DNS server. The following sections offer a quick review of DNS concepts. If your DNS knowledge is up to par, you can skip these sections. Subsequent sections in this chapter cover the installation, configuration, and management of a DNS server.

Understanding the DNS namespace

In order to understand DNS, you need to understand the DNS namespace. A *namespace* is an area that can be resolved. A postal address on a letter uses a namespace that contains a zip code, state, city, street address, and name. Because all letters follow this namespace, your mail reaches only you, out of the millions of possible addressees. (Well, most of your mail reaches you.)

To resolve the namespace used on a piece of mail, you start by examining the zip code, then the state, and then the city. This process narrows the resolution to one geographical area. Next, you resolve the address by narrowing it to one street and one street number. The final portion of the resolution process is your name.

This system works because all mail follows this namespace. If letter writers put whatever information they wanted on the envelope, your mail would probably never reach you. A namespace, then, is an area that can be resolved.

DNS functions in the same manner. Because host names follow a namespace, they can be resolved to IP addresses. For example, `www.microsoft.com` is a host name that represents an IP address. Because computers must have an IP address to communicate, the host name must be resolved to an IP address. In the past, this process was handled by Hosts files, which are static mappings of host name to IP addresses. Hosts files have been widely replaced by DNS, but they are occasionally still used.

Book II
Chapter 3

Installing and Configuring Access to Resources

To resolve a host name to an IP address, DNS starts by considering the root domain, which is represented by a period (.). Next, the address is read, beginning with the top-level domain, such as `com`, `edu`, `mil`, `gov`, `org`, `info`, `biz`, or `net`. For example, `microsoft.com` is a part of the `com` first-level domain, so at this point in the resolution process, all other first-level domains are excluded.

The second-level domain is usually a "friendly" name of a company, organization, or person. Microsoft is an original, unique, and friendly name, so it's resolved next. At this point, a particular server or group of servers, called *third-level domains,* can be resolved. For example, `sales.microsoft.com` may point to a particular server.

Using this method, any DNS name can be resolved to the host computer so that its IP address can be retrieved. The name-resolution process on the Internet usually requires numerous domain servers. For example, `com` servers would be used to resolve Microsoft, and so on.

Understanding DNS zones

The DNS name-resolution process uses DNS database files. Different servers in a network hold portions of the DNS database file so that name resolution can occur. In small networks, a DNS server may even hold the entire name-to-IP-address database file. When a DNS server is queried for name resolution, it checks its database file to determine whether it has an entry for the query. If not, the DNS server can forward the request to another DNS server.

To subdivide DNS duties and administrative control, DNS zones are often used in DNS networks. A *zone* is a discrete, contiguous portion of the DNS namespace. For example, `sales.tritiondev.com` and `acct.trition-dev.com` could be DNS zones. Servers in the `sales` zone hold all DNS records for that zone, while DNS servers in the `acct` zone hold all records for the `acct` zone. This feature enables different administrators to manage DNS servers in different portions of the namespace. By using the zone feature, you can partition the DNS namespace to make it more manageable.

Within a zone, you have two kinds of DNS database files: primary and secondary. One server in the zone contains the *primary zone database file*, and all other DNS servers in the zone contain copies of that primary database file called *secondary zone database files*. Only the primary zone database file can have updates or changes made to it. A process called *zone transfer* replicates any changes made to the primary zone database file to the secondary zone database files. The server that holds the primary zone database file is called an *authoritative server* because it has authority over the other DNS servers in the zone. Secondary database file servers in the zone are used to reduce the traffic and query load on the primary zone database server.

Windows 2000 DNS is Dynamic DNS (DDNS). In previous versions of Windows, DNS database files were *static* — an administrator had to change them manually. In Windows 2000, DNS can dynamically update its database when host-name-to-IP-address changes occur.

Installing DNS

You install DNS just as you would any other Windows 2000 server service. You can install DNS by using either the Configure Your Server tool in Administrative Tools or Add/Remove Programs in Control Panel.

DNS is automatically installed on domain controllers because DNS must be present for Active Directory. It isn't automatically installed on member servers, however. Keep this point in mind for tricky exam questions.

Setting Up DNS

After installation, DNS isn't operational until you set up the service. Fortunately, Windows 2000 Server provides a handy wizard to help you configure your DNS server for the role you want it to play in your DNS network.

Lab 3-1 walks you through the steps for using the Configure DNS Server Wizard. For the exam, you need to know the options that the wizard presents, so make certain you practice configuring DNS by using Lab 3-1.

Lab 3-1 Setting Up DNS

1. **Choose Start➪Programs➪Administrative Tools➪DNS.**

   This opens the DNS console.

2. **In the console's tree pane, select your DNS server and then choose Action➪Configure the Server.**

   The Configure DNS Server Wizard displays its welcome screen.

3. **Click Next.**

   The system collects setup information.

   The wizard displays the Root Server dialog box. In a DNS network, you must have a root server.

4. **If this is the first DNS server on your network, select the Create a Root Server radio button. If you already have other DNS servers running, click the Additional Server radio button and enter an IP address. (If you create an additional server, skip ahead to Step 7.)**

   If you choose to create a root server, the wizard prompts you to create a *forward lookup zone*, a name-to-IP-address database that helps computers resolve names to IP addresses. The zone also contains information about network services.

5. **Specify whether you want to create the forward lookup zone now by clicking either Yes or No.**

   The Zone Type dialog box gives you options for creating either an Active Directory-integrated zone, a standard primary zone, or a standard secondary zone. In pure Active Directory environments, you should select the Active Directory-Integrated option so that all zone and database data is stored in Active Directory. Selecting the Standard Primary option creates a new zone where the database is stored locally, and selecting the Standard Secondary option enables your server to become a secondary server in an existing zone.

6. **Select the type of zone you want to create and then click Next.**

7. **In the Zone Name dialog box that appears, enter the name of the zone and click Next.**

8. **In the Zone File dialog box that appears, you can choose to create a new zone database file or use one that you have copied from another computer by selecting the appropriate radio button; click Next.**

   The wizard prompts you to create a *reverse lookup zone*, which enables a computer to resolve IP addresses to DNS names. (Normally, DNS names are resolved to IP addresses.) You can choose to provide this capability now, or you can create a reverse lookup zone later.

9. **Indicate whether you want to create a reverse lookup zone and click Next.**

   If you choose to create a reverse lookup zone, the wizard displays the Zone Type dialog box. Otherwise, the wizard displays a summary dialog box. See Step 5.

10. **Review your selections and click Finish.**

Managing the DNS server

After you install and configure DNS (see the previous sections in this chapter), you must manage the server so that it performs in a desired manner. Exam 70-215 expects you to know how to perform several DNS server-management tasks, so this section points out those issues and shows you how to manage the DNS server.

To access the Properties dialog box that you use for configuring your DNS server, select your DNS server in the DNS Manager console's tree pane and then choose Action⇨Properties to access the Properties dialog box. The seven tabs in the Properties dialog box offer numerous configuration options; you need to know about several of these tabs for the exam:

✦ **Interfaces:** You can specify the IP addresses for which your DNS server answers DNS queries. With the default setting, your server listens to all IP addresses. However, you can select the Only the Following IP Addresses radio button and enter the desired IP addresses. This feature is useful if you want your DNS server to service only a select group of computers.

✦ **Forwarders:** You can select the check box to enable *forwarders*, which enable your DNS server to forward unresolved queries to other DNS servers that you specify on this tab. If your server is the root server, this option isn't available because your server is already at the top of the hierarchy.

✦ **Advanced:** This tab, shown in Figure 3-1, offers several server configuration options, which you can select by selecting the appropriate check boxes.

   By default, the BIND Secondaries, Enable Round Robin, and Enable Netmask Ordering options are selected. You can also disable recursion, which prevents a DNS server from carrying the full responsibility for name-to-IP-address resolution (allows forwarding). You can select Fail on Load if Bad Zone Data is detected by the DNS server when attempting to load, and you can select Secure Cache Against Pollution to use a cache method that prevents pollution from occurring. *Pollution* is the loading of outdated mappings.

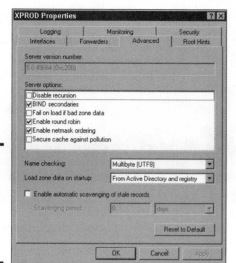

Figure 3-1:
The Advanced tab of the server's Properties dialog box.

For the Name Checking option on the Advanced tab, you can select the following methods, which you should remember for the exam:

- **Strict RFC:** Strictly enforces the use of RFC-compliant rules for all DNS names. Non-RFC names are treated as errors.

- **Non RFC:** Any names can be used, including names that aren't RFC-compliant.

- **Multibyte (UTF8):** Uses the Unicode 8-bit translation encoding scheme.

- **All Names:** Allows all names to be used with the DNS server.

You also can specify how you want the DNS server to load zone data at startup. Depending on your network configuration, you can make the appropriate selection from the following options:

- From Active Directory and the Registry

- From the Registry

- From the file \winnt\System32\boot.dns

You can also use the Advanced tab to enable automatic scavenging of stale records. This feature enables the server to automatically clean old records out of the database at an interval that you specify on the Advanced tab. The default automatic scavenge interval is every seven days.

✦ **Root Hints:** This tab specifies other DNS servers and IP addresses that your DNS server can use for query resolution. On the Root Hints tab, you can enter the names and IP addresses of other DNS servers that your server can contact for name resolution, or you can edit and remove them as necessary. This feature helps an authoritative zone server to find servers above it in the hierarchy.

✦ **Logging:** This tab gives you the option to log various events, such as query, notify, and update.

You use the logging feature to specify the kind of DNS activity you want written to dns.log, which the system stores in %SystemRoot%\ System32\DNS. This feature is useful for troubleshooting purposes.

However, you should only enable logging for monitoring particular problems or events. This feature consumes lots of disk space, and you may see performance problems on the server, so use logging of DNS events for troubleshooting only.

✦ **Monitoring:** With this tab, you can perform simple DNS tests against your server so that you can verify its configuration.

✦ **Security:** Like all other Security tabs in Windows 2000 Server, this one has options that enable you to configure who can access and configure the DNS service on this server.

Managing zone resource records

Each zone database file may contain any number of resource records. A *resource record* is simply an entry in the database — a record that helps the DNS server resolve queries.

When a new zone is created, two default resource records are automatically created. The first is the Start of Authority (SOA), which defines the authoritative server for the zone. The second is the Name Server (NS) record, which lists all DNS servers operating in the zone. DNS servers also use a SRV, or service, record that identifies them as a DNS server. Keep these in mind for the exam.

In addition to the SOA and NS records, you can create several other records. To create these records, simply expand the DNS server in the tree pane, select the appropriate zone, and then click the Action menu and choose the kind of record you want to create from the list that appears.

Table 3-1 explains the major resource records that you can create. You need to memorize them for the exam.

Table 3-1	Zone Resource Records
Resource Record	*What It Does*
Host (A)	Provides a host-to-IP-address mapping for a forward lookup zone.
Pointer (PTR)	Created with an A record, it points to another reverse lookup zone of the namespace where you can map an IP address to a host name.
Alias (CNAME)	Enables a host to have a different name. CNAME records are often used for load-balancing purposes, and each CNAME record contains a host's alias as well as the fully qualified domain name. CNAME records can be used to group DNS servers so they appear as one server.
Mail Exchanger (MX)	Identifies a mail server with a particular host or domain.

In addition to these standard resource records, you can also create specific records for your environment by choosing Action⇨Other New Records. When you choose this command, the console displays a list of possible records that you can create; you can even create custom records.

You don't need to know all about these other records for the exam, but you should remember that the option exists.

Examining Windows 2000 Print Features

For the most part, the printing process in Windows 2000 works the same as in down-level versions of Windows. However, Windows 2000 does have several new printing features that give your network print environment more flexibility and possibilities.

You should know the new Windows 2000 print features for Exam 70-215:

✦ **Standard port monitor:** Windows 2000 supports a standard port monitor that enables Windows 2000 computers to print to network interface printers by using TCP/IP. This feature replaces LPRMON for TCP/IP printers connected directly to the network with a network adapter card and is 50 percent faster than LPRMON.

✦ **Remote port support:** Windows 2000 supports remote port configurations that enable a print administrator to manage any remote network printers without physically visiting the printer or computer where it's connected.

✦ **Active Directory integration:** Windows 2000 computers can automatically store network printers in Active Directory so that network users can easily find the printers and use them.

✦ **Internet printing:** Windows 2000 allows client computers (running Windows 2000) to print to a print server using a URL. This feature further integrates the Internet or intranet with the local network.

✦ **Performance monitoring:** Performance Monitor in Windows 2000 contains a new Print Queue object that enables you to set up counters in Performance Monitor to troubleshoot printing problems.

✦ **Macintosh and UNIX support:** Windows 2000 supports printing to Macintosh and UNIX printers.

Installing Printers

All printer installation and configuration takes place in the Printers folder on a Windows 2000 member server. You access the Printers folder by choosing Start⇨Settings⇨Printers, or through Control Panel.

The Printers folder contains icons for any installed printers and an Add Printer Wizard, which takes you through the steps for installing a new printer. For the most part, installing a new printer is rather easy, but you do need to understand some new print features that Windows 2000 offers, which you can explore in the next section.

Configuring Printers

After you install a printer (see the preceding section), you can configure the printer as desired by accessing the printer's properties. In the Printers folder, select the printer and then choose File⇨Properties. The resulting Properties dialog box has numerous configuration options available for your printer, and the exam expects you to know what options you have and where you configure them.

The following sections examine each tab in a printer's Properties dialog box, pointing out only the information that you need to know for the test.

Understanding the General tab

The General tab in your printer's Properties dialog box gives you basic information about the printer, including the printer's name and location, and your comments, which you can add to or change if desired. Also, the second half of the General tab lists the printer's features, such as color printing, double-sided printing, and stapling capabilities.

If you click the Printing Preferences button at the bottom of the General tab, you can adjust such qualities as page layout and paper quality. Also, depending on your printer, clicking this button may enable you to use various utilities. The options available vary depending on the printer you have installed.

At first glance, the General tab may not seem very important, but you can store the information listed on the General tab in Active Directory. Then, users can search for printers that offer the capabilities they need — color, stapling, and so on — and find the desired printer. To ensure that Active Directory has accurate information about each printer, you must have the correct information on the General tab in each printer's Properties dialog box.

Using the Sharing tab

The Sharing tab in your printer's Properties dialog box enables you to share the printer so that other users can access it and print to it. To share the printer, you simply click Shared As and then give the printer a share name.

Only Windows 2000 computers can automatically publish printers to Active Directory. The Sharing tab includes a List in the Directory check box, which is automatically selected. With this setting, Windows 2000 computers can automatically publish shared printers to Active Directory. Printers connected to down-level computers (such as NT and 9*x*) can also be published in Active Directory, but an Active Directory administrator must manually add those printer objects to the directory. Watch out for tricky exam questions on this issue.

The Sharing tab also has an Additional Drivers button. Windows 2000 computers can connect to Windows 2000 print shares and automatically download the printer drivers. This process is invisible to users, who simply determine which printer they want to use and then connect to it. Because the print drivers are needed for network printers, Active Directory downloads the drivers to the client. If you have other clients — for example, NT and 9*x* — on your network, you need to click the Additional Drivers button and make drivers for those operating systems available for download to down-level clients. In the dialog box that appears after you click Additional Drivers, select the check box corresponding to each operating system to which you want to provide drivers. You may be prompted for an installation CD or disk for the printer driver.

Pulling in to the Ports tab

On the Ports tab in your printer's Properties dialog box, you select ports the printer can use. If you configure several ports, documents print to the first free port. You can also add new ports and delete ports. By clicking the Configure Port button, you open the Port Settings dialog box, where you can change settings for a selected port. Typically, however, you won't need to change port settings.

You also use the Ports tab to enable printer pooling. Printer pooling enables printing to two or more identical print devices that users see as one printer. For example, you could have three identical print devices and configure them so that they appear as one device. Users simply print to the one printer, yet three print devices are available to accommodate the tasks. This management option may help you reduce confusion for end-users. To enable printer pooling, select the check box and then select all ports that are in use by the print devices.

Configuring the Advanced tab

On the Advanced tab in your printer's Properties dialog box, you can configure various options that determine how the print device behaves. First, if desired, you can determine a time period each day when the printer is available, and you can set the printer's priority.

The printer device priority range is 1 (lowest) to 99 (highest). For example, if you have multiple print devices connected to the same port, a print device with a priority of 2 will always print before a print device with a priority of 1. You can use this feature to send critical documents to a printer that has the highest priority so that those documents always print first. For the exam, just remember that a higher number means a higher print priority.

You have several other check box and radio button options on this tab. You need to be familiar with these options for the exam:

+ **Spool Print Documents So Programs Finish Printing Faster:** With this option, a print job can be held in a spool so that users can get control of their programs and move on to other tasks. To start printing immediately, users can choose to begin printing as soon as the last page is spooled.

+ **Print Directly to the Printer:** This option skips the spooling process and prints directly to the printer. Use this option only if you can't print by using the spooling options.

+ **Hold Mismatched Documents:** This option tells the spooler to check the printer setup and match it with the document setup before the document goes to the printer. If the information doesn't match, the spooler holds the print job in the print queue. This action doesn't stop other properly matched documents from printing.

+ **Print Spooled Documents First:** If several print jobs are being spooled, this option tells the spooler to print the jobs as spooling is complete. This action can override priority settings, so you may not want to use it if your priority settings are very important.

+ **Keep Printed Documents:** This option tells the spooler to keep print documents after they're printed instead of deleting them. Then, documents can be reprinted directly from the print queue instead of the program from which the user originally printed.

✦ **Enable Advanced Printing Features:** Normally enabled by default, this option turns on metafile spooling so that advanced options, such as page order, booklet printing, and pages per sheet are available.

Configuring the Security tab

You can determine who can print to a particular printer and what additional rights users or administrators may have by using the Security tab in a printer's Properties dialog box.

By default, the available permissions are Print, Manage Printer, and Manage Documents. And by default, administrators, print operators, and server operators have rights to all these permissions. Also by default, all users in the Everyone group have Print permissions.

You can, of course, change these default permissions as needed. Use the Add and Remove buttons to make changes to the list as desired.

You can also configure Advanced permissions by clicking the Advanced button. This feature opens the Access Control Settings dialog box for the printer. Select a user or group in the list and then click View/Edit to make additional permission changes, or click Add to add new users or groups to the list.

When you click View/Edit, the Permission Entry dialog box opens, giving you the additional permission options of Read, Change, and Take Ownership.

By assigning the Take Ownership permission, you allow another user to take ownership of the printer, which essentially gives that person full control permissions to the printer. By default, administrators have Take Ownership permission, and you should think carefully before giving this permission to any other user.

Using the Device Settings tab

In a printer's Properties dialog box, the Device Settings tab shows you a tree structure of different device settings, such as paper tray configuration. Expand the list and click the drop-down menus to make changes as desired.

In addition to the tabs that we describe in the preceding sections of this chapter, a printer's Properties dialog box may include other tabs, such as Color Management and Utilities, depending on the printer you have installed. You won't see any questions about these printer-specific tabs on the exam.

Managing Printers

You manage printers by configuring the printer's properties (see the preceding sections in this chapter), or by simply selecting the printer icon in the Printers folder and choosing options from the File menu. The options presented to you are rather simple, but you need to know them for the exam.

Table 3-2 explains the options you can choose from the Printers folder's File menu. You should memorize these options for the exam.

Table 3-2	File Menu Options in the Printers Folder
Option	*What It Does*
Open	Opens the print queue, which shows a list of documents waiting to be printed. From this interface, you can cancel documents or pause the printing of certain documents as needed.
Set as Default Printer	Sets the selected printer as the default printer. All print jobs from your server will automatically default to this printer.
Printing Preferences	Opens the Preferences dialog box, which is also available from the General tab in the printer's Properties dialog box.
Pause Printing	Holds all documents in the queue.
Cancel all Documents	Deletes all documents from the print queue.
Sharing	Opens the Sharing tab in the printer's Properties dialog box so that you can make changes.
Use Printer Offline	Takes the printer offline so that you can troubleshoot problems or configure the printer before you use it.

Monitoring and Troubleshooting Printers

You can monitor printers in Windows 2000 by using Performance Monitor, which now contains print queue objects. This is an effective tool for troubleshooting printer problems. To access Performance Monitor, choose Start⇨Programs⇨Administrative Tools⇨Performance. Also see Book II, Chapter 5 to find out more about Performance Monitor.

In addition to knowing how to use Performance Monitor to monitor and troubleshoot print problems, the exam expects you to understand some of the more common printing problems and solutions. In particular, you should memorize the following common problems and solutions:

✦ **A printer connected to a computer doesn't print:** The failure usually involves a physical problem with the printer, an incorrect printer driver, a problem with the print server, or the application from which you want to print. Systematically examine each of these possibilities.

✦ **A printer connected directly to the network doesn't print:** The problem may be the physical printer or NIC, the logical printer setting on the client computer, or the application from which you're printing. Systematically examine each of these possibilities.

✦ **The printer doesn't automatically appear in Active Directory:** The printer is connected to a down-level server or client. Only Windows 2000 computers can automatically publish printers to the directory.

✦ **Windows 9*x* computers can't connect to a printer:** The printer doesn't have the drivers for Windows 9*x* installed. Use the Sharing tab on the printer's Properties dialog box to install the 9*x* drivers.

✦ **A document doesn't print or prints garbled text:** The driver is incorrect or corrupt. Update the driver by using the New Driver button on the Advanced tab in the printer's Properties dialog box.

✦ **Documents don't print and can't be deleted from the print queue:** The server may not have enough disk space for the print spooler, or the spooler may be stalled. Check for necessary disk space, and stop and restart the spooler.

Monitoring and Configuring Access to Shared Folders

In Windows 2000, you can easily share files and folders — even files and folders within folders. Typically, you manage shares by grouping files into appropriate folders and then sharing those folders with appropriate permissions. This method of organization simplifies your work as an administrator and reduces the number of shares you have to manage.

To share a folder, locate the folder on your computer by either browsing or using Windows Explorer, right-click the folder, and choose Sharing from the pop-up menu.

If an exam question indicates that the Sharing option isn't available when you right-click a folder, look for an answer that involves enabling File and Printer Sharing. To share folders or printers, you must enable File and Printer Sharing. This feature is enabled by default, but if necessary, you can enable it by right-clicking My Network Places, choosing Properties from the context menu that appears, and then right-clicking the Local Area Connection icon. Click Properties and then click the Install button and select File and Printer Sharing for Microsoft Networks.

After you choose File and Printer Sharing from the pop-up menu, Windows 2000 displays the Sharing tab in the Properties dialog box for the folder that you selected. On the Sharing tab, click Share This Folder and then enter a name for the share.

The Sharing tab offers some other options, too, as follows:

✦ If you want to create a hidden share, add the $ to the end of the share name (such as `share$`). Network users can't browse and find the hidden share, but they can map to it.

✦ You can also enter a comment about the share, if desired. Users that are using the Detail View can then see your comment about the share.

✦ To limit the number of users who can connect to the folder at one time, click the Allow button and then use the up- and down-arrow buttons to select the maximum number allowed.

✦ The Sharing tab also has a Permissions button. We discuss the Permissions button and the Security tab in the section "Controlling access to shared folders," later in this chapter.

✦ Finally, the Sharing tab has a Caching button. *Caching* is a new feature of Windows 2000 that enables users to cache network documents on their computers so that they can work with the documents when not connected to the network. By clicking the Caching button when you share a folder, you enable users to cache the folder or documents within the folder.

If you click the Caching button, Windows 2000 displays the Caching Settings dialog box, as shown in Figure 3-2.

To allow caching for the shared folder, select the Allow Caching of Files in This Shared Folder check box and then select a setting from the drop-down list.

Figure 3-2:
Use the
Caching
Settings
dialog box
to configure
offline
caching.

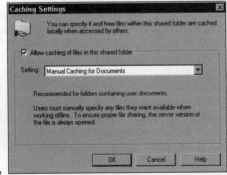

You can expect the exam to ask you a question about the options in the Settings drop-down list. You should memorize the three Settings options:

✦ **Automatic Caching for Documents:** This setting is recommended for folders containing user documents. Opened files are automatically downloaded and cached on the user's computer so that they're available when the user works offline. Older versions of the file are automatically deleted from the cache and updated with the newest version.

✦ **Automatic Caching for Programs:** This setting is recommended for folders with read-only data as well as for run-from-network applications.

✦ **Manual Caching for Documents:** This setting is also recommended for folders containing user documents. Users must manually specify any files they want available when working offline.

Controlling access to shared folders

NTFS is the file system recommended for Windows 2000 computers. NTFS is available in both Windows 2000 Server and Windows 2000 Professional. Although Windows 2000 supports FAT and FAT32 file systems, NTFS gives you exceptional security features in all aspects of networking, including file and folder security.

With NTFS permissions, you can control the security of a shared folder as well as each file within the folder. In this way, you can allow a user to access a folder, but not necessarily all the files within the folder. Or, a user may have full control over one file in a folder but only read permission on another file in the same folder. In other words, NTFS gives you complete control over which shares you make available to users and groups and what permissions those users and groups have with the shared file or folder.

NTFS permissions are available only on Windows 2000 hard disk volumes formatted with NTFS. You can't use NTFS permissions on volumes formatted with FAT or FAT32.

NTFS permissions function the same in Windows 2000 as they do in Windows NT. For the 70-215 exam, you need to have a firm understanding of the different file permissions that you can assign. Table 3-3 reviews these permissions.

Table 3-3	NTFS Permissions for Files
With this Permission . . .	*A User Can . . .*
Read	Read the file and view its attributes, permissions, and ownership.
Write	Perform any Read function and edit the file and change its attributes.
Read & Execute	Perform all the Read actions and run applications.
Modify	Perform all actions of Read and Read & Execute, as well as modify or delete the file.
Full Control	Perform any action permitted by other permissions and change the permissions and take ownership.

You also need to understand the different folder permissions that you can assign. Table 3-4 describes these permissions.

Table 3-4	NTFS Permissions for Folders
With this Permission . . .	*A User Can . . .*
Read	View the files and subfolders within the folder and view the folder ownership, attributes, and permissions.
Write	Create new files and subfolders within the folder, make changes to the folder attributes, and view folder ownership and permissions.
List Folder Contents	See the names of files and subfolders in the folder.
Read & Execute	Perform all actions of Read and List Folder Contents and move through the folders to other files and folders without permission for each folder.
Modify	Perform all actions of Write and Read & Execute and delete the folder.
Full Control	Perform all actions provided by other permissions and change the folder permissions, take ownership, and delete files and subfolders.

For each permission, both for files and folders, you can either grant the permission or deny the permission. If you deny all permissions for a user or group, the user or group has no access rights to the file or folder. For each file and folder, NTFS maintains an *access control list* (ACL) that lists the users and groups that have been granted access to a file or folder. If a user tries to access a file or folder, NTFS checks the ACL to see whether the user has any permissions for the file or folder.

When assigning permissions, you can view and edit the ACL by clicking the Advanced button found on the Security tab, which appears in the Properties dialog box of each shared folder. This option gives you a fine level of control when you need to customize the ACL to provide specific NTFS permissions for a particular share.

Understanding effective permissions

At first glance, assigning permissions may seem like an easy task, but you must be careful. You can assign users and groups permissions for a file or folder, but users may be members of several groups, each with different permissions. In such cases, a user who belongs to different groups with differing permissions will have *effective permissions*.

Effective permissions are combined NTFS permissions. For example, assume that a user is a member of two groups. One group has Read permission for a folder, and the other group has Modify permission for the same folder. In that case, the user's effective permission is Read and Modify. As you can see, effective permissions may give some users more permissions than you would like them to have. Planning is of key importance.

The exception to the effective-permissions rule is Deny. If a user has Read permission for a folder in one group, but is denied permission in another group, the user has no access. Deny overrides all other effective permissions. Keep this in mind for the exam.

Understanding inheritance

You need to understand the relationship between sharing folders and inheritance. By default, all files and folders within a folder inherit the permissions of the parent folder. You can prevent inheritance by assigning different permissions to a subfolder. When you perform this action, the subfolder becomes the new parent folder for all the files and folders that it contains.

Book II
Chapter 3

Installing and
Configuring Access
to Resources

Moving and copying shared files and folders

For the exam, you need to know how moving and copying files and folders affect permissions. These permission rules aren't difficult, but they can be confusing.

You should memorize these rules for the exam:

✦ If you copy a file or folder to a new folder on the same NTFS volume or a different NTFS volume, the file or folder inherits the permissions of the destination folder.

✦ If you copy a file or folder to a FAT or FAT32 volume, you lose all NTFS permissions.

✦ If you move a file or folder within the same NTFS volume, the file or folder retains its permissions.

✦ If you move a file or folder to a different NTFS volume, the file or folder inherits the permissions of the destination folder.

✦ If you move a file or folder to a FAT or FAT32 volume, you lose all NTFS permissions.

Monitoring shared folders

In many cases, you may need to monitor user access to shared folders and files. You can easily perform this action by using the Windows 2000 Server Shared Folder MMC snap-in.

To open the Windows 2000 Server Shared Folder MMC snap-in, follow the steps in Lab 3-2.

Lab 3-2   Opening the Shared Folder Snap-in

1. **Choose Start⇨Run.**

2. **In the Run dialog box, type MMC and click OK.**

3. **Choose Console⇨Add/Remove Snap-in.**

4. **Click Add.**

5. **In the snap-in list, select Shared Folders, and then click Add.**

6. **In the resulting Shared Folders dialog box, select Local Computer, choose to View All Sessions, and then click Finish.**

7. **Click Close.**

8. **Click OK.**

   The snap-in now appears in the console. If you expand Shared Folders in the console, you can see containers for Shares, Sessions, and Open Files.

The Shared Folders console enables you to view the shares on your computer, the sessions currently in progress, and the open files. Here's what else you can do with the Shared Folders console:

✦ Click each container to see the sessions and open files (or shares).

✦ Click Sessions, and you see the user connected to the share along with the number of open files, the amount of time connected, and the idle time.

✦ To disconnect a specific user, right-click the user in the right window, and then choose Close Session from the pop-up menu.

✦ To disconnect everyone, choose Action⇨Disconnect All Sessions.

The Open Files container displays the shared files that are open, which users have the files open, and the user's permissions for the file. You can right-click any file in the window and choose Close Open File to force the user to close the file, or you can choose Action⇨Disconnect All Open Files.

Understanding Dfs

In previous versions of Windows, users have to browse through different servers to find the shared folders they need to use. In large networks, this process can be time-consuming and frustrating. With the Windows 2000 Distributed file system (Dfs), you can organize shared folders in a network environment so that the folders appear as one, structured location to users.

Dfs and Active Directory free end-users from worrying about the network structure. In other words, while users can easily access and use resources, users don't need to know where those resources physically reside on the network.

Dfs organizes resources on the network in a tree-like structure that users can simply browse to find the shared folder they need. To end-users, all the folders appear as though they are located in one place. Users don't see where the folders actually reside on the network. Various servers may hold the shared resources, but in Dfs, they appear as though they reside in one location. This feature makes the network architecture transparent to users, and ultimately makes finding resources a much quicker and easier process.

Windows 2000 supports two kinds of Dfs:

+ **Standalone:** You store a standalone Dfs on a single server that network users access. The Dfs server holds the folder information for all other servers and presents that information to users in a tree-like structure. However, a standalone Dfs has no fault tolerance. If the server fails, Dfs won't be available to users.

+ **Domain-based (or fault tolerant):** A domain-based Dfs stores the folder structure in Active Directory. If one server fails, a domain-based Dfs is still available on other servers within the Active Directory environment. Domain-based Dfs roots must be stored on volumes formatted NTFS 5.0.

Only clients that support Dfs can use the Dfs features. Clients running Windows 2000, Windows NT, and Windows 98 have built-in support for a standalone Dfs. Windows 2000 and NT clients also have built-in support for a domain-based Dfs. Windows 98 clients can download the 5.0-compliant client, and clients running Windows 95 can download the Dfs client from www.microsoft.com.

The exam expects you to know about both standalone and domain-based Dfs. The following sections explore both types of Dfs and what you need to know for the exam.

Managing a standalone Dfs

Dfs is available on your Windows 2000 server after an initial server installation. Dfs functions as an MMC snap-in, but it doesn't appear in your Administrative Tools folder. Instead, you manually add the snap-in to an MMC and then the console for future use.

Lab 3-3 lists the steps for adding the Dfs snap-in.

Lab 3-3   Adding the Dfs Snap-in

1. **Choose Start⇨Run.**

2. **In the Run dialog box, type MMC.**

3. **Choose Console⇨Add/Remove Snap-in and click the Add button on the snap-in window that appears.**

4. **Select Distributed file system from the snap-in list, click Add, and then click Close.**

5. **Save the console after you have the Dfs snap-in loaded.**

Setting up the Dfs root

You set up Dfs by establishing a *Dfs root*, a container for files and Dfs links.

You can create a Dfs root on FAT or NTFS partitions, but FAT and FAT32 do not provide the security features of NTFS. If possible, you should always create the root on an NTFS partition.

A standalone Dfs root has some limitations:

✦ The standalone Dfs root doesn't use Active Directory, so it has no fault tolerance.

✦ A standalone Dfs root can't have root-level Dfs shared folders. In other words, you can have only one root, and all shared folders must fall under the hierarchy of the root.

✦ With a standalone Dfs, you have a limited hierarchy available. A standalone Dfs root can have only a single level of Dfs links.

Lab 3-4 explains the steps for creating a new standalone Dfs root. For the exam, you should know what options the New Dfs Root Wizard offers.

Lab 3-4   Creating a Standalone Dfs Root

1. **Starting from the MMC console, choose Action⇨New Dfs Root.**

   Windows 2000 displays the welcome screen for the New Dfs Root Wizard.

2. **Click Next to advance to the New Dfs Root Type dialog box.**

3. **Select the Create a Standalone Dfs Root radio button and then click Next.**

4. **In the Host Server dialog box, enter the name of the host server for the Dfs root and click Next.**

5. **In the Specify Dfs Root Share dialog box, choose to use an existing share, or create a new one by entering the desired share name and path; click Next.**

   The Dfs share holds the Dfs information, so you can simply use a share already available on your server, or you may want to create a new one strictly for the Dfs root.

6. **In the Name the Dfs Root dialog box, enter a name for the Dfs root and enter a comment, if desired; click Next.**

7. **Click Finish to complete the wizard.**

Creating a Dfs link

Dfs links provide a folder name to the users. When a user accesses the folder, the system transparently redirects the user to the server that actually holds the shared folder.

Lab 3-5 describes the steps for creating a Dfs link.

Lab 3-5	Creating a Dfs Link

1. **Select the Dfs root in the console and then choose Action⇨New Dfs Link.**

   The Create a New Dfs Link dialog box appears.

2. **Enter the desired name for the Dfs link and the network path to the shared folder.**

3. **If desired, enter a comment.**

   The comment box is provided for administrative notes that you may want to include.

4. **If necessary, change the amount of time that clients cache the link information on their systems and then click OK.**

   The default time is 1,800 seconds. If the link seldom changes, you can extend the cache timeout value if desired.

   After you establish the Dfs link, it appears in the Dfs tree.

Creating replicas

After you establish a Dfs link (see the preceding section), you can create additional replicas for the link. A *replica* is an alternate location of a shared folder. For example, the Dfs link Company Documents may reside in several locations.

By definition, a replica participates in replication, so you may have two more shared folders that hold the same information and replicate with each other as that information changes. The replica set keeps track of the possible locations that Dfs can use to service clients. The alternate must be stored on a Windows 2000 server running NTFS and the Dfs service.

To create a replica, select the desired Dfs link in the console and then choose Action⇨New Replica. In the dialog box that appears, enter the alternate for the shared folder and then click OK. Note that the standalone Dfs offers no replication or backup. You can create a replica, but file replication doesn't work.

Understanding Dfs security

Keep in mind that Dfs basically provides a link interface to users. When a user opens a Dfs link, Dfs redirects the user to the server that holds the shared folder. Dfs itself doesn't provide any inherent security because it only provides an interface for users to access shares. You set security for the shared folders on each folder on the server where the folder actually resides. Likewise, if you delete a Dfs link, you aren't deleting any shared information in the folder, you're simply removing the link to the shared folder in the Dfs tree.

Managing a domain-based Dfs

The domain-based Dfs is your best choice for implementing Dfs on a network. When you implement a domain-based Dfs, you provide fault tolerance for the Dfs. Also, you can have root-level shared folders and you have no Dfs hierarchy limit — that is, you can have multiple levels of Dfs links.

When you implement a domain-based Dfs root, you must use a domain member server as the host, and you must store the Dfs *topology* — that is, the structure of the Dfs (such as roots and links) — in Active Directory.

Setting up the Dfs root

Although you can create a Dfs root on either a FAT or an NTFS partition, FAT doesn't provide the security features of NTFS. Consequently, you should always create the root on an NTFS partition.

You create a domain-based Dfs root by using the New Dfs Root Wizard. Lab 3-6 shows you how to use the wizard to configure a domain-based Dfs root. You need to know these steps for Exam 70-215.

Lab 3-6   Creating a Domain-based Dfs Root

1. **To start the New Dfs Root Wizard, open the Dfs console and then choose Action⇨New Dfs Root.**

2. **Click Next on the wizard's welcome screen.**

3. **In the wizard's Select Dfs Root Type dialog box, select the Create a Domain Dfs Root radio button and then click Next.**

4. **Select the host domain for the Dfs root and click Next.**

5. **Enter the name of the server in the host domain that will host the Dfs root and click Next.**

6. **In the Specify Dfs Root Share dialog box, choose to use an existing share, or create a new one by entering the desired share name and path; click Next.**

    The DFS share holds the DFS information, so you can simply use a share already available on your server, or you may want to create a new one strictly for the Dfs root.

7. **Enter a new name for the Dfs root and a comment if desired; click Next.**

8. **Click Finish.**

Book II
Chapter 3

Installing and
Configuring Access
to Resources

Configuring the domain-based Dfs root

To configure a domain-based Dfs root, you use the same process as you use for a standalone Dfs. Refer to the section "Managing a standalone Dfs," earlier in this chapter, for information on creating Dfs links and replicas.

For a domain-based Dfs, you can also create a new root replica by using the Action menu. This feature enables you to create a root replica on another domain member server.

Understanding domain-based Dfs replication

Because one of the major purposes of a domain-based Dfs is to provide fault tolerance, replication must occur between Dfs roots and shared folders to ensure that replicas hold an exact copy. In a standalone Dfs root, you can create folder replicas, but you have to perform replication manually. In a domain-based Dfs, replication can occur automatically.

You can't use automatic replication on FAT volumes on Windows 2000 servers. By using only NTFS volumes for domain-based Dfs, you ensure that replication can occur automatically.

When you create a root replica in the Dfs console, a replica wizard appears that enables you to specify the server where the replica will reside. Dfs shared folders can also be replicated automatically on a domain-based Dfs. When you create a new replica for a shared folder, select the Automatic Replication radio button so that replication can occur automatically.

Dfs uses the File Replication Service (FRS) to perform replication automatically. FRS manages updates across shared folders configured for replication. By default, FRS synchronizes the folder contents at 15-minute intervals.

When you set up the automatic replication, the Dfs console displays a dialog box in which you configure the replication policy. You can specify one share as the primary (or initial master). The primary replicates its contents to the other Dfs shared folder in the set.

Of course, you can choose to perform *manual replication,* in which you manually update the folder contents if a change occurs. For replica sets that seldom change, this may be a wise choice to reduce unnecessary synchronization traffic.

Within a set of Dfs shared folders, don't mix automatic and manual replication. Use one or the other to ensure that replication occurs properly.

Monitor, Configure, and Control Access to Web Sites

In Windows 2000, you can share any folder as a shared Web folder on the Web site that you specify. The shared folder appears on your Internet or intranet site, where users can access the contents of the shared folder.

You share a Web folder in the same way that you share any other folder on your system. Lab 3-7 describes the steps for sharing a Web folder.

Lab 3-7 Sharing a Web Folder

1. **Right-click the folder you want to share and choose Sharing from the pop-up menu.**

2. **In the resulting Properties dialog box, click the Web Sharing tab.**

3. **Using the drop-down list on the Web sharing tab, select the Web site on which you want to share the folder.**

4. **Select the Share This Folder radio button.**

5. **In the Edit Alias dialog box that appears, give the Web folder an alias name, if desired.**

The Edit Alias dialog box also gives you options for assigning access permissions and application permissions. Under Access Permissions, you can select Read, Write, Script Source Access, or Directory Browsing. Under Application Permissions, you can select None, Scripts, or Execute (Includes Scripts).

6. **Select the desired permissions and then click OK to make the share active.**

Configuring Web folder properties

After you share a Web folder (see the preceding section in this chapter), you can access its properties from within Internet Services Manager. Choose Start⇨Programs⇨Administrative Tools⇨Internet Services Manager. Expand your server in the tree pane and then expand the desired Web site. You now see the shared folder within the Web site. Select the shared folder and choose Action⇨Properties. On the five tabs in the resulting Properties dialog box, you can further configure the shared Web folder.

For the exam, you need to know what you can do on each of the four tabs in the Properties dialog box for a shared Web folder. The following sections explore what you need to know for the exam.

Configuring the Virtual Directory tab settings

You use the Virtual Directory tab in a Web folder's Properties dialog box to configure the location and the way in which users access a Web folder. First, you need to specify the location of the content for the shared Web folder. Depending on the setting you choose in the top part of the Virtual Directory tab, the content of the shared Web folder may come from a directory on your local machine, a share on another computer, or a redirection to another URL. Your selection in the top part of this tab also determines what options you see in the lower part of the dialog box. For example, if you select another computer, you provide the path to that computer in the provided dialog box. If you specify that the content comes from a URL redirect, you enter information about the URL in the provided dialog box. If you specify sharing a Web folder on your local machine, you need to specify the path to that directory in the provided dialog box.

The middle part of the Virtual Directory tab contains the local path to the Web folder, which you can change by clicking Browse and then browsing to the desired folder.

If you subsequently move the shared Web folder to a different location on your computer, you need to change the local path setting accordingly, or Web users won't be able to access the directory.

**Book II
Chapter 3**

Installing and
Configuring Access
to Resources

The Virtual Directory tab also has several check boxes that you can select to determine what users can do with the shared folder and how it's configured on the Web server.

You need to know the following options for the exam:

+ **Script Source Access:** Allows users to access the source of any scripts that run with the directory.

+ **Read:** Allows users to read the directory information.

+ **Write:** Allows users to write directory information.

+ **Directory Browsing:** Allows users to browse the directory.

+ **Log Visits:** Creates a log of all visitors.

+ **Index this Resource:** Allows the index server to include this directory when the Web site is indexed.

Also, if you're sharing applications in the Web folder, you can configure an application name, determine execution permissions, and configure application protection. The execution permissions enable users to execute either scripts, executable files, or both. The Application Protection feature enables you to select low, medium, or high protection.

Managing the Directory Security tab

The settings on the Directory Security tab in a Web folder's Properties dialog box enable you to configure different kinds of security for the shared folder. You have three options:

+ Anonymous access and authentication control

+ IP address and domain name restrictions

+ Secure communications

For anonymous access and authentication control, you can click the Edit button and then select the desired authentication methods in the Authentication Methods dialog box that appears. In this dialog box, you can allow anonymous access to the directory by selecting the Anonymous Access check box. With this setting, users can access the directory without a username and password. Instead, they use a default username and password, such as iusr_*servername*. You can change this default account as desired by clicking the Edit button.

In the Authenticated Access section, you can configure the kind of authentication that's required when anonymous access is disabled or when access is restricted due to NTFS ACLs. You have three options, which you should remember for the exam:

✦ **Basic Authentication:** Users access the directory with a username and password that the system sends in clear text. You can also specify a default domain by clicking Edit.

✦ **Digest Authentication for Windows Domain Servers:** This feature allows IIS to manage authentication using user names and passwords from Windows domain controllers.

✦ **Integrated Windows Authentication:** This feature integrates the authentication process with Windows 2000 domain controllers.

Book II
Chapter 3

Enabling HTTP headers

With the options on the HTTP Headers tab in a shared Web folder's Properties dialog box, you can configure HTTP headers that Windows 2000 sends to a user's browser when the user accesses the directory. You can configure content expiration, content ratings, and additional MIME types.

For the exam, you only need to know about the content expiration option. You can select the Enable Content Expiration check box and then enter a day and time at which the Web folder content expires. This feature is very useful for time-sensitive documents or files.

Understanding the settings on the Custom Errors tab

On the Custom Errors tab in the Properties dialog box for a shared Web folder, you can create custom error messages for the directory. This feature is useful for particular kinds of directory files or applications. You can create a custom error message that Windows 2000 sends to the user for a particular error that may be encountered.

For the exam, you only need to know what this option does. You won't see detailed questions about creating custom error messages.

Prep Test

1 **How do you create a new scope for a DHCP server?**

   A ○ Select the server in the DHCP console and click the Scope link in the details pane.

   B ○ Select the server in the DHCP console and then choose Action⇨Properties.

   C ○ Select the server in the DHCP console and then choose Action⇨New Scope.

   D ○ You can only create a superscope.

2 **An administrator configures only a multicast scope on a newly installed DHCP server and then authorizes the server in Active Directory. The server, however, doesn't issue MADCAP IP addresses. What did the administrator do wrong?**

   A ○ The multicast scope isn't configured accurately.

   B ○ The administrator didn't configure a standard DHCP scope.

   C ○ The network contains no multicast clients.

   D ○ DHCP doesn't support multicasting on IP subnets.

3 **On a newly installed DHCP server, you configure a scope and then authorize the DHCP server in Active Directory. You wait for a period of time, but the server's icon remains red. What do you need to do?**

   A ○ Reinstall Windows 2000.

   B ○ Reinstall DHCP.

   C ○ Reauthorize the server.

   D ○ Refresh the server.

4 **You want to create a resource record for a zone that contains a mail-server-to-IP-address mapping. What kind of resource record do you need to create?**

   A ○ NS

   B ○ A

   C ○ MX

   D ○ CNAME

5 You want only a select group to be able to print to a particular printer. You don't want any other network users, except administrators, to use the printer. How can you configure this?

A ○ On the Advanced tab in the Server Properties dialog box, select the desired group and assign Print permission.

B ○ On the Advanced tab in the Printer Properties dialog box, select the desired group and assign Print permission.

C ○ On the Security tab in the Printer Properties dialog box, add the desired group and assign Print permissions.

D ○ On the Security tab in the Printer Properties dialog box, remove all undesired groups and then add the desired group and assign Print permissions.

6 An administrator installs a printer on a server. The administrator wants to share the printer and have it listed in Active Directory automatically. However, the printer is never published in the directory. Which of the following are possible solutions to the problem? (Choose all that apply.)

A ❑ The physical printer isn't working.

B ❑ The server isn't a Windows 2000 Server.

C ❑ The administrator never actually shared the printer.

D ❑ There isn't enough disk space for the print spooler.

7 You need to assign a particular user the permission to Write Attributes for a shared folder. This permission doesn't appear in the list on the Security tab. How can you configure this?

A ○ Configure the permission for individual files.

B ○ Place the user in a group and assign the permission.

C ○ Click the Advanced button and then assign the permission.

D ○ You can't assign this permission.

8 Which NTFS folder permission allows the user to delete the folder?

A ○ Write

B ○ List Folder Contents

C ○ Read & Execute

D ○ Modify

9 On a domain-based Dfs, automatic replication doesn't seem to be occurring. You make certain that the Dfs is domain based, and all other components appear to be configured correctly. What's most likely causing the problem?

A ○ The Dfs root isn't configured for automatic replication.

B ○ The Dfs links aren't configured correctly.

C ○ The Dfs is installed on a FAT volume.

D ○ Dfs doesn't support automatic replication.

10 You have a shared folder that users access via URL redirection. This folder is managed by another administrator on another Web site. Suddenly, users begin getting a 404 Not Found error. What has happened? (Choose all possible answers.)

A ❑ The URL has changed and has not been updated on your Web site.

B ❑ The shared folder has been removed.

C ❑ Higher security has been set on the folder.

D ❑ The Web site that hosts the folder is down.

Answers

1 **C.** You create new scopes by selecting the desired server in the console and then launching the New Scope Wizard from the Action menu. You can also right-click the server and click New Scope to launch the Wizard. *Review "Creating a standard scope,"* in Book III, Chapter 3.

2 **B.** DHCP and MADCAP work together, but DHCP servers must be configured to lease IP addresses to network clients. Clients can't obtain a multicast IP address without a typical IP address appropriate for the subnet. *Review "Configuring a multicast scope,"* in Book III, Chapter 3.

3 **D.** After authorizing the server with Active Directory, you should wait a few moments and then refresh the server to see whether it has been authorized. You can use the Action menu to refresh the server, or simply press F5. *Review "Authorizing the DHCP Server,"* in Book III, Chapter 5.

4 **C.** An MX (Mail Exchanger) record identifies a mail server's IP address. *Review "Managing zone resource records."*

5 **D.** By default, the Everyone group has Print permissions. You can change this setting by removing the group (and any other groups) and adding the desired group or users. Then, assign the group the desired permissions. *Review "Configuring Printers."*

6 **B and C.** To be published automatically to Active Directory, the printer must be shared on a Windows 2000 computer. Hardware or spooler problems would not affect Active Directory publication. *Review "Monitoring and Troubleshooting Printers."*

7 **C.** NTFS enables you to fine-tune permissions by using the Advanced button to access the Permission Entries for a user or group. The permission list enables you to assign the Write Attributes permission. *Review "Controlling access to shared folders."*

8 **D.** The Modify permission gives the user all permissions of Write and Read & Execute, as well as the permission to delete the folder. *Review "Controlling access to shared folders."*

9 **C.** In this scenario, the best answer is C. If automatic replication isn't functional on a domain-based Dfs, the Dfs may be installed on a FAT volume, which doesn't support automatic replication. *Review "Understanding domain-based Dfs replication."*

10 **A, B,** and **D.** A 404 error message occurs when a resource can't be found. Any of these could be the problem. Security would not be the problem because users would receive a different error message if they did not have access rights. *Review "Configuring the Virtual Directory tab settings."*

Chapter 4: Configuring and Troubleshooting Hardware Devices and Drivers

Exam Objectives

✔ **Configuring hardware devices**

✔ **Troubleshooting problems with hardware**

✔ **Configure driver signing options and updating drivers**

✔ **Using troubleshooting tools**

*T*he powers-that-be at Microsoft have smiled on us and provided a Plug and Play operating system in Windows 2000. Instead of forcing you to manually install and configure hardware devices, Windows 2000 automatically detects and attempts to install hardware on your system. Of course, this Plug and Play system doesn't eliminate all the possible hardware problems and issues, but it certainly makes the administrator's job easier.

In this chapter, we tell you what you need to know — and what you don't need to know — for the exam questions that relate to the relatively easy process of convincing Windows 2000 to play nicely with your hardware. You can review the following topics in this chapter:

✦ Installing hardware devices

✦ Troubleshooting installation problems

✦ Configuring hardware

✦ Solving problems with device drivers and driver signing

Installing Windows 2000 Hardware

Installing hardware devices in Windows 2000 computers involves the following steps:

1. **Physically attach the new hardware device to your computer, following the manufacturer's instructions.**

To avoid a potential electric shock and damage to your system, remember to turn off the power before you attach a new device.

2. Boot your system.

Windows 2000 should automatically detect the new hardware device and begin the installation wizard.

For the most part, hardware installation doesn't require any intervention from you, with the exception of providing a disk or CD that contains the drivers for the hardware device. In many cases, Windows 2000 can install generic drivers for the device if you don't have the manufacturer's drivers. Of course, you should always use the manufacturer's device drivers for Windows 2000 so that the device functions completely and properly.

Before purchasing a hardware device, check the Windows 2000 Hardware Compatibility List (HCL) to make certain that the device is compatible with Windows 2000. You can find the HCL on your installation CD-ROM or at `www.microsoft.com/hcl`.

Using the Add/Remove Hardware Wizard

In some cases, Windows 2000 may not automatically detect a new hardware device that you attach to your system. For example, you may have non-Plug and Play (legacy) devices. In such cases, you can use Control Panel's Add/Remove Hardware Wizard. Like Add/Remove Programs, the Add/Remove Hardware Wizard scans your system for devices and enables you to install or remove hardware from your system. Using the wizard, you can select an "unknown" device and install the drivers for it, or you can remove the device if desired.

You can also use the Add/Remove Hardware Wizard to troubleshoot devices. We explore this topic later in the chapter.

Lab 4-1 reviews the steps for installing a hardware device by using the Add/Remove Hardware Wizard. Lab 4-2 explains how to uninstall a device.

Lab 4-1   Installing a Device by Using the Add/Remove Hardware Wizard

1. **Launch the wizard by choosing Start⇨Settings⇨Control Panel⇨ Add/Remove Hardware.**

2. **Click Next on the wizard's welcome screen to bring up the Choose a Hardware Task dialog box.**

3. **In the Choose a Hardware Task dialog box, select the Add/ Troubleshoot a Device radio button and then click Next.**

Windows searches for new hardware and then displays the new hardware along with any problem hardware. You can then choose to install the new hardware or troubleshoot existing hardware, as shown in Figure 4-1. If you want to install new hardware, scroll through the list and select Install Device.

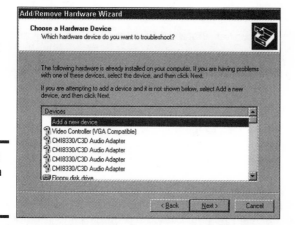

Figure 4-1:
Choosing a hardware device.

**Book II
Chapter 4**

Configuring and
Troubleshooting
Hardware Devices
and Drivers

4. **If Windows didn't detect your hardware, select the Add a New Device option so that you can manually install the hardware and click Next.**

   This brings up the Find New Hardware dialog box.

5. **In the Find New Hardware dialog box, select the No button so that you can manually install the hardware, and then click Next.**

6. **From the Select Hardware list that appears, select the type of hardware that you want to install and then click Next.**

   This brings up the Select a Device Driver dialog box.

7. **In this dialog box, select the manufacturer of the device and the model, or click the Have Disk button to install the drivers from a disk or CD.**

8. **Click Next and then click Finish.**

Lab 4-2   Uninstalling a Device by Using the Add/Remove Hardware Wizard

1. **Launch the wizard by choosing Start⇨Settings⇨Control Panel⇨ Add/Remove Hardware.**

2. **Click Next on the welcome screen to bring up the Choose a Hardware Task dialog box.**

3. **In this dialog box, select the Uninstall/Unplug a Device radio button and then click Next.**

4. **In the Choose a Removal Task dialog box that appears, select either the Uninstall a Device radio button or the Unplug/Eject a Device radio button, and then click Next.**

   Uninstall completely removes the device and its drivers, and the Unplug/Eject option temporarily disables a device.

5. **Select the device that you want to uninstall or unplug and then click Next.**

6. **Click Yes and then click Finish.**

Troubleshooting hardware installations

In a perfect world, you never have any problems installing hardware on a Plug and Play system. Alas, your network doesn't live in a perfect world, and hardware installation can pose a few problems.

For the exam, you are expected to know how to troubleshoot hardware installation problems. To help you prepare for these troubleshooting questions, this section describes the common problems and solutions that you are likely to encounter in the real world and on the exam. You should memorize this list before you take the exam:

+ **The system can't detect a device:** If your system can't detect a device, two problems may exist. First, check the device and make certain it is physically attached to your computer correctly. If the device has a separate power supply, make certain that the device is turned on. Second, make certain that the device is compatible with Windows 2000.

+ **A manually installed device doesn't appear on the system:** If you use the Add/Remove Hardware Wizard to manually install a device by selecting the device from the list, but the device still doesn't appear on the system or isn't operational, use the Add/Remove Hardware Wizard to troubleshoot the device.

+ **The system can't detect a device, and the device doesn't appear in the Add Hardware list:** If the system can't detect a hardware device, and the device doesn't appear in the list displayed by the Add/Remove Hardware Wizard, the device probably isn't compatible with Windows 2000. You can bypass this problem by using the hardware device's installation disk or CD-ROM to install it, but if the disk or CD isn't available, you will probably not be able to get the device to work with your system.

Configuring Hardware Devices

After you install a hardware device, you can further configure the device so that it performs on your system as desired. Depending on the device, you may find an icon for it in Control Panel. If so, you can double-click the icon to open the device's Properties dialog box and make the desired changes.

For example, by double-clicking Phone and Modem Options in Control Panel, you can configure your modem and dialing rules. On the Modems tab in the resulting dialog box, you can access properties for the modem and make any desired changes.

For study purposes, you don't need to know what you can do on each tab in each device's Properties dialog box. However, you should know how to access a device's properties and about troubleshooting the configuration of each device, which we discuss later in this chapter.

For other devices, you can access their properties by using Device Manager, which is a part of the Windows 2000 Computer Management console. Choose Start⇨Programs⇨Administrative Tools⇨Computer Management. In the console's tree pane, click the Device Manager, and a list of all device categories appears in the right pane, as shown in Figure 4-2.

**Book II
Chapter 4**

Configuring and
Troubleshooting
Hardware Devices
and Drivers

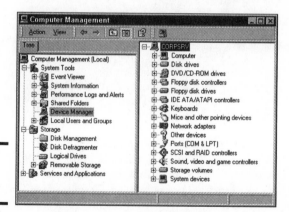

Figure 4-2:
Device
Manager.

If you expand the desired category, you can see a list of devices installed on your system for that category. To configure a device, right-click the device and choose Properties from the pop-up menu.

Each device may have different properties sheets, depending on the device. Also, devices that appear in Control Panel may have more configuration options (such as modems and keyboards). For most devices, the Properties dialog box includes General, Driver, and Resources tabs, as well as others — depending on the device.

The General tab for each device gives you information about the device and the status of the device. Figure 4-3 shows the General tab.

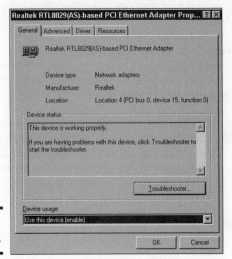

Figure 4-3:
General tab.

If you are having problems with a device, always check the General tab first. If the device isn't working properly, the Device Status window tells you so and often points out the problem.

You can also launch the Troubleshooter tool by clicking the Troubleshooter button. This action leads you through a series of steps to help you identify the problem, and you can read more about the Troubleshooter tool later in this chapter.

You can also disable the device by selecting this option from the drop-down list on the General tab. This feature is helpful in troubleshooting as well.

The Resources tab gives you information about which system resources the hardware device uses, such as I/O Range and IRQ, as shown in Figure 4-4. Fortunately, Windows 2000 does a good job of assigning system resources to hardware devices automatically, so you typically don't need to manually configure such resource allocations as IRQ and I/O Ranges. You can change these settings, if necessary — if the device has resource conflicts with other devices, for example. The Resources tab tells you about the conflict in the Conflicting Device List window.

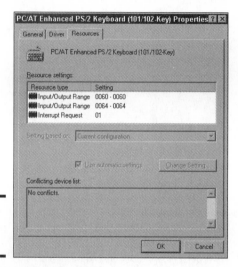

Figure 4-4:
Resources
tab.

Managing Drivers

A *driver* is software that enables the operating system to control a particular hardware device. You can think of a driver as the bridge between the operating system and the hardware. Typically, the company that makes the hardware device also manufactures the driver, which you get on a floppy disk or CD-ROM when you purchase the hardware.

The Windows 2000 operating system also contains an extensive list of generic drivers. When you install a new piece of hardware, Windows searches for the best driver for the device, including drivers that you provide with a floppy disk or CD-ROM. As we explain in the following sections, you manage drivers in two different ways: through the Driver tab in a device's Properties dialog box, or through your computer's system properties.

Using the Driver tab

Each hardware device has a Driver tab in its Properties dialog box. The Driver tab lists information about the driver and its manufacturer, and you have the options to view driver details, uninstall the driver, or update the driver, as shown in Figure 4-5.

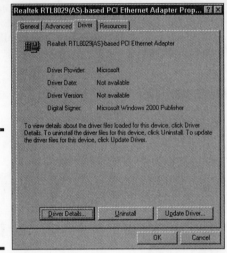

Figure 4-5:
Use the
Driver tab
to uninstall
or update
the device
driver.

To view the driver file, provider, file version, and copyright, click the Driver Details button.

If you click the Uninstall button, a warning message appears, telling you that you are about to remove the device from your system. If you remove the driver and then decide that you want to use the device after all, Windows 2000 must repeat the detection and installation process to install the hardware device.

For the exam, remember that removing a device's driver effectively removes the device from the system. Hardware can't function with your operating system without an appropriate driver.

By clicking the Update Driver button on the Driver tab, you open the Upgrade Device Driver Wizard. Because of the constant updates and refinements of device drivers, Microsoft provides this handy wizard so that you can update device drivers when updates become available. The wizard prompts you for the location of the new driver, searches for it, and then automatically installs it for the device. This wizard offers an easy way to make driver updates and changes.

Choosing driver signing options

Driver signing is the process that manufacturers use to digitally sign drivers so you can be assured that they come from the manufacturer and are safe for your system. Similar to the digitally signed software that you can download from the Internet, digitally signed driver files protect you from downloading a hidden virus or some other potentially dangerous piece of code.

By default, Windows 2000 checks all new software — that is, both system software and drivers — for a digital signature. If the system doesn't find or verify a digital signature, you receive a warning message. To ensure the integrity of your installation CD-ROM, all Windows 2000 CD files are digitally signed and checked during setup.

For the exam, you are expected to know how to change the driver signing options, which is an easy process:

1. **On the desktop, right-click My Computer and then choose Properties.**

2. **In the Properties dialog box, click the Hardware tab.**

Notice that you can launch the Hardware Wizard and Device Manager, and you can set up Hardware Profiles from this location.

3. **Click Driver Signing.**

Windows displays the Driver Signing Options dialog box, as shown in Figure 4-6.

Book II
Chapter 4

Configuring and
Troubleshooting
Hardware Devices
and Drivers

Figure 4-6:
Make
desired
driver
signing
changes
in this
dialog box.

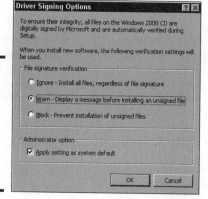

You have the following configuration options, which you should memorize for the exam:

* **Ignore:** This setting installs all files, regardless of the digital signature or whether one exists.

* **Warn:** This is the default setting, which gives you a warning message before installing an unsigned file.

- **Block:** This setting stops the installation of any unsigned file.

- **Administrator Option:** This option enables you to set the selected setting as the default for all users who log on to the computer. You must be logged on as an administrator to use this option.

4. **Make your selections and click OK.**

Using Hardware Profiles

You won't see lots of hardware profile questions on the exam because servers are typically not used by numerous people requiring different hardware settings.

By using hardware profiles, you can configure the system hardware to meet your needs. This profile is in effect each time you log on. If another user who accesses the same machine has different needs, you can create a different profile for that user. You often see hardware profiles used on laptop computers. You may have one profile in effect while connected to the network and another for use when you aren't connected to the network.

Hardware Profiles is accessible on the Hardware tab of System Properties. You can access System Properties by right-clicking My Computer, and then clicking Properties. By clicking the Hardware Profiles button on the Hardware tab in the System Properties dialog box, you access a simple interface in which you can easily create new profiles and define settings for laptop computers. You use the radio buttons in this Hardware Profiles dialog box to select the desired boot-up settings so that you can choose the hardware profile desired, as shown in Figure 4-7. This is all you need to know for the exam, so this section doesn't delve any deeper into the creation of hardware profiles.

Figure 4-7:
Use the
Hardware
Profiles
interface to
create or
configure
profiles.

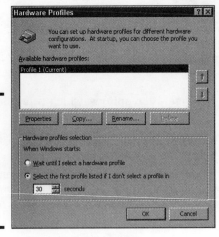

Using Hardware Troubleshooting Tools

Windows 2000 attempts to make hardware-problem resolution much easier than in previous versions by providing two troubleshooting tools: the Add/Remove Hardware Wizard and the Troubleshooter tool.

Troubleshooting with the Add/Remove Hardware Wizard

The Add/Remove Hardware Wizard can help you troubleshoot problem hardware. Lab 4-3 shows you how to use the troubleshooting feature of the wizard; you should be familiar with these steps for the exam.

Book II
Chapter 4

Configuring and Troubleshooting Hardware Devices and Drivers

Lab 4-3	Troubleshooting with the Add/Remove Hardware Wizard

1. **Choose Start➪Settings➪Control Panel.**

2. **Double-click Add/Remove Hardware.**

3. **Click Next to move past the welcome screen.**

   This brings up the Choose a Hardware Task dialog box.

4. **Select the Add/Troubleshoot a Device radio button and then click Next.**

   Windows searches for new or problem devices and presents you with a list of the devices that it finds.

5. **From the list, select the problem device and click Next.**

   The wizard displays a summary window that identifies the problem with the device.

6. **Click Finish to complete the wizard.**

   After you click Finish, the Troubleshooter opens automatically to assist you.

If the problem involves the device driver, Windows automatically launches the Upgrade Device Driver Wizard.

Using the Troubleshooter tool

Windows 2000 provides a Troubleshooter tool to help you resolve problems with hardware devices. The Troubleshooter walks you through a series of questions to attempt to find the problem and its solution.

You can access the Troubleshooter from the problem device's Properties dialog box. On the General tab, click the Troubleshooter button to launch the tool.

The Troubleshooter is a part of the Windows 2000 Help files. The Hardware Troubleshooter gives you a series of radio buttons, as shown in Figure 4-8. Select the problem that you are having and then click Next. You may walk through several of these screens until Windows 2000 determines the problem and presents you with a solution.

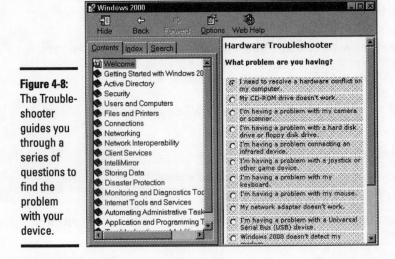

Figure 4-8:
The Trouble-
shooter
guides you
through a
series of
questions to
find the
problem
with your
device.

Prep Test

1 Windows 2000 can automatically detect and install which type of hardware devices?

- **A** ○ Modems
- **B** ○ Hard disks
- **C** ○ CD and DVD drives
- **D** ○ Any Plug and Play hardware

2 You want to install and configure a legacy device on a Windows 2000 computer. What will you probably need in order to complete the installation?

- **A** ○ IRQ settings.
- **B** ○ I/O settings.
- **C** ○ Device drivers.
- **D** ○ Legacy devices can't be installed on Windows 2000.

3 You want to temporarily disable a hardware device. How can you do this without removing the device from the system? (Choose all that apply.)

- **A** ❑ On the General tab in the device's Properties dialog box
- **B** ❑ On the Resource tab in the device's Properties dialog box
- **C** ❑ By manually removing the device from the system
- **D** ❑ By using the unplug option in the Add/Remove Hardware Wizard

4 You manually install a legacy device and assign an IRQ for the device. How can you easily determine whether this creates a conflict with another device?

- **A** ○ Use the General tab in the device's Properties dialog box.
- **B** ○ Use the Resource tab in the device's Properties dialog box.
- **C** ○ Use the Add/Remove Hardware Wizard.
- **D** ○ Uninstall the device to troubleshoot the problem.

5 You want to view properties for several different devices on your Windows 2000 Server. How can you use the Computer Management console to perform this action?

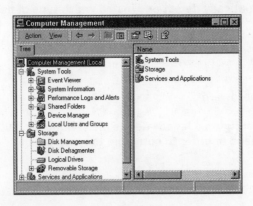

6 You attach a Plug and Play device to your Windows 2000 server, but the system can't automatically detect it. What should you do first?

A ○ Run the Add/Remove Hardware Wizard.

B ○ Make certain that the device is physically attached to your computer correctly.

C ○ Check the driver.

D ○ Manually install it.

7 You need to access the complete properties for a scanner attached to your computer. Where can you view the complete properties for the device?

A ○ Device Manager

B ○ Scanner Properties in Hardware profiles

C ○ Control Panel

D ○ Add/Remove Hardware Wizard

8 You are having a problem with a particular device and need to troubleshoot it. You want Windows 2000 to help you troubleshoot the device. Which options can you use to allow Windows 2000 to help you troubleshoot the device? (Choose all that apply.)

A ❑ Click the Troubleshooter button on the General tab in the device's Properties dialog box.

B ❑ Click the Troubleshooter button on the device's Resources tab.

C ❑ Use the Add/Remove Hardware Wizard.

D ❑ Access Windows Help files.

9. You want to change the default driver signing option on your Windows 2000 Server computer. Where can you perform this action?

A ○ Driver tab

B ○ Driver Properties

C ○ System Properties

D ○ Add/Remove Hardware Wizard

10 Which of the following actions can you perform using the Hardware tab in System Properties? (Choose all that apply.)

A ❑ Launch the Hardware Wizard.

B ❑ Access Driver Signing Options.

C ❑ Launch Device Manager.

D ❑ Access the Hardware Profiles dialog box.

Answers

1 **D.** Windows 2000 is a Plug and Play-compliant system that can automatically detect and install Plug and Play devices. *Review introduction to chapter.*

2 **C.** To install a non-Plug and Play device, you need the drivers for the device to manually install it when you run the Add/Remove Hardware Wizard. *Read "Using the Add/Remove Hardware Wizard."*

3 **A** and **D.** You may disable a device for troubleshooting purposes without removing the device from the system. You can accomplish this by disabling the device in the Device Usage drop-down list on the General tab in the device's Properties dialog box or by using the Add/Remove Hardware Wizard to unplug the device. *Review "Installing Windows 2000 Hardware."*

4 **B.** If you believe that a resource conflict exists, such as IRQ or I/O settings, access the Resources tab in the device's Properties dialog box. The Conflicting Device List window automatically lists any conflicting devices. *See "Configuring Hardware Devices."*

5 Device Manager is an integrated part of the Computer Management console. After you access the console, you can click Device Manager to access properties for various hardware devices. *Study "Configuring Hardware Devices."*

6 **B.** If you are installing a Plug and Play device and the system can't detect it, your first troubleshooting step is to make certain that the hardware is physically attached to your computer correctly. Running the Add/Remove Hardware Wizard will attempt another detection, but will mainly prompt you to manually install the hardware. *Study "Trobleshooting hardware installations."*

7 **C.** Several hardware devices, such as scanners, modems, and keyboards, have icons in Control Panel that you can use to fully configure the device on your system. *Study "Configuring Hardware Devices."*

8 **A** and **C.** Windows 2000 can assist you in troubleshooting hardware. Use the Troubleshooter button on the General tab in the device's Properties dialog box to start the troubleshooter, or use the Add/Remove Hardware Wizard to help you troubleshoot a problem device. *Study "Configuring Hardware Devices."*

9 **C.** You can configure driver signing options by accessing system properties, clicking the Hardware tab, and then clicking the Driver Signing button. *See "Choosing driver signing options."*

10 **A, B, C,** and **D.** The Hardware tab in System Properties provides an easy access point for all these operations. *Study "Choosing driver signing options."*

Chapter 5: Managing System Performance and Availability

Exam Objectives

- ✔ Monitoring and optimizing usage of system resources
- ✔ Setting priorities and starting and stopping processes
- ✔ Optimizing disk performance
- ✔ Managing and optimizing availability of System State data and user data
- ✔ Recovering System State data by using Windows Backup
- ✔ Troubleshooting system restoration by starting in safe mode
- ✔ Recovering System State data by using the Recovery Console

*O*ne of your jobs as a systems administrator is to make certain that your servers are functioning at their very best. This task includes monitoring your system, solving system resource problems, and even optimizing hard disks for better performance. These tasks don't have to be overwhelming or difficult, but they do require that you be aware of system processes and have a constant eagle eye on their performance.

For the exam, you'll need to know how to manage system and disk performance, and how to use Windows 2000 tools, such as Performance Monitor, MSINFO, and Disk Defragmenter. You can expect to review the following in this chapter:

- ✦ Managing system process and resource usage with Performance Monitor
- ✦ Using MSINFO32
- ✦ Configuring performance options and using Task Manager
- ✦ Optimizing disk performance
- ✦ Understanding System State data and user data

Managing System Process and Resource Usage with Performance Monitor

If you have ever used Windows NT on a system administration level, you are familiar with Performance Monitor. Performance Monitor is one of those tools you tend to avoid learning to use until you need it, which makes problem resolution much more difficult.

For the exam, you are expected to know how to use Performance Monitor, and more specifically, which performance counters you should use to monitor a number of processes and resources. Although you can use Performance Monitor to monitor a great number of system processes, we only focus on what you need to know for the exam in the following sections.

Using Performance Monitor

Like most other tools in Windows 2000, Performance Monitor is now an MMC snap-in and functions in the same manner as all other snap-ins. This streamlined approach to Windows 2000 tools should make any learning curve you need to master much easier.

To access Performance Monitor, choose Start⇨Programs⇨Administrative Tools⇨Performance. The Performance Monitor snap-in appears, as shown in Figure 5-1.

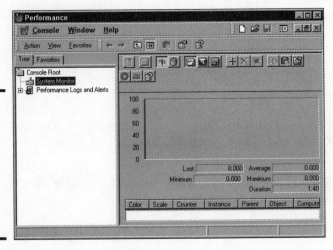

Figure 5-1: The Performance Monitor snap-in is used to monitor system processes.

You have two basic options when you use Performance Monitor — you can create charts for the System Monitor or you can generate logs and alerts. Notice in Figure 5-1 that both of these options are available under the console root.

The System Monitor portion of Performance Monitor is your tool for monitoring processes, such as memory and processor utilization, that are occurring on your system. You monitor your system by creating a chart of system processes you want to monitor. This is done by adding *counters*. To add counters, click the Add icon button above the chart in the right console pane (shown as a + sign). When you click the icon, the Add Counters window appears, shown in Figure 5-2.

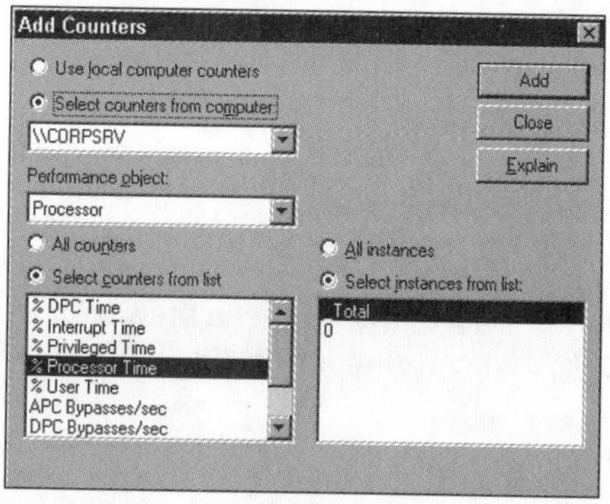

Figure 5-2:
Use the Add
Counters
window to
create per-
formance
charts.

In the Add Counters window, select the computer that you want to monitor by clicking the Use Local Computer Counters radio button, or clicking the Select Counters from Computer radio button and choosing a computer name from the drop-down list. Next select the performance object and click either the All Counters or the Selected Counters from List radio buttons. If you choose to select counters from the list, you must choose from among the many different performance objects in the drop-down list, including processor, system, memory, paging file, physical disk, and many others. For each object, select different counters that you want to monitor for that object. When you are done, click the Close button.

In the next section, "Reviewing important counters," we look at specific counters that you need to know for the exam.

After you add the counters for the object and close the Add Counters window, you can see the charting process taking place, as shown in Figure 5-3. Each counter is assigned a different color so that you can easily track each one. (We know this is a black-and-white book, but trust us on this one.)

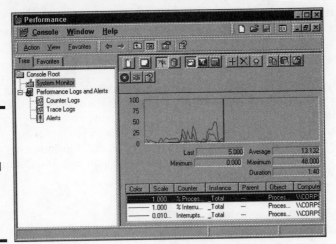

Figure 5-3:
Added
counters
are charted
in the Per-
formance
Monitor
window.

Using the buttons on the toolbar, you can also choose to view the counters in a histogram or report form instead of a chart.

In addition to creating counter charts that you can view, you can also create performance logs and configure performance alerts. To do so, simply follow these steps:

1. **Expand Performance Logs and Alerts in the console tree.**

2. **Right-click Counter Logs or Trace Logs that appear in the console.**

3. **Assign a new log name in the name dialog box that appears.**

4. **Create the log file as desired.**

Counter log files log activity for counters that you specify, and *trace* logs are designed to "trace" certain activities, such as I/O or page faults. You need a tool to parse trace logs so that you can extract the data you need, which is a developmental task. For each log type, you can create a new log setting by right-clicking the counter log and choosing Properties. When you create a new setting, a window appears, where you can configure the log (either add counters or trace providers) and where you can configure a schedule for the logs to run. By default, all log files are stored in `C:\PerfLogs`.

In much the same way that you create logs, you can create alerts. *Alerts* are used to let administrators know when particular system resources or processes reach a threshold value. To create an alert, follow these steps:

1. **Right-click Alerts and choose New Alert Settings.**

2. **Provide a name for the new settings in the Alert dialog box.**

3. **Click OK.**

This action opens the properties sheet. You can add a counter, and then assign a value limit when an alert will be generated.

4. **On the Action tab of the properties dialog box, determine what action should be taken when the value limit is triggered.**

Your options are

- Log an entry in the application event log
- Send a network message
- Start a performance data log
- Run a particular program

Make your selections by clicking the check boxes and click OK when you are done.

**Book II
Chapter 5**

**Managing System
Performance and
Availability**

Reviewing important counters

For the exam, you need to know the major performance counters. Exam questions may present a particular problem and ask you which performance counters you should use to attempt to find the problem. In the following sections, We examine several counter objects and the counters for those objects that you need to know for the exam. You'll need to memorize all of these, so make certain you study carefully.

Memory

System memory is a very important part of system performance. Without enough system memory, excessive *paging* occurs. Paging is the process of temporarily writing blocks of data to the hard disk when not enough RAM is available to keep the data in memory. As system resources call for the paged information, the data is read from the hard disk back into memory. Paging is an important part of Windows 2000 and you should expect paging to occur, but if you are experiencing excessive paging, your system responsiveness slows down, an indicator that you need more RAM.

You can use Performance Monitor to track system memory performance by choosing the memory object and using the following counters, which you need to know for the exam:

✦ **Memory\Available Bytes and Memory\Cache Bytes:** Use these counters to examine memory usage on your system.

✦ **Memory\Pages/sec, Memory\Page Reads/sec, Memory\Transition Faults/sec, and Memory\Pool Paged Bytes:** Use these counters to examine memory bottlenecks.

Processor

Your system processor manages all system processing and threads. In networking environments, the demands of the network often outgrow the processing power of your system processor. In many cases, you will see an overall system slowdown and a slowdown in services that meet the needs of network clients. If you are experiencing such a slowdown, you can either reduce the load on the server or upgrade to a higher processor.

You can use Performance Monitor to examine the activity of your system processor. You specifically need to keep in mind the following counters for the exam:

+ **Processor\% Processor Time:** Use this counter to examine the processor usage. A consistently high % Processor Time reading tells you that your processor is overworked and can't keep up with the demand placed on it.

+ **System\Processor Queue Length, Processor\Interrupts/sec, System\ Processor Queue Length, and System\Context switches/sec:** You can use all of these counters to examine the system processor and determine whether it has become a bottleneck.

Disk

Your hard disk is automatically a Windows 2000 Performance Monitor object, and you can use Performance Monitor to examine its performance.

For the exam, you need to know that logical disk counter data is not collected by Windows 2000 by default. If you want to get performance data for logical drives for storage volumes, you have to use the diskperf -y command at the command line.

Keep the following disk counters in mind for the exam:

+ **Physical Disk\ Dis Reads/sec, Physical Disk\ Disk writes/sec, LogicalDisk\ % Free Space:** Use these counters to examine disk usage.

+ **Physical Disk\ Avg. Disk Queue Length:** Use this counter to determine whether your disk has become a bottleneck.

Configuring Performance Options

In addition to using Performance Monitor to manage your system performance, you can also access the Advanced tab of System Properties to make further configuration choices. To do so, follow these steps:

1. **Right-click My Computer and choose Properties.**

   The System Properties dialog box comes up.

2. **Click the Advanced tab.**

3. **From this tab, click the Performance Options button.**

   This brings up the Performance dialog box, where you have two choices:

   - You can choose to optimize system performance for either applications or background services. By default, background services is selected. This allows your system to provide more priority to background services than to any applications that may be running. You can change this so that applications have priority by clicking the radio button, but this may slow down background processes.

   - You can click the Change button to make changes to your Total paging file size. The minimum paging file size is 2MB and the recommended size is 1.5 times the amount of RAM on your system. Your paging file is automatically set to the recommended setting, but you can change it if you want.

Generally, you should not change the total paging file size. Windows does a good job of managing its own paging file. If you reduce or increase the paging file too much, you may experience system performance problems.

Using Task Manager

Another important tool that allows you to manage system processes and performance is Task Manager. You can access Task Manager by right-clicking on an empty area of the taskbar and clicking Task Manager.

You can use three tabs on Task Manager: Applications, Processes, and Performance. The Applications tab contains a list of running applications. You can select any running application and use the End Task, Switch To, or New Task buttons. This tab is typically used to stop a malfunctioning application.

The Processes tab presents a list of all processes running on your system. You can select any process and click the End Process button to stop the process from running. This feature is also useful in troubleshooting system problems that you believe are caused by a system process.

You can right-click any task and change the priority of the task to High, Normal, or Low. This feature allows you to give certain processes more priority over others. Watch out for tricky exam questions concerning priorities and how to change a process's priority.

The Performance tab shows the percentage amount of CPU usage and Memory usage. This tab is useful to see how much CPU or Memory resources are currently in use and whether either appears to be a bottleneck.

Using MSINFO

If you ever took a peek at Windows 98, you may be familiar with the Microsoft Information tool (MSINFO) that was first introduced with that operating system. All Windows 2000 operating systems also include MSINFO, which can be an excellent tool to gain information about your system and to troubleshoot problems.

To access System Information, choose Start⇨Accessories⇨System Tools⇨ System Information, or choose Start⇨Run, then type **MSINFO32** and click OK. This brings up the System Information screen, shown in Figure 5-4.

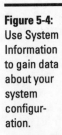

Figure 5-4: Use System Information to gain data about your system configur- ation.

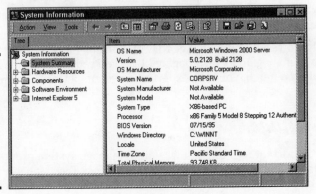

System Information provides you an MMC snap-in interface with categories for System Summary, Hardware Resources, Components, Software Environment, and Internet Explorer.

For the exam, all you need to know is what information is available in each category. You don't have to worry about many exam questions on System Information, so we have put the information about each category in the fol- lowing list so that you can easily memorize it.

✦ **Hardware Resources:** This container holds categories so that you can check your systems' IRQ usage, DMA allocation, memory resources, forced hardware, I/O configuration, and conflicts/sharing.

✦ **Components:** This container holds information about your system com- ponents, such as multimedia, display, network connections, modems, printing, and so on. Also available is a category for Problem Devices so you can determine the solutions to problems that you may be experiencing with system components.

✦ **Software Environment:** This container holds information about your system software configuration, such as drivers, environment variables, network connections, running tasks, services, and so on.

✦ **Internet Explorer 5:** This container holds your current settings for IE 5, which includes file versions, connectivity, cache, content, and security.

Optimizing Disk Performance

Windows 2000 Server contains several tools to help you optimize your disk performance. These tools are easy to use and are a vital part of managing your Windows 2000 Server. You can access some of the tools by choosing Start⇨Accessories⇨System Tools, and you can access all of them by clicking the Tools menu in System Information.

Don't worry about excessive questions concerning these tools, but you do need to know what each tool can do and when you should use each tool:

✦ **Disk Cleanup:** This is a handy utility that you can use to clean out old files on your hard disk in order to free up more storage space. Of course, you can delete these files manually, but Disk Cleanup provides a quick and easy way to perform the task because Disk Cleanup finds the files that you may want to delete. When you launch Disk Cleanup, the program scans your system and presents you with a list of files that you can choose to delete, such as cached Internet files and other files that are no longer in use.

✦ **Dr. Watson:** This is a program error debugger that you may have seen in previous versions of Windows. Dr. Watson logs program errors that can be used to diagnose and solve system problems. Dr. Watson logs errors in a text file called Drwtsn32.log whenever an error is detected. Dr. Watson is primarily used to log errors that can then be sent to support personnel for analysis.

✦ **Disk Defragmenter:** This is now available in Windows 2000 as an MMC snap-in. Over time, as you create, change, and delete files, information on your hard disk can become fragmented. This means that data is stored in a noncontiguous manner. Pieces of files are stored in any available location on your hard disk, which causes the system to run slower when reading those files from the disk. Disk Defragmenter reorganizes your hard disk data so that it is stored in a contiguous manner. If your system seems to be slow when reading data from the hard disk, you may need to run this utility.

Managing and Optimizing Availability of System State Data and User Data

For the exam, you must understand the difference between System State data and user data. *User data* simply refers to data on your system that is accessed by users; common examples include documents, files, applications, and so forth. *System State data* is used by your operating system and contains the following, which you need to know for the exam:

+ Registry

+ COM+ class registration database

+ System boot files

+ Certificate services database (if your server is a certificate server)

Windows 2000 domain controllers also contain the Active Directory services database and the SYSVOL directory; member servers don't contain this data because they don't run Active Directory. Watch out for tricky exam questions concerning the differences between member server and domain controller System State data.

Reviewing backup concepts

Like Windows NT, Windows 2000 has different types of backup that you can implement. In fact, both systems support the same backup types, and the following section reviews those concepts for you.

We can't define only one correct way to back up data. Your backup plan depends on the needs of your network, the type of data used, and the critical nature of the data. You don't need to back up files on a regular basis if those files rarely change, but you do need an effective backup plan for data that changes daily so that you can recover the most recent version of that data.

Windows 2000 enables you to use various backup media, such as tape drives, Zip drives, CD-ROM drives, and even hard drives on remote computers.

You need to know the different types of backups for the exam, so you should carefully review the following descriptions:

+ **Normal:** Backs up all files and folders that you select. A normal backup does not use markers to determine which files have been backed up. Each file is marked as having been backed up. A normal backup is the easiest type of backup to restore, but it can be slow, depending on the amount of data.

✦ **Copy:** Backs up all selected files and folders, but does not look at markers and does not clear any existing markers.

✦ **Differential:** Backs up only selected files and folders that contain a marker. A differential backup does not clear the existing markers.

✦ **Incremental:** Backs up selected files and folders with a marker and then clears the existing marker.

✦ **Daily:** Backs up all selected files and folders that have changed during the day. A daily backup does not look at or clear markers, but is an effective way to back up files and folders that have changed during the day.

Creating a backup plan is an important part of the planning process. Most network environments use a combination of normal backups and differential or incremental backups. For example, you may use a normal backup on Monday and then perform incremental backups throughout the rest of the week. The key is finding the balance between ease of data recovery and the amount of time required to perform the backup each day.

**Book II
Chapter 5**

Managing System
Performance and
Availability

Using Windows backup

Windows 2000 offers an easy-to-use Backup tool. You access the Backup tool by choosinging Start⇨Programs⇨Accessories⇨System Tools⇨Backup.

The Backup tool's interface has four tabs, as shown in Figure 5-5. You can start the Backup Wizard by clicking a button on the Welcome tab, or you can manually create a backup job by using the other tabs.

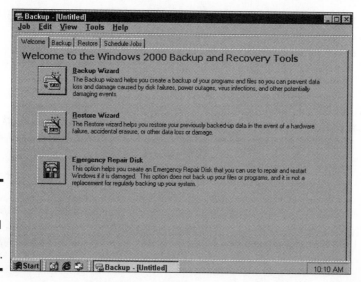

Figure 5-5:
Use the
Backup Tool
to configure
backup jobs.

For the exam, you need to know how the Backup Wizard works. You also need to know how to configure a backup job manually. You can review both processes in the following sections.

Working with the Backup Wizard

Lab 5-1 walks you through the steps for using the Backup Wizard. You should practice this lab on your server.

Lab 5-1   Using the Windows Backup Wizard

1. **On the Welcome tab, click the Backup Wizard button.**

2. **Click Next on the Backup Wizard Welcome screen.**

   This brings up the What to Back Up dialog box.

3. **Specify whether you want to back up everything on the computer, only selected files, drives, or network data, or only System State data by clicking the appropriate radio button.**

4. **Click Next.**

   For the exam, you need to know that System State data on a Windows 2000 member server contains the registry, the COM+ Class Registration database, system boot files, and the Certificate Services database (if the server is operating as a certificate server). On domain controllers, System State data also includes the Active Directory database.

   If you choose to back up only selected files, the wizard displays a dialog box so that you can select the files that you want to back up.

5. **If you've chosen to back up only selected files, select the desired files and then click Next.**

6. **Select the backup media that you plan to use by entering the drive path or by clicking the browse button and then selecting the desired path.**

7. **Click Next to bring up the Completion dialog box.**

8. **In the wizard's Completion dialog box, click Advanced to configure additional options in the Advanced Options dialog box (optional).**

9. **In the Type of Backup dialog box, shown in Figure 5-6, use the drop-down list to select either Normal, Copy, Incremental, Differential, or Daily Backup.**

   You can also click the Backup Migrated Remote Storage Data check box. Windows 2000 supports *remote storage,* which enables your computer to store data in a remote storage location — for example, a tape drive — if the storage space on your hard drive runs low. If you select the backup remote storage option, Windows Backup reads the data stored in remote storage and backs it up as well.

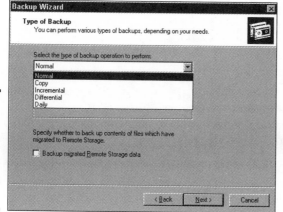

Figure 5-6:
Select the
backup type
as well as
remote
storage data
backup.

10. **Click Next to bring up the How to Back Up dialog box, which offers options for verifying data after backup and using hardware compression.**

   You can specify that the system should verify the backup data for integrity before the backup job completes. This option causes your backup job to take more time, but it does ensure that your backup job was successful. If hardware compression is available on your server, you can use hardware compression to reduce the amount of storage space that a backup job consumes. You can only restore compressed backups on drives that support compression. If your hardware does not support compression, this option is grayed out.

11. **Select the desired backup options and click Next.**

   In the Media Options dialog box that appears, you can choose to append the backup job to existing media, or replace the data on the backup media with this backup. If you choose to replace the media, you can also specify that only the owner or an administrator can have access to the backup data and to backups appended to the replacement data.

12. **Select the desired media options and click Next.**

13. **In the Backup Label dialog box that appears, provide a backup label and media label, if desired, and then click Next.**

   This brings up the When to Backup dialog box.

14. **In this dialog box, indicate whether you want to run the backup now or later by selecting the appropriate radio button.**

   If you choose later, enter a job name and start date.

   If you click the Set Schedule button, you can enter an exact start time and other minor options, such as beginning the backup when the computer is idle.

15. **Make your selections and click Next.**

16. **Click Finish to complete the wizard.**

    Depending on the options you chose, the backup job begins immediately or at the scheduled time.

Performing a manual backup

The Backup Wizard is a handy tool to help you configure backup jobs. After you become a pro at creating backup jobs, you may want to perform them manually. This is usually quicker, and you have the same options that the wizard provides.

To manually configure a backup job, access Windows Backup and then click the Backup tab, as shown in Figure 5-7.

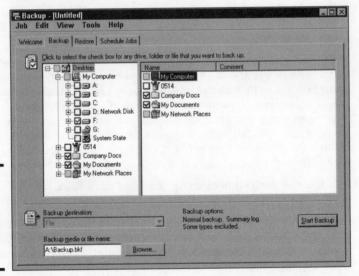

Figure 5-7:
Use the Backup tab to manually configure a backup job.

Specify what you want to back up by clicking the appropriate check boxes. You can back up individual files, System State data, or entire drives. At the bottom of the Backup tab, use the Browse button to select the backup media.

If you want to configure additional options for the backup job, choose Tools⇨Options. On the tabs in the resulting Options dialog box, you can select the type of backup, backup log, and other features that you also see when using the Backup Wizard.

After you select the desired options on the Backup tab, you can click the Start Backup button on the Backup tab, or you can click the Schedule Jobs tab to schedule the job. The Schedule Jobs tab displays a calendar on which you can select the backup dates and times.

Recovering System State Data and User Data

This section tells you everything you need to know about recovering lost data: restoring data, safe mode, and using the Recovery Console.

Restoring data

You realize the benefits of backing up data after you experience a system or disk failure. After your system becomes operational again, you can use the Windows Backup tool to restore the data that you previously backed up.

To restore data, you can use the Restore Wizard on the Welcome tab of the Backup utility, or you can use the Restore tab on the Backup Utility to manually run the restorable process. The wizard displays a few dialog boxes that enable you to determine what you want to restore and the location of the backup job. You can use the Advanced button to determine where on your hard drive to restore the data and if the restore operation should replace any of the same existing files on your system. The system then restores the data. You can manually select the same options all at once by choosing Restore All on the Restore tab.

Using safe mode

All Windows 2000 computers have safe mode capabilities, so you can attempt to solve problems with your server when it won't start.

About the ERD

The Emergency Repair Disk (ERD) is a tool that you can use to help start and recover your Windows 2000 Server system in the event of a system boot failure. You can easily create an ERD by accessing the Backup utility and clicking the Emergency Repair Disk button on the Welcome tab. You'll need a blank, formatted floppy disk to create the ERD.

The ERD is not a replacement for a backup plan, and the ERD can only help you repair system files, the partition boot sector, and the startup environment. You can also replace registry files using the ERD in conjunction with the Recovery Console.

You should keep a current ERD around at all times, so each time you make a significant system configuration change, you need to also create a new ERD.

Windows 2000 provides the following types of safe mode, which you need to know for the exam:

✦ **Safe Mode:** Starts Windows 2000 with only basic files and minimal drivers. With this type of safe mode, you can start the system so that you can troubleshoot and hopefully resolve the problem. If you still can't start your system by using safe mode, you probably need to use the Emergency Repair Disk (ERD) to correct system problems.

✦ **Safe Mode with Networking:** Starts Windows 2000 with only basic files and drivers, but also provides a network connection, so you can gain access to the network while in safe mode.

✦ **Safe Mode with Command Prompt:** Starts Windows 2000 with only basic files and drivers. After you log on, the system displays the command prompt instead of your Windows desktop.

✦ **Enable Boot Logging:** Starts Windows 2000 while logging all the drivers and services that are loaded or not loaded by the system. The log file is called ntbtlog.txt, and it is located in the %WINDIR% directory. By using this feature, you can review the boot log and determine the exact cause of your system problem.

✦ **Enable VGA Mode:** Starts Windows 2000 with the basic VGA driver. It is not uncommon to have problems after installing a new video card and driver, so this option installs the basic VGA driver. By using this option, you can resolve the VGA driver problem. Windows always uses VGA mode when you start the system in Safe Mode, Safe Mode with Networking, or Safe Mode with Command Prompt.

✦ **Last Known Good Configuration:** Starts Windows 2000 by using the registry information that Windows saved during the last shutdown. (Windows NT also offers this option.) This feature boots the system with the last good configuration that was saved and is only useful when incorrect configuration has caused the problem. Last Known Good Configuration doesn't solve problems with corrupt files or drivers, and any configuration changes made since the last successful startup are lost.

✦ **Debugging Mode:** Starts Windows 2000 while sending debug information to another computer through a serial cable.

Windows 2000 domain controllers also have a Directory Service Restore Mode, which you can use to troubleshoot Active Directory problems or restore the Active Directory database when a failure has occurred. For the exam, keep in mind that this option is available only on domain controllers and not on member servers.

To start your system in safe mode, turn on your server and hold down the F8 key. The Safe Mode menu appears, and you can select the type of safe mode that you want to use by pressing the arrow keys.

Using the Recovery Console

The Recovery Console is a command-line console feature of Windows 2000 that enables you to perform powerful administrative tasks on a system that won't start. Using the Recovery Console, you can start and stop services, read and write data to the local drive(s), format drives, and perform many other tasks. The Recovery Console is particularly useful if you need to replace corrupt system files with new copies from the installation CD-ROM. Only administrators have rights to use the Recovery Console.

Book II
Chapter 5

Managing System
Performance and
Availability

You can start the Recovery Console in two ways. First, if you can't start your server, you can launch the Recovery Console from the setup disks or from your installation CD-ROM (if your computer supports booting from a CD-ROM drive). Second, you can install the Recovery Console on your computer so that it is available as a boot menu option.

To install the Recovery Console so that it appears as a boot menu option, follow the steps in Lab 5-2.

Lab 5-2	Installing the Recovery Console

1. **Insert your Windows 2000 installation CD-ROM into the CD-ROM drive.**

2. **At the command prompt, type the letter of your CD-ROM drive and then type \i386\winnt32.exe/cmdcons.**

   A message appears, telling you about the Recovery Console.

3. **Click Yes to install it as a startup option.**

   File copy begins, and the console is installed.

When you boot your computer with the Recovery Console (either by startup disk, CD-ROM, or as a startup option), the basic console appears. You are prompted to select which Windows 2000 installation that you want to log on to (for dual-boot systems). Provide your administrator password, and you can then perform the desired actions, or type **Help** to see a list of available actions and proper syntax.

You don't need to know every syntax option for the exam, but you do need to know the basic options and what you can do with them. Table 5-1 describes those options so that you can easily memorize them.

Table 5-1	**Recovery Console Tasks**
Task	*What It Does*
Disable	Disables system services or device drivers
Enable	Enables system services or device drivers
Exit	Closes the Recovery Console and restarts your computer
Fixboot	Writes a new partition boot sector to the system partition
Fixmbr	Writes a new master boot record to the hard drive
Logon	Logs you on to an installation of Windows 2000
Map	Displays a mapping of drive letters to physical device names
Systemroot	Sets the current directory to the systemroot folder

In addition to the basic console tasks listed in Table 5-1, you can also choose from several Recovery Console commands that are available. Table 5-2 describes these commands, which you should memorize for the exam.

Table 5-2	**Recovery Console Commands**
Command	*What It Does*
Attrib	Changes the attributes of a file or directory
Batch	Executes the commands specified in a text file
ChDir (CD)	Displays the name of the current directory or changes the current directory
Chkdsk	Checks a disk and displays a status report
Cls	Clears the screen
Copy	Copies a single file to another location
Delete (Del)	Deletes one or more files
Dir	Displays a list of files and subdirectories in a directory
Diskpart	Manages partitions on your hard drives
Expand	Extracts a file from a compressed file
Format	Formats a disk
Listsvc	Lists the services and drivers available on the computer
Mkdir (Md)	Creates a directory
Rename (Ren)	Renames a directory
Rmdir (Rd)	Deletes a directory
Set	Displays and sets environment variables

Prep Test

1 There seems to be a lot of paging occurring on your system. You want to use Performance Counter to examine memory usage on your system. Which counters should you use? (Choose all that apply.)

A ❑ System\Context switches/sec

B ❑ Memory\Available Bytes

C ❑ Memory\Cache Bytes

D ❑ Memory\System Driver Total Bytes

2 You have several logical drives on a storage volume. You want to make certain that disk counters are available for those logical drives in Performance monitor. What command do you need to run at the command prompt to enable this object and the counters?

A ○ None — they are available by default.

B ○ diskperf -ld

C ○ disperf -dv

D ○ diskperf -y

3 Which performance option is in effect by default on Windows 2000 systems for application response?

A ○ Applications

B ○ Pagefile.sys

C ○ Background services

D ○ System processes

4 In the Windows Backup Wizard, you have the option of verifying the integrity of your backup job after it is complete. Which statement about verification is correct?

A ○ Verification ensures the integrity of your backup, but increases the time necessary to perform the entire backup operation.

B ○ Verification ensures the integrity of your backup job, but creates additional disk overhead.

C ○ Verification ensures the integrity of your backup job, but compresses the data on the backup media.

D ○ Verification ensures the integrity of your backup job, but removes the file markers.

5 You want to implement a backup type that backs up only selected files and folders that contain markers, but you don't want the existing markers cleared. What type of backup do you need to use?

A ○ Normal

B ○ Copy

C ○ Differential

D ○ Incremental

6 You want to implement a backup type that backs up only selected files and folders that contain markers, but you want the existing markers to be cleared. What type of backup do you need to use?

A ○ Normal

B ○ Copy

C ○ Differential

D ○ Incremental

7 Which of the following is not a component of System State data on a Windows 2000 member server?

A ○ Registry

B ○ Active Directory database

C ○ COM+ Class Registration database

D ○ System boot files

8 When configuring the Advanced options of a backup job, you notice that the hardware compression option is grayed out. Why is this option unavailable?

A ○ The backup job doesn't support hardware compression.

B ○ Windows 2000 doesn't support hardware compression.

C ○ Your server hardware doesn't support hardware compression.

D ○ Your backup media doesn't support hardware compression.

9 You enable Boot Logging on your server to troubleshoot a boot problem. What is name of the log file that Boot Logging generates?

A ○ bootlog.log

B ○ ntbtlog.log

C ○ ntbtlog.txt

D ○ ntbtlog.exe

10 When using the Recovery Console, you want to view the services and drivers available on the computer. What command do you need to use?

A ○ Diskpart

B ○ Expand

C ○ Ren

D ○ Listsvc

Answers

1 **B** and **C.** To examine excessive paging, these two counters are your best choice. *Study "Memory."*

2 **D.** The diskperf -y command enables performance counters for logical drives or storage volumes. To view a list of diskperf commands, type **diskperf** ? at the command prompt. *See "Disk."*

3 **C.** Concerning application response, you have the option to either select applications or background services to optimize performance. By default, background services is selected, but you can change this by accessing System Properties, Advanced Tab, and then by clicking the Performance Options button. *Study "Configuring Performance Options."*

4 **A.** Although verification does ensure the integrity of your backup job, it also increases the amount of time that a backup job takes. *Review "Workingiwth the Backup Wizard."*

5 **C.** A differential backup backs up selected files and folders that contain markers, but it does not clear the existing markers. *Study "Reviewing backup concepts."*

6 **D.** An incremental backup backs up selected files and folders that contain markers, and it clears the existing markers. *See "Reviewing backup concepts."*

7 **B.** The Active Directory database is a part of System State data on domain controllers, not member servers. *Study "Managing and Optimizing Availability of System State Data and User Data."*

8 **C.** If the hardware compression option is grayed out, the server hardware does not support hardware compression. *Study "Working with the Backup Wizard."*

9 **C.** `ntbtlog` is stored as a text file in the %WINDIR% directory. *Study "Using Safe Mode."*

10 **D.** You use the Listsvc command to list the services and drivers available on your computer. *Study "Using the Recovery Console."*

Chapter 6: Managing, Configuring, and Troubleshooting Storage Use

Exam Objectives

✔ Monitoring, configuring, and troubleshooting disks and volumes

✔ Configuring data compression

✔ Recovering from disk failures

✔ Monitoring and configuring disk quotas

As a systems administrator, you need to manage hard disks. Fortunately, Windows 2000 handles hard disks much better than Windows NT 4.0. However, this means you need to understand some changes and additions in the way that Windows 2000 uses hard disks. Windows 2000 and Windows NT 4.0 have many of the same options, such as fault tolerance support, but Windows 2000 also gives you some new features that you need to know for the exam and for your job as an IT professional.

For the exam, you need to know how to manage and configure hard disks. You also need to know about data compression and some tactics for recovering from disk failures. You can review the following topics in this chapter:

✦ Managing hard disks

✦ Configuring volumes

✦ Using data compression

✦ Configuring mounted volumes

✦ Configuring quotas

Examining Windows 2000 Disk Basics

As you may know, Microsoft loves to change things. Fortunately, these changes are often for the better, and disk management in Windows 2000 is no exception. You can manage your hard disk needs in Windows 2000 by using the Computer Management tool, which you access by clicking Start⇨ Programs⇨Administrative Tools⇨Computer Management. Expand the Storage container and then click Disk Management to access the Disk Management interface, as shown in Figure 6-1.

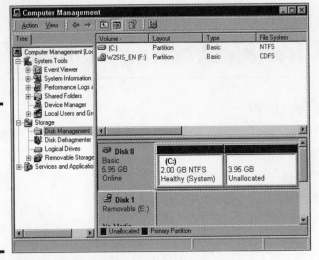

Figure 6-1:
You can
configure
hard disks
through the
Computer
Manage-
ment
console.

Choosing a file system

Windows 2000 supports FAT, FAT32, and NTFS file systems. The NTFS file system in Windows 2000 is an enhanced version that supports the security features of the Kerberos protocol. Unless you have a specific reason for using FAT or FAT32, you should format your drives with NTFS so you have the security features of Kerberos and the storage features of Windows 2000, several of which are available only with NTFS.

Understanding basic and dynamic disks

A new feature of Windows 2000 disk management involves the distinction between *basic* and *dynamic* disks. Basic disks consist of partitions and logical drives. If you upgrade from Windows NT 4.0, your disk configuration remains intact and it is a basic disk. With a basic disk, you can manage the partitions and the logical drives, and you can create additional partitions. However, you can't create any new volume sets, stripe sets, and so on. Windows 2000 manages dynamic disks and contains *dynamic volumes,* which are simply volumes that you create with the Disk Management console.

Dynamic disks don't contain partitions or logical drives; they contain volumes. With this design, disks are no longer limited to a certain number of partitions and they can contain multiple volumes. This design gives you greater flexibility for disk management without the restrictions imposed by previous versions of Windows. Also, you can make changes to your disk configuration on a dynamic disk without having to reboot your computer.

Previous disk management solutions and fault-tolerant solutions are still available on dynamic disks, but the names have changed. (More terminology!) You need to know the differences, so take the time to memorize the following terms:

✦ **Spanned volume:** A spanned volume, formerly called a *volume set,* is a collection of volume (formerly partition) "pieces" that the system treats as one volume. By using spanned volumes, you can make constructive use of small portions of disk space; however, spanned volumes have no inherent fault tolerance.

✦ **Striped volumes:** A striped volume, formerly called a *striped set,* stores data on two or more physical disks. Striped volumes allocate data evenly (in stripes) across the disks in the striped volume, so you must have the same amount of storage space on each disk. Striped volumes are an excellent storage solution, but they offer no fault tolerance. If one disk in the stripe volume fails, you lose all data on the entire striped volume.

✦ **Mirrored volumes:** Mirrored volumes, formerly called *mirror sets,* represent a fault-tolerant solution that duplicates data on two physical disks. One disk is the primary disk, and the other disk is the mirror (or a copy of the primary disk). If one disk fails, you can reconstruct data by using the mirror. In fact, in Windows 2000, if one of the disks fails, your system continues to operate as though nothing has happened by using the mirror. You can replace the failed disk and re-create the mirror for continued fault tolerance. However, the same controller is shared by the disks, so if the controller fails, the whole system goes down. Mirrored volumes are effective fault-tolerance solutions, but they are costly in terms of megabytes (50 percent). In other words, if you want to mirror a 2GB disk, you must have another 2GB disk available. This configuration requires twice as much disk space as you would normally use without the mirror. So, in terms of disk megabyte expense, you are only getting to use half of your total storage space.

✦ **RAID-5 volumes:** A RAID-5 volume, formerly called a *stripe set with parity,* requires at least three physical disks and up to 32 disks. Data is written in a stripe fashion across the disks and includes a parity bit that the system can use to reconstruct data in case of a disk failure. If a disk fails within the RAID-5 volume, the data can be regenerated with the parity bit. You can't mirror or extend RAID-5 volumes after you create them, but they are an effective fault-tolerant solution.

In order to manage your disks in Windows 2000, you need to upgrade each disk from basic to dynamic. To do so, simply right-click the disk (not the partitions) in the Disk Management console and then choose Upgrade to Dynamic Disk. You need to reboot your computer in order for the upgrade to take effect.

Book II
Chapter 6

Managing,
Configuring, and
Troubleshooting
Storage Use

After you upgrade to dynamic disk, you can't boot previous versions of Windows on the dynamic disk because these operating systems can't access dynamic volumes. Therefore, dynamic disks are a Windows 2000-only solution, but you should implement them as soon as possible in order to take advantage of the features that dynamic disks offer.

When you upgrade a basic disk to a dynamic disk, you must have 1MB of unformatted free space at the end of the disk, which Windows uses for administrative purposes. To maintain previous volume sets, striped sets, and similar items from a basic disk, you must upgrade all the basic disks to dynamic disks. Also, keep in mind that you can't upgrade removable media to dynamic disks.

Understanding online and offline disks

In addition to the distinction between basic and dynamic disks, Windows 2000 introduces two more disk-related terms: *online* and *offline*. The Disk Management console displays this status for each disk. *Online* means that the disk is up and running, and in contrast, an *offline* disk has errors and is not available.

To access the properties of either an online or offline disk, simply right-click the disk in the Disk Management console and click Properties. From the Properties dialog box for an offline disk, you can use the disk tools to attempt to repair the disk. Alternatively, you can attempt to repair the offline disk by right-clicking it and then choosing Reactivate Disk.

Understanding disk status

The Disk Management console provides several pieces of information about each disk volume, such as layout, type, file system, status, capacity, and free space. For the exam, you need to know about disk status and the possible status indicators that can occur.

You need to memorize these status indicators for the exam:

+ **Healthy:** The volume is accessible and has no problems.

+ **Healthy (At Risk):** The volume is accessible, but I/O errors have been detected. The underlying disk, which is the physical disk on which the volume is located, is displayed as Online (Errors). Usually, you can solve this problem by reactivating the disk (right-click the disk and choose Reactivate Disk).

+ **Initializing:** The volume is being initialized and will be displayed as Healthy after initialization is complete. This status does not require any action.

✦ **Resynching:** The system is resynchronizing mirrored volumes. After Windows 2000 completes the resynchronization, the status is displayed as Healthy, and no action is necessary from you.

✦ **Regenerating:** Data on RAID-5 volumes is being regenerated from the parity bit. This process occurs after a disk failure and disk replacement by an administrator. No action is required.

✦ **Failed Redundancy:** The underlying disk is offline on fault-tolerant disks. In this case, you no longer have any fault tolerance on either mirrored or RAID-5 volumes. You need to reactivate or repair the disk in order to avoid potential data loss if one of the disks fails.

✦ **Failed Redundancy (At Risk):** This status is the same as Failed Redundancy, but the status of the underlying disk is Online (Errors). Reactivate the disk so that it returns to Online status.

✦ **Failed:** The system can't start the volume automatically, and you need to repair the volume.

Book II
Chapter 6

Managing,
Configuring, and
Troubleshooting
Storage Use

Creating Volumes

You can easily create new volumes on your dynamic disks in Windows 2000 in the Disk Management console. Simply right-click the free space where you want to create a new volume and then choose Create Volume. This action launches the Create Volume Wizard.

You can create any volume, spanned volume, striped volume, mirrored volume, or RAID-5 volume (assuming that you have the number of drives required) by using the Create Volume Wizard.

The Create Volume Wizard is rather straightforward and easy to use, but the exam does expect you to understand how the wizard works. Review Lab 6-1, which creates a simple volume, to make certain that you understand how the wizard works.

Lab 6-1   Creating a Simple Volume

1. **In the Disk Management console, right-click the area of free space where you want to create the volume and then choose Create Volume.**

2. **Click Next on the Create Volume welcome screen that appears.**

   This brings up Volume Selection dialog box.

3. **Select Simple Volume from the list of options and click Next.**

   If you want to create a different kind of volume, select the desired type and click Next.

4. **Select the desired disk and click Add, as shown in Figure 6-2. You can also adjust the MB size for the volume in the Total Volume Size box, as desired. Click Next.**

   This brings up the Drive Letter dialog box.

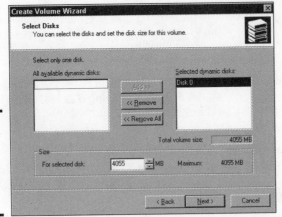

Figure 6-2:
Select the disk and volume size and then click Next.

5. **Select a drive letter for the volume or choose to mount the volume to an empty folder. You can also choose not to assign a drive letter or drive path at this time. Make your selection and click Next.**

   See the section "Using Mounted Volumes," later in this chapter for more information about mounted volumes.

6. **In the Format dialog box that appears, indicate whether you want to format the volume. If you choose to format it now, select a file system, an allocation unit size, and a volume label.**

   You can also choose to perform a quick format and enable file and folder compression, if desired.

   The data compression option enables the Disk Management console to compress data on the volume so that more storage space is available.

7. **Click Finish to complete the wizard.**

   The system creates the volume and formats it (if specified).

Checking Out Common Management Tasks

After you configure your volumes in the desired manner, disk management requires very little time on your part. Your basic tasks include occasional management and troubleshooting.

You can manage your disk volumes through the Disk Management tool. By right-clicking a dynamic disk or disk volume, you can perform several tasks. These tasks may vary depending on the type of disk or volume, but you should understand the following basic management actions, which you need to remember for the exam:

✦ **Open/Explore:** Enables you to open the disk or volume and view its contents.

✦ **Extend Volume:** You can dynamically extend a disk volume to incorporate more space from free disk space. You can only extend volumes with other NTFS volumes — not FAT or FAT32.

✦ **Change Drive Letter and Path:** You can dynamically change a volume's drive letter and path by entering the desired change.

✦ **Reactivate Volume/Disk:** Use the Reactivate feature to correct Online (Error) status readings.

✦ **Delete Volume:** Removes the volume from your computer.

✦ **Properties:** In the Properties dialog boxes for disks and volumes, you can see general information about the disk and its hardware, and you can access disk tools, such as Error Checking and Disk Defragmenter.

Using Mounted Volumes

By using mounted volumes in Windows 2000, you can easily replace drive letters so that a disk volume appears as a folder. In other words, by mounting a drive to a folder, you can give the drive a friendly name and you won't run out of available drive letters. To create the mounted volume, simply create an empty folder, name it as you desire, and then mount the volume to the folder by using Disk Management.

To create a mounted volume, follow the steps that we describe in Lab 6-2.

Lab 6-2   Creating a Mounted Volume

1. **Right-click the volume that you want to mount and choose Change Drive Letter and Path from the pop-up menu.**

2. **In the Change Drive Letter and Path dialog box, click Add.**

3. **As shown in Figure 6-3, click the Mount in This NTFS Folder option, enter the path to the shared folder, and click OK.**

    (You can also click Browse and then navigate to the shared folder.)

Figure 6-3:
Enter the
name of
the NTFS
folder and
click OK.

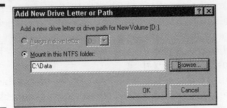

After you mount the volume to the NTFS folder, the folder appears as a drive on your system, as shown in Figure 6-4.

Figure 6-4:
The
mounted
volume now
appears as
a drive on
your system.

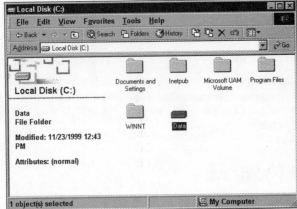

Configuring Disk Quotas

Disk quotas track and control disk space on Windows 2000 volumes. You can configure disk quotas to establish a limit of disk space usage and even log events when users exceed their disk space limit. In effect, using disk quotas controls the use of disk space and encourages network users to remove outdated information that they don't need to keep in storage.

Disk quotas function only on NTFS volumes on Windows 2000 computers, since Windows 2000 uses NTFS version 5. NTFS volumes on Windows NT computers don't support disk quotas.

When you configure disk quotas, you establish the actual disk usage limit and a warning level. For example, a user may have a disk space limit of 100MB and a warning level of 90MB. You can also allow users to exceed their disk space limit. In this case, you can use disk quotas to track disk usage by individual users without actually restricting the user's storage space.

For the exam, remember that data compression doesn't affect disk quotas. If a user has only 50MB of storage space, compression doesn't allow the user to store more than 50MB of data.

Disk quotas affect individual users and their disk usage. For example, if one user has 25MB of storage space on a disk, and another user also has 25MB of storage on the same disk, one user's consumption of 25MB doesn't affect the other user. In other words, each user has a quota. This design is particularly useful for network volumes in which multiple users have a quota that they can use on that volume.

Disk quotas apply to volumes — not the file or folder structure on the underlying disk. It doesn't matter how many folders or files a user saves — all the data collectively equals the storage space used. Also, disk quotas can apply to spanned volumes. Because the quota applies to the volume, it doesn't matter how much data is stored on each physical disk — the quota applies to the entire volume. Disk quotas are based on file ownership, so if a user takes ownership of a file, that file counts toward the user's disk quota.

Book II
Chapter 6

Managing,
Configuring, and
Troubleshooting
Storage Use

Enabling disk quotas

To enable disk quotas for a particular volume, access the volume through either My Computer or Disk Management, right-click the volume, and then choose Properties. In the Properties dialog box, click the Quota tab. To enable quotas on the volume, click the Enable Quota Management check box, as shown in Figure 6-5.

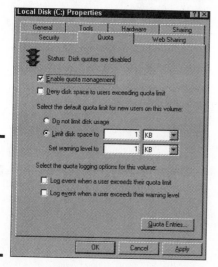

Figure 6-5:
Enable
quotas on
the Quota
tab of the
desired
volume.

After you enable quotas for the volume, you can configure the following options on the Quota tab, which you need to remember for the exam:

✦ **Decide whether to deny disk space to users exceeding the quota limit:** Remember that you don't have to deny disk space to users exceeding their limits, but you can use the disk quotas for monitoring purposes. However, you can deny disk space by selecting this check box.

✦ **Indicate whether you want to limit disk space:** If you choose to establish a limit, enter the limit and the warning level values in the provided boxes.

✦ **Specify whether to log an event when a user exceeds the quota limit or when a user exceeds the warning level:** You can choose either of these options, both of them, or neither.

Configuring quota entries

On the Quota tab, you can click the Quota Entries button to configure quota entries for the volume. Quota entries define the quota limits and warning levels for users of that volume. If you click the Quota Entries button on the Quota tab, the Quota Entries dialog box appears, as shown in Figure 6-6.

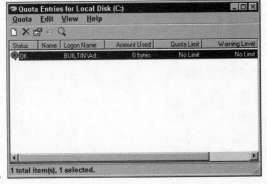

Figure 6-6:
Quota entries enable you to set quotas for users.

To configure a new quota entry, choose Quota⇨New Quota. This action opens the user list from Active Directory, from which you can select the user for whom you want to create the quota entry. Select the user, click Add, and then click OK. The Add New Quota Entry dialog box appears, as shown in Figure 6-7. In this dialog box, you can configure the disk space limit and warning level.

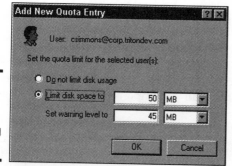

Figure 6-7:
Setting the
quota limit
and warning
for the user.

After you configure quota entries, you can easily edit them by selecting the user in the Quota Entries dialog box and clicking the Properties button on the taskbar. This action enables you to change the quota limit and the warning level. You can also perform standard management tasks such as copying and deleting users from the list.

For the exam, remember that you can't delete a quota entry until all the user's files and folders have been removed from the volume, or until another quota entry has taken ownership of them.

Book II
Chapter 6

Managing,
Configuring, and
Troubleshooting
Storage Use

Prep Test

1 Your server has three dynamic physical disks. Each disk has just over 1GB of free space. What storage solution can you implement that makes the best use of this free space?

A ○ Spanned volume

B ○ Striped volume

C ○ Mirrored volume

D ○ RAID-5 volume

2 You have four dynamic physical disks on your server. You want to implement a fault-tolerant solution that provides the best performance and uses the least amount of megabyte cost available. What solution do you need to implement?

A ○ Spanned volume

B ○ Striped volume

C ○ Mirrored volume

D ○ RAID-5 volume

3 You want to use a fault-tolerant solution that creates an exact copy of your primary hard drive. You have three physical disks on your computer. Which fault-tolerant solution should you use?

A ○ Spanned volume

B ○ Striped volume

C ○ Mirrored volume

D ○ RAID-5 volume

4 You notice that your RAID-5 volume is displayed as Regenerating after a recent disk failure. What action to you need to take?

A ○ No action is required.

B ○ Reactivate the disk.

C ○ Make the disk online.

D ○ The disk is not usable and needs to be replaced.

5 You notice that a particular volume is displayed as Healthy (At Risk). What action do you need to take?

A ○ No action is required.

B ○ Reactivate the disk.

C ○ Make the disk online.

D ○ The disk is not usable and needs to be replaced.

6 When creating a new volume, NTFS is the preferred file system. What other options do you have? (Choose all that apply.)

A ❑ FAT

B ❑ FAT32

C ❑ VFAT

D ❑ CDFS

7 You have a FAT32 volume that you want to extend, but the option doesn't seem to be available. What is the problem?

A ○ The disk is offline.

B ○ The disk needs to be reactivated.

C ○ You can only extend volumes formatted with NTFS.

D ○ The drive is mounted.

8 You want to mount a volume to a folder. What folder requirements must be met in order to accomplish this task? (Choose all that apply.)

A ❑ It must be an NTFS folder.

B ❑ The folder must be empty.

C ❑ The folder must reside in the root of C.

D ❑ There are no folder requirements.

9 You have a spanned volume that includes space on three physical disks. You want to implement disk quotas on this spanned volume, but you want to also make sure that users have a total storage limit of only 30MB on the spanned volume — not on each physical disk. What do you need to do after configuring the quota for the spanned volume?

A ○ Set limits on each physical disk.

B ○ Set limits on each volume in the spanned volume.

C ○ Install disk quotas for spanned volumes using Add/Remove Programs.

D ○ You don't need to do anything else.

10 You want to remove a quota entry for a particular volume, but you can't remove the entry. What is the most likely problem?

A ○ The user account is not available.

B ○ You need to edit diskqt.txt to manually remove the user.

C ○ The user's files and folders must be removed from the volume.

D ○ There is a general system error.

Answers

1 **B.** Because you have three disks with slightly more than 1MB each, your best solution is to create a striped volume, which makes better use of the storage space and provides the best performance. *Review "Understanding basic and dynamic disks."*

2 **D.** You need at least three physical disks to create a RAID-5 volume, which stripes data across the disks and writes a parity bit for data regeneration in the case of a disk failure. The only other choice is a mirrored volume, which has a 50 percent megabyte cost and slower write and read time, so your best answer choice is D. *Read "Understanding basic and dynamic disks."*

3 **C.** A mirrored volume creates a mirror, or exact copy, of one hard disk on another hard disk. In the case of a failure, you can recover the data from the copy. *Study "Understanding basic and dynamic disks."*

4 **A.** The Regenerating status indicator tells you that data on a RAID-5 volume is being regenerated. After regeneration is complete, the status will appear as Healthy, and you don't need to take any action. *Study "Understanding disk status."*

5 **B.** When a volume is displayed as Healthy (At Risk), you need to reactivate the disk by right-clicking it and then choosing Reactivate Disk. *Study "Understanding disk status."*

6 **A and B.** NTFS is the file system of choice, but when you create a new volume, the Create Volume Wizard also allows you to choose FAT and FAT32, if desired. *Study "Choosing a file system."*

7 **C.** Although you can use volumes formatted with FAT, only volumes formatted with NTFS can be extended. *Study "Checking Out Common Management Tasks."*

8 **A and B.** You can mount a volume to a folder, but the folder must be an NTFS folder and it must be empty. *Study "Using Mounted Volumes."*

9 **D.** Disk quotas apply to volumes — not physical disks. A spanned volume is treated as any other volume. In this case, after you set up disk quotas on the spanned volume, the users can't exceed their quota limit, regardless of how the data is stored across the spanned volume. *Study "Configuring Disk Quotas."*

10 **C.** Before deleting a quota entry, you must remove the user's files and folders from the volume, or another user must take ownership of them. *Study "Configuring Disk Quotas."*

Chapter 7: Configuring Windows 2000 Network Connections

Exam Objectives

- ✔ Installing, configuring, and troubleshooting network protocols
- ✔ Installing and configuring network services
- ✔ Installing, configuring, and troubleshooting shared access
- ✔ Installing, configuring, and troubleshooting network adapters and drivers
- ✔ Configuring, monitoring, and troubleshooting remote access
- ✔ Installing, configuring, and troubleshooting a virtual private network (VPN)
- ✔ Installing, configuring, monitoring, and troubleshooting Terminal Services

Managing Windows network connections requires a knowledge of Windows 2000 Server configuration and protocols. As you may guess, Windows 2000 Server provides all the functions and features necessary to manage and maintain connections on a Windows 2000 network.

Fortunately, Windows 2000 doesn't have too many new surprises concerning protocols and connections, and this chapter focuses only on what you may see on the exam. You can review the following topics in this chapter:

- ✦ Installing and configuring protocols
- ✦ Installing and configuring services
- ✦ Configuring shared access
- ✦ Configuring and troubleshooting remote access
- ✦ Installing and configuring Terminal Services
- ✦ Installing and managing network adapters and drivers

Installing and Configuring Protocols

You install and configure network protocols for any network interface card (NIC) that you have installed on your server. If you have multiple NICs, you can configure different protocols and services for each NIC, depending on how you want to use it for network communication. The process for installing and configuring protocols is rather easy, and the following sections point out what you need to know for the exam.

Installing protocols

To install new protocols for a NIC, access the Properties dialog box for that NIC by right-clicking My Network Places on your desktop and then choosing Properties. Windows 2000 opens the Network and Dial-up Connections dialog box, which shows Local Area Network (LAN) connections or dial-ups installed on your server.

To install and configure protocols for a NIC, right-click its icon and choose Properties. Windows 2000 opens the Local Area Connection Properties dialog box for that NIC, as shown in Figure 7-1.

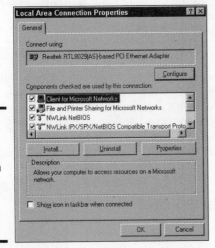

Figure 7-1:
Use the
Local Area
Connection
Properties
dialog box
to install
protocols.

To install a new protocol, follow the steps in Lab 7-1. You should remember how to perform this process for the exam.

Book II
Chapter 7

Configuring
Windows 2000
Network
Connections

Lab 7-1   Installing a Protocol

1. **In the NIC's Local Area Connection Properties dialog box, click Install.**

2. **In the resulting Select Network Component Type dialog box, select Protocol and then click Add.**

3. **In the Select Network Protocol dialog box, select the protocol that you want to install and click OK.**

   If you want to install a different protocol that doesn't automatically appear, click Have Disk. (You must have a disk or CD-ROM containing the protocol to use this option.)

   Windows 2000 installs the protocol on your system. The protocol now appears in the list that's displayed in the Local Area Connection Properties dialog box.

Configuring protocols

To configure a protocol after you install it, select the protocol in the Components window in the Local Area Connection Properties dialog box and then click Properties.

If you select a protocol and the Properties button appears gray (unavailable), that protocol has no configurable options. For example, NetBEUI doesn't have any configurable options, so you can't access a Properties dialog box for that protocol.

After you click the Properties button, various sheets may appear, depending on the protocol that you select. For example, the Properties dialog box for Internet Protocol (TCP/IP) has a General tab where you can configure the IP address, subnet mask, and default gateway, as well as preferred DNS server IP addresses. (You can also configure TCP/IP to obtain its IP address from a DHCP server.) If you select NWLink and click Properties, you see a General tab where you can manually enter the internal network number and frame type.

For the exam, you are expected to know the major options that you can configure for the more common protocols. You don't need to know all the details about each setting, but you do need to have a general understanding of what you may need to configure. Table 7-1 points out the major configuration options for each major protocol. You should memorize this information for the exam.

Table 7-1	Protocol Configuration
Protocol	*Configuration Options*
TCP/IP	Used for communication in a TCP/IP network. Configurable options are IP address, subnet mask, default gateway, DHCP option, and additional options, such as DNS or WINS servers.
NWLink	Used for communication with IPX/SPX networks (NetWare). Configuration options are the internal network number and frame type in use. (Typically, your server detects them automatically, but you can manually configure these settings for troubleshooting purposes.)
AppleTalk	Used for communication with Macintosh computers. The configurable option is the AppleTalk zone.

Removing protocols

To boost network communication performance, remove any protocols that you no longer use or need on your system. To remove a protocol, simply select it in the Components window of the Local Area Connection Properties dialog box and then click Uninstall. Click Yes in the dialog box that appears, and you are prompted to reboot your system after Windows 2000 uninstalls the protocol.

Common protocol problems

Generally, protocols are not problematic system components. For the exam, you need to know two basic problems and solutions for TCP/IP and NWLink.

✦ **You have configured an incorrect IP address or subnet mask:** The odds are pretty good that this is your problem if your server has a static IP and subnet mask but you don't have connectivity. In a TCP/IP network, you must have an appropriate IP address and subnet mask configured (if you are not using DHCP). If DHCP is in use, this information is automatically supplied to the server.

✦ **You have an incorrect frame type:** This is most likely your problem if you are using NWLink to communicate in a NetWare environment and you can't gain connectivity. Windows 2000 does a good job of automatically detecting this information, but if you have connectivity problems, check the frame type and make certain that the NetWare servers use the same one.

Installing Network Services

Depending on the configuration of your server, you can install additional client and service features on your server for a particular NIC by using the following steps:

1. **Right-click My Network Places and then choose Properties.**

This brings up the Network and Dial-Up Connections box.

2. **Right-click the connection icon and choose Properties to access the Local Area Connection Properties.**

3. **Click Install and select either Client or Service and click Add.**

4. **From the list that appears, select the type of service you want to install and then click OK.**

The network services that you can install from this location are specific services for the NIC.

Book II
Chapter 7

Configuring
Windows 2000
Network
Connections

Installing Other Connections

Windows 2000 Server can support many types of connections other than a typical network connection using a NIC. For example, you can install modem connections, VPN connections, serial, parallel, or infrared ports, and ISDN lines to accommodate your networking needs.

You can easily install these connections by first installing necessary hardware and using the Add/Remove Hardware Wizard, or by using the Make New Connection Wizard in the Network and Dial-up Connections dialog box, which you access by right-clicking My Network Places and then choosing Properties.

Configuring Shared Access

Windows 2000 servers can share access points with other computers on your network. Namely, Windows 2000 can share a modem or ISDN connection so that other computers can access information on the Internet using the share on the server. The server then provides the connection, address translation, and name-resolution functions to retrieve the Internet information and return it to the client who requests it.

This feature of Windows 2000 provides some of the functionality of a proxy server and is designed for small office or home networks. By configuring the server with the dial-up connection and modem, ISDN hardware, DSL connection, or some other kind of connection technology, only one computer on your network must have the hardware or configuration and all others can use it through the share.

Shared access isn't difficult to configure, but it is a new feature of Windows 2000 Server, so you can expect some exam questions on this topic. This section explores only the shared access topics that you are likely to see on the exam.

To set up shared access for an Internet connection, follow the steps in Lab 7-2.

Lab 7-2   Setting Up Shared Access

1. **Right-click My Network Places and click Properties.**

2. **In the Network and Dial-up Connections dialog box, right-click the connection that you want to share and choose Properties.**

3. **In the resulting Properties dialog box, click the Sharing tab, as shown in Figure 7-2.**

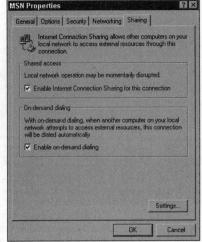

Figure 7-2:
Use the Sharing tab to configure shared connections.

4. **To enable shared access, click the Enable Internet Connection Sharing for This Connection check box.**

If desired, you can also select the Enable On-demand Dialing check box. On-demand dialing enables your server to automatically establish a dial-up connection when a user accesses the shared connection. For example, suppose that a user needs to retrieve an Internet document through the shared connection. When the user accesses the shared connection, the server automatically establishes a dial-up connection to service the user's needs.

After you select the desired settings on the Sharing tab, click OK to share the connection. Windows 2000 Server displays a message stating that your NIC will be set to use the IP address 192.168.0.1, which may cause your server to lose connectivity with other computers on the network. This safety feature protects your IP network from being compromised, so it is important to consider the TCP/IP connectivity implications of sharing a connection. The server now acts as a DHCP, or NAT server, for the other clients on the network who will be accessing the shared connection.

On the exam, you may see a question about a small office network that implements Internet connection sharing and then loses IP connectivity with the server. The problem involves the use of the new IP address of 192.168.0.1. You can reestablish your original TCP/IP settings by accessing your TCP/IP properties and manually changing the IP address back to the appropriate address for your network.

You can also configure applications and services for use with the shared connection. On the Sharing tab, click Settings. On the Applications and Services tab in the dialog box that displays, click Add or use the Edit and Delete buttons as needed to enable the use of various applications via the connection. The applications feature is designed for applications that you may have installed that can be shared over the Internet with another office or user. The services feature enables you to determine which services (such as FTP and SMTP) can be used over the connection. These features enable you to configure the connection sharing to meet the needs of your network users.

Connection sharing is designed for very small networks or home networks. It is not intended for use in networks with other Windows 2000 domain controllers or where DNS and DHCP servers are in use. ICS uses NAT rather than DHCP.

Watch out for tricky exam questions that combine the use of Internet connection sharing with large networks. This is not the intended use of connection sharing, and this configuration is certain to cause connectivity and even security problems.

Book II
Chapter 7

Configuring
Windows 2000
Network
Connections

Managing Network Adapters and Drivers

You manage network interface (adapter) cards (NICs) and drivers for these cards in the same manner as any other hardware device attached to your computer. If you access the NIC's properties in the Network and Dial-up Connections dialog box, you can click Configure to access the NIC's Properties dialog box. You can troubleshoot problems and manage the driver for the NIC by using the Driver tab.

Understanding Remote Access

Remote Access Service (RAS) allows remote network clients to establish a remote connection with a RAS server. After the connection is established, the remote client functions just like a locally connected network client. The user can browse the network, use permitted resources, connect to other servers — anything that a locally connected client can do — provided the RAS client has appropriate permissions. In recent years, RAS has become more and more important as more users work from laptops in different locations.

In Windows NT, remote access was called Routing and Remote Access (RRAS), which combined remote access and routing technologies. In Windows 2000, the routing portion is a built-in part of the RAS console and is simply called Routing and Remote Access.

The exam objectives don't focus on the configuration of routing interfaces on a Windows 2000 Server, but are focused on the remote access configuration. In light of this fact, this chapter primarily focuses on the remote access portion of Routing and Remote Access, and the term "RAS" refers to both routing and remote access.

Enabling Remote Access

RAS is installed by default on Windows 2000 Servers when you perform an initial installation. However, RAS is not enabled. In order to set up and implement RAS, you have to enable it, and you accomplish this through the Routing and Remote Access Server Setup Wizard.

You need to know the options presented in this wizard for the exam. To practice setting up RAS by using the wizard, follow the steps in Lab 7-3.

Lab 7-3   Enabling Routing and Remote Access

1. **Click Start➪Programs➪Administrative Tools➪Routing and Remote Access.**

   This brings up the RRAS console.

2. **In the console, select your server, click the Action menu, and then click Configure and Enable Routing and Remote Access.**

3. **Click Next on the wizard's welcome screen.**

4. **On the Common Configuration window, make a selection for the kind of remote access server that you want to install, and then click Next.**

   For this lab, select Remote Access Server, as shown in Figure 7-3.

5. **Verify the required protocols in the list provided and click Next.**

   Typically, you need TCP/IP, but may need other protocols, depending on your network clients.

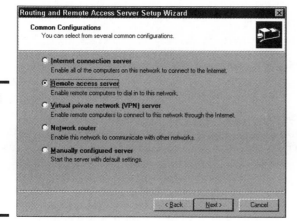

Figure 7-3:
Windows
2000 RAS
provides
you with
several
server
options.

**Book II
Chapter 7**

Configuring
Windows 2000
Network
Connections

6. **In the IP Address Assignment window that appears, choose how you want remote clients to be assigned an IP address by clicking either the Automatic radio button or the Specified Range radio button, and then clicking Next.**

   If you choose Automatic, remote clients are provided an IP address through DHCP. If you click Specified Range, you enter an IP address range to assign to remote clients.

7. **Next, click either No or Yes to determine whether to enable RADIUS, and then click Next.**

   Remote Authentication Dial-In User Service (RADIUS) provides a central authentication database for multiple remote access servers and collects accounting information about remote connections. This window allows you to set up this remote access server to use an existing RADIUS server if you so choose.

8. **Click the Finish button.**

   Windows 2000 starts the Routing and Remote Access Service.

Configuring Server Properties

After RAS is enabled, you can further configure the server by accessing the server's properties sheets. In the Routing and Remote Access console, select your server, click the Action menu, and then click Properties.

You need to know the configuration options on the tabs of the Properties sheet that we discuss in the next sections. You may have other tabs, such as AppleTalk for Macintosh clients — depending on your network configuration — but the following sections only explore the tabs that you need to know for the exam.

Configuring the General tab

The General tab gives you two options:

✦ **You can choose to enable your server as a router:** If you select this option, you can choose to allow only local LAN routing, or you can choose to allow LAN and demand-dial routing.

✦ **You can choose to enable your server as a remote access server:** This option simply allows you to use your server as either a routing or remote access server, or both.

Configuring the Security tab

The Security tab allows you to choose the security and accounting provider. You can select either Windows authentication and accounting or RADIUS authentication and accounting. If you choose to implement RADIUS, you use the Configure button to connect to a RADIUS server.

For Windows authentication, you can click the Authentication Methods button and select the type of Windows authentication you want to use for remote access. The following list details your options, and you need to know these for the exam:

✦ **Extensible authentication protocol (EAP):** Allows the use of third-party authentication software and is also used for Smart Card logon.

✦ **MS-CHAP V2:** Generates encryption keys during RAS authentication negotiation.

✦ **MS-CHAP:** An earlier version of CHAP that provides secure logon.

✦ **Shiva Password Authentication Protocol (SPAP):** Used by Shiva clients connecting to a Windows 2000 RAS Server. SPAP is more secure than clear text, but less secure than CHAP.

✦ **Unencrypted password (PAP):** No encryption required.

✦ **Unauthenticated access:** No authentication is required.

Configuring the IP tab

The IP tab allows you to enable IP routing and IP-based remote access and demand-dial connections. You can choose to implement either DHCP IP leases for remote clients or you can enter a static IP address pool. These are the same options you configured with the RAS Setup Wizard, but you can use this tab to make changes as necessary.

Configuring the PPP tab

The PPP tab gives you three main check boxes for Point-to-Point Protocol features that you can enable.

You need to know these check boxes for the exam:

✦ **Multilink Connections:** This feature allows you to use multilink, which connects several modems or adapters together to increase bandwidth. You can also choose to use dynamic bandwidth control with Bandwidth Allocation Protocol (BAP) or Bandwidth Allocation Control Protocol (BACP). These protocols allow the multilink connection to dynamically add or drop PPP links as necessary for the traffic flow.

✦ **Link Control Protocol (LCP) extensions:** You can use these to manage LCP and PPP connections.

✦ **Software Compression:** Uses the Microsoft Point to Point Compression Protocol (MPPC) to compress data sent on the remote access or demand-dial connection.

Book II
Chapter 7

Configuring
Windows 2000
Network
Connections

Configuring the Event Logging tab

The Event Logging tab provides you an effective way to monitor your remote access server through the use of log files.

The Event Logging tab provides you with several radio buttons so you can choose to log information, such as errors, warnings, PPP logging, and so forth. If you are experiencing problems with your remote access server, these different logging options can help you pinpoint the problem.

Monitoring Remote Clients

The Routing and Remote Access console provides you the ability to monitor the clients that are currently connected to the remote access server. In the console tree, expand your server, and then click the Remote Access Clients icon. A list of remote access clients appears in the details pane by user name, duration, and the number of ports in use. You can use this interface to manually disconnect clients if desired.

Configuring Inbound Connections

Inbound connections allow remote clients to connect to your remote access server. To allow the clients to connect, you must configure the hardware, such as a modem or ISDN adapter, in order to accept the inbound connection.

To configure the inbound connection, expand your server in the Routing and Remote Access console, select Ports, and then select Action⇨Properties. A window appears, listing the routing and remote access devices that are attached to your computer. You can select the desired device, and then click the Configure button. The Configure Device window appears, as shown in Figure 7-4.

Figure 7-4:
The
Configure
Device
window
allows a
device to
accept
inbound
connections.

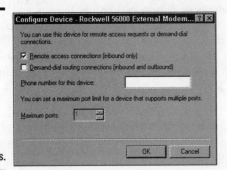

To allow the device to accept inbound-only connections, click the appropriate check box. You can also choose to use the device for demand-dial routing connections. After you enable the device for inbound connections, users can then dial the specified phone number to contact the device for inbound access.

Creating a Remote Access Policy

Remote access policies define how remote access can be used by remote clients. The policies create "rules" that must be followed for different remote access rights and permissions. For example, you specify certain dial-in numbers, dial-in hours, and even numbers that a user must dial in from.

To create remote access policies, select Remote Access Policy in the Routing and Remote Access console, click the Action menu, and then click New Remote Access Policy.

This action leads you through several steps in order to create the new remote access policy. Lab 7-4 guides you through these steps, and you need to know how to perform this task for the exam.

Lab 7-4   Creating a Remote Access Policy

1. **Select Remote Access Policy in the console tree, click the Action menu and select New Remote Access Policy.**

2. **In the Remote Access Policy dialog box, enter an easy-to-remember name for the policy and then click Next.**

3. **In the Conditions window that is displayed, click the Add button to see a list of conditions that you can use to create the policy.**

4. **Select the desired condition(s) and then click Add, as shown in Figure 7-5.**

5. **You may be asked to enter additional information, depending on the option you selected. Click Next.**

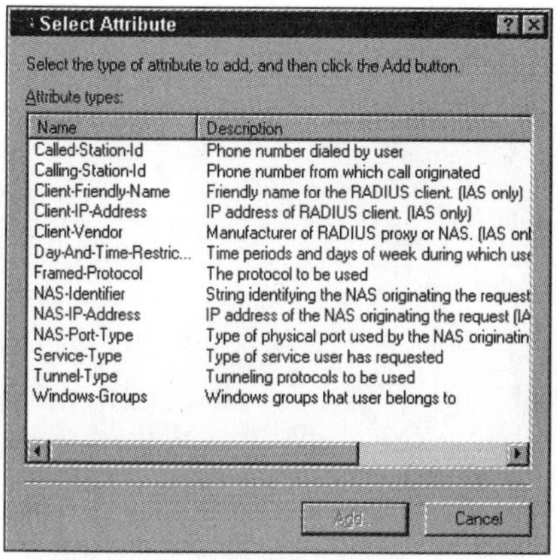

Book II
Chapter 7

Configuring
Windows 2000
Network
Connections

Figure 7-5:
Select the
desired
policy
attribute
from this
window.

6. **On the Permissions window that appears, choose to either grant or deny remote access permission, based on your attribute selection and then click Next.**

7. **Click Finish.**

   The new policy now appears in the details pane of the Routing and Remote Access console.

Editing a Remote Access Policy

After you create desired policies, you can easily edit them and change them as necessary.

To edit a policy, click the Remote Access Policies icon in the RRAS console tree, and then select the desired policy in the details pane. Click the Action menu, and then click Properties. The Properties option provides you a single Settings tab, shown in Figure 7-6, which shows how the policy is defined.

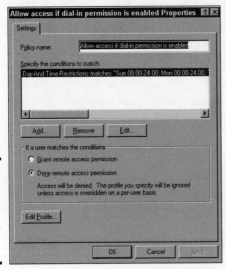

Figure 7-6:
Use the
Settings tab
to edit an
existing
policy.

Use the Add, Remove, or Edit buttons to make changes to the existing policy attribute, and you can also change the grant or deny feature for the policy by selecting the desired radio button. Basically, editing a policy gives you the same options when creating a new policy, but you can easily change existing policies without having to remove and re-create them.

Configuring a Remote Access Profile

For each remote access policy, you can configure the remote access profile. The profile defines settings for users who match the conditions that you specify in the policy.

You can create/edit a profile when you first create the policy by clicking the Edit Profile button during the policy steps. You can also edit it by accessing the properties of the policy and clicking the Edit Profile button.

This action opens the Profile window that contains six tabs. For the exam, you need to know what configuration options are available on each tab. The following sections point out what you need to know for the exam.

Configuring the Dial-in Constraints tab

The Dial-in Constraints tab, shown in Figure 7-7, allows you to set restrictions for the dial-in policy. You can choose to disconnect if the connection is idle for a certain period of time, restrict the maximum session time, or restrict access to certain days and times. You can also choose to restrict the kind of dial-in media used by the client.

Book II
Chapter 7

Configuring
Windows 2000
Network
Connections

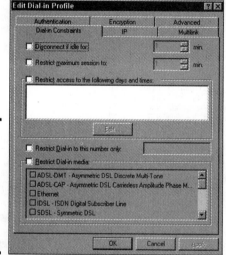

Figure 7-7:
Use the
Dial-in
Constraints
tab to place
restrictions
on the
remote user.

Configuring the IP tab

The IP tab allows you set a specific profile for the policy, such as a server-assigned or client-requested IP address. By default, the Server Settings Define Policy radio button is selected.

Configuring the Multilink tab

Using the Multilink tab, shown in Figure 7-8, you can also define multilink settings for this particular profile. By default, the profile uses the server settings, but you have the option to define multilink settings for this profile. You can choose to either allow or disable multilink and use Bandwidth Allocation Protocol (BAP) if desired. If you choose to use BAP, you specify when a link is dropped by the percentage of bandwidth usage and period of time. Additionally, you can require BAP for dynamic multilink requests.

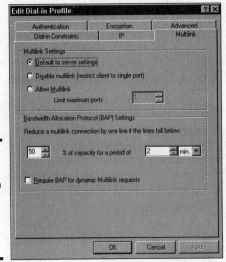

Figure 7-8:
Use the
Multilink tab
to configure
multilink
settings for
the profile.

Configuring the Authentication and Encryption settings

You can configure authentication and encryption settings for the RAS server by accessing the RAS server's properties. You can also configure Authentication and Encryption settings for the policy's profile. This feature allows you to implement different encryption and authentication settings for each profile, if desired. The Authentication and Encryption tabs both provide you with a list of check boxes where you can select the desired authentication and encryption settings. These are the same as the server properties, and you can review them in the "Configuring Server Properties" section located earlier in this chapter.

Configuring the Advanced Profile tab

The Advanced Profile tab allows you to specify additional attributes to be returned to the Remote Access sever. If you click the Add button, you can see a lengthy list of attributes that you can select, shown in Figure 7-9.

The Add Attributes option allows you to specify additional information for certain network client configurations. You don't need to know these attributes for the exam, but do keep in mind that you can configure specific client options on the Advanced Profile tab.

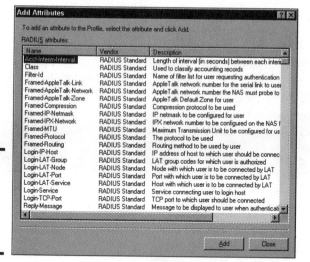

**Book II
Chapter 7**

Configuring
Windows 2000
Network
Connections

Figure 7-9:
Additional
attributes
can be
added for a
profile.

Configuring Virtual Private Networks

A VPN is an extension of a local private network that contains links across public networks, such as the Internet. With a VPN, you can establish a link between two computers across a public network and send information as if it were through a private point-to-point link.

To emulate this private link, data is encapsulated in a frame that provides routing information so the data can travel over the public network to its destination. At the receiving end, the outer frame is removed to reveal the actual data inside. The data in the frame is encrypted for safety as it travels over the private network.

VPNs are effective solutions in many scenarios where one office needs to send data intermittently to another office without maintaining an expensive WAN link. By using the Internet as a transport mechanism, data can be transmitted safely and inexpensively.

Windows 2000 offers several new features for VPNs. You should keep these new features in mind for the exam:

✦ **Layer Two Tunneling Protocol (L2TP):** Windows 2000 supports both Point to Point Tunneling Protocol (PPTP) and L2TP, which is used with Windows 2000's Internet Protocol Security, IPSec. This combination creates very secure VPNs. L2TP is a de facto standard for VPN security.

✦ **Remote Access Policies:** Remote access policies can be used to set connection conditions for VPNs. This feature allows you to enforce different kinds of authentication and security features.

✦ **MS-CHAP V2:** With MS-CHAP V2, VPNs are greatly strengthened in terms of security because you can send encrypted data that requires the use of encryption keys for decoding.

✦ **Extensible Authentication Protocol (EAP):** EAP is supported for VPN connections. EAP allows you to use new authentication methods with RAS and VPNs, specifically Smart Card logon.

✦ **Account Lockout:** Account Lockout after a specified number of failed VPN connection attempts is now supported, but is disabled by default.

After you've installed routing and remote access, you can enable VPN usage on the RAS server by accessing the Ports option in the console tree. Select Ports, click the Action menu, and then click Properties. In the Port properties sheet, you see a PPTP and L2TP Miniport available, as shown in Figure 7-10.

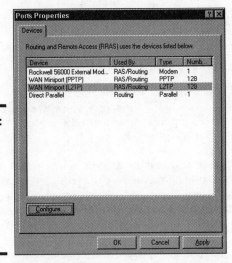

Figure 7-10:
Use the
Ports
properties
sheet to
configure
the PPTP
and L2TP
ports.

As with other Ports, select the desired port and click the Configure button to allow remote access connections and demand-dial connections (inbound and outbound). This feature allows your server to accept PPTP or L2TP connections for data transmission.

After you configure your VPN ports, you can then create VPN policies and profiles as desired to manage your VPN connections.

Understanding Terminal Services

Terminal Services provide remote access to a server desktop through software that serves as a terminal emulator. This feature transmits the user interface to the client. The client then manages the interface through keyboard and mouse clicks that are returned to the server for processing. A Terminal Server can host many sessions at one time, and each session user sees only his or her manipulation of the interface.

Terminal Services for clients can run on a number of platforms, including Windows platforms, and even Macintosh and UNIX platforms with additional third-party software.

You can deploy Terminal Services in either Remote Administration mode or Application Server mode, but not both at the same time. In Remote Administration mode, you can access your server from any terminal on your network and administer it remotely. In Application Services mode, terminals that may not be able to run Windows can connect to the Terminal Server and run applications as needed.

Terminal Services offer several benefits, one of which is the use of Windows 2000 and Windows 2000 applications on older computers that can't support Windows 2000. This feature allows users to "get to know" Windows 2000 before it is implemented on all client computers.

**Book II
Chapter 7**

Configuring
Windows 2000
Network
Connections

Reviewing Terminal Services Administrative Tools

Several administrative tools enable you to manage Terminal Services on your Windows 2000 Server.

You need to know the following for the exam and what you can do with each:

✦ **Terminal Services Manager:** Use this interface to manage and monitor users, sessions, and processes on any server running Terminal Services on the network.

✦ **Terminal Services Configuration:** Use this interface to change the Terminal Services TCP/IP connection clients use to access the Terminal Server. You can name a connection, specify a connection transport and its properties, enable or disable logons, and so forth.

✦ **Active Directory Users and Computers and Local Users and Groups Extensions:** This feature extends Active Directory Users and Computers on domain controllers and local users and groups so you can control Terminal Services features for each user.

✦ **Terminal Services Licensing:** Registers and tracks licenses for Terminal Services clients.

✦ **System Monitor Counters:** Terminal Services extends System Monitor by adding User and Session objects and their counters.

✦ **Task Manager Additional Fields:** Terminal Services provides two additional fields to Task Manager for monitoring and ending processes for all sessions.

✦ **Client Creator:** Use this interface to make disks that are used to install the Terminal Services client.

✦ **Client Connection Manager:** The Client Connection Manager is installed on the client computer when Terminal Services are installed.

✦ **Multi-user Support in Add/Remove Programs:** Ensures that applications are installed for use in a multisession environment.

Installing Terminal Services

You install Terminal Services just as you do any other Windows 2000 component: through either Add/Remove Programs in Control Panel or through the Configure Your Server tool.

When you choose to install Terminal Services, a window appears, asking you to select one of two modes, either Remote Administration mode or Application Server mode. You can choose to install either one, but the exam expects you to know about both of them. After you install Terminal Services, you will need to reboot your computer. We explore both of these Terminal Server modes in the next several sections.

Using Terminal Services Remote Administration Mode

You can use Terminal Services Remote Administration mode to remotely manage your Windows 2000 Server from virtually any computer on your network.

When you choose to install this mode, you should install it only on Windows 2000 Servers on an NTFS partition, and you don't need to enable Terminal Services Licensing for remote administration. Keep both of these points in mind for the exam.

After you install Terminal Services in Remote Administration mode, you can install Terminal Services on the desired client computer so that you can remotely administer your server.

To install Terminal Services on the client, you need to make the installation disks by clicking Start⇨Programs⇨Administrative Tools⇨Terminal Services Client Creator. Follow the instructions that appear (you will need two floppy disks).

Use the two floppy disks to install the client terminal service on the desired client computers. After the installation is complete, launch the Terminal Services Client application from the Programs menu, and then enter an administrator user name and password. The terminal appears on the remote computer where you can administer the Terminal Server. With appropriate administrator permissions, you can configure the server just as if you were sitting at it.

You can use the Terminal Services Manager on the Terminal Server by clicking Start➪Programs➪Administrative Tools➪Terminal Services Manager to manage sessions in progress, as shown in Figure 7-11.

Book II
Chapter 7

Configuring
Windows 2000
Network
Connections

Figure 7-11:
Use
Terminal
Services
Manager
to manage
sessions.

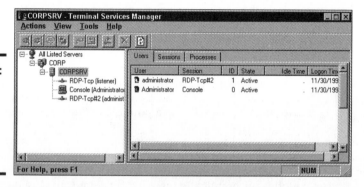

By selecting the desired user and clicking the Action menu, you can disconnect the user, send the user a message, reset the connection, log the user off, and examine the status. Although these actions are all simple, they are considered important monitoring features and you should keep them in mind for the exam.

You don't have to worry about licensing when using Terminal Services Remote Administration mode. Two concurrent connections are allowed and licenses for the connections are not needed.

Using Terminal Services Application Server Mode

Application Server mode allows users to connect to your Terminal Server and run applications. Keep in mind that all of the processing is performed on the server's end and users are simply provided a graphical interface. Though they are effective and very useful, you should consider the impact on system resources that several sessions can create. Your processor and system RAM must be able to handle running multiple applications and processes when clients connect to the Terminal Server. In short, use Application Server mode on a server that has high system resources and is not responsible for a multitude of other network tasks.

Installing Terminal Services Application Server mode

When you choose to install Terminal Services Application Server mode, a window appears where you can select permissions compatible with Windows 2000 users or permissions compatible with Terminal Server 4.0 users. The Windows 2000 option provides the most secure environment. By default, users have the same permissions as members of the users group, which may prevent them from running some legacy applications. If you are using legacy applications, you can choose to use permissions compatible with Terminal Services 4.0 users.

When you select the down-level permissions option, users have full access to critical registry and file system locations, which is required in many legacy applications. However, this is a potentially dangerous scenario.

After you make your selection, a window appears, listing any programs that may not function properly in Application Server mode, so take note of those. You are also prompted for the location for the license server database, which is automatically installed by default in C:\winnt\System32\Lserver.

For the exam, it is important to remember that Terminal Server licensing for Application Server mode can apply to either an enterprise or domain, depending on which option you selected during setup. Keep in mind that Terminal Servers can only access domain license servers if they are in the same domain as the license server. Terminal Services has its own method for licensing clients that log onto the Terminal Server. Clients must receive a valid license before they are allowed to log on in Application Server mode. Microsoft must activate the license by using Microsoft Clearinghouse, which is a database to maintain and activate licenses.

However, Terminal Server allows unlicensed clients to connect for 90 days. After that time, Terminal Servers won't allow clients to connect without appropriate licenses. You can use the Terminal Server Licensing tool, which is available in Administrative Tools, to activate the license with the Microsoft database.

Configuring Application Sharing

Once Terminal Services is installed in Application Server mode, you need to install and configure applications for sharing for multisession access. This allows multiple users to access the same application at the same time.

You have two ways to do this. The first method is to use Add/Remove Programs in Control Panel to install the desired applications. The second method is to use the `change user` command at the command prompt before and after installing the program. The `change user` command ensures that program files are installed in the system root rather than in the Windows subdirectory of the user's home directory. This makes the program available for multisessions. The `change user / install` command places the system in Install mode and turns off the `.ini` file mapping. After the program is installed, the `change user / execute` command returns the system to Execute mode, restores the `.ini` file mapping and redirects user-specific data to the user's home directory.

Book II
Chapter 7

Add/Remove Programs automatically runs the `change user` command in the background, so it is the preferred method for installing applications on Terminal Server for multisession use.

Configuring
Windows 2000
Network
Connections

After you install the applications, terminal service clients can then connect to Terminal Server and open multiple sessions of the program.

Applications that were installed before you installed Terminal Server in Application Server mode will need to be reinstalled so they will be available to users in Multisession mode. Keep this in mind for the exam.

When installing applications on your Terminal Server, you should disconnect any users to avoid potential problems. Also, it is important to test your application installations. Some 16-bit programs may have problems working with Terminal Services, so you should test all installations and note any problems.

Managing Terminal Services Connections

The Terminal Services Configuration tool, which is accessible by clicking Start⇨Programs⇨Administrative Tools⇨Terminal Services Configuration, offers an MMC interface to configure your Terminal Services connections and server settings. The Server Settings container gives you the attributes that you configured during setup, which you can change from this location.

For the exam, you are most likely to see a question or two about configuring your connections. If you click the Connections container in the console tree, you see an RDP-TCP connection in the details pane. Microsoft Remote Desktop Protocol (RDP) is the protocol used for Microsoft Terminal Services. If you use other terminal servers, you may use a different protocol, in which case you should check the third party's documentation.

To create a new connection, select the Connections container, click the Action menu, and then click Create New Connection. A wizard assists you in creating the connection, but you only need to do so if you are using third-party terminal services. If you are only using Microsoft Terminal Services, the RDP-TCP connection is all you need.

If you select the RDP-TCP connection, and then click the Action menu, you can access the properties pages for the connection.

Several tabs are available, but the following sections only examine the ones you need to know for the exam.

Configuring the General tab

The General tab reports to you the type of connection and the transport (TCP), and allows you to make a comment. The important point about the General tab is that you can change the Encryption settings by clicking the drop-down menu. Terminal Services in Windows 2000 Server supports the use of encrypted data between the client and the server.

You have three levels of encryption, which you need to know for the exam:

+ **Low:** Only data sent from the client to the server is protected by encryption, based on the server's standard key strength.

+ **Medium:** All data sent between the client and the server is protected by encryption, based on the server's standard key strength.

+ **High:** All data sent between the client and the server is protected by encryption, based on the server's maximum key strength.

Configuring the Sessions tab

The Sessions tab, shown in Figure 7-12, allows you to configure default settings to manage user sessions. None of these are enabled by default, but you can use them to place certain restrictions on users.

To create the restrictions, simply click the desired check boxes, drop-down menus, and radio buttons to configure the restrictions as desired. For example, you can choose to end a disconnected session after a certain period of time, limit active sessions, create an idle session limit, and even override user settings.

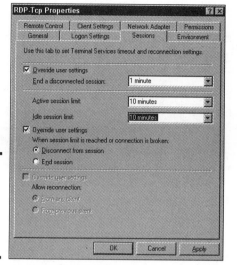

Book II
Chapter 7

Configuring
Windows 2000
Network
Connections

Figure 7-12:
Use the
Sessions
tab to set
sessions
limits.

Configuring the Environment tab

The Environment tab allows you to override settings from the user's profile and Client Connection Manager.

When you override the settings, you can choose to start a program when the user logs on and you can choose to disable wallpaper, which can greatly conserve server resources.

Reviewing Terminal Server Commands

Terminal Services offers several commands that you can use to manage the Terminal Server. You need to know these for the exam, as listed in Table 7-2.

Table 7-2	Terminal Server Commands
Command	*Explanation*
change logon	Temporarily disables logons to Terminal Server.
change port	Changes COM port mappings for MS-DOS program compatibility.
change user	Changes the .ini file mapping for the current user.
cprofile	Removes user-specific file associations from a user's profile.
dbgtrace	Enables and disables debug tracing.
flattemp	Enables or disables flat temporary directories.

(continued)

Table 7-2 *(continued)*

Command	Explanation
logoff	Ends a client's session.
msg	Sends a message to one or more clients.
query process	Displays information about processes.
query session	Displays information about Terminal Services sessions.
query termserver	Lists Terminal Servers on the network.
query user	Displays information about users logged on to the system.
register	Registers a program so that it has special execution characteristics.
reset session	Allows you to reset a session from Terminal Server.
shadow	Allows you to monitor or remotely control an active session of another user.
tscon	Connects a client from a Terminal Services session.
tsdiscon	Disconnects a client from a Terminal Services session.
tskill	Terminates a process.
tsprof	Copies user information and changes profile path.
tsshutdn	Shuts down a Terminal Services server.

Prep Test

1 You have several protocols installed for a particular network interface card (NIC). You want to configure one of the protocols, but the Properties button in the Local Area Connection Properties dialog box is grayed out. What is causing this?

   A ○ The protocol is not installed correctly.

   B ○ The protocol is not operative.

   C ○ The protocol is not configurable.

   D ○ The protocol is not functioning.

2 You are having problems communicating on a TCP/IP network. All other computers and servers in your IP subnet can communicate with each other, but you can't communicate with other computers, and they can't communicate with yours. The NIC is installed and functioning correctly, and TCP/IP is installed. What is the most likely problem?

   A ○ Incorrect DNS server

   B ○ Incorrect default gateway

   C ○ Incorrect frame type

   D ○ Incorrect subnet mask

3 An inexperienced administrator needs to install NWLink on a member server that will communicate with a NetWare server, but the administrator can't find the internal network ID number and is hesitant to install the protocol. When the administrator comes to you for help, what advice should you offer?

   A ○ Find the ID number on the NetWare server and use it for the Windows 2000 Server.

   B ○ The Windows 2000 Server should be able to automatically detect the internal network ID number.

   C ○ The Windows 2000 Server doesn't need an internal network ID number.

   D ○ The Windows 2000 Server doesn't need NWLink to communicate with the NetWare server because this capability is built into Windows 2000 Servers.

4 You have a small office network with 1 Windows 2000 Server and 10 Windows 2000 Professional clients. You have an ISDN connection established for the server but no connections for the clients. The clients need Internet connectivity, but you don't want the cost of installing IDSN hardware on all the client machines. What is an inexpensive solution?

A ○ Install modems on the client computers.

B ○ Use the server for all Internet communication.

C ○ Share the ISDN connection.

D ○ Create a multilink that the clients can use.

5 An administrator plans to share an ISDN connection to the Internet so that clients on a particular IP subnet in a medium-sized network environment can use the connection. The administrator comes to you for advice. What is the first thing you should tell the administrator?

A ○ Make certain that you use an appropriate IP address.

B ○ Make certain that you have a specific subnet mask.

C ○ Connection sharing should be used only in small office or home networks and is not designed for normal LAN environments.

D ○ Configure all clients with the connection sharing software.

6 When you configure shared access on a Windows 2000 Server for a modem, what happens to your NIC card?

A ○ Nothing.

B ○ The NIC becomes inoperative.

C ○ The NIC is assigned a different, static IP address.

D ○ The NIC is assigned a different subnet mask.

7 You want to make certain that if RAS clients dial a particular phone number, they are granted remote access, assuming they provide authentication. What do you need to do?

A ○ Create a policy.

B ○ Create a profile.

C ○ Use MS-CHAP.

D ○ Use MS-CHAP V2.

8 Which VPN protocol is used with IPsec to create highly secure VPN transmissions?

A ○ MS CHAP

B ○ EAP

C ○ L2TP

D ○ IEAP

9 You want to install both remote administration and application server modes on the same server, but can't seem to do so. Why?

A ○ Your server is not configured for application server mode.
B ○ Remote administration is active at the time of installation.
C ○ A conflict exists between multisessions.
D ○ You can't install both modes on one server.

10 Which Terminal Server command allows you to remotely control the session of another user?

A ○ register
B ○ shadow
C ○ tdiscon
D ○ tskill

Answers

1 **C.** Some protocols, such as NetBEUI, don't have Properties dialog boxes because you can't configure for these protocols. In these cases, the Properties button is grayed out. *Review "Configuring protocols."*

2 **D.** In this scenario, the only possible answer is an incorrect subnet mask. Incorrect DNS server and default gateway settings won't halt IP communication, and incorrect frame types refer to problems with the NWLink protocol. *Review "Common protocol problems."*

3 **B.** Windows 2000 requires NWLink to communicate with NetWare servers, but can generally auto-detect the internal network ID and frame type. The administrator should install the protocol and then perform troubleshooting if connectivity can't be established. *See "Configuring Protocols."*

4 **C.** You can share dial-up connections so that small offices or home networks can have one connected computer and the other computers can share the connection. *Study "Configuring Shared Access."*

5 **C.** Connection sharing shouldn't be used in networks that have other Windows 2000 Servers. It is designed for small office or home networks, and shouldn't be used in this scenario. *Study "Configuring Shared Access."*

6 **C.** When you enable shared access, your NIC card is automatically assigned a static IP address of 192.168.0.1. *Study "Configuring Shared Access."*

7 **A.** You can use policies to configure a number of connection items that either grant or deny access, such as particular phone numbers, times of day, and so forth. *Study "Creating a Remote Access Policy."*

8 **C.** Layer 2 Tunneling Protocol is used with IPsec to provide highly secure VPN transmissions. *Read "Configuring Virtual Private Networks."*

9 **D.** You can install either Remote Administration or Application Server mode, but not both on the same server. *Read "Installing Terminal Services."*

10 **B.** By using the shadow command, you can monitor or remotely control an active session of another user. *See "Reviewing Terminal Server Commands."*

Chapter 8: Implementing, Monitoring, and Troubleshooting Security

Exam Objectives

✔ Encrypting data on a hard disk by using Encrypting File System

✔ Implementing, configuring, managing, and troubleshooting policies in a Windows 2000 environment

✔ Implementing, configuring, managing, and troubleshooting auditing

✔ Implementing, configuring, managing, and troubleshooting local accounts

✔ Implementing, configuring, managing, and troubleshooting account policy

✔ Implementing, configuring, managing, and troubleshooting security by using the Security Configuration Tool Set

*T*his chapter examines the security features in Windows 2000 Advanced Server and the security issues that you are likely to see on the exam. This chapter also explores local and system policies in Windows 2000 as well as auditing, local accounts, account policy, and the Security Configuration Tool Set.

The exam expects you to know about these security features, so study this chapter carefully. You can expect to review the following:

✦ Encrypting File System

✦ Windows 2000 auditing

✦ Managing account policy

✦ Understanding policies

Understanding Encrypting File System

Encrypting File System (EFS) is a powerful security feature in Windows 2000. With EFS, you can encrypt your files and folders so that other users can't read, move, or delete them.

However, EFS only functions on NTFS volumes, so in order to implement EFS, you should convert any FAT or FAT32 volumes to NTFS.

EFS is invisible to the user. You can specify for a file or folder to be encrypted, but you work with the file or folder just as you normally do. In other words, you don't have to decrypt a file to use it, and then re-encrypt it again. You can open and close your files, move them, rename them — any action — without being aware of the encryption. However, if an intruder attempts to open, move, copy, or rename your file or folder, the intruder receives an Access Denied message.

For the exam, you should remember the following important points about EFS:

✦ Only files or folders on NTFS volumes can be encrypted.

✦ Compressed files or folders can't be encrypted. You must uncompress the file or folder to encrypt it, and you must uncompress compressed volumes in order to encrypt any files or folders on the volume.

✦ Only the user who encrypts the file or folder can open it.

✦ Encrypted files can't be shared. (Technically, they *can* be shared, but no one else will be able to open them.)

✦ Encrypted files moved to a FAT or FAT32 volume lose their encryption.

✦ System files can't be encrypted.

✦ Encrypted files are not protected against deletion. Anyone with delete permission can delete an encrypted file.

✦ Encrypt your Temp folder so that files remain encrypted while they are being edited. It is also a good idea to encrypt your My Documents folder.

✦ You can encrypt or decrypt files and folders stored on a remote computer that has been enabled for remote encryption. However, the data is not encrypted while it is in transit over the network. (Other protocols, such as IPsec, provide this feature.)

✦ You can't drag and drop files into an encrypted folder for encryption purposes. If you want to put files into an encrypted folder, use the copy-and-paste method so that the files will be encrypted in the folder.

Encrypting a File or Folder

You can encrypt a file or folder by accessing its Properties sheets. On the General tab, click the Advanced button, and then select the Encrypt Contents To Secure Data check box, as shown in Figure 8-1.

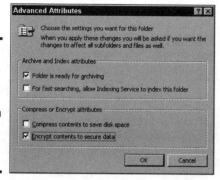

Book II
Chapter 8

Implementing,
Monitoring, and
Troubleshooting
Security

Figure 8-1:
Click the
Encrypt
Contents To
Secure Data
check box
to enable
encryption.

You can also decrypt a file or folder in the same manner. Keep in mind that you don't have to encrypt or decrypt your files and folders to work with them — the encryption feature is invisible to you.

When you encrypt a folder, you are asked if you want all files and subfolders within the folder to be encrypted as well. When you encrypt a file, you are asked if you want to encrypt the folder in which it is stored as well.

You can also encrypt files and folders by using the `cipher` command at the command line. Type **cipher /?** to see a list of options.

Recovering Encrypted Data

Data recovery is available for EFS as a part of the security policy for your system. A recovery policy is automatically generated when you encrypt your first file or folder. The recovery agent has a special certificate and associated private key that allows data to be recovered by the recovery policy. If you lose the file encryption certificate and private key, such as in the case of a disk failure, a recovery agent can decrypt the file or folder for you.

The system administrator is the default recovery agent when he or she logs onto the system for the first time. In the case of any employee leaving the company, the administrator can log onto the machine and recover any encrypted data.

To accomplish recovery, use the Export and Import commands from the certificate's MMC, which allows you to back up the recovery certificate and associated private key to a secure location. The default recovery policy is configured locally for standalone computers. For networked computers, the recovery policy is configured at either the domain, organizational unit, or individual computer level, and applies to all Windows 2000 computers within the scope.

You can specify a recovery agent for a local computer by opening the Group Policy MMC snap-in in Local Computer mode. Click Public Key Policies and then right-click Encrypted Data Recovery agents and click Add. This action opens a wizard that allows you to specify the user who is the recovery agent for the local computer.

Understanding Policies

Security settings determine how the computer implements and enforces various security behaviors. A *policy* is essentially a collection of settings that are applied to a computer that determines which security features are in effect.

In a Windows 2000 network, security policies are an important aspect of your overall security plan, just as they are in Windows NT. However, security policies in Windows 2000 are defined through Group Policy, a powerful feature that allows you to manage the security settings of computers within a domain or organizational unit.

You can create the following types of Group Policies:

✦ **Local policies** are local to the computer. They are based on the computer that you are logged onto and the rights you have on that local computer. Local policies affect a number of security components, such as the enabling or disabling of security settings, digital signing of data, user logon rights and permissions, and the audit policy.

✦ **Account policies** apply to the user account and the "rules" of security behavior for that account.

✦ **System policies** are applied to the computer system and are based on registry settings in Windows NT 4.0 and can be made by using the System Policy Editor. In Windows 2000, System Policy Editor is mainly replaced by Group Policy, but it is still useful in some specific circumstances, such as the management of Windows NT 4.0 computers, Windows 9x computers, and even the management of standalone computers running Windows 2000.

Windows 2000 computers have a local Group Policy object. With this feature, group policy settings can be stored on individual computers, even if they are not in an Active Directory environment. However, the local Group Policy settings can be overwritten by Group Policy objects on the site, domain, or organizational unit level.

You can make Group Policy settings for the local computer by opening the Group Policy snap-in and selecting local computer. From this interface, shown in Figure 8-2, you can configure local settings for the computer for both the computer configuration and the user configuration.

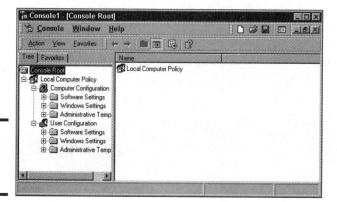

Book II
Chapter 8

Implementing,
Monitoring, and
Troubleshooting
Security

Figure 8-2:
The Group
Policy
snap-in.

Using Auditing

Auditing is the Windows 2000 Server security feature that monitors security events on your server. By using auditing, you can determine whether security breaches, such as break-ins, are occurring on your server.

You can audit many events on your system, including access to files and folders, management of user and group accounts, and logon and logoff activity.

The Windows 2000 auditing feature generates an audit trail to help you keep track of the security administration events that occur on the system. This feature is particularly useful because you can see how auditing has occurred. You can also determine whether other administrators with access to your server have changed any auditing of events.

To implement auditing on your server, complete the following three major steps:

1. **Determine which categories of events you want to audit by turning on auditing for those events (configuring an audit policy).**

2. **Determine the size of the security log that the auditing process will generate, as well as certain characteristics for the log.**

3. **Modify the security descriptors for certain objects that you plan to audit, such as folders or files.**

Configuring an audit policy

The first step in setting up auditing is to configure an audit policy. The policy tells the system what you want to audit.

TIP

To configure an audit policy, open an MMC and then add the Group Policy snap-in. Expand Computer Configuration, Windows Settings, Security Settings, and Local Policies, and then select Audit Policy, as shown in Figure 8-3.

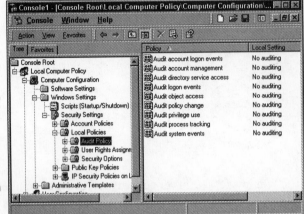

Figure 8-3:
Use the
Group
Policy
snap-in to
configure an
audit policy.

You can see in the details pane the different audit policies that you can configure. By default, auditing is turned off for all of them.

To enable auditing, double-click the desired audit policy and then click either the Success or Failure check boxes (or both) to audit the event, based on success or failure, as shown in Figure 8-4.

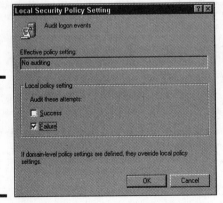

Figure 8-4:
Use the
Success or
Failure
check box
to enable
auditing.

Continue down the list and enable auditing for each event desired.

Auditing access to files and folders

You can audit access to files and folders on NTFS partitions. Before you configure the file or folder for auditing, you must enable the Audit Object Access event in the Group Policy MMC snap-in.

To configure auditing for a particular file or folder, follow the steps we describe in Lab 8-1.

Lab 8-1   Configuring Auditing for a File or Folder

1. **Right-click the desired file or folder and choose Properties.**

2. **In the Properties dialog box, click the Security tab and then click Advanced.**

3. **Click the Auditing tab and then click Add.**

   This brings up the Select User, Computer, or Group dialog box.

4. **From the Name box, select a user or group account for which you want to audit access to the file or folder and then click OK.**

   This brings up the Auditing Entry dialog box.

5. **In the Auditing Entry dialog box, shown in Figure 8-5, select the events that you want to audit by clicking the Successful or Failed check boxes, or both. Click OK.**

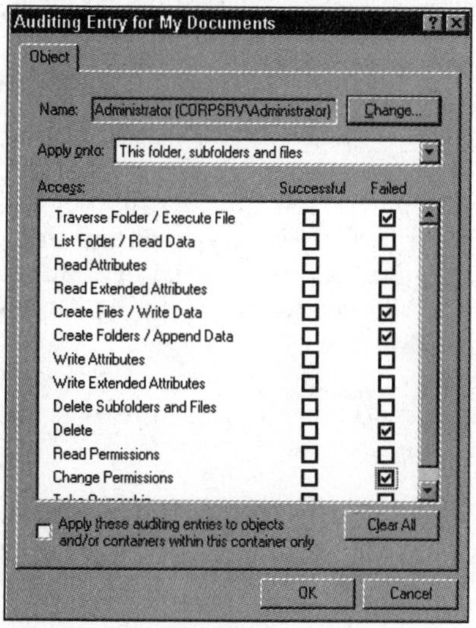

Book II
Chapter 8

Implementing, Monitoring, and Troubleshooting Security

Figure 8-5:
Click the Successful or Failed check boxes to configure auditing for the file or folder.

Auditing Entry for My Documents

Object

Name: Administrator (CORPSRV\Administrator)   Change...

Apply onto: This folder, subfolders and files

Access:	Successful	Failed
Traverse Folder / Execute File	☐	☑
List Folder / Read Data	☐	☐
Read Attributes	☐	☐
Read Extended Attributes	☐	☐
Create Files / Write Data	☐	☑
Create Folders / Append Data	☐	☑
Write Attributes	☐	☐
Write Extended Attributes	☐	☐
Delete Subfolders and Files	☐	☐
Delete	☐	☑
Read Permissions	☐	☐
Change Permissions	☐	☑

☐ Apply these auditing entries to objects and/or containers within this container only   Clear All

OK   Cancel

The auditing options that you configured appear in the Access Control Settings dialog box, as shown in Figure 8-6.

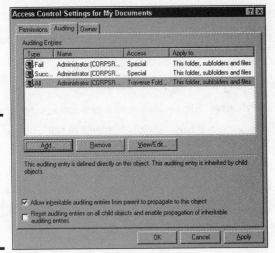

Figure 8-6:
Auditing
entries
appear in
the Access
Control
Settings
dialog box.

By selecting a check box at the bottom of the Access Control Settings dialog box, you can allow inheritable auditing entries from the parent to propagate to this object, or you can choose to reset auditing entries on all child objects and enable propagation. With these features, both the parent and the child objects can inherit auditing entries. You can disable both or either of these options by clearing the check boxes.

Viewing the Security log

After you implement auditing, you can view the Security Log by clicking Start➪Programs➪Administrative Tools➪Event Viewer and then clicking Security Log in the left console pane. You see the list of audited events, which you can use to determine whether your system has security problems or issues that you need to address.

The Security Log is limited in size, so you should choose carefully which events you want to audit.

Managing Local Accounts and Account Policy

You configure local accounts on Windows 2000 member servers for users who log on to the local machine. Accounts on domain controllers are stored in Active Directory.

On a Windows 2000 member server, you create and manage local accounts by using the Computer Management tool, which is available in Administrative Tools. In the Computer Management console, expand Local Users and Groups to see the Users and Groups containers. If you click either container, you see a list of users and groups in the details pane, as shown in Figure 8-7. By default, a Windows 2000 server has an administrator account and a guest account, which is disabled by default.

**Book II
Chapter 8**

Implementing,
Monitoring, and
Troubleshooting
Security

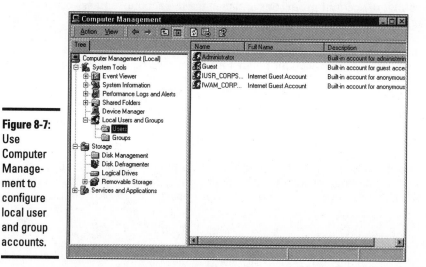

Figure 8-7:
Use
Computer
Manage-
ment to
configure
local user
and group
accounts.

To create a new user or group account, select the desired container and then choose either Action⇨New User or Action⇨New Group. In the dialog box that's displayed, you can enter the user name and password, and determine the following password-related settings:

✦ User must change password at next logon.

✦ User can't change password.

✦ Password never expires.

✦ Account is disabled.

Weak management of passwords translates directly into weak security. Microsoft recommends that all passwords conform to the following standards:

✦ Should be at least seven characters long

✦ Should not contain a user's name

✦ Should have a mixture of uppercase and lowercase letters, numbers, and symbols

For example, xjjb34!2 is an appropriate password in Windows 2000.

After you create user accounts, you can add them to groups as desired, and you can configure account properties. Right-click a user account and choose Properties to open the Properties dialog box for that account.

For the exam, you don't need to worry about the specifics of the Properties dialog boxes for user and group accounts. Just remember that you can configure account properties and manage the account's password, group memberships, and profiles from these dialog boxes.

In addition to creating accounts and configuring their properties, you can also configure the account policy for your server.

To configure your account policy, open an MMC and add the Group Policy snap-in. Expand Computer Configuration, Windows Settings, and Security Settings, and then select Account Policies. You see the policy entries in the details pane.

Double-click either the Password Policy container, the Account Lockout Policy container, or the Kerberos Policy container, and then double-click the entries to configure the desired policy settings. You can define various policy settings, such as account lockout duration, account lockout threshold, enforce password history, and maximum password age.

Using Security Configuration Tools

Windows 2000 Server includes a tool set that you can use to manage your security configuration. You can manually add a Security Configuration and Analysis snap-in and a Security Templates snap-in to an MMC.

You need to know about both of these snap-ins for the exam, and the following sections explain the issues that you are likely to see on the exam.

Using the Security Configuration and Analysis snap-in

You use the Security Configuration and Analysis snap-in to analyze and configure local computer security. The snap-in uses a security database, which you need to create before you use the snap-in for the first time. To create a security database, right-click the Security Configuration and Analysis object and choose Open Database. In the dialog box that's displayed, click Open. In the resulting dialog box, select the database template to open and then click Open.

After you open a database, you can perform three major tasks. Select the Security Configuration and Analysis object in the console and then click the Action menu to perform these tasks, which you need to remember for the exam:

✦ **Analyze Computer Now:** This process analyzes your security configuration and reports issues or potential problems to the database. This feature is an excellent troubleshooting tool.

✦ **Configure Computer Now:** This process applies any templates you have chosen to your computer.

✦ **Import Template:** This action enables you to import a security template that you want to apply to your system. After importing a desired template, choose Action⇨Configure Computer Now.

Using the Security Templates snap-in

The Security Templates snap-in contains a list of security templates that you can edit to configure your system security as desired. You can also create new templates and import other templates into this snap-in. For each template, you can define account policies, local policies, event logs, restricted groups, system services, and the registry and file system. For each category, you can open the templates and adjust the settings as desired.

Like the Security Configuration and Analysis snap-in, the Security Templates snap-in gives you an all-in-one location where you can implement and configure the desired security settings for your server.

**Book II
Chapter 8**

**Implementing,
Monitoring, and
Troubleshooting
Security**

Prep Test

1 You have a compressed volume in which you want to implement EFS. You can't seem to make this work, even though the volume is formatted with NTFS. What is the problem?

A ○ EFS doesn't work with compression.

B ○ You are not using Microsoft compression.

C ○ You need to install the EFS compression protocol.

D ○ The volume is formatted with Windows NT 4.0's version of NTFS.

2 You want to be able to use the command prompt to enable encryption on certain folders. What command can you use to gain a full list of command line compression options?

A ○ Compress /?

B ○ Encrypt /?

C ○ Cipher /?

D ○ Protect /?

3 Aside from the recovery agent and the user who encrypts the files, which other users can open encrypted files by default?

A ○ None

B ○ Backup operators

C ○ EFS operators

D ○ Replication administrators

4 You want to audit access to a particular folder. You access the advanced settings from the Security tab in the folder's Properties dialog box, but you receive an error message when you try to configure auditing. What did you forget to do?

A ○ Configure Event Viewer.

B ○ Configure the Audit Object Access Event.

C ○ Configure the Audit Folder Access Event.

D ○ Install auditing.

5 Which tool can you use to view the security log?

A ○ Group Policy snap-in

B ○ Event Viewer

C ○ Task Manager

D ○ Configure Your Server

6 When auditing a particular file, where can you block inherited auditing entries from the parent?

A ○ Security tab

B ○ Computer Management

C ○ Access Control Settings dialog box

D ○ Group Policy snap-in

7 What is Microsoft's recommended minimum password character length?

A ○ 5

B ○ 6

C ○ 7

D ○ 8

8 Which two accounts are configured on a Windows 2000 member server by default? (Choose all that apply.)

A ❑ Administrator

B ❑ Backup Operator

C ❑ IUSR

D ❑ Guest

9 What can you use to configure account policy?

A ○ Computer Management

B ○ Group Policy snap-in

C ○ Configure Your Server

D ○ Security Configuration snap-in

10 You want your computer to configure the policy templates you have decided to use. Which tool can automatically perform this action for you?

A ○ Templates snap-in

B ○ Group Policy snap-in

C ○ Security Configuration and Analysis snap-in

D ○ Active Directory Users and Computers snap-in

Answers

1 **A.** Compressed volumes, folders, or files can't be encrypted. To encrypt the volume, folder, or file, first remove the compression. *Review "Understanding Encrypting File System."*

2 **C.** The `cipher` command allows you to compress data at the command line. *Read "Encrypting a File or a Folder."*

3 **A.** Only the user who encrypts the file can open it, along with the recovery agent. *See "Understanding Encrypting File System."*

4 **B.** Before you can audit a file or folder, you have to enable the Audit Object Access policy in the Group Policy MMC snap-in. *Read "Auditing access to files and folders"*

5 **B.** Use Event Viewer to examine the security log. *Review "Viewing the Security Log."*

6 **C.** The Access Control Settings dialog box contains check boxes that enable you to block inheritance from parent objects and to child objects. You can block inheritance by clearing the check boxes. *See "Auditing access to files and folders."*

7 **C.** Microsoft recommends that all passwords have at least seven characters, with a mixture of letters, numbers, and keyboard symbols. *Study "Managing Local Accounts and Account Policy."*

8 **A** and **D.** The administrator and guest accounts are configured by default, but the guest account is also disabled by default. *See "Managing Local Accounts and Account Policy."*

9 **B.** You can use the Group Policy snap-in to configure account policies, as well as other policies for the local Windows 2000 computer. *Read "Managing Local Accounts and Account Policy."*

10 **C.** This tool can analyze your computer's security settings and configure your computer's security template settings. *Study "Using the Security Configuration and Analysis snap-in."*

Book III

Managing a Microsoft Windows 2000 Network Environment: Exam 70-218

The 5th Wave   By Rich Tennant

©RICHTENNANT

What helps the Windows 2000 operating
system communicate with hardware?

That's easy— a massive,
worldwide advertising
campaign.

Contents at a Glance

Chapter 1: About Exam 70-218

In This Chapter

✔ **What you should already know**

✔ **What objectives are covered**

✔ **What you can expect**

*E*xam 70-218, Managing a Microsoft Windows 2000 Network Environment, tests your knowledge of Windows 2000 network management by using Microsoft Windows 2000 Server. On this exam, you can expect to be tested on issues such as resource access, networking infrastructure, troubleshooting servers and client computers, managing Active Directory, and managing Remote Access. The exam covers standard problems and procedures that you are likely to face in a real networking environment using Windows 2000.

What You Should Already Know

Before you begin studying this book for Exam 70-218, we assume that you bring a few prerequisites to the certification table. If you are deficient in any of these areas, you should stop studying for this exam and learn some background information from other books devoted to these topics:

✦ **Windows 2000 Professional and Windows 2000 Server:** Although you can take the Microsoft exams in any order to achieve your MCSA, we recommend that you pass the Windows 2000 Professional exam (70-210) and the Windows 2000 Server exam (70-215) before taking the Windows 2000 Network exam. We say this because the Network exam tests your knowledge of using Windows 2000 Server to provide networking services to Windows 2000 Professional clients.

✦ **Networking:** This book assumes that you have some networking experience and are currently working with Windows 2000 Server in a networking environment. If you have no networking experience, you need to study networking first and try to get some hands-on experience. You may find this book difficult to understand without any prior networking knowledge.

✦ **Networking services:** In addition to basic networking skills, you should already be familiar with common networking services and protocols, such as DNS, DHCP, WINS, and other common services.

✦ **TCP/IP:** You need to have a strong understanding of TCP/IP. The Managing a Microsoft Windows 2000 Network Environment exam expects you to be able to manage and troubleshoot IP addressing. Entire books are devoted to the topic of TCP/IP, and you should study one of these if your IP skills are lacking.

What Exam Objectives Are Covered

The Windows 2000 Network exam objectives are available on the Microsoft Web site, and we also include them here for your convenience. This book strictly adheres to the exam objectives and covers the test material that you are most likely to see concerning the exam objectives. On the exam, you can expect to see the following issues:

Creating, Configuring, Managing, Securing, and Troubleshooting File, Print, and Web Resources

✦ Publish resources in Active Directory. Types of resources include printers and shared folders.

  • Perform a search in Active Directory Users and Computers.

  • Configure a printer object.

✦ Manage data storage. Considerations include file systems, permissions, and quotas.

  • Implement NTFS and FAT file systems.

  • Enable and configure quotas.

  • Implement and configure Encrypting File System (EFS).

  • Configure volumes and basic and dynamic disks.

  • Configure file and folder permissions.

  • Manage a domain-based Distributed file system (Dfs).

  • Manage file and folder compression.

✦ Create shared resources and configure access rights. Shared resources include printers, shared folders, and Web folders.

  • Share folders and enable Web sharing.

  • Configure shared folder permissions.

  • Create and manage shared printers.

  • Configure shared printer permissions.

✦ Configure and troubleshoot Internet Information Services (IIS).

  • Configure virtual directories and virtual servers.

  • Troubleshoot Internet browsing from client computers.

- Troubleshoot intranet browsing from client computers.

- Configure authentication and SSL for Web sites.

- Configure FTP services.

- Configure access permissions for intranet Web servers.

✦ Monitor and manage network security. Actions include auditing and detecting security breaches.

- Configure user account lockout settings.

- Configure user account password length, history, age, and complexity.

- Configure Group Policy to run logon scripts.

- Link Group Policy objects.

- Enable and configure auditing.

- Monitor security by using the system security log file.

Configuring, Administering, and Troubleshooting the Network Infrastructure

✦ Troubleshoot routing. Diagnostic utilities include the tracert command, the PING command, and the ipconfig command.

- Validate local computer configuration by using the ipconfig, Arp, and route commands.

- Validate network connectivity by using the tracert, PING, and pathPING commands.

✦ Configure and troubleshoot TCP/IP on servers and client computers. Considerations include subnet masks, default gateways, network IDs, and broadcast addresses.

- Configure client computer TCP/IP properties.

- Validate client computer network configuration by using the winipcfg, ipconfig, and Arp commands.

- Validate client computer network connectivity by using the PING command.

✦ Configure, administer, and troubleshoot DHCP on servers and client computers.

- Detect unauthorized DHCP servers on a network.

- Configure authorization of DHCP servers.

- Configure client computers to use dynamic IP addressing.

- Configure DHCP server properties.

- Create and configure a DHCP scope.

✦ Configure, administer, and troubleshoot DNS.

- Configure DNS server properties.
- Manage DNS database records such as CNAME, A, and PTR.
- Create and configure DNS zones.

✦ Troubleshoot name resolution on client computers. Considerations include WINS, DNS, NetBIOS, the Hosts file, and the Lmhosts file.

- Configure client computer name resolution properties.
- Troubleshoot name resolution problems by using the Nbtstat, ipconfig, Nslookup, and NetDiag commands.
- Create and configure a Hosts file for troubleshooting name resolution problems.
- Create and configure an Lmhosts file for troubleshooting name resolution problems.

Managing, Securing, and Troubleshooting Servers and Client Computers

✦ Install and configure server and client computer hardware.

- Verify hardware compatibility by using the qualifier tools.
- Configure driver signing options.
- Verify digital signatures on existing driver files.
- Configure operating system support for legacy hardware devices.

✦ Troubleshoot starting servers and client computers. Tools and methodologies include safe mode, Recovery Console, and parallel installations.

- Interpret the startup log file.
- Repair an operating system by using various startup options.
- Repair an operating system by using Recovery Console.
- Recover data from a hard disk in the event that the operating system won't start.
- Restore an operating system and data from a backup.

✦ Monitor and troubleshoot server health and performance. Tools include System Monitor, Event Viewer, and Task Manager.

- Monitor and interpret real-time performance by using System Monitor and Task Manager.
- Configure and manage System Monitor alerts and logging.
- Diagnose server health problems by using Event Viewer.
- Identify and disable unnecessary operating system services.

✦ Install and manage Windows 2000 updates. Updates include service packs, hot fixes, and security hot fixes.

- Update an installation source by using slipstreaming.

- Apply and reapply service packs and hot fixes.

- Verify service pack and hot fix installation.

- Remove service packs and hot fixes.

Configuring, Managing, Securing, and Troubleshooting Active Directory Organizational Units and Group Policy

✦ Create, manage, and troubleshoot user and group objects in Active Directory.

- Create and configure user and computer accounts for new and existing users.

- Troubleshoot groups. Considerations include nesting, scope, and type.

- Configure a user account by using Active Directory users and computers. Settings include passwords and assigning groups.

- Perform a search for objects in Active Directory.

- Use templates to create user accounts.

- Reset an existing computer account.

✦ Manage object and container permissions.

- Use the Delegation of Control Wizard to configure inherited and explicit permissions.

- Configure and troubleshoot object permissions by using object Access Control Lists (ACLs).

✦ Diagnose Active Directory replication problems.

- Diagnose problems related to WAN link connectivity.

- Diagnose problems involving replication latency. Problems include duplicate objects and the LostandFound container.

✦ Deploy software by using Group Policy. Types of software include user applications, antivirus software, line-of-business applications, and software updates.

- Use Windows Installer to deploy Windows Installer packages.

- Deploy updates to installed software, including antivirus updates.

- Configure Group Policy to assign and publish applications.

**Book III
Chapter 1**

About Exam 70-218

✦ Troubleshoot end-user Group Policy.

- Troubleshoot Group Policy problems involving precedence, inheritance, filtering, and the No Override option.

- Manually refresh Group Policy.

✦ Implement and manage security policies by using Group Policy.

- Use security templates to implement security policies.

- Analyze the security configuration of a computer by using the secedit command and Security Configuration and Analysis.

- Modify domain security policy to comply with corporate standards.

Configuring, Securing, and Troubleshooting Remote Access

✦ Configure and troubleshoot remote access and virtual private network (VPN) connections.

- Configure and troubleshoot client-to-server PPTP and L2TP connections.

- Manage existing server-to-server PPTP and L2TP connections.

- Configure and verify the security of a VPN connection.

- Configure client computer remote access properties.

- Configure remote access name resolution and IP address allocation.

✦ Troubleshoot a Remote Access Policy.

- Diagnose problems with Remote Access Policy priority.

- Diagnose Remote Access Policy problems caused by user account group membership and nested groups.

- Create and configure Remote Access Policies and profiles.

- Select appropriate encryption and authentication protocols.

✦ Implement and troubleshoot Terminal Services for remote access.

- Configure Terminal Services for remote administration or application server mode.

- Configure Terminal Services for local resource mapping.

- Configure Terminal Services user properties.

✦ Configure and troubleshoot Network Address Translation (NAT) and Internet Connection Sharing.

- Configure Routing and Remote Access to perform NAT.

- Troubleshoot Internet Connection Sharing problems by using the ipconfig and PING commands.

What You Can Expect

As you study this book and prepare for the exam, keep the following points in mind:

+ You can expect to see all of the exam objectives covered, but some will be hammered more than others. In fact, some objectives may appear more indirectly in questions supporting other objectives.

+ You can expect the exam questions to be complicated. Microsoft exams love to convolute information and make questions more difficult to read than necessary.

+ You can expect the networking exam questions to intersect with each other as combination questions, and you may even see issues that seem to come from the Windows 2000 Professional and Server exams. Because Microsoft expects your knowledge to be global and not product-specific, expect some questions that seem to cross over with the Windows 2000 Professional and Server exams.

The only real way to be successful on the Windows 2000 Server exam is to combine your existing knowledge and experience with the principles explored in this book. Then, practice, practice, practice, before taking the exam!

Chapter 2: Creating and Managing File, Print, and Web Resources

Exam Objectives

✓ Publishing resources in Active Directory

✓ Managing data storage

✓ Creating shared resources and configuring access rights

✓ Configuring and troubleshooting Internet Information Services

✓ Monitoring and managing network security

Two primary purposes for networking computers together are for information sharing and security. The first purpose, information sharing, is often the driving force for creating a network in the first place. When you think about it, even the Internet — the world's largest network — is basically a way to share information.

In Windows 2000 networks, sharing information and keeping it organized is easier than ever with the help of Active Directory. You can publish shared folders and printers quickly and easily so that they are available to network clients. Your job as the administrator is to keep those resources available and solve resource access problems that clients may experience.

In this chapter, you find out about managing and sharing file, print, and Web resources. This chapter, like all other chapters in this book, is focused on exam objectives and the issues that you are likely to see on the network administration exam. In this chapter, you find out about

✦ Publishing resources

✦ Managing data storage

✦ Working with Web resources

✦ Managing network security

✦ Managing IIS

Publishing Resources in Active Directory

Active Directory is a storehouse of information in Windows 2000 networks. The Active Directory database, which resides on Windows 2000 domain controllers, contains all user and group accounts, but it also contains information about shared resources. Users can easily search Active Directory and locate the shared resources as needed.

Publishing shared folders

Large environments may contain thousands of shared folders containing documents and even applications. Finding the folder that you need can be difficult, and for this reason, you can publish shared folders to Active Directory, where users can more easily locate the shared folder.

When you publish a shared folder to Active Directory, the shared folder doesn't actually reside in Active Directory. Rather, an Active Directory object is created that contains attributes about the shared folder so that users can find the folder they need. More simply, Active Directory works as a link to the shared folder. For example, suppose that a shared folder is located on a Windows 2000 Professional computer on the network. The Active Directory object for the shared folder contains the network path to the shared folder. When a user finds the shared folder in Active Directory and clicks it, the user is automatically redirected to the Windows 2000 Professional computer that actually holds the shared resource. If the user has permission to access the shared folder, the shared folder opens. If not, the user sees an Access Denied message.

As a network administrator, you may spend a fair amount of time publishing shared folders in Active Directory. The good news is that the process is easy. Just follow the steps in Lab 2-1.

Lab 2-1   Publishing a Shared Folder

1. **Click Start⇨Programs⇨Administrative Tools⇨Active Directory Users and Computers.**

   The Active Directory Users and Computers console appears.

2. **Right-click the desired organizational unit (OU) or container and click New⇨Shared Folder.**

3. **In the Shared Folder dialog box, give the shared folder a friendly name that network users will see, and then provide the path to the shared folder using the UNC convention, as shown in Figure 2-1.**

4. **Click OK.**

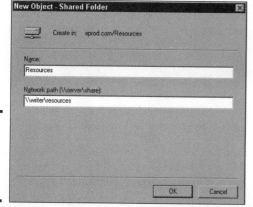

Figure 2-1:
Enter the shared folder name and path.

The shared folder now appears in the desired OU or container, as shown in Figure 2-2.

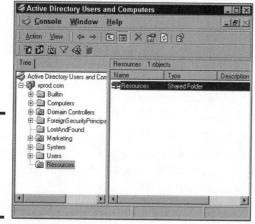

Figure 2-2:
The shared folder now appears in Active Directory.

If you right-click the shared folder object in Active Directory, you can access the Properties dialog box. Note that on the General tab of this dialog box, shown in Figure 2-3, you can click the Keywords button to add keywords for the object. For example, if your shared folder contains company documents, you may add keywords such as "corporate, documents, public, company," and so forth. Keywords help users locate the folder when searching Active Directory, so try to include keywords that users are likely to type when searching for the contents found in the shared folder.

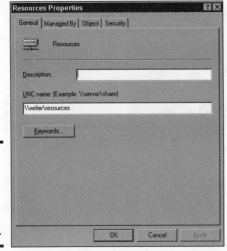

Figure 2-3:
Enter
search
keywords
on the
General tab.

You can easily search Active Directory from within the Active Directory Users and Computers console (refer to Figure 3-2), and users can search Active Directory from My Network Places. See Chapter 5 to learn more about searching Active Directory.

Publishing a printer

Publishing a printer in Active Directory works in the same basic way as publishing a shared folder. The main difference is that computers in the domain running Windows 2000 or even Windows XP can automatically publish shared printers in Active Directory. When a user on a Windows 2000 or XP computer shares a printer, a List in the Directory check box option appears in the printer's Properties dialog box on the Sharing tab, as shown in Figure 2-4. If the user selects this check box, the shared printer is automatically published to Active Directory without any intervention from you, the administrator.

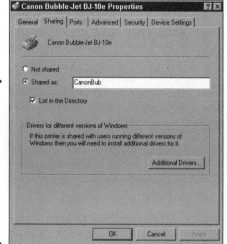

Figure 2-4:
Windows
2000 and XP
computers
can auto-
matically
publish
printers
to Active
Directory.

If client computers on your network run Windows NT, 9*x*, or Me, you have to manually add the shared printers attached to those computers to Active Directory. To do so, follow the steps in Lab 2-2.

Lab 2-2   Publishing a Printer

1. **Click Start⇨Programs⇨Administrative Tools⇨Active Directory Users and Computers.**

2. **Right-click the desired OU or container and click New⇨Printer.**

3. **Enter the UNC path of the Windows NT, 9*x*, or Me print share and then click OK.**

   The shared printer now appears in Active Directory.

Access the Properties dialog box for the shared printer to configure keywords so that users can locate the shared printer more easily.

Managing Data Storage

Data is stored on computer hard disks or some kind of removable media, such as CDs. From a network administration point of view, managing stored data involves the use of a file system, either FAT or NTFS, and several Windows 2000 features that can make data storage and access easier. The following sections take a look at a number of storage features.

Windows 2000 is optimized for NTFS, and most all of the features explored in the following sections only work on NTFS disks.

Implementing NTFS and FAT file systems

Windows 2000 computers support both NTFS and FAT file systems, both of which have their potential advantages. See Book II, Chapter 6 to learn more about FAT and NTFS.

Enabling and configuring quotas

Disk quotas track and control disk space on Windows 2000 volumes. You can configure disk quotas to establish a limit of disk space usage and even log events when a user exceeds his or her disk space limit. Basically, disk quotas allow you to help control and encourage network users to keep their disks clean by removing outdated information that doesn't need to be kept in storage.

Disk quotas only function on NTFS volumes on Windows 2000 computers. NTFS volumes on Windows NT computers don't support disk quotas.

When you configure disk quotas, you establish the actual disk usage limit and you establish a warning level. For example, a user may have a disk space limit of 100MB and a warning level of 90MB. You can also allow users to exceed their disk space limit. In this case, you can use disk quotas to track individual user disk usage, but not actually restrict the user's storage space.

Data compression doesn't affect disk quotas. If a user only has 50MB of storage space, compression doesn't allow the user to store more than 50MB of data by compressing the data.

Here are a few additional points to remember about disk quotas:

+ **Each user has his or her own disk quota:** For example, if a user has 25MB of storage space on a disk while another user has 25MB of storage on the same disk, one user's consumption of his or her 25MB doesn't affect the other user. This design is particularly useful for network volumes in which multiple users have a quota that they can use on that volume.

+ **Disk quotas apply to volumes, not the file or folder structure on the underlying disk:** It doesn't matter how many folders or files a user saves — the collective data equals the storage space used.

+ **Disk quotas can apply to spanned volumes as well:** Because the quota applies to the volume, it doesn't matter how much data is stored on each physical disk — the quota applies to the entire volume.

✦ **Disk quotas are based on file ownership:** If a user takes ownership of a file, that file counts toward his or her disk quota.

Enabling disk quotas

To enable disk quotas for a particular volume, follow the steps in Lab 2-3.

Lab 2-3   Enabling Disk Quotas

1. **Access the volume through either My Computer or Disk Management.**

2. **Right-click the volume, and then click Properties.**

3. **Click the Quota tab.**

4. **To enable quotas on the volume, click the Enable Quota Management check box, as shown in Figure 2-5.**

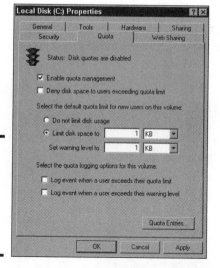

Figure 2-5:
Enable
quotas on
the Quota
tab of the
desired
volume.

After you enable quotas for the volume, you can then configure the following components on the Quota tab:

✦ **Deny disk space:** You can deny disk space by clicking the Deny Disk Space to Users Exceeding Quota Limit check box. However, remember that you don't have to deny disk space to users exceeding their limits, but you can use the Disk Quota tool for monitoring purposes.

✦ **Limit or not limit disk space:** Use the Do Not Limit or Limit radio buttons to either limit or not limit disk space. If you choose to establish a limit, enter the limit and the warning level values in the provided text boxes.

✦ **Log when user exceeds quota limit or warning level:** Use the logging event check boxes to log an event when a user exceeds the quota limit or when a user exceeds the warning level. You can choose either of these options, both of them, or neither of them.

Configuring quota entries

On the Quota tab, you can click the Quota Entries button to configure quota entries for the volume. Quota entries define the quota limits and warning levels for users of that volume.

To configure a new quota entry, follow the steps in Lab 2-4.

Lab 2-4   Configuring a New Quota Entry

1. **Click the Quota Entries button on the Quota tab of the volume's Properties dialog box.**

   The Quota Entries window appears, as shown in Figure 2-6.

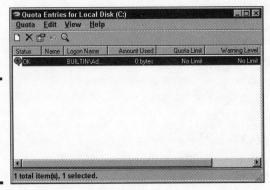

Figure 2-6: Quota entries allow you to set quotas for users.

2. **Choose Quota⇨New Quota Entry from the menu bar.**

   This action opens the user list from Active Directory where you can select the user for whom you want to create the quota entry.

3. **Select the user, click Add, and then click OK.**

   The Add New Quota Entry dialog box appears, as shown in Figure 2-7.

4. **Configure the disk space limit and warning level and then click OK.**

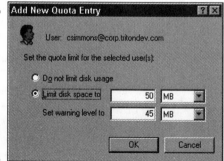

Figure 2-7:
Use the Add
New Quota
Entry
window to
set the
quota limit
and warning
for the user.

After quota entries are configured, you can easily edit them by selecting the user in the Quota Entries window and clicking the Properties button on the toolbar. This action allows you to change the quota limit and warning level. You can also perform standard management tasks such as copying and deleting users from the list.

You can't delete a quota entry until all of the user's files and folders have been removed from the volume, or until another quota entry has taken ownership of them. Also, quota entries are a great way to make exceptions to the standard quota rule that you configure on the Quota tab. If you have a quota of 25MB, but you want a certain user to have a greater or smaller quota, configure a quota entry for that user.

Implementing and configuring Encrypting File System (EFS)

Encrypting File System (EFS) is a powerful new security feature in Windows 2000. With encrypting file system, you can encrypt your files and folders.

EFS only functions on NTFS volumes, so to implement EFS, you should convert any FAT or FAT32 volumes to NTFS (see Book II, Chapter 6 for more information).

EFS is invisible to the user. You specify for a file or folder to be encrypted, but you work with the file or folder just as you normally do. In other words, you don't have to decrypt a file to use it and then re-encrypt it after you're done. You can open and close your files, move them, rename them — any action — without having to be aware of the encryption. However, if an intruder attempts to open, move, copy, or rename your file or folder, the intruder receives an Access Denied message.

For the exam, remember these important points about EFS:

✦ Only files or folders on NTFS volumes can be encrypted.

✦ Compressed files or folders can't be encrypted. You must uncompress the file or folder to encrypt it, and compressed volumes must be uncompressed to encrypt any files or folders on the volume.

✦ Only the user who encrypts the file or folder can open it.

✦ Encrypted files should not be shared.

✦ Encrypted files that are moved to a FAT or FAT32 volume lose their encryption.

✦ System files can't be encrypted.

✦ Encrypted files aren't protected against deletion. Anyone with delete permission can delete an encrypted file.

✦ Encrypt your Temp folder so that files remain encrypted while they are being edited. This action keeps temporary files created by some programs encrypted while they are in use. It is also a good idea to encrypt the My Documents folder.

✦ You can encrypt or decrypt files and folders stored on a remote computer that has been enabled for remote encryption. However, the data is not encrypted while it is in transit over the network. (Other protocols, such as IPsec, can provide this feature.)

✦ You can't drag and drop files into an encrypted folder for encryption purposes. If you want to put files into an encrypted folder, use the copy-and-paste method so that the files will be encrypted in the folder.

You can encrypt a file or folder by accessing its Properties dialog box. On the General tab, click the Advanced button, and then select the Encrypt Contents to Secure Data check box, as shown in Figure 2-8.

Figure 2-8:
Click the
Encrypt
Contents
check box
to enable
encryption.

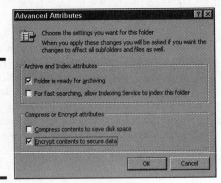

In the same manner, you can decrypt a file or folder as well. Keep in mind that you don't have to encrypt or decrypt your files and folders to work with them — the encryption feature is invisible to you.

When you encrypt a folder, you are asked if you want all files and subfolders within the folder to be encrypted as well. When you encrypt a file, you are asked if you also want to encrypt the folder in which it is stored.

You can also encrypt files and folders using the cipher command at the command line. Type **cipher /?** to see a list of options.

Configuring file and folder permissions

Also included in the exam objectives for this section is the configuration of file and folder permissions. In order to keep from repeating material in this book, see Book II, Chapter 8 to learn more about file and folder security.

Configuring volumes and basic and dynamic disks

A new feature of Windows 2000 disk management is "basic" and "dynamic" disks:

✦ A **basic disk** consists of partitions and logical drives. If you upgrade from Windows NT 4.0, your disk configuration is kept intact and is a basic disk. The basic disk contains partitions and logical drives, which you can manage and create additional partitions, but you can't create any new volume sets, stripe sets, and so forth.

✦ A **dynamic disk** is managed by Windows 2000 and contains dynamic volumes, which are simply volumes created with Disk Management.

Dynamic disks don't contain partitions or logical drives, but now contain volumes. With this design, disks are no longer limited to a certain number of partitions, but can contain multiple volumes. This design allows you more flexibility with your disk management without the previous restrictions. Also, you can make changes to your disk configuration on a dynamic disk without having to reboot your computer.

It is important to note that previous disk-management solutions and fault-tolerant solutions are still available on dynamic disks, but the names have changed (more terminology!). You need to know the differences, so we have put this information in the following list so you can easily memorize it.

✦ **Spanned volume:** A spanned volume, formerly called a *volume set*, is a collection of volume (formerly *partition*) "pieces" that are treated as one volume. Spanned volumes are storage solutions that allow you to constructively use small portions of disk space, but have no inherent fault tolerance.

✦ **Striped volumes:** A striped volume, formerly called a *striped set*, stores data on two or more physical disks. Striped volumes are storage solutions that allocate data evenly (in stripes) across the disks in the striped volume, so each disk must contain the same amount of storage space. Striped volumes are an excellent storage solution, but have no fault tolerance. If one disk in the striped volume fails, all data on the entire striped volume is lost.

✦ **Mirrored volumes:** Mirrored volumes, formerly called *mirror sets*, is a fault-tolerant solution that duplicates data on two physical disks. One disk is the primary disk and the other disk is the mirror (or a copy of the primary disk). If one of the disks fails, data can be reconstructed using the mirror. In fact, in Windows 2000, if one of the disks fails, your system continues to operate as though nothing has happened by using the mirror. You can replace the failed disk and re-create the mirror for continued fault tolerance. Mirrored volumes are effective fault-tolerance solutions, but do have a high cost in terms of megabytes (50 percent).

✦ **RAID-5 volumes:** A RAID-5 volume, formerly called a *striped set with parity*, requires at least three physical disks. Data is written in a stripe fashion across the disks and includes a parity bit that the system can use to reconstruct data in case of a disk failure. If a disk fails within the RAID-5 volume, the data can be regenerated with the parity bit. You can't mirror or extend RAID-5 volumes after they are created, but they are an effective fault-tolerant solution.

In order to manage your disks in Windows 2000, you need to upgrade the disk to dynamic. You can perform this action by right-clicking the disk (not the partitions) in Disk Management and clicking Upgrade to Dynamic Disk. You will need to reboot your computer for the upgrade to take effect.

After you upgrade to dynamic disk, you won't be able to boot previous versions of Windows on the dynamic disk because these operating systems can't access dynamic volumes. Dynamic disks are a Windows 2000-only solution, but one that you should implement as soon as possible to take advantage of their features.

Also, when you upgrade a basic disk to a dynamic disk, you must have 1MB of unformatted free space at the end of the disk, which Windows uses for administrative purposes. To maintain previous volume sets, striped sets, and so forth from a basic disk, you must upgrade all of the basic disks to dynamic disks. Also, it is important to note that removable media can't be upgraded to dynamic disks.

Understanding online and offline disks

Windows 2000 also introduces disk terminology of *online* and *offline*. This status is displayed in the Disk Management console for each disk. Online means that the disk is up and running, and an offline disk has errors and isn't available. You can access the properties sheet of either an online or offline disk and use the disk tools to attempt to repair an offline disk, or right-click the disk and click Reactivate Disk to attempt to repair it.

Understanding disk status

The Disk Management console provides several pieces of information about each disk volume, such as layout, type, file system, status, and capacity, and free space. For the exam, you need to know about disk status and the possible status indicators that can occur.

You need to memorize these for the exam, so we have put them in the following list that's easy to memorize:

✦ **Healthy:** The volume is accessible and has no problems.

✦ **Healthy (At Risk):** The volume is accessible, but I/O errors have been detected. The underlying disk is displayed as Online (Errors). You can normally solve this problem by reactivating the disk (right-click the disk and click Reactivate Disk).

✦ **Initializing:** The volume is being initialized and will be displayed as Healthy after initialization is complete. This status doesn't require any action.

✦ **Resynching:** This status occurs on mirrored volumes when resynchronization between the mirrored volumes is occurring. When the resynchronization is complete, the status is displayed as Healthy, and no action is necessary.

✦ **Regenerating:** This status occurs on RAID-5 volumes when data is being regenerated from the parity bit. This occurs after a disk failure and disk replacement by an administrator. No action is required.

✦ **Failed Redundancy:** This status is displayed when the underlying disk is offline on fault-tolerant disks. In this case, mirrored or RAID-5 volumes no longer have any fault tolerance. The disk needs to be reactivated or repaired in order to avoid potential data loss if one of the disks fails.

✦ **Failed Redundancy (At Risk):** This status is the same as Failed Redundancy, but the underlying disk is Online (Errors). Reactivate the disk so that it returns to Online status.

✦ **Failed:** The volume can't be automatically started and the volume needs to be repaired.

Creating volumes

You can easily create new volumes on your dynamic disks in Windows 2000 by right-clicking on the free space where you want to create a new volume and clicking Create Volume. This action launches the Create Volume Wizard.

You can create any volume, spanned volume, striped volume, mirrored volume, or RAID-5 volume (assuming you have the number of drives required) by using the Create Volume Wizard.

The Create Volume Wizard is rather straightforward and easy to use. You can review Lab 2-5, which creates a simple volume, to make certain you understand how the wizard works, which you need to know for the exam.

Lab 2-5 Creating a Simple Volume

1. **Right-click the area of free space where you want to create the volume and click Create Volume.**

2. **Click Next on the Create Volume Welcome screen.**

3. **Select Simple Volume from the list of options and click Next.**

   If you want to create a different kind of volume, select the desired type and click Next.

4. **Select the desired disk and click the Add button. You can also adjust the MB size for the volume as desired in the Size area of the dialog box. Click Next. (See Figure 2-9.)**

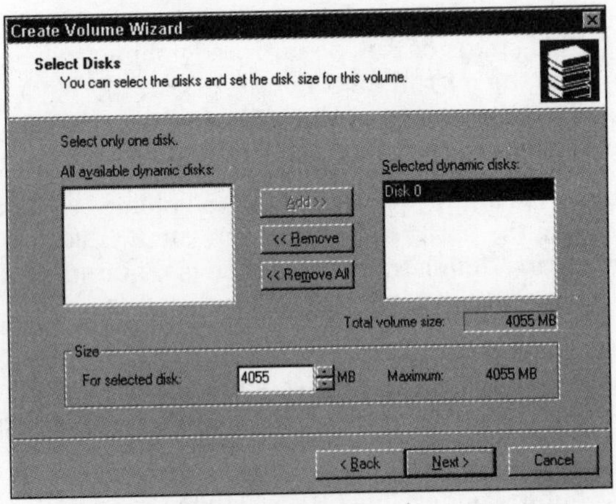

Figure 2-9:
Select the disk and volume size, and then click Next.

5. **Next, select a drive letter for the volume or choose to mount to volume to an empty folder. You can also choose not to assign a drive letter or drive path at this time. Make your selection and click next.**

   See the "Using mounted volumes" section later in this chapter for more information about mounted volumes.

6. **Next, choose to either format the volume or not to format it. If you choose to format it now, select an operating system, allocation unit**

size, and volume label by using the drop-down menus and dialog box. You can also to choose to perform a quick format and enable file and folder compression, if desired.

The data compression option allows Disk Management to compress data on the volume so that more storage space is available.

7. **Click Finish to complete the wizard.**

The system creates the volume and formats it (if specified).

Checking out common management tasks

After your volumes are configured in a desired manner, disk management requires very little time on your part. Your basic tasks include both occasional management and troubleshooting.

You can manage your disk volumes through the Disk Management tool. By right-clicking on a dynamic disk or disk volume, you can perform several tasks. These tasks may vary depending on the type of disk or volume, but your basic management actions are explained in the following bullet list, which you need to remember for the exam:

✦ **Open/Explore:** Allows you to open the disk or volume and view its contents.

✦ **Extend Volume:** You can dynamically extend a disk volume so that it incorporates more space from free disk space. You can only extend volumes with other NTFS volumes — not FAT or FAT32.

✦ **Change Drive Letter and Path:** You can dynamically change a volume's drive letter and path by entering the desired change.

✦ **Reactivate Volume/Disk:** Use the Reactivate feature to correct Online (Error) status readings.

✦ **Delete Volume**

✦ **Properties:** Properties sheets for disks and volumes give you general information about the disk, its hardware, and you can access disk tools, such as Error Checking and Disk Defragmenter.

Using mounted volumes

Mounted volumes in Windows 2000 are an easy way to replace drive letters so that a disk volume appears as a folder. In other words, you can mount a drive to a folder so that you can give the drive a "friendly" name and so that you don't run out of available drive letters. To create the mounted volume, you create an empty folder with a desired name, and then mount the desired volume to the folder using Disk Management.

To create a mounted volume, follow these steps:

1. **Right-click on the volume that you want to mount and click Change Drive Letter and Path.**

2. **In the Change Drive Letter and Path window, click Add.**

3. **Click the Mount in This NTFS folder, and then enter the path to the shared folder, or click the Browse button and select it, and then click OK. (See Figure 2-10.)**

Figure 2-10: Enter the name of the NTFS folder and click OK.

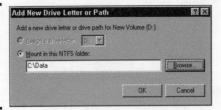

After you mount the volume to the NTFS folder, the folder now appears as a drive on your system, as shown in Figure 2-11.

Figure 2-11: The mounted volume now appears as a drive on your system.

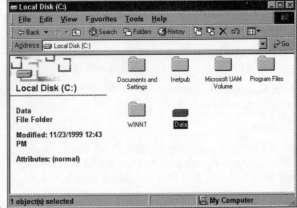

Configuring Dfs

Dfs (Distributed file system) enables you to organize shared folders in a network environment so they appear as one structured location to users. In the past, a user had to browse through different servers to find the shared folder that he or she needed to use. In large networks, this process can be time-consuming and frustrating. Along with Active Directory, one of the goals of Dfs is to remove the network structure from end-users — in other words, users don't need to know where resources on the network physically reside. They simply need to easily access those resources and use them.

Dfs is organized in a treelike structure in which users can simply browse the structure and find the shared folder that they need. To end-users, the folders appear to be located in one place — users don't see where the folders actually reside on the network. As shown in Figure 2-12, a number of different servers hold these shared resources, but in Dfs, they appear as though they reside in one location. This feature makes the network architecture transparent to users, and in the end, makes finding resources much quicker and easier.

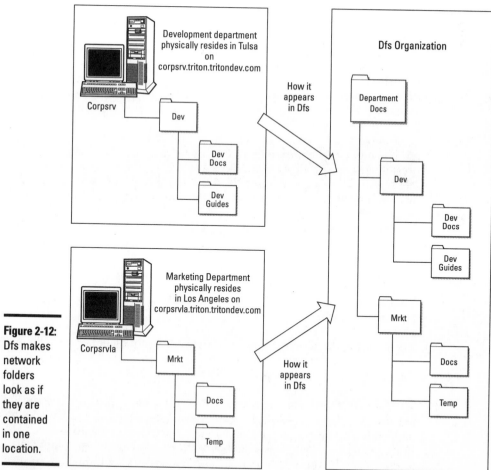

Figure 2-12: Dfs makes network folders look as if they are contained in one location.

The two kinds of Dfs are

✦ A **standalone Dfs** is stored on a single server that is accessed by network users. The Dfs server holds the folder information for all other servers and presents that information to users in a treelike structure. However, it has no fault tolerance, so if the server fails, Dfs won't be available to users.

✦ A **domain-based Dfs** stores the folder structure in Active Directory. If one server fails, Dfs is still available on other servers within the Active Directory environment.

Only clients that support Dfs can use the Dfs features. Clients running Windows 2000, Windows NT, and Windows 98 have built-in support for Dfs, and clients running Windows 95 can download the Dfs client from www.microsoft.com.

The exam expects you to know about both standalone and domain-based Dfs. The following sections explore both of these and what you need to know for the exam.

Managing a standalone Dfs

Distributed file system, or Dfs, is available on your Windows 2000 Server after an initial server installation. Dfs functions as an MMC snap-in, but doesn't appear in your Administrative tools folder. Instead, you manually add the snap-in to an MMC, and then you can save the console for future use. To add the snap-in, type **MMC** at the Run dialog box, and then choose Add/Remove snap-in from the Console menu. Choose Distributed File System from the snap-in list, and then you can save the console after you have the snap-in loaded.

Setting up the Dfs root

You set up Dfs by establishing a Dfs root. A *Dfs root* is simply a container for files and Dfs links.

It is important to note that you can create a Dfs root on either a FAT or NTFS partition, but FAT doesn't provide the security features of NTFS, so you should always create the root on an NTFS partition if possible.

When creating a standalone Dfs root, it is important to remember some limitations. First, the standalone Dfs root doesn't use Active Directory, so it has no fault tolerance. Second, a standalone Dfs root can't have root-level Dfs shared folders. This means that one root exists and all shared folders must fall under the hierarchy of the root. Also, you have a limited hierarchy available. A standard Dfs root can only have a single level of Dfs links.

To create a new Dfs root, click the Action menu and click New Dfs root. This action opens the New Dfs Root Wizard. Lab 2-6 explains the steps in this wizard, and you should know what options are available for the exam.

Lab 2-6   Creating a Standalone Dfs Root

1. **Click Next on the Welcome screen.**

2. **In the New Dfs Root Type window, select the Create a Standalone Dfs root radio button, and then click Next.**

3. **In the Host Server window, enter the name of the host server for the Dfs root and click Next.**

4. **In the Specify Dfs Root Share window, you can use an existing share, or create a new one by entering the desired share name and path. Click Next.**

   The DFS share holds the DFS information, so you can simply use a share already available on your server, or you may want to create a new one strictly for the Dfs root.

5. **In the name the Dfs root window, enter a name for the Dfs root and enter a command if desired. Click Next.**

6. **Click Finish to complete the wizard.**

Creating a Dfs link

Dfs links provide a folder name to the user. When a user accesses the folder, the user is transparently redirected to the server that actually holds the shared folder.

To create a Dfs link, select the Dfs root in the console, click the Action menu and click New Dfs Link. The Create a New Dfs Link window appears, as shown in Figure 2-13.

Book III
Chapter 2

Creating and
Managing File, Print,
and Web Resources

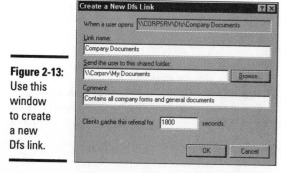

Figure 2-13: Use this window to create a new Dfs link.

Enter the desired name for the Dfs link and the network path to the shared folder. You can enter a comment if desired and you can change the amount of time that clients cache the link information on their systems. The default time is 1800 seconds. If the link seldom changes, you can extend the cache timeout value if desired.

After the Dfs link is established, it now appears in the Dfs tree, as shown in Figure 2-14.

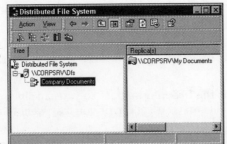

Figure 2-14: New Dfs link now appears in the Dfs tree.

Creating replicas

After a Dfs link is established, you can create additional replicas for the link. A *replica* is an alternate location of a shared folder. For example, the Dfs link Company Documents may reside in several locations. By definition, a replica participates in replication, so two more shared folders may hold the same information and replicate with each other as that information changes. The replica set keeps track of the possible locations that can be used to service clients. The alternate must be stored on a Windows 2000 Server running NTFS and the Dfs service.

To create a replica, select the desired Dfs link in the console, click the Action menu, and then click New Replica. Enter the alternate for the shared folder, and then click OK.

Understanding Dfs security

Keep in mind that Dfs basically provides a link interface to users. When a user opens a Dfs link, the user is redirected to the server that holds the shared folder. Dfs doesn't provide any inherent security because it only provides an interface for users to access shares. Security for the shared folders is set on each folder on the server where the folder actually resides.

Likewise, if you delete a Dfs link, you aren't deleting any shared information in the folder; you are simply removing the link to the shared folder in the Dfs tree.

Managing a domain-based Dfs

The domain-based Dfs is your best choice for implementing Dfs on a network. When you implement a domain-based DFS, you provide fault tolerance for the Dfs. Also, you can have root-level shared folders and no Dfs hierarchy limit — you can have multiple levels of Dfs links.

When you implement a domain-based Dfs root, it must be hosted on a domain member server, and the Dfs topology, or the structure of the Dfs (such as roots and links), is stored in Active Directory.

Setting up the Dfs root

You create a domain-based Dfs root by using the New Dfs Root Wizard.

It is important to note that you can create a Dfs root on either a FAT or NTFS partition, but FAT doesn't provide the security features of NTFS, so you should always create the root on an NTFS partition.

To run the New Dfs Root Wizard, open the Dfs console, click the Action menu, and then click New Dfs Root. Lab 2-7 shows you how to use the wizard to configure a domain-based Dfs root, and you need to know these steps for the exam.

| Lab 2-7 | Creating a Domain-based Dfs Root |

1. **Click Next on the wizard welcome screen.**

2. **On the Select Dfs Root Type window, click the Create a Domain Dfs Root radio button, and then click Next.**

3. **In the next window, select the host domain for the Dfs root, and then click Next.**

4. **Next, enter the name of the server in the host domain that will host the Dfs root. Click Next.**

5. **In the Specify Dfs Root Share window, you can use an existing share, or create a new one by entering the desired share name and path. Click Next.**

   The DFS share holds the DFS information, so you can simply use a share already available on your server, or you may want to create a new one strictly for the Dfs root.

6. **Enter a new name for the Dfs root and a comment if desired. Click Next.**

7. **Click Finish.**

Configuring the domain-based Dfs root

Configuration for the domain-based Dfs root functions in the same manner as the standalone Dfs. Refer to the "Managing a standalone Dfs" section earlier in this chapter for information on creating Dfs links and replicas. Note that for the domain-based Dfs, you can also create a new root replica by using the Action menu. This feature allows you to create a root replica on another domain member server.

Understanding domain-based Dfs replication

Because one of the major purposes of domain-based Dfs is to provide fault tolerance, replication must occur between Dfs roots and shared folders to ensure that replicas hold an exact copy. In a standalone Dfs root, you can create folder replicas, but replication must be manually performed. In a domain-based Dfs, replication can occur automatically.

Automatic replication can't be used on FAT volumes on Windows 2000 servers. You should use only NTFS volumes for domain-based Dfs so replication can occur automatically.

When you create a root replica in the console, a wizard appears that allows you to specify the server where the replica will reside. Dfs shared folders can also be replicated automatically on a domain-based Dfs. When you create a new replica for a shared folder, click the Automatic replication radio button, as shown in Figure 2-15, so that replication can occur automatically.

Figure 2-15:
Click the
Automatic
Replication
radio button
to use
automatic
folder
replica
replication.

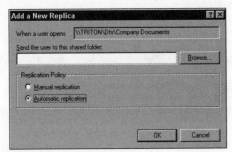

Dfs uses the File Replication Service (FRS) to automatically perform replication. FRS manages updates across shared folders configured for replication. By default, FRS synchronizes the folder contents at 15-minute intervals.

When you set up the automatic replication, a window appears that enables you to configure the replication policy. This allows you to specify one share as the primary (or initial master). The primary replicates its contents to the other Dfs shared folder in the set.

Of course, you can choose to perform manual replication where you must manually update the folder contents if a change occurs. For replica sets that seldom change, this may be a wise choice to reduce unnecessary synchronization traffic.

Within a set of Dfs shared folders, don't mix automatic and manual replication. Use one or the other to ensure that replication properly occurs.

Managing file and folder compression

Windows 2000 supports an internal compression feature that enables you to compress files and folders in order to conserve disk storage space. When you compress a file or folder, you can open and use that file as you normally would without having to manually decompress and recompress the file or folder. In other words, the process is seamless in Windows 2000 networks.

To compress a file or folder, right-click the file or folder and choose Properties. On the General tab, click Advanced and click the Compress Contents to save disk space check box in the Advanced Attributes dialog box.

For the exam, you should remember two major items concerning compression:

✦ Compression and encryption aren't compatible. You can compress a file or folder or encrypt a file or folder, but not both.

✦ You can only use compression if the file or folder is stored on an NTFS drive.

Creating Shared Resources and Configuring Access Rights

The exam expects you to know how to create a shared folder and printer, and how to assign permission to those shared resources. If you have studied for the Windows 2000 Professional and Windows 2000 Server exams, you know that permissions and resource configuration works the same way on all Windows 2000 computers. Because this objective repeats other objects found both within this book and Books I and II, we don't delve into these issues here. For the lowdown on shared resources, see Book II, Chapter 3, which is devoted to this topic.

Configuring and Troubleshooting Internet Information Services

In Windows 2000, you can share any folder so that it becomes a shared Web folder in the Web site that you specify. This action causes the shared folder to appear on your Internet or intranet site so that users can access the contents of the shared folder. You share a Web folder in the same way you share any other folder on your system. Follow the steps in Lab 2-8.

Lab 2-8   Sharing a Web Folder

1. **Right-click the folder that you want to share and click Sharing.**

2. **Click the Web Sharing tab.**

3. **Use the drop-down menu to select the Web site in which you want to share the folder, and then click the Share This Folder radio button, as shown in Figure 2-16.**

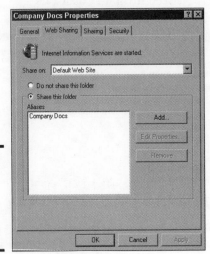

Figure 2-16:
Use the
Web
Sharing tab
to share a
Web folder.

When you click the Share This Folder radio button, the Edit Alias window appears. This window allows you to give an alias name to the Web folder if desired, and then you have the option to assign certain access permissions: Read, Write, Script Source Access, or Directory Browsing. Under application permissions, you can select None, Scripts, or Execute (Includes Scripts).

4. **Make your selections in the Edit Alias dialog box, shown in Figure 2-17, and click OK for the share to become active.**

Figure 2-17: Edit the Edit Alias dialog box for the desired share properties.

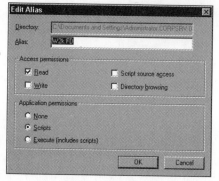

Configuring Web folder properties

After you share a Web folder, you can access its properties dialog box from within Internet Services Manager. Click Start⇨Programs⇨Administrative Tools⇨Internet Services Manager. Expand your server in the Tree pane and expand the desired Web site. You now see the shared folder within the Web site. If you select the shared folder and choose Action⇨Properties, you can further configure the shared Web folder.

The Properties dialog box for shared Web folders has five tabs. You need to know what you can do on each tab, and the following sections explore what you need to know for the exam.

Configuring the Virtual Directory tab

The Virtual Directory tab, shown in Figure 2-18, allows you to configure the location or the way a Web folder is accessed.

Book III Chapter 2

Creating and Managing File, Print, and Web Resources

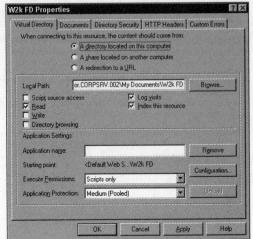

Figure 2-18:
Use the
Virtual
Directory
tab to mark
the
directory
location and
access
rights.

First, you can determine if the directory is located on this computer, another computer, or is a redirection to another URL. Depending on the selection you make, the rest of tab's content changes. If you select another computer, you provide the path to that computer, and if you select a URL redirect, you enter information about the URL. When you share a Web folder on your local machine, you select the Located on This Computer option.

The middle part of the window contains the local path to the Web folder, which you can change by clicking the Browse button.

If you later move the Web folder to a different location on your computer, you need to change the local path setting so it will be correct, or Web users won't be able to access the directory.

You can select several check boxes to determine what users can do with the shared folder and how it is configured on the Web server. You need to know these options for the exam:

✦ **Script Source Access:** Allows users to access the source of any scripts that run with the directory.

✦ **Read:** Allows users to read the directory information.

✦ **Write:** Allows users to write directory information.

✦ **Directory Browsing:** Allows users to browse the directory.

✦ **Log Visits:** Creates a log file of all visitors.

✦ **Index This Resource:** Indexes the Web file in the Web site.

Also, if you are sharing applications in the Web folder, you can configure an application name, determine execution permissions, and configure application protection. The execution permissions allow users to either execute scripts, executable files, or both. Application protection allows you to select low, medium, or high protection.

Configuring the Documents tab

The Documents tab allows you to select a default document that launches when a user accesses the shared folder. For example, you can create a default.htm document for the folder that contains links to the contents of the shared folder. This feature is optional, but is something you may want to use, depending on the structure of your Web site.

Managing the Directory Security tab

The Directory Security tab allows you to configure different kinds of security for the shared folder. You have three options: anonymous access and authentication control, IP address and domain name restrictions, and secure communications.

For anonymous access and authentication control, you can click the Edit button to select the desired authentication methods, as shown in Figure 2-19.

Book III
Chapter 2

Creating and
Managing File, Print,
and Web Resources

Figure 2-19:
Use the
Authenti-
cation
Methods
window to
configure
the desired
access
methods.

First, you can allow anonymous access to the directory by clicking the Anonymous Access check box. This allows users to access the directory without a username and password. Instead, they use a default username and password, such as IUSR_*servername*. You can change this as desired by clicking the Edit button.

In the Authentication access section, you can configure the kind of authentication when anonymous access is disabled or when access is restricted due to NTFS ACLs. You have three options, which you should remember for the exam:

+ **Basic authentication:** Users access the directory with a username and password that is sent in clear text. You can also specify a default domain by clicking the Edit button.

+ **Digest authentication for Windows domain servers:** This feature allows IIS to manage authentication using usernames and passwords from Windows domain controllers.

+ **Integrated Windows authentication:** This feature integrates the authentication process with Windows 2000 domain controllers.

Next, you can determine directory security based on IP address and domain name restrictions. If you click the Edit button, you can create an IP address domain acceptance or restricted list, as shown in Figure 2-20.

Figure 2-20:
Use the IP
address and
Domain
Name
Registrations
tab to
manage
access by
IP address.

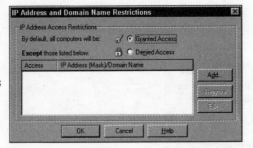

You have two options. First, you can click the Granted Access radio button so that all IP addresses are granted access except the ones you add to the list, or you can reverse this by clicking the Denied Access radio button, in which case all IP addresses are denied except the ones you provide in the list. Click the Add button to enter the desired IP addresses.

Finally, you can use secure communications through certificate services, if certificates are in use in your network. Certificate services requires a user to have a valid digital certificate in order to log on to the network or access the Web directory. You don't have to worry about this option for the exam, so no further explanation is provided here.

Enabling HTTP headers

The HTTP Headers tab allows you to configure HTTP headers that are sent to the user's browser when the directory is accessed. You can configure content expiration, content ratings, and additional MIME types.

All you need to know for the exam is the content expiration option. You can click the Enable Content Expiration check box and enter a day and time the Web folder content expires. This feature is very useful for time-sensitive documents or files.

Understanding Custom Errors

The Custom Errors tab allows you to create custom error messages for the directory. This feature is useful for particular kinds of directory files or applications. You can create a custom error message that is sent to the user for a particular error that may be encountered.

For the exam, you only need to know what this option does — you won't see detailed questions about creating custom error messages.

Using the Permissions Wizard

IIS 5 includes a handy wizard that allows you more control over Web directory access. Through the Permissions Wizard, you can control how users access the entire Web site or particular Web folders.

The Permissions Wizard allows you to control Web site access and permissions for the site or individual directories. You need to know what options are available, so you should practice Lab 2-9 to get familiar with the Permissions Wizard.

Book III
Chapter 2

Creating and
Managing File, Print,
and Web Resources

Lab 2-9   Using the Permissions Wizard

1. Open the Internet Services Manager.

Choose Start➪Programs➪Administrative Tools➪Internet Services Manager.

2. Start the Permissions Wizard.

You can click either the Web site in the Tree pane or a particular folder; choose Action➪All Tasks➪Permissions Wizard to start the wizard.

3. On the welcome screen, click Next.

The Security Settings window appears.

4. **You have the option to inherit all security settings or select security settings from a template. Make your selection and click Next.**

   If you selected to use a template, a list is provided from which you select. If you selected Inherit All Security Settings, the Windows Directory and File Permissions window appears (which is also what you are eventually led to if you choose a template). The window shows the basic rights provided.

5. **You have the option to replace all directory and file permissions with the ones listed, leave the current directory and file permissions intact and add the new ones, or leave the directory and file permissions as they are, shown in Figure 2-21. Make your selection and click Next.**

   The permissions that will be applied by your setting are listed in the Security Summary window.

Figure 2-21: Use this window to determine permission settings.

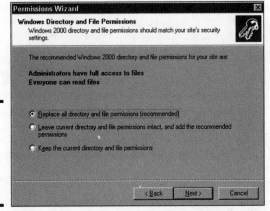

6. **Click Next to accept the permissions that are listed or use the Back button to make changes. Click Finish to complete the wizard.**

Monitoring and Managing Network Security

As a network administrator, monitoring and managing network security is an ongoing process that will require your attention. Specifically, the exam expects you to know about user account settings as well as auditing. Book II, Chapter 8 explores these topics in detail.

Prep Test

1 Which statement is true concerning Active Directory and shared folders?

- A ○ Shared folders are stored in Active Directory.
- B ○ Shared folder objects are stored in Active Directory.
- C ○ Active Directory provides link permissions to the shared resources.
- D ○ Users must be authenticated by Active Directory to access a shared resource.

2 Which operating system would require you to manually configure a printer object in Active Directory when a shared printer is attached to that computer?

- A ○ Windows XP Professional
- B ○ Windows 2000 Professional
- C ○ Windows Me
- D ○ Windows 2000 Server

3 You enable disk quotas on a particular volume. All users have a maximum quota limit of 10MB. However, for a certain user, you want a quota limit of 20MB. How can you configure this?

- A ○ Raise the volume limit to 20 MB.
- B ○ Use Group Policy to override the default limit for the user.
- C ○ Give the user domain administrative permissions.
- D ○ Use a quota entry for the user.

4 You want to encrypt a particular folder, but the encryption option doesn't seem to be available. What is the most likely explanation?

- A ○ Compression is in use.
- B ○ The folder is on a FAT volume.
- C ○ You don't have administrator privileges for the local machine.
- D ○ The folder is not managed by Group Policy.

5 Which kind of volume would you use to provide data fault tolerance with the least amount of wasted megabyte space?

- A ○ Spanned volume
- B ○ Striped volume
- C ○ Mirrored volume
- D ○ RAID-5 volume

6 **On a routine inspection of a server, you discover that one of the disks is listed as Healthy (At Risk). What should you do?**

A ○ Rescan the disk.

B ○ Reactivate the disk.

C ○ Replace the disk.

D ○ Create a mirror.

7 **How is fault tolerance provided in a domain-based Dfs?**

A ○ Manual backup

B ○ Active Directory

C ○ Automated backup storage

D ○ It has no fault tolerance.

8 **For a particular virtual directory in IIS, you want to make certain that users aren't able to browse through subdirectories. What do you need to do?**

A ○ Disable Read access.

B ○ Disable directory browsing for the folder.

C ○ Disable directory browsing for the Web site.

D ○ Disable browsing.

9 **Which type of IIS authentication uses clear text passwords and usernames?**

A ○ Anonymous

B ○ Basic

C ○ Digest

D ○ Integrated Windows

10 **For certain IIS content, you need the content to expire after a period of time. Which option enables you to configure content expiration?**

A ○ Custom Errors

B ○ HTTP Headers

C ○ HTML Tags

D ○ UDP Timestamps

Answers

1 **B.** The AD object contains the path to the shared network folder. *Review "Configuring Dfs."*

2 **C.** Operating systems earlier than Windows 2000 can't automatically publish resources in Active Directory. *Read "Publishing a printer."*

3 **D.** Quota entries allow you to set specific quota limits for individual users. *Review "Configuring quota entries."*

4 **B.** Encryption only works on NTFS volumes. *See "Implementing and configuring Encrypting File System (EFS)."*

5 **D.** The RAID-5 volume doesn't use as much disk space for redundancy as a mirrored volume. *Study "Configuring volumes and basic and dynamic disks."*

6 **B.** You can reactivate the disk to try and bring it back online. *Study "Understanding disk status."*

7 **B.** A domain-based Dfs resides on each domain controller, so fault tolerance occurs through the Active Directory. *Study "Configuring Dfs."*

8 **B.** Disable the directory browsing permission to prevent users from browsing the directory. *Study "Configuring the Virtual Directory tab."*

9 **B.** Basic authentication uses clear text passwords and usernames. *See "Managing the Directory Security Tab."*

10 **B.** Use HTTP Headers to configure header information, including expirations. *Study "Enabling HTTP headers."*

Chapter 3: Configuring and Troubleshooting the Network Infrastructure

Exam Objectives

- ✔ Troubleshooting routing
- ✔ Configuring and troubleshooting TCP/IP on servers and client computers
- ✔ Configuring, administering, and troubleshooting DHCP on servers and client computers
- ✔ Configuring, administering, and troubleshooting DNS
- ✔ Troubleshooting name resolution on client computers

*N*etwork management, client access, and name resolution are important troubleshooting and configuration issues that you'll face as a network administrator. The good news is that Windows 2000 networks are the easiest to configure of the Microsoft IP networks. IP configuration is more automatic and easier to troubleshoot than it has been in years past.

IP configuration and network management are important parts of your job, and the network administration exam certainly expects you to know your way around IP, DHCP, and DNS. All of these topics are lengthy and complex, but this chapter explores the exam objectives only. If you are new to network management, we strongly suggest that you study some background information on TCP/IP, DHCP, and DNS in order to tackle the tricky questions that the exam is likely to throw your way. In this chapter, you'll learn about

- ✦ Using tools to troubleshoot TCP/IP
- ✦ Configuring TCP/IP properties
- ✦ Configuring DHCP
- ✦ Configuring DNS and name resolution

Troubleshooting Routing

The concept of configuring, administering, and troubleshooting the network infrastructure primarily concerns the troubleshooting of client and server TCP/IP configuration, as well as router configurations on a network. With proper IP addressing, default gateways, and subnet masks, TCP/IP is a rather easy protocol to administer. However, this protocol must be configured correctly, and you must know what TCP/IP tools to use in order to both examine and solve configuration problems.

An entire book could be devoted to the topic of network infrastructure management, but the exam primarily expects you to know about a few TCP/IP tools and how and when to use them. For example, suppose that Jane uses a Windows 2000 Professional computer. Jane is unable to access other computers on the network and other computers on the network are unable to access Jane's computer. What do you do? First, you should perform a few ping tests to see whether Jane's computer has any connectivity at all, and then you should use ipconfig to inspect the computer's TCP/IP configuration.

For the exam, it is important that you know about these tools, what they do, and the basics of how to use them so that you can answer scenario questions that ask you what to do to solve a particular problem. You need to know what you can do with these tools, and you must have some hands-on experience using them. Fire up a Windows 2000 computer and check out the command line tools so that you'll have a better understanding of them. Here are the tools that you need to know for the exam:

✦ **PING:** PING is a command that you can use to test connectivity with another host or even a computer's NIC. You can ping other computers by IP address or host name, and you can even test a computer's NIC by typing the PING 127.0.0.1 command at the Windows command prompt.

When a computer doesn't seem to have connectivity, try pinging other computers on the same subnet, first by name, and then by IP address. If you can ping computers by IP address but not by name, the problem is typically with name resolution, such as DNS. If you can't ping anything, the problem is either in the IP addressing or a physical problem with the NIC. When you ping a computer, you get either a failure message or a reply message, as shown in Figure 3-1.

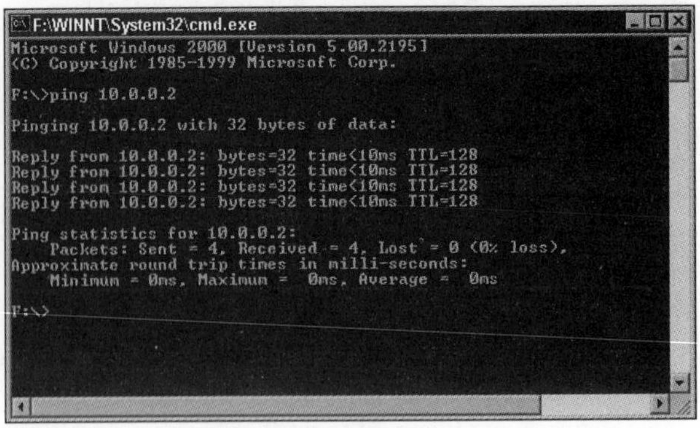

Figure 3-1:
Use the
PING
command
to test
connectivity
with other
computers.

✦ **Tracert:** Tracert traces the route to a particular host on a local network, remote network, or even the Internet. Tracert is a kind of PING program, but it also reports each hop to the location. In other words, when you use tracert, the route through each router to the desired host is traced. You can use tracert in the same way that you use the PING command, using the host's name, IP address, or even Internet URL. If connectivity to a particular host is slow, use tracert to see what route is being taken and if a particular router is very slow. This can help you to pinpoint the problem over the route and take appropriate action to correct the bottleneck.

✦ **PathPING:** PathPING is a combination of the PING and tracert commands. However, pathPING provides additional information about the path, specifically, the number of packets that are being dropped at any given router. Suppose that you are having problems on your routed Windows 2000 network, and you want to try to find the router that is causing the bottleneck. In this case, pathPING is a great tool to use because the packet loss at each router can help you find the bottleneck.

✦ **Ipconfig:** Ipconfig is a very helpful tool that displays the IP configuration of a computer, such as the IP address, subnet mask, default gateway, DHCP lease, and so forth. Simply type **ipconfig** at the command line to receive this basic information, or type **ipconfig /all** to receive complete TCP/IP data, as shown in Figure 3-2. Windows 9x and Me also have a version of ipconfig called Winipcfg that shows you this same information in a graphical interface. If you need to get IP addressing information about a computer, ipconfig or Winipcfg is the best tool to use. Ipconfig also contains a number of command line switches to manipulate information. To learn about them, type **ipconfig /?** at the command prompt. Also, you can release and renew DHCP leases by using ipconfig with ipconfig /release and ipconfig /renew. Keep these in mind for the exam.

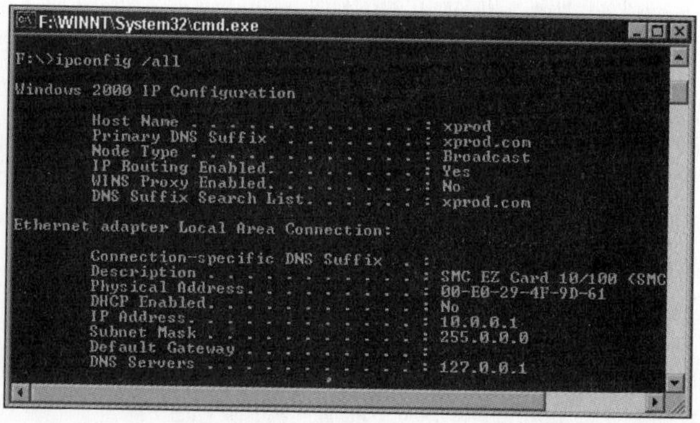

Book III
Chapter 3

Configuring
the Network
Infrastructure

Figure 3-2:
Ipconfig gives you IP configuration data.

✦ **Arp:** Arp, or Address Resolution Protocol, allows a computer to convert an IP address to a hardware address. The Arp tool allows you to manipulate the Arp cache in that you can add addresses that are frequently used. The cache is stored in memory, so it is flushed after a reboot. In cases where you want to speed up network access to a particular host, however, use Arp to add hardware addresses. You aren't likely to see many (if any) questions about Arp on the exam, but just keep machine address issues in mind for any questions you run across.

✦ **Route:** Route is a command that allows you to manipulate the routing table and enter static routes to desired hosts. For example, let's say that in a WAN, access to a certain host can be obtained over several paths, but you only want the host accessed over one particular path. Use Route to configure a static route to that host. If you want to see the routing table, type **ROUTE PRINT** at the command prompt.

Configuring and Troubleshooting TCP/IP on Servers and Client Computers

The TCP/IP configuration on client and server computers in Windows 2000 networks is typically handled by DHCP. (See the next section for more on DHCP.) DHCP servers can automatically assign an IP address, subnet mask, default gateway, and other IP configuration addresses, such as the addresses for DNS and WINS servers. However, you may encounter cases in which you manually need to look at a Windows 2000 computer's IP addressing data and even make manual cases. Or, in the case of server computers, you may want to assign a specific, static IP address to the server.

In either case, you can inspect the TCP/IP configuration of a server or client computer in a couple of ways. If you want a quick look at the IP configuration of a client computer, use ipconfig. (If you need to see this information on Windows 9*x* or Windows Me, use Winipcfg.) If you want to take a look at IP configuration on a Windows 2000 client, follow the steps in Lab 3-1.

Lab 3-1   Inspecting the TCP/IP Configuration

1. **Choose Start⇨Settings⇨Network and Dial-up Connections.**

2. **Double-click the Local Area Connection icon and click the Properties button.**

   The Local Area Connection Properties window appears.

3. **Select Internet Protocol (TCP/IP) and click the Properties button.**

   The Internet Protocol (TCP/IP) Properties dialog box appears, as shown in Figure 3-3.

4. The standard setting is to Obtain an IP Address Automatically. If you need to configure the IP addressing information manually, select Use the Following IP Address and enter the desired information. You can also enter the IP addresses of DNS servers on your network.

In networks where DHCP is in use, the IP addressing data is provided by the DHCP server. In non-DHCP networks, Windows 2000 computers can automatically assign themselves a TCP/IP address in a private IP address range appropriate for small workgroups.

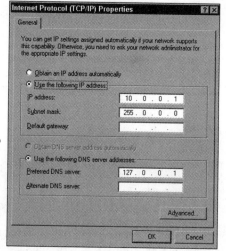

Figure 3-3:
The Internet
Protocol
(TCP/IP)
Properties
dialog box.

5. Click the Advanced tab to enter additional addressing information for DNS, WINS, and default gateways.

As you may imagine, in a Windows 2000 network, DHCP handles most all IP configuration, but the exam may ask you a question or two about manually configuring IP addressing data on the TCP/IP properties dialog box. Just be familiar with the setting options you find here.

Configuring, Administering, and Troubleshooting DHCP on Servers and Client Computers

DHCP (Dynamic Host Configuration Protocol) is a server service that dynamically assigns, or *leases,* IP addresses and related IP information to network clients. At first glance, this may not seem like an important task, but you have to remember that on a TCP/IP network, each network client must have a unique IP address and an appropriate subnet mask. Without these, the client can't communicate on the network. Also, two clients can't have the same IP address. If two clients have the same IP address, neither will be able to communicate on the network.

Back in its early days, TCP/IP gained the reputation of being a "high over-head" protocol — it required more configuration than other networking protocols. The prospect of having to physically visit each client machine and enter a correct IP address and subnet mask without making a duplication error was enough to give network administrators severe panic attacks.

DHCP handles all of this automatically. Clients are provided a unique IP address, subnet mask, and other IP information, such as default gateways and the IP addresses of WINS and DNS servers. DHCP makes certain that no clients have duplicate addresses, and this entire process is invisible to network administrators and network users. As you can see, DHCP is very important, and the exam expects you to know how to install and configure it.

How does DHCP work?

DHCP works by leasing IP addresses and IP information to network clients for a period of time. For the lease to happen, a "negotiation" process occurs, which we explain in the following list:

1. During the boot process, a client computer that is configured as a DHCP client sends out a broadcast packet called DHCPDISCOVER. The Discover packet contains the client's computer name and MAC address so that the DHCP servers can respond to it. In our language, the Discover packet basically says, "Looking for a DHCP server that can lease an IP address."

2. DHCP servers on the network respond to the broadcast with a DHCP-OFFER. The DHCPOFFER says in our language, "I am a DHCP server, and I have a lease for you." If several DHCP servers respond to the request, the client accepts the first offer it receives.

3. The client responds via a broadcast message called a DHCPREQUEST. This basically says, "I accept your lease offer and want an IP address." If other DHCP servers made offers, they also see that their lease offers weren't accepted by the broadcast message, so they rescind their offers. (There's nothing like getting snubbed by a client computer.)

4. The DHCP server whose offer was accepted responds with a DHCPACK message, which acknowledges the lease acceptance and contains the client's IP address lease, as well as other IP addressing information that you configure the server to provide. The client is now a TCP/IP client and can participate on the network.

Keep in mind that a lease is for a period of time. Typically, a client can keep its IP address for several days (or whatever you configure). After half of the lease time expires, the client attempts to gain a second lease for the IP address. After a client obtains an IP address, it attempts to keep the lease by requesting a new lease for the same IP address. If unsuccessful, the client simply has to get a new IP address lease.

Important DHCP terms

You need to know the DHCP terms listed in Table 3-1. You will work with these throughout the chapter and during any hands-on configuration of DHCP. The exam expects you to know these, so we have put them in Table 3-1 so that you can quickly memorize them.

Table 3-1	Important DHCP Terms
DHCP Term	*Definition*
Scope	A scope is a full range of IP addresses that can be leased from a particular DHCP server.
Superscope	A superscope is a grouping of scopes used to support logical IP subnets that exist on one physical IP subnet (called a *multinet*).
Multicast scope	A multicast scope contains multicast IP addresses, which treat multicast clients as a group. Multicast is an extension of DHCP (MDHCP) and uses a multicast address range of 224.0.0.0 to 239.255.255.255.
Address pool	An address pool is the IP addresses in a scope that are available for lease.
Exclusion range	An exclusion range is a group of IP addresses in the scope that are excluded from leasing. Excluded addresses are normally used to give hardware devices, such as routers, a static IP address.
Reservation	A reservation is used to assign a permanent IP address to a particular client, server, or hardware device. Reservations are typically made for servers or hardware devices that need a static IP address.
Lease	A lease is the amount of time a client may use an IP address before the client has to re-lease the IP address or request another one.

Book III
Chapter 3

Configuring
the Network
Infrastructure

Installing DHCP

You install DHCP in the same manner that you install other networking components in Windows 2000 Server: through either Add/Remove Programs in Control Panel or by using the Configure Your Server tool.

DHCP, as with most other Windows 2000 components, functions as a Microsoft Management Console (MMC) snap-in. After DHCP is installed, you must configure the service for operation. You can open the DHCP Manager by choosing Start⇨Program⇨Administrative Tools⇨DHCP. The right pane within the snap-in tells you that the service must be configured.

DHCP doesn't begin leasing IP addresses and it isn't functional until it is first configured by an administrator. You can learn how to configure DHCP for operation in the following sections.

Creating and Configuring DHCP Scopes

A *scope* is the full range of IP addresses that can be leased from a particular DHCP server. Each DHCP server has its own scope of IP addresses that are appropriate for the subnet on which the DHCP server leases addresses.

DHCP servers don't share scopes, and their scopes must not overlap with each other. Overlapping results in the same IP addresses being leased to different network clients, which will cause the clients to lose network communication ability.

Before the DHCP server can lease IP addresses to clients, a scope must be configured and the server has to be authorized by Active Directory. You can learn about authorization in the "Authorizing the DHCP Server" section, later in this chapter, and you learn how to create various scopes in the next few sections.

Creating a standard scope

To create a standard DHCP scope, complete the steps in Lab 3-2. The exam expects you to know how to create scopes, so study this lab carefully.

Lab 3-2	Creating a Standard Scope

1. **Open the DHCP Manager.**

   Choose Start⇨Programs⇨Administrative Tools⇨DHCP.

2. **Select the server in the console tree and then choose Action⇨New Scope.**

   The New Scope Wizard begins.

3. **Click Next on the Welcome Screen.**

   The Scope Name dialog box appears.

4. Enter a name for the scope and a description, if desired.

The IP Address Range window appears.

5. Enter the starting and ending IP addresses of the full scope for this server, and then enter the subnet mask for the IP subnet in the Subnet Mast dialog box, shown in Figure 3-4. Click Next.

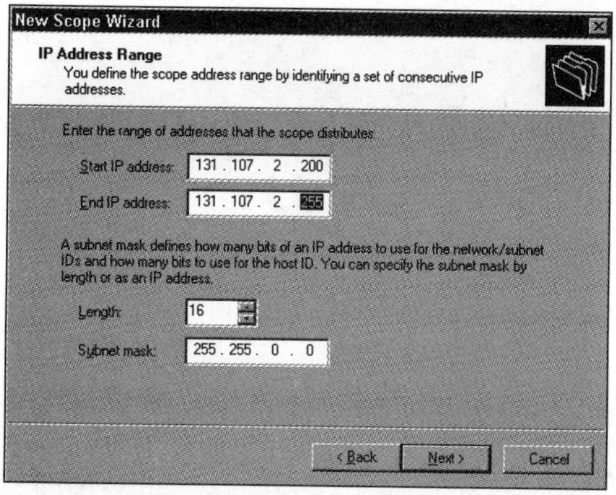

Figure 3-4:
IP Address
Range.

The Add Exclusions window appears.

6. Enter any exclusion ranges desired by entering the starting and ending IP addresses of the range(s). Click the Add button to add it to the list, and then repeat the process to define more exclusion ranges.

The Lease Duration window appears.

7. Enter the desired lease duration in the provided boxes and then click Next.

The default lease time is eight days. If you have primarily mobile computers, you may want to reduce the lease times to free up more IP addresses when those computers aren't connected. For stable, desktop networks, longer leases are fine. In most cases, the default setting is best.

The Configure DHCP Options window appears. DHCP options allow you to specify additional IP addressing information that is returned to clients with an IP lease, such as the address of the default gateway, WINS, and DNS servers.

8. Click the Yes button to accept the default settings, and then click Next.

The Router (Default Gateway) window appears, as shown in Figure 3-5.

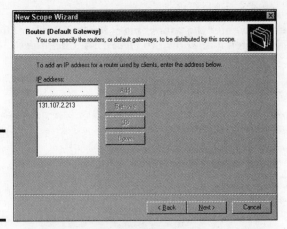

Figure 3-5:
The Router
(Default
Gateway)
window.

9. **Enter the IP address(es) of the routers for your subnet, if desired, and then click Next.**

The default gateway allows IP traffic to flow between different subnets. If you don't enter this information, client computers can still find the default gateway through broadcast packets, but network broadcast traffic can be reduced by providing the IP address.

The Domain Name and DNS Servers window opens, as shown in Figure 3-6.

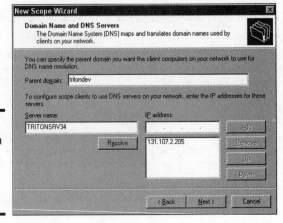

Figure 3-6:
The Domain
Name and
DNS
Servers
window.

10. **Enter the name of the parent domain and DNS server(s) name and IP addresses as desired. Use the Add button to enter the addresses that you provide, and then click Next.**

   The parent domain provides the name of the domain that clients use for DNS resolution, and the server names and IP addresses point the clients to appropriate servers.

   The WINS Servers window appears.

11. **Enter the server name(s) and IP address(es) of WINS servers on your network that you want sent to your client computers. Click the Add button to add the WINS servers to the list, and then click Next when you are done.**

   The Activate Scope window appears.

12. **Click the Yes button, and then click Next.**

13. **Click Finish to complete the wizard.**

Although the Scope Wizard helps you to configure the scope that you need, the DHCP manager also allows you to make changes to the scope easily. You can learn about these options in the "Managing Servers and Scopes" section later in this chapter.

After you complete the Scope Wizard, the scope is activated, but it still can't lease IP addresses to clients until the server is authorized by Active Directory. Watch out for tricky exam questions concerning this issue. You can learn how to authorize the server in the "Authorizing the DHCP Server" section later in this chapter.

Configuring a superscope

A network subnet has one scope in which IP addresses are leased to clients on that subnet from the scope. However, in some cases, you may need to extend the scope to provide additional IP addresses because of network growth. Instead of creating additional subnets with additional scopes, you can use a concept called *multinets*. A multinet allows you to combine several scopes so that they appear as one scope on an IP subnet. This scope combination is called a *superscope*. The multinet allows you to create logical IP subnets in which only one physical subnet exists. This is an administrative solution to extend the IP address range of a subnet without creating a new subnet.

You can easily configure a superscope in DHCP Manager, but as with all aspects of networking, you must first carefully plan in order to ensure that your multinet meets your administrative needs and ensures client connectivity. To create a superscope, follow the steps in Lab 3-3.

Lab 3-3	Creating a Superscope

1. **Open the DHCP Manager.**

2. **Select the server in the console for which you want to create a Superscope and then choose Action⇨New Superscope.**

   The New Superscope Wizard begins.

3. **Click Next on the Welcome screen.**

   The Superscope Name window appears.

4. **Enter the name of the superscope and then click Next.**

   The Select Scopes window opens.

5. **Select one or more scopes to add to the superscope and then click Next.**

6. **Click Finish to complete the wizard.**

Configuring a multicast scope

Multicasting is the process of sending multiple messages to network clients. In much the same way you can send an e-mail message to a group of people, multicasting allows a group of clients to appear as one client. Multicasting is used for a variety of purposes. For example, a multicast group can be configured so that a video conference is sent over the network to all members of the group. By using the multicast features in DHCP, the multicast IP address can be automatically assigned.

To accomplish multicasting, use a Class D IP address range that is reserved for multicasting purposes. The address range is 224.0.0.0 to 239.255.255.255, which you should remember for the exam. The Class D address allows you to use multicasting on your network without interfering with typical IP communication. In other words, multicast clients have a typical IP address appropriate for their subnet and they also have a multicast IP address.

Multicast DHCP (MDHCP) is an extension of the typical DHCP service, but they are still separate components. DHCP and MDHCP work together to dynamically assign multicast IP addresses to multicast clients. Each multicast client must have both a standard DHCP IP lease as well as a multicast IP address lease.

As with a typical DHCP scope or superscope, you can also configure a multicast scope if multicasting is in use on your network. Lab 3-4 shows you how to configure a multicast scope.

Lab 3-4   Creating a Multicast Scope

1. **Open the DHCP Manager.**

2. **Select the desired server where you want to create a multicast scope and then choose Action⇨New Multicast Scope.**

   The New Multicast Scope Wizard appears.

3. **Click Next on the Welcome Screen.**

4. **Enter a name for the multicast scope and a description, if desired, and then click Next.**

5. **Enter a valid IP address range for the multicast and, if you want, enter a Time to Live (TTL). Click Next.**

   The IP address must fall in the 224.0.0.0 to 239.255.255.255 range. The TTL is the number of routers that multicast traffic passes through on your network. The default is 32.

   The Add Exclusion window opens.

6. **Enter an exclusion range, if desired, by entering the starting and ending IP addresses of the exclusion range. Click the Add button to add the exclusion range to the list, and then click Next.**

   The Lease Duration window opens.

7. **Enter the desired multicast lease duration and then click Next.**

   The default is 30 days. Configure the lease duration depending on your multicast needs, based on the amount of time a multicast group may need to exist.

   The Activate Multicast Scope window appears.

8. **Click Yes to activate the multicast scope and then click Next.**

9. **Click Finish to complete the wizard.**

Authorizing the DHCP Server

After you have configured the desired scopes for your subnet, your next step is to authorize the DHCP server in Active Directory. DHCP servers can't lease IP addresses in Windows 2000 networks without being authorized. Keep this in mind for the exam!

In most cases, domain controllers that function as DHCP servers are automatically authorized by Active Directory, but member servers must be authorized manually. Watch out for tricky test questions on this issue — member servers must be manually authorized.

Authorization is a security precaution that ensures only authorized DHCP servers operate on the network. This prevents unauthorized, or "rogue" DHCP servers from coming online and issuing IP addresses. This security feature also prevents DHCP servers from "accidentally" coming online and leasing incorrect or inappropriate IP addresses to network clients. When a DHCP server is authorized by Active Directory, its IP address is added to a list of authorized servers. If an unauthorized server comes online, Active Directory can detect that the server isn't on the authorized list and shut it down. So, in order for a DHCP Server to lease IP address, it has to be authorized by Active Directory.

To authorize a DHCP server, follow the steps in Lab 3-5.

Lab 3-5   Authorizing a DHCP Server

1. **In the DHCP manager console, select the DHCP server that you want to authorize.**

2. **Choose Action⇨Authorize.**

    The authorization process may take a few moments.

3. **Choose Action⇨Refresh (or simply click F5) to refresh your server to see whether authorization has taken place.**

    If it has, the server object in the console appears with a green icon. The server can now lease IP addresses to clients.

Managing Servers and Scopes

After you have configured your desired scopes and authorized the member server with Active Directory, you can further configure the server or scope(s) in a number of ways. You can also use this information to manage the server and scopes as necessary. In general, DHCP doesn't need a lot of maintenance from network administrators, but the exam expects you to know about the following configuration issues.

Managing the DHCP server

You can manage the DHCP server by selecting it in the console and choosing an option from the Action menu. You have two major options:

✦ **Display Server Statistics:** Server statistics, as shown in Figure 3-7, give you statistical information about the server and provide information such as leases, releases, the percentage of the scope that is in use, and so forth. The Server Statistics option is a good way to gain quick information about the server's DHCP functions.

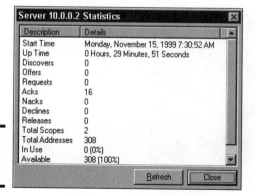

✦ **Properties:** You can also manage the server by accessing the server's properties, found on the Action menu. The Server Properties dialog box has three tabs: General, DNS, and Advanced. You can find out more about these tabs in the next few sections.

The General tab

The General tab features three check boxes that you can select or deselect:

✦ **Automatically Update Statistics:** You can change the statistics update time if desired. The default is every 10 minutes.

✦ **Enable DHCP Logging:** This option is selected by default and this feature writes a daily file that you can use to troubleshoot and monitor the DHCP service.

✦ **Show the BOOTP Table Folder:** You can enable this option so that you can see the BOOTP table folder if your network uses BOOTP clients. BOOTP clients are diskless workstations that obtain their IP addresses and boot programs from the server. BOOTP is an older technology solution that is supported in Windows 2000 for backward compatibility.

The DNS tab

On the DNS tab, you can make some selections about how the DHCP server interoperates with DNS. DNS and DHCP are integrated in Windows 2000, and because of the dynamic nature of Dynamic DNS, shown in Figure 3-8, DHCP can automatically update DNS when a client's IP address changes.

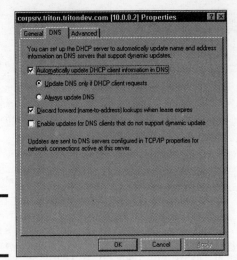

corpsrv.triton.tritondev.com [10.0.0.2] Properties

General | DNS | Advanced |

You can set up the DHCP server to automatically update name and address information on DNS servers that support dynamic updates.

☑ Automatically update DHCP client information in DNS

    ◉ Update DNS only if DHCP client requests

    ○ Always update DNS

☑ Discard forward (name-to-address) lookups when lease expires

☐ Enable updates for DNS clients that do not support dynamic update

Updates are sent to DNS servers configured in TCP/IP properties for network connections active at this server.

OK | Cancel | Apply

Figure 3-8:
Dynamic
DNS.

You can expect the exam to ask you some questions about this tab, so the following list details what you can configure. You should understand the importance of each, so you should memorize this list:

✦ **Automatically Update DHCP Client Information in DNS:** This option is selected by default and you should allow it to remain selected so DHCP can automatically update DNS. You have the options of updating DNS only if the DHCP client requests it (only Windows 2000 Professional clients can do this) or to always update DNS. The Update DNS Only if DHCP Client Requests option is selected by default.

✦ **Discard Forward (Name-to-Address) Lookups When Lease Expires:** This option is selected by default and allows the DHCP server to discard name-to-IP address lookups by the DNS server when the leases expire. This helps make certain that incorrect name-to-IP address information isn't returned to DNS.

✦ **Enable Updates for DNS Clients That Don't Support Dynamic Update:** This option is also selected by default. Previous, or down level, versions of Windows (such as NT and 9x) don't support dynamic updates, so the DHCP server can handle the updates with the DNS server when this option is selected. In pure Windows 2000 networks, this option isn't needed.

The Advanced tab

On the Advanced tab, you have a few configuration options. First, you can set conflict detection, if desired. Conflict detection allows the DHCP server to attempt to detect IP lease conflicts before leasing an IP address to a network client. Under normal circumstances, this option isn't needed, and if you choose to use conflict detection, the leasing negotiation between the server and client will operate more slowly.

You can also use the Advanced tab to change the audit log file and database paths, if desired. The default is C:\WINNT\System32\dhcp. You can also click the Bindings button to change the server network connection that communicates with network clients. This feature is useful for servers that have multiple Network Interface Cards (NIC).

Managing scopes

Just as you can manage the DHCP server, you have several options that enable you to manage the scope.

First, you can access the Properties dialog box for the scope just as you can for the server. Select the scope in the console and choose Action⇨Properties. The General tab of the Properties dialog box contains the scope name, starting and ending IP address, and the lease time. All of this information was configured when you created the scope, but you can easily change it as needed on the General tab. The DNS tab provides you the same tab as shown in the server properties, so refer to the previous section for more information. The Advanced tab contains three radio buttons; you can choose to assign IP addresses to DHCP clients only, BOOTP clients only, or to both. If you choose to lease IP addresses to BOOTP clients, you can set the lease duration for them on this tab as well.

You can also use the Action menu to delete or deactivate a scope. If you de-activate a scope, you can use the Action menu to reactivate it, but the scope won't be able to lease IP addresses to clients as long as it is deactivated.

If you expand the scope in the console tree, you see several subcontainers, as shown in Figure 3-9.

Book III
Chapter 3

Configuring
the Network
Infrastructure

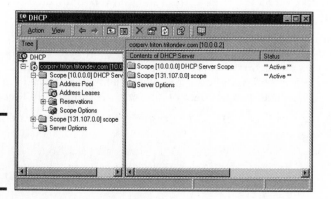

Figure 3-9:
DHCP
subcon-
tainers.

The following list tells you what you can do with each:

✦ **Address Pool:** If you click Address Pool, your current address pool appears in the details pane. If you choose Action➪Add Exclusion Range, you can add a new exclusion range, if desired.

✦ **Address Leases:** If you click Address Leases, a list of leased IP addresses and the clients who hold the leases appears in the details pane as well as the lease expiration dates.

✦ **Reservations:** If you click Reservations, a list of your current reservations appears in the details pane. You can add a new reservation by choosing Action➪New Reservation.

✦ **Scope Options:** If you click Scope Options, you can configure additional IP options for the scope. See the next section to find out more.

Configuring Scope Options

Scope Options are additional IP configuration information that you can have returned to clients when they lease an IP address. Just as you can have the IP addresses of the default gateways, WINS, and DNS servers returned to clients, you can also have a number of other server types and options returned. These options allow you to tailor DHCP to the needs of your network.

To configure Scope Options, follow the steps in Lab 3-6.

Lab 3-6   Configuring Scope Options

1. **In the DHCP console tree, expand the desired scope and select Scope Options.**

2. **Choose Action➪Configure Options.**

   The Scope Options page appears. It has a General and Advanced tab.

3. **On the General tab, you can browse through the list of available options, select the ones you want, and then enter the IP configuration information for those options.**

   For example, say a Cookie Server is in use on our network and we want that information returned to DHCP clients. We select the Cookie Servers check box, and then enter the server name and IP address in the bottom of the window. Now, when clients receive an IP address lease, the IP address of the Cookie Server is returned to them as well.

4. **On the Advanced tab, you can configure options for vendor and user classes.**

By default, standard DHCP options are selected for the vendor class, but you can access the drop-down menu and select Microsoft options, Windows 2000 options, or Windows 98 options. When you select a desired vendor class, a list of options appears that you can select to use. The same is true for the user class. A default user class is selected, but you can use the drop-down menu and select the BOOTP class or Routing and Remote Access Class. When you select a different class, a list of options appears that you can select for that class.

In most cases, the default settings are all you need for an effective DHCP implementation; however, you can configure different vendor and user classes to tailor your DHCP implementation to your network needs.

Enabling DHCP Clients

Windows 2000 Professional as well as down-level Windows clients (NT, 9*x*) can be DHCP clients in Windows 2000. To configure a client computer to act as a DHCP client, simply access the client's TCP/IP properties pages, and then select the Obtain an IP Address Automatically radio button. This option tells the client to contact a DHCP server for TCP/IP configuration at boot-up.

It is important to note that Windows 2000 Professional and Windows 98 client computers can autoconfigure themselves with a TCP/IP address if a DHCP server isn't available. If this occurs, the client continues to attempt to contact the DHCP server so that it can gain a leased IP address instead of using the one it has temporarily assigned itself. If autoconfiguration occurs, the clients use a reserved B class address in the 169.254.0.0 range with a subnet mask of 255.255.0.0. The client will test its autoconfigured IP address by using a "gratuitous ARP," which is broadcast using Address Resolution Protocol, to see if another client is using the address. If not, the client will use the address until it can reach the DHCP server. This entire process is transparent to end users who aren't aware of the client computer's DHCP configuration or autoconfiguration.

Configuring, Administering, and Troubleshooting DNS

Domain Name System (DNS) is an industry standard for resolving host names to IP addresses. DNS is integrated with Windows 2000 because DNS is widely used and is very extensible. This means the naming structure, or *namespace,* can grow as an organization grows with virtually no limits — it is used on the Internet, which hosts millions of computers.

DNS is fully integrated with Windows 2000 so that domains, such as `www.microsoft.com,` can also be the name of a local network. `KarenS@tritondev.com` is an e-mail address, but it can also be a user name in a Windows 2000 network. Windows 2000 networking with Active Directory is based on DNS and all Active Directory names are DNS names. This approach provides a global naming system so that the local network naming structure is the same as on the Internet. So, in short, you can't separate Windows 2000 and DNS.

Understanding DNS zones

DNS name resolution occurs by the use of DNS database files. Different servers in a network hold portions of the DNS database file so that name resolution can occur. In small networks, a DNS server may even hold the entire name to IP address database file. When a DNS server is queried for name resolution, it checks its database file to determine whether an entry for the query exists. If not, it can forward the request on to another DNS server.

To subdivide DNS duties and administrative control, DNS zones are often used in DNS networks. A *zone* is a discreet and contiguous portion of the DNS namespace. For example, `sales.tritondev.com` and `acct.tritondev.com` could be DNS zones. Servers in the sales zone hold all DNS records for the zone while DNS servers in the `acct.zone` hold all records for the `acct.zone`. This feature allows different administrators to manage DNS servers in different portions of the namespace. The zone feature is a way to partition the DNS namespace so that it is more manageable.

A zone contains two kinds of DNS database files: a primary database file and a secondary database file. One server in the zone contains the primary zone database file, and all other DNS servers in the zone contain copies of that primary database file, called *secondary zone database files*. Only the primary zone database file can have updates or changes made to it. Any changes made to the primary zone database file are replicated to the secondary zone database files through a process called *zone transfer*. The server that holds the primary zone database file is called an *authoritative server* because it has "authority" over the server DNS servers in the zone. Secondary database file servers in the zone are used to reduce the traffic and query load on the primary zone database server.

A final conceptual note about Windows 2000 DNS is Dynamic DNS (DDNS). In the past, DNS database files were static — they had to be manually changed by an administrator. In Windows 2000, DNS can dynamically update its database when host name-to-IP address changes occur.

Installing DNS

You install DNS just as you would any other Windows 2000 Server service. You can use either the Configure Your Server tool in Administrative Tools to install it, or you can use Add/Remove Programs in Control Panel.

DNS is automatically installed on domain controllers because DNS must be present for Active Directory. It is not automatically installed on member servers, however. Keep this point in mind for tricky exam questions.

Setting up DNS

After DNS is installed, it isn't operational until you set up the service. Fortunately, a handy wizard is provided to help you configure your DNS server for the role that you want it to play in your DNS network.

Lab 3-7 walks you through the wizard. You need to know what options are presented in the wizard for the exam, so make certain that you practice configuring DNS using Lab 3-7.

Lab 3-7   Setting Up DNS

1. **Click Start➪Programs➪Administrative Tools➪DNS.**

2. **In the Tree pane, select your DNS server and then choose Action➪Configure the Server.**

   The Configure DNS Server Wizard appears.

3. **Click Next on the Welcome screen.**

   The system collects setup information, and the Root Server window appears.

4. **A DNS network must have a root server. If this is the first DNS server on your network, select the appropriate radio button, and if other DNS servers are already running, select the appropriate radio button and enter an IP address.**

5. **If you chose to create a root server in Step 4, you are prompted for a decision concerning a forward lookup zone. Click either Yes or No to create it.**

   Forward lookup zone is a name-to-IP address database that helps computers resolve names-to-IP addresses and contains information about network services. You are encouraged to create the forward lookup zone now.

The Zone Type window appears next, as shown in Figure 3-10.

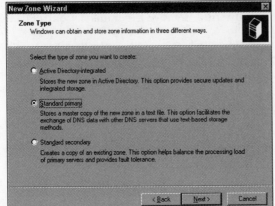

Figure 3-10:
Select the
Zone Type in
this window.

6. **You can choose to create an Active Directory integrated zone, standard primary zone, or standard secondary. Make your selection and click Next.**

   In pure Active Directory environments, the first option should be selected so that all zone and database data is stored in Active Directory. Selecting the Standard Primary option creates a new zone where the database is stored locally, and selecting Standard Secondary allows your server to become a secondary server in an existing zone.

   The Zone Name window appears.

7. **Enter the name of the zone and click Next.**

   The Zone File window opens.

8. **You can choose to either create a new zone database file or use one that you have copied from another computer. Make your selection by clicking the appropriate radio button, and then click Next.**

9. **You are next prompted to create a reverse lookup zone. Make your selection and click Next.**

   A reverse lookup zone allows a computer to resolve IP addresses to DNS names. Under normal circumstances, DNS names are resolved to IP addresses instead of in the reverse manner. You can choose to provide this or you can always create a reverse lookup zone later.

10. **If you chose to create a reverse lookup zone in Step 9, the Zone Type window appears. If you need to create a reverse lookup zone, enter the information to create the zone.**

    If you choose not to create a reverse lookup zone, a summary window appears.

11. **Review your selections and click Finish.**

Managing the DNS Server

After DNS is installed and configured, you have the task of managing the server so that it performs in a desired manner. The exam expects you to be able to perform several management tasks, so this section points out those issues and shows you how to manage the DNS Server.

To make this section easier to read, management tasks are broken into different subsections so that you can quickly review the various tasks.

Configuring server properties

To configure server properties, select your DNS server in the Tree pane and choose Action⇨Properties. The dialog box that appears contains seven tabs. You have a number of configuration options in the properties tabs, and you need to know about several of these for the exam.

Interfaces tab

On this tab, you can determine which IP addresses your DNS server listens to for DNS queries. The default is for your server to listen to all IP addresses, but you can select the Only the Following IP Addresses radio button and enter the desired IP addresses. This feature is useful if you want your DNS server to service only a select group of computers.

Forwarders tab

On this tab, you can click the check box to enable *forwarders*. Forwarders allow your DNS server to forward unresolved queries to other DNS servers that you specify on this tab. If your server is the root server, the option won't be available because your server is already at the top of the hierarchy.

Advanced tab

This tab, shown in Figure 3-11, presents you with several server options that you can select by clicking the appropriate check boxes.

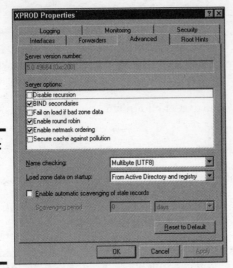

Figure 3-11:
Different
options
appear on
the server
properties
Advanced
tab.

By default, the BIND Secondaries, Enable Round Robin, and Enable Netmask Ordering check boxes are selected by default. You can also disable recursion, which prevents a DNS server from carrying the full responsibility for name-to-IP address resolution (allows forwarding). Besides this option, you can choose to Fail When the DNS Server Loads If Bad Zone Data is Detected, and you can use a cache method that prevents pollution from occurring.

Under Name Checking, you can use the following methods, which you should remember for the exam:

✦ **Strict RFC:** Strictly enforces the use of RFC-compliant rules for all DNS names. Non-RFC names are treated as errors.

✦ **Non-RFC:** Any names that aren't RFC-compliant can be used.

✦ **Multibyte:** Uses the Unicode 8-bit translation encoding scheme.

✦ **All Names:** Allows all names to be used with the DNS server.

You also choose how you want zone data to be loaded at startup. You have the option of using Active Directory and registry, registry, or from a file (Boot.dns in \WINNT\System32). Depending on your network configuration, you can make the appropriate selection.

Finally, you can also use this tab to enable automatic scavenging of stale records. This feature allows the server to automatically clean old records out of the database at an interval that you select on the tab. The default automatic scavenge interval is every seven days.

Root Hints tab

This tab contains DNS servers and IP addresses that can be used for query resolution. The Root Hints tab allows you to enter the names and IP addresses of other DNS servers that your server can contact for name resolution, or edit and remove them as necessary. This feature helps an authoritative zone server to find servers above it in the hierarchy.

Logging tab

This tab gives you the option to log a number of events, such as query, notify, update, and so forth, as shown in Figure 3-12.

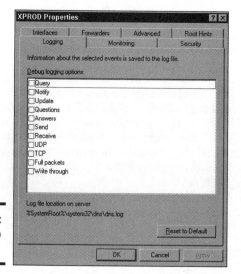

Book III
Chapter 3

Configuring
the Network
Infrastructure

Figure 3-12:
Logging tab
options.

The logging feature allows you to specify the kind of DNS activity that you want written to dns.log in %SystemRoot%\system32\dns. This feature is useful for troubleshooting purposes.

However, logging should only be enabled for monitoring particular problems or events. This feature consumes a lot of disk space and you may see performance problems on the server, so keep in mind that logging of DNS events is for troubleshooting *only*.

Monitoring and Security tabs

The Monitoring tab allows you to perform simple DNS tests against your server so that you can verify its configuration. The Security tab is like all others in Windows 2000 Server, where you can configure who can access and configure the DNS service on this server.

Managing the server's database

Aside from configuring the server's properties, you can also manually manage the server's DNS database and perform a few other actions by selecting the server in the Tree pane and choosing an option from the Action menu.

The following list reviews these options. You need to know these for the exam, so we recommend that you memorize this list:

✦ **New Zone:** This option launches the New Zone Wizard, which you use in Lab 3-7. You can use this feature to configure new zones as needed.

✦ **Set Aging/Scavenging for All Zones:** This option opens the Server Aging/Scavenging Properties dialog box, shown in Figure 3-13, where you can scavenge stale resource records. Scavenging is a server task that cleans old records out of the DNS database. You can configure the No-Refresh and Refresh intervals (both of which are seven days by default). The No-Refresh interval is the time between the most recent Refresh of a record timestamp and the moment when the timestamp may be refreshed again, and the Refresh interval is the time between the earliest moment when a record timestamp can be refreshed and when it can be scavenged.

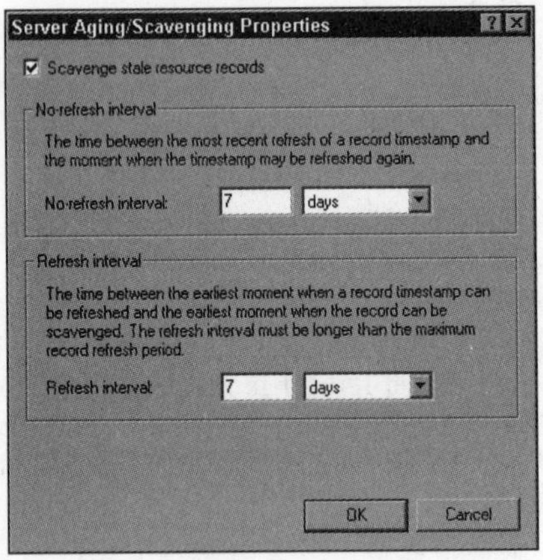

Figure 3-13: Use this Server Aging/Scavenging Properties dialog box to configure scavenging.

✦ **Scavenge Stale Resource Records:** This option allows you to manually scavenge the database. You don't need to perform this action because the database scavenges itself every seven days by default, but you can use it if you believe the database has old records that need to be cleaned.

✦ **Update Server Data Files:** Data files are normally updated at predefined intervals and when the server is shut down. You can manually force the action by choosing this option from the Action menu, which causes the DNS service to write all changes to the zone data files immediately.

Managing Zone Resource Records

Each zone database file contains any number of resource records. A *resource record* is simply an entry in the database — a record that helps the DNS server resolve queries.

When a new zone is created, two default resource records are automatically created. The first is the Start of Authority (SOA), which defines the authoritative server for the zone. The second is the Name Server (NS) record, which lists all DNS servers operating in the zone. Keep these in mind for the exam.

Aside from the SOA and NS records, you can create several other records. You can easily create these records by expanding the DNS server in the Tree pane and selecting the appropriate zone, and then clicking the Action menu.

Table 3-2 explains the major resource records that you can create, which are the ones you need to know for the exam. We have put them in a table format so that you can easily memorize them.

Book III
Chapter 3

Configuring
the Network
Infrastructure

Table 3-2	Zone Resource Records
Resource Record	*Explanation*
Host (A)	An A record provides a host-to-IP address mapping for a forward lookup zone.
Pointer (PTR)	A PTR record is created with an A record, and it points to another portion of the namespace where you can map an IP address to a host name.
Alias (CNAME)	A CNAME (Canonical Name) record allows a host to have a different name. CNAME records are often used for load-balancing purposes and contain a host's alias as well as the fully qualified domain name. CNAME records can be used to group DNS servers so that they appear as one server.
Mail exchanger (MX)	An MX record identifies a mail server with a particular host or domain.

Aside from these standard resource records, you can also choose Action⇨ Other New Records to create specific records for your environment. When you use this option, you are presented with a list of possible records that you can create; you can even create custom records.

Managing Zone Properties

You can access the Properties dialog box for each zone by expanding the zone in the Tree pane, selecting the desired zone, and choosing Action⇨Properties. You need to know what is available on each tab and the configuration options available, so study the following list carefully:

✦ **General tab:** This tab lists the status of the zone (such as running or paused) and the type of zone (primary, secondary, and so forth). If you click the Change button, you are presented with the Zone Type window described in "Setting up DNS," previously in this chapter. You can change the zone type to either Active Directory integrated, primary, or secondary as necessary.

The Allow Dynamic Updates drop-down menu allows you to select Yes or No. A big feature of Windows 2000 is dynamic DNS (DDNS), which allows the server to dynamically update records within a zone when they change (such as DHCP IP address lease changes). This feature should be enabled so that dynamic updates can occur.

✦ **SOA and NS tabs:** These tabs provide the resource records for the Start of Authority and Name Server records. These are configured automatically when you create a new zone, but you can make changes as needed by using these two tabs.

✦ **WINS tab:** This tab allows you to use WINS to resolve name-to-IP address mappings that DNS can't resolve.

This is a useful feature in networks that contain down-level clients and servers (such as NT, 9*x*, and so forth). Typically, you don't need this feature if your network is a pure Windows 2000 network.

✦ **Zone Transfers tab:** This tab allows you to enable zone transfer to occur (which is enabled by default). You can specify that zone transfers be sent to any server in the zone or only to servers that you specify.

Troubleshooting Name Resolution on Client Computers

Name resolution in Windows 2000 networks is primarily performed by DNS. In earlier Windows networks, name resolution was performed by Windows Internet Name Services, or WINS. WINS uses NetBIOS names, whereas DNS uses host names. The problem with WINS is that it didn't scale well in large environments, one of the main reasons for the shift to DNS in Windows 2000.

However, most networks don't have the luxury of immediately upgrading to a pure Windows 2000 environment. Because of this financial fact, you are likely to face managing a number of different client computers on the network, such as a mixture of Windows 2000 computers and down-level computers, such as Windows 9x and Me.

Name resolution tools

You can use a few command line tools to help solve name resolution problems on your network. When clients can't resolve a host or NetBIOS name to an IP address, or vice versa, you may need to use these tools to troubleshoot the problem. At the very least, you should memorize the following tools and get some hands-on experience with them before taking the exam:

✦ **Nbtstat:** Nbtstat, or NetBIOS Statistics, is a command line tool that lets you manage NetBIOS statistics on a computer using NetBIOS. You can view the NetBIOS cache, list names, and even reload the cache. If you type **Nbtstat** at the command line, you can see a list of available switches. For the exam, keep in mind the –RR switch, which sends a name release packet to a WINS server, and then refreshes. If a particular client computer seems to be having name resolution problems, this switch is a good one to use.

✦ **Nslookup:** Nslookup is a DNS tool that allows you to look up name-to-IP address mappings on a particular DNS server. This tool is useful if you want to test the service and accuracy of a DNS server.

✦ **NetDiag:** NetDiag is a utility that helps to isolate networking problems and connectivity problems by performing a series of tests to see whether the network client is functional. This test can also help to identify name resolution problems.

Creating and configuring hosts and lmhosts files

In the event that you need to use static mappings for NetBIOS or DNS clients, you can use any lmhosts file or host file, respectively. Lmhosts and hosts files are text files that contain static mappings for name resolution. Lmhosts files resolve NetBIOS names to IP addresses, and hosts files resolve host, or DNS names, to IP addresses. Under most circumstances, you will allow WINS or DNS to handle this automatically, but in some cases, you may need to use a static mapping.

The exam expects you to know what these files are and when you may use them; otherwise, they are primarily used to resolve special name resolution problems. The problem, of course, is that hosts and lmhosts files are static files — they must be manually created and manually updated, so as a networking solution, they are very ineffective. However, if a client is having problems resolving a certain server with a static IP address, a hosts or lmhosts file can be used to speed up name resolution. For example, think of these files as a last resort to solving name resolution problems that should otherwise be corrected in DNS or WINS.

Prep Test

1 A certain computer on your network is having problems connecting to other network hosts. You want to test the computer's NIC to make sure it is functioning properly. Which test would be best to use?

A ○ PING 127.0.0.1

B ○ Tracert

C ○ Ipconfig

D ○ Netstat

2 You want to perform a test on a network host at a remote location. There are several routers between the host and your computer, and connectivity to the host is slow. You want to see which router is dropping the most packets in order to determine the network bottleneck. What test should you use?

A ○ PING

B ○ Tracert

C ○ PathPING

D ○ Route

3 A certain Windows 2000 Professional computer should be getting an IP address lease from DHCP. However, the computer is configured with a static IP address. You want to make certain that the computer uses DHCP. You access the TCP/IP properties page. What should you do?

A ○ Select the Use DHCP option.

B ○ Select the Obtain an IP Address Automatically option.

C ○ C Remove the IP address.

D ○ Change the subnet mask to 255.254.0.0.

4 You want to group several scopes together that exist on one physical IP subnet. What kind of scope is this called?

A ○ Multicast

B ○ Superscope

C ○ Address pool

D ○ Reservation

5 On your network, DHCP is used. Four member servers need to have static IP addresses configured. You need to make certain that these static IP addresses are not leased to client computers on the network because this would cause an IP address conflict. What do you need to do?

A ○ Use multicast addresses.

B ○ Use a different subnet mask on the servers.

C ○ Create a reservation.

D ○ Create an address pool.

6 You install DHCP on a new member server, but after the installation, the server is unable to provide IP addresses on the network. What do you need to do?

A ○ Configure a multicast scope.

B ○ Create a multinet.

C ○ Change the IP address of the server.

D ○ Authorize the server.

7 What process is used to update secondary zone database files from changes made to the primary zone database file?

A ○ Zone transfer

B ○ Replication

C ○ Update

D ○ DNS rollover

8 When a new DNS zone is created in Windows 2000, what two records are created by default? (Choose two.)

A ❑ SOA

B ❑ CNAME

C ❑ RR

D ❑ NS

9 You need to create a DNS record so that several DNS servers act as one server in a round-robin fashion for load-balancing purposes. What kind of record do you need to create?

A ○ PTR

B ○ CNAME

C ○ MX

D ○ A

10 **You need to create several static mappings for a WINS client. What kind of file do you need to create?**

A ○ Lmhosts

B ○ Hosts

C ○ CNAME

D ○ RR

Answers

1 **A.** Use the PING command to test network connectivity against other hosts as well as the local computer. *Review "Troubleshooting Routing."*

2 **C.** PathPING gives you information about dropped packets at each router. *Read "Troubleshooting Routing."*

3 **B.** This option will have the computer request an IP address from a DHCP server. *Review "Configuring and Troubleshooting TCP/IP on Servers and Client Computers."*

4 **B.** A superscope contains several scopes within the same IP subnet. *See "Configuring a superscope."*

5 **C.** If you need to use some static IP addresses, create a reservation with those addresses so that DHCP doesn't lease them. *Study "Managing scopes."*

6 **D.** DHCP servers must be authorized by Active Directory before they can lease IP addresses. *See "Creating and Configuring DHCP Scopes."*

7 **A.** Zone transfers are used to update secondary zone database files from the primary zone database file. *Study "Understanding DNS zones."*

8 **A and D.** The Start of Authority and Name Server records are created by default. *Study "Managing Zone Resource Records."*

9 **B.** A CNAME record is an alias record used for load-balancing purposes. *See "Managing Zone Resource Records."*

10 **A.** An lmhosts file contains static NetBIOS-to-IP address mappings. *Study "Creating and configuring hosts and lmhosts files."*

Chapter 4: Managing and Securing Servers and Client Computers

Exam Objectives

✔ Installing and configuring server and client computer hardware

✔ Configuring an operating system for legacy hardware devices

✔ Troubleshooting starting servers and client computers

✔ Monitoring and troubleshooting server health and performance

✔ Installing and managing Windows 2000 updates

In any network administration job, a large portion of your daily tasks will consist of simply managing and solving problems on client and server computers. The tasks that you will face can range from the simple and mundane to the very complex.

Obviously, we can't possibly explore every potential task that you may encounter, but the network administration exam targets a few exam objectives under the category of managing and troubleshooting client and server computers. In this chapter, we take a look at these exam objectives, and you can expect to find out about

✦ Managing computer hardware

✦ Troubleshooting startup

✦ Managing performance

✦ Applying updates

Installing and Configuring Server and Client Hardware

If you have previously taken your Windows 2000 Professional and Server exams, you are essentially ready to take this exam in terms of the server and client hardware management. In other words, this exam contains no new information from that which you encountered on the previous exams. In fact, you've probably noticed a lot of repetitive exam objectives, which is why it's helpful to take the Professional and Server exams first.

If you haven't yet taken your Professional or Server exams, we encourage you to study Book I, Chapter 4, or Book II, Chapter 4, because both of these chapters are devoted to hardware configuration and management.

Configuring the Operating System for Legacy Hardware Devices

Legacy hardware devices are devices that aren't directly compatible with Windows 2000 or aren't Plug and Play-compliant. Obviously, at this late date, not too many hardware devices are in use that aren't Plug and Play, as this standard first emerged onto the scene in Windows 95.

However, for some reason, the exam wants you to know about using legacy devices on Windows 2000. Simply put, if you must use a legacy device on a Windows 2000 computer, follow these simple steps for device installation:

1. Manually install the legacy device to the correct port or slot.

2. Start Windows 2000. If Windows 2000 doesn't detect the device, use Add/Remove Programs in Control Panel to manually install the device. You may need to provide a driver.

3. Check the manufacturer's Web site for updated driver information and try to use the latest driver available. You are more likely to have better luck by using the latest driver.

4. After the device is installed, use Device Manager. You may have to adjust IRQ and resource settings if the device is conflicting with another existing device on your computer. See Book II, Chapter 4 to learn more about Device Manager.

Keep in mind that no surefire approaches exist to using legacy hardware. Your best solution is to locate the newest driver possible for the device, and to use Device Manager to adjust any IRQ or resource settings that seem to conflict.

Troubleshooting Starting Servers and Client Computers

The network administration exam expects you to know a few things about starting server and client computers that are giving you problems. In the event that a server or client operating system won't start, you have a few options that can help you get a Windows 2000 Server or Windows 2000 Professional operating system started. Because both Windows 2000 versions work in the same way concerning startup, the following sections apply to both versions.

Using safe mode

Safe mode is probably your easiest and most used method for starting a computer that won't start. For example, suppose that you install a new video card. On reboot, the screen is completely garbled and the computer is useless. What do you do? Boot into safe mode and replace the driver.

In order to access safe mode, hold down the F8 key when you start the computer. A boot menu with several safe mode options appears. Aside from the basic safe mode, you need to know some additional boot options for the exam:

✦ **Enable Boot Logging:** This option logs the loading and initialization of drivers and services. You can then inspect the boot log, called Ntbtlog.txt, found in C:\Winnt, and look for a service or driver that may be causing the problem.

✦ **Enable VGA Mode:** You can use this option when your video driver goes haywire. This option boots Windows 2000 in the normal manner, but a basic VGA driver is used for the display instead of the current driver.

✦ **Last Known Good Configuration:** This option starts Windows 2000 using the registry information Windows 2000 saved when the computer was shut down.

✦ **Debugging Mode and Directory Services Restore Mode:** Found on Windows 2000 Server only, Debugging Mode provides programming code troubleshooting while Directory Services Restore Mode is used for Active Directory restore.

Using the Recovery Console

The Recovery Console is a Windows 2000 command line tool that can help you repair an installation of Windows 2000. You can stop and start services, format disks, and even read and write data on NTFS drives. You can install the Recovery Console from the Windows 2000 installation CD. As you can imagine, the Recovery Console is a very powerful tool, but you need to get some hands-on practice in order to learn all of the commands. Fortunately, the exam expects you to simply have an awareness of the Recovery Console, not how to run it.

For the exam, remember that the Recovery Console gives you a way to repair a Windows 2000 installation that won't start, and if you are unable to use safe mode, the Recovery Console is your next best bet.

Book III
Chapter 4

Managing and
Securing Servers
and Client
Computers

Using a parallel installation

The exam objectives make mention of a parallel installation. A *parallel installation* simply uses two different partitions of the hard disk where Windows 2000 is stored on each. If one installation won't start, you can start from the other installation, which appears as a boot menu option each time you start up. You can then copy necessary files from the good installation to repair the failed installation. Of course, this method consumes a lot of disk space because you essentially have two drives that contain the same data, but keep this one in mind for the exam.

Recovering data from backup

In the event that you can't restart a Windows 2000 computer, or the data on the disk has been corrupted, you can recover data from Windows 2000 backup, assuming you have a backup plan in place. You can learn more about backup and recovery in Book II, Chapter 5.

Monitoring and Troubleshooting Server Health and Performance

As a network administrator in a Windows 2000 environment, you need to monitor your servers and consider how well those servers are performing in your network environment. To accomplish this, Windows 2000 provides you with some important tools. You should get some hands-on practice using these tools, which we describe in the following sections.

Using Event Viewer

Event Viewer is an easy-to-use Windows 2000 tool that gives you information about system events. Event Viewer is available in the Computer Management console, found in Administrative Tools in Control Panel. When you access Event Viewer, you see different log categories, such as Application, Security, and System. Just double-click an event to learn more about the problem or issue.

Using Performance Monitor

Like most other tools in Windows 2000, Performance Monitor is now an MMC snap-in and functions in the same manner as all other snap-ins. This streamlined approach to Windows 2000 tools should make any learning curve you need to master much easier.

To access Performance Monitor, choose Start➪Programs➪Administrative Tools➪Performance. The Performance Monitor snap-in appears, as shown in Figure 4-1.

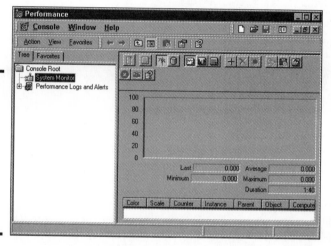

Figure 4-1: The Perform-ance Monitor snap-in is used to monitor system processes.

You have two basic options when you use Performance Monitor:

✦ You can create charts for the System Monitor.

✦ You can generate logs and alerts.

Notice in Figure 4-1 that both of these options are available under the console root.

System Monitor

The System Monitor portion of Performance Monitor is your tool to monitor processes that are occurring on your system. You create this monitor by creating a chart of system processes you want to monitor. You do this by adding *counters*. Lab 4-1 details this process.

Lab 4-1   Creating Performance Charts

1. **In the Performance Monitor, select System Monitor in the console tree.**

2. **Click the Add icon button above the chart in the right console pane (shown as a "+" sign).**

   The Add Counters dialog box appears, shown in Figure 4-2.

Book III Chapter 4

Managing and Securing Servers and Client Computers

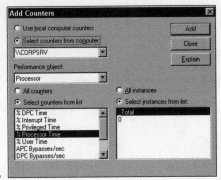

Figure 4-2:
Use the Add
Counters
dialog box
to create
perform-
ance charts.

3. **Select the computer that you want to monitor.**

4. **Select the performance object and either all counters for that object or selected counters.**

   Performance objects include processors, systems, memory, paging files, physical disks, and many others. For each object, you select different counters that you want to monitor for that object.

   See the "Reviewing important counters" section later in this chapter to review specific counters you need to know for the exam.

5. **After you add the desired counters for the desired object, close the Add Counters dialog box.**

   You then see the charting process taking place, as shown in Figure 4-3. Notice that each counter is assigned a different color so that you can easily track each counter.

Figure 4-3:
Added
counters
are charted
in the
Perform-
ance
Monitor
dialog box.

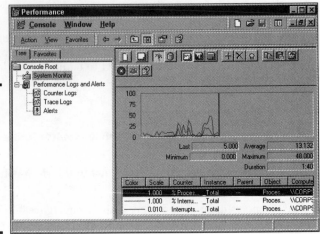

Using the buttons on the toolbar, you can also choose to view the counters in a histogram or report form instead of a chart.

Performance logs and performance alerts

Aside from creating counter charts that you can view, you can also create performance logs and configure performance alerts. Follow the steps in Lab 4-2 to create a performance log.

Lab 4-2   Creating Performance Logs

1. **In the Performance Monitor, expand Performance Logs and Alerts in the console tree. Then right-click counter logs or trace logs, depending on what log you want to create.**

    Counter log files log activity for counters you specify, and trace logs are designed to "trace" certain activity, such as I/O or page faults. You do need a tool to parse trace logs so that you can extract the data you need (this is a developmental task).

2. **Choose New Log Settings and then enter a new log name.**

    The Properties dialog box appears.

3. **Create the log file as desired. You can configure the log (either add counters or trace providers) and configure a schedule for the logs to run.**

    By default, all log files are stored in C:\PerfLogs.

In a similar manner, you can create alerts. *Alerts* are used so that administrators can be contacted when particular system resources or processes reach a threshold value. Follow the steps in Lab 4-3.

Lab 4-3   Creating Alerts

1. **In the Performance Monitor, right-click Alerts under Performance Logs and Alerts.**

2. **Choose New Alert Settings and then provide a name for the new settings.**

    The Properties dialog box appears.

3. **On the General tab, you can add a counter and then assign a value limit when an alert will be generated.**

4. **On the Action tab, you can determine what action should be taken when the value limit is triggered.**

    Your options are log an entry in the application event log, send a network message, start performance data log, or run a particular program.

**Book III
Chapter 4**

**Managing and
Securing Servers
and Client
Computers**

Reviewing important counters

For the exam, you need to know the major performance counters. Exam questions may present a particular problem and ask you which performance counters should be used to attempt to find the problem. In the following sections, we examine several counter objects and the counters for those objects that you need to know for the exam. You need to memorize all of these, so study carefully.

Memory

System memory is a very important part of system performance. Without enough system memory, excessive *paging* occurs. Paging is the process of temporarily writing blocks of data to the hard disk when not enough RAM is available to keep the data in memory. As system resources call for the paged information, the data is read from the hard disk back into memory. Paging is an important part of Windows 2000 and you can expect it to occur, but if excessive paging is occurring, your system responsiveness will slow, an indicator to you that you need more RAM.

You can use Performance Monitor to track system memory performance by choosing the memory object and using the following counters, which you need to know for the exam:

✦ **Memory \ Available Bytes and Memory \ Cached Bytes:** Use these counters to examine memory usage on your system.

✦ **Memory \Pages/sec, Memory \Page Reads/sec, Memory \ Transition Faults/sec, and Memory \Pool Paged Bytes:** Use these counters to examine memory bottlenecks.

Processor

Your system processor manages all system processing and threads. It is very common in networking environments for the demands of the network to outgrow the processing power of your system processor. In many cases, you will see an overall system slow-down and a slow-down in services that meet the needs of network clients. If this is occurring, you can either reduce the load on the server or upgrade to a higher processor.

You can use Performance Monitor to examine the activity of your system processor. You specifically need to know the following counters for the exam:

✦ **Processor\ % Processor Time:** Use this counter to examine the processor usage. A consistently high % Processor Time reading tells you that your processor is overworked and can't keep up with the demand placed on it.

✦ **Processor\ Processor Queue Length, Processor\ Interrupts/sec, System\ Processor Queue Length, and System\ Context switches/sec:** All of these counters can be used to examine the system processor and determine whether it has become a bottleneck.

Disk

Your hard disk is automatically a Windows 2000 Performance Monitor object, and you can use Performance Monitor to examine its performance.

It is important to note for the exam that logical disk counter data isn't collected by Windows 2000 by default. If you want to get performance data for logical drives for storage volumes, you have to use the diskperf -yv command at the command line.

Keep the following disk counters in mind for the exam:

✦ **Physical Disk\ Dis Reads/sec, Physical Disk\ Disk Writes/sec, LogicalDisk\ % Free Space:** Use these counters to examine disk usage.

✦ **Physical Disk\ Avg. Disk Queue Length:** Use this counter to determine if your disk has become a bottleneck.

Configuring performance options

Aside from using Performance Monitor to manage your system performance, you can also access the Advanced tab of System Properties to make further configuration choices. Just follow the steps in Lab 4-4.

Book III
Chapter 4

Managing and
Securing Servers
and Client
Computers

Lab 4-4	**Configuring Performance Options in System Properties**

1. **Right-click My Computer and choose Properties.**

2. **Click the Advanced tab and then click the Performance Options button.**

   The Performance Options dialog box appears.

3. **Choose to optimize system performance for either applications or background services.**

   By default, background services is selected. This allows your system to provide more priority to background services than to applications that may be running. Select the radio button to change this so that applications have priority, but this may slow down background processes.

4. **If you want to make changes to your Total paging file size, click the Change button and then make your changes in the dialog box that appears.**

The minimum paging file size is 2MB and the recommended size is 1.5 times the amount of RAM on your system. Your paging file is automatically set to the recommended setting, but you can change it if desired.

Windows does a good job of managing its own paging file. If you reduce or increase the paging file too much, you may experience system performance problems. Generally, this is a setting that you shouldn't change.

Using Task Manager

Another important tool that allows you to manage system processes and performance is Task Manager. You can access Task Manager by right-clicking on an empty area of the taskbar and clicking Task Manager.

The Task Manager has three tabs:

✦ **Applications:** On this tab, a list of running applications appears. You can select any running application and use the End Task, Switch To, or New Task buttons. This tab is typically used to end a malfunctioning application.

✦ **Processes:** On this tab, a list of all processes running on your system is presented. You can select any process and click the End Process button to stop the process from running. This feature is also useful in troubleshooting system problems that you believe are caused by a system process.

✦ **Performance:** This tab shows the percentage amount of CPU usage and Memory usage. This tab is useful to see how much CPU or Memory resources are currently in use and if there appears to be a bottleneck with either.

Using System Information

If you ever took a peek at Windows 98, you may be familiar with the Microsoft Information tool (MSINFO) that was first introduced with that operating system. All Windows 2000 operating systems also include MSINFO, and it can be an excellent tool to gain information about your system and troubleshoot problems.

To access System Information, choose Start⇨Accessories⇨System Tool⇨ System Information, or choose Start⇨Run, and then type **MSINFO32** and click OK.

System Information, shown in Figure 4-4, provides an MMC snap-in interface with categories for System Summary, Hardware Resources, Components, Software Environment, and Internet Explorer.

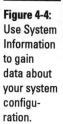

Figure 4-4: Use System Information to gain data about your system configuration.

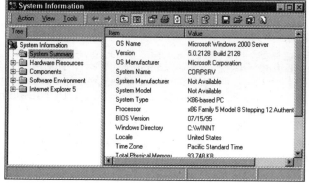

For the exam, all you need to know is what information is available in each category. You don't have to worry about many exam questions on System Information, so we have put the information about each category in the following list so you can easily memorize it.

✦ **Hardware Resources:** Contains categories so that you can check your system's IRQ usage, DMA allocation, memory resources, forced hardware, I/O configuration, and any conflicts/sharing that exist on your system.

✦ **Components:** This container holds information about your system components, such as multimedia, display, network connections, modems, printing, and so forth. This container also has a category for Problem Devices so that you can determine the solutions to problems that you may be experiencing with system components.

✦ **Software Environment:** This container holds information about your system software configuration, such as drivers, environment variables, network connections, running tasks, services, and so forth.

✦ **Internet Explorer 5:** This container holds your current settings for IE 5, which includes file versions, connectivity, cache, content, and security.

Optimizing Disk Performance

Windows 2000 Server contains several tools to help you optimize your disk performance. These tools are easy to use and are a vital part of managing your Windows 2000 Server. You access some of the tools by choosing

Book III
Chapter 4

**Managing and
Securing Servers
and Client
Computers**

Start⇨Accessories⇨System Tools, and you can access all of them by accessing the Tools menu in System Information. (Refer to the preceding section for more on System Information.)

You don't have to worry about excessive questions about these tools, but you do need to know what each tool can do and when you should use each tool. We have put this information in the following list so that you can easily memorize it.

✦ **Disk Cleanup:** Disk Cleanup is a handy utility that you can use to clean out old files on your hard disk in order to free up more storage space. Of course, you can delete these files manually, but Disk Cleanup provides you a quick and easy way to perform the task because Disk Cleanup finds the files that you may want to delete. When you launch Disk Cleanup, the program scans your system and presents you with a list of files that you can choose to delete, such as cached Internet files and other files that are no longer in use.

✦ **Dr. Watson:** Dr. Watson is a program error debugger that you may have seen in previous versions of Windows. Dr. Watson logs program errors that can be used to diagnose and solve system problems. Dr. Watson logs errors in a text file called Drwtsn32.log whenever an error is detected. Dr. Watson is primarily used to log errors that can then be sent to support personnel for analysis.

✦ **Disk Defragmenter:** Disk Defragmenter is now available in Windows 2000 as an MMC snap-in. Over time, as you create, change, and delete files, information on your hard disk can become *fragmented*. This means that data is stored in a noncontiguous manner. Pieces of files are stored in any available location on your hard disk, which causes the system to run slower when reading those files from the disk. Disk Defragmenter reorganizes your hard disk data so it is stored in a contiguous manner. If your system seems slow when reading data from the hard disk, you may need to run this utility.

Installing and Managing Windows 2000 Updates

From time to time, Microsoft releases service packs for operating systems. Service packs contain fixes for Windows 2000 as well as updates. Service packs are typically installed from CD, download, or from a network share. In the same manner, Microsoft sometimes releases hot fixes. A hot fix repairs some portion of Windows 2000, correcting some problem. For example, if a security hole is discovered, a hot fix is generally released, which can be installed in order to fix the security hole.

From an exam point of view, the only thing that you really need to remember about Windows 2000 updates is the concept of *slipstreaming*. Suppose that you need to install 1,000 Windows 2000 Professional computers, and you want to apply the latest service pack at the time of installation. You can use the service pack with the Windows 2000 distribution files for network installations in a process called slipstreaming. To run a slipstream deployment, follow these steps:

1. Obtain the service pack.

2. Extract the service pack files from the installation package. To do this, run the executable at the command prompt with the –x switch, as in w2ksp3.exe –x. You are then prompted to choose a directory to which the files can be extracted.

3. Choose the distribution folder to place the files into. This action slipstreams the update files with the original installation files for Windows 2000.

Book III
Chapter 4

Managing and
Securing Servers
and Client
Computers

Prep Test

1 You install a new camera on a Windows 2000 computer. After the installation, the camera does not work. What is most likely causing the problem?

    A ○ The connection

    B ○ The driver

    C ○ The camera software

    D ○ The registry

2 You are having problems installing a Plug and Play device. You have a disk containing the driver. What is the easiest way to install the device?

    A ○ Add/Remove Programs.

    B ○ Add/Remove Hardware.

    C ○ Run the driver exe.

    D ○ Manually load the driver into `C:\Winnt`.

3 You need to install a non-Plug and Play device on Windows 2000. You have the latest driver. What do you need to do?

    A ○ Install it as a USB device and install the driver.

    B ○ Use Add/Remove Hardware to install the device and driver.

    C ○ Load the driver into `C:\Winnt` and then physically connect the device.

    D ○ Boot into safe mode and run the DRVUPDATE command.

4 You install a new video driver. After reboot, the screen is garbled. You need to restart the computer as fast as possible. What should you do?

    A ○ Boot into VGA mode.

    B ○ Boot into Debugging mode.

    C ○ Reinstall a new driver.

    D ○ Use the Recovery Console.

5 A Windows 2000 Server computer has failed to start. You need to access the computer's disk and copy some critical files from the hard disk. You can't wait for the server to be repaired. What can you do?

    A ○ Use safe mode.

    B ○ Use the Recovery Console.

    C ○ Use debugging mode.

    D ○ Run the UPDATE command.

6 You want to use two partitions on your hard disk and install duplicate copies of Windows 2000 Server. What kind of installation is this called?

A ○ Parallel

B ○ Duplicate

C ○ Fault Tolerant

D ○ RIS

7 On a Windows 2000 Server computer, you want to monitor counters to determine whether the server has enough RAM installed. What is one counter that you could monitor?

A ○ Memory Pages/sec

B ○ Processor % Processor Time

C ○ Physical Disk Avg Disk Queue Length

D ○ Terminal Services connections

8 You want to easily see the current CPU usage and Memory usage on a Windows 2000 Server. What tool is the easiest to use?

A ○ Performance

B ○ MSINFO

C ○ Task Manager

D ○ Event Viewer

9 What tool can be used to log system errors and program errors?

A ○ MSINFO32

B ○ Dr. Watson

C ○ Performance

D ○ Task Manager

10 You need to extract the service pack files from an executable in order to slip-stream them into a Windows 2000 distribution folder. What switch can you use to extract the files?

A ○ -r

B ○ -z

C ○ -x

D ○ -n

Answers

1 **B.** Hardware devices must have a compatible driver. *Review "Installing and Configuring Server and Client Hardware."*

2 **B.** The Add/Remove Hardware Wizard can help you install problematic devices. *Read "Installing and Configuring Server and Client Hardware."*

3 **B.** Use Add/Remove Programs to install non-Plug and Play devices and drivers. *Review "Configuring the Operating System for Legacy Hardware Devices."*

4 **A.** VGA mode boots the computer normally, except a basic VGA driver is used instead of the current driver. *See "Using safe mode."*

5 **B.** The Recovery Console allows you to read the hard disk on a computer. *Study "Using the Recovery Console."*

6 **A.** Parallel installations contain duplicate operating system copies on different partitions. *See "Using a parallel installation."*

7 **A.** You can use the Memory object and examine pages/sec to determine whether the system is having to page a lot of data. *Study "Memory."*

8 **C.** Use Task Manager's Performance tab to view this information. *Study "Using Task Manager."*

9 **B.** Use Dr. Watson to log system and program errors. *See "Optimizing Disk Performance."*

10 **C.** Use the –x switch to extract the files for slipstreaming. *Study "Installing and Managing Windows 2000 Updates."*

Chapter 5: Managing Active Directory Organizational Units and Group Policy

Exam Objectives

✔ Creating, managing, and troubleshooting user and group objects in Active Directory

✔ Managing objects and container permissions

✔ Diagnosing Active Directory replication problems

✔ Deploying software by using Group Policy

*A*ctive Directory is Windows 2000's storehouse of information. You find all user accounts, group accounts, computer accounts, and shared resources in Active Directory. Active Directory provides a streamlining effect for the network, makes the network easier to use, and makes resources more readily available to network users. From an administration standpoint, Active Directory is your one-stop location to configure and troubleshoot many items in a Windows 2000 network.

In this chapter, you read about Active Directory management. As you might imagine, management of Active Directory is an entire book in and of itself, but because our main goal here is to prepare for the network management exam, we limit our discussion to the exam issues that you are most likely to run across. Let us also mention that your hands-on practice with Active Directory is extremely important. In this chapter, you find out about

+ Managing users, groups, and Organizational Units (OUs)

+ Managing permissions

+ Troubleshooting replication problems

+ Using Group Policy

+ Managing software with Group Policy

Creating and Managing User and Group Objects in Active Directory

All user and group accounts are configured in Active Directory and are referred to as *objects*. As a network administrator, you'll spend quite a bit of time setting up and managing group accounts in Windows 2000. The exam expects you to be able to manage these tasks and will ask you some questions so that you can prove your proficiency. The following sections examine the issues you are most likely to see.

Creating and configuring accounts for new and existing users

All user and computer accounts are created in Active Directory, and the creation of these objects is rather easy and quick. The main factor to keep in mind for the exam is where to create them. For your domain, you are likely to have default containers where user and computer accounts reside. However, your domain may also use Organizational Units (OUs) to store different user and computer accounts. The point is that you can store a user or computer account in a variety of locations in Active Directory, and most environments use either the default container or a special OU for storing these accounts.

Log on to a Windows 2000 domain controller with a domain administrator account or another account that has permission to create user and computer objects, and then follow the steps in Lab 5-1 to create a new user account.

Lab 5-1   Creating a User Account

1. **Choose Start⇨Programs⇨Administrative Tools⇨Active Directory Users and Computers.**

2. **In the Active Directory Users and Computers console, select either the Users container or choose a different OU where you want to create the new user account, as shown in Figure 5-1.**

3. **Right-click the desired container or OU and choose New⇨User from the right-click menu that appears.** The New Object — User dialog box appears, shown in Figure 5-2.

4. **Enter the desired information for the user and click Next.**

5. **On the next page, enter a default password and choose any account password policy that you want to enforce. Your choices require the user to change the password at the next logon; the user cannot change the password; the password never expires; or the account is disabled. Click Next.**

6. **Click Finish.**

   The new object now appears in the container.

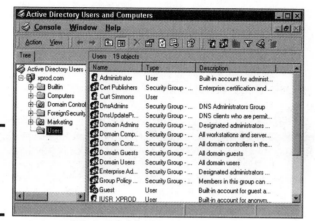

Figure 5-1:
The AD
Users and
Computers
console.

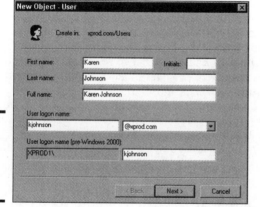

Figure 5-2:
The New
Object —
User
dialog box.

Book III
Chapter 5

Managing
Active Directory
Organizational Units
and Group Policy

You can create a computer account in Active Directory in basically the same
manner. As with creating a user account, you must have domain admin
rights to create a computer account in Active Directory, or your account
must have the right to create computer accounts. To create a computer
account, follow the steps in Lab 5-2.

Lab 5-2   Creating a User Account

1. **Choose Start⇨Programs⇨Administrative Tools⇨Active Directory
   Users and Computers.**

2. **In the Active Directory Users and Computers console, select either
   the Users container or choose a different OU where you want to
   create the new computer account.**

3. **Right-click the container and choose New⇨Computer.**

4. **In the New Object — Computer dialog box, enter the computer name, the pre-Windows 2000 computer name, and then click OK.**

Configuring user accounts

After a user account is created, you easily configure the user account as needed by accessing the user account properties. In Active Directory Users and Computers, select the container or OU that contains the desired user account. Right-click the user account icon and click Properties.

In the Properties dialog box that appears, you can configure a number of informational tabs, such as address, profile, telephones, organization, dial-in, environment, and so on. You should be familiar with all of these tabs for the exam, but the two primary tabs you should pay special attention to are the Account and Member Of tab.

The Account tab, shown in Figure 5-3, gives the user logon name (which you can change at any time), and you can configure logon hours and a preferred domain controller to logon. If the account is locked, you can clear the Account Is Locked Out check box in order to re-enable the account. You also see the account options where the user must change the password, account expiration option, and so on. These options are self-explanatory, but the exam expects you to know that these options are available on this tab.

If you need to reset a user's password, you can easily do so by right-clicking the user's account in Active Directory Users and Computers and clicking Reset Password.

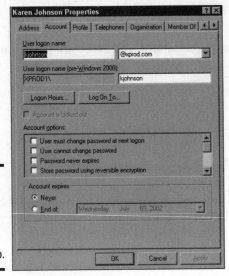

Figure 5-3:
Configure
account
properties
on the
Account tab.

On the Member Of tab, you can manage the user's group memberships by using the Add/Remove buttons. Memberships can be changed as needed at any time by accessing the Member Of tab.

Troubleshooting groups

Like user and computer accounts, you can create group accounts by using the Active Directory Users and Computers console. After you create a group, you can assign the desired permissions to that group and assign members to the group.

Groups are the primary management tool in Windows 2000 networks that enable you to manage users and computers. Using group memberships, you can easily control access to resources. However, groups can also cause you some difficulty. If you understand the types of groups and the management of them, however, you'll find that group management does not have to be complicated or difficult.

Types of groups

The exam expects you to know about the types of groups in Windows 2000 and how to apply those groups in a variety of situations. You can expect the exam to combine the group types and give you confusing scenario questions; however, if you keep the following definitions in mind, you can master group memberships easily:

✦ **Local groups:** A local group defines access to resources in a domain. For example, you might have a "printer" local group. Members of the printer local group have access to a particular shared printer(s) within the domain. Local groups can have global group members, universal group members, user accounts, or other domain local groups as members.

✦ **Global groups:** A global group is used to manage objects that change frequently, such as user accounts. Global groups are domain-specific and traffic is not replicated outside of the domain when global groups are changed. Typically, users are placed in global groups. You can then assign global groups to local groups so that global groups can access local resources.

✦ **Universal groups:** Universal groups are replicated across the entire forest and are most often used to consolidate groups that cross multiple domains. For example, say you have two domains and two different global groups in each. If you regularly apply the same permissions to both groups in both domains, you can create one universal group to simplify the administration of the two groups.

The exam will most certainly try to confuse you on the types of groups and the scope, or how they are used. Just remember that *local groups* are used to provide resource access. *Global groups* generally hold user accounts and are applied to local groups so that users can access the resource. The *universal group* is used to consolidate groups that function across a domain.

Nesting

A term you should keep in mind for the exam is group *nesting.* When you nest a group, you place the group inside of another group. Essentially, when you create a universal group, you are nesting other global groups inside of the universal group. While nesting has its place in Windows networking, you should be wary before nesting any groups because of permissions inheritance. Nested groups typically inherit the permissions of the parent container, so the more groups you nest, the more confusing group memberships can become. While nested groups can be useful and have their place in networking, be wary of exam questions that use complicated nesting as a viable troubleshooting solution.

Performing Active Directory searches

Users can easily locate objects in Active Directory by searching for them. In the past, users had to browse network folders and objects to find what they needed. With Active Directory, you can perform advanced search functions based on the object, attributes, or qualities about the object, or even by container.

The exam simply expects you to know that this option is available and how to perform the search. Your best bet is to get some hands-on practice by using the search feature so that you can experiment with all of the options available to you.

If you are working within Active Directory Users and Computers, you can simply click the search icon on the toolbar. You can also search directly from within My Network Places by clicking the search link options.

Either way, you arrive at the same search dialog box. Simply choose what you want to find, the desired search location (such as a container or all of Active Directory). Depending on the object you choose to search for, the search option changes. For example, Figure 5-4 shows a search for a printer. You can search by printer name, features, or you can configure advanced search options. Simply click Find Now to find the closest results for your search.

Using templates to create user accounts

The exam objectives point out the option of using a template to create user accounts. In actuality, the concept of the template is simply to copy an existing account and create a new account. You repeat this process over and over without having to enter additional information. To use the template process, you simply follow these steps:

1. **Create a user account (refer to Lab 5-2 if you need a refresher).**

2. **Access the account's properties and configure any desired basic information, such as group memberships, account settings, and so forth.**

3. **Right-click the account and click Copy.**

   The Copy Object — User dialog box appears, which is the same dialog box you first saw when you created the user account.

4. **Enter the next username and logon name to create the new account.**

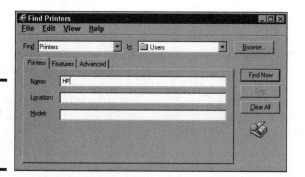

Figure 5-4:
Choose the desired search options.

Book III
Chapter 5

Managing
Active Directory
Organizational Units
and Group Policy

This new account retains all of the account settings you configured when you created the first account. You can repeat this process over and over in order to create user accounts with the same properties.

Although most functions of user account management are rather easy, keep in mind that the exam expects you to know how to perform the actions. You may see step-by-step questions that expect you to select a correct answer for completing a certain action. For this reason, hands-on practice is imperative!

Managing Object and Container Permissions

Permissions issues are one of those scary animals that can give administrators migraine headaches and users a lot of grief. The important rule about permissions is simply this: The more complex the permissions are, the more complications you are likely to have.

For example, say a user named Carla is a member of four groups, each containing different permissions to a particular shared folder. Permissions are based on NTFS permissions as well as folder permissions. What permission does Carla actually have? That can be a confusing question, both on the exam and in the real world. When NTFS permissions are in use, the permissions are cumulative and the most permissive permission applies. A user with full control and read access in NTFS permissions would have full control. However, when folder permissions are combined with NTFS permissions, the most restrictive permission applies. If the user has read folder permission but full control NTFS permission, the user has only read permission.

The exam may throw ridiculously complicated permissions questions at you. Simply remember the rules of how NTFS permissions and folder permissions are applied to a share, and you can sort through those difficult problems. You should use the scratch paper the exam administrator gives you to chart the permissions so that you can make sense of any tricky exam questions.

Using delegation of control

Windows 2000 Server provides a helpful feature called delegation of control. *Delegation of control* allows a domain or enterprise administrator to delegate control of a container or OU to another administrator or user. When you delegate control, you can give the administrator the desired permissions. The purpose of delegation of control is to diversify administrator responsibilities and make life easier on senior administrators, without giving complete administrator privileges away.

Consider an example: Suppose that user accounts are stored in the Users container. You don't want to spend your time creating new user accounts. Using delegation of control, you can train an employee to create new user accounts, and then use delegation of control that allows this user to create accounts. However, you don't have to give the user total control over the container. In fact, you don't have to give the user any control that you don't want. On the other hand, you could also give an administrator complete control over a particular OU or domain by using delegation of control.

You can configure delegation of control with the help of a wizard, so setting up delegation is rather easy. On the exam, you mainly need to know when to use delegation of control. Questions that give you situations with multiple administrators who need access to certain containers or OUs, but not others, almost always refer to delegation of control. For the exam, however, spending some time working with this feature is important so that you are familiar with using it. Follow the steps in Lab 5-3 to use the Delegation of Control Wizard.

Lab 5-3   Using Delegation of Control

1. **Choose Start⇨Programs⇨Administrative Tools⇨Active Directory Users and Computers.**

2. **In Active Directory Users and Computers, right-click the container, OU, or domain that you want to delegate and click Delegate Control.**

   The Delegation of Control Wizard appears.

3. **Click Next on the Welcome screen.**

4. **In the Users or Groups window that appears, use the Add button to select the User or Group that you want to delegate control to and click Next.**

5. **In the Active Directory Object Type window, shown in Figure 5-5, you can choose to delegate the entire folder, or only certain types of objects within the folder by selecting the desired check boxes. Make the desired selections and click Next.**

   For example, in the previous example concerning the creation of user accounts, you might restrict the delegate's access to only user objects.

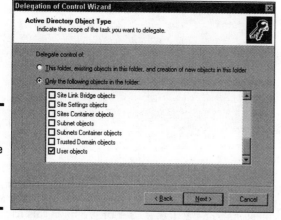

Figure 5-5: Choose to delegate the folder or certain objects.

Book III Chapter 5

Managing Active Directory Organizational Units and Group Policy

6. **In the Permissions window, choose the permissions that you want to assign to the user and click Next.**

7. **Click Finish.**

To make changes to any delegation, simply run the Delegation of Control Wizard again.

Configuring object permissions

Each object in Active Directory, whether a shared folder, a printer, an OU, or any other object, gives you the ability to control what users or groups access that object and what the users or groups can do with the object. The security settings are made by editing the Access Control List (ACL) of the object. The ACL is a listing of permissions that determines a user's or group's effective permission for an object.

You can right-click any object within Active Directory and click Properties. You see a Security tab option. If you do not see the Security tab, choose View⇨Advanced Features to enable the tab. As you can see in Figure 5-6, you see a standard Windows 2000 Security tab containing users and groups, as well as permissions.

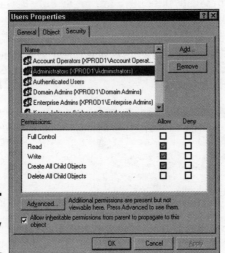

Figure 5-6:
The Security tab.

Under most circumstances, the default permissions are all you need to configure. However, say you have a situation where you need to apply specialized permissions to a particular user or group. In this case, you can edit the ACL by clicking the Advanced button. In the Access Control Settings window, select the user or group and click the View/Edit button. This opens the Permission Entry window, where you can allow or deny the permission entries, shown in Figure 5-7. Under most circumstances, you should not have to do this because the default permissions are all you need.

Although ACL entries can be helpful in certain circumstances, be wary of exam questions that use editing the ACL entries as an easy solution. Editing of these security attributes can be more confusing than helpful, so be careful.

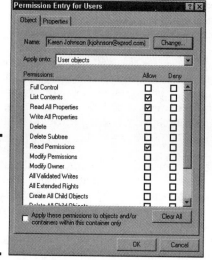

Figure 5-7:
Allow
or deny
permission
entries from
the Object
tab.

Diagnosing Active Directory Replication Problems

Replication is the process of exchanging update information among domain controllers on the network. Because Windows 2000 networks function in a peer fashion, there is no single master domain controller. Therefore, changes to the Active Directory database made on one domain controller must be replicated to the other domain controllers so that all domain controllers maintain a consistent view of the network. Without replication, the data between domain controllers would quickly become a worthless collection of varying data.

Active Directory replication occurs frequently and automatically in a single-site environment. In fact, Active Directory handles the initial configuration of replication when you install the network, and replication is not something that an administrator has to worry about in a single-site network. In a WAN environment, where two or more sites are used, Active Directory replication can become more of a problem, depending on the physical configuration of the network and the availability and size of the WAN links connecting the sites. Using sites, Active Directory determines what traffic should remain within the local site and what traffic should be replicated to a remote site.

Exam 70-218 is not likely to ask you many questions (if any) about replication. The questions you may see are generally easy and straightforward. However, we should note that replication is a complicated topic and Active Directory books often devote a chapter or more to the subject. Because the design of this book is to help you prepare for the exam, we assume that you are familiar

Book III
Chapter 5

**Managing
Active Directory
Organizational Units
and Group Policy**

with basic replication concepts. If not, you need to study a general Active Directory book, such as *Active Directory Bible,* by Curt Simmons (Wiley Publishing) to get the background information that you need.

The amount of time required to transfer replication data over WAN links determines the latency of replication. *Latency* is the amount of time that domain controllers are out of sync due to replication. For example, if you add a user account on a domain controller, the amount of time required to replicate that addition to other domain controllers throughout the forest is the latency value.

In multisite environments, latency primarily depends upon the site links. Slow or unreliable site links, such as 56 Kbps dial-up connections, may increase latency time. As a general rule, Active Directory does a good job of configuring replication schedules over WAN links, provided by the information about the WAN links that you configure in Active Directory Sites and Services, but the limitations of the WAN bandwidth still may have a negative effect on intersite replication. In other words, if your site links are slow, latency will be greater, and there is simply no workaround for the bandwidth problem except to upgrade the site links.

However, if you have two site links between two sites, such as a 256 Kbps and a 56 Kbps, use the Active Directory Sites and Services console to configure a cost for each link. Higher bandwidth links, such as the 256 Kbps link in this example, should have a lower cost than slower links, such as the 56 Kpbs. Active Directory tries to always use the lower cost link first. If the link is unavailable, the higher cost link is used. You can also use Active Directory Sites and Services to configure replication schedules and a frequency value, if you are having problems with link availability and latency. Using these tactics, you can get good replication results, even over slow links. The best solution for latency, however, is to simply upgrade site links to higher bandwidth links.

The exam might throw a couple of replication problems your way. In the real world, you are not likely to deal with these issues on a regular basis, but keep them in mind for the exam:

✦ **Duplicate Objects:** Depending on replication, you can create duplicate objects in Active Directory. Say one administrator adds a user account on one domain controller. Another administrator adds the account on a different domain controller before replication has occurred. Which object is used? The replication process will typically overwrite the second object because it was created last. These kinds of conflicts are generally resolved by Active Directory, but there can be instances where you may manually need to delete the object that is not desired.

✦ **Authoritative Restore:** Say you delete a shared folder from Active Directory by accident. Before you realize what has happened, the change is replicated to other domain controllers. In this case, you need to restore the shared folder that you deleted, but the problem is that replication from other domain controllers will continue to delete the folder. So, you have to perform an authoritative restore. The *authoritative restore* marks the restore as "authoritative" so that replication does not overwrite it. The authoritative restore is then replicated to other domain controllers, thus restoring the object. For the exam, you don't need to know how to run an authoritative restore; instead, you simply need to know when to use this option, and that NTDSUTIL is used to run the authoritative restore.

✦ **LostAndFound Container:** Say that an administrator on a one-domain controller is adding a printer object to the Marketing OU, while at the same time, an administrator on another domain controller moves all items out of the Marketing OU and deletes the OU. Where is the new printer object supposed to go? In this case, Active Directory does not know. So, Active Directory puts the new printer object in the LostAndFound container. The LostAndFound container is found in the Active Directory Users and Comptuers console, shown in Figure 5-8. If you can't see it, choose View➪Advanced Options. You should get in the habit of checking this folder from time to time to see whether you need to move any orphaned objects to appropriate containers.

Book III
Chapter 5

Managing
Active Directory
Organizational Units
and Group Policy

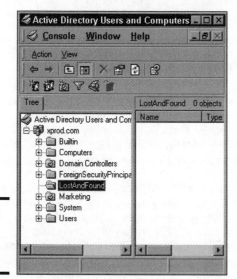

Figure 5-8:
LostAnd
Found
Container.

Using Group Policy

Group policy is a Windows 2000 feature designed to make the management of network computers and software easier and more flexible. Using group policy, administrators can control Windows 2000 computers on a Windows network and even install software on those computers. Like the subject of replication, group policy is a complicated topic and even entire books are devoted to the subject. Our purpose here is to examine the group policy issues and features you are likely to see on Exam 70-218. If you need a general tutorial on group policy, see the Windows Help files or a book devoted to this purpose.

If you have been around Windows 2000 at all, you have no doubt heard about group policy. Group policy basically replaces system policies in a Windows 2000 network and group policy provides you with some powerful features for desktop management. With group policy, you can enforce a standardized desktop and system setting configuration, install software, download documents to a client computer, and even configure Internet settings. Group policy is designed to lower the Total Cost of Ownership (TCO) by giving administrators more control over user desktops. With group policy, you can then enforce company policy regarding configuration and use of client computers.

The exam expects you to have some hands-on practice with group policy, as well as understand some basic features and functions of the software. The following sections review the group policy issues you are likely to see on the exam.

Group policy inheritance behavior

Before exploring group policy, it is very important that you understand group policy inheritance behavior. As soon as you understand how to apply group policy, you can then begin to plan a group policy implementation for your Active Directory infrastructure. You can apply group policy at the site, domain, or OU level. The inheritance structure is site to domain, and then domain to OU. In other words, inheritance works from the top down.

Say that you want to configure a single group policy that applies to all users and groups in your entire enterprise. You can create the group policy, and then implement the policy at the site level. Due to inheritance, the policy will be applied to all domains and OUs within the enterprise. Or, you may possibly have different group policies that are applied to domains. Domain A has a different group policy from Domain B. You create the group policy, implement it in the desired domain, and all users, groups, and computers in the domain receive the policy. You can perform the same process or individual OUs if necessary, so that inheritance is in effect from the site level down to the domain and OU levels. But what happens if there is a site policy, and a domain policy, and an OU policy?

Not to be confused with inheritance, *override* is also in effect by default. This simply means that if a site policy is in place, it is applied to all domains, unless a domain has its own group policy. In that case, the domain group policy overrides the site policy when there are conflicting settings. If an OU in that domain also has a group policy, it overrides the domain policy if there are conflicting settings. Here's the key: The policy closest to the user is one that is applied. There may be a site policy, but if there is an OU policy for a particular OU in which a user or computer resides, the settings in the OU policy override any conflicting site policy.

The term *group policy* may seem like a misnomer because you can't actually apply a group policy to a user or group of users. You can only apply it to a site, domain, or OU: Those are the only three levels of application. If a site, domain, and OU policy is applied to a user or computer object, each policy is implemented, and conflicting settings are overwritten by the policy closest to the user or computer object (OU, in this case). Keep this point in mind for the exam so that you can sort out tricky exam questions.

Now here's the tricky and ridiculously confusing part. While it's true that the policy closest to the user is applied, this does not mean that no components of the higher policy get applied. What it means is that if a site policy says to remove the Run command and a domain policy says to use the Run command, the Run command is used. If, however, a domain policy has "not configured" on a number of possible policies and a site policy has a configured setting, it is still applied at the domain level. The override behavior overrides conflicting policies. So, in order to completely stop a higher-level policy from becoming effective, you can block inheritance.

For example, say a domain policy is in place, but a particular OU has its own policy. You don't want the OU to receive any of the domain policy, so you can choose to block the domain policy at the OU level. This way, only the OU policy is applied. However, to keep the chain of command straight, a domain administrator can also configure "no override" so that a policy cannot be blocked. In this case, the no override "overrides" block inheritance. As you can imagine, this can quickly become a big mess. As with all configuration in Active Directory, simplicity is always best. Strive for only one or just a few group policies that you can apply at the highest levels possible. This reduces conflict problems and can help you avoid messing with group policy configurations.

**Book III
Chapter 5**

**Managing
Active Directory
Organizational Units
and Group Policy**

Working with group policy objects

Group policy has three major components. The first is group policy objects (GPOs), which contain the actual setting configuration that is applied to user and groups within Active Directory. When you create a group policy, you are in essence creating a GPO. GPOs are like all other objects in Active Directory. You apply the GPO to the site, domain, or OU where you want to implement the policy. The GPO stores its configuration information in a Group Policy Container (GPC) as well as in Group Policy Templates (GPT). Like GPOs, GPCs and GPTs are Active Directory objects, but they also reside in the SYSVOL folder of domain controllers. This place is good for them because you don't have to worry about replication. Windows 2000's File Replication Service (FRS) replicates them among domain controllers for you.

You can access the Group Policy console, an MMC snap-in, in three different ways. You can access it from the site, domain, or OU Properties sheets within Active Directory. For example, say you want to implement a site level group policy. In Active Directory Sites and Services, expand the Sites container, and then select the desired site. Choose Action⇨Properties and you see a Group Policy tab on the Properties page, shown in Figure 5-9.

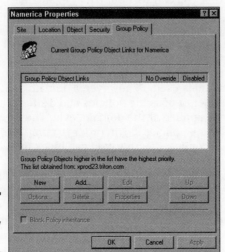

Figure 5-9:
Group policy
tab.

You see the same tab if you access your domain and OU properties sheets as well. You can select the Block Policy Inheritance check box at the bottom of the Group Policy tab, or click the New Button to create a new policy. You see the new Group Policy Object Link called New Group Policy Object appear in the window (you can rename it). If you select the Group Policy object and click the Options button, a window appears that enables you to select the "no override" option, and you can also disable the group policy from this window, shown in Figure 5-10.

Figure 5-10:
The New
GPO Object
Options
dialog box
enables you
to disable
group
policy.

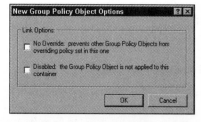

If you click the Properties button, you see a General, Links, and Security tab. The Links and Security tab are standard object tabs, but notice on the General tab that you can choose to Disable the Computer Configuration or the User Configuration portion of group policy. This an effective option because you could have a Group Policy where you only configure the user portion and not the computer portion. You could then disable the computer portion to speed the policy application process.

You can also click the Add button to add a different GPO to the console. This feature opens a window that enables you to select an existing site, domain, or OU policy that you can add and use.

Finally, the Edit button opens the Group Policy MMC console, shown in Figure 5-11, where you can actually configure the group policy. Notice that you have two categories: User Configuration and Computer Configuration.

Book III
Chapter 5

**Managing
Active Directory
Organizational Units
and Group Policy**

Figure 5-11:
The Group
Policy
console
enables you
to configure
the group
policy.

Aside from accessing the group policy from either the site, domain, or OU properties, you can also manually open the Group Policy MMC snap-in. To open the GPO in this manner, follow these steps:

1. **Choose Start⇨Run, type MMC, and then click OK.**

2. **Choose Console⇨Add/Remove snap-in.**

3. **On the Add/Remove snap-in window that appears, click the Add button.**

4. **From the snap-in list that appears, select Group Policy and click OK.**

5. **The Select Group Policy object window appears, shown in Figure 5-12.**

6. **By default, the group policy is focused on the local computer. To change this, click the Browse button.**

The Browse for a Group Policy object window appears, containing tabs for Domain/OUs, Sites, Computers, or All.

Figure 5-12:
Select the
Group
Policy
Object.

7. **You can browse the tabs and open the desired policy, and then click OK.**

8. **Click the Finish button, click Close on the Add Standalone snap-in window, and then click OK to open the snap-in.**

Configuring a Group Policy

After you open a group policy, either by using the site, domain, or OU properties sheets or by manually opening the console, you can then configure the group policy object as desired. You can configure either the user object or computer object (or both, of course) by clicking the icon in the left pane to expand them. You see that the categories are the same for the user and computer, and you even find that many of the policies overlap.

After you apply the policy, if the user policy and computer policy conflict, the user policy is applied.

Configuration is easy for the most part, but you do have quite a few options. The following two sections examine the Computer and User configuration. To create a group policy, you must be a member of the Administrators group or the Group Policy Creator Owners group.

Computer Configuration

If you expand Computer Configuration in the Group Policy console, you see that you have three containers: Software Settings, Windows Settings, and Administrative Templates. The following sections consider what is available in each of these.

Software Settings

The Software Settings container contains a software installation icon. If you select the icon, you can see any configured software packages displayed in the right pane. You can also create a new software package by selecting Software installation in the left pane and choosing Action⇨New⇨Package. This action opens a window where you can browse for a Windows Installer package (.msi) that you have previously created. Any installer packages that you add to the console then become a part of the group policy and install on client computers to which the policy applies.

If you select Software Installation in the left console pane, and then choose Action⇨Properties, you see the property sheet for software installation. On the General tab, you have a few basic options that determine how installation behaves when it is being deployed. For example, you can choose to display a deployment software dialog box as well as a basic or maximum user interface while installation is occurring. You also see an option to publish. This means that you want the new package to be published with the standard package options. As you can see in Figure 5-13, the published option is grayed out — because you can only publish to users, not computers. If you accessed this page from the User configuration, the Publish option would be available. You can also see that you can assign a software package to any user or computer. You also can select Advanced Published or Assigned, which enables you to configure the options at the time of deployment. You can also choose to uninstall any applications when they fall out of the scope of management by selecting the check box at the bottom of this tab.

Book III
Chapter 5

Managing Active Directory Organizational Units and Group Policy

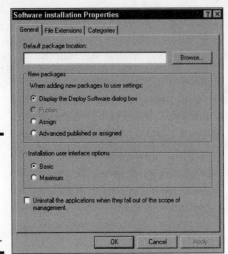

Figure 5-13:
You can
assign or
publish
software
from the
General tab.

Applications fall out of the scope of management when the applications are no longer needed, or when a computer is moved to a different domain. When a computer is moved, the application is automatically uninstalled because it no longer resides in the domain management by that particular GPO.

A File Extensions tab enables you to associate all extensions with particular applications. This option is useful to associate the correct files with their extensions for custom applications. The Categories tab enables you to add custom categories to Add/Remove Programs on the user's computer. These custom categories can store corporate software applications.

Windows Settings

If you expand Windows Settings, you see two categories, Scripts and Security Settings. If you select Scripts in the left pane, you see start up and shut down options appear in the right pane, and if you select one of the options and then choose Action⇨Properties, you can choose to use a desired script or you can add one as needed. When you add scripts, or remove them for that matter, the scripts become part of the group policy and run when the user boots the computer or shuts down.

If you expand the Security Settings container, you see a number of sub-containers that house different kinds of security policies. For example, if you select account policies in the left pane, the password policy and account lockout policy containers appear in the right pane. If you double-click one of the policy containers, you see a list of actual policies. For example, under password policy, you see such policies as enforce password history, maximum password age, minimum password length, and so on. If you double-click one of the policies, a simple dialog box appears, where you can define a policy. For example in Figure 5-14, you see the Security Policy Setting dialog box. To define the policy, simply select the Define This Policy Setting check box, enter the number of passwords a computer should remember in the Keep Password History box, and then click the OK button.

By default, most policies are not defined. This is a big design issue because you only need access and define the policies you want to implement. Many policies are available to you, but you won't use all of them for your implementation.

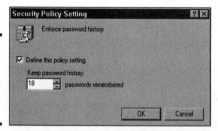

Figure 5-14:
Set the
password
history
policy here.

Book III
Chapter 5

Managing
Active Directory
Organizational Units
and Group Policy

To configure the policies you want, simply move through the different containers and access the desired policy container, and then the desired policy. You may have to spend some time wading around to find the exact policy that you want, but the following list reviews what is available in the Security Settings container, which you should keep in mind for the exam:

✦ **Account policies:** Contains subcontainers for password policy and account lockout policy.

✦ **Local Policies:** Contains subcontainers for audit policy, user rights assignment, and security options.

✦ **Event Log:** Contains policy settings for the Event Log.

✦ **Restricted Groups:** Contains security access policies for restricted group access.

✦ **System Services:** Contains security policies for system services on the computer, such as DHCP Client, FRS, and so on. This feature enables you to set security on various system services to prevent user tampering.

✦ **Registry:** Contains security policies for registry access and editing.

✦ **File System:** Contains security policies for file system configuration.

✦ **Public Key Policies:** Contains subcontainers for encrypted data recovery agents, automatic certificate request settings, trusted root certification authorities, and enterprise trusts.

✦ **IP Security Policies:** When IP Security (IPSec) is in effect, these policies define security settings client and server IP traffic.

Administrative Templates

The Administrative Templates container contains a number of templates and different categories that you can use to configure various system components. You can also import other templates as desired. Fortunately, policy templates all look basically the same. When you double-click the template, you have a Policy tab and an Explain tab. On the Policy tab, shown in Figure 5-15, you can choose to enable, disable, or keep the policy not configured.

For Computer configuration, you have quite a number of helpful administrative templates. We're obviously not going to list them all here, but the following list gives you an overview of the template categories available to you:

✦ Under Windows Components

- NetMeeting contains templates to configure NetMeeting.

- Internet Explorer contains templates to configure Internet Explorer and Internet connectivity settings.

- Task Scheduler contains templates to manage task usage and modification.

- Windows Installer contains templates to prevent or control the use of Windows Installer.

✦ Under System

- Logon contains templates to configure logon processes.

- Disk Quotas contains templates to enforce disk quota settings.

- DNS Client contains templates for DNS communication.

- Group policy contains templates to control the configuration of a local group policy.

- Windows File Protection contains templates to control the use of Windows File Protection.

✦ Under Network

   • Offline Files contains templates to control and configure offline file usage.

   • Network and Dial-up Connections contains templates to configure connection sharing.

✦ Under Printers, you have a number of templates that determine what users can do with a local printer when logged onto the computer.

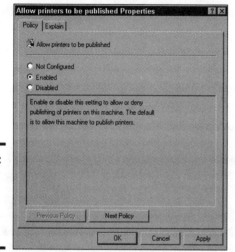

Figure 5-15:
Enable or disable policies from the Policy tab.

User Configuration

As you can guess, group policy user configuration places management restrictions or permissions on items directly associated with the user/group account. You have the same Software Settings, Windows Settings, and Administrative Templates containers as you saw in the previous sections, so we're only going to point out information that is different in User Configuration.

Under Windows Settings, you have a few additional categories, which are

✦ **Internet Explorer Maintenance:** This category of policies enable you to configure a number of custom Internet Explorer options, such as a custom title bar. You can also use animated bitmaps, custom logos, preconfigured connection settings, preconfigured URLs, security settings, and program settings.

✦ **Remote Installation Services:** This category gives you a Choice Options icon that presents you with a simple window so that you can define the level of user interaction during a remote installation, such as using custom setup, and so on.

✦ **Folder Redirection:** Folder redirection enables a user to log on to any workstation and receive his or her files and folders. You can choose the target location on the user's computer to redirect the folders.

Under Administrative Templates, you also have categories for the following:

• **Start Menu & Task Bar** enables you to configure Start Menu and taskbar items.

• **Desktop** enables you to control desktop settings including Active Desktop as well as Active Directory searches.

• **Control Panel** enables you to manage Control Panel items.

Refreshing Group Policy

For some reason, the folks who created the Windows 2000 and the networking exams like to ask you questions about group policy refresh rate. In order to answer the exam questions correctly, you simply need to remember these important points:

✦ By default, the computer policy is refreshed every 45 minutes. You can, however, configure a refresh rate interval that is lower or higher than this value within group policy in Computer Configuration\Administrative Templates\System\Group Policy.

✦ A user can refresh group policy manually if necessary by using the secedit command. To manually refresh the group policy, choose Start⇨Run and type **secedit/refreshpolicy USER_POLICY**.

Prep Test

1 On Windows 2000 Server, which MMC console do you use to create domain user accounts?

A ○ User Manager

B ○ Active Directory Users and Computers

C ○ Active Directory Domains and Trusts

D ○ Active Directory Sites and Services

2 In a certain domain, the marketing group needs access to a particular printer. The printer is shared in the local group Printers. What should be done to give the marketing group access to this printer?

A ○ Create a new local group called marketing and add it to the Printers local group.

B ○ Create a new universal group called marketing and add it to the Printers local group.

C ○ Create a global group called marketing and add it to the Printers local group.

D ○ Add marketing to the Printers local group, and then create a Universal group.

3 Your network consists of two domains. Marketing groups are in both domains that frequently require the same access to resources. You would like to simplify administration. What kind of group would be best?

A ○ Local group

B ○ Global group

C ○ Universal group

D ○ You cannot create one group because of domain replication.

4 An administrator trainee is in a particular domain. You would like for this new administrator to be able to control a certain OU. However, you do not want to give the new administrator full control. How can you perform this action?

A ○ Edit the administrator's ACLs.

B ○ Use group policy.

C ○ Use delegation of control.

D ○ Assign the administrator to the OU ADMINS universal group.

5 **A particular user needs access to a certain object. However, this is a special case where the user needs some specific kinds of access denied. You need to edit the ACL when assigning permission. What do you do?**

A ○ Access the Security tab and select the permissions.

B ○ Use secedit.

C ○ Click the Advanced button on the Security tab and edit the ACLs.

D ○ Use delegation of control.

6 **In your environment are two sites. Between the sites is a 56 Kbps modem connection and a T1 connection. You want to make sure that replication always tries to use the T1 connection instead of the 56 Kbps connection. What action should you take?**

A ○ Assign a cost of 100 to the T1 connection.

B ○ Assign a cost of 1 to the T1 connection and 50 to the 56 Kbs connection.

C ○ Assign a cost of 100 to the 56 Kbps connection.

D ○ Assign a cost of 1 to the 56 Kbps connection and 50 to the T1 connection.

7 **An administrator accidentally deletes an Active Directory container from a domain controller. Before the mistake is realized, replication deletes the container across the domain controllers in the forest. What do you need to do?**

A ○ Manually re-create the container.

B ○ Perform a restore from backup.

C ○ Perform an authoritative restore.

D ○ Copy the container from another domain controller.

8 **A certain user account receives a site, domain, and OU group policy. Conflicting settings are in the OU and domain policies. Which policy does the user actually receive?**

A ○ Site

B ○ Domain

C ○ OU

D ○ None

9 **In a certain environment, an OU administrator has used the Block Policy Inheritance option so that no domain policies are inherited to the OU. As a domain level administrator, you now want to make sure OU admins block policy inheritance. What should you do?**

A ○ Use "no override."

B ○ Block admin permissions.

C ○ Use the ndsutil/d command.

D ○ Remove the OU policies.

10 Group policy is in effect in three domains in your environment. Each group policy manages software installed on computers. You move one computer from one domain to another, but the software is uninstalled. What has happened?

A ○ The group policy is not applied across the domain.

B ○ The computer has fallen out of the scope of management.

C ○ The computer is not logged onto the domain.

D ○ The user does not have the correct permissions.

Answers

1 **B.** All user and group accounts are created in Active Directory Users and Computers. *Review "Creating and Managing User and Group Objects in Active Directory."*

2 **C.** Local groups provide resources, while global groups contain users. Add global groups to local groups. *Read "Types of groups."*

3 **C.** Universal groups contain users and/or groups from multiple domains in order to simplify administration. *Review "Types of groups."*

4 **C.** Delegation of control enables you to give rights as needed for OUs or domains. *See "Using delegation of control."*

5 **C.** The ACLs for an object can be edited by clicking the Advanced button on the Security tab. *Study "Configuring object permissions."*

6 **B.** Cost assignments tell Active Directory which connection should be favored. Lower cost connections are favored over higher cost connections, so that a cost of 1 for the T1 link ensures that it is used when available. *Study "Diagnosing Active Directory Replication Problems."*

7 **C.** An authoritative restore can be used to mark the restore so that replication does not delete the container again. *Study "Diagnosing Active Directory Replication Problems."*

8 **C.** The policy closest to the user is the one the user receives. *Study "Group policy inheritance behavior."*

9 **A.** "No override" stops a lower-level policy from blocking a higher level policy. *See "Group policy inheritance behavior."*

10 **B.** Software installed by group policy is typically removed when it falls out of the scope of the group policy's management. *Study "Software Settings."*

Chapter 6: Configuring, Securing, and Troubleshooting Remote Access

Exam Objectives

- ✔ Configuring and troubleshooting remote access and virtual private network (VPN) connections
- ✔ Troubleshooting a remote access policy
- ✔ Implementing and troubleshooting Terminal Services for remote access
- ✔ Configuring and troubleshooting Network Address Translation (NAT) and Internet Connection Sharing

*N*etwork connectivity and access to resources from remote locations can be a complex topic, and as a network administrator, you are likely to run into a number of situations using Windows 2000's remote access, as well as other services, such as Terminal Services, NAT, and ICS.

In this chapter, you read about these remote access issues that you are likely to face on the exam. As with all exam topics, remote access and Terminal Services can be difficult topics, with entire books devoted to these issues. If you do not have hands-on experience working with these services, you may need some additional study as well. In this chapter, you find out about

- ✦ Managing remote access
- ✦ Working with Terminal Services
- ✦ Using NAT
- ✦ Using ICS

Configuring and Troubleshooting Remote Access and Virtual Private Network Connections

Remote Access Service (RAS) allows remote network clients to establish a remote connection with a RAS server. As soon as the connection is established, the remote client functions just like a locally connected network client. The user can browse the network, use permitted resources, connect to other servers — anything a locally connected client can do — provided the RAS client has appropriate permissions. In recent years, RAS has become more and more important as more and more users work from laptops in different locations.

The exam objectives do not focus on the configuration of routing interfaces on a Windows 2000 server, but they do focus on remote access configuration. In light of this fact, this chapter primarily focuses on the remote access portion of Routing and Remote Access, and the term "RAS" refers to both routing and remote access.

Enabling remote access

RAS is installed by default on Windows 2000 servers when you perform an initial installation. However, it is not enabled. In order to set up and implement RAS, you have to enable it, which is accomplished through the Routing and Remote Access Server Setup Wizard.

You need to know the options presented in this wizard for the exam. To practice setting up RAS by using the wizard, follow the steps in Lab 6-1.

Lab 6-1   Enabling Routing and Remote Access

1. **Choose Start⇨Programs⇨Administrative Tools⇨Routing and Remote Access.**

2. **In the console, select your server, click the Action menu, and then choose Configure and Enable Routing and Remote Access.**

3. **Click Next on the wizard's welcome screen.**

4. **On the Common Configuration window, make a selection for the kind of remote access server that you want to install, as shown in Figure 6-1. For this lab, select Remote Access Server and then click Next.**

5. **Verify the required protocols in the list provided. Typically, you need TCP/IP, but may need another protocol depending on your network clients. Click Next.**

6. **In the IP Address Assignment window, select how you want remote clients to be assigned an IP address. Select either the Automatically radio button or the Specified Range radio button, and then click Next.**

   If you choose automatic, remote clients are provided an IP address through DHCP (see Book IV, Chapter 5). If you click the specified option, you enter an IP address range to assign to remote clients.

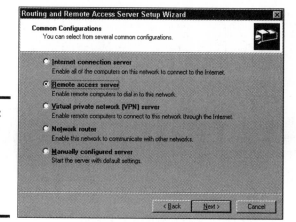

Figure 6-1: Windows 2000 RAS provides several server options.

7. **Next, you can choose to enable RADIUS or not. Select either No or Yes and then click Next.**

   Remote Authentication Dial-In User Service (RADIUS) provides a central authentication database for multiple remote access servers and collects accounting information about remote connections. This window enables you to set up this remote access server to use an existing RADIUS server if you so choose.

8. **Click the Finish button.**

   Windows 2000 Starts the Routing and Remote Access Service.

Configuring server properties

After RAS is enabled, you can further configure the server by accessing the server's properties sheets. In the Routing and Remote Access console, select your server, click the Action menu, and then choose Properties.

You need to know the configuration options on the tabs explored in the next sections. Depending on your network configuration, you may have other tabs, such as AppleTalk for Macintosh clients, but the following sections only explore those tabs you need to know for the exam.

Configuring the General tab

The General tab gives you two options. First, you can choose to enable your server as a router. If you select this option, you can choose to allow only local LAN routing, or you can choose to allow LAN and demand-dial routing. Next, you can choose to enable your server as a remote access server. These options simply allow you to use your server as both a routing and remote access server, or either one as desired.

Book III
Chapter 6

Configuring,
Securing, and
Troubleshooting
Remote Access

Configuring the Security tab

The Security tab allows you to choose the security and accounting provider. You can select either Windows authentication and accounting or RADIUS authentication and accounting. If you choose to implement RADIUS, then you use the Configure button to connect to a RADIUS server.

For Windows authentication, you can click the Authentication Methods button and select the type of Windows authentication that you want to use for remote access. The following bullet list tells you what options you have, which you need to know for the exam:

✦ **Extensible authentication protocol (EAP):** Allows the use of third-party authentication software and is also used for Smart Card logon.

✦ **MS-CHAP V2:** Generates encryption keys during RAS authentication negotiation. MS-CHAP only works with Windows clients.

✦ **MS-CHAP:** An earlier version of CHAP that provides secure logon. MS-CHAP only works with Windows clients.

✦ **Shiva Password Authentication Protocol (SPAP):** Used by Shiva clients connecting to a Windows 2000 RAS Server. SPAP is more secure than clear text, but less secure than CHAP.

✦ **Unencrypted password (PAP):** No encryption required.

✦ **Unauthenticated access**

Configuring the IP tab

The IP tab allows you to enable IP routing and allow IP-based remote access and demand-dial connections. You can choose to implement either DHCP IP leases for remote clients or you can enter a static IP address pool. These options are the same ones you configured with the RAS Setup Wizard, but you can use this tab to make changes as necessary.

Configuring the PPP tab

The PPP tab gives you three main check boxes for Point-to-Point Protocol features that you can enable.

You need to know these for the exam, so we put them in an easy-to-memorize bullet list:

✦ **Multilink Connections:** This feature allows you to use multilink, which connects several modems or adapters to increase bandwidth. You can also choose to use dynamic bandwidth control with Bandwidth Allocation Protocol (BAP) or Bandwidth Allocation Control Protocol (BACP). These protocols allow the multilink connection to dynamically add or drop PPP links as necessary for the traffic flow.

+ **Link Control Protocol (LCP) extensions:** Manages LCP and PPP connections.

+ **Software Compression:** Uses the Microsoft Point to Point Compression Protocol (MPPC) to compress data sent on the remote access or demand-dial connection.

Configuring the Event Logging tab

The Event Logging tab provides you an effective way to monitor your remote access server through the use of log files.

The Event Logging tab provides several radio buttons so that you can choose to log the kind of information desired, such as errors, warnings, PPP logging, and so forth. If you are experiencing problems with your remote access server, these different logging options can help you pinpoint the problem.

Monitoring remote clients

The Routing and Remote Access console provides you the ability to monitor the clients currently connected to the remote access server. In the console tree, expand your server, and then click the Remote Access Clients icon. A list of remote access clients appears in the details pane by username, duration, and the number of ports in use. You can use this interface to manually disconnect clients if desired.

Configuring inbound connections

Inbound connections allow remote clients to connect to your remote access server. To allow the clients to connect, you must configure the hardware, such as a modem or ISDN adapter, to accept the inbound connection.

To configure the inbound connection, expand your server in the Routing and Remote Access console, select Ports, and then choose Action⇔Properties. A window appears, listing the routing and remote access devices attached to your computer. You can select the desired device, and then click the Configure button. The Configure Device window appears, shown in Figure 6-2.

To allow the device to accept inbound-only connections, select the appropriate check box. You can also choose to use the device for demand-dial routing connections. After you enable the device for inbound connections, users can then dial the specified phone number to contact the device for inbound access.

Book III
Chapter 6

Configuring,
Securing, and
Troubleshooting
Remote Access

Figure 6-2:
The
Configure
Device
window
allows a
device to
accept
inbound
connections.

Troubleshooting Remote Access Policy

Remote access policies define how remote access can be used by remote clients. The policies create "rules" that must be followed for different remote access rights and permissions. For example, you specify certain dial-in numbers, dial-in hours, and even numbers from which a user must dial in.

You can create remote access policies by selecting Remote Access Policy in the Routing and Remote Access console, clicking the Action menu, and then choosing New Remote Access Policy.

This action leads you through several steps in order to create the new remote access policy. Lab 6-2 guides you through these steps, and you need to know how to perform this task for the exam.

> **Lab 6-2   Creating a Remote Access Policy**
>
> 1. **Select Remote Access Policy in the console tree and choose Action menu⇨New Remote Access Policy.**
>
> 2. **Enter a friendly name for the policy and then click Next.**
>
> 3. **In the Conditions window, click the Add button to see a list of conditions that you can use to create the policy, as shown in Figure 6-3. Select the desired condition(s) and then click Add.**
>
>   You may be asked to enter additional information, depending on the option you selected.
>
> 4. **Click Next.**
>
> 5. **On the Permissions window, choose to either grant or deny remote access permission, based upon your attribute selection.**
>
> 6. **Click Next and then click Finish.**
>
>   The new policy now appears in the details pane of the Routing and Remote Access console.

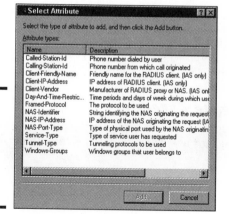

Figure 6-3:
Select the
desired
policy
attribute
from this
window.

Editing a remote access policy

After you create desired policies, you can easily edit them and change them
as necessary.

To edit a policy, click the Remote Access Policies icon in the console tree
and then select the desired policy in the details pane. Click the Action menu
and then choose Properties. The Properties option provides you a single
Settings tab that shows how the policy is defined. (See Figure 6-4.)

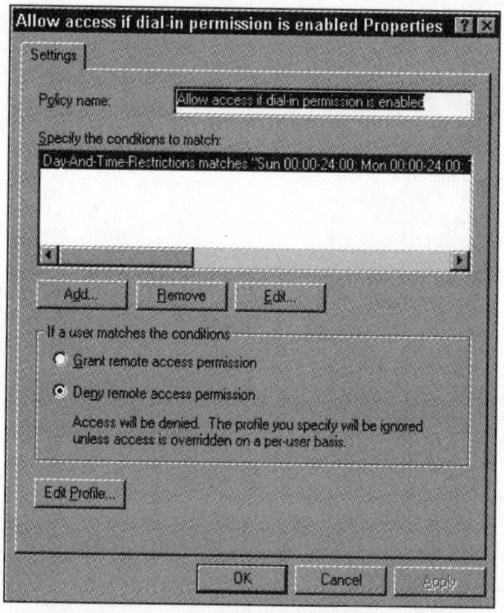

Book III
Chapter 6

Configuring,
Securing, and
Troubleshooting
Remote Access

Figure 6-4:
Use the
Settings tab
to edit an
existing
policy.

Use the Add, Remove, or Edit buttons to make changes to the existing policy attribute, and you can also change the Grant or Deny feature for the policy by selecting the desired radio button. Basically, editing a policy gives you the same options when creating a new policy, but you can easily change existing policies without having to remove and re-create them.

Configuring a remote access profile

For each remote access policy, you can configure the remote access profile. The profile defines settings for users who match the conditions you specify in the policy.

You can create/edit a profile when you first create the profile by clicking the Edit Profile button during the policy steps. You can also edit it by accessing the Properties of the policy and clicking the Edit Profile button.

This action opens the Profile window that contains six tabs. For the exam, you need to know what configuration options are available on each tab. The following sections point out what you need to know for the exam.

Configuring the Dial-in Constraints tab

The Dial-in Constraints tab, shown in Figure 6-5, allows you to set restrictions for the dial-in policy. You can choose to disconnect the connection if it is idle for a certain period of time, restrict the maximum session time, or restrict access to certain days and times. You can also choose to restrict the kind of dial-in media the client uses.

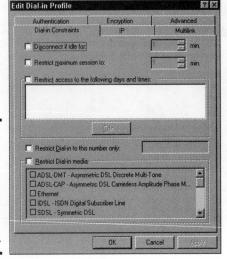

Figure 6-5:
Use the Dial-in Constraints tab to place restrictions on the remote user.

Configuring the IP tab

The IP tab allows you set a specific profile for the policy, such as server-assigned or client-requested IP address. By default, the Server Settings Define Policy radio button is selected.

Configuring the Multilink tab

You can also define multilink settings for this particular profile. By default, the profile uses the server settings, but you have the option to define multilink settings for this profile by using the Multilink tab, as shown in Figure 6-6. You can choose to either allow or disable multilink and use BAP, if desired. If you choose to use BAP, you specify when a link is dropped by the percentage of bandwidth usage and period of time. Additionally, you can require BAP for dynamic multilink requests.

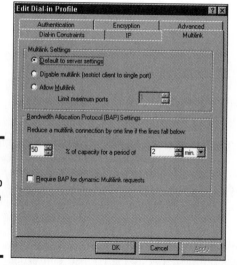

Figure 6-6:
Use the Multilink tab to configure multilink settings for the profile.

**Book III
Chapter 6**

Configuring,
Securing, and
Troubleshooting
Remote Access

Configuring the Authentication and Encryption tabs

You configure authentication and encryption settings for the RAS server by accessing the RAS server's properties. You can also configure Authentication and Encryption settings for policy's profile. This feature allows you to implement different encryption and authentication settings for each profile, if desired. The Authentication and Encryption tabs both provide you with a list of check boxes, where you can select the desired authentication and encryption settings. These are the same as the server properties, and you can review them in the "Configuring server properties" section earlier in this chapter.

Configuring the Advanced tab

The Advanced profile tab allows you to specify additional attributes to be returned to the Remote Access sever, as shown in Figure 6-7. If you click the Add button, you can see a lengthy list of attributes that you can select.

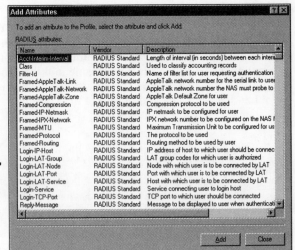

Figure 6-7: You can add additional attributes to a profile.

The Add Attributes option allows you to specify additional information for certain network client configurations. You don't need to know these attributes for the exam, but do keep in mind that you can configure specific client options on the Advanced profile tab.

Configuring virtual private networks

A virtual private network, or VPN, is an extension of a local private network that contains links across public networks, such as the Internet. With a VPN, you can establish a link between two computers across a public network and send information as if it were through a private point-to-point link.

To emulate this private link, data is encapsulated in a frame that provides routing information so that the data can travel over the public network to its destination. At the receiving end, the outer frame is removed to reveal the actual data inside. The data in the frame is encrypted for safety as it travels over the private network.

VPNs are effective solutions in many scenarios where one office needs to send data intermittently to another office without maintaining an expensive WAN link. By using the Internet as a transport mechanism, data can be transmitted safely and inexpensively.

VPNs have several new features in Windows 2000. You should keep these new features in mind for the exam, we've placed them in an easy-to-memorize bullet list.

✦ **Layer Two Tunneling Protocol (L2TP):** Windows 2000 supports both Point-to-Point Tunneling Protocol (PPTP) and L2TP, which is used with Windows 2000's Internet Protocol Security (IPsec). This combination creates very secure VPNs.

✦ **Remote Access Policies:** Remote Access policies can be used to set connection conditions for VPNs. This feature allows you to enforce different kinds of authentication and security features.

✦ **MS-CHAP V2:** With MS-CHAP V2, VPNs are greatly strengthened in terms of security because you can send encrypted data that requires the use of encryption keys for decoding.

✦ **Extensible Authentication Protocol (EAP):** EAP is supported for VPN connections. EAP allows you to use new authentication methods with RAS and VPNs, specifically Smart Card logon.

✦ **Account Lockout:** Account Lockout after a specified number of failed VPN connection attempts is now supported, but it is disabled by default.

After routing and remote access is installed, you can enable VPN usage on the RAS server by accessing the Ports option in the console tree. Select Ports, choose the Action menu, and then choose Properties. In the Port Properties sheet, you see a PPTP and L2TP Miniport available, shown in Figure 6-8.

**Book III
Chapter 6**

**Configuring,
Securing, and
Troubleshooting
Remote Access**

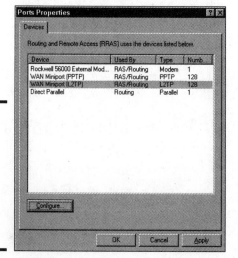

Figure 6-8:
Use the Ports properties sheet to configure the PPTP and L2TP ports.

As with other Ports, select the desired port and click the Configure button to allow remote access connections and demand-dial connections (inbound and outbound). This feature allows your server to accept PPTP or L2TP connections for data transmission.

After you configure your VPN ports, you can then create VPN policies and profiles as desired to manage your VPN connections. See the sections earlier in this chapter on policies and profiles.

Implementing and Troubleshooting Terminal Services for Remote Access

Terminal Services provides remote access to a server desktop through software that serves as a terminal emulator. This feature transmits the user interface to the client. The client then manages the interface through keyboard and mouse clicks that are returned to the server for processing. A terminal server can host many sessions at one time, and each session user sees only his or her manipulation of the interface.

Terminal Services for clients can run on a number of platforms, including Windows platforms and even Macintosh and UNIX platforms with additional third-party software.

You can deploy Terminal Services in either remote administration mode or application server mode, but not both at the same time. In remote administration mode, you can access your server from any terminal on your network and administer it remotely. In application services mode, terminals that may not be able to run Windows can connect to the terminal server and run applications as needed.

Terminal Services has several benefits, with a major one being the use of Windows 2000 and Windows 2000 applications on older computers that cannot support Windows 2000. This feature allows users to "get to know" Windows 2000 before being implemented on all client computers.

Reviewing Terminal Services administrative tools

Several administrative tools enable you to manage Terminal Services on your Windows 2000 server.

You need to know these tools for the exam and what you can do with each, so we list them here:

+ **Terminal Services Manager:** Use this interface to manage and monitor users, sessions, and processes on any server running Terminal Services on the network.

✦ **Terminal Services Configuration:** Use this interface to change the Terminal Services TCP/IP connection clients use to access the terminal server. You can name a connection, specify a connection transport and its properties, enable or disable logons, and so forth.

✦ **Active Directory Users and Computers and Local Users and Groups Extensions:** This feature extends Active Directory Users and Computers on domain controllers and local users and groups so that you can control Terminal Services features for each user.

✦ **Terminal Services Licensing:** Registers and tracks licenses for Terminal Services clients.

✦ **System Monitor Counters:** Terminal Services extends System Monitor by adding User and Session objects and their counters.

✦ **Task Manager Additional Fields:** Terminal Services provides two additional fields to Task Manager for monitoring and ending processes for all sessions.

✦ **Client Creator:** Use to make disks used to install the Terminal Services client.

✦ **Client Connection Manager:** The Client Connection Manager is installed on the client computer after Terminal Services are installed.

✦ **Multi-user Support in Add/Remove Programs:** Ensures that applications are installed for use in a multisession environment.

Installing Terminal Services

You install Terminal Services just as you do any other Windows 2000 component, through either Add/Remove programs in Control Panel or through the Configure Your Server tool. For specific instructions for installing this or any other Windows 2000 service, see Book III, Chapter 2.

When you choose to install Terminal Services, a window appears, asking to select one of two modes, either remote administration mode or application server mode. You can choose to install either one, but the exam expects you to know about both of them. After you install Terminal Services, you need to reboot your computer. Later sections explore both of these terminal server modes. You read about using both modes in the next several sections.

Using Terminal Services remote administration mode

You use Terminal Services remote administration mode to remotely manage your Windows 2000 Server from virtually any computer on your network.

**Book III
Chapter 6**

Configuring,
Securing, and
Troubleshooting
Remote Access

When you choose to install this mode, you should install it only on Windows 2000 Servers on an NTFS partition, and you don't need to enable Terminal Services Licensing for remote administration. Keep both of these points in mind for the exam.

After you install Terminal Services in remote administration mode, you can install Terminal Services on the desired client computer so that you can remote administer your server.

To install Terminal Services on the client, you need to make the installation disks by choosing Start⇨Programs⇨Administrative Tools⇨Terminal Services Client Creator. Follow the instructions that appear, and you need two floppy disks.

Use the two floppy disks to install the client Terminal Services on the desired client computers. After the installation is complete, launch the Terminal Services Client application from the Programs menu, and then enter an administrator username and password. The terminal appears on the remote computer, where you can administer the terminal server. With appropriate administrator permissions, you can configure the server just as if you were sitting at it.

You can use the Terminal Services Manager on the terminal server by choosing Start⇨Programs⇨Administrative Tools⇨Terminal Services Manager to manage sessions in progress, as shown in Figure 6-9.

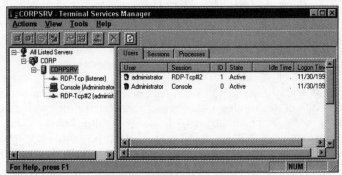

Figure 6-9:
Use
Terminal
Services
Manager to
manage
sessions.

By selecting the desired user and choosing the Action menu, you can disconnect the user, send the user a message, reset the connection, log the user off, and examine the status. Although these actions are all simple, they are considered important monitoring features, and you should keep them in mind for the exam.

You don't have to worry about licensing when using Terminal Services remote administration mode. Two concurrent connections are allowed and licenses for the connections are not needed.

Using Terminal Services application server mode

Application server mode enables users to connect to your terminal server and run applications. Keep in mind that all the processing is performed on the server's end, and users are simply provided a graphical interface. Though effective and very useful, you should consider the impact on system resources several sessions can create. Your processor and system RAM must be able to handle running multiple applications and processes when clients connect to the terminal server. In short, use the application server mode on a server that has high system resources and is not responsible for a multitude of other network tasks.

When you choose to install Terminal Services application server mode, a window appears, where you can select permissions compatible with Windows 2000 users or permissions compatible with Terminal Server 4.0 users. The Windows 2000 option provides the most secure environment. By default, users have the same permissions as members of the Users group, which may prevent them from running some legacy applications. If you are using legacy applications, you can choose to use Permissions compatible with Terminal Services 4.0 users.

However, when you select this option, users have full access to critical registry and file system locations, which is required by many legacy applications. However, this scenario can be dangerous, as you can see.

After you make your selection, a window appears, listing any programs that may not function properly in application server mode, so take note of those. You are also prompted for the location for the license server database, which is automatically installed by default in `C:\WINNT\System32\Lserver`.

For the exam, it is important to remember that Terminal Server licensing for the application server mode can apply to either an enterprise or domain, depending on which option you selected during setup. Keep in mind that terminal servers can only access domain license servers if they are in the same domain as the license server. Terminal Services has its own method for licensing clients that log onto the terminal server. Clients must receive a valid license before they are allowed to log on in application server mode. The license must be activated by Microsoft, which uses Microsoft Clearinghouse, a database to maintain and activate licenses.

However, terminal server allows unlicensed clients to connect for 90 days. After that time, terminal servers will not allow clients to connect without appropriate licenses. You can use the Terminal Server Licensing tool available in Administrative Tools to activate the license with the Microsoft database.

Book III
Chapter 6

Configuring, Securing, and Troubleshooting Remote Access

After you're all set up and ready to go, you need to install and configure applications for sharing for multisession access. This allows multiple users to access the same application at the same time.

You have two ways to set up sharing for multisession access. First, you can use Add/Remove programs in Control Panel to install the desired applications. You can also use the change user command at the command prompt before and after installing the program. The change user command ensures that program files are installed in the systemroot rather than in the windows subdirectory of the user's home directory. This process makes the program available for multisessions. The change user / install command places the system in install mode and turns off the .ini file mapping. After the program is installed, the change user / execute command returns the system to execute mode, restores the .ini file mapping, and redirects user specific data to the user's home directory.

Add/Remove Programs automatically runs the change user command in the background, so it is the preferred method for installing applications on a terminal server for multisession use.

After you install the applications, terminal service clients can then connect to the terminal server and open multiple sessions of the program.

Applications that were installed before you installed Terminal Services Application Server Mode will need to be reinstalled so that they are available to users in multisession mode. Keep this in mind for the exam.

When installing applications on your terminal server, you should disconnect any users to avoid potential problems. Also, testing your application installations is important. Some 16-bit programs may have problems working with Terminal Services, so you should test all installations and note any problems.

Managing Terminal Services connections

The Terminal Services Configuration tool, accessible by choosing Start⇨ Programs⇨Administrative Tools⇨Terminal Services Configuration, provides you an MMC interface to configure your Terminal Services connections and server settings. The Server Settings container gives you the attributes you configured during setup, which you can change from this location, if desired.

For the exam, you will most likely see a question or two about configuring your connections. If you click the Connections container in the console tree, you see an RDP-TCP connection in the details pane. Microsoft Remote Desktop Protocol (RDP) is the protocol used for Microsoft Terminal Services. If you use other terminal servers, you may use a different protocol, in which case you should check the third party's documentation.

You can create a new connection by selecting the Connections container, choosing the Action menu, and then clicking Create New Connection. A wizard assists you in creating the connection, but you only need to do so if you are using third-party terminal services. If you are only using Microsoft Terminal Services, the RDP-TCP connection is all you need.

If you select the RDP-TCP connection, and then choose the Action menu, you can access the properties pages for the connection.

Several tabs are available, but the following sections only examine the ones you need to know for the exam.

Configuring the General Tab

The General tab reports to you the type of connection, the transport (TCP), and allows you to make a comment. The important point about the General tab is you can change the Encryption settings by clicking the drop-down menu. Terminal Services in Windows 2000 server supports the use of encrypted data between the client and the server.

You have three levels of encryption, which you need to know for the exam:

+ **Low:** Encryption based on the server's standard key strength protects only data sent from the client to the server.

+ **Medium:** Encryption based on the server's standard key strength protects all data sent between the client and the server.

+ **High:** Encryption based on the server's maximum key strength protects all data sent between the client and the server.

Configuring the Sessions tab

The Sessions tab allows you to configure default settings to manage user sessions. None of these settings are enabled by default, but you can use them to place certain restrictions on users. (See Figure 6-10.)

To create the restrictions, simply select the desired check boxes, drop-down menus, and radio buttons to configure the restrictions as desired. For example, you can choose to end a disconnected session after a certain period of time, limit active sessions, create an idle session limit, and even override user settings.

Configuring the Environment tab

The Environment tab allows you to override settings from the user's profile and Client Connection Manager.

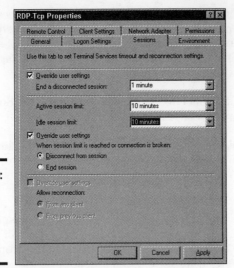

Figure 6-10:
Use the
Sessions
tab to set
sessions
limits.

When you override the settings, you can choose to start a program when the user logs on, and you can choose to disable wallpaper, which can greatly conserve server resources.

Reviewing Terminal Services commands

Terminal Services has several commands that you can use to manage the terminal server. You need to know these for the exam. See Book II, Chapter 7 to review the commands.

Configure and Troubleshoot Network Address Translation and Internet Connection Sharing

Network Address Translation (NAT) is an addressing scheme that allows the translation of private network addresses into a public IP address for use on the Internet. NAT is a common translation method often used by firewalls and related products. For example, say that on your network, users access a RAS server to access the Internet. The RAS server can translate those private IP addresses into public IP addresses so that the internal IP addresses are hidden from the public network. Should a hacker from the Internet attempt to use one of the public-translated IP addresses, the hacker cannot gain access to the private network because the real IP addresses of the clients are hidden.

You find NAT at work in many firewall products, including residential gateways and routers for small office or home networks. Windows 2000 RAS can also use NAT. You can use NAT with any routed connection to the Internet with a dial-up connection or even a network interface connection to the Internet.

To implement NAT on a Windows 2000 Server, simply open the Routing and Remote Access Server console (RRAS), right-click the server name, and then choose Configure and Enable Routing and Remote Access. In the wizard that appears, choose the Internet connection server option and click Next. In the Internet Connection Server setup, you can choose to use ICS or NAT, as shown in Figure 6-11.

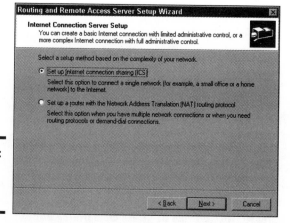

Figure 6-11:
Select either ICS or NAT.

Book III
Chapter 6

**Configuring,
Securing, and
Troubleshooting
Remote Access**

When you select the NAT option, you can either configure a LAN connection or a demand-dial interface. Follow the remaining steps in the wizard to configure the Internet NAT server. When clients access the server, NAT is used to translate private IP addresses to public IP addresses.

In the same basic manner, ICS shares a single Internet connection so that multiple clients can use the same connection. To the Internet, it appears as though a single client is accessing the Internet because a single public IP address is used. However, ICS is designed for the home or small office network, not a Windows domain. Both Windows 2000 Server and Windows 2000 Professional support ICS. You can set up ICS from the Network and Dial-up Connections folder. From an exam point of view, remember that ICS should not be used in a large Windows network where multiple servers are in use because ICS interferes with some of these services. ICS is designed to be a great home and small office solution, however.

Prep Test

1 A certain RAS server was previously configured to be a remote access server. However, you would like to change this configuration so that the RAS server functions as a router. How can you configure this option?

   A ○ Reinstall RAS.

   B ○ Access the General properties tab and select the router option.

   C ○ Access the Options properties tab and select the router option.

   D ○ Run the RASROUTE command.

2 Which RAS authentication protocol can use smart cards?

   A ○ EAP

   B ○ MS-CHAP

   C ○ Shiva Password Authentication Protocol

   D ○ PAP

3 Which PPP option uses the BAP protocol?

   A ○ Multilink

   B ○ LCP Extensions

   C ○ PPTP

   D ○ EAP

4 You have created several remote access policies. One policy should prohibit users from accessing the RAS Server during the hours of 10:00 a.m. and 12:00 p.m. each day. However, the policy grants users the right instead of denying users the right. What should you do?

   A ○ Select Remote Access Policies in the console, right-click the policy, and then choose Deny.

   B ○ Select Remote Access Policies in the console, right-click the policy, choose Properties, and then choose Deny.

   C ○ Select Remote Access Policies in the console, right-click the policy, choose Properties, and then choose Remote Permissions.

   D ○ Select Remote Access Policies in the console, right-click the policy, choose Properties, and then choose Delete.

5 You need to use a VPN connection on a Windows 2000 Professional computer, accessing a Windows NT 4.0 VPN server. What protocol can you use?

A ○ L2TP

B ○ PPTP

C ○ PPP

D ○ PPNP

6 In what two modes can you deploy Terminal Services?

A ❑ Application mode

B ❑ Server mode

C ❑ Workstation mode

D ❑ Remote administration

7 You want to use Terminal Services for remote administration. Which statement is true concerning licensing?

A ○ You need one licensing server.

B ○ You need two licensing servers.

C ○ You need three licensing servers.

D ○ Remote administration does not require a license.

8 You want to use Terminal Services in application server mode. You'll be using several legacy applications. Which permission should you use?

A ○ Windows 2000

B ○ Terminal Server 4.0

C ○ RRAS

D ○ Use no permissions.

9 You want to implement NAT on a Windows 2000 Server so that clients can use a demand-dial interface. Where can you enable NAT?

A ○ RRAS

B ○ Terminal Services

C ○ Active Directory Users and Computers

D ○ On the dial-up connection

10 Which statement is *not* true concerning ICS?

A ○ ICS provides a shared Internet connection, where one IP address is used on the Internet.

B ○ ICS is designed for small office or home networks and not Windows 2000 domains.

C ○ ICS requires a Windows 2000 Server.

D ○ ICS can provide a demand-dial interface.

Answers

1 **B.** You can change the RAS configuration on the General tab. *Review "Configuring the General tab."*

2 **A.** Extensible authentication protocol uses third-party authentication software, such as Smart Cards. *Read "Configuring the Security tab."*

3 **A.** Multilink uses the BAP or BACP protocols. *Review "Configuring the PPP tab."*

4 **B.** Access the properties to change allow or deny permission. *"Configuring and Troubleshooting Remote Access Policy."*

5 **B.** L2TP and PPTP are both VPN protocols. Hovever, Windows NT supports only the use of PPTP, so if you are connecting to a Windows NT VPN Server, PPTP is your only choice. *Study "Configuring Virtual Private Networks."*

6 **A** and **D.** Only these two modes are supported by Terminal Services in Windows 2000. *See "Installing Terminal Services."*

7 **D.** You can use remote administration mode without any licensing. *Study "Using Terminal Services remote admin. mode."*

8 **B.** Use Terminal Server 4.0 if you want to use legacy applications. *Study "Using Terminal Services application server mode."*

9 **A.** Use the RRAS Configuration Wizard to set up RRAS as an Internet server using NAT. *See "Configuring and Troubleshooting Network Address Translation (NAT) and Internet Connection Sharing."*

10 **C.** You can configure an ICS host on Windows 2000 Professional, as well as other operating systems, such as Windows 98, Me, and XP. *Study "Configuring and Troubleshooting Network Address Translation and Internet Connection Sharing."*

Book IV

The Network+ Exam

Contents at a Glance

Chapter 1: About the Network+ Exam

In This Chapter

✔ Checking out the format of the Network+ exam

✔ Knowing how to study: Preparing for the exam

✔ Scheduling and paying for the exam

CompTIA (the certification outfit for A+, Network+, Server+, i-Net+, and a vast array of other pluses) has revised the Network+ certification program for hard-working network technicians who have an excellent general knowledge of networks and internetworking technologies. Passing the Network+ exam certifies to the world that a technician possesses the knowledge required to configure and install TCP/IP clients.

Unlike other networking certifications — such as MCSE (Microsoft Certified Systems Engineer), CNE (Certified Novell Engineer), or CCNA (Cisco Certified Networking Associate) — Network+ certification covers all kinds of general network-technology knowledge and practices. It doesn't limit its scope to brand-specific stuff; Apple, Microsoft, Novell and other manufacturers and their products are included on the Network+ test, making it the true measure of a networking technician's overall grasp of networking and internetworking technology.

Meeting the Objectives

The Network+ exam is the result of an industry-wide analysis of what skills and knowledge a networking technician must have after 18 to 24 months of on-the-job experience. The final test, as published in January 2002, reflects the culmination of over five years of skill-set and test development by the IT Skills Project task force.

The questions on the Network+ exam cover four topic areas of networking technology knowledge, called *domains* in the exam objectives:

✦ Media and topologies

✦ Protocols and standards

✦ Network implementation

✦ Network support (also known as *troubleshooting*)

Table 1-1 lists and describes the four domains of the Network+ exam, the topics within each major area, and the percentage (and number of questions) that each area represents on the total test.

Table 1-1	Network+ Exam Domains	
Area	*Percentage of Test*	*Content*
1.0 Media and topologies	20%	Basic network terminology and knowledge of networking elements — including media, connectors, structure, topologies, and the OSI model.
2.0 Protocols and standards	25%	TCP/IP, IPX/SPX, and Apple protocols and the application of the OSI model.
3.0 Network implementation	23%	Network planning, design, configuration, and installation procedures.
4.0 Network support	32%	Network troubleshooting techniques, procedures, and tools.

The format of the Network+ exam is a hybrid of formats used for many other certification exams. Although the A+ exam has recently converted to an adaptive testing format, the Network+ exam (at least for the time being) remains a *serial exam* — what you might call your basic, standard, multiple-choice test. An *adaptive* test, on the other hand, bases the difficulty of your next question on whether you get the current question right or wrong.

For now, you can expect predominantly multiple-choice questions on the Network+ exam. You don't have to worry about not giving all the correct answers on multiple right-answer questions. There are no "choose all that apply" questions. Any question that has more than one correct answer has two tip-offs:

✦ The first tip-off is that instead of a round button beside each answer choice, you'll see a square box.

✦ The second tip-off is that at the bottom-left corner of the screen is the exact number of answers expected. This number has some importance; when you finish answering the exam questions, any that you haven't given enough answers for are highlighted as incomplete.

Expect at least one question that asks you to mark components and network types on electronic illustrations, as well as a couple of questions that ask you to identify a network component (or troubleshooting area) from an exhibit.

Counting up the questions

If you choose to do the optional test tutorial that can orient you to the question types you're about to encounter, the time you spend doesn't count against the time limit. Your actual testing time doesn't begin until you click the Start button for the test.

We recommend that you use the Item Review feature built into the test engine, pacing yourself to allow some time at the end of the exam for another look at any questionable answers or unanswered questions. (When you encounter a tough question, an immediate guess is usually better than no response at all; you may not get a chance to review everything you marked.)

During the life of the Network+ exam, the number of questions, the time allowed to take the exam, or the minimum passing score may change. For the latest information about the test, go to the CompTIA Web site (www.comptia.org).

As with all CompTIA tests, you know immediately how you did. After you completely signoff and exit the test engine, the test center administrator has a printout of your results waiting for you. The Score Report is a standardized format that shows you both a Gantt chart and a section-by-section breakdown of how you did. The Gantt chart shows your score represented as a bar plotted against a bar of the Required Score you must make (or beat) to pass the exam. Below that, you get a Section Analysis that shows for each section how many questions were on the test and how many you answered correctly. For any sections in which you answered incorrectly, the blueprint summary is printed.

Although the exam objectives are divided into four distinct sections, the questions on the test are not. Questions from all domains and all topics are intermixed throughout the test, often with more than one domain covered in a single question.

Drawing on your knowledge

You may encounter a question that asks you to mark items on illustrations with a crosshair-like cursor. You use this icon to pick which part of a network diagram includes a repeater, or to locate a bus topology, or to hone in on a network segment.

Working a Study Plan

Knowing your stuff is the key to passing the Network+ exam. So, how do you make sure you're ready and able to give certification your best shot? Use the questions in this book (or on a test simulator) to determine the parts of the test that you need to give the most study. Although you shouldn't ignore any test topic completely, focus on the areas in which you need to improve your knowledge.

At the end of each chapter in this book, you can find a Prep Test that covers the topics in the chapter. On the CD-ROM that accompanies this book, you'll find a test engine with hundreds of practice questions. The CD-ROM also contains five PDFs of Practice Exams, each focused on one of the five exams covered in this book. Also, many test simulators are commercially available.

Go through this book and mark the pages that have lists, tables, and diagrams. It's a fact of certification life that certain information requires memorization. For example, the maximum distance for a thinnet cable, the OSI layer of a particular device, or the address range for a Class B network are typical of the answers that nobody can figure out from the data in the question. You have to know this stuff inside and out. Begin committing this information to memory as soon as you can — and remember to refresh your quick recall regularly.

We also highly recommend using at least one (or more) of the commercially available practice test banks to help you prepare for the exam. You're better prepared if you can get a different perspective and interpretation of the exam and its questions.

You may want to use other resources as well. Sometimes a slightly different explanation or approach to a subject can bring the material into sharper focus. The CompTIA Web site (www.comptia.org) lists a number of companies offering study aids and practice tests.

Practice makes passing

Keep yourself focused on the topics that we identify as being on the test; avoid studying any new technologies that debuted within the six-month period before the release of the exam. The very latest, brand-new, cutting-edge stuff, such as Windows XP, won't be on the test — that's guaranteed. Hold off on studying the new stuff till *after* you're certified.

The benefits you enjoy from Network+ certification are well worth the time you invest in studying for and taking the test. Whatever method you use to prepare for the test, create a plan and then stick to it. Give yourself ample time to truly understand the material instead of relying purely on memorization. If you can grasp the concepts behind the details, the facts may start to make some sense.

Here are a few tips to consider as you prepare for the test:

✦ Focus on the exam objectives, which lay out the full landscape of the test's coverage. CompTIA is very good at staying within the boundaries established by the exam objectives; you can access the full exam objectives at `www.comptia.org/certification/networkplus/all_about_networkplus.htm`.

✦ Use the Prep Tests and sample exam questions throughout this book and on the accompanying CD, as well as any other practice tests to which you have access. You can't take too many practice tests.

✦ Take occasional short breaks, a day or two, from studying. You can overdo the intensity and burn out. This test is very important, but it isn't a life-and-death issue. Keep your perspective.

How much studying is enough, anyway?

It all depends on you. Gilster's Law of Test Preparation says: "You never can tell, and it all depends." You never can tell how much preparation you'll need, and it depends on your experience, your education, and so on. Seasoned veterans of the networking wars may need only to catch up on the very latest stuff, but someone just starting out in network technology may have a much greater challenge getting ready for the exam.

Because someone (probably you!) is investing real money to pay for this test, we suggest erring on the side of too much studying, if that's possible. If you're intent on passing, make your goal to pass the first time (unless you can afford to take the test just to find out what you should study). All we can say is, "This book is much less expensive than the test, and we tell you what to study." But, then again, it's your money! If you have any excess funds burning a crater in your pocket, you could always send them to us care of Wiley Publishing, Inc. (Just kidding. We think.)

Scheduling the Test

An important move toward grabbing that golden ring of certification (after repeating right out loud — with feeling — "I think I can, I think I can . . .") involves registration through either Prometric or VUE. To schedule an exam, access the Prometric Web site at `www.2test.com` or the NCS/VUE Web site at `www.vue.com`. If your company is a member of CompTIA, the test fees are a bit lower, so by all means take advantage of that.

Be ready with credit card information or plan to mail a check for the registration fee (not a great option if you're in a hurry). Schedule the exam as far as six weeks in advance, but at least two days before your desired test date. The Web sites of both testing companies allow you to set a date and time and pick a testing center near your home — or close to the vacation spot where you'll celebrate after the exam. Both companies have literally thousands of locations worldwide, so it shouldn't be too hard finding one near you.

We recommend contacting the testing service as soon as you think you're entering the final phases of your preparation for the exam. Some sites aren't available every day of the week, and some have only certain hours of the day available. The earlier you contact them, the better.

Paying the Price

If you are a corporate member of the CompTIA organization and you live in the United States, the Network+ registration currently costs $140. If you can round up about 50 or more of your friends or co-workers to take the test, the price can be even lower. Nonmembers pay $190, whether one person registers or a small army. International pricing varies, depending on the exchange rate. Of course, CompTIA could change its fees at any time (yet another great reason to contact it early), so don't hold us to these dollar amounts.

Prometric and VUE welcome all generally accepted credit cards. You may make other payment arrangements with the testing folks, such as paying by check or money order, but before you can take the test, you must be paid in full.

Chapter 2: Networking Basics

Exam Objectives

- ✓ Understanding basic network structures
- ✓ Defining network types
- ✓ Differentiating common network topologies
- ✓ Identifying common network media and connectors
- ✓ Listing the characteristics of common network media
- ✓ Describing the media and function of a network backbone
- ✓ Defining a network segment

The Network+ exam assumes you have fundamental knowledge of trouble-shooting, fixing, installing, designing, and upgrading networks. If you're not keen on networking topologies, media, networking technologies, and so forth, you may not do well on the Network+ exam (or the MCSA track exam, for that matter). Without a fundamental understanding of network concepts and principles, you may have some difficulty brilliantly deducing the right answer to a question about the best approach to configuring, installing, improving, or troubleshooting an Ethernet network, which is the focus of the Network+ exam.

Covering Networking Basics

Even if you know the Father of Ethernet personally and truly understand the basic concepts and usage of networking and network topologies, you should still review this chapter. A general knowledge can help you understand how networks work, but that knowledge may not be enough to answer some of the more complicated questions on a test. We recommend that you review the networking fundamentals in this chapter as a part of your test preparation. You should also give this info a quick review before you take the test, just in case.

Here's the most basic of network basics: *A network is two or more computers connected by a transmission media for the purpose of sharing resources.* This is on the test!

You absolutely must understand this concept. One computer (or even a computer just connected to a printer) cannot be a network. A *network* is two or more computers connected by some form of communications media that enables them to share data, software, or hardware resources. Think about it: What better reason to connect two computers than to enable one to access and use something the other one has? Sharing resources is what networks are all about.

Figure 2-1 illustrates this concept: Adam's computer is connected to Eve's computer so that Adam can use Eve's new killer laser printer. In this configuration, Adam and Eve can also share data on each other's hard drives. Although the configuration is extremely simple, the two computers in Figure 2-1 form a network.

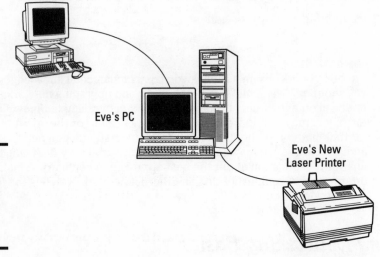

Adam's PC

Eve's PC

Eve's New
Laser Printer

Figure 2-1:
Two
computers
can form a
simple
network.

Whether the required resource is software, data, or access to a particular piece of hardware, such as Eve's printer, the network puts everything within fingertip reach of the user, as if each user were directly connected to every other user's PC.

Peer-to-peer and client/server networks

Essentially, there are really only two types of networks:

✦ **Peer-to-peer:** Also known as a peer-based network. In a *peer-to-peer network,* a user's PC is neither a master or slave. Peer-to-peer networks are voluntary, you-trust-me-and-I'll-trust-you affairs. A peer network user voluntarily shares his or her resources with the other network users.

✦ **Client/server:** Also known as a server-based network, a *client/server network* has a centralized server or *host* computer that services the resource requests of the network's users. Figure 2-2 shows a simple client/server network. Nearly all the questions on the Network+ exam are in some way related to client/server networks.

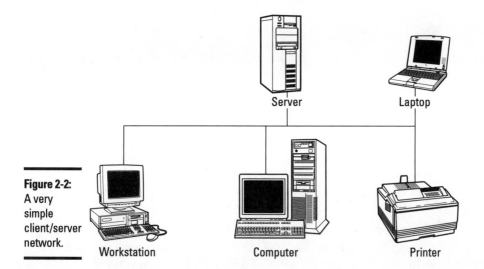

Server   Laptop

Figure 2-2:
A very
simple
client/server
network.

Workstation   Computer   Printer

Oh sure, there are many different network technologies and topologies and communication services, but all of the above exist in either a peer-to-peer or a client/server type of network.

Table 2-1 lists the major factors that differentiate peer-to-peer and client/server networks.

Table 2-1	Peer-to-Peer versus Client/Server Networks	
Factor	*Peer-to-Peer*	*Client/Server-Based*
Number of workstations	2-10	Limited only by the network hardware and software in use.
Relative cost	Inexpensive	Can be very expensive, depending on network size.
Security	User-managed	Centrally administered.
Administration	User-managed	Centrally administered.
Data backups	Each user responsible for backing up his or her own data.	Backups centrally created.

How many users can a network have?

Generally, a peer-to-peer network is effective only to a maximum of 10 workstations. Remember that on a peer-based network, each user has to manage his or her own resources and also who is allowed to access and use them. With more than 10 users on the network, this can become time-consuming and burdensome. Eventually, this effort can become so much that the network users (the peers) decide to install a client/server network and appoint someone as the central network administrator.

On the other hand, the number of user computers that can be supported by a client/server network is virtually unlimited. For an example of how large a client/server network can grow, consider the Internet, the granddaddy of all networks, and how it continues to grow and grow and grow.

Many factors can each impose a limit on the number of workstations on a network. These factors include such variables as the type of cable used, the network operating system, and how much money you're willing to spend on connectivity devices; see "Moving Around Network Cabling" later in this chapter.

Who controls security?

The real difference between peer-to-peer and client/server networks truly lies in security. In a peer-based network, *security* — that is, who can access a resource and what can they do with it — is controlled by the owner/operator of each workstation. Security is granted to individual users on the peer network individually and one resource at a time.

In the Windows world (meaning Windows 9*x*, Windows Me, Windows NT, Windows 2000, and Windows XP), the permission needed to share a printer, scanner, or a data folder is granted to individual users on the Network Neighborhood by the resource owner.

For example, in both Windows 9*x* and Windows 2000, file and folder permissions are granted through the Shared Files Properties function. You can access this function from Windows Explorer by right-clicking the folder to be shared (in this case, the My Documents folder) and choosing Sharing.

Server-based networks have a central administrator (or a group of administrators if it's a large network), who is responsible for the function, security, and integrity of the entire network, including the workstations. The central network administrator sets the permissions (which control the files, folders, and resources that network users can access) either on an individual or group basis, as well as manages the network configuration and troubleshoots problems that arise.

The client/server network users are relieved of these responsibilities for network-wide resources. However, users can still share their local resources by using the same mechanisms as used on a peer-based network.

Defining networks near and far

You need to worry about only two network classifications on the Network+ exam: local area networks (LANs) and wide area networks (WANs). You may actually see other network classifications here and there on the test (usually as a wrong answer), but your focus should be on the differences between these two:

✦ **Local area network (LAN):** A LAN, which enables users to share resources, connects workstations (also called nodes) in a relatively small geographical area — typically in a single office, department, or building.

✦ **Wide area network (WAN):** A WAN connects nodes and interconnects LANs that are located across geographically large areas, such as states, countries, and continents, by using dedicated long-distance, high-speed lines. The Internet is the *mother* of all WANs.

Please accept my topologies

If you have ever seen an aerial view of a city and its roads, you have the general idea of a network topology. Just like the streets, roads, and highways in a city provide its general layout, a network topology defines a network's general layout and shape. The pattern of connections that tie workstations to a network is its *topology*.

The four basic network topologies (and the ones you should know for the exam) are

✦ **Bus:** Nodes are connected to a central cable, called a *backbone*, which runs the length of the network.

✦ **Ring:** The primary network cable is installed as a ring or loop and workstations are attached to the primary cable through access points attached to the ring.

✦ **Star:** On a star topology (in its purest form), each workstation is connected with its own cable directly to a central server or other network device in a starburst-like pattern. However, as it is most commonly implemented, a star topology is used to connect workstations to a hub, which provides a connection to the network for each of its workstations.

✦ **Mesh:** Each workstation is directly connected to all other workstations of a network, creating a mess, we mean, mesh of network connections.

**Book IV
Chapter 2**

Networking Basics

This topology, which provides the most redundancy of the basic topologies, is not common, but you may encounter it on the exam.

Exam-wise, here's what you should remember about topologies:

✦ The **bus topology** is commonly used for Ethernet networks, especially coaxial cable implementations. Figure 2-3 shows a bus topology.

✦ The **ring topology** is the basis for the Token Ring network structure. Figure 2-4 illustrates a ring topology.

✦ In today's world, the **star topology** is used with both Ethernet and Token Ring networks to cluster workstations to hubs, switches, routers, or in the case of Token Ring, multistation access units (MAUs), which are in turn attached to the primary network cable. Figure 2-5 illustrates the star arrangement.

✦ **The mesh topology** is most commonly applied in a WAN environment. If you see a network topology diagram on the exam in which every node is connected to every other node, the diagram is depicting a mesh topology. Figure 2-6 attempts to illustrate the concept of a mesh network.

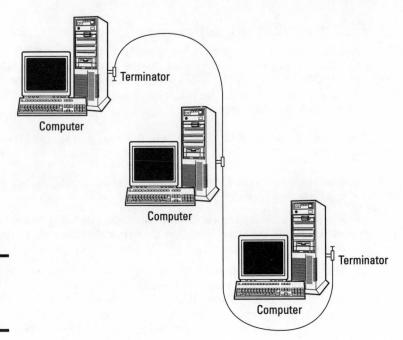

Figure 2-3:
A network in a bus topology.

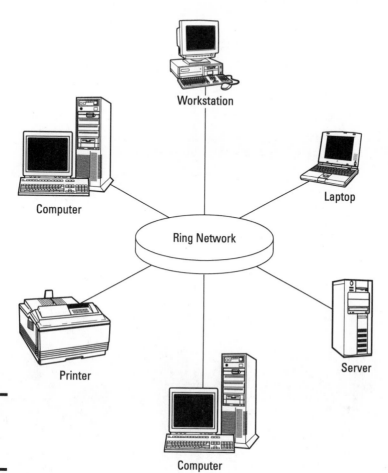

Workstation

Computer

Laptop

Ring Network

Printer

Server

Computer

Figure 2-4:
A network
in a ring
topology.

Riding the bus

In a network implemented on the bus topology, all nodes are connected to the network backbone. Remember that network backbone is the primary network cable and in a bus topology it runs the length of the network.

In its simplest form, a bus network consists of workstations that connect to the backbone in a daisy-chain arrangement as illustrated in Figure 2-3. This implementation is very common with Ethernet networks installed on either thinnet or thicknet cabling. (See "Coaxial cables through thick and thin" later in this chapter.)

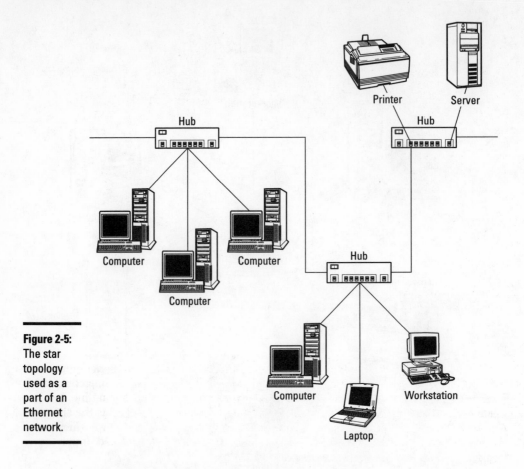

Figure 2-5:
The star
topology
used as a
part of an
Ethernet
network.

The defining characteristic of a bus topology network is the backbone cable that runs the length of a network. On a bus network, workstations and other networked devices typically attach directly to the backbone or are connected through a hub or another type of clustering device.

Bus topologies have three primary characteristics: signal transmission, cable termination, and continuity.

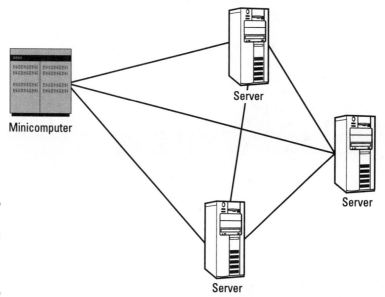

Figure 2-6:
A network in
a simplified
mesh
topology.

Minicomputer

Server

Server

Server

Signal transmission

To avoid communication problems, such as when two network computers or other devices try to transmit data at the same time, only one computer can transmit a signal on a bus network backbone at any given time. Politely, when one node is "talking," the other nodes are "listening." As the signal travels down the cable, the nodes examine the signal to see whether it was sent to them. The signal passes down the cable uninterrupted until it reaches the correct workstation.

Bus network nodes listen for messages sent only to them and do not pass signals along by regenerating the signal; therefore, the bus topology is considered a *passive* network structure.

The bus topology is commonly known as Ethernet. Ethernet networks are passive networks because they don't regenerate signals from one node to the next.

Cable termination

By definition, only one signal should be on the backbone of a bus-topology network at a time. So what do you do if a signal misfires? Or two signals are transmitted on the backbone at the same time? Without some electronic thingy to absorb the errant signals to prevent them from bouncing back and forth on the network backbone, a renegade signal would ricochet indefinitely, preventing any and every other signal from being sent. Terminating the cable at each end helps prevent a message from riding the bus indefinitely. The *terminator* is a resistor that's placed on each end of the backbone cable to absorb errant signals and clear the cable.

If the backbone cable breaks or has an open end (an open connection, for example), the network is sure to malfunction because signals are too busy bouncing around to reach the terminators.

If the network is connected to another network through a bridge, router, or other connectivity device, the terminated cable is also known as a *segment*. Two computers on the same wire are on the same segment. Two computers on two different wires may be on the same network, but they're on different segments of the network.

Continuity check

As long as a bus network's cable has no open ends and is properly terminated, the network continues to function properly and happily. However, even if one of the nodes on the network fails, as long as its cable connections are intact, the network cable is operable. This doesn't mean that any problems that the failed node is causing magically disappear; it means only that the network cable is still okay.

Problems on a bus topology network are typically caused by hardware devices, such as cable connectors, NICs, hubs, and the like.

Won't you wear my ring around your net?

As depicted in Figure 2-4, the ring topology looks like, well, a ring. The primary network cable forms a loop that has no beginning or end, which eliminates termination problems on the network. A signal placed on the network cable travels around the ring from node to node until it reaches its destination. A ring structure is rarely installed in a perfectly round shape, but you already guessed that amazing truth, right?

In contrast to the bus topology, the ring topology is an *active topology*. Each node on the ring network receives the signal, examines it, and then regenerates it onto the network. Therefore, if a computer on the network fails and is unable to regenerate the signal, the entire network is affected and continuity is lost.

The access control method used on a ring network is called *token passing*. A special kind of message is designated as a *token* and only the node in possession of the token, a kind of hall pass, has access to the network. When a message is sent out over the ring, the token is included so that the destination node can access the network to reply. When the originating node is finished transmitting, it releases the token and passes it upstream to the next active node wishing to transmit on the network.

Like the bus network, only one ring network node can send data at a time. Only the node with the token can transmit to the network. None of the other nodes can send messages to the network because they don't have the token. It's as simple as that!

I want to see stars!

Once upon a time, terminals were directly connected to mainframes by individual runs of wire that resulted in a configuration of wires sprouting from the central unit giving it the look of a starburst. Ah, the good old days! This same configuration is the basis for the star topology, in which network nodes are directly connected to the central server.

The star topology can be used as the structure for an entire network, but this setup is rare these days. ARCNet networks (a legacy networking type) use the star topology. Ironically, the primary reason ARCNet networks aren't popular these days is because of the star topology: Each workstation on an ARCNet network has a direct wire (called a *home-run*) to the server; when the server is down, so are the workstations' network services.

Mixed topologies

Today, the star topology is commonly used in conjunction with other topologies. You can use the star topology to improve the configuration and performance of the bus and ring topologies by creating clusters of workstations that attach to the bus or ring backbones through a clustering device, such as a hub or a switch. The result: hybrid or mixed topologies, such as the star-bus and the star-ring (also called the *ringed-star*):

✦ **Star-bus:** Used with bus (Ethernet) networks. A hub is used as the central or clustering device, which is then attached to the network backbone. This is the most common topology of Ethernet networks and is shown in Figure 2-5.

**Book IV
Chapter 2**

Networking Basics

✦ **Star-ring:** Used with ring (Token Ring) networks. An MAU is used to cluster workstations and to connect with the next MAU to complete the ring. Used in lieu of a pure ring structure, the star-ring is the most common form of ring networks.

Moving Around Network Cabling

Networks use cables made of three materials: copper, glass, and a special kind of plastic. (Yes, the same stuff you find in pennies, windows, and pop bottles.) All of these substances are relatively inexpensive and abundant, but more importantly, they're all excellent conductors, each in its own way. Copper is a great conductor of electricity, and glass and plastic are super conduits of light.

In order for one computer to carry on a conversation with another computer, both computers must be able to transmit and receive electrical impulses that represent the encoded data and commands being transmitted. Whether peer-to-peer or client/server (see "Peer-to-peer and client/server networks" earlier in the chapter), the computers and peripherals of a network are interconnected through a *transmission medium* (the technical term for a network cable) that enables the exchange of those electrical signals. Network media (the plural term for medium) comprise the foundation on which networks grow — literally.

The big three of cabling

Perhaps the best news in this book, beyond the fact that you don't have to memorize the name of every network operating system (NOS) that ever existed for the Network+ exam, is that you need to know just three cable media types for the exam:

✦ **Coaxial:** Also known as coax (co-axe), this type of cable is like the cable used to connect your television set to the cable TV outlet. Actually, networks use two types of coax cable: thick coaxial cable and thin coaxial cable. For a description of each type, see the upcoming section "Coaxial cables through thick and thin."

✦ **Twisted pair (No, not the upstairs neighbors):** Twisted pair cable is available in two types: unshielded twisted pair (UTP) and shielded twisted pair (STP). Head to the section "The twisted pair," later in this chapter, for more about — what else? — twisted pair cables.

✦ **Fiber-optic:** Glass or plastic strands carry modulated pulses of light to represent digital data in the form of electronic signals. See the section "You need your fiber" later in the chapter for more information on fiber-optic cables.

Technical cable stuff

All network cabling has characteristics that guide you in picking the most appropriate cable for a given situation. Here are definitions for the ones you may find on the Network+ exam:

✦ **Bandwidth (speed):** The amount of data a cable can carry in a certain period. Bandwidth is often expressed as the number of bits (either kilobits or megabits) that can be transmitted in a second. For example, UTP cable is nominally rated with a bandwidth of 10 million bits per second (10 Mbps).

✦ **Cost:** This is always a major consideration when choosing a cable type. However, the Network+ exam only deals with cost on a comparative basis. The relative cost comparisons are

- **Twisted pair cable** is the least expensive, but has distance limitations that may require additional hardware, such as a repeater or hub, which can add additional expense and offset part or all of the cable savings.

- **Coaxial cable** is slightly more expensive than twisted pair, but it typically doesn't require additional network hardware and is usually inexpensive to maintain.

- **Fiber-optic cabling** is the most expensive, requires skilled installation labor, and is costlier to install and maintain than the copper medium cables. However, because of its superior characteristics (see "You need your fiber" later in this chapter), it may be worth the added expense — when it is used in the right situations.

✦ **Maximum segment length:** Every cable is subject to a condition called *attenuation,* which is the weakening of a transmitted signal as it travels down the cable. Every cable type has an attenuation point at which the signal is so weakened that it is in danger of becoming unrecognizable and requires retransmission and regeneration. The attenuation point in any cable is stated as a distance-specific length (typically in meters) for every cable type. This distance is the maximum segment length for each specific cable medium, which means that a single segment of cable between two transmission points cannot exceed this length without being regenerated. For example, the maximum segment length for twisted pair cable is 100 meters.

✦ **Maximum number of nodes per segment:** Every time you add a device to a network, the effect is like another hole being put in the cable. Like too many leaks in a water hose, too many devices attached to a network cable reduces the "pressure" of the line and increases the impact of attenuation on the segment. So, in order to minimize the impact of attenuation, the number of devices that can be attached to a cable segment is also limited. Exceeding the maximum number of nodes on a cable segment can compromise the quality of the communications on a network.

✦ **Resistance to interference:** The different cable media have varying vulnerabilities to electromagnetic interference (EMI) or radio frequency interference (RFI) that are caused by electric motors, fluorescent light fixtures, your magnet collection, the radio station broadcasting from the next floor of your home or office, and so on. As the construction of the cable and its *cladding* (coverings) varies, so does its resistance to EMI and RFI signals.

Just for clarification, a *network segment* is created each time you add a network device that regenerates or redirects the message signals being transmitted over the network. Examples of such devices are routers, switches, bridges, hubs, and repeaters. We discuss these networking types in Book IV, Chapter 3.

Memorize the characteristics of thin and thick coaxial cable, unshielded twisted pair cable, and fiber-optic cable, especially because they're used in an Ethernet network as defined in the Institute of Electrical and Electronics Engineers (IEEE) 802.3 (which we cover in the later section "The Ethernet Cable Standards"). Be sure you know all of the other names coax cable goes by, which we list in the section "The coaxial cable standards."

The only way to remember the information in Table 2-2 is to memorize it. You can count on seeing a variety of questions that require you to regurgitate this information in one way or another.

Table 2-2	Cable Types and Their Characteristics			
Cable Type	Bandwidth	Max. Segment Length	Max. Nodes/ Segments	Nodes' Resistance to Interference
Thin coaxial	10 Mbps	185 meters	30 (uses 5-4-3 rule)	Good
Thick coaxial	10 Mbps	500 meters	100 (uses 5-4-3 rule)	Better
UTP	10–100 Mbps	100 meters	1,024	Poor
STP	16–1,000 Mbps	100 meters	1,024	Fair to Good
Fiber-optic	100–10,000 Mbps	2,000 meters (2 kilometers)	1,024	Best

Coaxial cables through thick and thin

Although recently deposed as the ruling network cable type, coaxial cable is still a popular choice for networks. Coaxial is inexpensive, easy to work with, reliable, and moderately resistant to interference, which makes it a good choice for many networking situations.

Coaxial cable is constructed with a single solid copper wire core, which is surrounded by an insulator made of plastic or Teflon. A braided metal shielding layer (and an additional metal foil layer in some cables) covers the insulator, and a plastic sheath wrapper covers the cable. The metal shielding layers increase the cable's resistance to EMI and RFI signals. Figure 2-7 illustrates the construction of a coaxial cable.

Thick coax is designated as RG-11 or RG-8 and thin coax as RG-58 (the coax used for television service is RG-59, by the way). The RG stands for Radio/Government and this is the cable's rating based on the type and thickness of its core wire.

The coaxial cable standards

The IEEE 802 project defines coaxial cable as thick or thin. Coaxial cable is used primarily in Ethernet networking environments, where folks refer to the cable as *thicknet* or *thinnet*. Coaxial cable also goes by the generic *coax* (pronounced co-axe); you can call thick coax cable 10Base5, thickwire, or yellow wire — they all mean the same thing. Aliases for thin coax cable include 10Base2, thinwire, and cheapnet.

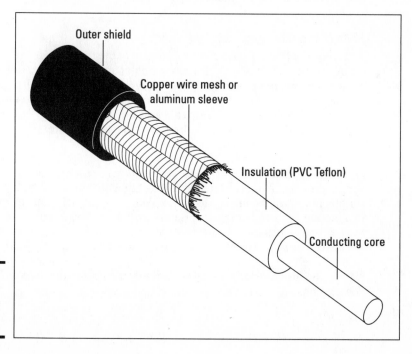

Outer shield

Copper wire mesh or aluminum sleeve

Insulation (PVC Teflon)

Conducting core

Figure 2-7:
The layers of a coaxial cable.

The 5-4-3 rule

Coaxial cable is subject to structure limitations under the IEEE 802 specifications that limit the number of segments, repeaters, and types of connections that can be used on a network. Specifically, the 5-4-3 rule, as it is commonly called, limits a coaxial network to five network segments with no more than four repeaters and only three of the segments can be connected to computers.

What's this 10Base stuff?

In the Ethernet world, the designation of cable is also descriptive of its characteristics. Thick coax cable is designated as 10Base5, thin coaxial cable is 10Base2, and twisted pair (UTP/STP) is 10BaseT.

The 10Base part indicates that these cables carry 10 Mbps bandwidths and that they carry baseband (digital) signals. For coax cable, the 5 and 2 mean 500 meters and 200 meters, respectively, which are the approximate maximum segment lengths of each cable type. Actually, the maximum segment length of thin coax is 185 meters, but the 200 is easier to remember. The T in 10BaseT refers to twisted pair cable. See "The Ethernet Cable Standards" later in this chapter for more information.

Does this cable make me look fat?

Thick coax is the more rigid of the coaxial cable twins (fraternal, no doubt). It's about 1 centimeter (about four-tenths of an inch) in diameter and is commonly covered in a bright yellow covering, the origin of its "yellow wire" nickname. The thicker hide makes the cable more resistant to interference and its thicker core wire increases its attenuation distance. This results in a longer segment length and the ability to support a greater number of nodes on a segment compared to its thinner sibling.

Connecting thick coaxial cable to workstations is a fairly complicated, simple process. What this means is that the whole business really is simple, but darned complicated to explain. An external transceiver attached to a piercing connector (appropriately called a *vampire tap*) is clamped on the thick wire, making a connection directly into the central core wire. A transceiver cable (called a drop cable) is used to connect the transceiver to a PC's network adapter with an attachment unit interface (AUI) connector. Figure 2-8 illustrates how simple this really is, despite the convoluted description.

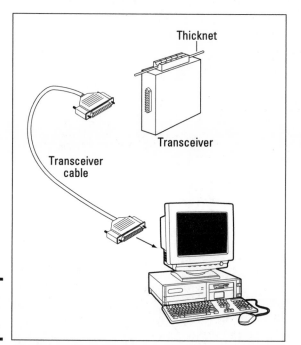

Thicknet

Transceiver

Transceiver
cable

Figure 2-8:
A thicknet
connection.

Table 2-3 details the characteristics of thick coaxial cable.

Table 2-3	Thick Coaxial Cable Characteristics
Characteristic	*Value*
Maximum segment length	500 meters (about 1,640 feet)
Bandwidth (speed)	10 Mbps
Number of nodes per segment	100
Connector type	AUI
Resistance to interference	Good

You can never be too thin

In contrast to thicknet, thin coaxial cable — commonly called *thinnet*
cable — is lightweight and flexible. Thinnet is about two-tenths of an inch in

diameter, and very flexible, which makes it is easy to install. Second only to UTP in popularity among network cabling, thinnet is typically installed in a daisy-chaining fashion to connect computers together by using a British Naval Connector "T" (BNC-T) connector (shown in Figure 2-9). *Daisy-chaining* refers to connecting computers in a series by running the thinnet cable from one computer to the next. Figure 2-3 (earlier in the chapter) illustrates a daisy-chained network.

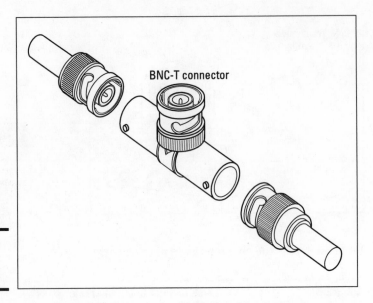

BNC-T connector

Figure 2-9:
A BNC-T
connector.

Table 2-4 summarizes the characteristics of thin coaxial cable.

Table 2-4	Thin Coaxial Cable Characteristics
Characteristic	*Value*
Maximum segment length	185 meters (a little over 600 feet)
Bandwidth (speed)	10 Mbps
Number of nodes per segment	30
Connector type	BNC
Resistance to interference	Good

The twisted pair

Although its title sounds like the bad name of an even worse movie, this section covers the most popular cabling in use on Ethernet and Token Ring networks — twisted pair copper wire. Twisted pair wire has all the attributes of a truly popular cable: It's the lightest, most flexible, least expensive, and easiest to install of the popular network media. The bad news is that it's vulnerable to interference and has a relatively short attenuation distance.

You can use two types of twisted pair wire in networks: unshielded (UTP) and shielded (STP), both shown in Figure 2-10. Of the two, the more common choice is unshielded, which is particularly popular in Ethernet networks.

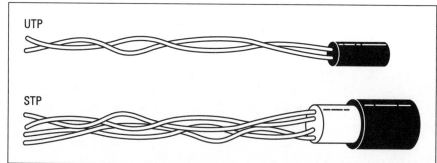

Figure 2-10: UTP and STP cables.

Unshielded cable

Unshielded twisted pair wire is just about what its name implies: two unshielded wires twisted together. Rather ingenious, isn't it?

Unshielded twisted pair (UTP) cable is the most commonly implemented cable on Ethernet networks. UTP is commonly referred to as *10BaseT* Ethernet cable, which translates to 10 Mbps bandwidth using baseband transmission over twisted pair copper lines.

Categorizing TP cable

The Electronics Industries Association and the Telecommunications Industries Association (EIA/TIA) define UTP cable according to five categories, or *cats,* as the real techies call them (as in Cat 3 or Cat 5):

✦ **Category 1 and 2:** Not used in networking. This isn't here and you didn't see it, so just walk away slowly, and you won't get hurt on the test.

✦ **Category 3:** A 4-pair cable supporting bandwidth up to 10 Mbps — the minimum standard for 10BaseT networks.

✦ **Category 4:** A 4-pair cable commonly used in 16 Mbps Token Ring networks.

✦ **Category 5:** A 4-pair cable with bandwidth up to 100 Mbps, used for 100BaseTX and asynchronous transfer mode (ATM) networking.

EIA/TIA recognizes some additional categories as well, such as Cat 6 and Cat 7, but — like Cat 1 and 2 — don't sweat them for the exam.

Table 2-5 summarizes the characteristics of UTP cable.

Table 2-5	Unshielded Twisted Pair Cable Characteristics
Characteristic	*Value*
Maximum segment length	100 meters (just over 320 feet)
Bandwidth (speed)	10–100 Mbps
Number of nodes per segment	1,024
Connector type	RJ-45
Resistance to interference	Poor

Shielded cable

The copper wires of the shielded twisted pair (STP) cable are covered with a grounded copper or foil wrapper intended to shield them from EMI and RFI. Because of its interference protection, STP is more expensive than UTP. The benefit of STP cable over UTP cable is that it is less susceptible to interference and can be used in certain installations where UTP would not be practical.

STP is commonly used in Token Ring networks. In fact, IBM has its own standards for twisted pair cable for ring networks. The IBM cable standard includes nine categories that range from a two-pair shielded cable (Type 1) to a UTP cable (Type 3), a fiber-optic cable (Type 5), and a fire-safe cable (Type 9).

Don't confuse UTP Category 3 or 5 (Cat 3 and Cat 5) with IBM Type 3 or Type 5 cabling. Cat *n* cables are used in Ethernet networks and IBM Type *n* cables are used in Token Ring networks.

Isn't that a phone plug?

UTP uses an RJ-45 connector, shown in Figure 2-11, which looks like the little clip connector on your telephone (an RJ-11), only the RJ-45 is a bit bigger.

The RJ-11 connector of your phone connects four wires (two pairs) and the RJ-45 network connector connects eight wires (four pairs).

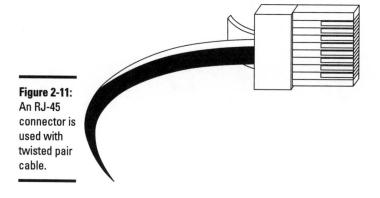

You need your fiber

A fiber-optic cable carries data in the form of modulated pulses of light. Imagine turning a flashlight on and off a couple of million times a second: That strobe effect demonstrates how data travels through this kind of cable.

The core of fiber-optic cable consists of two (or more) extremely thin strands of glass or plastic. Cladding (also of glass or plastic) covers each strand, helping to keep the light moving through the strand inside. Signals are transmitted between stations using two strands: one each for carrying light up and down the cable. A plastic outer jacket covers the cable. Figure 2-12 shows the makeup of a fiber-optic cable.

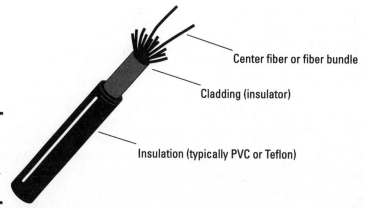

Center fiber or fiber bundle

Cladding (insulator)

Insulation (typically PVC or Teflon)

Figure 2-12:
The layers
of a two-
strand fiber-
optic cable.

**Book IV
Chapter 2**

Networking Basics

Because it uses light and not electrical signals, fiber-optic cable isn't susceptible to EMI or RFI, which gives it incredibly long attenuation and maximum segment lengths. Network backbones commonly use fiber-optic cable because of these properties.

Table 2-6 summarizes the characteristics of fiber-optic cable.

Table 2-6	Fiber-Optic Cable Characteristics
Characteristic	*Value*
Maximum segment length	2 km (just over a mile)
Bandwidth (speed)	100 Mbps to 2 Gbps
Resistance to interference	Excellent

Don't fret over the fact that Table 2-6 doesn't have all the same entries included in those for UTP and coaxial cables. Table 2-6 highlights the characteristics that you need to know for the test.

Working without a wire

The need for flexibility and mobility of network devices is making wireless networking options much more popular. Even CompTIA, which tends to operate slightly behind the technology curve, has included wireless technology in the latest version of the Network+ examination. That's as clear an indication as ever there was that wireless networking has arrived and is here to stay.

In terms of network media, wireless networks don't use wire. (Or was that already painfully obvious?) Instead, wireless systems use a radio frequency (RF) or infrared (IR) frequency or channel to transmit data.

In essence, as far as the basic networking functions are concerned, a wired network isn't much different from a wireless network. An Ethernet network (the primary network focus of the Network+ exam) on a wireless system operates virtually the same as one installed on a physically wired network.

The real difference is in the access points. Nodes on a wireless network connect to a *network access point* (NAP), which serves the same function as a hub in a wired network. Typically, a NAP is connected to the network backbone with a cable, but not always. At some point, a cable must be used to connect the wireless network to communications services, at least until the whole world goes wireless (but don't hold your breath). Figure 2-13 illustrates a typical wireless network implementation.

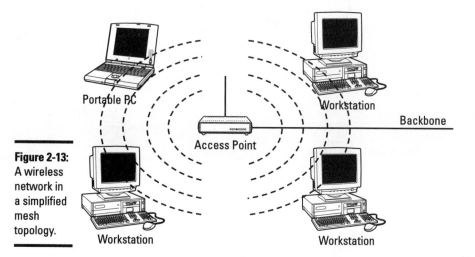

Figure 2-13:
A wireless
network in
a simplified
mesh
topology.

For the most part, the wireless media used to connect a wireless network is known as *ISM (Industrial, Scientific, and Medical)*. ISM media operates in the 2.4-gigahertz (GHz) frequency band, which is an unlicensed frequency set aside by the U.S. Federal Communications Commission (FCC) for commercial use. *Unlicensed* means that the space is wide open and available for use by just about anyone who wants to use it. Many bands fall within the ISM frequency range besides networking — garage door openers, baby monitors, and many public band radio communications also use it.

Networking on the 2.4 and 5 GHz bands is defined in the IEEE 802.11 standard that defines network bandwidth up to 54 Mbps.

The Ethernet Cable Standards

So, what's in a name, you ask? If you're talking Ethernet cable, the name tells it all: bandwidth/speed, transmission mode, and segment length (coaxial cable) or cable type (TP or fiber-optic). The IEEE 802.3 standards specify Ethernet cabling and assign each of the various cable compositions and capability combinations a separate designation. Table 2-7 breaks down the meaning of each of the Ethernet cable designations that you're likely to see on the Network+ exam. The "10Base" part of each standard indicates that it supports a 10 Mbps transmission speed and uses a baseband (digital) transmission mode.

Table 2-7		Basic Ethernet Cable Standards	
Cable	*Bandwidth*	*Maximum Distance*	*Cable Material*
10Base2	10 Mbps	185 meters (the 2 is for approximately 200 meters)	Thinnet coaxial
10Base5	10 Mbps	500 meters	Thicknet coaxial
10BaseF	10 Mbps	2,000 meters	Fiber-optic
10BaseT	10 Mbps	100 meters	UTP
100BaseFX	100 Mbps	400 meters	Fiber-optic
100BaseT	100 Mbps	100 meters	UTP
1000Base*x*	1 Gbps	Varies with media	Fiber-optic or copper

The 1000Base*x* designation defines *Gigabit Ethernet* media that is able to provide 1 Gbps bandwidth. The commonly used designations are 1000BaseSX (short-wave fiber optic), 1000BaseLX (long-wave fiber-optic), and 1000BaseCX (special copper cable).

To complicate life further, variations of 10BaseF and 10BaseT standards are likely to show up on the exam. Here are the ones you may encounter on test day:

+ **100BaseT:** The generic term for *Fast Ethernet.*

+ **100BaseTX:** The two-pair version of Fast Ethernet.

+ **100BaseT4:** The four-pair version of Fast Ethernet.

+ **100BaseFX:** Fast Ethernet using two-strand fiber-optic cable.

+ **100BaseVG:** A new 100 Mbps standard over Category 3 cable.

+ **100BaseVG-AnyLAN:** The Hewlett Packard proprietary version of 100BaseVG.

Backbones and Segments

Affectionately called the *backbone,* the cable that runs the entire length of a network interconnects all the computers, printers, servers, and other devices of the network. Visualize the skeleton of a fish: All the little catch-in-your-throat bones attach to one big ol' backbone. A network backbone serves the same purpose (without the smell): connecting and interconnecting all a network's resources. The backbone serves as the trunk line for the entire network.

IEEE 802.3 cable designations commonly used for backbones are 10Base5, 10BaseF, 10BaseT, Fast Ethernet, and Gigabit Ethernet.

FDDI ditty dee

Network backbones commonly use Fiber Distributed Data Interface (FDDI) technology. FDDI is pronounced "F-D-D-I," but some folks insist on making the letters into the word "fiddy." Is nothing sacred? FDDI is a 100 Mbps fiber-optic network access method that is excellent for moving traffic around the trunk of a network.

FDDI implements networks as two rings. You can attach workstations to one or both rings of the backbone. The two rings serve as redundant network trunks — if one ring breaks or fails, the other takes over, routing around the trouble spot. If both rings break, the remaining pieces bond together to form a new ring. Although the regrowth potential sounds like something akin to lizard tails or space aliens, FDDI's ability to regenerate the network backbone is what makes it so popular.

Differentiating networks and segments

Throughout the Network+ exam, the term *segment* pops up as a reference to discrete portions of a network, usually represented by a single run of cable, a group of workstations, or even a local area network within a WAN. The most common reason for creating a network segment is to improve network performance or security by installing bridges or routers (which we discuss in Book IV, Chapter 3) in strategic locations around the network.

A cable segment is a single run of cable with terminators at each end. A network segment is a group of workstations, servers, or devices that are isolated on the other side of a bridge or router to improve the network's performance or security.

**Book IV
Chapter 2**

Networking Basics

Prep Test

1 Networks on which of the following topologies fail when a cable breaks? (Choose two answers.)

A ❏ Star

B ❏ Bus

C ❏ Ring

D ❏ Star-bus

2 Which of the following topologies must be terminated?

A ○ Star

B ○ Bus

C ○ Ring

D ○ Star-bus

3 An Ethernet network most commonly uses which topology?

A ○ Star

B ○ Bus

C ○ Ring

D ○ Star-bus

4 A network implementation that's installed using thinnet cabling that's directly connected to a hub, which is in turn connected directly to a server, is using which of the following topologies?

A ○ Bus topology

B ○ Ring topology

C ○ Star topology

D ○ Mesh topology

5 The method used to control the transmission of signals to a ring network is

A ○ Backbone termination.

B ○ Segment termination.

C ○ Token passing.

D ○ Token termination.

6 Which of the following are characteristics of 10Base2 cable?

A ○ 10 Mbps bandwidth
B ○ 500 meters maximum segment length
C ○ 1,024 maximum nodes per segment
D ○ Poor interference resistance
E ○ None of the above

7 A Fast Ethernet standard that uses four-wire UTP cable is

A ○ 10BaseT.
B ○ 100BaseTX.
C ○ 100BaseFL.
D ○ 100BaseT4.

8 Which of the following are 100 Mbps Ethernet standards that use Category 3 cabling? (Choose two.)

A ❑ 100BaseT
B ❑ 100BaseVG
C ❑ 100BaseVG-AnyLAN
D ❑ 100BaseFX

9 Which of the following characteristics apply to FDDI? (Choose three.)

A ❑ 100 Mbps
B ❑ Fiber-optic backbone technology
C ❑ Implements only one ring similar to Token Ring.
D ❑ Implements two network rings.

10 UTP cable uses which type of connector?

A ○ RJ-11
B ○ AUI
C ○ RJ-45
D ○ RG-58

Answers

1 **B** and **C.** Bus backbone cables continue to operate even if a node fails, but are not available if the cable is broken between the termination points. A ring cable cannot operate if the cable or a node fails. *Review "Cable termination."*

3 **D.** The bus topology is the basic topology used in nearly all Ethernet networks, but the star-bus hybrid is the specific topology used in most implementations. *Review "Mixed topologies."*

4 **C.** The first clue to this answer should be the thinnet cable, but Ethernet (bus) networks can also be installed by using thinnet cabling. However, any network that involves direct connections to a server (or at least connections almost directly to a server, hub, or switch) is most likely using a star topology. *Review "I want to see stars!"*

5 **C.** The node in possession of the token is the only one that can send a message. The other workstations must wait until the token is available. *Review "Won't you wear my ring around your net?"*

6 **A.** Thick coax has a 500-meter maximum segment length, and UTP supports 1,024 nodes per segment and has poor resistance to interference. *Review "Technical cable stuff."*

7 **D.** Fast Ethernet is any of the 100BaseX standards. 100BaseT4 uses four-wire cable to implement Fast Ethernet. *Review "The Ethernet Cable Standards."*

8 **B** and **C.** Essentially, these two standards are the same. 100BaseVG-AnyLAN is the Hewlett Packard proprietary standard for Fast Ethernet using Category 3 cabling. *Review "The Ethernet Cable Standards."*

9 **A, B,** and **D.** FDDI implements two counter-rotating rings. *Review "FDDI ditty dee."*

10 **C.** RJ-11 connectors are used on telephone (two-pair) cable, AUI connectors are used with coaxial cable, and RG-58 is the standard for thinnet cable. *Review "Categorizing TP cable."*

Chapter 3: Protocols and Standards

*A*t the core of the Network+ exam is the OSI model, the TCP/IP protocols, and network security, all of which we cover in this chapter. The OSI model provides a standard blueprint for designing, implementing, and operating networking hardware and software. The model also provides the basic operating and interconnection rules for all network operating systems, network messaging, and communications connectivity devices.

Networks are exposed to evildoers within an organization as well as from outside hackers, crackers, and the like. These folks perpetrate the theft, damage, and attacks on a network that pose a real and serious threat to its integrity. In the real world, mean and nasty evildoers are out there with nothing better to do than to attack your network and its security. You should know, both for real life and the exam, how to apply security measures to protect a network and its users.

OSI: The Networking Supermodel

As a standard, the OSI model, illustrated in Figure 3-1, functions more like a blueprint or framework for the ways in which networking devices, protocols, and services should interact with one another. There is some wiggle room in how protocols and devices within a network layer interact with each other, but the basic skeleton of the OSI model never changes.

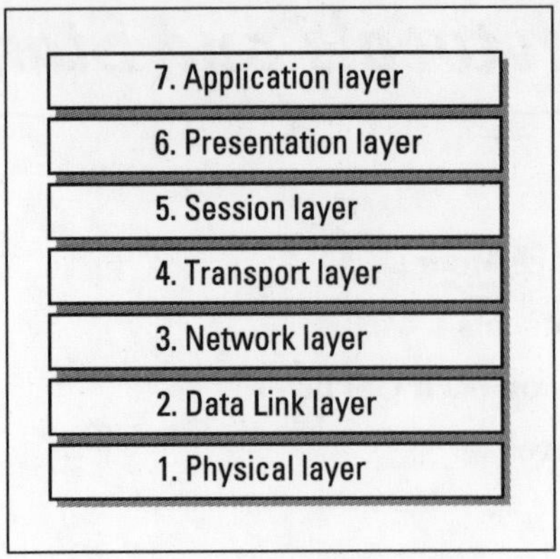

Figure 3-1:
The layers
of the OSI
reference
model.

The OSI model is made up of seven layers. The OSI model is less like a seven-layer cake, however, than it is like the layers of an onion. Each layer of the OSI model (see Figure 3-1 and Table 3-1) defines a standard for one or more of the specific formats and actions that must be used to move data from its source to its destination across a network.

Table 3-1 gives you the lowdown on what you need to know about each layer of the OSI model.

Table 3-1		OSI Model Layers
Level	*Layer*	*How Much You Need to Know*
7	Application layer	Not much besides the protocols, network devices, and encapsulation it defines.
6	Presentation layer	Not a heck of a lot besides the basic protocols, devices, and encapsulation it defines.
5	Session layer	Relatively little aside from the essentials — you guessed it — protocols, network devices, and encapsulation.
4	Transport layer	Quite a bit. Check out "Transport me to the gateway" and "Transport protocols" later in the chapter.
3	Network layer	A bunch. Skip to "Internetworking devices" and "Network protocols" later in the chapter.
2	Data Link layer	Lots. Take a look at "Linking up on the Data Link layer" later in the chapter.
1	Physical layer	Ooodles. See "Gettin' physical" later in the chapter.

Examining the layers of the OSI

Primarily the Network+ exam is concerned with the bottom four layers of the OSI model. However, you should know the protocols, network devices, and encapsulation defined on all seven layers, just in case.

Here's a brief overview of each OSI layer starting from the lowest (bottom) layer and working up to the highest (top) layer:

✦ **Physical layer (Layer 1):** As its name suggests, this layer is concerned with the physical nature of a network, which includes cabling, connectors, network interface cards, and the processes that convert bits into signals for sending and signals to bits when receiving.

✦ **Data Link layer (Layer 2):** This layer is concerned with providing context to the Physical layer's bits by formatting them into packets, providing error-checking and correction services, and avoiding transmission conflicts on the network.

✦ **Network layer (Layer 3):** This layer addresses data for delivery and converts network addresses into physical addresses. Routing of messages on the network and internetwork also occurs at this layer.

✦ **Transport layer (Layer 4):** This layer of the OSI model handles the connection between network computers as they talk and match messages to the capabilities and restrictions of the network medium. At this layer, network messages are chopped into smaller pieces for transmission and reassembled at their destination, ostensibly in the correct order. The Transport layer supports the delivery of messages as well as error detection and recovery.

✦ **Session layer (Layer 5):** This layer manages communication *sessions*, including *handshaking* (which connection-oriented devices use to establish a session), security, and the mechanics of an ongoing connection.

✦ **Presentation layer (Layer 6):** This layer is where raw data messages are packaged in generic form so that they can withstand the rigors of being transmitted over a network. Incoming messages are broken down and formatted appropriately for the receiving application.

✦ **Application layer (Layer 7):** As its name suggests, this layer interfaces with applications that want to gain network access. Don't confuse the Application layer with end-user application software, such as Microsoft Office, WordPerfect, or Corel Draw. Applications, such as Windows NT Server or NetWare, and certain network services, such as FTP, HTTP, TELNET, and SMTP, function at this layer.

**Book IV
Chapter 3**

**Protocols and
Standards**

So, what does a PDU do?

The official OSI name for a packet of data passed around a network is *PDU*, which stands for, take your pick, the original *protocol data unit*, the easily remembered *packet data unit*, or the heavyweight *payload data unit*. You won't see a test question asking you what PDU stands for, but you should know what a PDU does.

A PDU is a unit of data that is packaged for movement from one OSI layer function to another. On the lower OSI layers, PDUs are given specific names, such as *packets, datagrams, data frames, segments,* or *frames*. These terms are specific to a particular layer and help you to know the type of activities being discussed. Table 3-2 lists the various PDU terminology associated with each OSI layer.

Table 3-2	PDU Names by OSI Layer
OSI Layer	*PDU Name*
Application, Presentation, Session	PDU
Transport	Segments/datagrams
Network	Packets
Data Link	Frames
Physical	Bits

Remembering the OSI layers: Bring the pizza

Remembering the layers of the OSI model is as easy as memorizing a clever little saying. Here are a few possibilities:

✔ **"Please Do Not Throw Salami (or Sausage if you prefer) Pizza Away:"** This works for memorizing the layers from bottom to top: PDNTSPA. (This saying is our favorite. So is the pizza.)

✔ **"APpS Transport Network Data Physically:"** APS refers to Application, Presentation, and Session. This one spells out, from top to bottom, the layers that the Network+ test emphasizes, with the upper three layers grouped together.

✔ **"All People Seem To Need Data Processing:"** Another top-to-bottom reminder.

✔ **"Please Do Not Tell Secret Passwords Anytime:"** This one goes bottom-to-top.

We know — the mnemonic magic is waning!

Up one side and down the other

The OSI model itself is never actually implemented directly. Rather, its layers define how protocols and services should transfer data units between the hardware and software of a network and on to other networks. As depicted in Figure 3-2, when data is sent over the network, it travels down through the OSI layers of the originating network beginning from the Application layer and down to the Physical layer. At the Physical layer, the data is physically transmitted to the Physical layer of the receiving network, at which point the data passes back up through the layers from the Physical layer to the Application layer.

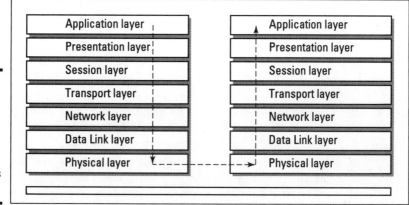

Figure 3-2: The path data takes through the OSI model from its source to its destination.

As data passes down through the sending-side layers, each layer performs its own brand of magic on the packet: formatting it, adding error-checking mechanisms, breaking it into smaller pieces, and more. Each of the lower layers also adds a header block that includes information for the corresponding layer on the receiving end to each piece of the data. For example, the Transport layer of the sending side provides a header with instructions for sequencing and reassembling the message for the receiving-side Transport layer. When transmitted by the Physical layer, each piece of the original message can have up to six headers attached to it.

As the packet passes up through the receiving-side layers, the packets are stripped away until the original message is delivered to the destination application. By the way, a packet gathers only six headers instead of seven because the Application layer is too lazy to add one before sending the packet to the Presentation layer. However, it does format the data for use by the other OSI layers.

Layers of Hardware

Each of the networking devices on a network operates on one or more layers of the OSI model. Remember that the OSI model is a framework or blueprint for the way things *should* work, and some hardware strictly conforms and other hardware conforms a bit more loosely. Some conformity is required, however, if *interoperability* (the ability for devices to communicate smoothly) with other networks and network devices is expected.

Gettin' physical

The Physical layer is concerned with moving bits on the physical media. Therefore, it deals only with the hardware affecting the physical movement of data from point A to point B. The networking devices that operate at the Physical layer are

+ **Network interface cards (NIC):** The NIC by itself — that is, the hardware device without its software drivers — operates at the Physical layer.

+ **Network media (cabling):** The medium used to transport the message bits on the network is also a Physical layer element. This is true with all media — copper wire, glass fiber, or wireless signals.

+ **Repeaters:** These devices, much like Aunt Sally, repeat everything they hear, energizing the message with new life in the process. Repeaters are used to solve attenuation problems in cables.

+ **Hubs:** Hubs come in two flavors: passive and active. A *passive hub* receives data on one of its ports and passes the data along to its other ports without regenerating the signal. An *active hub* combines the actions of the passive hub with a repeater to regenerate the signal passed along.

Linking up on the Data Link layer

The devices that operate on the Data Link layer forward data units by applying physical addressing, such as the MAC (Media Access Control) address. The devices that operate on the Data Link layer (at least as far as the Network+ exam cares) are bridges and Layer 2 or LAN switches.

Bridging across the network

A *bridge* connects two or more network segments — often dissimilar ones — to form a larger individual network. Using a bridging (also known as routing) table, a bridge determines on which network segment a destination address is located. A bridge examines the source address in a message and records on which of its interfaces a message arrived. This identifies the location of the source MAC address should a message arrive for it. Should a destination address not be in the bridging table, the bridge sends out a broadcast message to find the addressee. When the addressee replies with its MAC address, this too is recorded in the bridging table.

Switching around the network

A *switch,* also called a *multiport bridge,* is in effect a smart bridge, but it can also be likened to a very smart hub. Like a bridge, a switch also uses MAC addresses to determine on which of its interfaces a message should be forwarded and then sends it only to that interface.

Internetworking devices

Networking devices that operate at the Network layer (Layer 3), such as routers, focus on applying, verifying, and routing logical network addressing. Using logical addressing, such as the IP addressing scheme, Layer 3 devices effectively join separate networks and segments into larger internetworks. See Book IV, Chapter 5 for more information on IP addressing.

A *router,* which is more intelligent than a switch or bridge, uses its smarts to calculate the most efficient route for a packet to use to reach its destination. Another Network layer device is a *brouter* (pronounced *brow-ter*), which is a hybrid of a bridge and a router.

Transport me to the gateway

A gateway consists of hardware or software or both, but its main purpose is to provide an interface between two or more dissimilar systems or networks with similar functions that could not otherwise communicate. For example, take a PC workstation and a mainframe. Those are two pretty different devices. A gateway allows them to communicate like old friends.

Although a gateway is defined on the Transport layer, it can operate on any of the top four OSI model's layers.

In summary . . .

Table 3-3 summarizes the OSI model layers and the hardware that operates at each layer.

Table 3-3	The Hardware at Each OSI Model Layer
OSI Layer	*Devices*
Physical	Network adapter, cable and transmission media, repeater, and hub
Data link	Bridge and switch
Network	Router, brouter
Transport	Gateway
Upper layers	Gateway

Ain't It Suite?

Networking protocols are typically defined as a grouping of separate protocols that perform the actions and activities defined on each layer of the OSI model. Each of the protocols included in the most common protocol suites, such as TCP/IP or IPX/SPX, can be identified with a specific layer of the OSI model.

Three types of protocols are defined in the OSI model: application protocols, transport protocols, and network protocols. For the exam, you should know what each protocol does and the OSI model layer on which it operates. Figure 3-3 illustrates the general relationship of the three protocol types to the OSI model's layers.

Figure 3-3:
OSI
protocols
can be
defined into
three
groups.

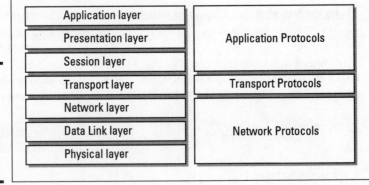

A *protocol* defines the rules that control how two computers, networking devices, or programs transfer data between themselves.

Network protocols

Network layer protocols provide for packet addressing and routing information, error checking and correction, and enforce the rules for communicating within a specific network environment. These protocols provide link services to other protocols operating at other layers.

The primary Network layer protocols are

- ✦ **IP (Internet Protocol):** You know, the IP of the famous TCP/IP duo. IP provides addressing and routing information.

- ✦ **IPX (Internetwork Package Exchange):** The Novell NetWare proprietary Layer 3 protocol used as the native routed protocol on NetWare versions before NetWare 5.0.

- ✦ **NWLink (NetWare Link):** NWLink is the Microsoft version of the IPX/SPX protocol for Windows Server systems.

- ✦ **NetBEUI (NetBIOS Extended User Interface):** Provides transport services for NetBIOS.

- ✦ **DLC (Data Link Control):** Used for network-connected mainframes and Hewlett Packard printers.

Transport protocols

Transport layer protocols provide for the reliable end-to-end transport and delivery of data, error detection, and flow control. Common transport protocols are

- ✦ **TCP (Transmission Control Protocol):** TCP is the TCP/IP protocol responsible for guaranteeing the transport and delivery of packets across networks. TCP is a universal protocol that runs on virtually any system, which is one of its major strengths.

- ✦ **SPX (Sequenced Packet Exchange):** In the Novell IPX/SPX protocol suite, SPX is the TCP, and IPX is the IP. Like TCP, SPX is used to guarantee data delivery.

- ✦ **NetBIOS/NetBEUI (Network Basic Input/Output System/NetBIOS Extended User Interface):** NetBIOS manages communications between computers, and NetBEUI provides the data transport services. NetBIOS and NetBEUI are Microsoft protocols used on Windows networks.

Application protocols

Application layer protocols provide application-to-application services to the upper layers of the OSI model. Some common application protocols are

**Book IV
Chapter 3**

**Protocols and
Standards**

✦ **SMTP (Simple Mail Transport Protocol):** This member of the TCP/IP gang is responsible for transferring electronic mail.

✦ **FTP (File Transport Protocol):** Another one wearing the TCP/IP colors, FTP transports files from one computer to another.

✦ **SNMP (Simple Network Management Protocol):** YATP (yet another TCP/IP protocol) that is used to monitor network devices.

How TCP/IP stacks up

The most commonly used protocol suite is TCP/IP. Although TCP/IP has been around for about 10 years longer than the OSI model, it matches up very nicely with the layers of the OSI model. Funny how that works out, huh?

Table 3-4 contains a layer-by-layer breakdown of the TCP/IP suite.

Table 3-4	TCP/IP and the OSI Model
OSI Model Layer	*TCP/IP Protocol(s)*
Physical layer	Physical hardware device connectivity
Data Link layer	NIC driver and ODI/NDIS
Network layer	IP, ICMP, ARP, OSPF, and RIP
Transport layer	TCP, DNS, and UDP
Upper layers	Telnet, FTP, and SMTP

The TCP/IP suite protocols included in Table 3-4 are

✦ **ODI/NDIS (Open Data-Link Interface/Network Driver-Interface Specification):** A Data Link layer interface that enables NIC drivers to connect to dissimilar networks and make them operate seamlessly as one interface. ODI is the Novell protocol, and NDIS is the Microsoft protocol for NIC interconnection.

✦ **IP (Internet Protocol):** A Network layer protocol that provides source and destination addressing and routing.

✦ **ICMP (Internet Control Message Protocol):** A Network layer protocol that carries control messages, such as error or confirmation messages.

✦ **ARP (Address Resolution Protocol):** A Network layer protocol that converts IP addresses to MAC physical addresses.

✦ **OSPF (Open Shortest Path First):** Used by TCP/IP routers to determine the best path through a network.

✦ **RIP (Routing Information Protocol):** Helps TCP/IP routers use the most efficient routes to nodes on the network.

✦ **TCP (Transmission Control Protocol):** The primary TCP/IP transport protocol that accepts messages from the upper OSI layers and provides reliable delivery to its TCP peer on a remote network.

✦ **DNS (Domain Naming System):** A Transport layer Internet name-to-address resolution service that allows users to use human-friendly names.

✦ **UDP (User Datagram Protocol):** Another Transport layer that can be used in place of TCP to transport simple single-packet messages.

Securing the Network

Few would argue that you must secure network resources from unauthorized access. Only those users authorized to access network resources should have access to them. Restricting access helps ensure that network resources aren't corrupted or misused and remain available to network users.

This section includes a discussion of various means that can be applied to provide security for a local area network.

Logon account authorization

Most network administrators agree that without users, their jobs would be a whole lot easier. Unfortunately, networks exist to enable users to share resources, and sharing inherently includes accessing. Access to a network most commonly involves using a logon account and password.

Logon names

A logon account name is usually a code word easily remembered by the user it identifies. A logon name can be just about anything the network administrator can get users to accept. Users' logons are normally something like their initials, name, or both. For example, jdoe, csimmons, rgilster, johnd, curts, and rong (although I personally avoid this one for obvious reasons) are examples of how login names are commonly constructed.

However, some network administrators believe that simple logon names can look like an open door to somebody wanting to access the network for nefarious reasons. Instead, these network administrators use randomly assigned logon names, such as *lges0qnz*.

Practicing safe passwording

Until such time that you can use retinal scanners, thumbprint verification, and saliva-sample DNA analysis (no chewing tobacco, please) on network workstations, passwords are the gatekeepers of the networking world. Even after the real techie stuff becomes available, passwords are most likely to still play a very valuable part in network security policies.

What you *do* need to know for the Network+ exam are the types of policies that a sound password security plan includes:

✦ **Changing passwords frequently:** Users should change passwords regularly to prevent the risk of discovery. However, users should not change passwords too often because users are prone to forgetting passwords that are changed too frequently. Changing passwords every 30 to 60 days is usually sufficient.

✦ **Minimum password length:** A single-character password is only slightly more secure than no password at all. For each character in its length, a password becomes exponentially more difficult to guess. The other side of this policy is that a password shouldn't be too long either because longer passwords are harder to remember. If users can't remember their passwords, you have the ultimate security — no one, not even network users, can log on to the network — which is a bad thing, we're told.

The most recent Gilster poll says that four out of five experts agree that six to eight characters is an acceptable length for a password.

✦ **Password uniqueness:** Users should not reuse passwords too frequently. Many users want to recycle the same three or four passwords repeatedly. A determined mean-and-nasty hacker can figure out the pattern of these passwords easily. Force your users to dream up new passwords and use them before you let them return to the safety of using *password* as their password again. Call it tough love, but it's for their own good. The experts in the Gilster poll say that eight is a safe number of passwords to use before repeating one.

✦ **Password strength:** You can require certain characters to be included in a password, if for no other reason than to make the password less predictable, and therefore harder to crack. Including special characters, uppercase, lowercase, or numbers (all four is best) in a password greatly reduces the chances of it being compromised.

✦ **Password protection:** Somebody with unauthorized access to your network can wreak havoc on you and your company's resources. Counsel users on protecting the secrecy and sanctity of their passwords. They should know that taping their password to the monitor or the outside window is not the best way to keep it secret. You should also explain the dangers of sharing passwords with friends and coworkers.

Setting account policies

An *account policy* is a set of rules that defines which access rights are assigned to which users on a network. Windows Server (NT and 2000) has a formal mechanism (called, of all things, *Account Policies*) to set the default account policies for all user accounts. On a Windows server, account policies are just one of the many system policies that the administrator must set.

A series of user-account parameters can be combined to create the account policy. The account policy is then applied to each account as it logs in. Account policies are *restrictive*. In other words, you're defining the parameters of acceptable behavior and allowable travel for users of the network: what they can do and where they can go.

The types of settings that you set and the questions you should ask to determine the correct setting to create an account policy are as follows:

✦ **Password restrictions:** The restrictions allow you to set parameters that control when passwords expire, how often users must change passwords, a password's minimum length, and how many different passwords must a user use before a password can repeat.

✦ **Account lockout:** Sets the number of chances a user (or hacker) gets to enter a password before the account is locked out.

✦ **Lockout duration:** If an account gets locked out, you can indicate whether the administrator must manually reset it or allow it to reset automatically after a certain period.

✦ **Forced disconnect:** Under Windows NT/2000, system policies also set the network's login hours — the maximum number of hours users can be logged on to their accounts.

Sharing network resources

In the same way that you verify users' accounts and passwords before granting them access to the network in general, share-level security can be applied to restrict access to specific network resources. In share-level security, passwords are assigned to resources instead of users. If the user knows the password for a shared network resource, he or she is able to access the resource on a shared basis.

Share-level security is built on the concept that any network user who knows the password can access the resource.

User-level security

User-level security is assigned to groups of users or individually to a single user for a particular shared resource. On a peer-to-peer network, each workstation owner must grant the access right, but on a client/server network, users are assigned their access rights centrally by the administrator in the user's profile. The bottom line on user-level security is that individual users can be given the right and permission to access certain network resources.

In addition to share-level security, user-level security defines what a user can do with a resource, provided he or she is given permission to access it. For example, using user-level security on a shared folder, you could grant Uncle Harry full access rights to the folder and restrict Aunt Sally to read-only on the folder contents.

In nearly all network operating systems (NOS), user-level security is often assigned to groups rather than to individual users. Users with common resource needs and access rights can be grouped together and administered and modified as a single entity.

Encrypting Data to Keep Network Secrets

Beyond restricting who can log into the network, you can also protect your network data resources by using a secret code. Encrypting data before transmitting makes its safe and secure arrival more likely. It may sound like something out of a James Bond flick, but the latest 007 poll suggests that encrypting data is becoming very common, especially in networks carrying e-commerce (credit card numbers, bank accounts, and the like).

Data encryption, or *cryptography*, converts data into a secret code so that you can transmit it over a public network. Some private networks also use encryption, but they usually use it on specialized and highly secure systems only. To encrypt a file, you use an *encryption algorithm* to convert the plain-text data into a *cipher*, also called *cipher text*. The cipher text is transmitted, and at the receiving end, it is decrypted back into plain text by using an *encryption key*, the basis for the original encryption.

The keys to encryption

An encryption key is a 40- to 512-bit binary number. Plain text is encrypted mathematically by combining the encryption key with its bits. Decryption involves extracting the key from the cipher-text bits to return the data to its original form.

The three encryption methods you should know for the Network+ exam are

✦ **DES (Data-Encryption Standard):** Both the sender and receiver use the same key to encrypt and decrypt. This encryption method, which uses a 56-bit encryption key, is the fastest and easiest method, but the key itself also must be transmitted. There are several versions of DES in use:

    • **DES-EEE3:** Three DES encryptions with three different keys.

    • **DES-EDE3:** Three DES operations in the sequence encrypt-decrypt-encrypt with three different keys.

    • **DES-EEE2** and **DES-EDE2:** Similar to the three key methods, except that the first and third operations use the same key.

✦ **RSA (Rivest, Shamir, and Adleman):** This method, which is named for its creators, is also called the public-key algorithm. It uses both a private and a public key to encrypt and decrypt data. Each recipient holds a private and unique key that's used in conjunction with a published public key. The sender uses the recipient's public key to encrypt the message, and then the recipient uses his private key to decrypt the message.

DES uses a 56-bit encryption key and RSA uses a two-part key: a private key that is kept by the owner and a public key that is published.

Digital certificates

A *digital certificate,* or digital ID, is your identity card on the Internet. You use it to supply your public encryption key to those to whom you send encrypted data. Certification authorities — such as Verisign, Inc. (www. verisign.com) — issue digital certificates. To have a digital certificate issued to you requires lots of documentation verifying who you are, such as a driver's license, a notarized statement, and fingerprints.

A digital certificate contains the following data:

✦ The certificate owner's name

✦ The name and address of the owner's company

✦ The company's public key

✦ The owner's certificate serial number (which is supplied by the certificate issuer)

✦ The certificate's validity dates

✦ The ID code of the certifying authority

✦ The digital signature of the certifying authority

For more information on encryption, visit the Electronic Frontier Foundation (www.eff.org).

Keeping safe with Kerberos

Kerberos is a security system and encryption method that was originally developed at the Massachusetts Institute of Technology. This system authenticates users as well as encrypting the data passed to and from users.

Microsoft has adopted Kerberos as its default encryption and security system for Windows 2000.

Hiding Safely behind a Firewall

The best way to keep a network secure is to make sure that only those authorized to share its resources have access to the network. Restricting access is an easy task if the network is only a LAN, but everything changes if you connect to the outside world. Opening a door for LAN users to exit also opens the door for others to enter.

One method for keeping your network secure is to implement a *firewall*. In general, a firewall — a set of programs running on your network's gateway server — monitors outgoing and incoming network traffic to allow authorized packets in or out. Commonly, firewalls allow users access to the Internet and to securely separate a network's public Web server from the internal network. Network administrators also use firewalls to secure internal subnetworks from unauthorized internal users.

In a nutshell, you use firewalls to keep unauthorized users out of the internal network and to block internal users from accessing unauthorized outside locations. Here are some firewall techniques that you may run into on the Network+ exam:

✦ **Packet filter:** A packet filter, also called a screening router, screens packets looking for certain IP addresses or port numbers.

✦ **Proxy server:** In addition to caching Web pages for a LAN, a proxy server acts as a switch between the LAN and the WAN, breaking the connection if necessary to prevent access.

✦ **Network Address Translation (NAT):** NAT serves as a translator to convert and conceal all internal IP addresses into a single IP address that is publicized to the world.

✦ **Stateful inspection:** This process matches outgoing requests to incoming responses and blocks any incoming messages without a matching request.

Security over the Internet

The Network+ exam, in its latest version, finally has recognized that the Internet may not be the safest place in the world to be transmitting personal data, such as your name, address, phone number, and especially your credit card and bank account numbers. Several protocols are used on the Internet to provide security and privacy for this sensitive data. Here's a list of the security protocols you should know for the exam:

✦ **IP Security (IPsec):** An Internet security protocol that provides both authentication and encryption. IPsec (pronounced as "eye-pea-sec") is a Network layer (Layer 3) protocol. Because it secures every part of a network transmission, it is fast becoming the standard security protocol.

✦ **Point to Point Tunneling Protocol (PPTP):** PPTP is a security protocol that uses RSA encryption to transmit other protocols over an IP network. PPTP is commonly used to implement VPNs over the Internet.

✦ **Secure Sockets Layer (SSL):** SSL is probably the best known and most commonly used security protocol on the Internet. SSL, which is a Transport layer (Layer 4) protocol, works like this: The SSL server sends its public key to your browser; the public key is then used by the browser to send a secret, randomly generated private key back to the SSL server to set up the key exchange for the SSL session.

Prep Test

1 Applications use which of the following layers of the OSI model? (Choose three.)

A ❑ Network layer

B ❑ Application layer

C ❑ Transport layer

D ❑ Session layer

E ❑ Presentation layer

F ❑ Physical layer

2 As a PDU is passed from layer to layer, what is added or removed from the packet by each succeeding layer?

A ○ Header

B ○ Trailer

C ○ Error-checking bits

D ○ Protocol ID bits

3 Which of the following is NOT a Physical layer device?

A ○ Network interface card

B ○ Repeater

C ○ Hub

D ○ Bridge

4 The device used to join two dissimilar network segments is a

A ○ Router.

B ○ Switch.

C ○ Bridge.

D ○ Hub.

5 Which of the following are Transport layer protocols? (Choose two.)

A ❑ SMTP

B ❑ TCP

C ❑ FTP

D ❑ IPX

E ❑ NetBEUI

6 The Network layer device that determines and sends packets over the most efficient route available is a(n)

A ○ Bridge.

B ○ Switch.

C ○ Active hub.

D ○ Router.

7 A good password policy should include (choose two)

A ❑ Changing passwords frequently.

B ❑ A maximum length for passwords.

C ❑ A standard for password uniqueness.

D ❑ A minimum reliance on passwords.

8 A user calls, complaining that she can't log into the network. She tried to enter her login and password three times, and then the system would no longer let her log in. What could be the reasons for this? (Choose two.)

A ❑ A network error occurred.

B ❑ The user was entering an incorrect account name or password.

C ❑ The user's workstation or network connection is faulty.

D ❑ The user's account was locked out after three tries.

9 Which of the following are commonly used encryption methods? (Choose two.)

A ❑ NSA

B ❑ DES

C ❑ U812

D ❑ RSA

10 A _____ is a set of programs running on the network gateway server that filters incoming and outgoing mail for appropriate and allowable destinations. (Choose two.)

A ❑ Proxy server

B ❑ Packet filter

C ❑ Default gateway

D ❑ Router

Answers

1 **B, D,** and **E.** The upper layers of the OSI model are grouped together as the application-oriented layers. *Review "Application protocols."*

2 **A.** Each layer adds its layer to the outbound PDU to provide instructions to its counterpart layer on the receiving end, which strips the header away. *Review "Up one side and down the other."*

3 **D.** A bridge is a Data Link layer device. *Review "Gettin' physical."*

4 **C.** A bridge joins two dissimilar network segments that perform similar functions but cannot otherwise communicate into a single network. *Review "Bridging across the network."*

5 **B** and **E.** This is not a trick question: NetBEUI includes NetBIOS and is used to mean both. Another common Transport layer protocol is SPX. *Review "Transport protocols."*

6 **D.** Plain as the nose on your face: Routers route packets over networks on the Network layer. *Review "Internetworking devices."*

7 **A** and **C.** Some systems have password length maximums, but they aren't typically included in the password policy. *Review "Practicing safe passwording."*

8 **B** and **D.** If an account policy has been established that limits account logins to three tries, the account lockout policy may have been engaged, locking the account to any additional tries. More than likely the account name is good, and the password is wrong. *Review "Setting account policies."*

9 **B** and **D.** DES and RSA are commonly used encryption models that use different types of keys and codes to encrypt data transmitted over the Internet. *Review "The keys to encryption."*

10 **A** and **B.** Proxy servers and packet filters are types of firewall implementations. You use a firewall to screen incoming and outgoing messages to prevent unauthorized access to the local network and to ensure that local users don't visit unauthorized sites. *Review "Hiding Safely behind a Firewall."*

Chapter 4: Remote Connections and WAN Technologies

In This Chapter

- Defining packet, circuit, and cell switching
- Explaining modem operations
- Differentiating WAN technologies

The Network+ exam includes a number of questions dealing specifically with remote connectivity and the communication services it uses. For the exam, you should know and understand data communications in general, and the protocols and transmission modes used in local and wide area network implementations.

Switching Packets and Circuits

In the world of broadband communications, eventually you have to deal with the telephone company. Most of the communication services used by the typical network to connect to the outside networking world are provided (controlled) by the same companies that provide telephone services.

Switching, like the processes used to move data across a local network, is the underlying process used to move data across the global communications network. In fact, the official name of the phone companies' network is the Public Switched Telephone Network, or PSTN (no, it isn't pronounced as "piston"; just say the letters P-S-T-N).

Technically, your home or office doesn't connect directly to the PSTN. Between your house or building and the telephone company's local switching system is a sublayer of service that connects you to the PSTN, called Plain Old Telephone Service or POTS (you can pronounce this one as it looks).

Getting from point A to point B

Two modes are used to carry data (and some voice) signals from point A (source) to point B (destination) through the global communications network:

- ✦ Packet switching
- ✦ Circuit switching

Packet switching

Packet switching is about what it sounds like. Data is transmitted across a network in what are called *protocol data units* or PDUs. On the Transport and Network layers of the OSI model, your request to download a Web page from www.dummies.com is broken up into several smaller message units for transmission over the network. The communications services that transport the message units (packets), forwarding them from router to router based on the destination address, are packet-switching services.

Circuit switching

If you prefer a more predictable path for your data than is likely to be used on a packet-switching service, you can use a circuit-switching service. A circuit-switching service builds a dedicated and virtually permanent path through the WAN. When you subscribe to a circuit-switching service, a virtual circuit (VC) is created between one end of your WAN connection and the other end of your WAN connection. In telecommunications parlance, this circuit is "nailed up" and dedicated to your sole and private use.

Data still travels as packets on a circuit-switching service, but instead of using the unpredictable path of a packet-switching service, it travels over a private circuit through the WAN. If the packet-switching system is the cloud, a circuit-switching system is a pipeline through the cloud.

When you dial up your Aunt Sally, her phone number (area code, local exchange, and number) is used to construct a virtual circuit over the PSTN that exists only for the duration of the call. However, in a WAN situation, the virtual circuit (the path through the PSTN) is made permanent to create what is called a permanent virtual circuit (PVC). We're not making this stuff up!

Working with Modems

The term *modem* is formed from the words *mo*dulate and *dem*odulate, the two actions that this device performs. A modem modulates the computer's digital signal into an analog signal that can be sent over the Plain Old Telephone Service (POTS). POTS is the standard telephone system that is available just about everywhere in some form. The other half of the modem's action occurs at a receiving end of a transmission where the modem demodulates the POTS analog signal — converts it back into a digital signal — and sends it on to a computer.

Modems don't make up a large portion of the Network+ test. You should focus on the point-to-point protocols, which we discuss in this chapter. However, don't skip over the rest of the material in this chapter. Study each area marked with an icon carefully because this information will likely appear on the test in a different context.

Modem standards

Since the late 1980s, the International Telecommunications Union (ITU), formerly known as CCITT (Consultative Committee for International Telegraphy and Telephony), has been producing the standards used for modems. The CCITT/ITU standards are the *V* standards that you've probably heard of.

Table 4-1 lists the *V dot* modem standards that you may see referenced on the Network+ exam.

Table 4-1	ITU Modem Standards
Standard	*Bits per Second (bps)*
V.32	9,600
V.32bis	14,400
V.34	28,800
V.34bis	33,600
V.42	57,600
V.90	56,000

The suffix *bis* means *second* in French, and it indicates the second version of a modem standard. Some standards also have *terbo*, which are third versions.

Another common modem standard is the Microcom Networking Protocol (MNP), which is defined as a series of classes (Class 1 through Class 5) that offer differing levels of error-detection and correction capabilities. MNP Class 5 protocol is common on modems because it includes data compression that doubles the data transmission rate.

The V.90 standard is the latest modem standard. It transfers data to the modem by using a technology that uses a modified modulation technique involving significant data compression at a speed of 56 Kbps. However, when sending data *up* the line, a V.90 modem transfers data at a speed of up to 33.6 Kbps, which must be modulated.

Asynchronous modems

An *asynchronous* (called *async* for short) modem is the most commonly used modem type largely because it's the most widely used communications type. Async data is transmitted in a serial stream, which has start and stop bits embedded in the stream to mark the beginning and end of each character.

Asynchronous communication isn't controlled by a clocking device that synchronizes the transmission of data to the specific timing used in synchronous communication. Instead, the slower of the two computers controls the flow by interrupting the transmission whenever it needs to catch up. The sending computer just sends its data stream, and the receiving computer just receives it. You always face a potential for error with async communications, so a parity bit and parity checking are used for error control.

In addition to the speeds listed in Table 4-1, many of the V.*xx* standards also include error control and data-compression techniques, which asynchronous communications apply. Often, a communications link to a local area network employs a number of protocols that incorporate several standards. For example, a typical LAN-to-LAN link using dial-up modems may employ V.32bis signaling, V.42 error checking, and V.42bis data-compression techniques.

Synchronous modems

A *synchronous* (or *sync*) modem uses a timing scheme that coordinates the transmission between the two computers. Data is grouped in blocks of characters, called frames, and synchronizing characters precede each frame. If the sync characters arrive at the correct point, everything's cool. Otherwise, the frame is retransmitted.

Synchronous communications use a number of primary protocols. Following are the ones that you should know for the exam:

+ **SDLC (Synchronous Data Link Control):** A versatile point-to-point and multipoint protocol that designates one station as the controlling node and the other station(s) as the controlled node(s).

✦ **HDLC (High-Level Data Link Control):** A high-level, bit-oriented protocol that sends messages in frames of variable sizes.

✦ **BSC (Binary Synchronous Communications):** Also known as *bisync*, a protocol in which the communicating devices are synchronized before data transmission begins. The data frame includes a header and trailer for synchronization.

Connecting a modem

Modems connect to a computer either internally, in the form of an expansion card, or externally through a serial port. In either case, you use an RJ-11 plug — which is a smaller lookalike of the RJ-45 connector used with 10BaseT media — to attach the modem to the telephone service.

Regardless of whether it's internal or external, a modem communicates through a serial port. The serial ports on most computers are COM1 and COM2. (*COM* refers to communication.) Some computers also have COM3 and COM4 ports as well.

The modem itself usually requires little in the way of configuration. Most modems are preset to the general communications standards. Some minor configuration settings may need adjusting, but most modems are good to go right out of the box. If a modem does need configuration, you can configure it by using software, AT commands, or DIP switches, depending on the modem.

Setting up a modem connection in Windows

Lab 4-1 provides you with some background and helps you internalize some of the terminology and processes that you use when you set up a modem connection. In this lab, you use Windows 9*x*, Windows Me, or Windows 2000 Professional tools to set up modem communications.

A modem connection is created in two phases: setting up the modem itself and configuring the dial-up networking properties.

Book IV
Chapter 4

Lab 4-1	Setting Up a Modem Connection

1. **Access the Windows Control Panel and double-click the Modems icon.**

   The Modem Properties dialog box appears.

Remote
Connections and
WAN Technologies

2. **Click Add.**

   The Modem Installation Wizard appears.

   You have the choice of letting the Wizard detect the new modem (assuming that you've already installed the modem into an expansion slot or connected it to a serial port) or picking the modem from the list of supported modems (our recommendation).

3. **Check the modem's configuration settings by clicking the Properties button in the Modems Properties window.**

   On many newer systems, a modem is standard equipment and already installed and configured.

4. **Open the My Computer window from the My Computer icon on the Windows Desktop and configure a dial-up destination by clicking the Dial-Up Networking icon.**

   In the Dial-Up Networking window, you should see a New Connection icon and possibly some existing connections.

5. **Click the New Connection icon.**

   The Make New Connection Wizard appears to guide you through the creation of a new dial-up remote connection.

Modem AT commands

The AT command set is common to nearly all modems, although most users never come into contact with it. You may see a question or two on the Network+ exam that refers to AT commands indirectly.

Except for the special character commands, the code *AT,* which stands for attention, precedes each AT command. For example, the command to dial 555-1212 is ATDT5551212. Table 4-2 contains only a few of the more common AT commands, but these are the ones that you may run into on the Network+ exam.

Table 4-2	AT Commands
Command	*Meaning*
, (comma)	Pause.
*70	Turn off call-waiting feature on telephone line.
AT	Attention command that precedes each command line (the source of the name AT commands).
DT	Dial using touch-tone mode.
H	Hang up.

Analog modems and digital codecs

You'll never guess which type of modem carries an analog signal. Ah, you peeked! Most modems in use are analog modems, so named because they connect to and modulate signals for the analog telephone system. Because the analog system uses sound waves to send data, any extra noise or interference on the line can corrupt the data that's being transmitted.

A digital signal, on the other hand, is far less affected by interference. To transmit digital data over digital lines, you don't really need a modem. However, sometimes you need the reverse of an analog modem — a device that encodes the analog signal into a digital signal. You use a *codec,* for example, to transmit an analog video image over digital lines. Codec is a contraction of *co*der/*dec*oder.

The Network+ exam refers to all protocols, standards, and technologies by only their initials or abbreviations. Make sure that you know their initials or abbreviations as well as their names.

PPP versus SLIP

When you connect to a remote network (such as the Internet) by using a modem, you most commonly use PPP (Point-to-Point Protocol) or perhaps SLIP (Serial Line Internet Protocol). You can use these protocols over ISDN (see the section "ISDN: It Should Do Networking" later in this chapter) or on dedicated high-speed lines as well as to connect some routers to other routers.

Getting to the point: PPP

PPP is the current standard protocol for point-to-point connections. It provides both Physical and Data Link layer connections to a variety of network protocols, including TCP/IP, NetBEUI, AppleTalk, and IPX. In effect, PPP enables your modem to act like a network adapter, seamlessly connecting you to a remote network protocol.

PPP also inherently supports compression and error checking, making it a very fast and reliable protocol.

Giving it the SLIP

SLIP is an older, legacy protocol, common to UNIX systems, that operates only at the Physical layer. You use SLIP primarily to connect to the Internet via a modem. Because its only connection is to TCP/IP, SLIP provides no addressing and relies on the connecting hardware to provide any error checking and correction performed in the transmission.

PPTP, VPN, ABC, NBC, and Other Networks

Tunneling a protocol means that one protocol, such as IPX or AppleTalk, is routed over another protocol, such as TCP/IP. This arrangement enables two networks to connect and communicate with their native protocol, such as AppleTalk, with their packets transmitted in a TCP/IP format.

One of the most common of the tunneling protocols is PPTP (Point to Point Tunneling Protocol). PPTP tunnels PPP over an IP network to create a network connection. PPTP uses the Internet as a network connection. PPTP enables you to encapsulate a variety of protocols (IP, IPX, or NetBEUI) inside of IP packets for transmission. As you would plain brown shipping paper, the receiving end discards the outer IP packet (the one used as the shipping container), and the original packet is forwarded on to its destination.

PPTP creates a virtual connection for remote users. The users perceive that they are directly connected to the network, as if they were local to it. This PPTP connection creates a *virtual private network* (VPN). Although the connection is made over the public Internet, the connection is virtually private because IP packets are essentially double-wrapped inside PPTP packets. PPTP itself doesn't create a connection. The connection is actually made by the carrying protocol, PPP or the like.

Analog and Digital Carrier Services

Within a LAN, you use a digital signal, but when the LAN is expanded or attached to a WAN, a different type of digital carrier or, very commonly, an analog service may be necessary. Digital and analog communications are available on a variety of carrier services.

Analog carrier services

You will hear telephone service referred to with two acronyms: POTS (Plain Old Telephone Service) and PSTN (Public Switched Telephone Network). These two acronyms are often used interchangeably, but they are a bit different. The service used to connect your home or business's telephone service to the telephone company's switching center (called a Central Office or CO) is POTS. The service that carries your call across the city, state, or around the world is the PSTN. However, for the Network+ exam, they are essentially the same thing.

The telephone company typically provides analog carrier services, but some other companies offer data networking services called *public data networks* (PDNs). The most common type of analog carrier service, however, is a dial-up switched line. The public telephone system is a switched service that you connect to by using dial-up access. Switching occurs as the signal travels from your telephone connection to the central office — the central office uses the telephone number as an address to switch the call to its destination.

Digital carrier services

You're likely to see the most common digital services referenced on the Network+ test. You aren't asked any questions directly about these items, but you can count on seeing them in a situational question or as part of a question's information.

The most common digital carriers are DDS (Digital Data Service) lines that provide a direct point-to-point synchronous connection. In general, these lines are all leased lines. A *leased* line is a dial-up line that is reserved for a single user or company for private use. This type of service is also called a *dedicated line.*

Because the DDS line is private and dedicated to connecting two points, you don't use a modem. Instead, you place a CSU/DSU (customer service unit/data service unit) at each end of the line. Leased lines use PPP (Point-to-Point Protocol) and HDLC (High-level Data Link Control) protocols.

T-carriers and DS levels

High-speed DDS lines are designated in a couple of different ways, the most common of which are T-carriers (T-1, T-2, and so on) and DS-level specifications (DS-0, DS-1, DS-2, and so on). Generally, you use these two line designations interchangeably, where a T-1 line is essentially the equivalent of the DS-1 specification.

TIP

Should you encounter either T-1 or DS-1 on the exam, just remember that for the exam's purposes, they mean the same thing.

The most widely used high-speed digital service is the T-1 line, which uses two pairs of wires to send signals at a maximum data rate of 1.544 Mbps. A T-1 line is a full-duplex carrier that uses one pair of wires to send and the other pair to receive. It consists of 24 individual 64 Kbps channels that can be used individually or in groups to create what is called *fractional T-1* service. Table 4-3 lists the three primary T-carrier categories you should know for the exam.

Table 4-3	T-Carrier Categories		
Level	*Number of Channels*	*Number of T-1s*	*Bandwidth*
T-1	24	1	1.54 Mbps
T-2	96	4	6.31 Mbps
T-3	672	28	44.74 Mbps

Instead of memorizing Table 4-3 for the exam, just remember the T-1 line's characteristics and the number of T-1 lines that each succeeding T-carrier level represents.

The DS (Data Signaling or Digital Service) scale categorizes DDS lines. The relationship to the T-carrier lines is that a DS-0 represents the data rate of a single T-1 channel, and the data rate of the full T-1 line (all 24 channels) is categorized as DS-1.

Table 4-4 lists the DS specifications and their T-carrier equivalents.

Table 4-4	DS Specifications	
DS Level	*T-Carrier*	*Data Rate*
DS-0	N/A	64 Kbps
DS-1	T-1	1.54 Mbps
DS-2	T-2	6.31 Mbps
DS-3	T-3	44.74 Mbps

In Europe, DDS lines are categorized as E-series carriers. An E-1 line is capable of transferring data at 2.048 Mbps. The Network+ test may refer to the E-series lines in conjunction with T-carrier lines.

Choosing the Right WAN Service

For the Network+ exam, you need to know the characteristics, in terms of speed, bandwidth (capacity), and media, of the following WAN services:

✦ ATM

✦ DSL

✦ Frame Relay

✦ ISDN

✦ X.25

Cell switching with ATM

Asynchronous Transfer Mode (ATM) is a Layer 2 (Data Link layer) network technology that can be used for both local and wide area networks. Originally designed to carry voice traffic, it is now used for video and data as well.

ATM is a physical switching technology that is hardware-based. A virtual circuit is created and data, which is organized into fixed-length cells, is forwarded from switch to switch along the circuit until it reaches its destination.

ATM uses a 53-byte cell that is transmitted digitally over physical media. This is why ATM is referred to as a cell-switching technology. Because ATM is a physical switching technology, which means it's hardware- rather than software-based, it's able to achieve faster switching speeds.

ATM is commonly used as a backbone technology in large carrier or enterprise networks. ATM is very scalable and supports transmission rates that range from 9.6 Kbps to 1.5 Mbps to 155 Mbps, 622 Mbps, 2.5 Gbps, and 10 Gbps. ATM commonly runs as an administrative layer on top of the SONET transmission technology.

Soaring with SONET

The Synchronous Optical Network (SONET) was originally developed to bridge the Baby Bells (the offspring created when the Bell system, also known as Ma Bell, was broken up) to long-distance carriers. SONET is a WAN technology implemented on fiber-optic cabling that supports data rates defined by the OC (optical carrier) levels, detailed in Table 4-5.

Table 4-5	Optical Carrier Transmission Speeds	
OC Service	Speed	Equivalents
OC-1	51.84 Mbps	1 DS-3
OC-3	155.52 Mbps	3 OC-1s
OC-12	622.08 Mbps	12 OC-1s or 4 OC-3s
OC-48	2488.32 Mbps	48 OC-1s or 4 OC-12s
OC-192	9953.28	192 OC-1s or 4 OC-48s
OC-768	38813.12 Mbps	768 OC-1s or 4 OC-192s

Running with DSL

Digital Subscriber Line (DSL) service is a dedicated always-on broadband technology that is carried to a home or business over existing POTS lines. In effect, DSL service turns the baseband POTS line into a broadband line that is able to carry both data transmissions and voice calls at the same time.

DSL comes in many flavors, but they are all either an asynchronous or synchronous service. Asymmetric DSL (ADSL) gets its name from the fact that it provides different data speeds for upload and download transmissions. Commonly available ADSL service provides 384 Kbps of download (data you receive) speed and 168 Kbps of upload (data you send) speed. Symmetric DSL (SDSL), which usually requires the installation of dedicated POTS lines, provides the same data speed for upload and download transmissions.

The customer premise equipment (CPE) used for ADSL is a DSL bridge (also known as a modem) and SDSL uses a DSL router, which provides many, but not all, of the features of a standard network router.

Connecting over Frame Relay

Frame Relay is a packet-switching telecommunications service that is used to connect two fixed points, such as two LANs or end-points on a WAN. Frame Relay transmits data in variable-length frames by using the packet-switching technology of the older X.25 service over a permanent virtual circuit (PVC). Typically, Frame Relay is available as a full T-1, but can also be subscribed as a fractional T-1 (256 Kbps, 512 Kbps, or 784 Kbps).

Broadband versus baseband

Just in case you're dying of curiosity, there's a difference between broadband and baseband communications. For example, the telephone line uses baseband signaling, allowing only one call per session, while the cable TV lines use broadband so that more than one channel (not to mention cable Internet access) can be received at one time.

Without getting too technical, *baseband* communications (the kind used on virtually all local area networks, or LANs) essentially use the entire bandwidth of a media to transmit a single digital signal. On the other hand, *broadband* is, well, broader in scope and transmits multiple signals over a single medium. If the telecommunications world only used baseband, first there would be a lot more wires on the telephone poles, and second, communications would be a lot slower.

Frame Relay service requires the use of a CSU/DSU (channel service unit/data service unit) at each end. This device converts the frame-based signal of the PVC to the digital formats used on the local network.

Networking with ISDN

Integrated Services Digital Network (ISDN) service is a digital transmission standard that, like DSL, transmits data over standard POTS lines to homes and offices, but it can also be carried over other dedicated media as well. While ISDN isn't as fast as some services, it can carry data at speeds up to 128 Kbps.

Two types of ISDN service are available: Primary Rate Interface (PRI) and Basic Rate Interface (BRI). BRI is the service a home or office is most likely to subscribe from the phone company and it's the one you will also see on the exam. For more detail about ISDN, see "ISDN: It Should Do Networking" later in this chapter.

Getting connected with X.25

One of the older communications services is X.25, which is an international standard that allows computers and LANs connected to the PSTN to communicate through a central or intermediary controller. You don't really need to know anything about X.25 services, but you may see it on a question or two on the exam.

ISDN: It Should Do Networking

ISDN (Integrated Services Digital Network) is a digital data service that has been bursting onto the scene since 1984. It is a completely digital communications networking specification that is capable of carrying voice, data, images, video, or just about anything that can be digitized — which is just about anything.

ISDN services are available in two formats:

+ **BRI (Basic Rate Interface):** This service consists of two B-channels, each of which carries 64 Kbps, and one D-channel that carries control signals at 16 Kbps. You can use the two B-channels independently or multiplex them together to reach a 128 Kbps data speed.

+ **PRI (Primary Rate Interface):** This ISDN type uses 23 B-channels and 1 D-channel. You can use the B-channels independently or combine them to attain the equivalent of a T-1 service. You use the D-channel for control and signaling.

For the Network+ exam, remember the number and type of lines that make up each of the two ISDN types. Don't worry about speeds, but remember that ISDN PRI service is the rough equivalent of a T-1 line.

Inverse multiplexing

An ISDN channel adapter, which is also called an inverse multiplexer (mux), is required at the customer end of an ISDN service connection. This device combines the signals carried on the separate B- and D-channels for use by your computer or LAN.

Another way to look at this inverse multiplexing is the technology used to combine multiple ISDN B-channels to achieve data speeds higher than 64 Kbps. In general, you implement inverse multiplexing methods outside of the ISDN technology. You use the following three methods for inverse multiplexing:

✦ **BONDING (Bandwidth On Demand Interoperability Group):** The most common method used, BONDING combines up to 63 56 Kbps channels or 64 Kbps B-channels.

✦ **Multilink PPP (Point-to-Point Protocol):** Routes IP over ISDN. A single logical connection is multiplexed across several physical connections.

✦ **Multirate service (also known as Nx64 service — pronounced as "N by 64" service):** Usually included as a part of PRI service. The service provider, usually the telephone company, combines as many channels as needed to give you the speed required on demand (in multiples of 64 Kbps) each time that you make a connection.

Advantages of ISDN

Here's a list of some of the advantages of using ISDN over PSTN:

✦ ISDN offers data speeds of two to four times faster than what is available on PSTN using an analog modem.

✦ ISDN provides a relatively low-cost, moderately higher-speed service to home or small office/home office (SOHO) users.

✦ ISDN is cost-effective when used as a dial-up nondedicated WAN service.

✦ ISDN service is available on a per usage basis from most Internet Service Providers (ISPs).

Disadvantages of ISDN

A few disadvantages of ISDN when compared to PSTN are as follows:

✦ ISDN data transmission speeds don't offer great improvements over those available on an analog modem and PSTN.

✦ ISDN dedicated services can cost much more than nondedicated services.

✦ ISDN requires a special adapter (called an inverse multiplexer) to translate between analog and digital signals.

✦ With at least 50,000 possible configuration combinations, ISDN is very complex to configure.

Prep Test

1 What is the data transmission rate of a T-3 carrier?

A ○ 784 Kbps

B ○ 1.54 Mbps

C ○ 25.74 Mbps

D ○ 44.74 Mbps

2 What is the data transmission rate defined by a DS-0?

A ○ 64 Kbps

B ○ 64 Mbps

C ○ 64 Gbps

D ○ 128 Kbps

3 The command string used to dial the telephone number 555-8812 from a modem is

A ○ ADT5558812&F

B ○ ATX555,8812+++

C ○ ATDT5558812

D ○ +++AT,DT,5558812

4 The protocol that is most commonly used with dial-up connections is

A ○ SLIP.

B ○ PPTP.

C ○ ISDN.

D ○ PPP.

5 The protocol that tunnels point-to-point communications over an IP network is

A ○ SLIP.

B ○ PPTP.

C ○ ISDN.

D ○ PPP.

6 The bandwidth available on a T-1/DS-1 service is

A ○ 64 Kbps.

B ○ 1.54 Kbps.

C ○ 1.54 Mbps.

D ○ 44.74 Mbps.

7 If a modem connection using SLIP is experiencing repeated transmission errors, which of the following actions should you take to help eliminate many of the errors?

A ○ Reset the modem.

B ○ Change the protocol to PPP.

C ○ Replace the serial cable.

D ○ Reconfigure the modem by using the ATZ command.

8 ISDN BRI service provides

A ○ 23 B-channels and 1 D-channel.

B ○ 2 D-channels and 1 B-channel.

C ○ 23 D-channels and 1 B-channel.

D ○ 2 B-channels and 1 D-channel.

9 What is the terminating device used at each end of a Frame Relay connection?

A ○ CSU/DSU

B ○ Router

C ○ Modem

D ○ Inverse mux

10 The process used to combine multiple ISDN channels to achieve higher bandwidths is called

A ○ Multiplexing.

B ○ Inverse multiplexing.

C ○ Rate services.

D ○ Binding.

Answers

1 **D.** Make sure that you memorize the data speeds of the different carrier types. *Review "T-carriers and DS levels."*

2 **A.** A DS-0 is the speed rating on a single T-carrier channel. *Review "T-carriers and DS levels."*

3 **C.** AT is the command for attention; DT stands for dial using touch tone; and what follows is the telephone number. Don't worry too much about memorizing all the AT commands, but do be familiar with those we've included in this chapter. *Review "Modem AT commands."*

4 **D.** The Point-to-Point Protocol (PPP) is by far the most commonly used protocol for modem communications. The Network+ test refers to all protocols only by their initials or abbreviations. *Review "Getting to the point: PPP."*

5 **B.** The Point to Point Tunneling Protocol (PPTP) enables you to encapsulate one protocol inside of IP packets so that you can use the Internet as a part of your network. *Review "PPTP, VPN, ABC, NBC, and Other Networks."*

6 **C.** Watch that qualifier very carefully. Be absolutely sure that any specific data speeds that you choose for answers have the correct speed abbreviations on them. *Review "T-carriers and DS levels."*

7 **B.** This doesn't mean that only changing the protocol to PPP will solve the problem. However, because PPP implements error checking and correction and SLIP doesn't, changing the protocol may eliminate many of the errors. *Review "PPP versus SLIP."*

8 **D.** BRI (Basic Rate Interface) is the most commonly available ISDN service, which naturally means it's the less capable of the ISDN formats. B-channels bear bytes, and D-channels carry directives. BRI has two Bs and one D. Just remember my high school report cards. *Review "ISDN: It Should Do Networking."*

9 **A.** You may be asked a question or two from the Troubleshooting domain of the exam regarding Frame Relay connection problems. Examine the question to know where the problem exists and never rule out the CSU/DSU and the problem source. *Review "Connecting over Frame Relay."*

10 **A.** Multiplexing involves combining multiple outbound lines onto a single line. Conversely, inverse multiplexing combines multiple inbound lines to connect to your computer. *Review "Inverse multiplexing."*

Chapter 5: TCP/IP and Network Addressing

In This Chapter

✔ Listing the main protocols in the TCP/IP protocol suite

✔ Identifying the OSI model layers of the TCP/IP protocols

✔ Describing the purpose and use of DNS, WINS, and hosts files

✔ Differentiating physical and logical addressing schemes

✔ Defining IP address classes

✔ Comparing IPv4 and IPv6 addressing

✔ Explaining subnetting and the use of a subnet mask

TCP/IP is not just one or two protocols, but rather a suite of protocols that work together to enable Internet, intranet, and networking communications over local and wide area networks and internetworks. You must know the use and function of each of the major protocols in the TCP/IP protocol suite. In addition, you really ought to be familiar with the layers of the OSI model on which each of the TCP/IP protocols operate.

You won't go far in your understanding of how the TCP/IP protocols work together if you don't know how Internet addressing works to get a message from point A to point B over the Internet. That's why, in this chapter, we cover addressing, subnetting, default gateways, DNS, WINS, and other client- and server-based tools and resources.

IP addressing schemes play a significant role on the Network+ exam. The good people at CompTIA expect you to know the address ranges for IP Class A, B, and C addresses. Not only that, but you need to know how subnet masks are derived for each class and applied to identify the host or the server of an IP address. Piece of cake!

The TCP/IP Protocols

We can't say it enough: TCP/IP is actually a suite of protocols that work together to provide for reliable and efficient data communications across an internetwork, which is a network of networks, local and wide area. To their friends, the TCP/IP protocols are more commonly known by their initials, but you should try to remember their full names.

The major protocols of the TCP/IP protocol suite are

✦ Address Resolution Protocol (ARP)

✦ Domain Name System (DNS)

✦ File Transfer Protocol (FTP)

✦ Hypertext Transfer Protocol (HTTP)

✦ Interactive Mail Access Protocol (IMAP)

✦ Internet Control Message Protocol (ICMP)

✦ Internet Protocol (IP)

✦ Open Shortest Path First (OSPF)

✦ Post Office Protocol (POP3)

✦ Routing Information Protocol (RIP)

✦ Simple Mail Transport Protocol (SMTP)

✦ Transmission Control Protocol (TCP)

✦ User Datagram Protocol (UDP)

Don't waste time memorizing all the protocols in the TCP/IP protocol suite. Look over the preceding list and mentally log them away. Being able to recognize what a protocol does (typically the name is a dead giveaway) and when it is used is more important than memorizing this list.

The TCP/IP protocols that we discuss in the next few sections are the ones you definitely need to know for the Network+ exam. To help make it relative, we cover these protocols in the order of their importance.

Transmission Control Protocol (TCP)

TCP (Transmission Control Protocol) is one of the namesake and foundation protocols of the TCP/IP protocol suite. TCP is a Layer 4 (Transport layer) protocol that manages and controls the transmission of data between the sending and receiving stations.

TCP is the primary transport protocol of the TCP/IP suite. TCP is a connection-oriented and reliable delivery protocol that ensures that message packets arrive at their destinations error-free.

In a nutshell, TCP accepts messages from the upper-layer OSI model protocols, fragments them for use by the Network layer protocols (primarily IP), and then directs the transport of the data to the TCP protocol operating on the Transport layer of the destination network.

TCP has the following characteristics and features:

+ **Connection-oriented:** Establishes and manages a direct connection to the remote network.

+ **Reliable:** Guarantees the delivery of message packets to their destinations by acknowledging those that arrive and requesting retransmission of late or erroneous packets.

+ **Packet handling:** Performs message fragmentation, sequencing, and reassembly.

+ **Error checking:** Before transmission, TCP uses a *checksum* (a count of the total number of bits in the complete message). On the receiving end, TCP ensures that packets are reassembled in the correct order and verifies that no bits are missing.

User Datagram Protocol (UDP)

The User Datagram Protocol (UDP) is TCP's evil twin. UDP is a connectionless and unreliable message delivery protocol that makes no guarantees that packets will arrive at all or, if they do, that they will be in the correct sequence. It even uses a different name, *datagrams,* for the packets it sends.

UDP is generally used in situations where the message packet doesn't need to be fragmented and where the speed of the delivery is more important than the overhead required to ensure the delivery. UDP is often used with Simple Network Management Protocol (SNMP) and TCP/IP utilities, such as TRACERT and PING.

Internet Protocol (IP)

The Internet Protocol (IP) is a connectionless protocol that provides two very valuable services: logically assigning destination address and routing (see "Routing protocols" later in this chapter), which involves determining the better way to get a message to its destination address.

Because IP is connectionless, it is therefore unreliable, especially when compared with TCP. However, IP is fast. Like all connectionless protocols, IP is called a *best-effort* protocol and relies on the kindness of other protocols, such as TCP, to handle reliability and other delivery issues.

IP addresses, such as 206.175.162.18, are called *logical addresses* because their assignment to workstations and network nodes is relative to other nodes on a network. For example, one node may be assigned a node address of .18 and another .19, and so on.

Address Resolution Protocol (ARP)

When delivering an IP segment over a network, the Address Resolution Protocol (ARP) picks up where DNS leaves off. DNS resolves the text domain name of a destination to its logically assigned numerical IP address, translating the human-friendly domain name to its IP address equivalent. ARP then resolves the IP address to the physical MAC address of the destination node.

IP works on the level of a directory in a large office building, like the one where your lawyer Gray N. Balding works. When you enter the building, you look at the directory to find Gray's office number. When you reach Aging, Rich, and Practicing (your lawyer's firm), you need to find the room where Gray actually hangs out, so you ask the ARP receptionist, who directs you to the specific physical location.

If ARP doesn't know the physical address of a node, it broadcasts a request packet to the network that contains the IP address it was provided. This is something like shouting to a large room of people, "Is Gray Balding here?" The workstation or device that is assigned the IP address in question then identifies itself by sending back its MAC address (the physical address, that is), just like Gray would identify himself by shouting back, "Yo!"

IP, DNS, and the big MAC

In contrast with the logical addressing scheme used by the IP protocol, physical addresses are assigned Media Access Control (MAC) addresses in the Data Link layer's MAC sublayer. MAC addresses are physically and permanently assigned to network adapters, routers, and other networking devices. Usually, IP addresses are assigned to nodes and workstations, while networking devices have MAC addresses.

We don't know if you noticed, but IP addresses such as 206.175.162.18 may be *logical* but they sure don't make a whole lot of sense. That's why

DNS (Domain Name System) came into existence. DNS uses a distributed database of Internet domain names and their corresponding IP addresses. The DNS databases enable Internet users to work with human-friendly system names, such as www.dummies.com or www.makemyday.info, rather than less friendly IP addresses, such as 206.175.162.18 (the Dummies IP address). Address Resolution Protocol (ARP), which we discuss in a nearby section, picks up where DNS leaves off. We also get into names and addresses later in this chapter in the section appropriately titled "Names and Addresses."

ARP stores the physical address along with the IP address in a table called the ARP cache, which is completely refreshed every two minutes, just to be sure that it has the very latest IP and MAC associations.

File Transfer Protocol (FTP)

The File Transfer Protocol (FTP) is used to transfer files from one computer to another and manage directories and folders on remote computers. At one time or another in your networking life, you've probably downloaded a file or two by using FTP. FTP is supported in virtually every network operating system and Web browser. If you want to transfer files independent of your Web browser, a variety of FTP clients, both shareware and freeware, are available.

When you transfer a file from your computer to a remote computer with FTP, you are *uploading* the file. *Downloading* a file is the reverse action — the file originates at the remote computer and is copied to your computer's hard disk. FTP clients (the software running on your computer) communicate with the FTP server (the software running on the remote host) to perform a variety of file management actions in addition to file transfers.

Of all the protocols that can possibly pop up on the Network+ test, FTP was the last one we expected to see, but appear it did — complete with a question fully devoted to the FTP topic.

Mail delivery protocols

The primary TCP/IP mail transport protocol is the Simple Mail Transport Protocol (SMTP), but other protocols are used at both the sending and receiving ends. You need to memorize exactly how the Internet e-mail system works, and know what each of the protocols involved are and which part of the process each handles.

Simple Mail Transport Protocol (SMTP)

The Simple Mail Transport Protocol (SMTP) provides foundation services for e-mail transfer across the Internet. By foundation, I mean the basics — SMTP makes sure that e-mail messages are delivered from the sender's server to the addressee's server. It doesn't deal with the delivery to the addressee's mailbox.

SMTP is like the postal service's trucks and airplanes that move mail from post office to post office, where those loving letters from Aunt Sally are sorted and delivered to you by the loyal, hardworking postal workers.

Book IV
Chapter 5

TCP/IP and Network Addressing

Routing protocols versus routed protocols

Don't let similar-looking terms screw you up on the Network+ exam. There is a difference between routing protocols and routed protocols.

Routing protocols are used between routers to provide updated information concerning the availability or health of a particular route over a network or the Internet. On the other hand, *routed* protocols are native network protocols (protocols that were created especially for a specific network or network environment) that can be transmitted across a network or the Internet. Say your network's native protocol (such as IP and IPX) provides necessary information to routers on the Internet so that the routers can more efficiently process your network's data packets. This data is a routed protocol.

After SMTP transfers e-mail across the Internet, mail servers hold the mail for users in their mailboxes. What happens to e-mail from this point on depends on the specific mail client being used.

Post Office Protocol (POP3)

To retrieve e-mail from Internet providers and download it to individual computers on the network, the Post Office Protocol (POP3) is by far the most commonly used send-and-receive protocol. The number 3 in POP3 refers to the latest version of this popular e-mail protocol. POP mail stores e-mail until users log on, at which time the mail is transferred to users' computers and removed from the e-mail server.

POP works well in situations where users log on from the same permanently assigned workstation.

Internet Mail Access Protocol (IMAP)

If you are using the Interactive Mail Access Protocol (IMAP), users' e-mail remains on the server even after it's been downloaded to their computers. E-mail is stored on the server indefinitely — that is, until users decide to manually remove it.

IMAP e-mail works very well in situations where clients regularly access their mail from various locations on the network or via remote access.

Internet Control Message Protocol (ICMP)

The Internet Control Message Protocol (ICMP) acts as a sort of intercom system for the TCP/IP protocol suite. ICMP, which is a Network layer (Layer 3) protocol, carries control, status, and error messages between systems. ICMP messages are encapsulated inside IP datagrams for transport over the network.

Internet gateways and servers use ICMP to transmit datagram problem reports back to the message source. Internet utilities, such as PING and TRACERT (see Chapter 7), send out ICMP echo requests and track the time it takes for the ICMP echo responses to verify and trace the route used to reach a remote location, respectively.

Routing protocols

Routers maintain the most efficient route to a remote destination at any given moment. In addition to communicating with each other about the most efficient pathways, routers also must manage statistics (called *metrics*) about the number of hops (how many routers and bridges and hubs and whatever else a packet must travel through), and about other route information. Only by using all this information can routers calculate the best path for a packet to take.

Of course, there are protocols specifically designed to do this essential work: the Routing Information Protocol (RIP) and the Open Shortest Path First (OSPF) protocol.

Routing Information Protocol (RIP)

The Routing Information Protocol (RIP) counts the number of routers and network devices (called *hops*) a packet must pass through to reach its destination. The number of hops is used to calculate the best and most efficient path available to a packet.

The lower the number of hops a packet makes, the faster and more efficient the path.

Open Shortest Path First (OSPF)

The Open Shortest Path First (OSPF) protocol uses other factors in addition to the number of hops to determine the best path, including the speed of the network between hops and the amount of network traffic on each segment.

**Book IV
Chapter 5**

TCP/IP and Network Addressing

Hypertext Transfer Protocol (HTTP)

No doubt you're keenly aware of Hypertext Transfer Protocol (HTTP), but have you considered that it's one of the TCP/IP protocols? HTTP, the underlying protocol of Web browsers, is hopelessly devoted to transferring documents encoded in the Hypertext Markup Language (HTML) or the Extensible Markup Language (XML) over the Internet. That's all it does.

Names and Addresses

Networked computers, like people, must have a unique identity by which other computers can refer to them. "Hey, you," just doesn't work any better on a network than it does in a group of people. Depending on the protocol or process communicating with a computer, the ID may be a number, a "friendly" name, or an IP address. Just like we have government-assigned Social Security numbers, our given names, phone numbers, and home addresses, a computer has a MAC address, an IP address, and perhaps a share name.

MAC addresses

The Media Access Control sublayer of the Data Link layer uses MAC (Media Access Control) addresses to physically address network devices. (By the way, virtually all network devices, such as network interface cards [NICs], routers, bridges, brouters, and switches, are assigned a MAC address.) MAC addresses, also called Ethernet addresses, are assigned by manufacturers and burned into the electronics.

A MAC address is a 6-byte (48-bit) hexadecimal number in the form of six two-digit numbers separated by colons or dashes, for example 00-11-22-33-44-55. Each digit of the MAC address can be in the range of the hexadecimal values 0-F.

The first 24 bits (3 bytes) of the MAC address contain a manufacturer's code. The last 3 bytes (24 bits) contain a unique serialized device ID number. The combination of the two IDs is intended to create a universally unique ID for every individual piece of networking equipment, such as NICs, router interfaces, and other network devices. The IEEE (Institute for Electrical and Electronic Engineers) globally assigns and administers MAC manufacturer codes.

On a Windows 2000 system, you can use the ipconfig utility to display most of the information displayed by the WINIPCFG command.

UNC names

On the Network+ exam, you're likely to encounter a list of sample names and be asked to pick the one that conforms to UNC (NetBIOS) syntax. NetBIOS is the native networking protocol used on a Windows network that provides services that include the management and cross-referencing of logical names (network names). (Read on to find out more about NetBIOS naming conventions.)

You should understand that UNC names (the term used on the exam) are really UNC *paths* that represent the path to a particular network resource.

The Universal Naming Convention (UNC) is not pronounced like a short-form of uncle, but rather by its initials (U-N-C). UNC is the generally accepted network naming syntax used to reference network resources, such as printers, disk arrays, servers, workstations, and so on. UNC names take the form of

```
\\SERVER_NAME\SHARE_NAME or PATH
```

where the computer name and the share name are names that have been assigned by the network administrator or the users who own a shared resource. For example, in the Windows UNC name

```
\\MAGOO\OPTICIANS
```

Magoo is the network, or "friendly," name for the computer, the name used by the network to refer to that device, and Opticians is a shared folder name on that computer. Users on other computers can request access to both the computer and its resources by using the UNC name format.

For the exam, be sure you know which way the slashes go in UNC names. Windows uses backward slashes and UNIX uses forward slashes, and no matter which operating system you use, two slashes appear at the beginning of a name.

NetBIOS and NDS names

Because it is so difficult for users to remember the MAC and IP addresses of nodes on a LAN, Windows and NetWare systems support user-friendly names that can be used to reference the network's resources, such as printers, other computers, and the like.

A UNC name is mapped to the device first and then to the shared resource, if it isn't the device itself. Only the first part of the UNC corresponds to the

MAC or IP address. In fact, UNC names (share names), which reference the shared server or computer, can be combined with IP addresses to reach a resource or folder. For example, on a Windows network, \\10.10.1.1\folder will get you to the "folder" folder on the computer with the IP address of 10.10.1.1.

NetBIOS names: For Windows networks

Every computer on a Microsoft network has a NetBIOS name assigned to it. The computer name is also a NetBIOS name. NetBIOS is the standard network basic input/output system used by Windows systems.

NetBIOS is actually an application programming interface (API). An API is something like a library or set of commands that can be used by application software to request services from the operating system. The commands in an API can be used to manage names, conduct sessions, and send datagrams between nodes on a LAN. Don't confuse an API with a protocol, which is one or more programs that provide support for a specific action or set of actions.

NetBIOS names follow the UNC format that we describe in the previous section. The format that Microsoft Windows uses is

```
\\SERVER\FOLDER
```

NDS names: For NetWare networks

Like NetBIOS, every resource you want to reference on a NetWare network must have a specific name; NetWare's is aptly called a NetWare Directory Services (NDS) name. NDS supports a database that contains the names of the users, devices, and computers on the network.

Under NDS, a resource name is something like this:

```
\\SERVER\VOLUME\DIRECTORY\SUB-DIRECTORY
```

Comparing names and addresses

The examples in Table 5-1 summarize and contrast UNC names (made up of share names), MAC addresses (device physical addresses), and IP (Internet Protocol) addresses.

Table 5-1	Examples of UNC Names and MAC and IP Addresses		
Actual Name	*UNC Name*	*MAC Address*	*IP Address*
Primary network server	\\SERVER1	00.00.0C.33.56.01	10.0.100.1
Susan's Accounting folder on Server1	\\SERVER1\ ACCTG_SUSAN	00.00.1D.78.21.09	10.0.100.22
The Documents folder on Susan's computer	\\SERVER1\ ACCTG_SUSAN\ DOCUMENTS	00.00.1D.78.21.09	10.0.100.22

Table 5-1 illustrates the following three principles of network naming and addressing:

✦ The UNC format is used to designate servers and network shared resources.

✦ No relationship exists between MAC and IP addresses.

✦ MAC and IP addresses are assigned to the device, and accessing resources (folders and files) on a device does not change these values.

DNS and WINS: What's in a Name?

Every device on a TCP/IP network has two pieces of identification: an IP address and a Fully Qualified Domain Name (FQDN), which consists of a host name and a domain name. The network administrator assigns a *host name* to uniquely identify the device, usually a computer, on the network.

Network Solutions (www.networksolutions.com), the company that assigns domain names on the Internet, assigns a *domain name* to a network (server). For example, for the FQDN www.dummies.com, the network administrator assigned the clever and unique name *www* to the network host, and the officially sanctioned, blessed, ordained, and registered domain name *dummies.com* to the network server's assigned gateway IP address. Together, www.dummies.com, the host name, and the domain name create the fully qualified domain name for this Internet site.

Domain Name System (DNS)

If the host to which you want to connect is on a remote network, you must know the host's IP address in order to properly route your data over the Internet. This is where name resolution and the Domain Name System (DNS) enter the picture. DNS can search through its database to find the FQDN you want to reach and supply its IP address to your system.

Domain names are registered in the DNS database that is distributed around the Internet and used to look up a domain name and convert it into its IP address. The DNS database literally contains all the domain names and their IP addresses for the entire Internet, a collection of information that requires frequent updating. However, the DNS database is considered a static database because domain name registrars, such as Network Solutions, along with Internet service providers, manually enter its updates periodically.

You can use the DNS database to look up names on any TCP/IP network, including a LAN using TCP/IP, but DNS comes into play mostly for finding names on a WAN.

The effect of name resolution is as follows: If you enter the command

`telnet www.dummies.com (before name resolution)`

the name changes to

`telnet 206.175.162.18 (after name resolution)`.

In this example, the FQDN www.dummies.com is converted into its IP address. (Just for the record, you don't need to know the Dummies IP address for the Network+ exam.)

If a URL can't be resolved, there's probably a human to blame. Maybe the client typed the domain name into the Web browser incompletely or misspelled it.

Some systems use local files and services in place of the DNS database. These local files provide an abridged and more relevant database of names-to-IP-address and names-to-MAC-address conversions. Generically, these files are called *hosts files* because they contain a list of network hosts and their corresponding addresses. The most commonly used local name resolution service is WINS (Windows Internet Name Service).

Windows Internet Name Service (WINS)

The Windows Internet Name Service (WINS) is a dynamic service used to resolve NetBIOS computer names to their IP addresses on Windows-based networks. Whenever a Windows network client computer boots up, it registers its name, IP address, the account name of its user, and whatever network services it's using with the WINS server. Note the word *Windows* in the name of this service. It tells you that this is a Microsoft product, and that other network operating systems (UNIX, NetWare, and so on) don't support its use.

Windows 2000 and XP support both WINS and DNS. A WINS server is any Windows server on a TCP/IP network on which WINS has been installed. It processes requests from client computers to register or look up IP addresses.

Another hosts file associated with NetBIOS name lookup is the LMHOSTS file. This static file, which requires manual maintenance, was essentially replaced by the WINS service, but many administrators use LMHOSTS as a backup name resolution technique. The LM in its name stands for LAN Manager, which may give you some insight into its age. The LMHOSTS file is also used to map NetBIOS names to their IP addresses.

The IP Gateway

A *gateway* is a mechanism used to connect two dissimilar networks that operate independently of one another, such as a LAN and the Internet WAN. The gateway is also the demarcation point of routing over the Internet.

To the clients on a LAN, the *default gateway* is the IP address of the router or other device used to connect to the Internet or WAN. The gateway provides the real connection to the Internet at the Physical layer and is the addressable device to which the network's IP address is actually assigned and mapped.

These two addressing concepts may help you understand the workings of an IP gateway:

- ✦ **Static IP address:** This IP address is permanently assigned to a computer, server, or device. Usually network servers supporting TCP/IP are assigned a static IP address, making them a stationary target for the rest of the Internet.

- ✦ **Dynamic IP address:** On many networks, IP addresses are dynamically assigned to workstations when they connect to the network using the Dynamic Host Configuration Protocol (DHCP).

Setting Sail for TCP/IP Ports and Protocols

The Internet Assigned Numbers Authority (IANA) registers service ports for use by the various TCP/IP protocols. Ports are used for interprocess communications between two connection points. Port numbers and key-words are used to designate the ends of the logical connections created when protocols, such as TCP (remember that TCP is a connection-oriented protocol), connect over the Internet for long-term interaction. Ports are especially handy for providing services to unknown callers, such as during an anonymous FTP session.

Ports are numbered and assigned keywords for easy reference. Some of the more common TCP/IP ports are port 80 (HTTP), port 21 (FTP), and port 25 (SMTP). The port number assigned to a service by IANA is usually the server-side contact port, also called the *well-known* port.

IANA divides port numbers into three groups:

✦ **Well-known ports:** These are the most commonly used TCP/IP ports and are in the range of 0 through 1023. Only system processes or privileged programs use these ports. Well-known ports are TCP ports, but they're usually registered to User Datagram Protocol (UDP) services as well.

✦ **Registered ports:** The ports in the range of 1024 through 49151. On most systems, user programs use registered ports to create and control logical connections between proprietary programs.

✦ **Dynamic (private) ports:** Ports in the range of 49152 through 65535. These ports are unregistered and can be used dynamically for private connections.

Have you ever noticed ports in use in the location bar (navigation bar) of your Web browser? A URL of something like the following:

```
http://www.dummies.com:80
```

may appear as you're navigating between some sites. The 80 indicates that this port is being used to track the connection to a remote site.

Prepare yourself: The Network+ exam is bound to ask you to identify the port assignment of several common TCP/IP protocols. If you know the ports that we've listed in Table 5-2, you'll definitely know more than you need for the test. Table 5-2 lists most of the commonly used port assignments.

Table 5-2	TCP/IP Well-Known Port Assignments
Port Number	*Assignment*
21	FTP (File Transfer Protocol)
23	Telnet
25	SMTP (Simple Mail Transfer Protocol)
53	DNS (Domain Name System)
69	TFTP (Trivial FTP)
80	HTTP (Hypertext Transfer Protocol)
110	POP3 (Post Office Protocol)
119	NNTP (Network News Transfer Protocol)
123	NTP (Network Time Protocol)
137	NetBIOS name service
161	SNMP (Simple Network Management Protocol)
520	RIP (Routing Information Protocol)

The port number identifies the service to which an incoming or outgoing packet should be passed. Memorize the ports listed in Table 5-2 and be ready to identify them by number on the exam.

Assigning IP Addresses Dynamically

Every client workstation on a TCP/IP network must be assigned an IP address so that it can send and receive Internet packets during an Internet session. IP addresses can be assigned to a client computer in one of two ways: manually, by the network administrator, or automatically, by a server. A manually assigned IP address is also called a *static* address. A static IP address is permanently assigned to a workstation or other network node and, for the most part, never changes, at least not until the network administrator decides to change it manually. On the other hand, a dynamic IP address is one that is automatically assigned and could very well change each time a node connects to the network.

There isn't much to say about static IP addresses, so in this section, we focus on dynamic addresses.

For the Network+ exam, you need to thoroughly understand the terminology and processes of DHCP (Dynamic Host Configuration Protocol). Know why to use DHCP, how it works, and which TCP/IP tools can be used to display and manage dynamic addresses.

To DHCP or not to DHCP

If you're the administrator of a fairly small network that has an ample number of IP addresses for its workstations and devices, assigning each node its own static IP address is probably not a problem. However, if you must configure a network with 50, 100, 200, or more workstations, or if the network has outgrown its IP address allocation and there just aren't enough IP addresses available to permanently assign the IP addresses to each node, consider using the Dynamic Host Configuration Protocol (DHCP).

The use of DHCP is fairly common on just about any network, large or small. DHCP provides you, the network administrator, with a number of benefits, including

✦ **Automatic configuration:** At minimum, a DHCP server provides a client with its IP address, subnet mask, and normally the default gateway option when the client identifies itself during logon.

✦ **Configuration control:** DHCP assignments are defined by a DHCP scope, which is an administrative tool that enables you to set the range, value, and exceptions for client configurations. The DHCP scope usually defines a range of available IP addresses, the subnet mask, and gives the option to configure the default gateway (router) for a range of addresses, and any IP addresses that have been set aside or reserved for other devices. Other values that can be configured into a scope for its IP addresses are

  • Default gateway

  • DNS server

  • WINS server

  • Lease time

  • Renewal time

✦ **Length of use:** DHCP IP address assignments are called *leases*. When a client receives assignment of an IP address, the length of time that the client can use that particular address is also set. A three-day time period is a common default lease period. The length of the lease is a configurable value controlled by the network administrator.

How DHCP works

Don't sweat the details, but do review the sequence of events that the DHCP uses to control IP address assignments on its clients. The DHCP process is divided into four phases: initializing, selecting, requesting, and binding. The following describes the actions of each phase:

✦ **Discovery (Initializing):** The DHCP client boots up with a null IP address and broadcasts a BOOTP discovery message that contains the client's MAC address and logical computer name to the DHCP server. The source address of the discovery message is 0.0.0.0 and its destination is 255.255.255.255, which are reserved IP addresses. (See "Special network addresses" later in this chapter.)

✦ **Selecting (Offer):** The DHCP server receives the discovery message and, if it has a valid configuration available for the client, responds with an offer message that contains the following information:

  • The client's MAC address (for delivery purposes).

  • The offered IP address.

  • The subnet mask.

  • The default gateway's IP address.

  • The address of the DHCP server.

  • The time duration of the DHCP lease; 72 hours is the typical default lease duration.

  If the server doesn't have an IP address available to the client, the client nags the server four times in the following five minutes. If it still doesn't have one, it waits five minutes, and then repeats the discovery cycle.

✦ **Requesting:** To accept the IP address offered to it, the client responds with a request message. Some networks can have multiple DHCP servers, all of which may have made offers to the client. The request message is a broadcast message so that all other DHCP servers know to withdraw their offers.

✦ **Binding:** This phase is also called the *bound* phase. The DHCP server that had its offer accepted politely sends a request message that includes an acknowledgment of the client's acceptance. When the client receives this acknowledgment, it proceeds with its initialization of TCP/IP and becomes a bound DHCP client.

Renewing your lease

After the DHCP lease expires, the client is in effect evicted and loses its IP address. To prevent the client from becoming homeless, a truly sad state of affairs, the client uses a renewal process. The renewal process involves the client sending the same type of request message it used to get its lease in the first place to the DHCP server that issued the original lease. The renewal request message is first sent out when the lease is 50 percent expired. If the server can renew the lease, it does. If the lease isn't renewed at the 50 percent point, however, the request message is sent out again at the 87.5 percent point. If the lease isn't renewed, the client reverts to the initializing phase and begins requesting an IP address to be assigned. The primary reason a lease wouldn't be renewed is there are more workstations than IP addresses available, which means workstations are waiting to grab a lease the moment it expires.

Dissecting the IP Class System

When the Network+ exam talks about IP addressing, it's referring to the current dominant version: Internet Protocol (IP), version 4 (IPv4). We discuss the newest version of IP addressing (IPv6) later in the chapter (see "Moving Up to IPv6"). If you see IPv6 on the exam, it will be specifically identified as such. So, if you see IP, think IPv4; if you see IPv6, shift gears.

IP addressing refresher

IP addresses are divided into five classes, each of which is designated with the alphabetic letters A through E. As you read about the different IP address classes, bear in mind that the inventors of this class system expected the Internet to remain a fairly small and exclusive club.

Although organizations such as Network Solutions (www.networksolutions.net) register domain names and assign and track network IDs for use on the Internet, another agency, ARIN (American Registry for Internet Numbers — www.arin.net) allocates IP addresses according to organizational need and size.

Here are some IP address facts to remember:

✦ IP addresses are made up of four binary numbers that are represented as four decimal numbers connected by periods (dots).

✦ IP addresses are 32 bits in length, with each of the four octets using eight bits.

✦ Each 8-bit number is called an octet.

✦ The value for each octet is based on the class of the address and the corresponding subnet mask used. See "Who Was That Subnet Masked Man?" later in the chapter.

✦ IP addresses are organized into five classes (labeled A through E) based on the size of the network. The biggest networks are Class A, and the classes get smaller as you progress through the alphabet. An example of a Class C IP address is 206.175.162.18, which is the address associated with the URL (Uniform Resource Locator) www.dummies.com, either of which will connect you to an excellent site for buying outstanding certification study guides. We're so shameless!

Memorize the ranges of the Class A, B, and C IP addresses. On the exam, you may be asked to pick a Class A or B address from a list. Watch out for trick answer choices that are in the overall range of a Class but are reserved for special purposes. (See "Special network addresses" later in the chapter.)

Class A IP addresses

Class A IP addresses are awarded to large networks. These addresses range from 1.*hhh.hhh.hhh* to 127.*hhh.hhh.hhh*, where all of the hhh's are used to identify a host computer by its unique address. Fifty percent of all IP addresses are Class A addresses.

Class A addresses use 8 bits to identify as many as 126 Class A networks. Each network can address as many as 16 million network nodes. There are 128 network (0 to 127) values available, but the network addresses with all 0s or 1s and network address 127 are reserved as special network addresses (see "Special network addresses" later in this chapter).

Class B IP addresses

Class B IP addresses are assigned to medium-sized networks. Twenty-five percent of all available IP addresses are in this class. A Class B address uses 16 bits to identify the network, which limits it to 16,382 networks using the range of 128.0.*hhh.hhh* (*hhh* represents the host address) to 191.255.*hhh.hhh*. A Class B network can address up to 65,534 IP addresses.

Class C IP addresses

Class C networks are relatively small networks and account for 12.5 percent of all available IP addresses. Class C addresses use 24 bits to identify the network, enabling identification of more than 2 million networks in the range of 192.0.0.*hhh* to 223.255.255.*hhh*. Eight bits are used to identify the host computer, but host addresses with all 0s or 1s are special host addresses (see "Special network addresses" later in this chapter). Each Class C network can address a maximum of 254 IP addresses.

Classes D and E addresses

Class D is reserved especially for IP multicasting, or sending multibroadcasts (communication across a network from one source to several). Class D addresses are in the range of 224.*hhh.hhh.hhh.hhh* to 239.*hhh.hhh.hhh*. Address 224.0.0.0 is reserved and cannot be used, and address 224.0.0.1 is reserved for addressing all hosts participating in an IP multicast.

Class E addresses are reserved for future use. A little over 3 percent of all IP addresses are in the range from 240.0.0.0 to 247.255.255.255. However, essentially all addresses above 240.0.0.0 may as well be Class E addresses. In fact,

**Book IV
Chapter 5**

TCP/IP and Network Addressing

in different references, you may see a variety of address blocks for Class E addresses, but just remember the 240.0.0.0 as the starting point.

Yes, we know that the percentages don't add up to 100 percent. Don't worry about why. In fact, don't worry about these percentages at all. We include them to give you a sense of scale. But, if you're still wondering, the remaining addresses are special IP addresses or unassigned addresses.

Table 5-3 summarizes the characteristics of the IP address classes. Memorize this information, especially the address range for each IP address class.

Table 5-3				Characteristics of the IP Address Classes	
Class	Bits in Network ID	Number of Networks	Bits in Host ID	Number of Hosts/Network	Address Range
A	8	126	24	16,777,214	1.0.0.0–126.255.255.255
B	16	16,382	16	65,534	128.0.0.0–191.255.255.255
C	24	2,097,150	8	254	192.0.0.0–223.255.255.255

Don't sweat Class D and E characteristics; they aren't on the exam. But, you need to know the address ranges of Classes A, B, and C, so study them until you're able to identify the IP address class of any IP address.

Special network addresses

Network addresses that are all binary 0s, all binary 1s, and network addresses beginning with 127 are set aside as special-purpose addresses. These addresses are used by networks as shortcut addresses to specific locations, such as the current host, the local network, to broadcast to a LAN or WAN, or to perform testing. Table 5-4 offers the list of special network addresses that you should know.

Table 5-4		Special Network Addresses	
Network Part	Host Part	Example	Description
0s	0s	0.0.0.0	This host
0s	Host address	0.0.0.34	Host on this network
1s	1s	255.255.255.255	Broadcast to local network
Network address	1s	197.21.12.255	Broadcast to network
127	1s or 0s	127.0.0.1	Loopback testing

The IP address 127.0.0.1 is reserved for loopback testing. The address 255.255.255.255 is used to send a broadcast message to the entire local network.

Public versus private addresses

Except for the addresses that we list in Table 5-5, all IP addresses are considered public addresses — addresses used to communicate over the Internet. Because some local networks want to use TCP/IP protocols as well, even if the networks don't connect to the Internet, blocks of IP addresses within the Class A and B ranges are reserved for this purpose. Another common reason is simply that private IP addresses are more readily available than public addresses. Even publicly accessible networks may use private IP addresses because under the IPv4 structure, public addresses are harder to come by. And yet another reason for using private IP addresses is security — it's much harder to hack into a network that is using private IP addresses.

Table 5-5	Private IP Address Ranges
IP Address Class	*Private Address Range*
A	10.0.0.0–10.255.255.255
B	172.16.0.0–172.31.255.255
C	192.168.0.0–192.168.255.255

Private addresses are used on a LAN and are ignored if sent out on the Internet. If a network using private IP addresses wants to access the Internet, the gateway router must perform the Network Address Translation (NAT) service. NAT creates a pointer to the internal address that is used to identify the requesting node when its download is received and sends out the address of the gateway to the Internet. NAT serves two purposes: protecting the internal networks and nodes and extending the pool of IP addresses that can be used to identify the internal network nodes.

Moving Up to IPv6

Several versions of the Internet Protocol (IP) have been used since the Internet was first introduced as the Arpanet. The version most predominantly used today is version 4 (commonly called *IPv4*), which has been in use for over 20 years. In 1997, The Internet Engineer Task Force (IETF), having the foresight to realize that the world would soon run out of IPv4 addresses, began the development of a new IP addressing specification called IP*ng* (or IP next generation). After a great deal of discussion and the abandonment of IPv5, this new generation of IP addressing has been designated as *IPv6* or IP version 6. IPv6 resolves the limited number of IPv4 addresses available with virtually an unlimited number of available addresses and includes many of the features optional in IPv4.

So, what do you need to know about IPv4 and IPv6 when you sit down to take the Network+ exam? Good question. You don't have to be fluent in the ins and outs of IPv6, but you should be able to identify the significant differences between versions. If you need to refresh your memory on IPv4 addressing for this discussion, take a look at the section "IP addressing refresher" earlier in the chapter. Here's the short version:

✦ **More is better:** IPv6 addresses have 128 bits in 16 octets, compared to the 32 bits and 4 octets of an IPv4 address. An IPv6 address includes a variety of addressing elements, such as the address type, which can be IPv4, OSI NSAP (network service access point), Novell IPX, geographic-based, or multicast. The addresses also include values reserved for protocols yet to come.

An example of an IPv6 address is

    4000:0000:0000:0000:FEDC:BA09:8765:4321

In comparison, an IPv4 address is

    192.150.101.206

✦ **The proof is in the colon:** In addition to the extra digit in each addressing element, IPv6 uses a colon (:) to separate each of its elements. Make sure you wear your glasses, if you use them, so that you can clearly see whether an IP address has dots or colons. You really have to watch those CompTIA rascals.

✦ **Way more is *way* better:** IPv6 addressing provides what amounts to an unlimited supply of IP addresses with over 10^{38} possible addresses available. IPv4, once thought to offer more addresses than would ever be needed, provides only 10^9 addresses. We would have given you the exact number of addresses for IPv6, but our calculator was unable to display it.

Who Was That Subnet Masked Man?

IP addresses contain both a network ID and a host ID that facilitate the routing of a message across the internetwork. The ability for a router to pull out only the network ID from an IP address enables it to identify the network and route messages appropriately.

To extract the network ID from an IP address, a filter mechanism is applied that masks out the host ID and exposes only the network number in the destination address. The filtering mechanism used is a *subnet mask,* which is also called a *network mask.*

The subnet mask enables a server, router, or switch to determine whether an IP address exists on the local network or beyond on a remote network.

After the network ID is extracted, it is compared to the local network ID. If the two match, the host ID must be on the local network. Otherwise, the message requires routing outside of the local network.

Default subnet masks

Table 5-6 lists the commonly used subnet masks for each IP address class. Take the time to memorize these.

Table 5-6	IP Class Default Subnet Masks
IP Address Class	*Subnet Mask*
Class A	255.0.0.0
Class B	255.255.0.0
Class C	255.255.255.0

Here's an example of how a subnet mask is applied:

1. On the Dummies Class C network, an IP address is 206.175.162.18, and its binary equivalent address is 11001110 10101111 10100010 00010010.

2. The common Class C subnet mask is 255.255.255.0, and its binary equivalent is 11111111 11111111 11111111 00000000.

3. These two binary numbers (the IP address and the subnet mask) are combined by using Boolean algebra, yielding the network ID of the destination:

Address: 206.175.162.18 11001110 10101111 10100010 00010010

Subnet mask: 255.255.255.0 11111111 11111111 11111111 00000000

Network ID: 206.175.162.0 11001110 10101111 10100010 00000000

4. The resulting ID is the IP address of the network, which means the message is for a node on the local network.

If you think that there has to be a simpler way to list these addresses, you're pretty bright because there is! All the binary 1s in a subnet mask extract the network ID, and the 0s yield the node ID. Subnet masks apply only to Class A, B, or C IP addresses.

Subnetting a network

Unfortunately, the founding mothers and fathers of the Internet and the IPv4 protocol had a much smaller Internet in mind than the one that has emerged. Companies that have only one network address assigned now may have need for multiple networks, which creates an addressing problem. A very good solution to this problem is *subnetting*.

Subnetting a network can solve or control several network problems by

+ Reducing network congestion
+ Providing better network throughput
+ Improving WAN performance
+ Simplifying LAN management

Subnetting IP addresses typically follows on the heels of network segmentation, and many of the benefits listed for subnetting hold true for segmenting the network as well. Breaking the network into smaller pieces helps deliver the promise of "less is more." However, segmenting a network usually introduces the problem of subnet addressing, which is the real challenge in developing and applying a subnet mask.

A classless approach to subnets

The standard or default application of subnet masks is a classful approach to subnetting. Another approach is the Classless Internet Domain Routing, or CIDR, which is pronounced as "cedar" or "cider," depending on whom you ask.

CIDR uses a numeric designator to indicate the number of bits that have been used to identify the network ID in an IP address. For example, if a network address uses 16 bits to identify the network ID, the address is indicated as 161.172.10.51/16. The "/16" indicates that 16 bits are used for the network ID. Another example is 206.172.10.30/28, which means that 28 bits are used for the network ID.

Here's an example of how an IP address (and its subnet mask) are represented in both classful (standard IP address designation) and classless representations:

```
Classful address: 161.172.10.1
Classful subnet mask: 255.255.0.0
Classless address: 161.172.10.1/16
```

The "/16" in the classless address represents that 16 bits are used to determine the network ID in the address, which represents the same thing as the "255.255." in the classful address subnet mask.

Using an Internet Proxy Server

A *proxy server* placed on a local network often acts in place of the Web server for the network's clients, but the real benefit of a proxy server is what it adds to network security. Proxy servers protect the outside world from internal network users — remember this, even though it may seem backward. A proxy server acts as a logical barrier between your local network users and the rest of the Internet.

I'm sorry, but you're not on the list

Proxy servers, and firewalls for that matter, maintain access control lists. These lists, which you manually create and maintain, include the URLs that network clients are blocked from visiting. The access control list on a proxy server may also contain IP addresses and ports from which requests are not accepted.

A proxy server intercepts all IP and Web-based requests for data outside the local network from the local network's clients. If a request is for an allowed Web page that was previously visited, the page is provided from the proxy server's storage cache. However, if the requested Web page isn't in the proxy server's cache and isn't on the access control list, the request is processed normally, and the Web page is passed on to the requesting client. If the requested page or site is on the access control list, the requesting user receives a message indicating that the site isn't authorized or accessible. Unauthorized incoming requests receive the same responses.

Putting up the proxy

You have three reasons to implement a proxy server:

+ A dial-up connection gives you Internet access. Proxy servers can handle multiple phone lines, providing an avenue to a single Internet access point.

+ You have only one connection point to the wide, wild world of the Internet (as opposed to separate connection points). This limits your exposure to unauthorized entry to your network and enables you to protect your network from the sites of evildoers.

+ You can enjoy the benefits of shared caching. Frequently visited sites may be in the cache, perhaps eliminating connection to the Internet service altogether. Proxy servers often cache FTP and HTTP pages.

Configuring a Workstation for TCP/IP

The first rule of setting up a workstation is plain and simple: Have an operating system that is compatible with the network operating system (NOS). With either Windows NT or NetWare, you usually have no problem with any of the more-common client operating systems, such as DOS or any of the Windows panes. But, these aren't the only client systems, so before using a nonmainstream operating system on a network, check it out.

You can expect to see questions on the Network+ exam regarding the process and settings used to configure a network client for the TCP/IP protocol. Be familiar with the steps used to configure the following settings on a Windows client:

✦ Choosing the TCP/IP redirector

✦ Static or dynamic (DHCP) IP address

✦ DNS and/or WINS server

✦ Default gateway address

✦ Host and domain name

Lab 5-1 details the steps that you take to configure a Windows workstation for these settings.

Lab 5-1   Installing the TCP/IP Client on a Windows *9x* Workstation

1. **Choose Start➪Settings➪Control Panel.**

2. **Double-click the Networks icon to open the Network Properties window.**

   If TCP/IP isn't installed, you're likely to see only the Dial-Up Adapter listed.

3. **Click the Add button to open the Select Network Component Type window; choose Protocol and click Add.**

   The Select Network Protocol window appears.

4. **Select Microsoft from the list of supported protocol families and then choose TCP/IP from the list that appears on the right side of the window.**

   The Network Properties window reappears, with Microsoft Family Logon and TCP/IP added to the list of network components that are now installed.

5. **Select TCP/IP in the protocols list and then click the Properties button.**

   The TCP/IP Properties window appears. Use the tabs across the top of the window to access each of the properties types you want to configure.

6. **Click the IP Address tab.**

   In most situations, you choose Obtain an IP Address Automatically. In those situations where a static IP address is assigned, click the indicator for an assigned (static) IP address and enter it in the box provided.

7. **Click the DNS Configuration tab.**

   If you want to use DNS lookup on the network, click the adjacent radio button to indicate that choice, and then enter the host ID, the domain ID, and IP address of the DNS server. You can enter more than one DNS server, and you can set an order of access.

8. **Click the Gateway tab and type the IP address of the gateways on the network.**

   You can set the access order for gateways. (The first one listed is the default gateway.)

9. **Click the WINS Configuration tab.**

   The WINS Configuration tab is strictly a Microsoft thing, used to indicate whether or not the network supports WINS services. If so, you must enter a WINS service ID.

**Book IV
Chapter 5**

TCP/IP and Network Addressing

Prep Test

1 The TCP/IP utility used to display the entire TCP/IP configuration of a Windows NT/2000 computer is

  A ○ PING.

  B ○ ROUTE.

  C ○ NETSTAT.

  D ○ IPCONFIG.

2 Which of the following is a valid MAC address?

  A ○ 000-123-456

  B ○ 00.00.0D.11.22.33

  C ○ HK.11.22.33.44

  D ○ ABC123456

3 Which of the following is a valid UNC name on a Windows network?

  A ○ //COMPUTER_NAME/SERVER_NAME

  B ○ \\COMPUTER_NAME\SERVER_NAME

  C ○ //SERVER_NAME/COMPUTER_NAME

  D ○ \\SERVER_NAME\SHARE_NAME

4 The Windows-based TCP/IP service that processes requests from client workstations to dynamically register or look up IP addresses and NetBIOS names is

  A ○ DNS.

  B ○ WINS.

  C ○ LMHOSTS.

  D ○ MAC.

5 To clients on a LAN, the IP address assigned to a router used to access another physical or logical network is designated as the default

  A ○ DNS server.

  B ○ HCP server.

  C ○ IP gateway.

  D ○ WINS server.

6 IP addresses in the range of 128.0.0.0 to 191.255.0.0 are in which class of IP addresses?

A ○ Class A
B ○ Class B
C ○ Class C
D ○ Special IP addresses

7 Which of the following is the default subnet mask for a Class C address?

A ○ 255.0.0.0
B ○ 255.255.0.0
C ○ 255.255.255.0
D ○ 255.255.255.255

8 What is the purpose of a proxy server?

A ○ To protect the Internet from internal users
B ○ To protect internal users from the Internet
C ○ To block all incoming port 80 traffic
D ○ To prevent DoS attacks

9 What is the TCP/IP protocol used to automatically assign IP addresses and other configuration information to network clients?

A ○ SNMP
B ○ ICMP
C ○ DHCP
D ○ IPCONFIG

10 The well-known TCP/IP port assigned to FTP is

A ○ 21.
B ○ 25.
C ○ 80.
D ○ 110.

Answers

1 **D.** There are versions of the TCP/IP utility IPCONFIG for different clients. *Review "MAC addresses."*

2 **B.** A MAC or Ethernet or adapter address is made up of six two-digit numbers connected by periods or dashes. The first three two-digit numbers identify the manufacturer and the remaining numbers represent a serialized unique ID assigned by the manufacturer to each NIC. *Review "MAC addresses."*

3 **D.** Expect to see a question like this on the Network+ exam. Remember that UNC slashes are backward slashes and the server precedes the share name. *Review "UNC names."*

4 **B.** The trick to this question is the word *dynamic.* DNS and host name resolutions are static systems where WINS is a dynamic service. *Review "Windows Internet Name Service (WINS)."*

5 **C.** The gateway server houses the default IP gateway. Understand that the IP address is tied to the MAC address of the NIC that serves as the gateway. *Review "The IP Gateway."*

6 **B.** Class B IP addresses are in the range of 128.x.x.x to 191.x.x.x. *Review "Class B IP addresses."*

7 **C.** The default subnet mask of an address class has the value of 255 in each octet used to identify the network in that class. A Class C address uses 24 bits (3 octets) to identify the network ID. *Review "Class C IP addresses."*

8 **A.** You can expect to see at least one question like this on the exam. If you are really intent on getting a perfect score, know the reason and benefits of a proxy as well as those of a firewall. Otherwise, forget it and focus on the rest of what you expect on the test. *Review "Using an Internet Proxy Server."*

9 **C.** The Dynamic Host Control Protocol (DHCP) is used to automatically configure TCP/IP clients as they log on to a network. *Review "To DHCP or not to DHCP."*

10 **A.** TCP/IP ports are used to designate the ends of a logical connection and enable interprocess communications between the connecting processes. *Review "Setting Sail for TCP/IP Ports and Protocols."*

Chapter 6: Implementing a Network

Exam Objectives

- ✔ Differentiating the major network operating systems
- ✔ Identifying popular client operating systems
- ✔ Configuring a network client
- ✔ Dealing with viruses
- ✔ Defining fault tolerance systems
- ✔ Implementing storage area networks

The Network+ exam deals with network operating systems (NOSes) in a rather strange way. Apparently, Network+ concedes testing of specific Microsoft Windows operations to the MCSA/MCSE tests, preferring to target itself to generic functions and administrative tasks common to just about any network operating system. However, you should know something about the major NOSes: Windows NT/200/XP, Novell NetWare, UNIX, and Linux. On NOSes, Network+ is more of a networking essentials exam, with a few choice tidbits thrown in, that allows you to demonstrate just what you've learned in your 18 months of experience as a network technician.

The value of the NOS is that it controls and manages what network users can do from their workstations. Many a network technician has uttered the words, "If it weren't for the users, this wouldn't be a half-bad job!" Unfortunately, without users, there is no network, which translates to no network technician jobs. So users — and especially their workstations — are an integral part of virtually every network.

On the Network+ exam, much of what you're expected to know concerns the installation, configuration, and troubleshooting of network client workstations. Thus, another important area of the exam is how to configure a network client to operate on a network. This chapter doesn't include everything about configuring a network client, but it does give you a good overview. Those users are here to stay . . . and each time that you get your paycheck, you should say a silent "Thank you" to them.

What You Need to Know about NOSes

Here are the key points to remember about network operating systems:

+ In alphabetical order, the most commonly used NOSes are Apple Macintosh OS, Novell NetWare, Windows NT Server, Windows 2000 Server, Windows XP Server, and UNIX/Linux.

+ Windows 9*x*, Me, 2000 Pro, and XP Pro and Home versions are the client operating systems most commonly used on network clients. However, Windows XP isn't included on the current version of the Network+ exam.

+ NetWare uses NDS (NetWare Directory Services) and Windows NT uses the Explorer and NT File System (NTFS) and other file systems for directory and file services. You won't find much about Windows 2000 on the exam, either.

A network operating system (NOS) is a specialized piece of system software that runs on a network server to provide the following services:

+ Connects computers and peripheral devices into a local area network (LAN) and services their requests for resources

+ Manages who can access data and shared network resources (such as printers, CD-ROM, disk drives, software, and so on)

+ Monitors the performance and activities of the network

You specifically need to know about four NOSes for the Network+ test: Apple Macintosh, Novell NetWare, Microsoft Windows NT/2000, and UNIX (or its little brother, Linux). Additionally, you need to know the features that these two Windows versions have in common, but also expect some questions specifically about each version. The focus of the Network+ exam and NOSes is primarily in network services, administration functions, configuration, and protocols. As you prepare for the Network+ exam, concentrate only on their NOS functions.

Examining the NOS Core Services

Network operating systems provide a range of core services:

+ **File services** provide shared access to directories and files and fault-tolerance services on network storage devices.

+ **Print services** provide a common utility for local and remote printing on shared network printers and also manage print queues, devices, forms, and user access.

✦ **Directory services** provide users with *transparent access* to network resources and services, which means that users don't need to know where data or resources are physically located. Directory services create the illusion that all resources are local. Novell NetWare includes NetWare Directory Services (NDS), and Windows NT uses its Explorer.

✦ **Security services** provide network security and data protection for local and remote access, including user-level (password-based), share-level (permissions-based), and data encryption services.

✦ **Messaging services** provide message (e-mail) storage and forward services and support for mail-enabled applications. This service, along with security services, is fast becoming a primary NOS service as internetwork computing continues to evolve.

✦ **Routing services** provide multiprotocol routing services, including options for common LAN protocols (IP, IPX, and AppleTalk).

✦ **Network administration services** provide SNMP (Simple Network Management Protocol) and resource and directory structure management tools.

Scoping Out Novell NetWare

Novell NetWare is a popular LAN operating system that can support a variety of LAN technologies, including Ethernet and Token Ring networks. Like most operating system (OS) software, Novell has gone through some changes, enhancements, and fixes in its history. In fact, Novell has a variety of versions, including NetWare 3.*x,* NetWare 4.*x,* and recently NetWare 5.*x.* Most NetWare questions on the Network+ test aren't version-specific, but you'll need to know one or two facts about Netware 5 and the versions that preceded it. If you have a good general understanding of NetWare functions and services, you'll be prepared for any NetWare questions.

Here's a summary of the NetWare facts that you should know for the exam:

✦ The *IPX protocol,* also known as the IPX/SPX protocol, is the primary protocol of NetWare versions prior to NetWare version 5 (see "IPX/SPX messaging services" later in this chapter). NetWare 5 supports Transmission Control Protocol/Internet Protocol (TCP/IP) as its native protocol, but it can still support IPX/SPX, if needed.

✦ NetWare arranges files and dates in both physical and logical file systems (see the following section).

✦ NetWare uses the NetWare Directory Services (NDS) to manage resources on the network (see "NetWare Directory Services [NDS]" later in this chapter).

NetWare file systems

A *file system* is the way that an NOS handles and stores files. NetWare organizes its file systems and the physical disk media into logical groupings called volumes. A *volume,* which represents a fixed-size amount of hard drive space, is the highest level in the NetWare file system. A volume may be created on any hard drive that has a NetWare partition, and a NetWare server can support up to 64 volumes on a network.

The NetWare file system contains two kinds of volumes: physical and logical. A *physical volume* is made up of as many as 32 volume segments that can be stored across one or more hard drives. To further complicate this, a disk drive can hold as many as eight volume segments from one or more physical volumes. A *logical volume* is divided into directories and is used to locate files. The NetWare installation creates the first volume, which is named SYS.

NetWare uses a unique designation for its file system volumes. A colon follows the volume name in directory paths; for example, the path to the PUBLIC directory on the SYS volume is SYS:PUBLIC. This format is much like the MS-DOS device designator (such as A:).

NetWare file and directory attributes

You can protect data on two levels: what can be done to files and directories (the subject of this section) and who has access to them. (We cover this hot topic in the upcoming "NetWare security services" section.) File and directory attributes indicate what actions can be performed on the file to which they're attached.

Table 6-1 compares a few of the file attributes used in NetWare and Windows NT/2000. As shown in the table, minor differences exist between NetWare rights and Windows file permissions. For the Network+ exam, you should know the file attributes that we list in Table 6-1.

Table 6-1		File Properties Used in NetWare and Windows NT	
NetWare Attribute	*Windows NT Permission*	*Meaning*	*Purpose*
A	A	Archive	Directory or file is new or has been changed and needs to be backed up.
H	H	Hidden	A file that can't be viewed with directory list commands.
RO	R	Read-only	Restricts access to read-only and prevents changes to the file.

NetWare Attribute	Windows NT Permission	Meaning	Purpose
RW	-*	Read-write	Directory or file can be viewed, changed, or deleted. No direct Windows NT equivalent (absence of read-only attribute enables same action).
SH	-*	Shareable	More than one user can access the file at a time; handled in Windows NT by creating a network share.
SY	S	System	Operating system files.

*The entries marked with a dash (-) in Table 6-1 indicate NetWare rights that aren't supported by or are implemented differently in Windows NT/2000.

NetWare print services

Network print services are a part of the transparent world created for network users. Figure 6-1 is a simplistic illustration of the difference between what the user believes and network reality.

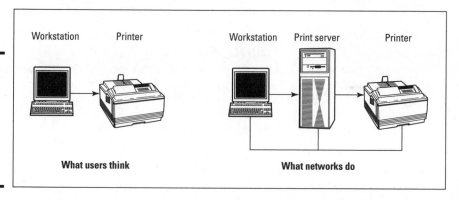

Figure 6-1: The perception of the user and the reality of networked printers.

NetWare controls printing through a server dedicated to print jobs, called a *printer queue* or *print server*. The queue accepts and holds requests for print services until the printer in question becomes available. A network may have one or more print servers. Print servers hang on to incoming print jobs until the printer is free.

The PCONSOLE utility manages NetWare printer queues. PCONSOLE is a command line utility that allows you to monitor and administer the network printer queues.

NetWare Directory Services (NDS)

In general, an NOS directory service is used to identify the resources on a network, such as e-mail addresses, computers, and printers, and make them accessible to users and server- and client-based applications. Ideally, the directory service shields the user from the network's physical topology and protocols, creating a transparent working environment. The Windows 9x Explorer is an example of a simple directory service.

NetWare Directory Services (NDS) delivers most NetWare core services. NDS serves as an agent for the user in requesting and accessing network resources. When the user logs on, NDS captures information about the user to facilitate any requests that the user makes — then or later — for system resources. Users can go blissfully about the business of what they want to do rather than concern themselves with how their wishes are carried out.

From a network administrator's point of view, NDS helps manage users, applications, and the network resources that users can access. Through NDS, the administrator creates and controls a database of users and resources, including resources in remote locations. Although NDS is an integrated part of a NetWare installation, it can be installed on a Windows NT network and on several flavors of UNIX as well.

NetWare security services

Any NOS worthy of that designation must provide some means for keeping out the mean-and-nasties while enabling the good-and-deserving to access the resources that they require. NetWare is no different: It uses a two-level model of SUPERVISOR and non-SUPERVISOR (also known as users, peons, pests, nags, and so on) accounts.

The all-knowing, all-powerful SUPERVISOR

Supervisor-level accounts (SUPERVISOR and ADMIN) are the omnipotent, anointed rulers of the NetWare network. Supervisor accounts have the power to add and remove users from the network and to set which network resources each user can and cannot access. Supervisor accounts also have the ability to run administrative software utilities for a wide range of security, fault-tolerance, and user-management functions.

Groups and users

On a NetWare system, a login account represents each user, and every account can have its own set of resource access rights. You turn to group accounts to collectively administer users who rely on the same software and access the same directories and files. On all NetWare systems, all users automatically belong to the PUBLIC group. However, to restrict access to accounting files, you could create a group named BEANCNTR that includes only the accounting office users. All file rights and permissions assigned to BEANCNTR are then automatically extended to the users in this group.

You can protect data not only by assigning file attributes (see "NetWare file and directory attributes" earlier in this chapter), but also by giving specific groups or individual users access to certain volumes, directories, and files. Assigning rights to group or user accounts is the mechanism by which you can keep all other users out of the accounting files — except those in the BEANCNTR group.

User security rights work with file attributes to determine who has access to a file and what they can do with it. Table 6-2 provides a list of the NetWare user security rights that you can assign to NetWare files and directories.

Review Table 6-2 for background information only. What you need to know about user rights is this: Much of data resource security is set through assignment of user rights, also known as *user-level security*.

Table 6-2	NetWare Security Rights
Name	*Description*
ACCESS CONTROL	This is like granting supervisor-level rights to a user for a particular directory or file.
CREATE	This enables a user to make subdirectories and create files.
ERASE	This enables a user to delete a file or directory, provided that the file isn't read-only.
FILE SCAN	The user can use the DIR command to view the contents of a directory.
MODIFY	The user can change files, including renaming them, and change their attributes.
READ	The user can open or execute files.
SUPERVISOR	The user has all other rights.
WRITE	The user can write to files that don't have read-only attributes set.

User account restrictions

By using NWADMIN, NWADMN32, NETADMIN, or SYSCON, depending on the NetWare version, you can set a variety of other access and login limits on a user account. These restrictions include the number of active login accounts that a user can open, a designated workstation for a user, and the time of the day or the days of the week that an account is valid. You can also set password characteristics, an account expiration date, or a limit on disk space used.

IPX/SPX messaging services

Although most people think of e-mail when they hear the term *messaging,* the word actually refers to the technology employed by the network to move service requests and data around the network. As far as e-mail goes, NetWare supports the protocols that enable e-mail clients and mail-enabled applications, but its primary messaging functions are carried out through the IPX protocol.

The Internetwork Packet eXchange (IPX) and its companion protocol Sequenced Packet eXchange (SPX), commonly referenced as IPX/SPX, provide a combined function that ensures that a network message — a *packet* — gets to its intended address. To help you remember what this protocol suite is and does, it provides essentially the same support to legacy NetWare versions (those before NetWare 5) as TCP/IP does to other NOSes, including NetWare 5.

IPX routes packets across the network to their destinations, directing replies and returning data to their appropriate locations; SPX verifies arrival of routed material. The IPX protocol works well with many different network topologies, which is one reason why Microsoft created its own version of IPX for Windows (see "IPX and TCP/IP" later in this chapter).

IPX is a *best-effort protocol,* which means that it doesn't include a message acknowledgment system to guarantee delivery of a message. This is where SPX comes in. SPX enhances IPX by supplying acknowledgment services. SPX requests verification (in the form of a check sum or calculated control sum) from the destination location and then compares that value with the sum that it calculated before sending the message. If the two match, the packet reached its destination intact. If the two sums don't match, SPX has IPX resend the packet. SPX also manages larger messages that must be broken into smaller packets, verifying their sequencing as well.

One of IPX's stronger features is its ability to support different frame types and formats. However, this feature can be a problem when two NetWare servers try to communicate by using different frame types. Unless two NetWare networks or servers use the same frame types, they can't communicate. For the test, you don't necessarily need to know the different packet formats supported by NetWare, but do remember that in order to communicate, two NetWare systems must use the same packet type.

Don't confuse IPX with IP (Internet Protocol). IP is the TCP/IP protocol that provides the mechanism for addressing and moving data across an internetwork, and IPX is the native transport protocol of NetWare versions prior to NetWare 5 (just in case we haven't mentioned that).

Checking Out the Windows Servers

Like NetWare, the Windows Server NOS has several versions. As far as the Network+ exam is concerned, the versions that you should concentrate on are Windows NT Server and Windows 2000 Server. Microsoft has announced its most recent take-the-world-by-storm version, Windows .NET (XP) Server. The questions on the Network+ exam are primarily on the Windows NT and 2000 versions; for the MCSA exams, you need to have a fairly broad base of Windows Server OS knowledge. Because the Network+ exam is focused on what a network technician needs to know when setting up and connecting a TCP/IP client, you won't be asked about Active Directories or Microsoft Exchange.

Whereas NetWare has NDS to provide the lion's share of its core services, Windows NT and 2000 rely on a family of specialized services to provide their core functions. In Table 6-3, we list the Windows services that provide each of the NOS core services.

Don't memorize this table. We include this information as background material and as a tool to compare the Windows NT architecture with Novell.

Table 6-3	Windows Server Core Services
Core Service Area	*Windows NT/2000 Service*
File services	NTFS (new technology file system)
Print services	Windows NT File and Print Services
Directory services	The Windows NT Explorer and the User Manager for Domains
Security services	The Security Access Manager and the Remote Access Services
Messaging services	Microsoft Exchange, Outlook, Mail, and other add-on products
Routing services	Routing Information Protocol (RIP)
Administration services	User Manager for Domains and Windows NT Control Panel

Windows client operating systems

The client operating system also includes many networking and messaging services that allow the user's computer to interact with the network operating system over the network. See "Setting Up a Windows Client" later in the chapter for more information on network client operating systems.

The mechanism that allows the software running on a client workstation to interact with a specific network protocol is called a *redirector,* which is another name for the protocol clients running on a network workstation. When you configure a workstation for a network, you add services and protocols, each of which has its own redirector that allows it to interact with the network OS.

**Book IV
Chapter 6**

**Implementing a
Network**

Windows file systems

Windows NT gives you a choice of two file systems: FAT (file allocation table) or NTFS (new technology file system). In terms of hardware and labor, FAT is the easier and less-expensive way to go. The FAT file system enables users to store and read files on server disk drives, but little data protection exists beyond basic user-level security. Because of this limitation, NTFS is the file system of choice for Windows NT/2000 Server servers. Windows 2000 supports the two file systems of Windows NT and adds support for FAT32, the 32-bit version of the FAT file system, as well.

NTFS is a driver that loads at the I/O (input/output) layer of Windows NT to process input/output requests for its files, directories, and volumes and provides file- and directory-level security.

FAT also provides share-level security identical to that offered by Windows *9x*. Network shares located on an NTFS drive provide additional share-level security features to the network administrator. (See "Share and share alike" later in this section.)

The disk bone is connected to the partition bone . . .

Windows NT/2000 supports a fairly simple hierarchical organization of hard disk drives. At the top of the storage tree is the physical storage media itself. By using FDISK.EXE (yes, the old DOS FDISK), you can divide the hard disk into one or more partitions. No matter how many disks are installed on a computer, at least one primary partition (usually designated drive C:) must serve as the boot partition for the system. Any other partitions created on the disks are *extended partitions*.

Here's the wrinkle in this otherwise simple hierarchy: Each extended partition can also be subdivided into as many as 23 logical partitions, each of which can be assigned a drive letter. One or more partitions form a volume, which is assigned to a file system, such as NTFS or FAT. And that brings you back full circle.

Share and share alike

Network shares enable users to access data and resources on the network. Although they're part of the file system, network shares create a new level of security called *share-level security*. Users can access data on the network only after assignment of the appropriate user-level security and creation of a network share for the directory or file that the user wants to access. In the peer-based network, the workstation owner administers the network shares. On a Windows network, both the network administrator *and* the workstation or resource owner may grant share-level access.

The share name for a file or directory is usually the same as its file system name, but different names can be assigned. For example, if you're so inclined, you can assign the directory BEANCNTR the share name ACC-TONLY. Users can then use the shorter name to access the shared resource by using the following syntax:

`\\SERVER_NAME\SHARE_NAME`

or

`\\THUNDER_BIT\ACCTONLY`

The general syntax used for share names is the Universal Naming Convention (UNC), which consists of two backward slashes followed by the server name followed by a backward slash followed by the share name, as shown in the first example. The second example shows the share for the ACCTONLY share (folder) on the THUNDER_BIT server.

Windows print services

Windows NT Server print services involves four components: print servers, print queues, print jobs, and oddly enough, printers. Actually, two types of printers exist: physical printers and logical printers. To confuse things further, you have three types of physical printers: server-attached, network-attached, and workstation-attached. These three configurations are also known as server printer, network printer, and remote printer, respectively. The good news is that beyond the naming quagmire, Windows NT printing works very well. It's just a matter of organization.

Print servers are either computers dedicated to that task or a network workstation that takes on an additional duty. Print queues form the line of print jobs (stuff to be printed) submitted by the user, with each job awaiting its turn on the printer. When the user sends something to the printer, the print server stores it in the queue for the destination printer until the printer is available.

For the exam, know the following three printer configurations for printers on a Windows Server network:

✦ **Server-attached (server printer):** This is just what it sounds like: a printer attached directly to the server computer.

✦ **Network-attached (network printer):** You can attach several printers directly to the network as an addressable node on the network. These printers use special network adapters, such as the HP JetDirect card, to connect to the network.

✦ **Workstation-attached (remote printer):** This is a printer cabled directly to a network workstation. In order for other network users to access the printer, the workstation user (owner) must make the printer available via share-level permissions. (See "Exploring Windows file services" later in this chapter.)

Windows client workstations still require a printer driver installed locally for a network- or server-attached printer. Windows NT/2000 print services manage the queue for client print jobs.

Exploring Windows file services

Veteran Windows users, those folks who have experience with a Windows version that includes a number 9 in it, are likely to be familiar with Windows Explorer. At first glance, NT Explorer looks exactly like the Explorer found in Windows 95, 98, and Me. Beneath its facade, though, Windows NT Explorer clearly separates itself from the Explorer pack. Windows 2000 Professional also includes Windows Explorer but doesn't feature it.

Windows NT Explorer is the file and directory management tool for Windows NT Server. By using a special set of tools and utilities found only on the Windows NT version, you can add or delete directories (called *folders*) and network shares or alter the structure of the network. With NT Explorer, you can also manage file permissions, auditing, and ownership properties.

File permissions (refer to Table 6-1) control the actions that a user can perform on a file or directory. Auditing sets up a tracking procedure that logs access and other activity on a share, file, or directory. Only the owner of a network resource can change its properties. On occasion, the administrator must take ownership of a resource to solve a problem.

The default permissions assigned to a new file by NTFS running on Windows NT depend on where the file is created and who is creating it. But, for the most part, they are

```
account operators - special (rwxd)
administrators - special (rwxd)
everyone - list (rx)
system - full control
```

Table 6-4 lists the six basic permissions that can be assigned to a file on a Windows NT system. Notice that these permissions, while assigned individually, are often grouped for convenient display.

Table 6-4	Six Basic Windows NT File Permissions
Permission	*Meaning*
R	Read
W	Write
D	Delete
X	Execute
P	Change Permissions
O	Take Ownership

Permissions on a directory (folder) indicate the user-level access that a user or group has to a directory and its contents. The permissions assigned to a directory extend to the subdirectories and files beneath it. When you create new files and subdirectories in the directory, they inherit their permissions from the directory. However, if you change a directory's permissions, any subdirectories and their files won't be changed unless you specifically indicate that the permission change should also apply to them. A directory's permissions are cumulative, with one exception — the No Access permission overrides all other permissions. See Table 6-5 for a listing of the Windows NT directory permissions.

Table 6-5	Windows NT Directory Permissions
Permission	*Meaning*
No Access (None)	User/group has no access to the resource.
List (RX)	User/group can only view the directory and the filenames.
Read (RX)	User/group can open files in read-only mode and execute programs.
Add (WX)	User/group can create new files to the directory but can't read or change the contents of the directory.
Add & Read (RWX)	User/group has read and add permissions.
Change (RWXD)	User/group has read and add permissions and can change contents and delete files.
Full Control (All)	User/group can do anything.
Special Directory Access	Allows customization of the basic permissions set for a user/group on the current directory.
Special File Access	Allows customization of the basic permissions set for a user/group on files in the current directory.

Windows security services

Security on Windows NT/2000 Server and Novell NetWare operates in much the same way, with three levels: user-level, share-level, and resource permissions. Users and groups are assigned rights to access shared network resources. Permissions govern the type of actions permitted on a resource. User rights are re-established with each logon. Permissions can be assigned to a file or directory as listed in Tables 6-4 and 6-5.

Another feature of security on a Windows Server system is encryption. For the exam, remember that Kerberos is the default security and encryption method for Windows 2000.

Clinging to the NetBEUI

At its most basic levels, Windows NT uses two protocols, NetBIOS (Network Basic Input/Output System) and NetBEUI (NetBIOS Extended User Interface) that have a singular purpose: to carry network messages around the network. However, NetBEUI is somewhat limited if you want the network to grow or connect to the outside world through, for example, the Internet.

NetBEUI is a nonroutable, connection-oriented protocol that works well on small networks. *Nonroutable* means that the protocol can't be used to connect with another physical network without the nonroutable protocol first passing through a bridge or being encapsulated in another protocol, such as PPP (Point-to-Point Protocol) or IP. *Connection-oriented* means that the protocol operates with a form of point-to-point connection much like the connection used to dial up another computer over a modem. One benefit of a connection-oriented protocol is that the sender receives confirmation when a packet arrives at its destination.

IPX and TCP/IP

Windows NT Server also supports virtually every one of the popular networking protocols in use, including IPX, TCP/IP, and AppleTalk. This support is provided through three protocol bundles: NWLink (NetWare Link), Microsoft Services for Macintosh, and Microsoft TCP/IP. NWLink is the Microsoft version of the NetWare IPX. Often called Microsoft IPX, NWLink is fully compatible with IPX.

Microsoft TCP/IP (Transmission Control Protocol/Internet Protocol) implements the hugely popular open-protocol suite used primarily for the Internet, and TCP/IP is gaining some favor as a LAN protocol as well.

For the Network+ test, you need to know that Windows NT/2000 Server supports and implements TCP/IP protocols and IP address resolution as its default protocol.

Other Windows NT protocols

Windows NT/2000 also supports Data Link Control (DLC) and AppleTalk. These protocols may show up on the exam in situation-type questions and multiple-choice answer lists. *DLC* is a protocol used to connect networks and workstations to mainframe computers or to network-attached printers. *AppleTalk* is the Apple Macintosh networking protocol. This protocol is implemented on a Windows NT Server network as Services for Macintosh. Another Apple Macintosh network protocol that you may see on the test is TokenTalk, which is the Token Ring equivalent of the Ethernet AppleTalk.

Getting around with Windows routing services

Routers are either dynamic or static. *Dynamic routers,* such as a TCP/IP or IPX router, are protocol-dependent.

Windows NT implements dynamic routers for both IPX (RIP IPX) and TCP/IP (RIP) by using a choice of frame (packet) standards: IEEE 802.2, IEEE 802.3, or autodetect. IEEE 802.2 and 802.3 are standards for Logical Link Control formats and bus networks, respectively. The autodetect method looks at the packet and determines which format it uses.

On the other hand, a Windows NT static router requires network addresses to be entered and managed individually. On a large network, this is not a good choice because of the amount of maintenance the network administrator must perform to keep the network routing information up to date. Any change to the network topology could invalidate the fixed (static) routing information of the static router. Static routing is more appropriate for small networks or a network with only a single point of access to the Internet or a wide area network (WAN).

Managing users and not much else

The User Manager for Domains utility is the Windows NT tool used to manage group and user accounts, rights, and permissions on a Windows NT Server network with multiple domains. Beyond this, Windows NT administrative services aren't specifically covered on the Network+ exam. Instead, the Network+ exam covers network administration activities in a general way without specifically mentioning particular network operating systems.

Giving UNIX (and Linux) the Once-over

For the Network+ test, you don't need to know a whole lot about the UNIX or Linux operating systems. What you do have to keep in mind is the way that this operating system supports networking, especially internetworking.

UDP and ICMP, and we all get along

TCP/IP on UNIX is no different than TCP/IP on any other operating system or NOS. However, in UNIX networking services, you have some alternatives, the most common of which are the User Datagram Protocol (UDP) and the Internet Control Message Protocol (ICMP). The UNIX world calls data packets *datagrams*.

UDP is a connectionless protocol designed for applications that don't need messages divided into multiple datagrams or that don't care about the sequence in which messages are received. UDP, which works with IP, is a direct replacement for TCP. However, UDP doesn't track what has been sent so that messages can be resent if necessary.

ICMP serves to transmit error messages and messages intended for TCP/IP itself. For example, if you attempt to connect to an Internet host server, you may receive an ICMP message that states `Host unreachable.`

Sharing files on NFS

The Network File System (NFS) provides network services by using a mechanism called *remote procedure call* (RPC). NFS enables users to access files on remote hosts in the same way that they access files on their local systems. The remote file access is completely transparent to the user and is compatible with a variety of server and remote host architectures. The true benefit of NFS is that centrally stored files can be mounted, or linked, to the local workstation when it's logged on. To the user, the file is just as close at hand as any local file. Using NFS to access files is very effective for sharing large or commonly accessed files, which can be installed in a single location and then shared throughout the network.

Creating one from many with NIS

The *Network Information System* (NIS) is a UNIX service that distributes information, such as that contained in the user accounts and groups files, to all servers on a network. NIS makes the network appear to be a single system, with the same accounts supported on all servers. Using NIS to organize a network eliminates the need for the user to know, or to find out, just where on the network that resources are located. Resources all appear to be present on what seems to be a single network.

Cross-Platform Connectivity

Windows Server and NetWare on the same network, you say? Surely not. Actually, the scenario isn't unusual, especially if the network is being migrated to one or the other. And because this is included in an MCSA book, you know which is being migrated to which. Both NOSes include utilities and services packages that provide for cross-platform connectivity on the network.

Windows Server includes a variety of cross-platform connectivity services to enable all Windows clients to access a NetWare server. These services are

+ **Gateway Service for NetWare (GSNW):** Enables Windows Server to act as a gateway for Windows clients to access resources on a NetWare server.

+ **Client Service for NetWare (CSNW):** Included in most Windows clients (especially NT Workstation). CSNW enables a client to access and use file and print services from a NetWare server.

+ **File and Print Services for NetWare (FPNW):** Enables Windows Server to be seen as a Novell NetWare 3.*x*-compatible server by NetWare clients for file and print services.

+ **Directory Service Manager for NetWare (DSMN):** Enables user and group accounts to be managed on both the Windows and NetWare servers, with the changes of one updated automatically to the other.

Building in Fault Tolerance

Another important part of setting up a server is to build in some form of fault tolerance on the server to ensure that the server and the network remains highly available when something unexpected — and always bad — happens.

One way to prevent network disasters of the hardware-failure kind is to build fault tolerance into the network. The purpose of *fault-tolerant systems* is to prevent hardware or software failures from removing the availability of network resources. In fact, fault-tolerant systems are also commonly called *high-availability systems*. These systems work by providing back-up hardware that kicks in if a network device malfunctions.

Networks that don't include fault-tolerant systems have several single points of failure: hard drives, power supplies, or others. Fault-tolerant systems help eliminate the points of failure from a network. Two common fault-tolerant techniques (at least on the Network+ exam) are adapter teaming and load balancing. Read on through the following sections for more on both.

Book IV Chapter 6

Implementing a Network

Speaking the high-availability lingo

On the test, you may run into a few of the terms used to describe fault-tolerant and high-availability systems, so you need to know them:

✦ **Failover:** A system has *failover protection* if a replacement or redundant component is immediately available for a failing or failed component. The benefit of a failover system is that it minimizes the downtime of a system. Failover can be as simple as having a spare hard drive to plug in if one fails, or as sophisticated as having an online server that automatically picks up the processing if a server goes down.

✦ **Hot-plug (hot-swap):** Failed devices on a server chassis that supports hot-plug components can be replaced without taking the server offline or shutting it down. Hot plugs can be useful when you replace an adapter, such as a PCI (Peripheral Component Interconnect) card, while the server is running and without interrupting the network. (See the upcoming section "Adapter teaming.") Another example is when disk duplexing is implemented on a server and one of the disk controllers fails: The controller can be replaced while the system is up and running.

✦ **Clustering:** Although RAID (Redundant Array of Independent Disks) protects the data resource, it doesn't protect the server itself. *Clustering* connects two or more servers to enhance data availability, reliability, scalability, and server manageability. Clustering is a kind of RAID for servers. Clustered servers are connected so that when one server fails, the other server or servers take over support for users and any running processes from the failed server. In most cases, clustering is completely transparent to the user. Clustering also provides scalability; servers can be added to the cluster without network downtime. Two types of clustering can be used in a couple different ways:

  • **Shared storage clustering:** Shared storage cluster servers are connected by SCSI (Small Computer System Interface) adapters. One server is designated as the primary server that carries the processing load as long as it's active. All the servers in the cluster are designated as secondary servers. All the servers in the cluster also have full access to the same shared storage devices, which means that if the primary server fails, a secondary server is ready and able to take up the role of the primary server. The failover process takes only a few seconds, typically from 5 to 15 seconds, because of the SCSI connection. The clustering ensures that very little downtime or performance degradation is involved in the failover. Because of the physical distance limitations of the SCSI standards, the servers must be relatively close to one another.

  • **Server mirroring clustering:** In this clustering form, mirrored servers are connected over a network. The advantage of this type of clustering is that the primary and secondary servers can be separated over longer distances. The downside is the failover time, which can take from 15 to 90 seconds before a secondary server is able to take over the I/O tasks. Data loss can happen during the failover process.

In either form of clustering, the administrator determines the events that can trigger a failover. For example, you may want the clustered servers to switch over when a program or process hangs, when a peripheral device fails, or you may want to manually perform the switch-over yourself.

✦ **Adapter Fault Tolerance (AFT):** *AFT* is a form of adapter teaming (see the next section) that provides network connection redundancy by supporting failover for two network interface cards (NICs) in a single server. When one of the server's links to the network fails, the redundant NIC automatically begins handling all incoming and outgoing network traffic. Most AFT adapters are also hot-plug devices.

Adapter teaming

If a server is being bombarded by user authentication requests and directory service traffic is drowning the server's network card, you should consider incorporating adapter teaming. *Adapter teaming*, also known as *Adapter Fault Tolerance* (AFT), is implemented by adding an additional network interface card to a server. However, to get the total effect of AFT, you must connect each NIC to a different network link, which gives you total redundancy. This gives you two separate links over which network traffic can flow. And if one of the links fails, you already have a link up and running.

Adapter teaming provides extra bandwidth and fault tolerance to the server. The two NICs share incoming and outgoing traffic, effectively cutting the network traffic of each card in half. If one of the links to the server fails, or if one of the NICs dies, the remaining card automatically steps up and takes care of all incoming and outgoing network traffic — perhaps not as fast, but one NIC is certainly better than none.

Many NICs on the market are *AFT compatible*, which means that they have built-in features to facilitate adapter teaming. AFT adapters are *hot-plug* devices; that is, they can be inserted and replaced while the server is running. If an AFT NIC fails, just take the bad NIC out and insert the new one. (I describe hot-plug devices in the previous section "Speaking the high-availability lingo.")

Load balancing

Load balancing is a technique used to provide scalability and high availability to network servers, such as Web servers and e-mail servers. Load-balancing servers (also called *hosts*) are configured in a cluster, which enables the servers to communicate with one another. The cluster is transparent to network users. As far as the user knows, only one server is responding to requests.

Load balancing can greatly increase performance of server-based applications, such as an e-mail server or printer server, by distributing user requests across multiple servers in the cluster. The load balancing is used to spread the wealth, so to speak. Another great benefit of load balancing is that it can detect whether a server in the cluster fails and thus automatically delegate the traffic to the remaining servers in the cluster.

As network traffic increases, the administrator can simply add additional servers to the cluster. Windows 2000 Advanced Server is capable of load balancing up to 32 servers in any one cluster. Standard versions of Windows NT/2000 Server don't include the capability of load balancing.

Swapping Drives

Having spare components on hand, such as adapter cards and hard drives, is an excellent idea so you're ready if a drive or card fails. For the Network+ exam, you should know the different ways to swap a hard drive and why one way may be better than another in a given situation. You also need to know how to rebuild a disk array after the replacement drive is installed. Here are the disk-swap techniques that you should know:

✦ **Cold swap:** Hard drives that require a *cold swap* can be installed only when the server is shut down and powered off. The problem that this poses for a high-availability system is that the server is offline while you're cold-swapping a hard drive.

✦ **Warm swap:** To *warm-swap* a disk drive, you must stop the device driver of the bus on which the hard drive is to be installed. The server can be powered on and the operating system running. Although the server is available, none of the data on disk drives installed on the affected bus is available. A warm swap device is certainly a better choice than a cold swap device for keeping the system available.

✦ **Hot swap:** *Hot-swappable* disk drives, power supplies, and other components can be removed and installed while the system is running — without downtime. In many server-case designs, hot-swap devices can be removed and replaced without opening the server case. As you know, rebooting a server can take an eternity, and while the system is down, all eyes are on you. So the faster the system is back online, the better. You may also hear hot swap devices referred to as *hot-plug* devices.

✦ **Hot spares:** Hot spares are an improvement on hot-swap devices. A *hot spare* is a device that's installed in the server, attached to a controller, and put in standby mode. If a drive fails, the device controller automatically recruits the hot spare as a replacement for the failed device. When a hot spare disk drive is used to back up a disk array, the disk controller automatically starts rebuilding the data on the spare drive as soon as it senses that another disk drive has failed. Hot spares are excellent for unattended servers or servers that absolutely cannot have downtime.

Preventing Storage Issues

For the most part, networks rely on traditional media and software technologies to attach storage solutions to networks. Commonly, the data-storage technology used for the network data resource is one or more hard drives physically located inside one or more of the network's servers. In situations where a large amount of storage capacity is required, it may be necessary to dedicate a server with several RAID-enabled hard disks to this purpose. If you need to provide high gigabyte or even terabyte (trillion) levels of storage, you may find yourself with a disparate array of disk storage and media hardware.

The drawback that is inherent in attempting to solve storage capacity problems using a traditional approach is that you still have to contend with traditional storage (hard disk drives), media (typically copper), network adapters (NICs), and backups (tapes).

Incorporating a storage area network

A *storage area network* (or SAN) is a very high-speed special-purpose subnetwork that interconnects different brands and types of data storage equipment and a network's servers to provide fast and dependable access to the network's users. A SAN isn't typically something that you find on a smaller network, but this technology is becoming very commonplace on larger, enterprise networks.

SAN technology clusters data-storage resources, typically very close to the servers, of a network. However, because it uses networking technology, a SAN can also include resources from offsite locations as well, such as backup and archival services, using wide area network (WAN) technologies, such as ATM (asynchronous transfer mode) or SONET (synchronous optical networks).

SAN technology supports many of the same techniques that you might use in a traditional data-storage approach, including disk mirroring, data backup and restore processes, data migration from one device to another, and the sharing of the data resource to multiple servers on the network.

SAN is commonly confused with NAS (network-attached storage). A *NAS* device or system is disk storage that can be attached to the network as a node with its own IP addressing. SAN technology supports the inclusion of NAS devices.

Putting Fibre in your network diet

Fibre channel technology allows for the transmission of data between network computers at 1 Gbps (gigabits per second) or higher speeds. Fibre channel is commonly used to connect shared storage devices, like NAS, and their related controllers together and to the network. Because of its speed, Fibre channel is used on large networks to replace SCSI as the transmission interface of choice on clustered storage arrangements. Another benefit to Fibre channel is that the devices that it interconnects can be as much as 6 miles (10 kilometers) apart over fiber-optic cabling. However, Fibre channel can also be implemented on coaxial and copper cabling as well for shorter distances.

A storage area network (SAN) uses the Fibre channel media technology and ATM communications to provide high-speed access to a network's data resources.

Configuring the Network Client

No matter which network operating system is running on the network servers, each workstation requires its own operating system, preferably one that's compatible with the NOS and its protocols. In some situations, the NOS has to adjust to the OS running on its clients, which is typically done through a service running on either the server or the client.

Windows systems (Windows 3.*x*, Windows 9*x*, Windows NT Workstation, and Windows 2000 Professional, for the Network+ exam) include client software that enables workstations to communicate with a network running the IPX, TCP/IP, or NetBEUI protocol. The later versions of the Windows clients (that is, Windows 9*x*, Windows Me, and Windows 2000) include clients and services providing cross-platform support for file, directory, and print services for NetWare and Macintosh AppleTalk networks.

Configuring a network client to connect to a network is slightly different for each of the client operating systems that the user may be using. The results, however, are essentially the same: a network workstation that's configured to interact with the NOS and the resources that it manages and protects.

In the following sections, we break down the steps used to configure a Windows 9*x* client and a UNIX/Linux client to a TCP/IP network, which are the situations that you're most likely to encounter on the Network+ exam. One other situation that we cover briefly is configuring a Mac/OS client to operate on a Novell network, which is also something that you may run into on the exam.

Setting Up a Windows Client

Because the Network+ exam focuses primarily on Ethernet networking, the process that we describe here is to configure a TCP/IP client. Also remember that the processes that we describe in this section for setting up a Windows 9*x* client aren't the same as those used for a Windows 2000 (or later versions) client. Don't worry, though; any configuration questions on the exam are about Windows 9*x* (meaning Windows 95 and 98) clients.

Checking out the installed components

Because the majority of network clients are running on a Windows 9*x* operating system, that is the example used in Lab 6-1, which details the steps that you use to check whether the network adapter is properly installed and configurable.

Lab 6-1	Checking Installed Network Components on a Windows 9*x* Client

1. **From the Start menu, choose Settings and open Control Panel.**

2. **In the Control Panel window, select and open the Network icon.**

   The Network configuration dialog box appears, as shown in Figure 6-2.

   On the Configuration tab is a list of installed network components. What you're hoping to find are

   • Client for Microsoft Networks (assuming that the client is being connected to a Windows network)

   • At least one network adapter, such as a Fast Ethernet adapter (see Figure 6-2)

   • TCP/IP, either by itself or configured to the adapter (as shown in Figure 6-2)

3. **If these three components are listed, you can proceed with configuring the client.**

   You may see other components listed, such as Client for NetWare Networks or IPX/SPX. If so, leave them. If the NetBEUI component is listed, check with the network administrator or the ISP (Internet Service Provider) to see whether it should be removed.

Figure 6-2:
The
Windows 9x
Network
configuration
dialog box.

Installing and configuring TCP/IP

If TCP/IP isn't listed on the Network configuration dialog box, you must install it, as we describe in Lab 6-2.

Lab 6-2   Installing TCP/IP on a Windows 9x Client

1. **On the Network configuration dialog box (refer to Figure 6-2), click Add.**

2. **From the Select Network Component Type dialog box list that appears, highlight Protocol and then click Add.**

   The Select Network Protocol dialog box appears (see Figure 6-3).

3. **Choose Microsoft from the Manufacturers list.**

   The available protocols provided by Microsoft appear in the right panel under Network Protocols.

4. **Select the TCP/IP option from Network Protocols and click OK.**

   You're returned to the Network configuration dialog box (refer to Figure 6-2); TCP/IP should now be listed in the components list there.

The process used to install the Client for Microsoft Networks is very similar to the preceding process, except that you choose Services and then add the client service instead of choosing Protocols from the Select Network Component Type dialog box.

Before your configuration changes are registered on the system, you'll likely have to restart the client.

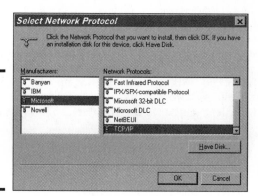

Figure 6-3:
The
Windows
Select
Network
Protocol
dialog box.

Configuring TCP/IP

The process used to configure the TCP/IP settings on a client can vary by network, depending on the topology in use, whether subnetting is implemented, and a few other factors. You aren't expected to know this procedure for the exam, but you should know some of the terminology used to configure TCP/IP on a client workstation.

The terms that you should know are

✦ **DHCP (Dynamic Host Configuration Protocol):** *DHCP* is commonly used on LANs to eliminate the need to hard-configure (you know, like, permanently, dude) network clients. When a DHCP client connects to the network, a DHCP server supplies it an IP address, subnet mask, and default gateway, which are the primary TCP/IP configuration elements of a client.

✦ **DNS (Domain Name System):** This is an IP address that points to the location used to look up and translate domain names into IP addresses.

✦ **Gateway (also known as default gateway):** This entry is the IP address of the device, typically a server or a router, used to connect outside the client's network segment or to a WAN (like the big WAN — the Internet).

✦ **Subnet mask:** This is typically the default subnet mask used for the IP address class of your network. On many LANs, either a Class B or Class C private IP addressing scheme is used, so the subnet mask will either be 255.255.0.0 or 255.255.255.0, respectively. However, if the network has been subnetted, the subnet mask will most likely not be a default value.

✦ **WINS (Windows Internet Naming Service):** In most cases, WINS is disabled on network clients. If you want to enable it, however, you must enter an address for the WINS server.

**Book IV
Chapter 6**

**Implementing a
Network**

Setting Up a Linux/UNIX Client

Although most network clients these days are running some version of the Windows operating system, a growing number of clients are running one of the many available Linux and UNIX versions. Setting up a Linux client to run on a TCP/IP network is different from setting up a Windows client (see "Setting Up a Windows client" earlier in the chapter), so I feel obligated to mention it here.

Getting the tools

Virtually all versions of Linux come with a bundle of networking tools that includes such essential services as arp, ifconfig, netstat, rarp, nameif, and route. (Notice that Linux/UNIX commands are all in lowercase.) Usually, the bundle has a creative name — something like net-tools. Typically, the net-tools bundle also contains utilities particular to many hardware types, such as plipconfig and slattach, and utilities for advanced IP configuration, such as iptunnel and ipmaddr.

Configuring a UNIX/Linux client

Assuming that both the network adapter and the net-tools bundle have been installed on the client hardware, you can follow the steps in Lab 6-3 to set up a UNIX/Linux client.

Lab 6-3   Configuring a UNIX/Linux Client

1. **Log on as root or in supervisor mode.**

   You need the root or supervisor password to do so — obviously.

2. **Edit the** /etc/sysconfig/network-scripts/ifcfg-eth0 **file.**

   The eth0 part of the file name refers to the network adapter that's being configured and could vary by system.

   The file probably contains entries something like these:

   ```
   DEVICE="eth0"
   BOOTPROTO="dhcp"
   ONBOOT="yes"
   IPADDR=""
   NETMASK=""
   ```

   The second line of this example shows how DHCP is enabled on a UNIX/Linux workstation.

3. **Enter the value for the** IPADDR **entry (the IP address) to the assigned address.**

4. **Enter the network or subnet mask in the** `NETMASK` **entry, which for a majority of local area networks will be something like 255.255.255.0.**

   Although not shown in the example, you can also enter a value for the default gateway by typing **GATEWAY="*xx*"**.

5. **Close and save the** `ifcfg-eth0` **file and run the** `network restart` **command to start the network routines.**

6. **Check the configuration by running** `ifconfig` **and try running a PING on the IP address assigned to the client.**

Setting Up an Apple Client on a Windows Network

Despite the ongoing war between Windows and Macintosh zealots, you might often find it necessary to connect an Apple computer to a Windows or NetWare network. For those of you familiar with the Macintosh operating system, the actions that we describe in the following sections probably make some sense. For the rest of you, review the steps in Lab 6-4 to gain a general understanding of configuring a Macintosh client for connecting to a TCP/IP network.

Lab 6-4	Configuring TCP/IP on a Macintosh Client

1. **From the Apple menu, choose Control Panels and open the TCP/IP Control Panel.**

   The Control Panel appears.

2. **Choose User Mode from the Edit menu on the toolbar at the top of the screen and select Advanced.**

   The Advanced dialog box appears.

3. **Choose Connect Via and select Ethernet from the pull-down menu.**

4. **Make sure that the box next to the Use 802.3 option is not checked.**

   If it's checked, clear it. (But you knew that.)

5. **Choose Configure and then select Manually from the pull-down menu.**

6. **Enter the IP address assigned to the client in the box labeled (what else?) IP Address, the network or subnet mask in the (duh!) Subnet Mask box, and the gateway address in the (you guessed it!) Gateway box.**

   If required, you can also enter the name server (DNS) entries and router address (typically the same as the gateway address).

7. **Click Options to open another dialog box that enables you to set TCP/IP as active or inactive.**

8. Select Active to automatically start the TCP/IP services.

You may want to also select (check) the Load Only When Needed option to allow the user to conserve system resources when not running network applications.

In order for a Macintosh client to operate on a NetWare network, it must be running the NetWare Client for Mac/OS.

Protecting the Network from Viruses

Viruses are nasty pieces of software that take on the characteristics of an infectious disease, spreading and infecting unsuspecting and unprotected PCs. You can expect at least one question on the exam that deals with the threat of a virus or how a virus is detected.

The following characteristics define a computer virus:

✦ A virus attaches itself to another piece of programming code in memory, on a floppy disk, or on a downloaded file.

✦ A virus infects a system when a user executes the infected file or program (and, in turn, inadvertently executes the virus's program code).

✦ A virus's code is programmed to replicate itself and infect other programs when users execute the virus-infected file, program, or disk.

✦ As a virus spreads, it may modify its form and manifest other behaviors as well.

Not all viruses do catastrophic damage to a system. Many viruses are just nuisances or pranks, playing music, simulating system meltdowns, or displaying misinformation during the system boot. However, many viruses are malicious and can cause considerable damage to the network in the form of lost data or altered program code.

Viruses and how they spread

Computer viruses are a form of electronic warfare developed solely to cause human misery. The evil, sick, and quite-talented minds that develop computer viruses would like nothing better than for all the boot sectors in a network to catch cold or for all the disk drives to develop dysentery. Four major virus classes exist, each with many subclasses as we describe in the following list:

✦ **Boot sector viruses (system viruses):** These viruses target the boot program on a hard drive. By attaching themselves to the boot sector program, the viruses are guaranteed to run whenever the computer starts up. Boot sector viruses spread mostly by jumping from disk drive to disk drive either on removable media or over a network.

✦ **File viruses:** *File viruses* modify program files, such as .EXE or .COM files. Whenever the infected program executes, the virus also executes and does its nastiness. File viruses spread when users pass infected floppy disks and files across networks and the Internet.

File viruses infect program files, not document files. That means that a simple e-mail can't be infected, but an e-mail program can be infected by an infected file attachment.

✦ **Macro viruses:** *Macro viruses* take advantage of the built-in macro programming languages of application programs, such as Microsoft Word and Microsoft Excel. Macro languages enable users to create *macros,* which are script-like programs that automate formatting, data entry, or frequently repeated tasks. A macro virus, most commonly found in Microsoft Word and Excel documents, can cause as much damage as other viruses and can spread by jumping from an open document to other documents on a hard drive and when users pass infected files and disks across networks and the Internet.

✦ **E-mail viruses:** The latest craze in viruses is the e-mail virus, and some particularly nasty ones have surfaced in the past couple of years, notably Klez Worm, BadTrans, Bubble Boy, Melissa, and their friends. You should also be aware that many e-mail viruses are just hoaxes.

Because a virus is a program, it can infect only programs. A virus can't hide where it doesn't blend into the scenery. A common myth is that viruses can infect graphic files, e-mail, or simple text files. Hiding viruses in those places would be like trying to hide a bright red ball among bright white balls because the infected code doesn't have anywhere to hide.

However, viruses can be attached to a text file or e-mail message and transmitted or copied to a new host system. And some of these viruses (called *worms* or *self-replicating viruses*) can devastate entire networks. When users execute the infected worm application (which often comes attached to an e-mail message), the worm replicates and sends itself to every e-mail address in the user's Address Book, slowing down (and often entirely halting) valuable network resources. You don't need to know this for the test, but you will deal with it in real life (if you haven't already).

We recommend that you temporarily stop your antivirus software while you update an operating system or install a fairly major piece of software, especially system software. The antivirus software wants to protect programs from being changed, which is exactly what an update is attempting to do. So, stopping your antivirus program will allow your upgrade to proceed unabated.

**Book IV
Chapter 6**

Implementing a
Network

Recovering from Disaster

Disaster recovery is an important topic for network administrators; one that you should take seriously. What you need to know for the Network+ exam is the purpose and characteristics of disaster recovery processes. Expect to see at least one disaster recovery question on the exam.

Disaster recovery must be implemented when a natural or external event crashes the network and makes its resources, especially the data resources, unavailable to its users.

The purpose of disaster recovery is to restore the critical data that support the operational needs of the organization.

Of course, the best recovery plan is to keep disasters from happening in the first place. That's why arguably the most important part of a disaster-recovery plan is the procedure that details how the network and its resources are to be protected against loss. And second only to prevention is how files will be restored if they *are* lost. If your disaster-recovery plan includes agreements that allow you to use another company's computers in the event of an emergency but you don't have a backup copy of the current data resources, there isn't much point to the recovery plan.

Although you need to know about most aspects of disaster prevention, one part of disaster preparedness that you don't need to worry about in detail is taking data backups. This is reserved for the CompTIA A+ and Server+ exams. (See Book V of this book for more about Server+.)

Preventing data disasters of the hardware kind

For the most part, hardware is very reliable these days, especially hard drives. But hard drives can and do fail, and the thought of losing everything, including the operating system, application programs, and system and user data from one fatal failure is the network technician's (and the user's) nightmare.

You can prevent data loss from hard drive failure. The most commonly used is RAID (Redundant Arrays of Independent [or Inexpensive] Disks), which you will see many questions about on the exam. RAID stores data in multiple locations so that even in the event of a serious crash, all the important data is still available. As cool as RAID is, however, don't put all your disaster-preparedness eggs in one basket. You also need to protect against the failure of several other hardware components. Here are the ones that you're likely to encounter in the situations that exam questions on disaster planning will pose:

✦ **Power loss:** A loss of power at the wrong time can be devastating. Even if you use RAID, the data in RAM and even cache memory is lost when the power source is lost. An appropriately sized UPS (uninterruptible power supply) — and, of course, a data backup — are the best ways to protect against a power failure.

✦ **Resource conflicts:** If two peripheral devices are set up with conflicting system resources, which include IRQs (interrupt requests), I/O (input/output) addresses, and DMA (direct memory access) channels, the conflicts can cause a network device and any data that it's holding to be lost.

Data disasters of the software kind

You should expect to see a question or two about software-related data disasters on the Network+ exam. *Software-related data disasters* are those caused by buggy software, viruses, and file-system failures. Data backups are the best defense against software-related data loss. Don't sweat the details of data backups, but you should know their worth.

Unfortunately, many software developers believe that they're forced to push out their programs as fast as possible to stay ahead of the competition. The result is software that can be buggy and unpredictable. In fact, for as melodramatic as you may think we're being, these days buggy software is almost the norm. We're sure that you've heard the rule about waiting until the first service pack is released before installing new software versions. Definitely one of the top two reasons to have a solid data backup program is to handle the devastating effect of buggy software. (The other reason is hardware, if you couldn't guess.)

Another potential software disaster is infection by a virus. Most of the antivirus software programs that you would use on your server include utilities that enable the software to keep itself (and all user workstations on the network) current automatically over the Internet. Virus attacks can be very malicious and result in severe data loss.

Remember that even the best antivirus software is no guarantee that servers and individual workstations are safe. Be prepared to answer at least one or two questions on the Network+ exam about antivirus software. See "Protecting the Network from Viruses" earlier in this chapter for more information on viruses and antivirus software.

Data disasters of the other kind

Because of faulty hardware or bad or malicious software, computers and servers can lose data electronically. But data can also be stolen or destroyed by network users or even by outside evildoers. Many studies have shown that the largest threat to a network is from within — meaning from a logged-on network user. The safeguards against data catastrophes caused by people are a well-defined and administered password security program and an active data backup program.

Locking out thieves

Theft prevention is one area that many administrators overlook when they set up disaster prevention plans. Although a server can't get up and walk away, a workstation, laptop, or storage media device can walk off with assistance from a bad person. This fact is another good reason for users to save data on the file server. The stolen equipment can be replaced, but replacing any data taken along with the equipment may be virtually impossible.

The best way to protect a server against outside intrusion is to secure it in a locked cabinet inside a locked room to which there is limited access.

Securing against sabotage

A disgruntled employee, a hacker, or maybe a competing company can also cause data loss by intentionally deleting or infecting the data files on your network file server. Backups are the only protection that you have against an individual who is determined to cause data loss. (And sometimes even the backups aren't enough.)

Understand that firewalls, virtual private networks (VPNs), and other network-related security measures can help to protect your data. But what we're talking about here is the protection that you have should these measures fail, thus compromising your data.

Monitoring the Network

Immediately after completing the implementation of a new or modified network — even if only the server is involved — you should create a network baseline. A *network baseline* is a record of a network's characteristics and performance prior to placing a load (such as users accessing resources or the Internet) on it. The purpose of the network baseline is to provide you with a benchmark to use in the future when troubleshooting what appear to be network performance problems, such as network or server bottlenecks.

By collecting information for a baseline of the network servers and network devices, such as routers and switches, you create an accurate picture of network traffic flow to the servers and network devices as it was initially installed.

A network baseline can come in handy when you're troubleshooting a network to determine the source of any performance problems. Baselining the network server or servers and network devices can help you to monitor the increase (or decrease) of activity on the network and to plan for adjustments in network capacities.

Baseline information is used to track the following characteristics of a server and network:

+ Server availability
+ Response times
+ Number of users throughout a given period
+ Number of application transactions
+ Network response based on per second
+ Responses from network nodes
+ CPU utilization
+ Memory utilization
+ Network availability

A lot of information can be gathered and used to assess the current condition of the network. The information that you need in the baseline depends on the roles of the servers and the type of devices on the network. The baseline's information can help you plan for upgrades and identify trouble spots before they become more than just a nuisance. In many cases, a network will show signs of slowing down well before it becomes a problem. When users complain that the network seems slow, you need to compare the current performance of the servers and network devices with their baselines. This comparison will point out the performance discrepancies that are the source of the network slowdown, and you can take care of the problem by upgrading server components or network devices.

To create a baseline, document the processor's current usage levels under a normal workload. On a Windows server, you can use the Performance Monitor utility to establish a reference point for processor usage. A baseline is normally more than a single value; generally, a *baseline* is a range within which processor usage, or other activity, can fluctuate and still provide acceptable performance. Typically a baseline is established over at least a one-week period.

You can use the baseline to identify trends, such as increasing memory and processor demands over a specified period, or to recognize problems that arise from a sudden change in the server or to the network.

**Book IV
Chapter 6**

Implementing a
Network

Building the Baseline

Most applications running on the server have one or more counters. To see an application's counters, open the Windows NT/2000 Task Manager and select the Process tab. Use these counters to record the activity of applications and system services.

Expect a question on the exam regarding processor usage and its monitoring. The best way to monitor processor activity is to log data from counters of the system, processor, process, thread, physical disk, and memory for at least a week (preferably longer) at an update interval ranging from 15 minutes to an hour. For the test, you won't need to know exactly what to monitor, but you need to know how long you should collect data to get the most accurate information.

After you baseline your network, you should have a good idea of what's normal behavior for your servers and network devices. The data that you collect to create your baseline should be recorded and kept in a safe place for future reference. Document everything that you do to a server or network device. Documentation is a very important part of the systems administrator's job, and the test hits hard on documentation.

From the day that you build a server, you should document everything that you feel is important in case a situation arises in which you might need to troubleshoot the server, or worse, rebuild the server.

Prep Test

1 Which of the following is a valid NetWare path to the public directory on the SYS volume?

A ○ \\SYS\PUBLIC

B ○ \PUBLIC\SYS

C ○ SYS\\PUBLIC

D ○ SYS:PUBLIC

2 NetWare printer queues are managed by which utility?

A ○ PRINTERS

B ○ PCONSOLE

C ○ PDIRECTOR

D ○ QUEUEMGR

3 A valid example of a Windows NT share name is

A ○ \\SERVER\SHARE_NAME

B ○ \SHARE_NAME\\SERVER

C ○ /SERVER/SHARE_NAME

D ○ /SHARE_NAME//SERVER

4 Microsoft's version of NetWare's IPX protocol is called

A ○ Client Services for NetWare.

B ○ Gateway Services for NetWare.

C ○ NWLink.

D ○ TCP/IP.

5 To set up the configuration for a TCP/IP connection to a LAN on a Windows 9x system, you would use which of the following Control Panel icons?

A ○ Dialup Networking

B ○ Modems

C ○ Networks

D ○ System

6 Which of the following does the DHCP server provide to a network client? (Choose three.)

A ❑ IP address

B ❑ Default gateway

C ❑ Subnet mask

D ❑ ISP dialup information

7 Which TCP/IP utility can be used to test the ability of a newly configured network client to see other elements on a LAN?

A ○ WINIPCFG

B ○ PING

C ○ WINS

D ○ ARP

8 What is the client service that must be installed to connect a Macintosh client to a NetWare network?

A ○ Client for Microsoft Networks

B ○ NetWare Services for TCP/IP Clients

C ○ NetWare Client for Mac/OS

D ○ NetWare NDS Client

9 Restoring critical mission-required data to a failed network is called

A ○ Fault tolerance.

B ○ High availability.

C ○ Disaster recovery.

D ○ Baselining.

10 Preventing hardware or software failure from interrupting the availability of network resources is called

A ○ Fault tolerance.

B ○ High availability.

C ○ Disaster recovery.

D ○ Baselining.

Answers

1 **D.** The volume name is used in directory path names. Following the MS-DOS device pattern, a colon follows the volume name. *Review "NetWare file systems."*

2 **B.** PCONSOLE manages NetWare printer queues. *Review "NetWare print services."*

3 **A.** Network shares enable users to access data and shared devices on the network. *Review "Share and share alike."*

4 **C.** Microsoft reverse-engineered IPX/SPX to create its own version of this popular network protocol. *Review "IPX and TCP/IP."*

5 **C.** Remember that the process used for Windows 9*x* clients isn't the same for Windows 2000 Professional clients. *Review "Installing and configuring TCP/IP."*

6 **A, B,** and **C.** The exam expects you to know the answers to this question — so you'd better remember this. *Review "Configuring TCP/IP."*

7 **B.** Know each of the utilities and protocols listed as answers to this question for the exam; know when each is applied and why. *Review "Configuring a UNIX/Linux client."*

8 **C.** You're likely to encounter an exam question that expects you to know this answer, so know it! *Review "Setting Up an Apple Client on a Windows Network."*

9 **C.** Make sure you know the purpose of disaster recovery and when it is done for the exam. *Review "Recovering from Disaster."*

10 **A.** You need to understand the differences in the purpose, application, and timing of fault tolerance, disaster recovery, and the use of a firewall. You will definitely see questions on the exam about these three things. *Review "Building in Fault Tolerance."*

Chapter 7: Network Support and Troubleshooting

Exam Objectives

✔ Using standard troubleshooting methods

✔ Isolating common network problems

✔ Troubleshooting with TCP/IP utilities

✔ Verifying the IP network with TCP/IP utilities

*D*epending on your outlook and what part of the network administration job you like, troubleshooting network problems is either what you love or what you hate about networks. No network administrators have mixed feelings about this job; everyone has an opinion one way or the other. Those who enjoy troubleshooting claim it's an art; those who don't enjoy it claim they spend too much time worrying about trivial matters. The enjoyment of solving the puzzle of why a workstation, server, or entire network is malfunctioning — especially when the solution is exactly right — is why some network administrators do the job. Or is it the money?

Regardless of how you feel about it, troubleshooting is a fact of networking life, and you must do it all too often. Networks usually combine a wide variety of hardware and software technologies and vendors to create the perfect environment for conflicts. (Have you ever noticed that networks have a strange habit of breaking down just when a user wants to perform or access something very important? It could very well be a conspiracy.)

Troubleshooting network problems is such a large and important part of the network administrator's job that the Network+ test allocates over 30 percent of the test to what it calls *Network Support*, making it one of the two top areas of the exam. The tools, resources, and procedures described in this chapter provide you all the troubleshooting-related information that you need to know for the test.

Troubleshooting and the Network+ Exam

The Network+ exam attempts to measure your problem-solving abilities along with how well you can identify and isolate a problem. To this end, this chapter reviews systematic procedures you should use to determine the source of a problem, decide on a response, and carry out the appropriate corrective action.

On the exam, expect to see four basic types of questions about troubleshooting:

✦ Content questions that ask about the steps of a systematic approach to troubleshooting and fixing network problems.

✦ Course-of-action questions that describe a situation and the steps performed so far. Your task is to pick the action that's most appropriate in the given situation.

✦ Troubleshooting questions that describe the symptoms of a network problem and ask you to identify the next network resource or element to check.

✦ Scenarios that require you to identify the likely source of a network connectivity problem and the troubleshooting tools you apply to verify the problem source.

Using a Systematic Approach to Network Problems

The Network+ exam objectives offer an eight-step systematic approach for troubleshooting network problems:

1. **Identify the symptoms:** In most situations, the symptoms of the problem clearly identify the source of the problem. However, before you jump in and merely tell the user to reboot his or her workstation, you may want to investigate a bit further — are other areas of the network affected?

2. **Identify the area of the network affected:** After you know all the symptoms (or at least all you can identify), you should isolate the part of the network being affected by a particular problem. With luck, it will be only one workstation or segment — occasionally, however, a problem that affects the entire network may actually be easier to solve.

3. **Identify any recently applied network changes:** Typically, things just don't go south unless a change is made to something. One of the reasons documenting network changes is so important (as we describe in Step 8) is so that you can easily identify the last change made to the network or a workstation. Unfortunately, problems created by a change to a network may not show up immediately — and it's possible that you may not have made the change yourself.

4. **Choose the problem source most likely causing the problem:** In many cases, more than one network element can cause a problem. You must apply your vast knowledge of networking hardware and software to pick the condition or element *most likely* creating the problem you're troubleshooting.

5. **Implement the corrective action:** In a process not to be confused with trial-and-error, you apply the solution you believe will correct the situation.

6. **Test the correction:** Verify that the correction you applied actually solved the problem. The testing should include a process that attempts to re-create the problem after you've made the correction. If you can't get the problem to emerge again while your solution is in place, you've made the right choice.

7. **Analyze the potential effects of the solution:** Your testing should include verifying that the corrective action doesn't *cause* future problems on the network. In many cases, any change made to a network can have a ripple effect and cause problems in other areas.

8. **Document, document, document:** All the way through the troubleshooting and correction processes, you should write down exactly what's going on. If you document as you go, this task won't loom quite as large after you complete your testing. Document every problem, large or small, and exactly what you did to fix it. Most problems do happen again, and your troubleshooting documentation may save you, or your replacement, time and trouble.

Finding the Source of a Problem

Network users report a significant number of network troubles. The range of problems that users report is directly related to the range of network and computer knowledge and experience of the users themselves. Complaints and questions such as "The network is slow today," "I can't log on to the server," or "Is the network down?" are commonplace, and we're sure you recognize them. These questions, though seemingly easy to remedy, may be the catalyst of a major system fix that you hadn't known was needed.

The obvious first place to look for the source of a problem is with (or at least in the vicinity of) the person reporting it. You know the saying about the skunk smelling its own scent first? This process is like that, and you need to proceed politely — because, in effect, you're telling the skunk that it stinks. The first tool to pull out of your bag is your interpersonal skills.

Eliminating user errors: The impossible dream

Your first action is to eliminate any user errors as the cause of the problem. As we're sure you're aware, most reported problems are user errors, or what we ascribe to user-training problems. Politely ask the user what he or she was doing when the error happened and to retrace the steps used (keystrokes and mouse actions). If the user is nearby, visit the user personally. If (as is becoming commonplace) the user is remotely located, follow these steps:

**Book IV
Chapter 7**

**Network Support
and Troubleshooting**

1. Ask another user on an equivalent workstation to perform the same action.

2. Ask another user to perform the same action on the original user's workstation.

3. Verify that the users performing the task are using the appropriate (or the most efficient) procedure.

4. Determine whether the users are using the appropriate versions of the hardware and software required for the action being performed.

Simply restarting the Windows computer can solve many user problems. Even before you begin your troubleshooting process, you may want to have the user reboot his or her computer.

If it isn't the user, it must be . . .

For the Network+ test, you need to know the various network elements that may cause a network problem and how each element manifests itself. Some of the more common contributors to network problems are

✦ **Account names and passwords:** Not all logon problems are system problems. Users may simply forget their usernames or passwords. Even the network administrator (although much less likely to do so) may enter a username and password incorrectly.

✦ **Access rights and permissions:** Even if users can log on to the network, the problem may be that they can't access files, folders, or directories they think they need. This problem may show up if a username changes, the user changes jobs, or if the network administrator recently added or reorganized user accounts or groups.

✦ **Faulty network media:** If network media (cabling) is installed correctly, it usually doesn't suddenly go bad. More likely, improper installation or configuration of connectors and connectivity devices — such as hubs, repeaters, and patch panels — cause intermittent problems that later manifest as a connection failure to a single workstation, workgroup, or network segment. However, the wrong cable (rolled versus straight, for example) can cause some immediate network problems.

✦ **Network configuration:** Another reason that connections to network resources, e-mail, or the Internet have problems is that the configuration may have changed. Network configurations don't change by themselves, but they can be inadvertently changed by other administrative changes. Configuration areas that can affect network operations are DNS (Domain Name System), DHCP (Dynamic Host Configuration Protocol), WINS (Windows Internet Naming Service), and hosts file designations.

✦ **Network servers:** The network's servers can potentially cause a wide variety of problems on the network. If the network's shared resources are no longer available, or users cannot log on or access e-mail, or Internet access suddenly stops, the problem is most likely on a network server or one of its connections.

+ **Physical conditions:** The physical environment includes environmental conditions, such as heat, cold, humidity (or the lack of it), or dust. The outside environment can also affect network operations — for example, thunderstorms, humidity levels, and other outside weather or natural phenomena, such as earthquakes, tornadoes, and so on. The quality and stability of the power source is another consideration. Physical conditions can directly affect the operation of the network, especially if they change rapidly. Of the conditions listed, power is most likely where the problems manifest themselves.

+ **Viruses:** If a user's workstation or a server suddenly cannot boot up, or if files are becoming corrupted, a virus is the likely cause — and immediate action is required.

Looking for Physical and Logical Indicators

In any network troubleshooting situation, physical or logical indicators are always present to help you figure out what's happening (or not happening, as the case may be). In Westerns and jungle movies, the native guides can always determine the day and time that a person walked by a bush — along with that person's shoe and hat size and date of birth — by looking at bent and broken twigs. If you know where to look and what to look for, you can find some bent twigs on the network to help you determine a problem's cause. We don't mean that literally. If you actually do have twigs in your network, you really need to do some housekeeping. (It does give a completely new meaning to the term *cable plant,* doesn't it?)

Checking out physical connections

Some of the more telling indicators available to you on the network are the little *link lights* (usually green or amber) on the network-connectivity devices — NICs (network interface cards), hubs, switches, and so on. Link lights indicate when a connection is working from one point to another. Most network devices have link lights in one form or another.

Should you run into a question about connection problems, consider the use of link lights on Physical-layer devices. After you've installed a workstation — or if a user reports that he or she cannot connect to the network — you should check the link lights on the face of the network adapter (NIC) to see if the workstation is seeing the network media.

A fairly complex network can have a variety of possible failure points. On the Network+ exam, you need to be able to identify possible network failure points from sample network diagrams, like the one shown in Figure 7-1.

**Book IV
Chapter 7**

Network Support and Troubleshooting

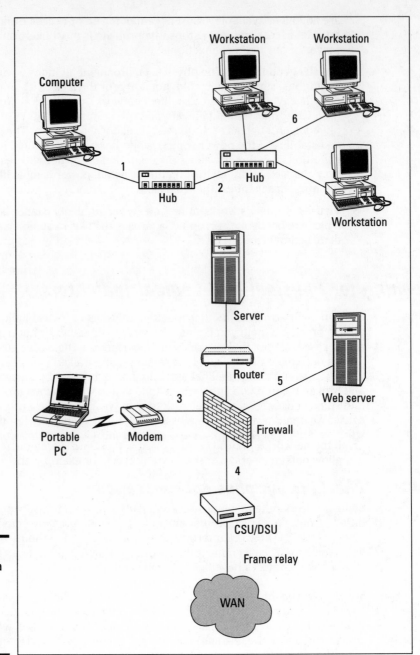

Figure 7-1:
Points on a
network
where
problems
commonly
occur.

On Figure 7-1, we've numbered a few of the possible points of physical or configuration failure. They are as follows:

1. To connect a computer workstation to a hub, a straight cable is used. If, for some reason, a *rolled* cable (one that has the send and receive wires crossed and is also called a *crossover* cable) is used, the hub won't see the computer, and the computer won't be able to connect to the network. Another problem could be that the computer is connected erroneously into a rolled (crossed or stack) port, which is used to connect one hub into another or to another network device.

2. Connecting one hub to another (or to any other network device) requires the use of a rolled cable. If a straight cable is used, any devices connected to the incoming device can't see the network, and vice versa.

3. If a computer is connecting to the network through a modem, a variety of configuration problems could prevent physical connection and block the ability to interact with the network. Typically, the problem is with the configuration in the dial-up settings of the computer, but it may also be in the serial cable or connection of the modem to the server or firewall if the access is via a VPN (virtual private network).

4. If Frame Relay service is used to connect to the WAN or the Internet, a CSU/DSU (channel service unit/data service unit) is required. If the connecting cable from the CSU/DSU to the next inline networking device is not properly connected, the LAN can't see the WAN. The same holds true for other WAN services that require interface devices, such as xDSL, ISDN (Integrated Services Digital Network), or SMDS (Switched Multimegabit Data Service). The range of line-limited services (such as xDSL) could also introduce network-access issues.

5. If the network's firewall is configured with a DMZ (demilitarized zone) to allow outside users to access a Web server, for example, the permit/deny configuration on the firewall could be letting in the wrong users and blocking the right ones.

6. Each type of cable media has a maximum segment length (100 meters for copper twisted pair). If the actual cable (including all cable pieces between two points) exceeds the maximum length, a workstation may have intermittent access problems — or fail to connect altogether.

Checking the readout

Other physical indicators that help you troubleshoot a network problem are error-code or message displays. The workstation operating system may display a message that indicates that the user can't log on because the domain server is unavailable to verify the username and password. This message is a surefire clue that a connection problem exists, or that the domain controller or server for the workstation isn't operating correctly, if at all.

**Book IV
Chapter 7**

**Network Support
and Troubleshooting**

Some higher-end network devices, such as routers, switches, or bridges, also have error displays to indicate a fault. More commonly, these devices have only an alarm light to indicate a problem, but some have little green screens, like copiers have, to display error codes and messages. Of course, you must have the manual memorized (or at least very handy) to know what the code means. In most cases, you can bet that if an error light or a code is displayed, you have a problem.

Logs, alerts, events, and other records

When network, workstation, or server problems occur, in most cases they're recorded as logical indicators in a log file. Most network operating systems, including Windows NT and NetWare, create and constantly update system actions, events, alerts, and errors as they're reflected in log files. The three general types of log files are as follows:

✦ **Application log files:** Contain events, messages, and errors posted by network applications and services

✦ **Security log files:** Contain security-related events and alerts generated by administrator-enabled auditing services of the NOS

✦ **System log files:** Contain messages, events, and errors posted by the NOS internal services and drivers

If you don't use them, generating endless log files wastes system resources *and* important information about the network's performance. Windows NOS systems (Windows NT and 2000) have a special tool, the Event Viewer, which enables you to (what else?) view log file events. The Windows NT Event Viewer has a built-in filter to help you select events from a particular time, date, workstation, device, segment, domain, and so on, rather than perusing all the log files.

Looking at logical connections

As we describe earlier in the section "Using a Systematic Approach to Network Problems," you need to analyze any recent network changes for their possible effect on the network. Moving a workstation or creating a new network segment can alter the existing setup or configuration of the network, especially in three network service areas:

✦ **DHCP:** Adding a workstation to a network can specify more IP addresses than the maximum number available in the DHCP pool. In this case, a user may not be able to connect or function on the network until another user logs off. To solve this problem, you may need to reconfigure the DHCP settings. Another solution may be to use one of the network utilities to release or renew the workstation's DHCP assigned configuration.

✦ **DNS:** If for some reason the network DNS server IP address has changed for all or part of a LAN, a workstation may not be able to reach beyond the local network until its DNS settings are also changed. DNS can also be the problem if a new Internet domain is launched and the world cannot find it. It does take some time to affect a DNS database addition, but working with your ISP or forcing the change yourself typically solves the problem.

✦ **WINS:** Problems with computer names are typically attributable to bad information in the WINS database. If a user can't find a resource on the local or wide area network, the WINS data should be reviewed.

Eliminating bottlenecks

We're sure you know the term *bottleneck* (a constricting point). A *network bottleneck* is any place in the network where a device restricts the network from operating at optimal performance levels. Every system has a bottleneck or two. The art of performance-tuning a network is finding and eliminating bottlenecks. However, technically, when you find and eliminate one bottleneck, another one appears instantly. Bottlenecks create and guarantee network administrator job security.

Eliminating a bottleneck may require adding more memory, a faster hard drive, faster NICs, more processors, or the like. However, after you eliminate the more serious bottlenecks on a network, you can still find some performance areas on a network to improve or fine-tune.

You can improve performance on many areas of the network by improving or implementing the following:

✦ **Disk caching:** This feature reduces the amount of disk I/O traffic on the system. Frequently accessed data is stored in physical memory, eliminating unnecessary I/O activity.

✦ **Multiprocessors:** Upgrading a server to multiple microprocessors enables the NOS to take advantage of multiprocessing capabilities. Applications don't have to compete for processor time on a system that supports multiprocessors, so multiprocessors enable a server to run applications faster. However, before adding a second or third multiprocessor to a system, verify that the motherboard, BIOS, and operating system can support multiple processors. The operating system, for example, absolutely must have Synchronous Multiprocessing (SMP) or Asynchronous Multiprocessing (AMP) support.

✦ **Physical memory:** Network operating systems that use smaller physical memory page sizes tend to reduce the problem of memory fragmentation and increase the amount of memory available to applications. For example, NetWare is very memory-dependent to support larger hard disk drives and Windows operating systems are just generally memory hogs. Adding more memory to a server can often improve its performance.

✦ **Virtual memory:** You distribute virtual memory swap files (reserved portions of the hard disk used exclusively for extending RAM) across several logical disk drives to increase the overall memory available to the server. Although the virtual memory process can effectively increase memory, it can also create another kind of bottleneck. Depending on the situation, distributing virtual memory swap files across two or more *physical* disk drives can improve a server's perform-ance; distributing such swap files across *logical* drives won't improve performance.

Performance monitoring

An integral step of performance tuning is *performance monitoring*, which tracks the usage of resources by network components and applications. Performance monitoring is an excellent method for determining just where bottlenecks and utilization problems are present on a system. After you identify them, you can improve or eliminate these problems.

You can use tools such as Windows Performance Monitor to track and report a variety of system resources, including

✦ Bottlenecks in CPU, memory, disk I/O, or network I/O activities

✦ Utilization trends on certain devices for different periods of time

✦ The impact of changes to system configurations or upgrades

✦ The system's real-time performance

Isolating Network Problems

Here is a brief overview of the different categories of network tools that help you isolate a network problem:

✦ **Network monitors:** These software packages track and report all or a certain portion of a network's traffic. Network monitors track network traffic by packet types, errors, or traffic to and from a certain computer.

✦ **NOS event and alert logs:** Whereas the three preceding categories are physical devices, this category is data-based and software-oriented. Most network operating systems (NOSs) maintain log files in which they record system events and alerts set by the administrator. You use reporting tools to display the log file contents for analysis purposes.

✦ **Physical media testers:** This category of tools includes digital volt-meters (DVM), time-domain reflectometers (TDR), tone generators, oscilloscopes, and advanced cable testers. These devices help you find and isolate problems at the Physical level of the network.

✦ **Protocol analyzers:** This category of network troubleshooting devices, which are also called *network analyzers,* enables you to evaluate the overall condition of the network by monitoring all network traffic. Protocol analyzers are commonly used to determine problems in the Network layer's operations.

Vendors, technical groups, and users provide a wide variety of information and advice on the Internet and World Wide Web that may save you troubleshooting time and effort. Before tackling a new and difficult troubleshooting project, you may want to check the Web for related information.

Applying Vendor Updates and Making Repairs

Unfortunately, an operating network can be much like a house of cards — making even the simplest change can upset the network's operations. Most of the changes to a network are made at the workstation as users change their hardware and software needs. Each workstation change can have adverse effects on the network and the workstation.

Errors caused by changes at the workstation level

You can expect to see at least one question on the Network+ test that deals with errors introduced into a network by changes made at a workstation. Changes at the workstation level can introduce four types of network problems:

✦ **Changes to the logon procedure:** New software may cause changes to the boot or logon procedures used at the workstation. In this case, you should inform the user of the changes and train that person to connect to the network successfully.

✦ **The network client software is missing a key element:** Installing new application software in the Windows environment can mean that older or newer versions of network-related software can be installed over any versions that are already on the system. Common victims in software installations are .DLL files, which are shared by many Windows-based programs. In the process of the installation, older or incompatible .DLL files can overlay them.

✦ **Unable to connect to the network:** A new network interface card (NIC) that isn't properly configured or is incompatible with the network media can prevent the workstation from connecting to the network. Also, if the user's network account name or password is configured incorrectly, the user will have difficulty connecting.

✦ **Workstation does not boot:** New hardware installed incorrectly may prevent the workstation from booting. In some network situations, this problem can affect other users relying on shared resources that are on or connected to the workstation.

Errors caused by changes at the network level

You should carefully analyze vendor updates to network hardware and software before you apply them to your network. After you decide to make the changes, however, you must be alert to their possible effects on the network and its workstations. You should thoroughly test all network updates and upgrades before releasing them for network operations — particularly if you're installing new Layer 3 (network) equipment such as a router, firewall, switch, or the like.

A few of the problems that may arise from changes made at the server or network level are

✦ **Loss of Internet access:** The network is not properly configured to see a new router, firewall, switch, DNS, or other Internet access device. Network users will likely report this problem.

✦ **User cannot log on:** Required network services aren't starting up or the connection to the user is linking end to end. A new NIC in the server or a new connectivity device, such as a hub or switch, is not properly configured or connected.

✦ **Missing segments:** If several users on a newly created network segment are reporting problems, more than likely you have a problem with configuration or addressing in the router or bridge creating the segment — or on the server.

Remember that a *segment* is a subset of a network created by the insertion of a router, switch, or bridge. Another way to view a segment is that by itself, it doesn't contain a router or bridge. You're likely to be asked to identify a segment by choosing it from a diagram. Just look for a group of workstations separated from the server by a router, switch, or bridge.

Other common sources of network errors

Experience is probably the best tool you have for recognizing common network errors. Eventually, as you gain experience with a network, you can recognize common errors and know their solutions without performing many, if any, tests. For example, when a group of users, all of whom are connected to a certain hub, report a loss of network connectivity, you may recognize that the hub needs to be reset. Because you've been religiously writing these things down, you know the problem is now happening quite frequently.

Here are some troubleshooting situations that you should be familiar with for the Network+ exam:

✦ **Installation problems:** If server or client software is installed improperly, it can cause unpredictable errors that may be hard to replicate, which is always a pain. When problems occur on a network server or client workstation immediately after you install new software, guess where you should look first?

✦ **Boot failures:** The range of problems that show up as boot failures would be too long a list to include here. The Network+ exam asks about two kinds of boot failures: system startup and virus-related failures. (A corrupted disk, bad video driver, or even a stuck key on the keyboard can cause a system startup problem, and must be overcome to get a user connected — but these are not usually *network* problems.) The virus-related failure may be caused by a corrupted master boot record or other essential system resources.

✦ **Cabling:** The vast majority of network problems (and headaches) happen on the OSI model's Physical layer. The problems are usually in the NIC, cabling, or connectors. A problem in the Physical layer must be first isolated to a particular computer or network segment. One way to eliminate the computer (including its NIC) as a suspect is to plug a different computer, like a notebook, onto the cable and see if you can log on and transfer files. If you can't log on, the problem is the cable. If you can log on, the original computer is the problem.

✦ **Performance issues:** You can easily solve performance issues — such as excessive traffic, cabling failures, and poorly operating hubs, routers, or switches — after you identify them. Excessive traffic may require segmentation of the network, and you can reconfigure bad devices and replace bad cable.

✦ **Power:** Expect to see some questions on the Network+ exam that relate to network power problems. Power-related problems are often difficult to isolate because they show up as hardware-operation troubles. Even with a surge suppressor or UPS in use, network servers and clients face other power-related problems. For example, if a workstation works fine during daylight hours (when the lights are off) but performs badly at night (when the lights are on), you should suspect that the voltage on the computer's line is dropping too low when the room lights are on for proper operation.

✦ **Hardware changes:** Changing hardware components can be no less problematic than adding new software. If a workstation — or a network — fails immediately after you add new hardware devices to the network, the network body is likely rejecting its new organ. However, some faults may take a while to show up. When a problem occurs, your lineup of suspects should always include the last hardware change made to the network.

✦ **Software updates:** Vendor updates, upgrades, or patches that are intended to solve current or future problems can and do cause system problems at times. If a system update or patch is applied, you should test the system each step of the way — and verify that the changes work. You may need to restore a backup if you can't fix the problem easily.

You can resolve most network-related problems on a workstation or client computer by merely restarting the workstation and having the user log on to the network.

Isolating Common Network Problems

Solving a problem that shows up on two workstations is far easier than solving one that occurs randomly across 100 network workstations and in different segments. By isolating the problem to its source, most of the network can continue to operate while you're testing.

Here are some common methods used to isolate network problems:

✦ **Same connection, different workstation test:** If a different computer doesn't have the problem when it's attached to the original workstation's cable, the problem is in the original workstation. Otherwise, the problem is in the network.

✦ **Same workstation, different connection test:** If the problem reoccurs when the original workstation is connected to a different line, the problem is in the workstation. Otherwise, the problem is in the original connection.

✦ **Replacing components test:** If the problem is thought to be in the connectivity of the workstation, begin replacing the components that are most likely causing the problem, including the NIC, patch cords, patch panel connection, hubs, and so on. After you resolve the problem, independently test the component that is isolated as the cause.

✦ **The terminator test:** On thinnet coax networks (10Base2), you can use terminators to isolate a workstation by removing the network cable from one side of its BNC-T connector and replacing the cable with a terminator. If the network problem goes away, you've found the source of the problem.

Troubleshooting Utilities

TCP/IP includes utilities that determine whether and where a problem exists. The TCP/IP (and a Windows utility or two) can be used to find and diagnose specific network or workstation problems.

A number of questions on the exam require you to recognize from a diagram the output of several of the software utilities that can be used to troubleshoot network status or problems. The utilities for which you should know both the application and displays are

✦ **ARP:** The `ARP` command can be used to modify or display the current contents of the ARP (Address Resolution Protocol) cache on a computer. This is helpful in tracking down a faulty IP-address-to-Mac-address mapping in the ARP cache. To display the ARP cache, enter the following command:

```
arp -a
```

✦ **IPCONFIG:** The `IPCONFIG` command, which is a standard TCP/IP utility, is useful for displaying the current IP configuration of a workstation. It can also be used to diagnose DHCP problems. By default, `IPCONFIG` lists the IP address, subnet mask, and default gateway of a workstation's network adapter. To display the details of a computer's IP configuration (see Figure 7-2), enter this command:

```
ipconfig /all
```

Several versions of `IPCONFIG` are available, all of which provide you with essentially the same information. In Windows NT/2000/XP, the command `IPCONFIG` is executed from the command prompt. On a UNIX or Linux system, the command `IFCONFIG` is executed from the command prompt. On a NetWare system, the command-line command is `CONFIG`.

```
C:\WINNT\System32\cmd.exe

C:\>ipconfig /all

Windows 2000 IP Configuration

        Host Name . . . . . . . . . . . . : RONGILSTER
        Primary DNS Suffix  . . . . . . . :
        Node Type . . . . . . . . . . . . : Hybrid
        IP Routing Enabled. . . . . . . . : No
        WINS Proxy Enabled. . . . . . . . : No

Ethernet adapter Local Area Connection:

        Media State . . . . . . . . . . . : Cable Disconnected
        Description . . . . . . . . . . . : Xircom CreditCard Ethernet Adapter 1
0/100
        Physical Address. . . . . . . . . : 00-10-A4-EC-B0-46

PPP adapter Verizon Internet-GTE:

        Connection-specific DNS Suffix  . :
        Description . . . . . . . . . . . : WAN (PPP/SLIP) Interface
        Physical Address. . . . . . . . . : 00-53-45-00-00-00
        DHCP Enabled. . . . . . . . . . . : No
        IP Address. . . . . . . . . . . . : 4.47.221.160
        Subnet Mask . . . . . . . . . . . : 255.255.255.255
        Default Gateway . . . . . . . . . : 4.47.221.160
        DNS Servers . . . . . . . . . . . : 4.2.2.1
                                            4.2.2.2
C:\>
```

Figure 7-2:
The display
produced by
the
IPCONFIG
utility.

✦ **NBTSTAT (NetBIOS on TCP/IP status):** The NBTSTAT utility (a Windows tool) is used to determine the cause of a connection failure to a specific server over NetBIOS connections. This command displays and verifies the computer names cache created and used by NetBIOS for forwarding TCP/IP packets over the network. NBTSTAT also troubleshoots problems in the Lmhosts (LAN Manager Hosts) file and other host files. NBTSTAT is used on Windows NT/2000/XP server-based networks running TCP/IP to display identifying information of a workstation or server (see Figure 7-3). It can be used to display the Mac address that corresponds to an IP address (or vice versa), or to display the NetBIOS names that have been recorded into the name-resolution services running on the network. The actual command you enter at a command prompt is

```
nbtstat -n
```

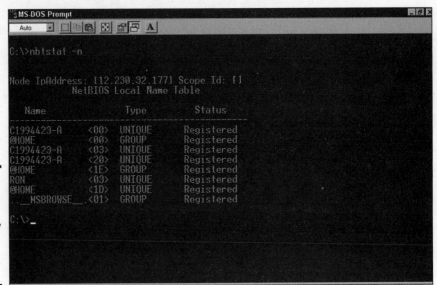

Figure 7-3: A sample of the output produced by the NBTSTAT utility.

✦ **NETSTAT (Network Statistics):** The NETSTAT utility, available on both Windows and UNIX systems, includes a number of display options that enable you to list statistics on an active network (see Figure 7-4). These options include active connections on a TCP/IP network, the status of Ethernet connections, and the current contents of the system's routing table. The command you enter on the command line is

```
netstat /a
```

The NETSTAT utility is used to test why a TCP/IP connection to a remote computer is not working properly. This utility displays the status of any activity on the TCP/UPD ports of a workstation. If any data is in the Sent or Received queues, chances are the connection is having problems. However, the problem could be caused by network delay, which should also be checked out.

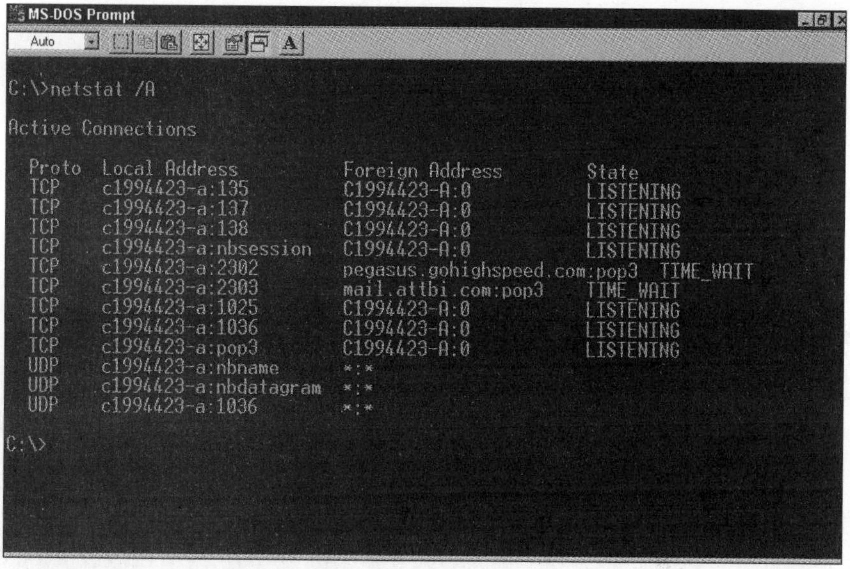

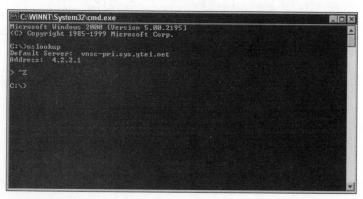

Figure 7-4:
The NETSTAT /A command displays information on active connections.

✦ **NSLOOKUP:** This command queries Internet domain name servers to display information about various hosts and domains or to list the hosts in a domain. Figure 7-5 shows the output of the NSLOOKUP command. The command used at the command prompt is

    nslookup

Figure 7-5:
The output of the NSLOOKUP utility produced on a Windows 2000 system.

✦ **PING:** The TCP/IP PING utility is used to determine if a local computer can reach a particular IP address (local or remote) over the network. PING sends out a 32-byte ICMP (Internet Control Message Protocol) echo request that should generate an echo response message from the target site. Figure 7-6 shows the display produced by PING. The command you enter should be something like this:

```
ping 4.56.78.1
```

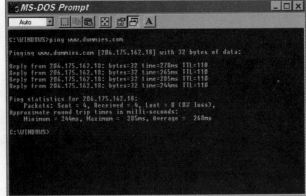

Figure 7-6:
A sample of the results produced by the PING utility.

✦ **TRACERT:** This TCP/IP utility (see Figure 7-7) is used to track the path of a forwarded packet from router to router between a local computer and a remote destination. This utility is often used to determine why a remote host (using its domain or IP address) cannot be accessed. The command entered is something like this:

```
tracert 4.47.220.13
```

This utility is most commonly used to pinpoint problems on a TCP/IP path. Like PING, TRACERT uses ICMP echo request packets to follow the route that packets use to reach a certain destination. Although PING can tell you whether a destination address is good, TRACERT also displays the hops that a packet has to make, along with the TTL (Time-to-Live) values of each hop.

Not all network firewalls permit TRACERT (or PING) to trace through the firewall, and the echo requests sent out by TRACERT and PING may appear to dead-end there.

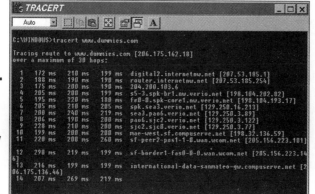

Figure 7-7:
A sample of the output produced by the TRACERT utility.

✦ **WINIPCFG:** On Windows 98 (and later) systems, another utility you can use to view the IP configuration (refer to Figure 7-8) is the WINIPCFG command. If a computer has more than one network adapter, you can choose which NIC you want to view from a pull-down list on the display. WINIPCFG can also be used to manage the DHCP settings for a workstation. To display the IP configuration on a Windows 9*x* system, enter the following command in the Run box on the Start menu:

```
winipcfg
```

Figure 7-8:
The dialog box displayed by WINIPCFG on a Windows 98 system.

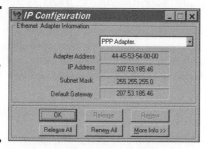

Using SNMP to manage a network

Another TCP/IP tool that can be applied to manage (and troubleshoot) a network is the Simple Network Management Protocol (SNMP). SNMP can save you time and effort when performing network configuration and maintenance tasks. Any network administrator who has ever configured a router, bridge, or switch in another part of a building, campus, town, state, or country — and wasted a goodly amount of time getting to it — can fully appreciate the benefits of SNMP.

SNMP provides a client/server environment for network management and monitoring — and is endorsed and supported by virtually every network equipment manufacturer and software provider.

SNMP levels, agents, and communities

SNMP works at two levels: the central management system and the management information base (MIB). The central management system software runs on the central server, and the MIB software runs on each managed device. The SNMP structure includes

✦ **SNMP manager:** This software collects messages from SNMP agents and enables administrators to view and configure network devices from a central location.

Any computer running the SNMP management software is an SNMP management system. Most SNMP management systems collect data on network devices, which can be viewed as text or graphics. SNMP management data is collected from SNMP agents by using a set of three commands:

- **Get:** Used to request a specific fixed or variable value, such as the number of maximum users or the current CPU utilization rate.

- **Get-next:** Used immediately after a get command to retrieve the next value in sequence following the get command.

- **Set:** Used to send a configuration value to a managed device.

✦ **SNMP agent:** This software monitors and communicates the activities of network devices. SNMP agents respond to requests from the central management system and report any errors or problems. SNMP uses a mechanism called a *trap* to capture and send information back to the management system.

Any network device running SNMP agent software is an SNMP agent.

✦ **SNMP communities:** These logical groups (those created by the administrator, as opposed to those that exist physically) of managers and agents formed to serve the needs of an individual network. An SNMP community groups certain managers with certain agents, which limits the number of managers to which the agent must send its traps. SNMP communities are often created as a security precaution because they limit SNMP access to a network segment.

A network administrator may want to cluster certain SNMP managers and agents for any of the following reasons:

- To limit the number of managers to which agents must respond.

- To limit the number of agents that managers control.

- To restrict the SNMP access points to a system. The public SNMP community that is created by default may have additional access points, but when managers are clustered, you have more control over which devices can access the system.

Management information bases (MIBs)

Every SNMP-managed device has a table called a *management information base* (MIB) that contains information on what that device can do. The table contains a list of the network management information and objects used by SNMP to manage, configure, and interact with the device.

Different systems support different MIBs. Several standard MIBs are found on Windows-based systems, including

✦ **Internet II MIB:** This standard Internet MIB contains a standard set of objects used for fault tolerance and system management in an Internet environment.

✦ **DHCP MIB:** This standard MIB manages and monitors Dynamic Host Control Protocol (DHCP) activities.

✦ **WINS MIB:** Windows NT/2000 enables an SNMP management system to monitor the Windows Internet Name Server service.

The Troubleshooting Toolkit

For all you troubleshooting nerds who are wondering when we're going to talk about tools that you hold in your hands or wear on a tool belt — with apologies to Tim Allen — it's Tool Time! Network troubleshooting hardware tools cover a wide range of uses and functions, ranging from voltage testers to devices that diagnose a network's overall health.

Here are some tools mentioned on the Network+ test:

✦ **Cable testers:** A cable tester not only determines if any breaks are in a cable, but also tells you everything about the cable, including performance data, such as frame counts, packet collisions, broadcast storms, and more.

✦ **Crossover cable:** This network cable crosses the transmit and receive wires and eliminates the need for a hub when connecting two computers. Crossover cables enable you to test the computer in a peer-to-peer fashion off the network. You also use them to connect hubs and switches using MID-X connections.

✦ **Digital voltmeter (DVM):** A DVM measures a cable's continuity and determines if any breaks are in the cable. It can also indicate whether a coaxial cable has been crushed and whether its sheathing is in contact with the copper core wire.

✦ **Hardware loopback plug:** A *loopback test* checks to see whether an NIC can communicate with the network and whether the cable and interfaces are working. It works very similarly to the way PING works over the network — sending out an echo signal and then treating the incoming echo as an incoming signal.

✦ **Protocol analyzers:** The most advanced tool in the troubleshooting tool belt is the protocol analyzer. Protocol analyzers monitor network traffic in real time, capturing network packets and decoding them to track network performance and determine the cause of network problems and bottlenecks. Protocol analyzers commonly include another major tool — a time-domain reflectometer (TDR) — as well. Popular protocol analyzers include the Internet Advisor (Hewlett Packard), the Sniffer (Network Associates), and the Network Probe (Network Communications Corporation). Microsoft's Network Monitor is a lightweight protocol analyzer. (It has fewer features than the others.)

✦ **Time-domain reflectometer (TDR):** You use this tool to determine whether a cable has a break or short circuit. A TDR has some advantages over a DVM — for example, a TDR can measure the distance from itself to a detected break. If you study the name of this device, it tells you how this task is done: The TDR measures how long it takes a signal to reflect back and then computes the distance (according to cable type).

✦ **Tone generator and tone locator (fox and hound):** These two devices are compact, handheld instruments. The tone generator generates a tracer tone down a wire that can be heard by an inductive amplifier (the tone locator) to locate the wire. If you've ever tried to locate a single wire in the bundle of spaghetti usually located in the floor or ceiling, you'll appreciate this set of tools. Look for a question on the exam that applies a tone generator to test wire continuity.

Expect to be asked about the pin configuration of an RJ-45 loopback plug. As shown in Figure 7-9, pins 1 and 5 are looped together, and pins 2 and 4 are looped together. This configuration allows the send signal to be looped back and received on the same port.

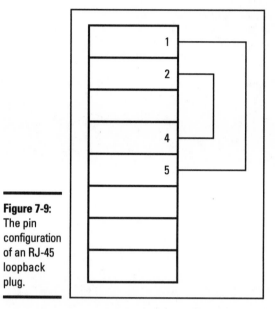

Figure 7-9:
The pin
configuration
of an RJ-45
loopback
plug.

Prep Test

1 A network device that supports SNMP monitoring and has software to communicate its activity to an SNMP server is an

A ○ SNMP agent.

B ○ SNMP manager.

C ○ SNMP community.

D ○ SNMP node.

2 To verify that an IP address is a valid address and can be reached from a particular workstation, which TCP/IP utility should you use?

A ○ TRACERT

B ○ PING

C ○ ROUTE

D ○ IPCONFIG

3 The Windows NT/2000/XP TCP/IP utility used to display a computer's host name, DNS server, MAC address, IP address, DHCP status, subnet mask, and other configuration details is

A ○ TRACERT.

B ○ PING.

C ○ WINIPCFG.

D ○ IPCONFIG.

4 Which TCP/IP utility is commonly used to locate path problems between a source and a destination IP address?

A ○ TRACERT

B ○ PING

C ○ ROUTE

D ○ IPCONFIG

5 After a recent reorganization in which many people moved their computers to new offices, a workstation is not functioning properly. The network is a 10BaseT Ethernet network with workgroups arranged in hubs. Which of the following is likely to be causing the problem? (Choose two.)

A ❑ The hub is faulty.

B ❑ The NIC is using the wrong drivers.

C ❑ A cable has been damaged.

D ❑ The workstation isn't connected to the network.

6 A user contacts you to report an application error on his workstation. Which of the following could you use to isolate the user's workstation problem?

A ○ Ask the user to restart his computer.

B ○ Ask another user to perform the same action on the original user's computer.

C ○ Ask another user to perform a related action on an equivalent workstation.

D ○ Ask the user to reinstall the NIC in the workstation.

7 After installing a new version of a word-processing application, the NOS client fails to start up, giving the error, Bad or Missing .DLL file. What has likely caused this error?

A ○ The Windows client wasn't restarted.

B ○ The new software has installed an incompatible version of the missing file.

C ○ The NOS client is corrupted.

D ○ The NIC is faulty.

8 A workstation has been giving you fits. It seems to work just fine early in the day when the room lights are off, but later in the day, when the room lights are on, it has trouble connecting to the network or holding an established connection. What do you think is the problem?

A ○ The NIC should be replaced.

B ○ The room is cabled incorrectly.

C ○ Low-voltage power.

D ○ User error.

9 Which of the following are indicators that a workstation is connecting to the network and functioning properly? (Choose three.)

A ❑ Link light on the NIC

B ❑ User logon successful

C ❑ Username account in domain username database

D ❑ File transfer between workstation and server

10 Which device checks to see whether an NIC can communicate with a network and whether the cables and interfaces of a workstation are working?

A ○ Hardware loopback

B ○ PING

C ○ Tone generator

D ○ TDR

Answers

1 **A.** An SNMP agent is any network device running SNMP software that enables the device to maintain a management information base (MIB) about itself as well as report its activities to an SNMP server. *Review "SNMP levels, agents, and communities."*

2 **B.** PING works like an Internet equivalent of SONAR (the underwater detection system used in all the submarine movies); it sends out a signal that bounces back from a remote location. In this case, the echo indicates that the Internet location is there and operating. *See "Troubleshooting Utilities."*

3 **D.** IPCONFIG has a number of options and switches that can be used to alter its display, which can include virtually everything about a Windows NT/2000 computer's TCP/IP configuration. *Review "Troubleshooting Utilities."*

4 **A.** TRACERT displays address and timing information about each hop that an ICMP packet must take to reach the destination IP address entered on the command line. *Check out "Troubleshooting Utilities."*

5 **C and D.** If the network and the workstation functioned together before the move — and unless severe damage was introduced — the likely causes are that the workstation is not connected or, if it is connected, that the cabling was damaged in the move. *Review "Other common sources of network errors."*

6 **C.** Restarting the computer is more of a way to resolve problems than to isolate problems. To determine the scope of a problem, you must use the same actions on all workstations. In order to determine the scope of a problem, you must use the same actions on all workstations. *Review "Eliminating user errors: The impossible dream."*

7 **B.** This question, or one very close to it, is on the Network+ exam. When installing new software, you must be alert to possible network or workstation effects. *Review "Errors caused by changes at the workstation level."*

8 **C.** If a computer's performance coincides with an environmental situation — such as power on or off, heaters in use, the pop machine coming on, and so on — most likely the problem is in the environmental factors and not the computer. *Review "If it isn't the user, it must be...."*

9 **A, B,** and **D.** A username should always be in the domain user database, if valid. Link lights that are on indicate that the connection is established. Logging on and transferring data are two surefire ways to tell whether a connection is good. *Review "Troubleshooting and the Network+ Exam."*

10 **A.** You will encounter questions on the Network+ exam that differentiate loopback tests from hardware loopback devices. Lookback tests are performed by hardware loopback devices, so be careful that you know what's being asked on any loopback questions. *Review "The Troubleshooting Toolkit."*

Book V

The Server+ Exam

The 5th Wave   By Rich Tennant

JAWS OF LIFE

"Here's a little tip on disassembly that you won't find on the Server+ Certification test."

Contents at a Glance

Chapter 1: About the Server+ Exam

In This Chapter

✔ Checking out the format of the Server+ exam

✔ Knowing how to study: Preparing for the exam

✔ Scheduling and paying for the exam

CompTIA (the group that gave you A+, Network+, i-Net+, and more certification) has launched another of its job skills-related certification programs — the Server+ exam. This exam is designed to certify the knowledge and skills of the server and network technician who already has an A+ certification, or an equivalent IT (information technology) certification from companies such as Compaq, Novell, Microsoft, or Hewlett Packard, and at least 18 months of on-the-job experience with network servers. The Server+ exam assumes experience that includes installation, configuration, troubleshooting, and diagnosis of server hardware, as well as familiarity with the potential problems of network operating systems.

Passing the Server+ (#SK0-001) exam certifies to the world that you are a server and networking professional who possesses the knowledge required to perform a full range of server-related technical activities. The Server+ certification was developed by a team of subject-matter experts from around the world and is a global certification that has been endorsed by such companies as 3Com, Adaptec, IBM, Intel, Hewlett Packard, and StorageTek.

You'll find no other certification like the Server+. The first of its kind, it's brand- and platform-neutral. Products from Microsoft, Novell, and other manufacturers are referenced on the Server+ test, but only to represent what the server technician works with in the real world and to make the test a true measure of the server technician's overall knowledge.

Meeting the Objectives

The Server+ exam consists of 80 questions that cover seven specific knowledge areas of server-related technologies, as listed in Table 1-1. As is indicated by the percentage each area represents of the whole test, some areas are emphasized more than others, and accordingly the number of questions varies with this emphasis.

Table 1-1 lists and describes the seven major knowledge areas (called *domains* by CompTIA) of the Server+ exam, the topics within each major area, and the percentage (and number of questions) of the total test each area represents.

Table 1-1	Server+ Exam Knowledge Areas	
Domain	*Number of Questions*	*Percentage of Test*
1.0 Installation	13	17%
Performing preinstallation planning activities		
Installing hardware using ESD best practices		
2.0 Configuration	14	18%
Upgrading BIOS levels		
Configuring RAID storage		
Installing a NOS		
Configuring external peripherals		
Updating a NOS		
Updating hardware-specific device drivers		
Installing service tools		
Preparing a server baseline		
Documenting a server's configuration		
3.0 Upgrading	10	12%
Performing system backups		
Adding processors to a server		
Installing hard disk drives		
Upgrading system memory		
Upgrading the BIOS		
Upgrading device adapters		
Upgrading peripheral internal and external devices		
Upgrading system-monitoring agents		
Upgrading service tools		
Upgrading a UPS		
4.0 Proactive Maintenance	8	9%
Performing data backups		
Creating a server baseline and comparing system performance		
Setting SNMP thresholds		
Performing physical housekeeping		

Domain	Number of Questions	Percentage of Test
Performing hardware verification		
Establishing remote notification		
5.0 Environment	**4**	**5%**
Recognizing and reporting on physical security issues		
Recognizing and reporting on server room environmental issues		
6.0 Troubleshooting	**21**	**27%**
Determining the source of a problem		
Using diagnostic hardware and software tools and utilities		
Identifying bottlenecks		
Identifying and correcting configurations or upgrade problems		
Determining whether problem is related to hardware or software, or is virus related		
7.0 Disaster Recovery	**10**	**12%**
Planning for disaster recovery		
Restoring data from backup		

The exam includes questions about commonly used terminology, practices, components, and protocols, along with questions about little-known facts on obscure services, devices, or activities — an obvious attempt to separate the truly worthy from the pretenders.

The format of the Server+ exam is strictly multiple choice — questions that have one or more correct answers. If a question has multiple answers, you're told how many answers you need to choose. You'll see one or two pick-the-object-from-the-diagram questions, but no true-or-false questions or required-objective/optional-objective scenario questions (such as those found on the MCSE and CCNA exams).

Getting Certified

The first step toward getting certified is to contact either Prometric (www.prometric.com) or VUE (www.vue.com) — the testing authorities — and register to take the Server+ exam (Test #SK0-001). On these Web sites, you can locate a testing center near your home (or the vacation spot in which you want to celebrate after the test). You can register online or over the telephone (using a credit card) or mail them a check or money order (not a great option if you're in a hurry).

The second step is to study for the exam; you can make excellent progress by reading this book. See the section "Preparing for the Exam" later in this chapter for more on how to go about your studies.

The third, and final, step is to arrive at the test location and take the test. The test is online and interactive. It's very well designed, providing you with every possible opportunity to pass. Each question is presented on-screen, one at a time, in an easy-to-read format; help is always available. Unfortunately, you won't find any subject-matter help available on the test. If you don't know what a word means on the exam, you're stuck; you can't look it up.

You can use a check box to mark questions you would like to review later. In fact, you're allowed to review the entire test if you want. The test even goes so far as to mark any questions for which you didn't provide an answer (or enough answers). Contrary to what you may have heard or believe about certification tests, the folks who created the Server+ exam *want* you to pass, if you have the right knowledge. The test really attempts to eliminate itself as a barrier to that goal. (What a concept.)

Passing the Test

To become Server+ certified, you must score at least a 75% on the Server+ Certification examination. This means you must get 60 correct of the 80 questions on the exam. Think of it this way — you can miss, incorrectly interpret, misconstrue, or choke on 20 questions and still pass. The test is a straight-line test; it's not adaptive, and doesn't get harder or easier according to whether you get a question right or wrong. One bit of caution on the passing score: CompTIA has adjusted the passing score on its exams upward in the past as the test matures. So, if you plan to study just enough to get anything less than 100%, you should check the CompTIA Web site (www.comptia.org) for the current passing score before you complete your studies.

You have 90 minutes to complete the test — plenty of time to work through the entire test, with perhaps a little bit of time left for reviewing some troubling questions. However, you must also understand that when time is up, the test is over! Bam, zoom, no last-minute guesses — over; done; finis! So watch the time — in the upper-right corner of the screen — carefully.

One other thing about taking the test. The physical setup of the testing facility varies from site to site. The test centers are in training companies, community colleges, universities, and the like. Regardless of how the testing center is organized, you'll be assigned to a specific computer workstation to take the test. You're not allowed to take breaks, talk to anyone, or get up and move around. Many test centers have open microphones and video cameras in the room to monitor the test-takers. This is intended to prevent anyone from cheating or disturbing other test-takers. As strict as this all sounds, your best bet is to forget about it and plan on sitting at your work-station for the duration, quietly taking your exam, knowing everybody else is in the same boat.

Where to Go

The Server+ Certification examination is conducted by Prometric and VUE testing centers. Both have centers in literally thousands of locations world-wide. To schedule an appointment to take the Server+ test, go online or call one of these testing centers. Schedule your test at least two days before your desired test date — at a date, time, and location convenient for you. The test is not given only at specific times or dates. You pick the date, time, and place, subject to availability. Some testing sites are not available every day of the week, or even every month of the year; some have limited testing stations; and some offer testing during only certain hours of the day. Our point: The earlier you contact your testing center, the better. We recommend going online or calling as soon as you enter the final stages of your exam preparation.

Preparing for the Exam

The best way for you to prepare for the exam depends on *you*. Gilster's Law of Test Preparation is this: "You never can tell, and it all depends." You need to find the tools that work best for you. If you have a good deal of experience with servers, you may need only to bone up on certain areas. If you are new to servers, networking, or computing, you should delay this certification until you have completed the A+ certification. As it happens, an excellent book to use to prepare for that exam is *A+ Certification For Dummies*, 2nd Edition, by Ron Gilster (that's me), and published by Wiley Publishing.

However, if you're ready and able to proceed, get hold of as many sample tests as possible — and keep taking them until you pass consistently. The sample tests included on the CD with this book are a good starting point — but they shouldn't be the only sample tests you use if you're fairly inexperienced (or even if you have loads of experience, for that matter). You can easily locate a number of interactive study aids available — some for purchase and some free to download. The more of them you master, the better your preparation.

Chapter 2: Servers under the Microscope

Exam Objectives

✔ Identifying common server types

✔ Detailing the type and speed of the bus structures

✔ Defining processor stepping

✔ Explaining multiple processor server concepts

✔ Identifying the major features and functions of common NOS

✔ Explaining cache memory systems

There are as many types of servers as there are services that network users want to have supported on a network. Understanding the role a server is to play in a network should be your guide to the requirements of its hardware and software configuration. For the Server+ exam, you should understand the role played by the different server types, including when, where, and why you would use a particular server. A server can be set up to "serve" many different functions.

The configuration of a server should be chosen to support its function. This includes its bus structures, its multiprocessing capabilities, memory, chipset, and caching, among other hardware components and features. The Server+ exam doesn't expect you to be a systems engineer with a deep nanotechnology-level understanding of how exactly the processor, bus, RAM, and I/O devices interrelate and operate, but you do need to know the basics.

On the softer side of servers, the network operating system (NOS) is another essential component in configuring a server to meet the performance requirements dictated by a network's users. The services provided by the NOS can vary from simple file sharing to more advanced remote access support. The test doesn't expect you to be an expert with every NOS, but you should know the fundamental differences between them and the more common commands used to get around in each of them.

There Are Servers and There Are Servers

Depending on the type, topology, and purpose of a network, the word "server" can have several meanings. The following few sections should help to clear up the semantics and provide some insight as to what it is you need to know for the Server+ exam concerning servers and their roles in different situations.

In general usage, a *server* is a centralized computer that provides common services to network users. A server is typically thought of as a hardware component of a network when in reality, it is a specific piece of software, running on a centralized computer, which supports a specific application or set of services. However, that's not all of the story, so read on.

A server is not absolutely required to create a network. A *peer-to-peer*, or *peer-based*, network can be created without a server. Networks without servers are not a big topic on the Server+ exam, obviously, but you should understand how the lack of a server on a peer-based network (see Figure 2-1) relates to a client/server network and its server.

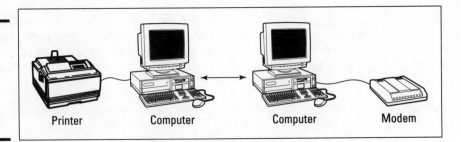

Figure 2-1:
A peer-to-peer network does not require a server.

Printer   Computer   Computer   Modem

As you can see in Figure 2-1, a peer-to-peer network allows users to share resources directly. Ron is able to share Curt's nifty new full-color laser printer, and Curt can share Ron's modem to connect to the Internet to check his stock portfolio. On a peer-based network, all shared resources are inside or attached to the client computers and are individually shared by their owners with the other users on the network.

Managing the permissions and passwords required to set up the sharing of resources among peer-based network users is quite a job for each of the network users. In effect, each user is the network administrator for his or her little part of the network. It didn't take long for people to figure out that peer-based networks can be too much work to maintain and administer.

Sharing on a Client/Server Network

A client/server network provides a centralized set of administrative services to network users. As shown in Figure 2-2, the network users are connected to the central server, in one form or another, and access shared resources through the network server. A central server controls the shared network resources under the management of a network administrator or a team of network administrators. Another important aspect of a centralized server is network security. Because all user accounts and their permissions are centralized, unauthorized users are easily blocked from accessing network resources.

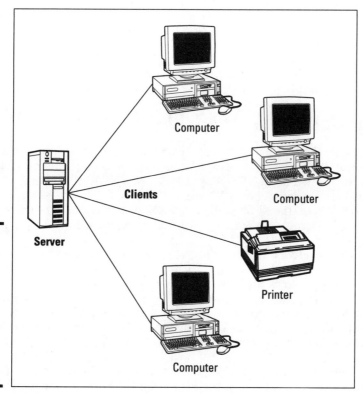

Figure 2-2:
A client/
server
network
shares
resources
under the
control of a
centralized
authority.

A client/server NOS provides user-level security to the network users. User-level security manages the access rights and permissions of the network resources and the access granted to the network users that is tied to each user's authenticating identifier, or username and password. Users cannot access network resources until they have been given permission individually or added to a group that has been assigned the appropriate permissions and rights.

Forming users into a *group* is a way to simplify a network's security management and administration. A group provides an easy way to assign access permissions by first creating a group and assigning it certain permissions and then adding the users to which you want to assign that specific set of permissions. For example, if the six people in Accounting all need the same access permissions, it is far easier to create a group named ACCOUNTING and add the six users to that group.

Differentiating the Majors

The current version of the Server+ exam unfortunately focuses on Microsoft Windows NT (which has many similarities to Windows 2000), but includes some questions on other major NOSes. You don't need to be an expert on all the major NOSes, but you do need to know the basics of each. To that end, the following sections give you just enough information to get by on the test — or in other words, just enough information for you to be dangerous.

Checking Out Windows NT/2000

The Server+ exam focuses mostly on the Microsoft network operating systems: Windows NT Server and Windows 2000 Server. Windows NT has two versions: Windows NT Server and Windows NT Workstation (the client OS you should know about). Windows 2000 also has two versions: Windows 2000 Server (the NOS) and Windows 2000 Professional (the client). Until the Server+ exam is updated, you won't see questions on Windows XP or .Net.

A *client-operating system* is one that is installed on a networked computer primarily to support the computing usage of the computer's user. Examples of client operating systems are Windows 9x, Windows 2000 Pro, Windows Me, UNIX/Linux, and OS/2. The latter two can be configured as either a client or a server. A client contrasts to a NOS in that the NOS is designed specifically to support the needs of the entire network and to provide centralized services, and a client is designed (in most cases) solely to support a user's PC.

All the Windows NT/2000 versions use TCP/IP as their native networking protocol. Remember that the NOS and the clients must all use the same protocols in order to communicate. A client that does not support TCP/IP is unable to connect to a Windows NT/2000 server.

Windows security accounts

Windows NOS applies security through user accounts and groups. The two types of user and group accounts used for administration are

+ **Local accounts:** Local users and groups are accounts that apply to each particular workstation or server. These accounts are created in a separate security database on the workstation or server, so the security settings that apply to the local users and groups have no influence with any other workstations or servers. The security for local users and groups pertains to resources on the local machine only.

+ **Global accounts:** Global users and groups are accounts that are created in the Security Account Manager (SAM) on the Primary Domain Controller (PDC). Unlike local user and group accounts, the global users and groups can travel outside their own workstations or servers. Global users and groups can access workstations and servers on other domains, given the proper permissions.

Global and local user and group accounts are administered by using the Windows NT Server utility User Manager for Domains and on Windows 2000, the utility used is Active Directory Users and Computers (see the section "Administering the Windows server" later in this chapter).

Building domains

In the Microsoft server world, a *domain* is typically what we define as a *subnetwork domain*. Microsoft uses domains to organize users, computers, and peripheral devices on the network. In the domain scheme, each user has a member account for the domain that is centrally administrated from the PDC (Primary Domain Controller), which supports the SAM (Security Accounts Manager) that holds the permissions and access levels for each network users account. Client computers are added as members to a domain and become accessible to the other domain elements, subject to the defined security and permissions of the domain and the member. Domain members cannot typically access a computer that is not a member of the domain unless a trust arrangement is established (see "Setting up a trust" later in the chapter).

A network domain can be one of two different things, depending on the network and the operating system in use:

+ **Subnetwork domain:** On a local area network (LAN), the clients and servers that are controlled by a single security database.

+ **Communications domain:** In this type of domain, all the resources under the control of a single server.

A Windows NT system can have only one PDC per domain, but a domain can have additional domain controllers for redundancy purposes. The redundant domain controller is a Backup Domain Controller (BDC) and should the PDC fail, the BDC steps in to fill the role of the PDC, just like the first runner-up in the Miss America pageant.

Windows 2000 treats all domain controllers as peers so there are no PDCs or BDCs. All domain controllers have a read/write copy of the SAM, and as soon as a change occurs on any domain controller, the SAM is replicated to all other domain controllers.

The Windows domain scheme is a logical organization, so the physical location of a computer is not a concern. The only concern is bandwidth. If you have two offices that are a good distance apart, you can still use one domain for both offices, but you want to make sure you have enough bandwidth to support the traffic between the two sites. Placing a BDC at the remote location is a good idea so that users can authenticate to that local BDC rather than over the campus area network (CAN) or wide area network (WAN) link that connects the two offices. Multiple offices can lead to more complex domain configurations.

Computers running Windows NT workstation, Windows for Workgroups, Windows NT Server, Windows 2000 Professional, or Windows 2000 Server can be members of a domain. Windows 9x clients treat domains like workgroups, so they don't actually join a domain.

Setting up a trust

If a network design requires multiple domains, you need to establish a *trust* between domains. A trust allows the users of one domain to access resources on a different domain by allowing a user's logon authentication to permit access to other domains.

A trust between two domains is a one-way thing. If domain A is set up to trust domain B, the users of domain B can access resources on domain A. However, the users on domain A can't access resources on domain B unless domain B is set up to trust domain A. A trust must be established for both directions between two domains if you want to share resources freely between them.

Administering the Windows server

Microsoft Windows NT/2000 Server includes several administration utilities included with Microsoft Windows Server. For the test, you should be familiar with the following utilities:

✦ **User Manager for Domains:** This utility, which is included with Windows NT Server, is used to create and administer user and group accounts. A similar utility — Active Directory Users and Computers — is included with Windows 2000 Server.

✦ **Server Manager:** This utility, which is also included with Microsoft Windows NT Server, is used to manage domain computers and their shared resources. The tasks that can be done through the Server Manager include

- Synchronizing the domain (replicating the SAM to all BDCs on demand)

- Viewing the list of users connected to any computer on the domain

- Viewing shared resources

- Managing the services running on any domain computer

- Sending a console message to any or all computers on the domain list

✦ **Network applet:** The Network icon on the Windows Control Panel is another very important utility. This utility is used for much more than just configuring a server's TCP/IP protocols and network adapters. The Network icon can also be used to install and configure services, such as Windows Internet Naming Service (WINS), Dynamic Host Configuration Protocol (DHCP), and Remote Access Service (RAS) and configuring the server by changing or adding protocols.

✦ **Performance Monitor:** This utility provides performance monitoring and fault management of the server's resources. A special value of this utility is that it provides real-time graphs of server performance.

✦ **Event Viewer:** The Event Viewer is a critical troubleshooting tool. Any time an error occurs, the system records information about the error to an event log. The Event Viewer allows the administrator to view the event logs. Depending on the severity of the error, one of three icons will be displayed with the error message. Red alert icons indicate the most serious error.

Check the Event Viewer security logs for failed logon attempts, providing that you turned on event auditing.

✦ **DHCP (Dynamic Host Configuration Protocol) Manager:** On larger networks, using the DHCP service to assign the IP configuration to the network clients is common. The DHCP Manager is used to manage the scope of addresses and additional options the administrator would like to use for the network's clients.

On a Windows 2000 Server system, you must authorize the DHCP server and activate the IP address scope before the DHCP clients will begin receiving DHCP configuration information.

✦ **DNS (Domain Name System) Manager:** This utility is used to maintain the DNS database.

✦ **SNMP Service (Simple Network Management Protocol):** Although it's not really "simple," SNMP is used to monitor and manage network devices. A server, which may be an SNMP agent, sends messages (called *traps*) to the SNMP manager on the network any time it encounters an error.

Using TCP/IP utilities

Windows NT/2000 systems include a suite of TCP/IP protocols and utilities that can be used to help monitor and manage a network. Table 2-1 lists the TCP/IP utilities you must know for the exam.

Table 2-1	Windows NT/2000 TCP/IP Protocols
Protocol	**Function**
ARP (Address Resolution Protocol)	Resolves IP addresses to MAC (media access control) or physical addresses.
IPCONFIG	Displays IP configuration of the server.
LPQ	Displays the status of an IP-based print queue.
Finger	Displays information about a user who is logged in to a host that is running the Finger service.
FTP (File Transfer Protocol)	Transfers files using TCP/IP.
NBSTAT	Displays NetBIOS over TCP/IP protocol statistics and current connections.
NETSTAT	Displays TCP/IP protocol statistics and current connections.
PING	Verifies network connectivity by sending an acknowledgment request to a remote host.
ROUTE	Makes changes to the routing table on a server that is configured as a router.
TRACERT	Traces the route taken between the server and a remote host.
Telnet	Accesses a Telnet host as a remote terminal.
TFTP (Trivial File Transfer Protocol)	Transfers files using UDP (User Data Protocol).

The PING utility is used to verify network connectivity.

Running with UNIX

UNIX was originally developed by Bell Laboratories as a peer-to-peer network operating system for use with minicomputers. A number of UNIX-like operating systems are available today, including, SCO, Linux, Solaris, and others. Each version is slightly different, but they all provide essentially the same core features and benefits. UNIX works equally well on a peer-to-peer network or a client/server network. As with any major NOS, TCP/IP is the default protocol stack for UNIX systems.

UNIX is powerful, flexible, and very reliable. The only real downside to UNIX is that the commands are somewhat awkward and they vary among the different versions of UNIX because it uses one of three different shells, or command interfaces: Korn, Bourne, and C shells. Okay, no seashore puns, please!

UNIX does provide a graphical user interface (GUI) as well to compliment the command line interface. The most popular GUIs are X-Windows and Motif, which are similar to Microsoft Windows.

The superuser, or root, account is the master administrator account used in UNIX. Administration utilities vary with each version of UNIX, but the core of UNIX administration tools is contained in the /etc (pronounced *et-cee*, not *et cetera*) directory.

Here are the UNIX administration utilities you should know for the exam:

✦ **/etc/passwd:** This file contains the user information for all user authentications. To create a new user, the administrator can edit the /etc/passwd file or on some UNIX systems use the mkuser command (or adduser or useradd, depending on the UNIX in use). The logon and authentication information for a user takes up one line in this text file. The information consists of fields separated with colons. The fields included are

- **Login-id:** The user's logon name or account name.

- **Password:** You guessed it — the user's password.

- **User information:** The user's full name.

- **User account number (UID):** A numerical identifier for the account.

- **Group account number (GID):** The group to which the user account is assigned.

- **Home directory:** The path to the user's home directory.

- **Shell:** Used for the user's initial shell program; if left empty, the default user shell is used.

✦ **/etc/group:** This file holds the information about the system's groups. One line in the file is used to define one group. The entry for a group consists of four fields separated by colons. They are

- **Group name:** Um . . . the name of the group — for example, Sales.

- **Password:** Um, again . . . the password.

- **Group account number (GID):** The GID is created in this file and is cross-linked to the /etc/passwd file. The user's login ID in the /etc/passwd file is applied in the comma-delimited list of users in the /etc/group file.

- **Comma-delimited list of users:** A list of the users assigned to the group.

✦ **/etc/hosts:** This configuration file stores a table of hostnames (computer names) and their corresponding IP addresses. Entries in this file look something like this:

```
#IP-Address Hostname Alias

192.168.2.10 BDC1

192.168.2.40 Hercules Herc
```

✦ **/etc/services:** The services that are configured on a UNIX server are listed in this file, which is very similar in format to the `/etc/hosts` file. Here is what the entries in this file look like:

```
#services port/protocol

smtp 25/tcp #Simple Mail Transfer Protocol

www 80/tcp #Hypertext Transfer or World Wide Web

ftp 21/tcp #File Transfer Protocol
```

✦ **ifconfig:** Like the Windows `IPCONFIG` and the Novell `CONFIG`, the `IFCONGIF` command is used to configure and manage an interface on the UNIX server, including enabling and disabling a TCP/IP interface, assigning addresses, and configuring protocols for the interface.

✦ **netstat:** The `netstat` command displays the network status for the server, including the status of sockets and server processes, management statistics, and the routing table.

✦ **ping:** This utility is the same on every operating system. It tests the network connectivity of a remote host.

The command used to shutdown a UNIX server is `shutdown` plus a grace period. If you want to shut down immediately, use `shutdown -g0`.

Operating with Novell NetWare

Novell NetWare has evolved through its 3.*x*, 4.*x*, and 5.*x* versions, which have very similar core features and services. All versions of NetWare support the use of the proprietary IPX/SPX (the meaning of which is no longer valid, and it's nothing you need to know anyway) protocol, but NetWare 5.*x* uses TCP/IP as its default protocol. The older NetWare versions support TCP/IP, but they use IPX/SPX as their native protocol suite. Novell NetWare supports all major clients, including Windows 3.*x*, Windows 9.*x*, Windows NT/2000, OS/2, Macintosh, and UNIX.

NetWare manages network resources through the Novell Directory Services (NDS), which is a database that tracks network resources. To edit the information in the NDS, the administrator uses the NetWare Administrator program.

The *NetWare Admin* utility organizes and displays network resources by using a tree hierarchy. At the top is the tree [root] object and under the [root] is the list of *container* units, which are like folders or directories that can be used to navigate through the resources on a hard drive. Each container holds either other containers or leaf objects, as well as the contents of any expanded container units. *Leaf objects* are the graphical representations of network resources or services; these objects are displayed as icons in the NDS tree. Unlike a container object, a leaf object does not contain any other objects. The default administrative account, which is ADMIN, is normally located in the Organizational container.

NetWare 5.*x* has many great improvements over its predecessors, but because the purpose of this book is to help you pass the Server+ exam and not to teach you to administer a NetWare network, we're going to gloss over a lot of the details. Remember that Novell NetWare 5.*x* uses TCP/IP natively, meaning it doesn't require IPX to be installed, although it can be.

Table 2-2 has a summary of the NetWare administration utilities you may encounter on the Server+ exam:

Table 2-2	Novell NetWare Administration Utilities	
Utility	*NetWare Version*	*Function*
CONFIG	All versions	Command-line utility used to display adapter configuration (similar to the TCP/IP IPCONFIG command).
ConsoleOne	NetWare 5.*x*	Java-based display of NDS tree information.
DNS/DHCP Manager	NetWare 5.*x*	Graphical application used to manage DNS and DHCP functions.
MONITOR	All versions	Display of performance stats in text menu.
NDPS Manager	NetWare 5	Text-menu utility used to display NDPS printer functions and stats.
NDS Manager	NetWare 4/5	Windows graphical application used to administer all NDS database replication.
NetWare Administrator	NetWare 4/5	Windows graphical application used to administer all NDS (NetWare Directory Services) objects.
PCONSOLE	All versions	Text-menu utility used to display printer functions and stats.
SET	All versions	Command-line utility used to set configuration parameters.

Use the CONFIG command to display the current network adapter configuration. To shut down a Novell server, use the DOWN command.

Flying at OS/2 Warp Speed

Yes, OS/2 is still out there. Chances are that you have heard of it, but may not have had the opportunity to actually work with it. You probably won't see any questions specifically on OS/2, but we'll provide you some background information so you can determine whether any mention of OS/2 is a correct or incorrect choice.

OS/2 is a 32-bit operating system that uses the same domain concept used by Windows NT. Domain controllers are used to store the network user and group database, which is replicated from a PDC to one or more BDCs, just as we describe in the section "Building domains" earlier in this chapter.

OS/2 Warp Server uses NetBEUI (Network BIOS End User Interface) as its native protocol, but supports TCP/IP as well. OS/2 is compatible with DOS, all Windows versions, Macintosh, and of course, OS/2 clients. That's really all you need to know about this NOS for the exam.

A DOS network boot disk can be used to install all versions of Windows, UNIX, NetWare, and OS/2.

The test focuses on Windows NOS but you may see a question or two on the other NOSes we discuss. Pay particular attention to the shutdown commands and the commands used to check network adapter settings. For example, IPCONFIG is used to check network configuration on a Windows NT/2000 server.

Serving the Network

Servers can be configured to do many functions. When people talk about a server, they usually refer to the major function that the server performs. For example, your boss comes running into your office in a panic while yelling that the file server has crashed (fun, huh?). Right away, you know that the file server is actually a server named FILESRV, and you quickly take action. Of course, you simply reboot the server and save the day.

Your boss was right, the file server was down; but did he know that the file server also runs the Dynamic Host Configuration Protocol (DHCP) service and that anyone trying to log on to the network at that time was thinking about throwing his or her workstation down a flight of stairs? A hardware server can actually be running many software servers.

Some of the more common servers and their features are

✦ **Application server:** A centralized computer that provides network-enabled versions of application software to network clients.

✦ **File server:** A server that stores user data files in a centralized location on the network.

✦ **Database server:** A centralized server that manages a common database or multiple databases for the network.

✦ **Print server:** A centralized server that manages the printers connected to the network and the printing of user documents on the network printers.

✦ **Communications server:** A communications server is a centralized computer that handles many common communications functions for the network, such as e-mail, fax, remote access, or Internet services.

✦ **Web server:** A Web server is a program that serves the files that form Web pages to Web users. Each computer on the Internet that contains a Web site must have a Web server program in order to provide the http service to clients. The most common example of a Web server is the Microsoft Internet Information Server (IIS). Other Web servers include the Novell Web Server for users using NetWare operating systems and the IBM family of Lotus Domino servers, primarily for IBM's OS/390 and AS/400 customers.

Remember that a server's "type" is just a general statement about its primary function. Each type of server is running a program or server service that provides the system with the specific function.

Serving the domain

You definitely need to understand the function of a domain server. The test likely includes a question or two concerning the use of a PDC and a BDC. Your understanding the role of both domain controllers and the steps used to configure a server either as a PDC or as a BDC is important. A server on a network that is not designated as a PDC or a BDC is only a *member server*. Here is a brief description of these network elements:

✦ **Primary Domain Controller (PDC):** A PDC manages the master user database for the domain. When the network administrator makes a change (such as adding a new user), the change is made only on the PDC.

✦ **Backup Domain Controller (BDC):** The master user database is periodically replicated in read-only form to a BDC, if one or more exists. This allows a user to be authenticated by any domain controller when he or she logs on to the network. The BDC can also be promoted to act as a PDC, should the PDC fail.

✦ **Member server:** Any network server running Windows NT Server, not designated as either a PDC or a BDC, that fulfills client/server functions for network clients.

To set up a Windows NT domain controller, you must specify during the installation whether a particular server is to be one of the following:

✦ Primary Domain Controller (PDC)

✦ Backup Domain Controller (BDC)

✦ Member server

If you choose to configure a PDC, you are stuck with it until you demote it to a BDC. A PDC is typically demoted because of network problems or a redesign of the network structure. This process involves first promoting a BDC to a PDC, which forces the pre-existing PDC to the role of a BDC — a process referred to as a *graceful demotion*.

Installing WINS servers

A *Windows Internet Naming Service* (WINS) server is used to translate NetBIOS (Network Basic Input/Output System) computer names to IP (Internet Protocol) addresses. A WINS server automatically creates a computer name-IP address mapping table that ensures that a computer name is unique on the network. If a computer is moved to another geographic location, the subnet part of an IP address is likely to change. WINS automatically updates the new subnet information in the WINS table. (See Book IV, Chapter 5 for information on subnets.)

You might see a question or two on the exam regarding troubleshooting name resolution problems. If a computer can reach other computers by IP address but not by name, the problem is likely in either the WINS setting or DNS.

Resolving names with DNS

The *Domain Name System (DNS)* is a system of name-server computers that store domain name-to-IP mappings. DNS servers are organized in a hierarchy based on domain names. DNS servers are organized at the highest level by top-level domains (`.biz`, `.com`, `.info`, `.gov`, `.org`, and so on).

Top-level DNS databases hold the most reliable source of information about top-level domains. Other DNS servers hold information on *lower-level domains* (also called *subdomains*). For example, a top-level DNS server contains information on `.com` domains and a DNS server at Microsoft has authority over the `microsoft.com` domain that contains information the Web server `www.microsoft.com`, and its third-level domains, such as `sales.microsoft.com`.

DNS is the name-resolution method used for Internet addressing and on many TCP/IP-based NOSes as well. DNS resolves domain names, such as `wiley.com`, to their IP addresses, such as `208.215.179.100`.

Configuring clients with DHCP

The Dynamic Host Configuration Protocol (DHCP) is used to automatically assign the IP configuration information, such as IP, WINS, DNS, and default gateway addresses, domain names, and the like, to a network client. The Server+ exam includes a question or two about DHCP. However, instead of questions specifically about DHCP, you may be asked how the `IPCONFIG/RENEW` command is used to request a DHCP configuration renewal from the DHCP server.

In order to be used as a DHCP server, a Windows server must meet the following requirements:

✦ The server must be running Windows NT Server or Windows 2000 Server (and yes, non-Windows DHCP servers do exist, and just not on the exam) on a TCP/IP network.

✦ A DHCP scope (the assignable IP address range and its network/subnet mask) must be defined on the DHCP server.

✦ If you are using Windows 2000 Server, the server must be authorized (watch for this one on the test).

DHCP uses a *lease time*, which refers to the amount of time that a given IP configuration can be used by a DHCP client. On a network that has more clients than IP addresses, the DHCP server can be configured to assign short lease times so that when a user logs off, the lease soon expires, making the IP address available for use by another client.

Providing Internetworking Services

An internetwork is created through the connection built between the routers of networks connected to the public network (Internet). Perhaps the most important services a LAN that connects to the Internet can provide are its routing and security services. The exam asks some general questions on routing and how to troubleshoot the problem when a client can't reach a network destination.

Using a server as a router

A server can be configured to serve as a router. By installing multiple network interface cards (NICs) or adapters, a server can be configured to forward outbound traffic and filter inbound traffic much like a router. *Routing* is the process of sending data from a host on one network to a host on a remote network. A router/server can be convenient and cost effective on a small LAN, but servers lack the performance and functionality needed to handle routing on a large network.

Protecting your valuables

Firewall software provides network security on a network's router or gateway server and is used to protect the resources of a private network from external network users. A firewall works in conjunction with a gateway (router) and examines each network packet to determine whether to forward it to the destination address.

A firewall is installed to prevent incoming requests from accessing private network resources. Firewalls allow mobile users remote access to the private network by the use of secure logon procedures and authentication certificates. Firewalls feature security logging, reporting, and automatic alarms at given thresholds of attack.

Using proxy servers

Another type of service that a network server can provide is a proxy server. A *proxy server* is an intermediary between a client and the Internet to maintain network security, administrative control, and perhaps provide a caching service. A proxy server is associated with (or part of) a gateway and a firewall server to achieve the task of keeping outside intruders from accessing the network.

When a user requests a Web page, the proxy server (assuming it's also configured as a cache server) looks in its local cache of previously downloaded Web pages. If the server finds the requested Web page in its cache, it forwards the page to the user without downloading the page from the Internet. If the proxy server does find the page in its local cache, the server downloads the page on behalf of the user, using one of its own IP addresses to make the request. A proxy server reduces the amount of Internet and network traffic and reduces download time.

Dialing up the network

A server may also be configured as a communications server. There are many different types of communications servers, but, in the context of the Server+ exam, the important type is RAS (Remote Access Services). A RAS (pronounced as "razz") server usually includes, or functions in conjunction with, a firewall and a router. RAS servers provide dial-in or modem access to a computer or network to remote users, which is typically how a dial-up customer reaches his or her ISP (Internet Service Provider).

Controlling the gateway

If you set up your server as the network router, it is typically also set as the network gateway. A network gateway is a TCP/IP host that has been configured with two or more network connection interfaces, which creates a *multi-homed host* (the term that refers to more than one interface).

Part of a client's configuration is the assignment of a default gateway, which is the router that connects a network to remote networks. In most cases, the gateway is a hardware router or firewall. However, configuring a server with a software router and installing firewall software to create a gateway may be more cost-effective.

Moving data over the network

The File Transfer Protocol (FTP) service is used to transfer files between the server and clients. FTP is similar to the HyperText Transfer Protocol (HTTP) that is used to transfer displayable Web pages.

To use an FTP utility, you need to log on to an FTP server. FTP utilities come in a variety of flavors. An FTP client can be as simple as a command line interface (for example, from the Windows MS-DOS Prompt window), a commercial program with a GUI, or a function built in to a Web browser. All these can make FTP requests to download files and programs that you select from the Internet.

You can also use FTP to update (delete, rename, move, and copy) files at a server. FTP utilities are commonly used to transfer Web page files and images from a host computer to the Web server for access by everyone on the Internet. FTP is also commonly used to download programs and other files to your computer from other servers.

Reviewing Bus Basics

The Server+ exam deals with bus structures in several areas: processors, memory, expansion cards, and the like. You must know the bus widths, speeds, and compatibilities of Pentium-class processors and the impact of these characteristics on memory and processor upgrades.

Basic busing

A *bus* is a path or channel used to transfer data between the processor, memory, and device controllers and adapters. The bus structure of a computer is like a multilane highway with each bus comprising wires that carry traffic to and from the various system components. The bus interconnects the components on the motherboard and serves as the conduit to transport data from one component to another. The bus consists of a system of parallel wires to which the CPU, memory, and all input-output devices are connected. The bus carries data between two system devices, with data traveling in either direction. Figure 2-3 depicts the major bus structures on a Pentium-class motherboard.

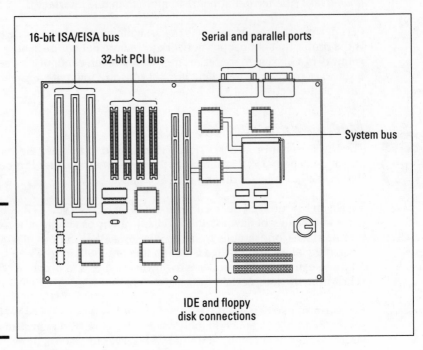

16-bit ISA/EISA bus

32-bit PCI bus

Serial and parallel ports

System bus

IDE and floppy disk connections

Figure 2-3: The bus structures on a Pentium computer mother-board.

Sorting out the buses

A typical computer has a system bus, an internal bus, a motherboard bus, a front-side bus, an address bus, a data bus, a local bus, an I/O bus, an expansion bus, and more. Not all of these bus structures are on the motherboard, but that is where the primary bus structures are located. What is commonly called the "bus" is the *system* or *internal bus*.

The system bus

The system/internal bus connects the CPU (central processing unit) to the various bus controllers, as illustrated in Figure 2-4. Bus controllers direct traffic to the devices attached to their buses. For example, when the CPU requests data from the network adapter, which is installed in a PCI expansion slot on the PCI bus, the request is transmitted to the system bus. The request stops at each bus controller to determine whether its bus is the route it needs. When the request reaches the PCI bus controller, it gets off the system bus and heads down the PCI bus to the network adapter.

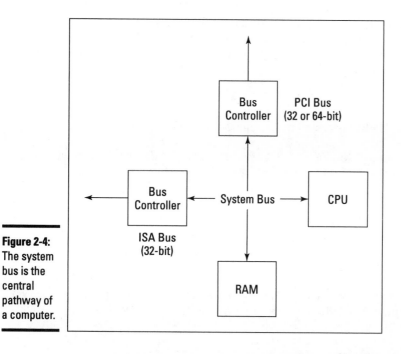

Figure 2-4:
The system
bus is the
central
pathway of
a computer.

As shown in Figure 2-4, all other buses branch from the system bus. The I/O
buses that support system (such as the processor, chipset, memory, and
Level 2 cache memory) and peripheral devices are connected to the internal
bus. The system bus is matched specifically to the capabilities and speed of
the processor.

The bus that connects to the CPU is the local bus, which carries the data
transmitted into and out of the processor. An I/O bus — also called the
expansion bus — carries data coming from or going to peripheral devices.

Bus parts

Regardless of its name and purpose, every bus is made up of two smaller
buses: an address bus and a data bus. The *address bus* carries information
about where the data came from or should go. The *data bus* carries the data
being transmitted from one system device to another.

The size and speed of the bus

Many varieties of buses exist, each with a different speed, width, and bandwidth. For the Server+ exam, you need to know the characteristics and compatibilities of the bus structures found in servers. You also need to know the
purpose of each bus and the peripherals typically attached to each.

Data is transmitted across the bus in parallel mode, which means that all the bits in a bus-sized piece of data travel on parallel wires simultaneously. The number of bits a bus can transmit in parallel is its width and a wider bus carries more bits. For example, a 64-bit bus can carry the equivalent of 8 characters (64 bits) at one time, and a 32-bit bus is wider than a 16-bit bus, which means more data can be transmitted at one time.

A bus is characterized by two measurements:

✦ **Bandwidth:** Bandwidth, also referred to as *throughput*, is measured in millions of bits (megabits) per second (Mbps).

✦ **Speed:** Most buses transmit one bit per clock cycle per wire (imagine one car per lane per green light). Some newer technologies allow multiple bits to be transmitted per clock cycle, which, of course, increases the performance of the bus (see "Taking the local bus" later in this chapter). The speed of a bus is measured in millions of cycles (megahertz) per second (MHz).

The different speeds used on the motherboard can be confusing. A server can have a 266 MHz processor with a 66 MHz bus. The data transmitted from the CPU at 266 MHz must be adjusted to the slower 66 MHz speed of the bus by the bus controller. The actual speed of the overall system is determined by the speed at which data moves over the bus.

66 MHz buses

The early Pentium processors had a 64-bit wide system bus with speeds of 60 or 66 MHz. Table 2-3 lists the bus width and speeds for the early Pentium-class processors.

Table 2-3	System Bus Characteristics on Early Pentium Processors	
Processor	*Width (bits)*	*Speed (MHz)*
Intel Pentium 60	64	60
Intel Pentium 100	64	66
Intel Pentium 150	64	60
Intel Pentium 166	64	66
Pentium Pro 200	64	66
Cyrix 6X86 P200	64	75
Pentium II	64	66

100 and 133 MHz buses

PC100 SDRAM (Synchronous Dynamic Random Access Memory) and PC133 SDRAM allow system bus speeds to increase to 100 MHz and 133 MHz, respectively. SDRAM synchronizes itself to the processor's bus to run at much higher speeds than conventional EDO DRAM (Extended Data Output Dynamic Random Access Memory) memory.

Rambus

Many of the very latest processors don't actually have a system bus in the sense of what made up a system bus in the past. On the very latest processors (such as the Pentium 4, and the AMD Athlon and Duron), the bus between RAM (memory) and the processor is separated from the other buses to form what is called a Rambus.

Taking the local bus

The local bus is a direct data bus expressway between the processor and one or more peripheral device controllers to provide a direct line to the processor. Nearly all Pentium-class motherboards include a PCI (Peripheral Components Interconnect) local bus and a legacy ISA (Industry Standard Architecture) expansion bus for those devices that don't require high-speed throughput.

The local bus architectures and standards you can expect to see on the Server+ exam are

✦ **Video Electronics Standards Association (VESA) Local Bus (VL-bus or VLB):** This was the first bus designed using the local bus concept. A VL-bus is a 32-bit bus that runs at 33 MHz on 486 processor motherboards.

✦ **Peripheral Component Interconnect (PCI) bus:** PCI is a 66 MHz, 32-bit bus that is a standard bus on virtually every PC motherboard manufactured today. The 32-bit PCI expansion slots (usually four per motherboard) can be used for SCSI adapters, NICs, video cards, and other device controllers that require a high-speed interface. See Figure 2-5 for an illustration of PCI slots and their placement on a motherboard.

✦ **Accelerated Graphics Port (AGP) bus:** The AGP bus was developed specifically for high-performance video adapters. AGP is a 66 MHz, 32-bit bus that provides data throughput between 266 Mbps and 2 Gbps. A single AGP slot is common on Pentium-class motherboards. See Figure 2-5 for an illustration of where an AGP slot is typically placed on a motherboard.

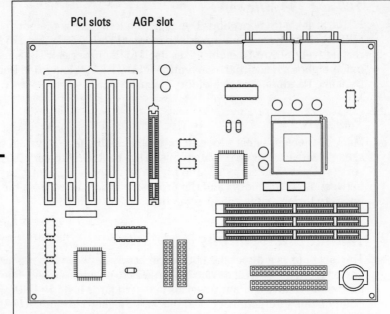

Figure 2-5:
The
placement
of PCI and
AGP
expansion
slots on a
typical
mother-
board.

Chatting about Chipsets

You may encounter a question or two about chipsets and PCI controllers on the Server+ exam. Here is a brief overview of chipsets and their role with the PCI bus.

Today's technology has combined what, in the early days of the PC, was dozens of chips each with its own special purpose and function, such as a clock generator, bus controller, system timer, keyboard controller, and so on, into a either one or two integrated circuits or chips, called a *chipset*.

The two chips of a chipset are designated as the North Bridge and South Bridge. The North Bridge contains the cache and main memory controllers and the interface between the high-speed processor bus and slower speed AGP and PCI buses and operates at system bus speed.

The South Bridge is the slower speed component of the chipset. The South Bridge connects to the 33 MHz PCI bus and contains the interface to the slower 8 MHz ISA bus as well. Normally the IDE hard disk controller, USB interface, CMOS RAM, and clock functions — and even the DMA and IRQ controllers — are included in the South Bridge.

Riding the Expansion Bus

The *expansion bus*, also known as the *I/O (input/output) bus* or the *peripheral bus*, is based on the ISA and other legacy bus architectures. The Server+ exam includes only the more modern and common bus architectures, but you should be familiar with some of the legacy interfaces to help you eliminate incorrect answers. Figure 2-6 includes an illustration of the expansion bus card types you need to be able to recognize on the exam.

REMEMBER

The PCI bus is also considered part of the expansion bus. Here are the I/O bus architectures you should be familiar with for the Server+ exam:

✦ **Industry Standard Architecture (ISA) bus:** Originally an 8-bit, 4.77 MHz bus that was later upgraded to 16 bits and 8 MHz.

✦ **Micro Channel Architecture (MCA) bus:** The MCA bus is a legacy architecture with a 32-bit architecture. The MCA architecture is largely outdated but is mentioned on the Server+ exam once or twice.

✦ **Extended Industry Standard Architecture (EISA) bus:** EISA extended the ISA bus to 32-bits and EISA slots are still found on some motherboards to provide backward compatibility. The EISA slot is a two-part affair, half of which is able to support an ISA expansion card.

Table 2-4 compares the buses found on a typical server.

Table 2-4	A Comparison of Bus Characteristics		
Bus	**Width (bits)**	**Bandwidth (Mbps)**	**Speed (MHz)**
8-bit ISA	8	4	2
16-bit ISA	16	8	8
EISA	32	8	33
VL-bus	32	33	133
32-bit PCI	32	33	133
64-bit PCI	64	66	266
AGP	32	66	266
AGP (x2 mode)	32	133	533
AGP (x4 mode)	32	266	1,066
AGP (x8 mode)	32	533	2,133

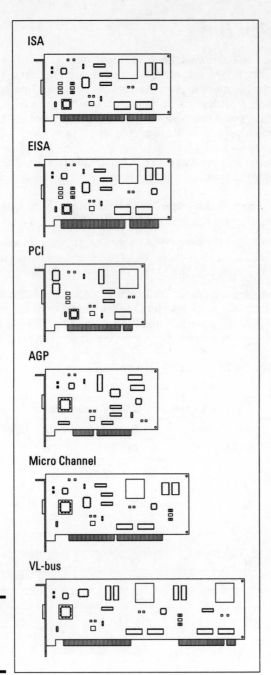

ISA

EISA

PCI

AGP

Micro Channel

VL-bus

Figure 2-6:
Common
expansion
card types.

Understanding the Processor

For the exam, you need to know the characteristics and compatibilities, particularly memory and bus structures, of the various Pentium-class processors. And you definitely need to know what memory and bus systems are compatible with each processor.

The Pentium processor

The first generation Pentium was a 273-pin chip that mounted in the Socket 7 ZIF (zero insertion force) socket and was available in 60 and 66 MHz versions. The second-generation Pentium, which was packaged in a Pin Grid Array (PGA), mounted in a 296-pin Socket 5 mounting, ran between 120 MHz to 200 MHz, included 16K of Level 1 (L1) cache, and was the first Pentium processor to run on 3.3 volts (V).

The Pentium's address bus is 32-bits wide, which translates to an ability to address only 4GB of memory, and its data bus is 64-bits wide.

The Pentium MMX processor

The important detail to remember about the Pentium MMX, which had clock speeds ranging from 166 to 233 MHz, is the added MMX (multimedia extensions) instructions. The Pentium MMX includes a set of 57 instructions that use matrix math (another definition for MMX) to support graphic compression and decompression algorithms (such as JPEG, GIF, and MPEG) and 3-D graphic renderings. MMX allows the floating-point math unit (FPU) to act on several pieces of data at the same time through a process called SIMD (single instruction multiple data).

Pentium Pro processor

The Pentium Pro processor was designed for use in high-end workstations and servers. The primary innovation of the Pentium Pro, which does not include MMX capabilities, was up to 1MB of Level 2 (L2) cache, with 256K being standard, into its PGA package.

The Pentium Pro is a 32-bit processor, but it is capable of addressing up to 64GB of memory, has processor speeds of 150 MHz or 200 MHz, and can be configured to run with up to four processors. For more information on multiple processor systems, see "Upgrading to Multiple Processors," later in this chapter.

Pentium II processor

The 387-pin Pentium II introduced a completely new processor chip and packaging designs. The Pentium II combines the Pentium Pro's scalability of multiple processors with MMX technology and 512KB of L2 cache. Like the Pentium Pro, the Pentium II is able to address up to 64GB of RAM.

The Pentium II is packaged in the Single Edge Contact Cartridge (SECC) that mounts the processor and several L2 cache chips on a small circuit board that is encased in a plastic outer shell. SECC packages mount to a motherboard Slot 1 connection. The original SECC was improved later to the SECC2 that places components on just one side of the mounting circuit, which provides for better cooling and the attachment of heat sinks and fans.

Pentium III processor

The Pentium III incorporates streaming SIMD extensions (SSE), which adds 70 new instructions to enhance the performance of advanced imaging, streaming audio/video, 3-D, and speech recognition applications. The Pentium III comes only in the SECC2 package. The Pentium III uses a 133 MHz bus speed that is 64-bits wide and has processor speeds that range from 400 MHz to over 1 GHz (gigahertz).

Pentium Xeon processors

The Xeon processors add more and faster cache memory to the Pentium II and Pentium III processors. The Xeon processors also include an additional L2 cache, available in 512K, 1MB, and 2MB versions. The L2 cache of the Xeon processor runs at processor speed using a high-speed bus that is internal to the processor package.

Intel's latest offerings, the Pentium 4 processor and Itanium technology, are not covered on the Server+ exam.

Matching processors to bus speeds

Expect to see questions on the Server+ exam that require you to match processors, bus speeds, and memory. Memory is categorized by the bus speeds to which it is compatible. To ensure compatibility to higher bus speeds, Intel has developed the PC100 (100 MHz) and PC133 (133 MHz) memory standards. Memory that is compatible with either of these standards is interoperable with motherboards, chipsets, and processors on that standard as well.

Should you mix the memory types — for example, put a PC100 memory in a PC133 system — the memory will run at the slower speed. You can also put a PC133 memory in a PC100 system with the same result, but should you ever upgrade to a PC133 system, you are that much memory ahead.

Table 2-5 lists the bus speeds of the later Pentium-class processors.

Table 2-5	System Bus Speeds on Newer Pentium Processors		
Processor	*Standard*	*System Bus (MHz)*	*CPU Speed(s) (MHz)*
Intel Pentium II	PC100	100	350, 400, 450
AMD K6-2	100	PC100	100, 250, 300, 400
Intel Pentium II Xeon	PC100	100	400 or 450
Intel Pentium III	PC133	133	450–1130
AMD Athlon	PC200 (PC100 x 2)	200	600–1000
Intel Pentium III Xeon	PC133	133	600–1000

Ensuring Memory Compatibility

Most modern servers use PC100 SDRAM or PC133 SDRAM modules. Some older systems may use PC66, but not many are left in production. The test will ask you questions about what RAM you can use with a specific processor or speed of data bus. For example: Will PC100 work with a Pentium III system that has a 133 MHz data bus? Using a memory module in a system it's not designed for results in a number of problems, including

✦ The system may not boot at all.

✦ System performance decreases significantly.

✦ Installing faster, more expensive memory does not result in faster system performance.

Table 2-6 provides a quick summary of the different processors, bus speeds, along with the type of memory that is compatible with each. Know this chart well for the test; you will see questions concerning processor compatibility.

Table 2-6	Processor/Memory Compatibilities	
Processor	*Memory Bus Speed (MHz)*	*Compatible Memory*
Pentium	66	66 MHz EDO
Pentium/MMX	66	66 MHz EDO or 66 MHz SDRAM
Pentium Pro	66	66 MHz EDO or 66 MHz SDRAM
Pentium II	100	100 MHz SDRAM
Pentium III	133	133 MHz SDRAM
Pentium II Xeon	100	100 MHz SDRAM
Pentium III Xeon	100	100 MHz SDRAM

Upgrading to Multiple Processors

Don't confuse multitasking and multiprocessing. *Multitasking* is an operating-system technique for sharing a single processor to execute multiple instructions. *Multiprocessing* refers to a system with more than one processor. A multiprocessing computer can execute multiple threads at the same time by using the multiple processors — one thread for each processor in the system.

At some point, you may find that your single processor server has become inadequate for the job it's performing and you need to upgrade it with an additional processor, providing it's configured for multiple processors. You should expect to see at a couple of questions about multiprocessing on the exam.

Stepping with the processor

You see stepping referred to on the test in reference to each of the processors in a multiple processor system needing to be on the same stepping level in order to function together properly. *Stepping* refers to the process of installing new microcode on a processor. Just as software updates and bug fixes are released as newer versions, processors are sometimes released with bugs and features that need upgrades or fixes.

Servers with multiple processors can operate if their processors have mixed stepping levels. However, the system operates at the feature level of the least capable processor. For example, if the first processor supports features A, B, and C, and the second CPU supports only feature A, features B and C of the first CPU must be disabled before the processors can be used together. Obviously, you're better off using processors of the same stepping. Some BIOS programs have support for processors with different steppings, but it isn't recommended.

Software support for multiprocessing

Multiprocessing operating systems can be either asymmetric or symmetric. The main difference between the two is in how the processors operate:

✦ **Asymmetric multiprocessing (ASMP):** An ASMP system uses one or more processors to run the operating system, and the remaining processors are dedicated to running only user applications. On a two-processor ASMP system, one processor runs the OS, and the other processor runs user applications.

✦ **Symmetric multiprocessing (SMP):** SMP is a multiprocessing architecture that supports from 2 to 32 processors on a single server that communicate with one another through shared memory. One major problem with the SMP system is that if one processor fails, the entire system is down. SMP processors can be combined into clusters to provide fault tolerance. Windows NT and 2000 operating systems are SMP systems.

Carrying Around Some Cache

On the Server+ exam, you may encounter a question or two that either asks about or references cache memory. You should know what cache memory is, how it is used, and the impact on a system's performance when cache is added.

Cache memory is essentially a small amount of SRAM. SRAM doesn't require the normal periodic refreshing common with other types of RAM, especially DRAM (Dynamic RAM). SRAM eliminates the need for refreshing because it uses transistors to store the electrical charges that represent 1s or 0s. SRAM is very fast with access speeds of two nanoseconds (ns) or less. A *nanosecond* is one-billionth of a second. Because it uses SRAM, cache memory is fast enough that it can keep pace with the processor; for this reason, computer designers have found that caching can greatly improve overall system performance.

This performance increase is a result of the processor not having to access system memory for data that's frequently requested. By storing this frequently requested data in the cache, the processor can read and write to and from the cache memory, which eliminates wait states. *Wait states* are durations in which the processor is standing still, waiting for the slow system memory to retrieve data.

Outguessing the processor

Cache memory, and most other caching systems on the computer, operates on a best-guess basis. That is, the caching system guesses as to what the next block of data to be requested by the CPU might actually be, and then reads it into cache memory. If the caching guesses correctly, a bunch of time is saved because the data is passed to the CPU from the very fast cache memory instead of waiting out the process that moves the data from the storage device into RAM and then to the CPU. When the caching guesses correctly — which it does over 95 percent of the time — a *cache hit* is scored. The effectiveness of cache memory is expressed as a *hit ratio*. A successful hit is calculated when the cache memory successfully anticipates the data next requested by the processor.

Missing in action

If the data requested isn't in cache, it is considered a *cache miss*. Precious clock cycles have been wasted looking for it. Obviously, if the data is not found in the cache, the data will be requested from RAM. A cache miss affects system performance because the clock cycles used looking for the data in cache must be added to the time required to find and transfer the data from main memory. If 10 total clock cycles are normally required to transfer a data burst from RAM and a cache miss takes 2 clock cycles, each cache miss actually results in 12 clock cycles required to get the requested data to the CPU. You can prevent cache misses by adding more Level 2 cache — that is, if your system can support the upgrade. Adding more Level 2 cache has no impact on the time used to look in the data store for requested data; adding more Level 2 cache will only improve the rate of cache hits.

Leveling with the processor

Two types, or levels, of cache memory are used on a server. You should be well acquainted with both levels for the test, including where each level is physically located, and why and how the location affects system performance.

The two levels of cache memory are

✦ **Level 1 (L1):** *Level 1 cache*, or *primary cache*, is a small (typically around 16K) amount of high-speed cache that's installed physically on the processor chip. This cache is used to store recently used data and instructions from memory.

✦ **Level 2 (L2) cache:** *Level 2 cache*, or *secondary cache*, holds recently used data in reserve for the smaller L1 (primary) cache. Level 2 is larger — usually 64K to 2MB in size — and slightly slower than Level 1 cache. Typically, Level 2 cache is located on the motherboard, but it can be included on the processor chip, or in some systems on a daughterboard that's installed in a slot on the motherboard.

Keeping up with the clock

Cache memory (as well as system memory) uses a variety of timing methods. For the test, you need to know the difference between the following timing methods and why one is better than the other.

✦ **Asynchronous:** Asynchronous memory uses an assigned minimum time period that is long enough to ensure that its operations are completed without regard to clock cycles.

✦ **Synchronous:** Synchronous memory is tied to the clock cycles of the system bus and runs at bus speeds.

✦ **Pipeline burst:** This type of synchronous memory is the caching technology found on most Pentium-class motherboards. Pipeline burst cache can be read from, or written to, with a succession of four data transfers (or bursts). Pipeline burst cache is used for both L1 and L2 cache.

Keeping everyone current

Not only does the processor read the data in cache, but it also makes changes to the data, as well. When a user makes changes to and saves data to the hard drive, the data is updated in RAM from the cache and then written back to the hard drive. The data must be synchronized between cache and RAM so that an outdated version of the data isn't passed to the CPU or hard drive.

Two basic cache write policies are used to regulate these actions to make sure that the data mirrored in cache and RAM stays in sync:

✦ **Write-back cache:** If any of the data mirrored in cache is updated in RAM, only the affected part is updated in cache. When data is no longer in use, only the changed portion is written back to RAM. This saves write cycles to memory.

✦ **Write-through cache:** Any time that data held in cache is changed, it is immediately written to both cache and RAM. This method ensures that cache is never out of sync with main memory.

Investing cache into the system

Some motherboard types have soldered SRAM on the board but also provide an open socket that enables you to upgrade by using cache modules. Adding SRAM usually requires that you change a jumper setting or two. If you can add SRAM to your system, its size and type are determined by the motherboard. Visit the motherboard manufacturer's Web site for details on what type of cache you can add and how, if possible.

A *COAST* (Cache on a Stick) is a commonly used form of cache-packaging module. These modules look something like the SIMM (Single Inline Memory Module), but vary in size depending on the manufacturer. COAST modules are mounted to the motherboard by using a special socket known as a *CELP* (card edge low profile).

Caching In on the Disk

Most hard drives contain an *integrated cache*, also known as a *buffer*. The function of disk cache is to act as a buffer between a relatively fast device and a relatively slow one. In hard drives, the cache is used to hold the results of recent reads from the disk, and also to store anticipated data (prefetch) that is likely to be requested in the near future. An example of this anticipation is the retrieval of the data from the sector or sectors immediately after the one just read from.

Disk caching is used to reduce the number of accesses by saving recently read data in a cache. The next time that the data is requested, the hard drive doesn't need to go to any particular sector on the drive because the data is waiting patiently in the cache. This prevents repeated reads from the sector the data is located on, and also enables data to stream uninterrupted from the disk when the bus is busy. The use of disk cache improves the performance of any hard drive. Most modern hard drives have between 512K and 2MB of internal cache memory, and some high-performance SCSI drives have as much as 16MB.

Increasing the size of the disk's cache is not overly significant to the performance of the system. In fact, many benchmarks have shown that the performance difference is very insignificant. When comparing the same drive using 512K or 1MB of internal cache memory, the difference is definitely nothing worth hollering about.

Caching In on the Internet

Another type of caching is a *cache server*, which actually has nothing to do with cache memory other than their operations are somewhat similar. Cache servers are all about bandwidth. Many companies that use the Internet are using cache servers as an intermediary between a workstation user and the Internet to provide caching service. Internet Service Providers (ISPs) use cache servers in the same manner. When a request is made for a Web page, the cache server looks at its store of previously downloaded Web pages. If the server finds the page in cache, it forwards the Web page to the user, thus saving the user from having to go out over the Internet to download the page. If the Web page is not found in cache, the server will cache the page so that the next time the page is requested, the server can respond to that request much quicker.

Prep Test

1 What is the default network protocol used by Microsoft Windows NT and 2000?

A ○ NetBEUI

B ○ IPX/SPX

C ○ NetBIOS

D ○ TCP/IP

2 What utility is used to display the network configuration of a Novell server?

A ○ IPCONFIG

B ○ IFCONFIG

C ○ CONFIG

D ○ NETCONFIG

3 Which type of server stores a copy of the master user database on a Windows NT network?

A ○ Router

B ○ Communications server

C ○ DNS server

D ○ PDC

4 What is the name resolution service that is used to translate host and server names to their Internet addresses?

A ○ IP

B ○ IPX

C ○ DNS

D ○ WINS

5 Name the pathway that connects peripheral devices to the processor.

A ○ Internal bus

B ○ Backside bus

C ○ SCSI bus

D ○ Expansion bus

6 A Pentium III is compatible with which memory standard?

A ○ PC66

B ○ PC100

C ○ PC133

D ○ PC200

7 It is recommended that the processors on a multiprocessing server all have which feature in common?

A ○ HAL

B ○ L1 cache

C ○ L2 cache

D ○ Stepping

8 _____ cache is located on the CPU.

A ○ Level 2

B ○ Level 3

C ○ Secondary

D ○ Level 1

9 _____ caching was designed to run with no concern for system clock cycles.

A ○ Synchronous

B ○ Pipeline burst

C ○ Asynchronous

D ○ Fast

10 When a customer of a user requests a Web page, the _____ looks in its cache of previously downloaded Web pages.

A ○ Cache server

B ○ Application server

C ○ File server

D ○ Web server

Answers

1 **D.** TCP/IP is the native protocol stack for virtually any new NOS. *Look at "Checking Out Windows NT/2000."*

2 **C.** The CONFIG utility is used to display the network configuration of a Novell server. *Study "Operating with Novell NetWare."*

3 **D.** Actually, the answer should be domain controllers in general. Maintaining the master user database is a function of a domain controller. *Take a look at "Serving the domain."*

4 **C.** DNS is the global protocol used to translate URLs (Uniform Resource Locators) into IP addresses. *See "Resolving names with DNS."*

5 **D.** The expansion bus lies beyond the bus controllers for a particular bus, such as the ISA or PCI buses. *Look at "Riding the Expansion Bus."*

6 **C.** The memory standards, PC100 and PC133, reflect the bus speeds to which they are compatible. PC100 memory works in a PC133 system, just more slowly, and the entire memory is slowed to the slower speed. *Check out "Matching processors to bus speeds."*

7 **D.** If the processors have different steppings, then only the lowest-level stepping will be used. *Take a look at "Stepping with the processor."*

8 **D.** Level 1, or primary, cache is located on the CPU. This type of cache is the fastest and most effective. *Check out "Leveling with the processor."*

9 **C.** Asynchronous caching does not work in conjunction with the system clock. In fact, the asynchronous method determines its own timing that chooses when data moves in and out of cache. *Review "Keeping up with the clock."*

10 **A.** The cache server is used to store frequently requested Web pages. *Study "Caching In on the Internet."*

Chapter 3: Memory, BIOS, and Storage

Exam Objectives

✔ Identifying memory technologies by their characteristics

✔ Explaining BIOS and ROM chips

✔ Determining when the system BIOS needs to be upgraded

✔ Performing a BIOS upgrade

✔ Identifying SCSI modes by their characteristics

✔ Explaining disk partitioning and physical versus logical disk drives

✔ Listing common file systems and their features

*I*f you've been working with computers for any length of time, you've installed a memory module or a hard drive or two. Your job as an IT guru is to provide, secure, and maintain data integrity and storage for network users.

One of the more basic components of a server is its memory. We're sure you know what RAM (random access memory) is, and most likely you know the different memory types available, because you should already have your A+ Certification, the prerequisite to the Server+ exam. On the Server+ exam, expect questions on the compatibility of certain memory types with processors and motherboards.

The BIOS is important for both real-world applications and the exam. The BIOS is very delicate, and without proper handling and maintenance, you can find yourself in big trouble.

If there is one single topic you really must know for the Server+ exam, the Small Computer System Interface (SCSI), followed closely by RAID (see Book V, Chapter 4 for more information on RAID) is it. Including the questions from all the exam domains, we estimate that as much as one-fourth of the exam concerns SCSI and RAID (Redundant Array of Independent Disks).

Refreshing Your Memory

This first part of the chapter is devoted to defining some of the foundation concepts and terminology used to describe memory characteristics and technologies. You should review this section to refresh your understanding of the terms and definitions provided, if for no other reason than to get an idea of the kind of information you're expected to know for the Server+ exam.

Before getting into the details of memory, we need to go over a few common components and terms. The following brief descriptions for each component or term refreshes your memory before getting into the really deep and technical stuff:

+ **Memory controller:** An essential component of any computer is the hardware logic circuit known as the *memory controller.* This component controls the memory by generating the signals needed to control the reading and writing of all information to and from the memory, and provides an interface between the memory and the other components of the computer. The memory controller is normally integrated into the motherboard's *chipset,* which integrates many of the standard functions and controllers on the motherboard, and is not something that Beaver Cleaver's mom used to serve snacks.

+ **Access method:** A *memory access* occurs when data is written to or read from memory. A procedure is used to control each occurrence of the memory being accessed. This procedure consists of having the memory controller generate the signals that specify which memory location needs to be accessed, and then presenting the data to the processor or device that made the request.

+ **Access time:** *Access time* is the time required to read or write data: The measure of time from when the address and proper control signals are given until the information is stored or stored in the device's output(s). Memory is designed in a variety of speeds, such as 100, 70, 60, 53, 50 nanoseconds (ns), and newer memory chips run at 6 ns and faster. Random access memory (RAM) speeds are typically expressed in nanoseconds: the lower the number, the faster the memory. Speeds for some newer forms of RAM are measured in megahertz (MHz), such as the system microprocessor.

+ **Write time:** The *write time* is the time expended from the instant data is entered for storage to the time it is actually stored in the physical memory location.

+ **Interleaving:** A technique known as *interleaving* was developed to help speed up the performance of FPM DRAM (Fast Page Mode Dynamic RAM — see "Random access memory (RAM)" later in this chapter). DRAM requires constant refreshing to maintain the electrical charge that indicates a bit. By using interleaving technique, the read/write speed can be increased fairly substantially.

✦ **Buffered and unbuffered memory:** All systems use a buffer in one way or another. A *memory buffer* is used to store data that's waiting to be transferred. Because the processor must manipulate the data it receives, sometimes it needs a second (actually much less) to catch up with the rest of the data coming down the pipe. Not using a buffer can create chaos for the chip set because it may not be able to keep up with the system memory. Think of a sink: The buffer is the faucet, and the water is incoming data. Run the faucet full blast, and the less you buffer the stream of water. In an unbuffered memory system, the chipset controller deals directly with the memory. If nothing is between the memory and the chip set as they communicate, the chipset could become overwhelmed with data, thus causing the system to become unstable and crash.

✦ **Registered memory:** Some dual inline memory modules (DIMMs) come with registers located on the memory module itself. These registers are used to redrive the signals through the memory chips. This added redriving of the signal allows the modules to be built with more memory chips. The computer's memory controller determines which type of memory the computer requires. When using registered memory, you must use only registered memory. Be sure not to mix unbuffered and registered memory; they don't play well together.

Recognizing Memory Types and Functions

Memory (RAM and ROM) has come a long way in the past several years. Not long ago, a small amount of RAM cost a fortune. Now you can purchase what used to be phenomenal amounts of RAM at a more affordable price. In this section, we provide a quick description of the different types of memory, and then we get into the gruesome details of it all.

Random access memory (RAM)

Random access memory (RAM) is the memory that serves as the workspace for your computer's processor. RAM is a temporary storage area used to store data as the processor uses it. RAM is also known as physical memory and main memory because it's installed in a memory slot on the motherboard. Remember that RAM is lost as soon as you turn off your computer or the computer's power is interrupted by, for example, a power outage. For this reason, RAM is referred to as *volatile memory*. When you launch a software program, it's loaded into RAM.

For example, say you open a new document in Word and you type the best love letter in your life (not that you've ever done anything to warrant the need for one). Gee, your significant other is going to love it! While you're taking a break to get another cup of coffee (or whatever), a storm is brewing outside and lightning strikes nearby, causing the lights to flicker. Because you haven't saved your masterpiece of a letter to your hard drive — which means that the only copy of it is in RAM — you go back to your desk to find Microsoft asking whether you want to try to recover the file. Good luck with that, and enjoy sleeping on the couch later that night.

The type of memory slot available on the motherboard determines the type of RAM your system accepts. As with every other computer component, RAM has evolved significantly over the years. You see the following types of RAM on the test:

✦ **Dynamic random access memory (DRAM)**: *Dynamic random access memory* (DRAM) is commonly used as system RAM. It's capable of storing many bits into a single chip and yet is relatively inexpensive. DRAM is made up of tiny capacitors that hold a charge to indicate a bit. By design, DRAM must constantly refresh in order to maintain the electrical charges in each individual memory capacitor: A charge equals a bit. This constant refreshing creates overhead for the system and slows down the memory read/write speed. A few different types of DRAM have evolved over the years. For the test, you should know the differences between the following flavors of DRAM.

   • **Fast page mode (FPM) DRAM:** FPM is the slowest form of DRAM available and is all but extinct. FPM DRAM runs at speeds between 100 ns and 80 ns and is not compatible with high-speed memory buses over 66 MHz, which most newer CPU and motherboard bus speeds have long surpassed.

   • **Extended data out (EDO) DRAM:** EDO, which is also called hyper page mode (HPM) DRAM, is an asynchronous DRAM type that requires support from the system chipset. EDO can be used in most of the original Pentium systems, some of the later PCI-based 486 motherboards, and older systems that are EDO-tolerant, which means EDO works, but it runs at FPM speeds. EDO timing circuits allow a system to access the memory before the previous request has finished. This translates to transfer speeds of 55 ns or faster and compatibility with 100 MHz memory bus systems.

   • **Burst extended data out (BEDO) DRAM:** Pronounced like "BEE-dough," BEDO DRAM uses a pipelining technology that allows it to operate with much faster bus speeds than the original EDO DRAM.

✦ **Synchronous DRAM (SDRAM)**: Because SDRAM works in unison with the system clock, it is able to read and write in burst mode and support much faster speeds than earlier forms of DRAM. SDRAM is designed to operate with newer 66 MHz and faster bus speeds (12, 8, and 6 ns, and faster — remember a lower number indicates a faster speed). On the test, you'll probably see a question or two concerning memory — don't confuse SDRAM with SRAM! SDRAM is used for system memory while SRAM is far too expensive to be used for this purpose. SRAM is used for the special functions I discuss in the upcoming bullet point "Synchronous RAM (SRAM)."

✦ **Rambus DRAM (RDRAM):** RDRAM, also known as Direct RDRAM (DRDRAM), is a newer memory design designed for use with high-end computer systems. RDRAM is capable of speeds more than twice as fast as SDRAM.

✦ **Synchronous RAM (SRAM):** SRAM is in a memory category of its own. Unlike DRAM, SRAM memory doesn't require periodic refreshing because it does not use capacitors. Instead, transistors are used to store electrical charges that represent 1s or 0s. SRAM is much faster than DRAM with access speeds as fast as 2 ns or less. SRAM is made up of six transistors per bit of storage, which requires up to 30 percent more space than DRAM and also makes it much more expensive.

Comparing DRAM and SRAM

You need to remember a few of the basic differences between DRAM and SRAM for the test. These differences are key when remembering what type of RAM is going to be used for system memory or cache memory. Table 3-1 compares the characteristics of DRAM and SRAM.

Table 3-1	Comparison of DRAM and SRAM Characteristics
DRAM	*SRAM*
Slower	Faster
Simple design	Complex design
System memory	Cache memory
Requires constant refreshing	Doesn't require constant refreshing
Inexpensive	Expensive
Small footprint	Larger footprint

Read-only memory (ROM)

Although many flavors of ROM are available, the test probably won't ask you specifics. For the most part, EEPROM (Electronically Erasable Programmable Read-Only Memory) is used most often nowadays, but you should know the types of ROM, if only to eliminate incorrect answers on the test.

ROM is constructed from hard-wired logic, encoded in the silicon itself, similar to the way that a processor is. ROM is programmed to perform a specific function and, in its most basic form, cannot be altered. This feature is inflexible, and thus regular ROM is used particularly for programs that don't require changes or updates, such as the system or adapter BIOSes.

The following sections describe the various types of ROM used in the PC presently or at one time. Each has its application, but don't worry specifically about the application of each. We are including this information only so you will recognize the terms should they be included in a question on the exam.

✦ **Programmable read-only memory (PROM):** PROM is a blank ROM chip that can be programmed with data. On a PROM, the programming process is irreversible, so what you burn (program) is what you get.

✦ **Erasable programmable read-only memory (EPROM):** An EPROM adds the ability to erase and reprogram the data on the PROM. The EPROM chip looks identical to the PROM with the exception of the quartz crystal window on the top of the chip. However, you need an EPROM eraser, EPROM burner, and/or some other nifty tools to reprogram an EPROM.

✦ **Electronically erasable programmable read-only memory (EEPROM):** Also referred to as Flash ROM, EEPROM is now commonly used for BIOS memory chips. EEPROM can be reprogrammed without removing the chip from the motherboard by using a process of called *flashing* (see "Upgrading the BIOS" later in the chapter).

✦ **Complimentary Metal-Oxide Semiconductor (CMOS):** CMOS is not actually a type of ROM and the BIOS is not stored in CMOS, but CMOS memory is where the BIOS system configuration is stored. Virtually all integrated circuits (ICs) in the server are made by using CMOS technology; but originally this technology was too expensive for anything other than holding the BIOS setup configuration data, and the name stuck. The CMOS memory requires very low voltage and can store data for a significant period with a lithium battery.

Be cautious when upgrading your EEPROM BIOS software because the ROM is hardware specific: You must get the ROM BIOS update from the motherboard manufacturer rather than the ROM manufacturer. The ROM manufacturer only makes the chip, not the software installed on the chip. To obtain the specific EEPROM BIOS update, you must call the motherboard manufacturer or download the software from its Web site. After you have the software, be sure to follow the installation instructions because they will be specific to your motherboard. This procedure is in most cases similar, but it is not at all the same for each manufacturer.

ROM memory is slow and generally appears in small amounts. ROM is ideal for storing the computer's start-up instructions but that's about the extent of it. ROM memory can't keep up with the systems processor and bus speeds. That is what RAM is for — RAM is much faster with larger memory that's just right for the job. See "Upgrading the BIOS," later in this chapter for more information on the flashing process.

Packaging Memory

For the Server+ exam, you should know the packaging types used for memory and how each type is installed on a motherboard. For the test, you need to know the following three common types of memory packages:

✦ **Dual inline package (DIP):** A DIP chip, not the kind with ridges that are great with salsa, are made of plastic or ceramic and are a rectangular shape with rows of pins running across the length of the bottom edge of the chip (see Figure 3-1). More common on older systems, DIP memory was either soldered on the motherboard or inserted into a socket on the motherboard.

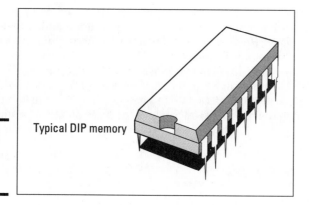

Typical DIP memory

Figure 3-1:
A DIP
memory
chip.

✦ **Single inline memory module (SIMM):** A SIMM is a small circuit board that plugs into a special socket (SIMM socket) on a motherboard. A SIMM chip combines several memory chips on one side of a circuit card. A SIMM has a notch at one end and a notch on its bottom edge near the center of its connector contacts (see Figure 3-2). SIMMs are available in two sizes: 30-pin and 72-pin and either single-sided or double-sided. The 30-pin SIMM is rare these days and the 72-pin SIMM is more common. A 72-pin SIMM is typically double-sided and ranges in size from 1MB to 128MB.

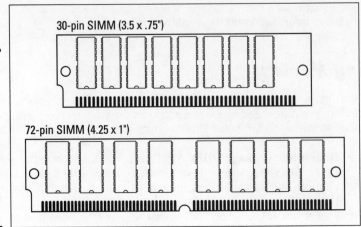

Figure 3-2:
A comparison of the 72 pin SIMM and the 30-pin SIMM. Note the notch in the center of the 72-pin SIMM.

30-pin SIMM (3.5 x .75")

72-pin SIMM (4.25 x 1")

✦ **Dual inline memory module (DIMM):** DIMMs are common in Pentium systems. A DIMM has about the same construction and general appearance of a SIMM. However a DIMM has two notches along the bottom edge of the chip (see Figure 3-3). DIMMs provide a huge speed increase because they are 64 bits in width, which yields the advantage of using a single DIMM rather than a pair of SIMMs. Compare a DIMM with a SIMM in Figure 3-3. Installing a DIMM is as easy as lining up the two notches and pushing the module straight down into the socket — nothing to it.

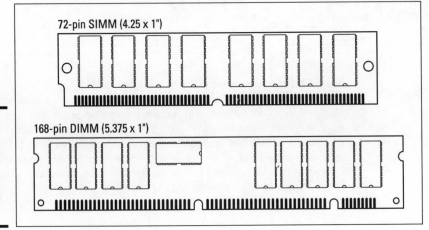

72-pin SIMM (4.25 x 1")

Figure 3-3:
A comparison of the 72-pin SIMM and the 168-pin DIMM.

168-pin DIMM (5.375 x 1")

DIMMs come in buffered and nonbuffered forms, and both 3.3 and 5 volts (V), so you need to be cautious that you install the DIMM supported by your motherboard, chipset, and processor. Install a DIMM by inserting the module into a socket at a slant and then tilting it up until it locks into the upright position. Most DIMM sockets are keyed specifically to a single type of DIMM to prevent the installation of the wrong type.

A buffered DIMM has extra buffer chips that are used to interface with the motherboard. Buffered DIMMs are not very common because the buffers slow the memory down quite a bit, and they're not very effective with today's higher-speed systems. Most systems use standard 3.3V, unbuffered DIMMs, and you could damage the memory if you put a 5V DIMM in a 3.3V socket.

Matching Memory Speeds and Motherboards

The memory modules or chips added to a server must be compatible with the bus speeds of the processor and motherboard. Expect to see questions on the Server+ exam that deal with memory, processor, and motherboard compatibility.

To obtain the best system performance, memory must be matched to the bus speed of the computer. Pentium system bus speeds range from 66 MHz to 100 MHz (PC100) to 133 MHz (PC133). As shown in Table 3-2, a PC133 bus requires 133 MHz memory.

Table 3-2	Memory Compatibilities		
Processor	*CPU Speed (MHz)*	*Bus Speed (MHz)*	*Memory Module Compatibility*
386	25/33	25/33	25/33 MHz FPM
486	50/100	33/50	33/66 MHz FPM/EDO
Pentium	166/200	66	66 MHz EDO
Pentium MMX	166–233	66	66 MHz EDO/SDRAM
Pentium Pro	200	66	66 MHz EDO/SDRAM
Pentium II	233–400	100	100 MHz SDRAM
Pentium III	450–1,130	133	133 MHz SDRAM

Filling a memory bank

Essentially, you should remember two memory-sizing facts for the exam:

✦ A Pentium motherboard with SIMM sockets requires two SIMMs to fill one bank. This is because a Pentium specifies each memory bank at 64 bits and 72-pin SIMMs are only 32 bits each, which means you need to combine two SIMMs to fill one memory bank.

✦ A Pentium motherboard with DIMM sockets needs only one DIMM to fill a bank because 168-pin DIMMs are 64-bit devices.

Unless specifically mentioned, the term Pentium refers to all Pentium-class motherboards and processors, which includes Pentium, Pentium MMX, Pentium Pro, Pentium II, Pentium III, Pentium 4, K6, and 6x86MX (AMD or Cyrix). But, be careful, sometimes Pentium only means Pentium — you know, the original 886 processor.

Matching the metals

If you've spent any time at all working with memory, you've probably noticed that SIMMs and DIMMs have either tin- or gold-plated contacts. If you look closely at the memory socket on the motherboard, you notice that it, too, is either gold or tin. You need to pay attention to the type of contacts when upgrading or replacing memory. When memory is installed on the motherboard, these contacts are under great pressure in the tight-fitting memory sockets. If you install a DIMM with gold contacts into a memory socket with tin contacts, you may run into problems down the road called fretting.

Fretting is a form of corrosion that causes a high resistance path between the DIMM's connectors and the motherboard's socket connectors over time. For optimal performance, use memory that matches the connection surface of the motherboard's memory sockets. Ideally, gold-to-gold should be used, but if your motherboard's memory sockets are tin, then you're stuck using tin-plated memory modules (which isn't really a bad thing).

Detecting memory errors

Diagnosing and correcting memory-related system errors can be a real pain. Following is a list of some of the most common types of memory errors. You should know and understand the types of memory errors and how to diagnose and fix them. Working with network servers requires quick troubleshooting skills, and knowing how to diagnose a problem is key to keeping downtime to a minimum, not to mention extraordinary interpersonal skills to deal with the boss or the user looking over your shoulder giving you pointers.

Here are the most common types of memory errors:

✦ **Hard errors:** A *hard error* is a repeatable error that is the result of defective hardware, incorrectly installed memory, or a failed memory module. A physical flaw, such as a bad capacitor or transistor, a loose memory module, a system that is running too hot, a blown memory chip, or a system board defect are common causes of hard errors. Because this type of error is consistent and repeatable, you have a better chance to isolate the problem. Memory errors that occur during the boot process are usually related to physical defects or problems with the installation of the RAM chips and can be identified by the POST beep codes or text messages. Memory errors that occur after the OS has loaded can be identified by a variety of messages. Some of the more common software memory error messages are listed here:

  • **Divide error:** Indicates that a division by zero or an operation too large to fit into the destination register has occurred.

  • **General protection fault error:** Indicates that a program occupying memory space has become corrupt and has been terminated.

  • **Fatal exception error:** Indicates that a software program executed an illegal instruction or tried to access memory beyond its allocated space. It is not actually a memory fault, but too many fatal exception errors with different programs should prompt you to check out the memory.

✦ **Soft errors:** A *soft error* is a transient error that occurs when a bit reads back a wrong value yet otherwise continues to function correctly. These errors are moving targets and are much harder to diagnose. Soft errors are the result of such factors as poor quality memory, motherboards, or ESD (electrostatic discharge).

Parity and error checking

Many memory systems include provisions to help verify when data being transferred in or out of memory is correct. The primary mechanisms are parity and error checking, both of which you need to know for the Server+ exam.

Non-parity and parity memory

Non-parity is plain old memory; eight bits are used to store each byte of data, containing exactly one bit of memory for every bit of data stored. On the other hand, *parity memory* uses nine bits to store each byte with the extra bit used only for error detection and correction.

Parity memory can use either an even or odd parity scheme. Even parity requires an even number or one bit, and odd — well, we're sure you guessed it. Table 3-3 illustrates how the parity bit is used to create odd and even.

Table 3-3		How the Parity Bit Is Used	
Data Bits	One Bit	Even Parity Bit	Odd Parity Bit
11111111	8	0	1
00000000	0	0	1
11111110	7	1	0
01001000	2	0	1

When a parity error is detected, an error message appears, asking you whether you want to reboot or continue working. Usually you're given three options:

✦ Press S to shut off parity checking and continue working.

✦ Press R to reboot the system and lose any unsaved work in the process.

✦ Press any key to resume your work with parity checking still enabled.

In most cases, you want to press S to shut off parity checking, save your work, and then reboot the system. Then, save your files with a different filename, and if possible, save to a floppy disk to avoid overwriting any files with corrupt data.

The process of parity checking is processor intensive and does slow down overall system performance, and memory errors are to be expected when using DRAM. To enable parity checking, you normally have to go into the BIOS settings and make the appropriate change. Parity does not correct memory errors; it only detects them and prompts the system to stop.

Error checking and correcting

Error checking and correcting (ECC) is a form of memory error detection that also attempts to correct errors as well. ECC can detect and correct single-bit memory errors and detect double-bit errors.

For the exam, you need to remember that unlike parity checking, ECC not only detects single-bit errors but it can correct them as well.

Troubleshooting Memory

Before you begin testing memory, you must disable the system's write-back cache. Disable the write-back cache in the BIOS menu. Memory-testing programs write data and then immediately read it back, but with write-back cache enabled, you may get false results when data is read from cache rather than main memory.

As shown in Lab 3-1, troubleshooting the system memory consists of the following practices:

Lab 3-1   Troubleshooting System Memory

1. **After disabling the write-back cache, restart the system.**

   If errors are detected during the POST, the memory chip itself may be defective or installed incorrectly.

2. **Check the BIOS setup to see what speed is indicated in the timing parameters.**

3. **If the BIOS setup provides a memory timing parameter, select BIOS or setup defaults that are usually the slower of the available options.**

4. **Save changes and reboot the system.**

   If the system successfully reboots, the source of the problem is an incorrect BIOS setting.

5. **If the POST still returns the error message, you probably have a bad SIMM/DIMM or the SIMM/DIMM is not seated properly.**

   The modules may not be matched up properly, and in some cases, SIMMs must be installed in matching pairs.

6. **Remove all memory modules with the exception of the first bank and reboot the system.**

   Removing the memory modules helps you pinpoint exactly which module is bad. If the system still doesn't boot, replace the memory in the first bank and reboot again to verify that the memory in that bank is working properly. If you replace the SIMM/DIMM and the system still will not boot, the motherboard itself may be bad. You'll need to replace the motherboard, too, to verify the integrity and retest.

If the memory errors occur while working in the OS, disable the write-back cache and boot the system to a floppy disk containing the memory-testing application. Follow the instructions to continue the tests. If the testing application does encounter an error, try using the troubleshooting sequence in Lab 3-1. If the memory still tests okay, you'll want to check for any updated software drivers, patches, and updates. If the testing application does not encounter any problems with the memory but you're still encountering memory errors, you may want to take the modules to a PC repair shop that can test the modules with a SIMM/DIMM tester. You may also want to test your power supply, and check the environment for excess static, radio transmitters, EMI (electromechanical interference), or other environmental factors that may be interfering with the components of the PC.

After determining the source of the memory errors, be sure to enable the write-back cache — if you forget to enable it, your system is going to run very slowly.

Upgrading the BIOS

BIOS, which stands for Basic Input/Output System, provides the basic interface between the operating system and the software device drivers of the peripheral devices on a server. The BIOS also contains the instructions used to boot the server, verify its hardware, and start the operating system and device drivers. The BIOS in nearly all server-class PCs is stored on an EEPROM.

On virtually all Pentium-class servers, no special equipment is needed to upgrade the BIOS stored on the Flash ROM. An EEPROM is updated through a process called *flashing*, which involves the use of a specialized (and often proprietary) software utility that either the BIOS manufacturer or the motherboard manufacturer usually supplies.

Upgrading the BIOS typically implements bug fixes or adds new features to the BIOS — features that may not have been available at the time your system was manufactured.

For the exam, know what the system BIOS is and does and know why, when, and how you update the BIOS with a flashing operation, as well as what can go wrong and how to recover. The best source for a BIOS update (flashing file) is the BIOS manufacturer or the motherboard manufacturer, which on some BIOS programs may be the same.

Flashing or not flashing

The first question involved in the process of flashing the BIOS ROM is deciding whether you need to upgrade at all. Many reasons to upgrade the BIOS are valid, the least of which is simply because a new version is available. Other reasons are

- ✦ **Operating system support:** New releases of operating systems often include features not supported by your version of the BIOS.

- ✦ **New CMOS settings:** A newer release of the BIOS may add features to the BIOS setup configuration data, such as Wake-on-LAN or booting from a CD-ROM or a SCSI drive.

- ✦ **Enhanced hardware support:** Updating the BIOS may add support for new hardware devices or hardware accessibility features.

- ✦ **Bug fixes:** This is a very important reason to upgrade the BIOS, especially if BIOS bugs are affecting your server's performance. However, follow the adage: "If it isn't broke, don't fix it."

Preparing to flash

Using a checklist of the actions required to upgrade the BIOS on a server is a very good idea. The checklist could be one prepared by the manufacturer or one of your own making. The important thing is that you do not forget a vital step that could damage the server.

A BIOS upgrade checklist should include the following:

✦ **Manufacturer:** Include the name of the BIOS manufacturer and, if different, the manufacturer and model number of the motherboard, along with the URL for each manufacturer's Web site.

✦ **Processor:** Also identify the processor or processors in the server, which should automatically also identify the manufacturer.

✦ **Current BIOS version and ID:** This information appears on the monitor after the video BIOS is loaded and the POST displays the system messages. At this point of the boot, pressing the Pause key on the keyboard should cause this information to display. If not, reboot until you have the version number. You can also use a software product, such as the BIOS Wizard from Unicore Software (www.unicore.com/bioswiz) to display your BIOS ID and other facts.

✦ **New version of BIOS:** Using the information already gathered for your checklist, you should be able to get the information on the new BIOS version number from the manufacturer's Web site or by calling the manufacturer directly.

✦ **A list of the features or bug fixes the upgrade will provide:** This part of the checklist should be transferred to the server maintenance logbook when the upgrade is completed.

✦ **A list of the actions of the flashing process:** This part of the checklist is actually a checklist itself. It should list the steps to be performed to update the BIOS. The steps should include the following:

 • Decompressing software, such as WinZip or the like, that's available. BIOS files are often compressed for downloading purposes.

 • The flash utility that you can download from the motherboard, computer, or BIOS manufacturer.

 • The upgrade BIOS file that you can download from the motherboard, computer, or BIOS manufacturer.

 • The key or keys used to access the BIOS Setup.

 • A boot disk that you create to boot the server to a real-mode DOS prompt that excludes memory drivers, such as HIMEM.SYS and EMM386.EXE.

Never flash the BIOS from a Windows DOS prompt command box. Remember that if the system locks up, your BIOS may be only partially upgraded and virtually useless.

- Verification that the server is connected to power through a UPS (Uninterruptible Power Supply) of sufficient size to keep the server powered up until the flashing process completes. The flashing process usually takes much less than a minute.

- A paper backup that you create of the BIOS configuration settings. Enter the BIOS Setup and copy down all settings, including all advanced menu functions. Flashing the BIOS resets all settings to their default values.

After you begin the flashing operation, absolutely — under no circumstances — disturb the server. This operation doesn't take long, and as long as you don't have a major power failure, have lightning strike the building, or a similar catastrophe, you should have no worries.

Other flashing considerations

Another BIOS setting that you should disable before flashing the ROM is ROM Shadowing (or *Shadow RAM*, as it is also called). RAM is much faster than ROM, and many systems copy the BIOS into RAM when the server is booted to gain some speed during the boot process.

You can also use the DOS DEBUG command to reset the BIOS Setup configuration to its default settings. The command varies by manufacturer; but for the majority of BIOS programs (meaning AMI and Award), you can enter the following command on a DOS command line prompt (not in a Windows DOS box):

```
C:\DEBUG
-O 70 17
-O 71 17
Q
```

Entering the BIOS setup

To enter the BIOS CMOS setup program, you must press the predefined key or keys. Some of the more common keystrokes appear in Table 3-4. As shown in Table 3-4, these keys can vary by manufacturer. Check the motherboard's documentation or watch the monitor very closely during a boot sequence to get the key or keys for your system.

Table 3-4	Keys Used to Access BIOS Setup
Manufacturer	*Keys*
AMI BIOS	Delete
Award BIOS	Delete or Ctrl+Alt+Esc
IBM Aptiva	F1
Phoenix BIOS	F2
Compaq	F10

Reacting when things go wrong

You should be very cautious and be sure that you have the exact software version for your specific BIOS. Installing the wrong BIOS software is a great way to corrupt your BIOS. The BIOS program that you are most likely to be using, such as Award and AMI, includes features to double-check the flash file's version against the motherboard model, processor, and chipset and to warn you of any mismatches. Be very careful because not all manufacturers include this type of safety feature to prevent the wrong BIOS version from being flashed to the wrong BIOS ROM.

Should any of the possible disasters that could happen when you are flashing your BIOS actually happen, you can make a few recoveries:

✦ **Boot-block:** Virtually all server motherboards have a boot-block BIOS, which is a small part of the BIOS that is not overwritten when you flash the ROM. The boot-block is a block of the BIOS programming that provides support for the floppy disk drive and ISA video cards that can reboot the system from a floppy disk.

✦ **Flash-recovery jumper:** Intel motherboards include a jumper that can be used to enable and disable access to the boot-block BIOS. After moving the jumper to the enable position, boot the system to the DOS boot disk. No video is available, so you must wait for a single beep code and the drive LED to go out, which indicates that the recovery has been completed; then you can restart with the boot disk and reattempt the flashing operation.

✦ **New BIOS chip:** Most manufacturers will either sell or give you a new BIOS chip. In fact, you can purchase chip replacement kits from companies such as Unicore Software (www.unicore.com) or Micro Firmware (www.firmware.com). This option is not available for all systems, however.

Setting up BIOS security

Virtually all BIOS settings include options for a user password and a supervisor password. With the user password set, the computer will not be allowed to boot until the proper password is entered. The supervisor password is used when accessing the BIOS settings. Without the supervisor password, users can't access the BIOS settings; however, the system is allowed to boot.

By setting either of these passwords, you are committing yourself to always remembering the passwords. If you forget the user password but know what the supervisor password is, you can enter the BIOS and clear the password by pressing the Enter key when prompted to do so.

If you forget a password, you will be unable to boot the server (without the user password) or unable to gain access to the BIOS (without the supervisor password). To clear the passwords and reset the CMOS settings to their default values, you can adjust the password-clear jumper. Check the motherboard's documentation for the appropriate settings to use.

On many motherboards, this jumper is located near the lithium battery or the BIOS ROM chip. Another way to clear the password is by removing the CMOS battery and allowing the CMOS memory to clear. By doing either of these procedures, you should be aware that any existing BIOS settings will be lost. Be sure to have this information documented in case the situation arises. Another way of resetting the CMOS is to remove the CMOS battery for five minutes or so. It takes about that long for the CMOS to drain away any power it holds.

The Other BIOS

Many of the system components contain their own BIOS programs. A good example is the video card. Without a set of drivers in a ROM on the video card, you wouldn't be able to see the video display until the drivers were loaded from the hard drive. Many devices have a ROM onboard, and keeping the BIOS in each ROM up to date is a very good idea. The most common devices with onboard ROM are the following:

+ **SCSI adapters:** In general, the SCSI adapter with onboard ROM is going to be for the system's hard drives. If your system has SCSI CD-ROM, Zip, tape drive adapter, and the like, those devices can wait until the OS loads the necessary drivers from the hard drive.

+ **Network adapters:** Those network adapters that allow a PC to be started up from a server have a boot ROM or IPL (Initial Program Load) ROM on the adapter. For example, with Windows 2000 server or the many disk-imaging programs on the market, you can boot from the system's network card and obtain an IP address from a DHCP server. After the system has IP connectivity, the system can download and install a disk image from a server on the network. Smart terminals act in the same manner; they boot directly from the network server.

✦ **IDE and floppy upgrade boards:** In order for the system to boot from CD or floppy disk, the drives must be connected to an adapter that has its own ROM. On most newer systems, the motherboard supplies the ROM and the BIOS, which includes the drivers needed to boot the PC from the IDE or floppy devices. If you add an adapter to support additional floppies and IDE devices, the onboard ROM is needed to allow the devices to be active during startup; otherwise, the devices connected to that adapter will not be available until the OS loads the adapter drivers from the hard drive.

Making the Hard Disk Easy

Hard disk drives connect to the PC through one of its I/O buses, typically the PCI (Peripheral Components Interconnect) bus for most newer drives. Some older disk drives use the VL-bus (Video Electronics Standards Association [VESA] Local Bus) and ISA (Industry Standard Architecture) buses. Disk drives use a signal interface that controls how data is sent to or received from the hard disk. The type of interface used to communicate with the motherboard is how hard disks are classified. If you want to upgrade the hard disks in your server, you need to know the type of drive interface the server supports, assuming you want to install the drives inside the system case.

The most common disk drive interface in use is the IDE interface. This interface and drive type is more properly called the *AT Attachment* (ATA) *interface* (AT once stood for Advanced Technology as a reference to the original IBM PC AT, but it simply means AT these days). You often see these interfaces paired up as IDE/ATA or ATA/IDE. The IDE/ATA interface specification is based on the ISA 16-bit bus and defines power usage and the data signal formats used between the I/O bus controller and the disk drive controller that is integrated into the disk drive, which is where IDE gets its name. A faster version of the IDE/ATA is the Extended Integrated Drive Electronics (EIDE) interface, which is also called the ATA-2 interface. EIDE processes data and interfaces to 32-bit buses.

The IDE/ATA bus in its standard form can support two hard disks or other IDE/ATA devices, such as a CD-ROM or a tape drive, on one channel. On the IDE/ATA channel, one device is designated as the master and the other is a slave. The Master/Slave designation is configured with jumpers on the drive. The EIDE/ATA-2 interface supports up to four devices on one channel. Like IDE/ATA drives, there must be one Master on the channel with the other drives designated as Slaves. Most motherboards support either two IDE/ATA or EIDE/ATA-2 channels. More information is available on IDE/ATA and EIDE/ATA-2 later in this chapter in the section, "Working with the IDE/ATA interface."

The IDE/ATA and EIDE/ATA-2 interfaces are used for hard disk drives installed inside the system case. Larger disk arrays that are typically located outside the server in its own chassis or cabinet use either the SCSI or the Fiber Channel-Arbitrated Loop (FC-AL) interface. FC-AL, commonly called the Fiber Channel interface, uses fiber-optic cables to connect its disk drives to a disk controller and the server. Fiber channel can support up to 127 devices, and because it uses fiber-optic cabling, the devices can be as far as 10 kilometers apart. FC-AL devices can be hot-swapped, which means that they can be inserted and removed without interfering with the operation of the system. For more information on the SCSI interface, see the section "Serving with the SCSI Interface" later in this chapter.

Moving data

Many people get confused at this point. A disk drive connects to a system I/O bus (such as the PCI) using an interface standard (mostly IDE/ATA), but it also uses a protocol to transfer data from the disk drive to system memory. The transfer protocols are used to format the data and handle problems that can arise during the data transfer.

The transfer protocols commonly used on hard disk drives are

✦ **Programmed I/O (PIO):** This is data transfer protocol used with older disk drives. PIO depends on the CPU to move data from the disk to RAM.

✦ **Direct Memory Access (DMA):** Devices that use DMA use built-in controllers to handle the transfer of data to and from memory without assistance from the processor.

✦ **Ultra DMA (UDMA):** UDMA, which is also known as Ultra ATA, ATA-33, ATA-66, ATA-100, and other acronyms, is an enhanced version of the IDE/ATA interface that transfers data between the disk drive and RAM at 33 Mbps, 66 Mbps, or 100 Mbps.

The data cable

IDE/ATA uses a standard 40-wire/40-connector cable to connect to the IDE connector on the motherboard or an adapter card. UDMA/ATA-66 transfer protocols use an 80-wire/40-connector cable. The extra 40 wires are used as grounding wires to provide a buffer between each of the 40 wires carrying data signals. With less cross talk between the wires in the cable, the data can be moved faster. Figure 3-4 compares the two cable types.

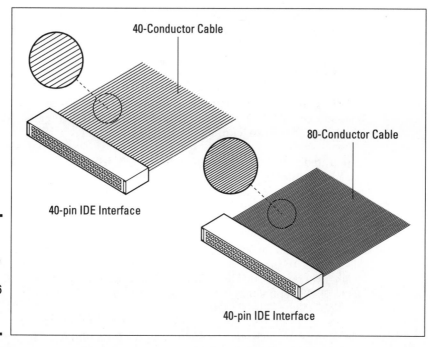

Figure 3-4:
An IDE/ATA
40-pin cable
compared
to an ATA-66
(UDMA)
cable.

IDE/ATA data cables have a red or blue stripe down the edge of the cable that indicates Pin 1 on the connector. Having the correct orientation is very important. If the data cable is installed incorrectly, you can definitely expect POST errors, such as "No disk detected" or "No boot device present."

Data addressing

Just as your house has an address that's relative to its neighboring houses, the block of your street, and the street itself, data is located on a disk drive in an addressing scheme that identifies its relative position. Data on a disk drive is addressed using one of two methods:

✦ **CHS (Cylinder-Head-Sector):** The CHS data addressing method locates data on the disk by cylinder (track), head (which side of the platter), and sector. For example, a file can be located at cylinder 250, head 2, and sector 33. CHS addressing is used by most IDE drives.

✦ **LBA (Logical Block Addressing):** LBA data addressing assigns a sequential logical block number to each sector on the disk. This number is a logical block number rather than physical block number because unusable disk sectors are not included. LBA addressing lists a single logical location for each file. LBA is used on EIDE/ATA-2 and SCSI drives.

You can look in the BIOS setup configuration data to find the number of cylinders, heads, and sectors on the hard disk drive in a server.

Working with the IDE/ATA interface

You'll encounter several questions on the Server+ exam regarding the IDE/ATA interface. Concentrate on formatting and the configuration of masters and slaves and pay close attention to any section that you see in this chapter with an icon.

Integrated Drive Electronics/AT Attachment (IDE/ATA) is the most common disk drive interface used on PCs, as well as on many low-end servers. IDE/ATA integrates the disk controller into the disk drive, which allows the drive to connect directly to the motherboard, or in some cases to a pass-through adapter board installed in an expansion slot.

A user or a technician should never do a low-level format on an IDE/ATA disk drive. To prepare the drive for use, only a high-level format is needed. High-level formatting can be done by using operating system utilities, such as the DOS command FORMAT.COM.

If a server or PC uses an adapter card, the IDE/ATA adapter card is typically a multifunction card that includes support for a floppy drive, a game port, and perhaps a serial port. Most motherboards include connectors for two IDE/ATA interfaces: one for a primary channel and the other for a secondary channel. Each IDE/ATA interface channels support two devices.

IDE/ATA drives are not compatible with SCSI drives; these are two completely different critters.

Serving with the SCSI Interface

The SCSI standard is a collection of interface standards covering a range of peripheral devices, including hard drives, tape drives, optical drives, CD-ROMs, and disk arrays. SCSI allows multiple SCSI devices to be connected to a single SCSI controller and share a common interface.

Like IDE/ATA devices, device controllers are built into SCSI devices. The devices connected to a SCSI channel interface to the server through a host adapter that's typically installed in a PCI slot on the motherboard. The host adapter supports both internal and external channels, allowing it to support hard disks and CD-ROM drives mounted inside the server's case, as well as tape drives, CD-ROMs, and other devices external to the server. Figure 3-5 illustrates this arrangement.

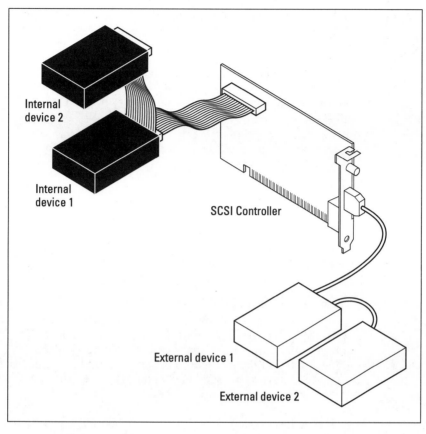

Figure 3-5:
A SCSI host
controller
can support
both internal
and external
devices.

Each SCSI channel, whether internal or external, connects its devices in a series sequence to a single cable, which is referred to as a *SCSI chain*. Each chain has the SCSI host adapter at one end and a terminator at the other end. In order to avoid confusion on the chain, each SCSI device is assigned a unique device number that differentiates it from the other devices on the chain. A device's SCSI ID is configured physically on the device through a jumper.

For example, on a SCSI chain, the host controller is assigned device ID 7 (the ID reserved for the host adapter) and the other devices are assigned numbers that indicate their priority on the SCSI chain. The lower the number, the higher the priority. Slower devices should be assigned higher ID values, so that they are accessed after faster devices. SCSI devices are accessed using a priority scheme. Device ID 7 has the highest priority, as it should, followed by devices 6 through 0 and then devices 15 through 8, if they are in use.

The termination on the SCSI chain prevents messages from bouncing back onto the bus if a message is not picked up by one of the devices on the chain.

Remember that SCSI cables are 50-pin (narrow) low-density or 68-pin (wide) high-density. You'll encounter a few questions on the Server+ exam about external storage devices connected to a server or servers with a SCSI connection.

Maintaining high standards

Yes, there *are* many different SCSI standards, thanks to all of the proprietary and trade association marketing programs. For the Server+ exam, however, you only need a good understanding of only a few of SCSI standards. You don't need to memorize all the different standards, but you should study them enough to gain a basic understanding of each. Table 3-5 summarizes the width, speed, and throughput of each of the SCSI modes. Don't sweat all of the details, but learn which ones are faster than others.

SCSI-1 and SCSI-2

SCSI-1 is now obsolete, but remember that SCSI-1 devices are still compatible with almost all newer SCSI host adapters and devices. SCSI-2 is an improvement on the SCSI-1 specification. SCSI-1 and SCSI-2 devices are compatible, but SCSI-1 devices ignore the additional SCSI-2 features. If you connect a SCSI-1 device to a SCSI-2 host adapter, the SCSI-1 device will work fine, but it will run at its own slower speed.

+ **SCSI-1/Standard SCSI:** SCSI-1 used an 8-bit bus (referred to as *narrow*), had a 5 Mbps transfer rate (slow), and used single-ended (SE) signaling (check out the section "Signaling the SCSI" later in this chapter).

+ **Wide SCSI:** SCSI-2 has many names, but it's known commonly as Wide SCSI and Wide SCSI-2. Wide SCSI devices use a 16-bit (wide) bus on the standard 5 MHz SCSI signaling (slow) and are capable of transferring up to 10 Mbps.

+ **Fast SCSI:** Fast SCSI, or Fast SCSI-2, is based on SCSI-2. Fast SCSI uses 10 MHz (fast) SCSI signaling on the standard SCSI 8-bit (narrow) bus to transmit as fast as 10 Mbps.

+ **Fast Wide SCSI:** Also called Fast Wide SCSI-2, this SCSI mode is the fastest of the SCSI-2 modes. It implements 10 MHz bus speeds (fast) on a 16-bit (wide) bus to provide a maximum transfer rate of 20 Mbps.

You must upgrade both the SCSI host adapter and the SCSI devices to benefit from the speed increase of a newer, faster SCSI solution. Slow drives on a fast host adapter still equal slow.

SCSI-3 modes

The main SCSI-3 flavors you need to know for the exam are

✦ **Fast-20 Wide SCSI/Wide Ultra SCSI/Ultra Wide SCSI:** These are all terms that refer to devices using 20 MHz SCSI signaling on a 16-bit bus to produce data throughput of up to 40 Mbps.

✦ **Fast-40 SCSI/Ultra2 SCSI/Narrow Ultra2 SCSI:** Ultra2 SCSI is the marketing term for the devices defined by the SCSI-3 Parallel Interface-2 (SPI-2) standard. These devices use an 8-bit bus with 40 Mhz signaling to produce a maximum throughput of 40 Mbps.

✦ **Wide Fast-40 SCSI/Wide Ultra2 SCSI:** These modes run on a wide (16-bit) bus by using Fast-40 (40 MHz) signaling that nominally runs at 40 MHz, but can produce a maximum throughput of 80 Mbps.

✦ **Ultra3 SCSI:** This marketing term refers to devices that support a maximum throughput of up to 160 Mbps using Fast-80 (80 Mhz) signaling on a wide (16-bit) bus.

✦ **Ultra160 SCSI:** This marketing term defines devices that support a 160 Mbps transfer speed.

Table 3-5		SCSI Standards			
Mode	*Standard*	*Width (Bits)*	*Speed (MHz)*	*Transfer (Mbps)*	*Cable (Pins)*
SCSI	SCSI-1	8	5	5	50
Wide	SCSI-2	16	5	10	68
Fast	SCSI-2	8	10	10	50
Fast Wide	SCSI-2	16	10	20	68
Ultra	SCSI-3/SPI	8	20	20	50
Wide Ultra	SCSI-3/SPI	16	20	40	68
Ultra2	SCSI-3/SPI-2	8	40	40	50
Wide Ultra2	SCSI-3/SPI-2	8	40	80	50
Ultra3	SCSI-3/SPI-3	16	40	160	68
Ultra160	SCSI-3/SPI-3	16	40	160	68

Ultra2 SCSI uses a narrow bus requiring a 50-pin connector and a LVD (low-voltage differential) or HVD (high-voltage differential) terminator. Ultra3 SCSI uses a wide bus and a 68-pin connector with a LVD terminator.

Don't get Ultra2 SCSI confused with SCSI-2. Ultra2 SCSI is newer, bigger, and allegedly better. Ultra2 SCSI is actually a marketing term for SCSI devices corresponding to the SCSI-3 Parallel Interface — 2 (SPI-2) standard that runs on a narrow (8-bit) bus. SCSI-2 is the SCSI standard that includes Wide, Fast, and Wide Fast SCSI modes.

Connecting SCSI devices

SCSI connectors come in a variety of shapes and sizes. The connector is, obviously, the physical mechanism used to attach a SCSI cable to a SCSI device. In an effort to keep matters as complicated as possible, the SCSI manufacturers use just enough different connectors to create the potential for mismatching connectors between devices. Over the years, the SCSI interface has seen dramatic changes; along with the changes to SCSI interfaces comes plenty of change with regards to the connector types used for SCSI. In Table 3-6, we list the connectors used internally and externally for each of the various SCSI standards. Figures 3-6 and 3-7 illustrate the connectors referenced in the table. (Just in case you're curious, IDC stands for Insulation Displacement Connector.)

Table 3-6	SCSI Standards and Connectors	
SCSI Standard	*External Connector*	*Internal Connector*
SCSI-1	50-pin Centronics	50-pin IDC
SCSI-2	50-pin High Density	50-pin IDC
Ultra SCSI	50-pin High Density	50-pin IDC
Fast SCSI	50-pin High Density	50-pin IDC
Wide SCSI	68-pin High Density	68-pin High Density
Fast Wide SCSI	68-pin High Density	68-pin High Density
Ultra SCSI-3	68-pin High Density	68-pin High Density
Ultra2 SCSI-3	68-pin Very High Density	68-pin High Density

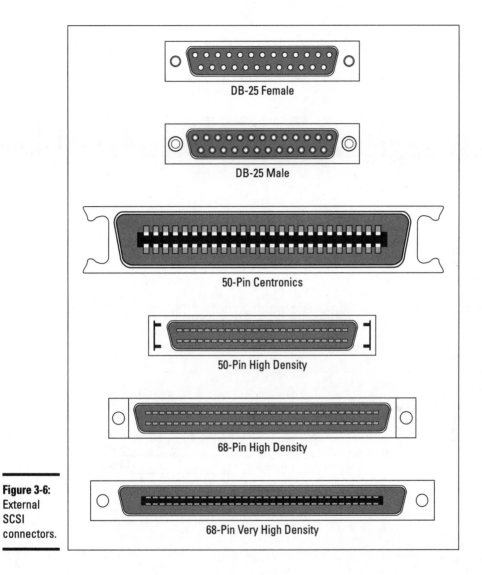

DB-25 Female

DB-25 Male

50-Pin Centronics

50-Pin High Density

68-Pin High Density

Figure 3-6:
External
SCSI
connectors.

68-Pin Very High Density

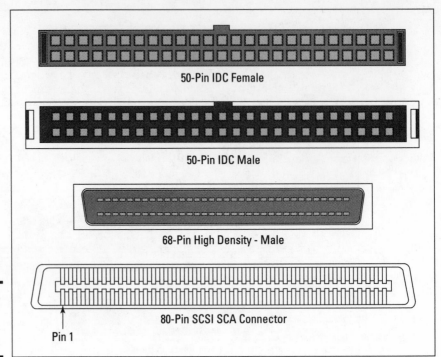

50-Pin IDC Female

50-Pin IDC Male

68-Pin High Density - Male

80-Pin SCSI SCA Connector

Pin 1

Figure 3-7:
Internal
SCSI
connectors.

Connecting to the SCA

One additional SCSI connector you should know for the exam is the 80-pin SCA (Single Connection Attachment), as shown in Figure 3-7. SCA is a high-density connector that includes the power connection as well. The device, such as a hot-swappable hard disk RAID drive, plugs directly into the SCA connector rather than a cable. After the device is plugged into the SCA connector, it uses the flexibility of its 80 pins to take care of all the configuration required for the device, including its ID.

The SCSI connectors most commonly used are the 50-pin Centronics; 50-pin high density (the "A" connector); the 68-pin high density ("P" connector); and the 80-pin SCA connector.

Signaling the SCSI

Expect a question or two on the signaling schemes used with SCSI systems. You need to know which signaling technique is preferred and the limitations of the different SCSI signaling methods. Table 3-7 summarizes the signaling used by each SCSI mode, the number of devices each supports, and the SCSI chain maximum distance.

Single-ended (SE) signaling

Standard SCSI (normal SCSI) uses a signaling technique known as single-ended (SE) signaling that uses a very simple signaling scheme. In the SE signaling scheme, a positive voltage represents a one and nonpositive voltage represents a zero. Because SE signaling is an unbalanced signaling scheme, it is very prone to interference and grounding problems. As a result, a normal SCSI chain is limited to a maximum distance of 6 meters in standard modes and as little as 1.5 meters for faster modes.

High voltage differential (HVD)

For the exam, HVD signaling is virtually obsolete, but here's a bit of background: HVD signaling is much less prone to interference than SE signaling, which allows for SCSI chains with lengths up to 25 meters. The problem with HVD is that its devices and host adapters are larger and more expensive, and they are not compatible with SE signaling devices.

Low voltage differential (LVD)

LVD, which is a combination of the best of SE and HVD signaling, is a differential signaling method designed to provide long cable lengths, lower cost, and electrical compatibility with the still-popular SE devices, to which it is compatible. If you connect an LVD SCSI device to a SE SCSI chain, the device automatically detects it on an SE bus and defaults to SE mode. Thus, regardless of its SCSI level, it performs just like an SE device with data speeds of 20 MHz (Ultra SCSI) and a cable length of 1.5 to 3 meters.

To get the best performance from a SCSI chain, the host adapter and devices should all use LVD signaling. If just one SE device is on the chain, the entire chain defaults to SE signaling mode. LVD is used primarily in Ultra2 (40 MHz) and Ultra3 (80 MHz) SCSI, but it is backward compatible.

Table 3-7		SCSI Signaling	
SCSI Mode	*Signaling*	*Devices*	*Maximum Length*
SCSI-1	SE	8	6 meters
	HVD	8	25 meters
Wide	SE	16	6 meters
	HVD	16	25 meters
Fast	SE	8	3 meters
	HVD	8	25 meters
Fast Wide	SE	16	3 meters
	HVD	16	25 meters

(continued)

Table 3-7 *(continued)*

SCSI Mode	Signaling	Devices	Maximum Length
Ultra	SE	8	1.5 meters
	HVD	8	25 meters
Wide Ultra	SE	8	1.5 meters
	HVD	4	3 meters
Ultra2	LVD	8	12 meters
	HVD	8	25 meters
Wide Ultra2	LVD	16	12 meters
	HVD	16	25 meters
Ultra3	LVD	16	12 meters
Ultra160	LVD	16	12 meters

High voltage differential (HVD) is considered obsolete. Low voltage differential (LVD) signaling is used in the Ultra2 and Ultra3 modes to increase performance and extend cabling lengths.

Terminating the SCSI

Termination is important because of how a SCSI bus transmits data from device to device. Better termination methods help to produce more reliable SCSI chains. Slower SCSI buses are not particular about the kind of termination used, but a faster bus has more demanding requirements and must be terminated properly. In addition, differential signaling (HVD or LVD) requires special termination. Here are the termination methods you should know for the exam:

✦ **Passive termination:** Passive termination is the original terminator, Arnold Schwarzenegger not withstanding. It is the simplest and least reliable termination type. Passive termination uses simple resistors to terminate the bus. Passive termination works great for short, low-speed SE signaling, but it is very rarely used anymore.

✦ **Active termination:** Active termination adds voltage regulators to the resistors to create termination that is more reliable and consistent. This method of termination is the minimum required for any of the faster-speed SE signaling buses (see "Signaling the SCSI" earlier in the chapter).

✦ **Forced perfect termination (FPT):** This type of active termination incorporates the use of diode clamps that force the termination to the correct voltage. This method provides the best form of termination for a SE signaling bus.

✦ **High voltage differential (HVD):** A system using HVD signaling requires the use of special HVD terminators.

✦ **Low voltage differential (LVD):** SCSI implementations using LVD signaling requires a terminator made specifically for the LVD bus.

Passive termination is no longer used with current SCSI devices, including Ultra2 and Ultra3 SCSI.

Terminators must be installed at ends of both the internal and external chains. Many SE signaling SCSI devices have internal terminators that can be used if the device is the last device on a chain. LVD and HVD devices do not have built-in termination and the chain must be terminated with a separate terminator. Some SCSI cables have built-in termination, though.

Host adapters can terminate each bus segment they are supporting. However, the host adapter must be the last device on the chain or segment. If the host adapter is in the middle of an external segment and an internal segment, it is not on the end of either chain; both should be terminated separately, and the host adapter's termination should be disabled.

Is your SCSI getting enough fiber?

You need to know that fiber channel is actually another flavor of SCSI and defined in the SCSI-3 standards. The most common implementation of fiber channel is the Fiber Channel-Arbitrated Loop (FC-AL), which is used to build a storage area network (SAN). A SAN consists of several servers and storage devices interconnected to provide high reliability, performance, and flexibility on an enterprise network.

Preparing the Hard Disk for Work

Expect to see several questions on the Server+ exam that deal with the process used to prepare a disk for use. Hard disk drives must be formatted and in many cases partitioned before you can begin storing data on them. Here is a quick review of the commands and utilities applied in the setup and maintenance of server hard disk drives.

Disk formatting

A hard disk can be formatted by using two formatting levels. Make sure you know what each one does, when it's done, and who should or shouldn't do it. Remember that formatting is done on other disks besides the hard disk — the floppy disk drive, for example.

Low-level formatting

The low-level format erases the disk at the media level (physical erase). Therefore, in most cases, the disk should only need to be cleaned off by using a high-level format (logical erase). A low-level format performs a destructive scan of the disk media, looking for defects in the recording media that would prevent it from holding data. The location of any bad places is recorded to avoid problems in the future. A low-level format should not be necessary on an IDE or SCSI hard disk outside of the factory. Low-level formatting is performed during manufacturing and should not ever be needed again. However, if one is absolutely necessary, the manufacturer of the hard disk drive can provide a low-level formatting utility.

High-level formatting

Any time that a disk drive needs to have its contents removed — or should need to be repartitioned — you must high-level format the drive before it can be used by the operating system. A high-level format erases all the data on the disk and prepares it for use. In most cases, the disk should first be partitioned, and then each partition can be formatted. A high-level format prepares the disk's partitions by creating a root directory and the File Allocation Table (FAT). The FAT is used to record the location and relationships of files and directories on the each partition. When you perform a high-level format, it erases the FAT; this, in effect, erases the disk because all references to the files stored on the disk are erased. If only there were high-level formatting to erase FAT for humans, huh? Entering the DOS utility FORMAT.COM on a command line prompt is commonly used to format a disk.

A low-level format should not be performed on a hard disk drive outside of the factory. A technician or user should never have to do a low-level format on a hard disk drive.

Partitioning the disk

In the previous section, we describe that before data can be stored on a disk, it must be partitioned and high-level formatted. The partitioning of the disk accomplishes two major functions: It reduces very large disk drives to multiple partitions of a more manageable size, and it creates divisions on the hard disk that can be managed and used as separate logical disk drives. Partitioning also supports the installation of two or more operating systems and the creation of multiple file systems (see the section "Creating File Systems" later in the chapter).

You find two types of partitions on a disk, each with its own purpose (know this for the exam):

✦ **Primary partition:** A bootable partition that holds at least the startup portion of an operating system. A hard disk can be divided into a maximum of four primary partitions, but most operating systems can only have one primary partition active at a time.

✦ **Extended partitions:** Any nonbootable partition is an extended partition. This type of partition can be divided into as many as 23 logical partitions, each of which can be assigned its own drive identity. Extended partitions can be used for any purpose. For example, you can set up a D: drive for the purpose of storing data separate from the operating system. Of course, this partition is not active, and it doesn't need to be because there is no operating system on it.

✦ **Logical partitions:** A logical partition is a subdivision of an extended partition. An extended partition can be divided into logical partitions, each of which can be assigned a drive identity. For example, it is conceivable that you could have drives X:, Y:, and Z: on a network server, which are each a logical partition carved out of an extended partition.

The DOS command FDISK is used to partition hard disk drives.

Deciding on a partition size

Disk space is allocated in clusters (groups of disk sectors) and the size of the cluster is directly determined by the size of the disk partition. A bigger partition yields bigger clusters. This is one case where bigger is not better. Big clusters result in fairly large unused spaces throughout the partition. A cluster is assigned a set size. So, if a partition has 16K clusters and most of the data is 10K or less, the result is at least 6K of wasted disk space for each file saved on the disk. Reducing the effective size of the disk, by creating several smaller partitions, results in smaller cluster sizes and less wasted space. On the other hand, if you are working with very large file sizes, you need to size the partition accordingly.

Partition sizes and cluster sizes are determined by the operating system in use. For example, DOS, Windows 3.*x*, and Windows 95a use the FAT (also known as FAT16) file system that requires that partition sizes be smaller than 2GB. This means that a 10GB hard disk must be divided into multiple 2GB partitions. Windows 95b, Windows 98, and Windows 2000 have file systems that allow partitions up to 2 terabytes (TB). Because we don't yet have disk drives quite that large readily available, whatever partition size you want to use should not be a problem for the operating system.

Disk compression

Older servers with disk drives smaller than 1GB commonly use disk compression to extend the capacity of the drive. A disk compression utility, such as Windows DriveSpace, operates in memory and works between the operating system and the disk controller much like a device driver. When a file is saved to the compressed drive, the compression utility intercepts it and compresses the file before saving it to disk. When the file is requested, the compression utility retrieves the file, decompresses it, and sends it on to memory. The downside to a compression utility is that it adds processing time to the read/write process.

Creating File Systems

All operating systems use at least one file system to track the usage of the disk and the placement of files. A file system manages the allocation and utilization of the disk storage on a server. The file system, which technically amounts to the tables used to track both the files stored on the disk and the unassigned space on the disk, is created during the high-level formatting of a partition. The more popular file systems, and the ones included on the Server+ exam, are

+ **FAT, or FAT16 (File Allocation Table):** DOS, Windows 3.*x*, and Windows 95a use this file system to track the location of each file on the hard disk. This file system does not support partition sizes over 2GB. For backward compatibility reasons, Window NT and Windows 2000 also support FAT, but typically FAT is used with these operating systems only for purposes of dual booting with one of the operating systems to which FAT is the native file system.

+ **FAT32 (32-bit FAT):** FAT32, found in Windows 95b (OSR2) and Windows 98, supports hard drive partitions as large as 2TB and uses a smaller cluster size for more efficient utilization of the disk.

+ **HPFS (High Performance File System):** HPFS is the file system used on OS/2 systems. Its architecture is the basis for many new file systems, including NTFS. HPFS features improved reliability, security, speed, and efficiency over FAT.

+ **NTFS (NT File System):** The native file system for Windows NT, NTFS includes such features as transaction logs to help recover from disk failures; the ability to set permissions at the directory or individual file level; and the ability of files to span across multiple disks or partitions.

+ **UNIX File System/Linux File System:** The UNIX and Linux files systems are the same and use a hierarchical branching-tree file structure that can have an unlimited number of subdirectories and sub-subdirectories, all emanating from a root directory on each partition (file system).

✦ **VFAT (Virtual File Allocation Table):** VFAT, which is supported by
Windows for Workgroups, Windows 95, Windows 98, and Windows NT,
serves as an interface between applications and the actual (physical)
FAT. VFAT is invoked when the processor switches into protected mode
during the protected mode phase of the boot process. Technically, VFAT
is a file system that uses the same directory structure, format, and partition type as ordinary FAT. VFAT is simply a way to store more information in the FAT directory.

VFAT, which has always sounded something like a villain in a Kung Fu
movie, was the first file system to offer support for long filenames.
Because it's built on ordinary FAT, each file has to have an eight-character
name and three-character extension. However, VFAT then allocates additional directory blocks to hold a longer file name. Programs running in
DOS, OS/2, and Linux (and old 16-bit Windows programs) do not use or
see the longer filename. Only Windows NT or Windows 9x make use of the
longer name. Because VFAT uses the old FAT directory to add some
unusual new entries, the VFAT additions can be damaged if the disk is
manipulated by a DOS or OS/2 disk utility that does not understand the
new structure. Even a simple DEL command under OS/2 for a FAT dataset
with a long filename can leave the extra blocks in the directory.

Table 3-8 lists the operating systems that support each of the common file
systems.

Table 3-8	File Systems and Operating Systems
File System	*Operating Systems*
FAT	DOS, Windows 3.x, Windows 9x, Windows NT/2000
FAT32	Windows 95b and greater, Windows 2000
HPFS	OS/2
NTFS	Windows NT/2000
UNIX/Linux File System	UNIX/Linux
VFAT	Windows 3.x, Windows 9x, Windows NT/2000

Prep Test

1 A DIMM has a total of _____ pins.

A ○ 30

B ○ 64

C ○ 72

D ○ 168

2 ECC is able to detect errors and _____ them.

A ○ Duplicate

B ○ Log

C ○ Correct

D ○ Prevent

3 When troubleshooting memory problems, you must first disable _____ in the BIOS.

A ○ ECC

B ○ Parity checking

C ○ Write-back cache

D ○ Power management

4 Where must terminators be installed on a SCSI bus?

A ○ On the adapter

B ○ On the device

C ○ On the controller

D ○ On both ends

5 Your server has an existing host adapter and Ultra2 SCSI drives. You want to upgrade the server to use Ultra3 drives. What will you have to do in order to achieve the best performance?

A ○ Replace only the Ultra2 drives.

B ○ Replace only the Ultra2 adapter.

C ○ Replace the drives and the adapter.

D ○ Change the jumpers on the drives.

6 Ultra ATA drives are _____ with Ultra3 SCSI drives.

A ○ Compatible

B ○ Not compatible

C ○ Compatible using cable adapters

D ○ Compatible using the same controller

7 _____ termination works great for short, low-speed SE SCSI, but is not suitable for modern SCSI buses.

A ○ Active

B ○ Forced Perfect Termination (FPT)

C ○ Low Voltage Differential (LVD)

D ○ Passive

8 How do you clear the CMOS settings and any unwanted or forgotten BIOS passwords?

A ○ Format the hard drive.

B ○ Run FDISK utility.

C ○ Edit the `AUTOEXEC.BAT`.

D ○ Adjust the CMOS/password-clear jumper.

9 What is the name of the process used to upgrade a BIOS on an EEPROM chip called?

A ○ Booting

B ○ Firming

C ○ Flashing

D ○ Pipelining

10 During a flashing operation, the power fails on a Pentium-class server that is not attached to a UPS. The server has a PCI video card. Attempts to reboot the server end with no video display and no beep codes sounding. What is likely to be the problem?

A ○ The power supply was damaged by the power failure and must be replaced.

B ○ The BIOS ROM is physically damaged and must be replaced.

C ○ The boot block should be activated and the flashing operation retried.

D ○ The video card is damaged and must be replaced.

Answers

1 **D.** DIMMs are made with a total of 168 pins along the bottom edge of the module. *Review "Random access memory (RAM)."*

2 **C.** Unlike parity checking, ECC can detect and correct single bit errors. *Check out "Error checking and correcting."*

3 **C.** Anytime that you're going to use memory-testing software, you need to disable the write-back cache function in the BIOS. *Take a look at "Troubleshooting Memory."*

4 **D.** Each end of a SCSI bus must be terminated to prevent messages from bouncing back onto the bus. Don't be fooled by the placement of the host adapter — if it's in the middle of two devices, it's not at the end of the bus. *Check out "Terminating the SCSI."*

5 **C.** You need to replace the drives and the adapter because Ultra2 drives use 50-pin (narrow, 8-bit) connectors, and the Ultra2 adapter is not as fast as the Ultra3 adapter. *Look over "Maintaining high standards."*

6 **B.** Ultra ATA is an IDE interface that is not compatible with SCSI technology. *Review "Maintaining high standards."*

7 **D.** Passive termination is rarely used with today's SCSI standards. *Take a look at "Terminating the SCSI."*

8 **D.** Resetting the CMOS jumper on the motherboard causes CMOS values, including password settings, to be reset to their default values. *See "Setting up BIOS security."*

9 **C.** Flashing is used to upgrade the BIOS ROM (also known as Flash ROM) under software control. *Look over "Upgrading the BIOS."*

10 **C.** The boot-block BIOS is never overwritten and allows the system to boot to the floppy disk and an ISA video. *Take a look at "Reacting when things go wrong."*

Chapter 4: RAID and High Availability Systems

Exam Objectives

✔ Defining the concepts and practices of high availability systems

✔ Listing the features, capabilities, and configuration of RAID systems

✔ Explaining the use and operation of RAID implementation levels

The strange aspect about network users is that they fully expect the resources of a network to be available whenever they want to access them. As unreasonable as this expectation may seem at face value, it's your job to make sure the network and its resources are actually available at all times. This is why the Server+ exam focuses around 12 percent of the test on disaster recovery, RAID, and other high availability and fault-tolerant hardware, software, and procedural areas. The focus of this chapter is RAID (Redundant Array of Independent [or Inexpensive] Disks) and high availability systems, which you should expect to account for at least five or six exam questions.

The need for high availability data storage is booming, and IT professionals are scurrying to keep up with the storage needs of our users. Storage space is not our only concern, however. We must also put our beady little minds to work to figure out just the right configuration to meet the needs of our users while concurrently providing high availability of the data. You need to make many choices when planning your server configuration and what method of fault tolerance you want to implement. Each choice is determined by need, cost, performance, data availability, and scalability.

Because RAID is common in servers, you need to know the ins and outs of RAID for the Server+ test. In this chapter, we review the different features, functions, and RAID levels available. If you don't have a lot of experience with RAID, strongly consider setting up a lab to get some hands-on experience to reinforce the content of this chapter.

Understanding RAID

Redundant Array of Independent (or Inexpensive) Disks (RAID) is a prime topic on the Server+ exam. RAID is one of the high availability techniques you can use to protect a network's data resource against hardware failure.

RAID is a data storage method that distributes data over two or more hard drives to guard against losing the data should one of the hard disk drives fail. All self-respecting servers use RAID in one form or another. RAID is a fault tolerance technique that protects the integrity of the data stored on the hard disks. *Fault tolerance* means that resources are structured so that they are able to withstand hardware faults and failures.

Understanding RAID concepts

By distributing the data across two or more drives, RAID lessens the impact of a disk drive failure. The Server+ exam expects you to have a very good understanding of RAID, including when, why, and how RAID is applied. You definitely need to understand these very important RAID concepts:

✦ **Mirroring:** A fault tolerance technique that duplicates all read/write processes to two separate (mirrored) disks. Writing duplicate data segments or files to more than one disk provides data redundancy. If one drive goes to hard drive heaven, the data on the mirrored drive is still available, and the system is able to continue running. As illustrated in Figure 4-1, mirroring writes data to two separate hard disk drives connected to a single RAID controller.

✦ **Duplexing:** An enhanced version of mirroring that duplicates data on two separate hard drives, but uses a separate RAID controller for each hard disk drive. This arrangement adds another layer of fault tolerance for your data. Not only is the data protected against a hard drive failure, but it's also protected against one of the RAID controllers failing as well. Check out such a structure in Figure 4-2.

✦ **Striping:** A disk read/write technique that writes data across multiple disks in what are called *stripes*. Data striping uses disk drives in parallel by having each disk drive read or write a piece of a file at the same time. The data is divided into stripes, and each drive writes or reads its stripe at the same time as the other drives are reading their stripes of the file Striping works something like this: Instead of saving a large file on one disk, the file is divided into byte-sized pieces (yes, we mean that literally) and saved across several disks.

Striping is a read/write technique used to improve disk performance and is not a fault tolerance technique. To get fault tolerance from striped data, you must add parity; see Figure 4-3.

✦ **Parity:** Often added to striping to gain the benefits of performance and fault tolerance because mirroring doubles the disk space required. The parity used with RAID structures is very much like that used with DRAM (Dynamic Random Access Memory — see Book V, Chapter 3). The parity information, which also contains error correcting code (ECC) data, is calculated for each disk and then mirrored on another disk. If a drive should fail, the data on the lost drive can be re-created from the parity information on the remaining drives.

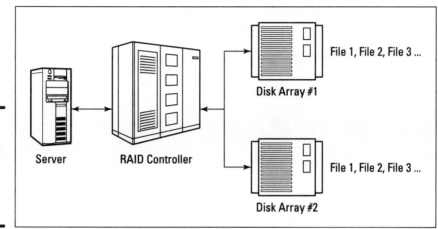

Figure 4-1:
A RAID
system that
implements
mirrored
hard disk
drives.

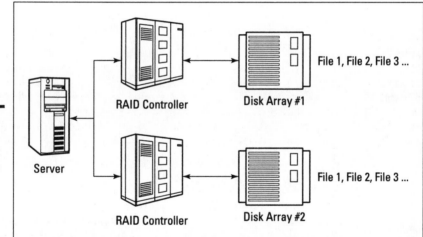

Figure 4-2:
A RAID
system that
implements
duplexed
controllers
and disk
drives.

For the test, remember that mirroring and parity are the two RAID techniques that provide fault tolerance and that duplexing and striping are used to increase read/write performance to and from hard disk drives.

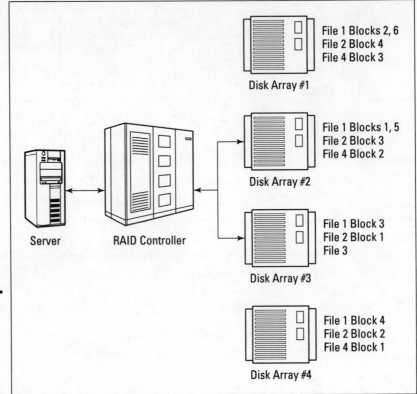

Figure 4-3:
A RAID
system that
implements
data
striping.

Reviewing RAID levels

There are ten different RAID levels, 0 through 7, 10, and 53. Each one is more complex than its predecessor. However, for the exam you need to be familiar only with RAID levels 0, 1, 3, 5, and the 0+1 combination. Here is a quick review of these RAID levels:

✦ **RAID 0 (data striping):** A striped volume combines areas of free space from multiple hard disks into one logical volume that can be spread over as many as 32 disks. Striped sets are very much like extending a simple volume or creating a spanned volume. If any of the disks in a striped volume fail, the data in the entire volume is lost. Remember that RAID 0 is not fault tolerant.

✦ **RAID 1 (data mirroring or duplexing):** Under RAID 1, data is stored in mirror sets. A *mirror set* contains two identical copies of a file or partition that are physically written to two separate hard disk drives. The logic behind RAID 1 is should either of the disks fail, the data can be recovered from the other disk. Mirror sets offer the fastest data recovery with very little impact on system performance because the mirrored partition contains all the data. When you configure your boot partition on a mirror set, you don't have to reinstall the Windows NT Server to restart the computer: Just swap the disks and reboot. RAID 1 does require more disk space than other RAID levels.

✦ **RAID 3 (data striping with single-disk parity):** This RAID level adds parity to RAID 0. An entire dedicated disk is used to store the parity information, which can be used to reconstruct lost data should a hard disk fail (provided that the failed drive is not holding the parity information).

✦ **RAID 5 (disk striping with distributed parity):** This combines the best of RAID performance and fault tolerance. RAID 5 uses the equivalent of one dedicated disk drive to store parity strips. Figure 4-4 illustrates how RAID 5 distributes not only the data but the parity as well. RAID 5 requires at least 3 disks and supports up to a maximum of 32. If a disk in the set fails, none of the data will be lost, but the system will be substantially slower because the system must read both the old parity and data stripes and compute the new parity stripe before writing data.

✦ **RAID 0+1 (striping and mirroring without parity):** RAID 0+1 combines the mirroring of RAID 0 with the data striping of RAID 1 to provide both excellent performance and fault tolerance. This special RAID implementation stripes data across the drives in the same manner as RAID 0 and then mirrors the striped drives with an equal number of drives. If the RAID 0 part of this implementation is set up on five disk drives, you must have five additional drives for the RAID 1 part. RAID 0+1 provides data redundancy for the striped data sets. However, be aware of this problem: After you invoke the fault tolerance, you no longer have redundancy when any one of the drives fails.

✦ **RAID 1+0 (mirroring and striping without parity):** This special type of RAID, which is also called RAID 10, uses mirroring and striping like RAID 0+1, but the implementation is reversed. Under RAID 1+0, disks are mirrored to create a series of mirrored sets. The mirrored sets are striped across the six disk drives so that each disk is mirrored and all of the mirrored sets are striped — therefore, you can lose half of the disks and still likely survive.

Although RAID helps to keep the data on a server available and current in a fault-tolerant disk configuration, the importance of data backups does not diminish. RAID cannot help you with user errors, sabotage, software malfunctions, and catastrophic disasters, such as fire, earthquakes, tornadoes, and floods. Hard disk fault tolerance is not an alternative to a sound backup strategy that includes offsite storage (see Chapter 8 for details on tape backup and disaster recovery).

Figure 4-4:
RAID 5
divides both
data and
parity
information
into stripes
that are
stored
across
multiple
hard disk
drives.

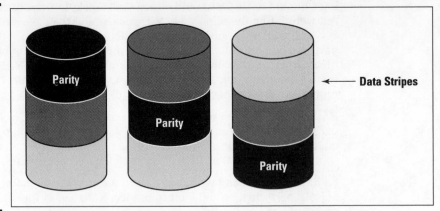

Data Stripes

Comparing hardware and software RAID

RAID can be implemented on a server through either software RAID or hardware RAID. The difference is where configuration and control for a RAID implementation comes from.

✦ **Software RAID:** Many server operating systems, including Windows NT, Windows 2000, NetWare, and UNIX, include utilities that allow you to logically configure the hard disks for RAID. The downside to software RAID, which isn't major, is that the RAID controller (like many device drivers) isn't available until the operating system is loaded and running. Thus, you can't boot the system from a RAID disk drive; you must configure a separate non-RAID boot drive with a boot partition.

✦ **Hardware RAID:** Hardware RAID does not require the operating system to be running to access the disk drives. A server with hardware RAID can boot the system from the disk array, but it could (if need be) boot the system with a drive missing.

Keeping the Server Highly Available

For the test, you should understand the importance of high availability and how to keep a server online and its resources available. *High availability* systems are just what their name implies: systems that are highly available, resistant to hardware and software failures, and stubbornly ready even in the face of a power outage. Another term used to describe high availability systems is *fault tolerant*, which means that a system can handle component, connection, or electrical faults and failures.

Expect to see questions on the test regarding what you should do when a server experiences a drive failure. Here are some high availability and fault tolerance terms you should know for the test:

✦ **Failover:** A system has failover protection if a replacement or redundant component is immediately available for a failing or failed component. The benefit of a failover system is that it minimizes the downtime of a system. Failover protection can be as simple as having a spare hard disk to plug in should a hard disk fail or as sophisticated as having an online server that automatically picks up the processing if a server goes down.

✦ **Hot plug (hot swap):** Failed devices on a server chassis that supports hot plug components can be replaced without taking the server offline or shutting it down. A common implementation of this technology is Adapter Fault Tolerance (AFT) that lets you replace an adapter, such as a PCI (Peripheral Components Interconnect) card, while the server is running and without interrupting the network. For example, if disk duplexing is implemented on a server and one of the disk controllers fails, you can replace the controller with the system up. See "Swapping devices" later in the chapter for more information on hot swap devices.

✦ **Clustering:** Although RAID protects the data resource, it doesn't protect the server itself. Clustering connects two or more servers to enhance data availability, reliability, scalability, and server manageability. Clustering is a kind of RAID for servers. Clustered servers are connected so that when one server fails, the other server or servers take over support for users and any running processes from the failed server. In most cases, clustering is completely transparent to the user. Clustering also provides scalability; servers can be added to the cluster without network downtime.

Here are the two types of clustering, used in different ways:

• **Shared storage clustering:** Definitely expect to see this type of clustering on the exam. Shared storage cluster servers are connected by SCSI (Small Computer System Interface) adapters. One server is designated as the primary server that carries the processing load as long as it is active. All the servers in the cluster are designated as secondary servers. All the servers in the cluster have full access to the same shared storage devices; thus, if the primary server fails, a secondary server is ready and able to take up the role of the primary server. The failover process takes only a few seconds (typically from 5 to 15 seconds) because of the SCSI connection. The clustering ensures that there is very little downtime or performance degradation involved in the failover. Because of the physical distance limitations of the SCSI standards, the servers must be relatively close to one another.

- **Server mirroring clustering:** In this clustering form, mirrored servers are connected over a network. The advantage of this type of clustering is that the primary and secondary servers can be separated over longer distances. The downside is the failover time, which can take from 15 to 90 seconds before a secondary server is able to take over the I/O (input/output) tasks. You also face the risk that data may be lost during the failover process.

In either form of clustering, the administrator determines the events that can trigger a failover. For example, you may want the clustered servers to switch over when a program or process hangs, when a peripheral device fails, or you may want to manually perform the switch-over yourself.

When two or more devices are connected into a cluster using a SCSI cable, or if more than one server shares an external disk array using a SCSI controller, any boot or disk access problems are likely to be the result of an improperly configured SCSI bus. That should be the first thing you check.

✦ **Adapter Fault Tolerance (AFT):** AFT is a form of adapter teaming (see Chapter 10) that provides network connection redundancy by supporting failover for two network interface cards (NICs) in a single server. If one of the server's links to the network fails, the redundant NIC automatically begins handling all incoming and outgoing network traffic. Most AFT adapters are also hot plug devices.

Swapping devices

Having spare components on hand, such as adapter cards and hard disk drives, is a great idea so that you're ready if a drive or card fails. For the Server+ exam, you should know the different ways to swap a hard drive and why one way may be better than another in a given situation. You need to know how to rebuild a disk array after the replacement drive is installed (see the section "Rebuilding the data" later in this chapter). Here are the disk swap techniques you should know:

✦ **Cold swap:** Cold swap devices can only be installed when the server is shut down and powered off.

✦ **Warm swap:** Warm swap devices can be installed while the server is running, but you must stop the device driver on the component's interface bus.

✦ **Hot swap:** Hot-swap components can be removed and installed while the system is running.

✦ **Hot spares:** Hot spares, which are also referred to as failover devices, are installed in a server, attached to a controller, and in standby mode ready to be activated should another device fail.

For more information on the different types of swap devices, see Book IV, Chapter 6.

Rebuilding the data

Expect a question on the actions used to rebuild the RAID structure on a server after you have replaced a failed drive, regardless of the type of swap used. As you might expect, the procedures used are different for software and hardware RAID.

Software RAID

Under software RAID, the system begins rebuilding the missing data as soon as the disk drive is detected with data copied from the other disks in the array. Depending on the RAID level in use, the disk either receives mirrored data from another disk or begins receiving data stripes as they are written to the disk, or both. Restoring RAID while the system is active can seriously impact the performance of the system because users have to compete with the RAID rebuilding process to get data. You're better off waiting until after the peak usage hours for the network to begin the rebuilding process. Many software RAID systems allow the administrator to indicate whether the rebuild should begin automatically or wait for a release from the administrator.

Hardware RAID

Remember that hardware RAID is not a service of the operating system. The administration of hardware RAID must be done either before the operating system is loaded during the boot sequence in the BIOS Setup utility or with a dedicated utility. However, like most software RAID systems, a hardware RAID generally rebuilds or restructures its array automatically when it senses that a new drive has been inserted.

The test asks several questions concerning RAID, so be prepared. If you have very little experience building or rebuilding RAID configurations, definitely take a look at the Windows NT or Windows 2000 Disk Manager or the Novell NetWare Disk Manager to get an idea of the interface used when setting up software RAID. The Windows and NetWare Disk Manager utilities are similar enough that you only need to work with one of the two to get the general idea of how they work.

Prep Test

1 Data mirroring is a common method of _____.

- A ○ Parity
- B ○ Fault tolerance
- C ○ Imaging
- D ○ Increasing read/write performance

2 Data striping is used to increase _____.

- A ○ Fault tolerance
- B ○ Parity
- C ○ Read/write performance
- D ○ Storage space

3 Disk striping is known as _____.

- A ○ RAID 0
- B ○ RAID 1
- C ○ RAID 3
- D ○ RAID 5

4 Which of the following RAID levels does not provide fault tolerance?

- A ○ RAID 0
- B ○ RAID 0+1
- C ○ RAID 1+0
- D ○ RAID 5

5 RAID 5 requires a minimum of _____ disks.

- A ○ 2
- B ○ 3
- C ○ 5
- D ○ 32

6 A feature of most server-level operating systems is a utility that implements _____, which can be used to configure an array of disks.

- A ○ Hardware RAID
- B ○ Disk formatting
- C ○ Disk compression
- D ○ Software RAID

7 When a second server is installed in a cluster with an existing server, both are connected to an external disk array over a SCSI connection. However, when the servers are started, only one or the other succeeds to boot. What should you check?

A ○ RAID controllers

B ○ SCSI bus

C ○ Cluster controller

D ○ Setup on the newest server in cluster

8 Use this technique to provide NIC redundancy and fault tolerance.

A ○ Clustering

B ○ Hot plug

C ○ Hot swapping

D ○ Adapter fault tolerance

9 Which of the following devices is an excellent choice for unattended servers?

A ○ Hot spare

B ○ Hot swapping

C ○ Cold swapping

D ○ Warm swapping

10 When a drive in a RAID structure fails, how is the performance of the server and network impacted while the RAID structure is rebuilt?

A ○ You see no impact on performance, which is the beauty of RAID.

B ○ Performance is degraded because incoming I/O requests must compete with the rebuild activities.

C ○ Performance is improved for a period, but no fault tolerance is available.

D ○ The RAID structure is unavailable to the network until the rebuild activities complete.

Answers

1 **B.** Mirroring is used to provide fault tolerance but is more expensive because it doubles the drive space required. *Review "Understanding RAID concepts."*

2 **C.** Striping is used to increase read/write performance, which does not provide fault tolerance. *Look at "Understanding RAID concepts."*

3 **A.** RAID 0 implements disk striping. Remember that it does not provide fault tolerance. *See "Reviewing RAID levels."*

4 **A.** Okay, we've beaten this dead horse long enough. But, you should know that RAID 0 does not provide fault tolerance. *Check out "Reviewing RAID levels."*

5 **B.** RAID 5 requires a minimum of 3 and maximum of 32 disks. *Look at "Reviewing RAID levels."*

6 **D.** A utility that implements and supports software RAID is included in Windows NT, Windows 2000, and NetWare operating systems. *Review "Comparing hardware and software RAID."*

7 **B.** It is very likely the SCSI adapters are competing for access to the disk and the clustering circuit and are canceling each other out. *See "Keeping the Server Highly Available."*

8 **D.** Adapter fault tolerance provides NIC redundancy and an automatic failover for access to LAN and WAN links. *Check out "Keeping the Server Highly Available."*

9 **A.** A hot spare is a device that is installed and powered but maintained in a standby state. The spare is automatically put online should another device fail. *Study "Swapping devices."*

10 **B.** When a drive fails, system performance is degraded and even more so during the rebuilding process. *Look at "Rebuilding the data."*

Chapter 5: Installing a Server

Exam Objectives

✔ Listing the steps of preinstallation planning

✔ Defining the tools used to verify hardware compatibility

✔ Explaining the various environmental conditions affecting a server

✔ Describing the procedures for installing hardware in a server

✔ Detailing the steps to install a server in a rackmount system

✔ Explaining the need to document a server's configuration

*B*efore you can install a new network server, you must carefully plan its configuration and installation. In this chapter, we explain the things you should consider when planning, installing, configuring, verifying, and documenting a network server. Along with this discussion, we also provide an overview of the tools, software, and documentation required during and after the server installation.

The Server+ exam expects you to know the steps involved in configuring and installing a server in a server room. The test seems to favor the use of lockable rackmount cabinets, so if your experience involves only servers that stand in a corner or in a locked closet, you really should review this chapter.

We have included the configuration of external Small Computer System Interface (SCSI) devices in this chapter, as well. The Server+ exam has several questions on configuring and troubleshooting both internal and external SCSI storage devices. (See Book V, Chapter 3 for the details on SCSI devices.) How important is SCSI on the exam? Well, the Server+ exam could easily be renamed the SCSI+ exam.

The information in this chapter includes several best practices that you should be using in the real world — you know . . . the world that exists outside the exam and its objectives. But, then, you're already using all of this stuff and more, aren't you?

Planning the Server Installation

In most cases, "needs" determine the role that a server plays on a network. A server must address the needs of the organization, the network users, and the system administrator (you). Unless you're really bored, don't have enough to do, or have way too much time available, chances are that you wouldn't be configuring a server just for the exercise. The point is that if you're considering the installation of a server, you should do some planning before actually installing and configuring it.

The role of the server also determines its configuration and what components it should have. A mail server, file server, domain controller, RAS (remote access server) server, or print servers are all configured differently and require a different configuration of the components they typically share. Some servers need more processing power, memory, hard drive, and network cards more than other servers. However, before you make your trip to the server superstore, you should figure out exactly what components each server to be configured needs to fulfill the job you have assigned it.

What purpose a server is to serve is the most important factor when planning its configuration.

Checking the list

If you're lucky, you may be able to purchase a server in the exact configuration needed. However, if you're recycling an existing server, you'll probably be adding and removing components to and from the server. The bad news is that not every operating system is compatible with every type of hardware you can install in the server. The good news is that the major network operating systems (NOS), at least the ones you should know for the exam, all provide a list of the components — and software in some cases — with which they are compatible.

The *Hardware Compatibility List (HCL)* lists the hardware (and software) with which an NOS is compatible. Microsoft, Novell, Red Hat, and most other NOS manufacturers maintain an up-to-date HCL on their Web sites. The HCL should be used to check whether the hardware components you plan to use are verified for use with the NOS and if so, you can be reasonably assured that you shouldn't have problems using them. However, keep in mind that the HCL is not a guarantee that any component (even if it is listed in the HCL) will work. The hardware or its device driver could have changed since the list was produced.

Use the HCL to verify that the server's hardware components are compatible with the NOS you're planning to install.

Gathering the parts

After you determine that the server components on your wish list are listed as compatible on the HCL, you can go ahead and gather the components you want to use. Don't start assembling the server until you have all of the components together, along with all of the associated documents and manuals (and software product keys, if needed) for every component.

Always use the vendor-specific device drivers that came with the device. Check the manufacturer's Web site for updated drivers. Device drivers that are packaged with a product can sit on the shelf for a while and become out-dated. As a matter of routine, you should regularly check the manufacturer's Web site for updated device drivers.

A very common hardware installation problem is the use of incorrect device drivers.

You should also have any service packs, firmware updates, and software updates on hand so that you can update your NOS, drivers, and applications before putting the server into production. The last thing you want to do is to bring down the server and interrupt service just to do a quick driver update or application update. In most cases, you'll have to reboot the server after applying an update of any sort.

Before you begin installing the components, you should be sure you have the proper tools for the job. Generally, you can do just about any hardware install or upgrade by using a multibit screwdriver, an anti-static strap, a piece of paper, and a pen. Of course, you may need many other tools but these are the core four. For test time, you need to remember that it's very important to document, document, document. Document the planning; document the installation; and document any changes or attempted changes you make to the server. In most cases, if an exam question asks about what you should do before or after making a change to a server, it's a pretty safe bet that the answer will involve documenting what you're about to do or what you've done.

After you have all of the parts, software, and tools gathered, a couple of steps remain before you actually install the server: identifying and preparing the physical location of the server, and making sure that you have a network connection for the server.

The room in which the server is to be located should be secure (see Book V, Chapter 9 for more information on securing the server room and the server), environmentally friendly, and have adequate power. (Read all about these details in the next section, "Setting the Environment.") Then, verify that a network connection is available and that you don't also need to reconfigure the network infrastructure to add the new server. You should have the server connected to the network during its installation and configuration. This is especially true with Windows NT/2000/XP (and most other operating systems as well). To join a domain (Windows NT) and configure a network interface card (NIC), you must be able to interact with the network. Thumb through Book V, Chapter 6 for more details about this part of the process.

Setting the Environment

Before you can install a server, you must verify the design and environment of the room or space in which you plan to place the server. The Server+ exam includes questions about how a server room should be configured and what to avoid when it comes to designing and maintaining a server room.

The first things you need to determine are the environment and conditions of the room in which the server will be located. A room's environment is its overall air quality (such as humidity and dust), heating, cooling, and the electrical supply system. The electrical supply is especially important because it has a direct bearing on how well the server's power supply performs.

It's the heat <u>and</u> the humidity

Like humans, servers prefer moderate humidity as opposed to very dry or very damp conditions. Computers aren't as sensitive to humidity as they are to temperature, but they are still affected by it. In a warm and humid environment, the chances are greater that moisture will condense out of the air onto the internal components of a server and cause them to short out.

If you notice that the room you're planning to use as the server room has stained ceiling tiles, you should check it out for water problems, such as humidity, ceiling leaks, or leaking water pipes. Your server room shouldn't be at risk for water, or worse yet, flood damage. You should also avoid placing a server in a basement or a subterranean cave, unless you work for Dr. Evil or one of James Bond's archrivals, of course.

News flash: Servers and water don't mix well. Keep the server room dry and avoid using the CD-ROM trays as cup holders. As for the air itself, although using a server in a humid area can cause problems, the climate has to be extremely humid to really cause you any grief. A room with moderate humidity, say between 40 and 60 percent, is ideal. In most cases, humidity isn't a real concern. The biggest danger with humidity is that it can lead to corrosion and possible condensation, which can damage electrical equipment. High humidity can also make cooling the server and server room more difficult.

On the other hand, air that's too dry (not humid enough) can also cause problems in a couple of ways. First, drier air (below 40 percent humidity) increases the amount of static electricity in the room, which of course increases the chances of damaging the server's components through electrostatic discharge (ESD). Second, very dry air can also cause some components to wear out faster, such as some capacitors, the rollers on laser printers, and the feed rollers on tape drives.

Dry air can produce static electricity, which opens the door to electrostatic discharge (ESD) that can damage computer components. You should always use and wear anti-static protection (like an anti-static strap) when working inside the server's system unit, no matter what the humidity may be.

Avoiding ESD

Electrostatic discharge is caused by the buildup of electrical charge on one surface that is suddenly transferred to another surface when it's touched. Here's your fun fact for the day: An ESD discharge typically carries several thousand volts — it just has very little current, which is why it doesn't knock you on your caboose.

Other than the annoying zap, ESD won't harm you, but it can certainly damage the server's components. Integrated circuits, which include circuits such as processors, memory, cache chips, and expansion cards, are especially sensitive to ESD.

Here are two primary ways to control ESD:

✦ **Reduce ESD buildup:** One way to reduce the buildup of ESD is to increase the humidity in the server room, but not by too much. Static builds up more readily in a dry environment than in more humid ones; this is why you get zapped much more often in the wintertime, especially if you live in northern climates.

✦ **Draining ESD away:** Draining static can be as simple as touching something that is grounded, such as the metal chassis of the server's case when it's plugged in. By touching the chassis, you drain off any static that has built up in your body through the ground system of the server. If you don't ground yourself before touching the server's electronic components, you're likely to damage them.

No matter what the fashionistas clamor for this season, *never* go strapless when working on your computer. Always wear an anti-static strap! For the test, you need to know how to prevent electrostatic discharge (ESD) from damaging your server components while you handle them. ESD is basically static, and as you know, static can zap and ruin your processor, memory, or other components instantly. For the test, remember that the best way to avoid static and the danger of ESD is to work at a static-safe workstation and to wear an anti-static strap (also called a commercial grounding strap).

An anti-static wrist or heel strap is absolutely a minimum requirement when you're working inside a server. You should also *not* take off your shoes and wander around the nylon carpet in your wool socks when working on a server.

Don't try to make your own anti-static strap. Commercial anti-static straps, made with a large resistor that helps to keep you from being shocked if you touch a live power source, are inexpensive and easy to use. Considering their low cost and how easy they are to use, it's amazing how many people don't bother with anti-static straps — all you have to do is wrap one around your foot or wrist, and both you and your computer are better protected.

In addition to wearing an anti-static strap, you can further protect yourself and the computer by grounding yourself to the exterior metal case on your computer's power supply by touching the case somewhere near the fan before you unplug the computer from its power source. And, by all means, unplug the server before you begin working inside the case. After the case is open, you should occasionally touch the computer's metal chassis to ground yourself.

Handle all components by their edges and avoid touching any pins, contact edges, chips, or anything else electronic or made of metal other than the case chassis. This further decreases the chance you will zap, bend, or break anything.

Dealing with dirty environments

For the best results and longevity of the system, ensure that the server room is a clean environment. Not only does this mean that you should pick up your dirty laundry, but more importantly it means that the server room has to have clean air. Most office environments are clean enough that the computer equipment only needs an annual or biannual blast from a can of air as part of a regular preventive maintenance program.

However, if the server room is in an industrial environment or the air is dusty or full of pollutants, such as oil mist, metal filings, dust, or water vapor, you should move the server to a better location. If that's not an option, at least maintain a regular cleaning schedule to keep it and the server room clear of air problems. One easy preventive measure is to use an air cleaner in the server room. You can also buy special cases and enclosures for server hardware designed for industrial environments to prevent damage from dirt and pollutants.

If you find that dust bunnies are continually causing a server to heat up and shut down, you should perform a weekly or at least monthly preventive maintenance schedule that includes cleaning the cooling system elements and the interior of the system case.

Keeping it cool

Keeping the server cool is very important. A cool server is going to run more reliably and last longer than a system that runs hot. How can you tell if your system is cool enough? It's the one with the Armani leather case and the

Ray-Bans over its intakes. (Sorry . . . too tempting.) When planning a server room, you should definitely check for adequate cooling and ventilation in the room.

Yes, the server does have internal cooling fans, but the server's fans and cooling system won't do it much good if the server room itself is too hot. Follow this general guideline: If you're too hot, the server may have a problem. So, if you sweat bullets every time you enter the server room, you can bet the server's processor, memory, and other delicate electronics are heating up. If the internal components get too hot, you run the risk of data loss, an erratically performing processor, and memory errors, not to mention degradation of other components. Each server manufacturer has an environmental guideline that specifies the tolerance levels of the server, including the ambient temperature of the server room. Most recommend the room be cooled to 60 to 75 degrees Fahrenheit.

Beware of the two types of damage — degradation and catastrophic — that heat and ESD can cause to the electronics of a server:

+ **Degradation:** This type of damage occurs when a component is being continually damaged a little at a time until it finally fails completely and in a way that is near impossible to troubleshoot and isolate. An overheated system typically causes degradation in a number of interior components; unfortunately, it's usually the expensive ones, such as the processor, memory, or chipset.

+ **Catastrophic:** Although this type of damage sounds worse, it's actually easier to handle because a component dies all at once, and then you can easily pinpoint the problem.

If a server is placed in a rackmount cabinet — something the exam recommends and so do we — the cabinet should have ventilation fans installed at the top of each bay to exhaust the heat out of the rack. A cabinet without an exhaust fan can be dangerous to the server because in addition to locking away the server, it also locks in the heat.

Listing the benefits of a rackmount cabinet

In addition to organizing your server and other networking equipment, a rackmount cabinet has three very important features:

+ **Security:** Any cabinet worth buying has locking doors that can be a vital part of the server's security. Avoid cabinets that use the same keys for the doors on every bay, though.

+ **Environmental controls:** The better cabinets also have exhaust fans over each bay to pull the heat up and away from the servers and other devices, helping to maximize the cooling systems of this equipment.

✦ **Power:** Rackmount cabinets can also be equipped with surge suppressor power strips, but in most situations, you're much better off installing a UPS (uninterruptible power supply) in the bottom of the rack and using it to power the devices mounted in the rack.

Keep the server rackmount cabinet doors closed and locked, but also make sure that the ventilation fans are operating properly.

Quieting the noise

All electronic devices give off electromagnetic interference (EMI), which is radiation caused by electrical or magnetic activity. EMI is also known as *electrical noise*. The problem with EMI is that emissions from one device can interfere with other devices and potentially cause problems. EMI can lead to such things as data loss in memory, distortion of the display on a monitor, as well as other problems on a server or network clients.

EMI problems are a two-way street because servers *generate* EMI emissions even though they are *affected* by the EMI emissions from other devices. Servers can definitely be affected by EMI from other devices. If a server is located close to a noisy device, it can directly affect the server.

However, servers and PCs don't typically cause much interference to other devices because the Federal Communications Commission (FCC) requires them to be certified as Class B devices. This FCC certification is used to verify that a system conforms to standards that limit the amount of EMI that a computer can produce. EMI is contained by the metal lining of the case and cover of a server or PC — this limits the amount of EMI that escapes from the chassis.

More common, though, is electrical interference that's transmitted over the electrical power lines. EMI problems are not all that common, but a server affected by EMI can be incredibly frustrating to troubleshoot. EMI problems can be avoided by spacing the devices in a rack a few inches apart (see the manufacturer's recommendations for rack spacing) or by never, never placing a server next to a pop machine or a power transformer.

Of the many ways you can protect your server from electrical interference, here are the three you should know for the exam:

✦ **Physical isolation:** Systems should be kept at a reasonable distance from one another. However, server rackmount cabinets limit your ability to spread devices apart too far. Typically, a rack bay allows you around 48 rack units (1.75 inches to a rack unit) and depending on the size of the server or servers, UPS, patch panels, switches, routers, and anything else you need to install along with the spacing between devices and the cable management, it can often be a tight fit. However, most rackmount servers are designed to withstand EMI from the devices above and below it. Very thick metal chassis, especially on the top and bottom, help to prevent EMI radiation from escaping or entering the server chassis.

✦ **Use dedicated circuits:** Employ separately grounded and isolated power circuits dedicated for use in the server room. You don't want your servers sharing the same circuit as the breakroom vending machines or the air-conditioning unit. Separating the server room circuits from others in the building removes the threat of interference being passed to the server room equipment from other electrical devices. Plus, isolating the server room electrical supply also improves the quality of the power used by the equipment in your server room.

✦ **Install a UPS:** The use of an uninterruptible power supply (UPS) is a definite must-have when planning your server room. A UPS filters out interference caused by other devices that share a line with your servers and also provides backup power in case of an unexpected power interruption.

Powering the Server

As with any electrical equipment, servers require a good, clean power source in order to run optimally and reliably. Before you get carried away installing a raised floor and setting up server racks, you should determine where the existing power is in the room and where power needs to be available for the server and, more appropriately, the UPS.

Make sure that you have enough electrical outlets in the server room to connect the power supplies, surge suppressors, and cabinet fans and that the outlets are on separate circuits from the rest of the building. If the room you want for your potential server room only has one or two outlets, please don't try to save money by using power strips and extension cords. The better thing to do is to have an electrician install more electrical outlets (on dedicated circuits) or, in the least, use a multioutlet UPS or surge suppressor. We're talking about servers, switches, tape drives, and other very sensitive and expensive electrical equipment here.

Purifying the power

In addition to providing an adequate power supply for your server room, you also need to provide good, clean, reliable power. As the old computer saying goes, "Garbage in, garbage out." If your servers and server room equipment are being supplied poor-quality power, you may as well buy an industrial-size bottle of aspirin because you're setting yourself up for Migraine City. If your data is important — it must be if your company is spending the money and time to set up a server room — you must pay attention to the quality of your power! Most people aren't aware that power issues are probably responsible for more computer problems than any other single source.

Begin by looking at the power delivered to the server. The power that comes into your office is normally quite reliable, but you'd be surprised how many quality problems you can find with the power you use daily. Spikes, surges, blackouts, brownouts, and line noise are all very common power problems that we don't notice. (Okay, most of the time we do notice a blackout.)

For the most part, servers and other computer equipment can deal with these power problems. The power supplies in servers have some tolerance to these problems. And the more expensive the system, the more the power supply fluctuations it can tolerate without failure. However, you can't expect the power supply to protect your server day in and day out: That's not its role. The power supply's role is to provide rectified (converted) power, not to clean it up. Poor power can and will lead to system problems that manifest themselves in ways that would never lead you to suspect power as the culprit.

When planning the installation of a server and preparing the server room, you can take some steps to improve the quality of the power. You should review each of the following sections because these issues show up on the exam as questions and answers, both right and wrong.

Line noise

Line noise is basically small variations in the voltage level delivered to the server. A certain amount of line noise is expected; no power generation circuits are perfect. Most power supplies can deal with line noise without any problem. On the other hand, the power quality in some areas is worse than others. We repeat: It's not the power supply's role to deal with crummy power. EMI is the leading source of line noise problems. The server should not be sharing a circuit or be physically located near devices that cause EMI. Motors, heavy machinery, radio transmitters, refrigerators, and microwaves are all EMI culprits. Line noise that the power supply cannot handle will be passed on to your motherboard or other internal devices, creating problems that can be nearly impossible to diagnose.

Surges and spikes

The electrical company rates the power coming from the wall to be within a certain voltage range. The nominal voltage for circuits in North America is 110 volts (V). However, the voltage can unexpectedly increase (*surge*) because of disturbances such as distant lightning strikes and problems within the electrical grid. A voltage surge, also called a *spike,* can certainly make its way down the line. This temporary increase of voltage normally lasts only a few thousandths of a second, but this is plenty of time for the voltage to increase from 110V to 1,000V or even higher.

As with line noise, the power supply is subjected to and deals with many of these surges, but these spikes are bad news because the power supplies internal components. These high-voltage surges can disrupt or even damage the power supply and/or internal server components. Over time, the surges will ultimately degrade the power supply and cause it to fail prematurely.

Brownouts

A *brownout*, also called a *sag*, is a dip in the voltage level of the power line. A brownout happens when the voltage drops from its normal level and then bounces back up. It's almost the opposite of a surge. Power supplies can handle a reduction in the expected nominal voltage. The capability of the power supply to deal with brownouts is dependent upon its allowable input voltage range. For example, a power supply may be rated for 120V of alternating current (AC) but may tolerate anything from 95V to 130V. Any reduction of voltage below 95 volts for more than a fraction of a second will likely result in the power supply shutting down or malfunctioning in strange, unpredictable ways.

Brownouts are very common, and just like surges, they can lead to mysterious and hard-to-diagnose problems. The lights flickering or dimming are definite signs of a brownout. Brownouts occur more frequently during heavy load periods, such as a late afternoon on a hot summer day, and also during storms.

Brownouts are extremely hard on computer systems. They are worse than a blackout in many ways because in a blackout, the power just goes off; with a brownout, the device will try to continue to get power but at a reduced level. In most cases, the system will malfunction rather than fail completely.

Blackouts

A *blackout* occurs when the power to the facility is totally lost. Server damage caused by a blackout depends a great deal on timing. Your best-case scenario is that the system is idle when the blackout occurs. If the system is idle, you probably won't encounter any problems with the system when the power comes back on. Your worst-case scenario is when the power goes out while you're working on the hard disk and the drive was updating your file allocation tables. If you're doing anything of a fragile nature when a blackout happens, you're more likely to have trouble!

When a blackout does occur, it's not pretty. When the power goes off, it often doesn't go out cleanly. In most cases, spikes, surges, and other power jitters occur when the power is cut and when it comes back on. In most situations, a system will survive the power going off and coming back on without too much fuss. The potential for significant damage does exist, however, and you can count on losing any unsaved data that was being worked on when the power went out.

The best way to prevent damage from the aforementioned power pitfalls is to install an uninterruptible power supply (UPS) along with your servers and other server room equipment.

Planning the UPS

You'll definitely see a question or two about the use and installation of an uninterruptible power supply (UPS). You should be aware of why you should use a UPS, the advantages of using a UPS, and how a UPS works.

Different types of backup power supply solutions are available, but the Server+ exam focuses on the UPS. The purpose of a UPS is to provide a connected device, such as a server, with a constant and unwavering source of power. A UPS can be used to protect many different types of equipment, but for the exam, you only need to worry about protecting a server.

The standard power supply system in the United States and Canada provides 110V of AC power. Other parts of the world have the same power standard, or use 220V or higher. Most computer power supplies include a voltage source switch that allows it to be set for the voltage level of the incoming electricity.

The UPS is inserted between the electrical power source and the server's power supply; as far as the power supply knows, the UPS is the electrical system that is supplying it with AC power. Two types of UPS systems can be planned into your system:

✦ **Standby UPS:** This type of UPS is commonly called a *battery backup*. It provides the server with protection against a power failure (blackout) or a low-voltage event (brownout). In standby mode, the UPS draws off a small amount of power to charge its battery and passes unfiltered AC power on to the server. In the event of a blackout, the standby UPS provides the PC with an AC power source. A downside to a standby UPS is that large surges, spikes, or low-voltage events are likely to be passed through the UPS to the server.

✦ **Online (or inline) UPS:** An online UPS provides AC power to a server from its battery that's constantly recharged from the actual AC power source. The incoming AC power is rectified into direct current (DC) power that recharges the battery. Another system provides power to the server by converting the DC power from the battery into AC power through an inverter. An online UPS requires no switchover because it's already online. Online UPS units also include surge suppression and line conditioning to protect the UPS itself. An extended brownout would begin discharging the battery of the UPS, which would eventually fail without the AC power being restored.

Laser printers in particular can draw large amounts of power and should never be used on a UPS. You shouldn't connect a laser printer to a UPS because it produces a lot of EMI and draws a fluctuating amount of power, which can in time damage the UPS.

One little known fact about a UPS is the possible equipment failure and even safety hazards that can result from plugging surge suppressors into the output jacks of a UPS. ***Do not*** plug a surge suppressor into a UPS; they're not designed to be used this way and doing so could lead to the surge suppressor smoking or catching fire, neither of which it was designed to do.

The most important factor in deciding on a UPS is its load. You must be sure that the UPS will support the equipment connected to it. The volt-amp capacity of the UPS should be slightly more than the peak power demands of the equipment connected to it. So, before buying a UPS, add up the peak power requirement for each device, which should be indicated on the device or available in its documentation, and then buy accordingly. Most top-line UPS manufacturers have an online calculator to help you to determine the best UPS for your needs, such as the one from American Power Conversion at `www.apcc.com/sizing/`.

Verifying the Network Connection

Another important step in the planning process is checking for adequate network connections in the server room, or what is the proposed server room. Unbelievably, you may find a question on the exam that asks whether you need to have a network connection available in order to connect the server to the network. (If you get this one wrong, you're doomed to a life of cleaning floppy disk drives for a living.)

When planning the installation of a server, you should ensure that you have an open port on the switch or router to which you plan to connect. If so, you're good to go. However, if no connection is available, you need to stop the planning and rework the network to make a network connection available. After you resolve this, resume the planning for your server installation.

If the network is an entirely new network, your planning must include the cabling that will interconnect the server and its clients.

Connecting the server to the network

A server without a network connection is a very high-priced standalone PC. As a part of your planning, make sure that adequate cabling is available to connect the server to the network. You should be familiar with the following situations for the exam.

Network and power cables

As a part of your preparations, you should verify that adequate cabling is available. If you're preparing a new server room, for example, you won't have any pre-existing cabling. If your server room has raised flooring, though, you can run new power and network cables fairly easily. If you can't configure the cabling, you'll have to choose a new location for the server.

After installing cabling (or if you were fortunate enough to already have it), make sure that the cables that connect the server to the network switch, router, or patch panels are long enough to reach the location you've chosen for the server. Also bear in mind that you need to stay under the segment length limitations of the cable type you're using or you'll add the headache of attenuation to this.

Telephone connections

Your planning should also include making sure you have a telephone connection nearby that can be reached without creating a safety hazard with a cable strung across the room (a *tripnet*). A telephone connection is used on a server for many purposes, not the least of which is remote access for remote administration.

Bandwidth

You'll find a question or two on the exam concerning bandwidth. Bandwidth should be a part of your system planning as well. Depending on the role of your server, it may need a connection to the outside world, such as to a wide area network (WAN) or the Internet. Perhaps a telephone connection is sufficient, but if you need (or may someday need) more bandwidth, you should plan for this. A frame relay, ISDN (Integrated Services Digital Network), ATM (asynchronous transfer mode), DSL (Digital Subscriber Line), or wireless connection may have some lead-time before it's available.

How much bandwidth you need depends on the size of your company (how many users), how much traffic will be coming and going on the link, and how much growth is expected. You aren't asked to configure the bandwidth of a broadband communications line on the exam, but you will encounter the T-carrier (telecommunications carrier) and DS (digital signal) systems. A T-carrier is defined in terms of the number of 64 Kbps channels (also referred to as DS0s) it includes.

Review Table 5-1 for the exam.

Table 5-1	T-Carrier and Digital Signals Systems		
T-Carrier	**DS Type**	**Channels**	**Bandwidth**
-	DS0	1	64 Kbps
T-1	DS1	24	1.544 Mbps
T-2	DS2	96	6.312 Mbps
T-3	DS3	672	44.736 Mbps
T-4	DS4	4,032	274.186 Mbps

The T-carrier and DS systems provide digital transmission services from a common carrier. You may see references to T-1, E-1 (the European approximate equivalent to the T-1), and DS3 on the exam. Don't be confused by the E-1. The E-carrier system is used in Europe and is close enough to the T-carrier lines to be interchangeable.

Installing the Components

After you've prepared a well-documented plan and you've assembled all the hardware, software, tools, and documentation you need, you're ready to start configuring your server. The first step in doing so, of course, is to install all the server's hardware components. In this section, we take you through all the hardware-related information you should know for the exam. Be prepared for test questions about the installation of server components.

In the following sections, we discuss the precautions, actions, and procedures involved with configuring a server and its hardware. Review them all to make sure that when you encounter a question that describes a similar activity, you'll be able to project to the next step (which in many cases is what the question is asking for) or understand the ramifications of each process.

Storing server components

When working with server components, you should keep them in their original packaging or an anti-static bag until you're ready to install them in the server. If you don't have a component's original packaging, store all static-sensitive components — which is just about everything that goes inside the server — in an anti-static bag.

Anti-static bags do not repel static. In fact, they do just the opposite. Anti-static bags are partially conductive. Never put an anti-static bag inside of a server, and absolutely never power up a component that's lying on top of an anti-static bag — unless, of course, you're trying to fry the component and the server.

Keeping track of the gozintas

The trick to installing hardware in a server is to know where it goes and why. On the exam, you can expect a few questions about where certain components connect to the motherboard. You may even encounter a diagram that asks you to identify the location of a few of the different expansion slots on the board. (See Book V, Chapter 2 for information on a motherboard's bus structures.) Just for a refresher, study Figure 5-1 to familiarize yourself with the location of ISA (Industry Standard Architecture), PCI (Peripheral Component Interconnect), AGP (Accelerated Graphics Port), memory (SIMM or DIMM) sockets, and the processor socket or slot.

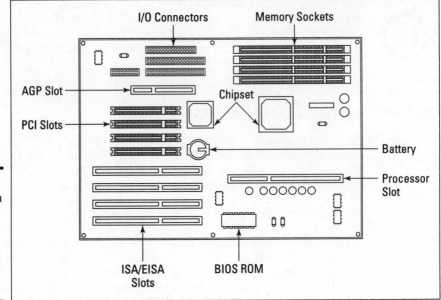

Figure 5-1: The location of the various expansion bus slots on a motherboard.

Form factors

Another characteristic of a server is its form factor, which defines the shape, size, and fit of the motherboard, power supply, and case. Many form factors are used in servers these days, including ATX, Baby AT, NLX, and WTX, but for the Server+ exam, you only need to recognize that ATX and Baby AT are in fact form factors for the server's motherboard and case.

Document, document, document

Just in case we haven't mentioned this before: If you encounter a question on the Server+ exam that asks whether you should document every change, update, or modification made to a server, your answer is a definitive *Yes*. You should always document any changes — including any attempted changes that are made to a server — and specifically, any jumper changes you make.

Testing with a POST

Now that you have the components installed and the server is ready to power up, you need to be sure that the system sees all the devices. The second step to installing hardware components is to test them. You do this with a Power-On Self-Test (POST). At this point, the hard drive has no operating system on it, and you need to check that your installed components are going to play well with the others. You will probably also need to make changes in the BIOS setup program to accommodate the new components that you've added to the motherboard.

Lab 5-1 lists the steps used to perform the first test of newly installed components in a server. These steps may vary slightly from system to system. However, for the Server+ exam, the steps listed are generic enough to cover all bases.

Lab 5-1   Using the POST Process to Complete the Installation

1. **Be sure that you don't have any floppy disks or bootable CD-ROM discs in those drives. Begin with the server and monitor powered off.**

   Now it's time to bring your creation to life, Igor.

2. **Plug the server in to a power source and hit the power button. Turn on the monitor.**

   Please don't scare your fellow employees by yelling, "It's alive! It's alive!"

3. **Listen for early POST beep codes and carefully watch the POST messages displayed on the monitor.**

4. **If all is well, the server runs through the POST with no problems.**

   The POST includes tests on the components and devices listed in the BIOS Startup configuration data, including the video BIOS, memory, hard disk, keyboard, and so on.

   If any problems are encountered, the POST will sound beep codes or display error messages on the monitor, depending on when the problem is detected in the POST process. Refer to the BIOS or motherboard documentation to determine exactly what the beep code or message is signaling. Ignore the little voices in your head and pay attention to the beeps.

5. **If the POST is successful, the BIOS displays the keystroke used to enter the BIOS Setup program, which is typically the Del, F1, or F2 key.**

   Press this key to enter the BIOS Setup and enter and save any necessary adjustment required by the new hardware components.

6. **After you save the new setup configuration, the BIOS will continue with the boot process and load the operating system.**

   If the system boots clean, the new hardware component should be detected by the operating system. If a new hardware component is a Plug and Play device, it will be automatically configured or you may be asked for a device driver disk. Follow the on-screen instructions to complete the installation.

Remember to copy down the BIOS settings in a manual record. This is very important in case you or someone else needs to restore the system should the BIOS settings ever get wiped out by accident, or otherwise.

If your BIOS doesn't support the new device or device driver, you may need to update the system BIOS or that on the device controller, such as a SCSI (Small Computer System Interface) host adapter. Visit the BIOS or device manufacturer's Web site for update instructions, software, and an update file. Book V, Chapter 10 also includes information on this process, which is called *flashing the BIOS*.

Putting the Server on the Rack

The passwords and other authentication procedures that run on the network provide for a server's logical security. However, the Server+ exam is very interested in whether you understand the means used to secure a server physically.

Security is always a top priority with network servers. For the exam, you should remember that the best physical security involves a rackmount server installed in a locking cabinet in a locked room. Both the cabinet and the room should have very limited access.

For added security, the doors of the server rack should be kept locked at all times.

Most rackmount kits include side rails that are attached to the server's case that allow you to slide the server out of the rack for maintenance. The rackmount kit typically includes a pair of mating rails: one that mounts to the server rack or cabinet, and another set that attaches to the side of the server. When attaching the side rails to the rack, cabinet, or server, be careful not to trap any of the cables or cords that will attach to the server.

Normally the cabling is run along the top and down the sides of the rack in a compartment of sorts. Also make sure that you provide enough slack in the cables and cords so that when a server slides out, the cables and cords aren't strained or unplugged.

You need to plan a little for installing a server in a rack or cabinet. Place heavy devices toward the bottom of the rack to prevent the rack from tipping over. The cabinet or rack should be arranged so that the server's UPS (uninterruptible power supply) is located nearby. Typically, a rackmount UPS is very heavy and would be at the bottom of the rack or cabinet bay. If the UPS includes a feedback or interactive capability, it must also be connected to the server with an RS-232 serial cable.

When planning the installation of devices in a rack or cabinet, you should always follow the methods prescribed in the manufacturer's documentation of the rack or cabinet.

One rack unit, or U, is equal to 1.75 inches of vertical height in a rack.

Switching between Servers

Connecting a mouse and monitor to the server inside a rack or cabinet can pose some space and human-engineering challenges. Some rackmount monitors, keyboards, and mice take up as little as one or two rack units, but these are expensive and only typically found in high-volume server farms or companies with unlimited technical budgets, or the like.

In situations with only a single server to manage, you can install extension cables for the peripheral devices you need so that you can place them on a worktable or desk outside of the cabinet or rack. If you have multiple servers to which you need a connection, the best tool to use is a KVM (keyboard, video, and mouse) switch. A KVM switch enables you to switch the attachment of a single monitor, keyboard, and mouse to two or more computers. On the back of the KVM switch is a series of PS/2 and VGA connections for the devices from each server to be managed to attach to the KVM switch. On the front of the KVM are push buttons that enable you to select the device you want to activate.

A KVM switch allows the network administrator to manage multiple devices from a single location. The KVM switch also supports the security of the system because the cabinet doors can remain locked while the servers are being managed, administered, and monitored.

To connect four servers to a KVM switch, you will need four sets of cables, one for each of the servers.

Configuring External SCSI Devices

The time to add external devices that are supported by an internal interface bus is after the server is online with all its BIOSes, service packs, and programming updated to current and compatible levels. The server's configuration is now stable and ready to support whatever else you want to throw on or at it, including external Small Computer System Interface (SCSI) devices. The SCSI bus and SCSI devices can be finicky and a real pain to troubleshoot. You definitely want the server to be in its tiptop shape so that when you're faced with a SCSI challenge — and you will be — you can concentrate on solving SCSI problems and not other system issues.

Connecting to the SCSI bus

The SCSI bus and SCSI devices are most commonly used in network servers and high-end workstations because their performance and reliability are often crucial to the needs of these systems. However, SCSI systems are typically more expensive and complex than standard Integrated Device Electronics/AT Attachment (IDE/ATA) devices commonly found in end-user PCs. SCSI devices provide a higher level of performance, data integrity, and reliability over other device interfaces. Expect to see more than a few questions about external SCSI devices — and especially external redundant array of independent disks (RAID) systems connected to a server using SCSI technology.

External SCSI devices are connected to a SCSI host adapter that's typically installed in a Peripheral Component Interconnect (PCI) slot inside the server. Because the SCSI host adapter plugs into a system expansion bus, it requires the assignment of several system resources. The resources used by a SCSI host adapter can vary depending on the system bus used and the transfer method used to transfer data over the bus. The following resources are typically assigned to a SCSI host adapter:

✦ **Interrupt Request Line (IRQ):** All SCSI host adapters require an IRQ. Generally the host adapter uses IRQ 9, 10, 11, or 12. If one of the IDE/ATA channels is not in use, the host adapter could be also assigned either IRQ 14 or 15. However, a PCI-based host adapter doesn't explicitly use an IRQ of its own. Instead, it uses the IRQ, called a *system IRQ*, mapped to a PCI slot. Remember this fact about PCI SCSI host adapters for the exam.

✦ **DMA channel:** Older SCSI host adapters typically use either the Industry Standard Architecture (ISA) or the VESA local bus (VLB) expansion bus and use a direct memory access (DMA) channel to transfer data directly to system memory from SCSI devices, bypassing the processor. These devices usually use DMA channels 1, 3, or 5. PCI-based host adapters use PCI bus mastering, which doesn't use a regular ISA DMA channel. Don't sweat bus mastering beyond the fact that it allows a device to take control of the PCI bus and move data to and from devices directly.

✦ **Input/Output (I/O) address:** All SCSI host adapters require an I/O address resource assignment, just like all other I/O devices.

If the server fails to recognize a SCSI device, or if a SCSI device is acting abnormally, check the device's SCSI ID. The device must be assigned a unique device ID. See Book V, Chapter 3 for more information on this and other SCSI characteristics.

PCI SCSI host adapters are typically Plug and Play devices and are automatically configured by the system BIOS during the boot process.

Before connecting the SCSI device, you need to power off the server and the device. Connect the device to the server's SCSI host adapter by using the indicated external SCSI cable. After the SCSI cable is in place and the device has the terminator attached to its second SCSI interface, you can begin powering up the peripheral devices and the server. First power on the SCSI device and then the server. When you power up the server, the host adapter should detect the new SCSI device and configure the necessary resources. However, before you do, power up the external device and the server to double-check that the SCSI chain is properly terminated.

Terminating the chain, gang

When connecting multiple SCSI devices to a SCSI chain, remember that each device in the chain must be configured with a unique SCSI ID, and the devices at each end of the chain must be terminated. The ID will be 0-7 or 0-16 depending on the SCSI standard you're using. A single SCSI channel with a narrow SCSI host adapter can include eight devices (well, actually only seven, because the host adapter counts as a SCSI device on that channel). A single SCSI channel with a newer, wide SCSI host adapter can have up to 16 SCSI devices (okay — actually 15, because the host adapter is counted as SCSI host on the channel).

Some host adapters have dual channels that enable you to double the number of drives per host adapter. Most systems allow up to four SCSI host adapters. The host adapter is normally 0 or 7 (with narrow SCSI) or 0 or 15 (with wide SCSI). The attached devices are automatically detected by the SCSI host adapter during the system boot and are assigned an ID that isn't being used by another SCSI device or the host adapter itself. On some older SCSI systems, you may need to configure the device IDs on the device itself by using jumpers or DIP (dual inline packaging) switches.

After you've successfully configured any external devices, you're ready to bring the server online. When you build a new server, you should take the time to create a baseline to help you track system performance.

If devices on a SCSI chain are having strange and random problems, make sure that the SCSI chain is terminated properly.

For the Server+ exam, you definitely need to understand how, where, and why a SCSI chain is terminated. Remember that the devices at each end of the chain need to be terminated to prevent the electrical signals from bouncing back and forth on the chain. The terminating block includes a resistor that absorbs signals that reach the end of the chain.

One thing to watch for on the test is termination of the host adapter. If the host adapter is at the beginning of the chain, the chain must be terminated at the host adapter and at the last device on the chain. The test will try to trip you up and propose that the host adapter is in the middle of the SCSI chain with SCSI devices connected to it both internally and externally.

The answer lies in how many channels are being used. If the host adapter has only one channel, you want to terminate the chain at the SCSI device at the end of the internal and external channels. The host adapter is simply in the middle of the chain. However, if the SCSI host adapter has dual channels and it is stated that the external and internal devices are on separate channels, you'll want to terminate both of those channels (SCSI chains) at the host adapter and at the last device of each chain.

Mixing and matching SCSI modes

Host adapters that have dual channels can provide multiple channels (or segments). Multiple channels also enable you to configure the host adapter to support both of the current signaling standards (single-ended, or SE; and low-voltage differential, or LVD) on the same host adapter. Many newer SCSI host adapters are multimode adapters, meaning they can operate SE, LVD, or a combination of both on one chain. Remember that multimode host adapters will default to the degraded performance of the SE mode if you connect an SE device to the chain. You could have a number of high-performance LVD devices on the chain, but if you add a single SE device to the chain, all the devices will perform like SE devices.

SE SCSI is slow SCSI. The preferred SCSI signaling is LVD. If you use even one SE device on a LVD SCSI chain, all devices will operate at the degraded SE operation.

Establishing a Server Baseline

After any necessary external storage devices are connected and configured and the system is online, you should create a server baseline. By collecting information for a baseline of the network servers and network devices, such as routers and switches, you will have an accurate picture of network traffic flow to the servers and network devices. A network and server baseline provides you with the data needed to evaluate the growth of the network and to pinpoint network or server bottlenecks.

Running the baseline

A baseline can also come in handy when you're troubleshooting the network to determine the source of any performance problems. Baselining a server and its network devices helps you to monitor the increase (or decrease) of activity on the server and network and to perform capacity planning.

Use baseline information to track the following characteristics of a server and network:

+ CPU utilization

+ Memory utilization

+ Network availability

+ Network response based on per second

+ Number of application transactions

+ Number of users throughout a given period

+ Response times

+ Responses from network nodes

+ Server availability

Much information can be gathered and used to assess the current condition of the server and network. The information you need to record as part of the baseline depends on the role of the server or the type of network device. This information can help you plan for upgrades accordingly, and it can also help you identify trouble spots so that you can prevent the problem from becoming more than just a nuisance. In many cases, a network will show signs of slowing down well before it becomes a problem. When your users complain that the network seems slow, you need to compare the servers' and network devices' current performance with their baselines. This comparison will point out the performance discrepancies that are the source of the network slowdown, and you can take care of the problem by upgrading server components or network devices.

By comparing your server's current performance with its baseline, you can plan for future growth. For example, if you notice that your server is running at 40 percent CPU utilization compared with 10 percent a month earlier, you know that either the server is having problems or that the demand on the server is beginning to increase. If you discover that demand is increasing, you may consider upgrading or adding additional servers to support the traffic.

To create a baseline, document the processor's current usage levels under a normal workload. On a Windows server, you can use the Performance Monitor utility to establish a reference point for processor usage. A baseline is normally more than a single value; generally a baseline is a range within which processor usage, or other activity, can fluctuate and still provide acceptable performance. Typically a baseline is established over at least a one-week period.

You can use the baseline to identify trends, such as increasing memory and processor demands over a specified period, or to recognize problems that arise from a sudden change in the server or to the network.

Building the baseline

Most applications running on the server have one or more counters. To see an application's counters, open the Windows NT/2000 Task Manager and select the process tab. Use these counters to record the activity of applications and system services.

Expect a question on the exam regarding processor usage and how to monitor it. The best way to monitor processor activity is to log data from counters of the system, processor, process, thread, physical disk, and memory for at least a week, preferably longer, at an update interval ranging from 15 minutes to an hour. For the test, you won't need to know exactly *what* to monitor, but rather *how long* you should collect data to get the most accurate information. You should also include network data, such as Bytes Total/sec, if you suspect that network traffic might be bogging down the processor with constant interruptions.

When gathering the baseline data, you should track the values reported at various times of day, especially when users are logging on or off, as well as while backups are being done. You want to get the most accurate representation of a day in the life of the server. While monitoring values for these counters, you'll probably see occasional spikes. The spikes can typically be excluded from your baseline data. The range of values that appear consistently, day to day, are the ones that represent your baseline. When developing your baseline, you need to remember that the longer you log data for your baseline, the more accurate your baseline will be.

After you establish a baseline for your network, you should have a good idea of what normal behavior is for your servers and network devices. The data you collect to create your baseline should be recorded and kept in a safe place for future reference. Document everything you do to a server or network device. Documentation is a very important part of the systems administrator's job, and the Server+ exam hits hard on documentation.

Creating a Paper Trail

On the exam, you should fully expect to find questions concerning troubleshooting and repair to which the answer is generally "Check the server documentation for any changes that may have taken place," or words to that effect. Unlike real life, the test assumes that you (and your users) keep, and file in an organized way, every bit of documentation for every component and device included in or attached to your server or network. Of course, this is in addition to all the manual records from you (and every other technician that has worked on a server) detailing every maintenance, configuration, and monitoring event that has ever taken place. From the day you build a server, you should document everything that you feel is important in case you may need to troubleshoot the server — or worse, rebuild the server.

Documentation is essential for keeping your systems up to date, and it can be your lifeline when it comes to troubleshooting. Here's another (often overlooked) reason for faithfully documenting your server's configuration and any changes or problems it's experienced: Because systems administrators come and go, this paper trail is a wonderful thing for the new systems administrator. Just imagine going into a new job and having all these wonderful documents full of everything you need to quickly get up to speed and down to business. Without this documentation, you'd spend weeks or even months to ramp up.

When documenting the configuration of the server, you should include everything that is needed to rebuild the server if you or another tech ever has to. Plan for the worst and try to be as prepared as possible. By documenting as much information as you can, you'll be ready for anything — well, almost anything. Not only does the documentation help you with maintenance, but it also provides a quick reference for new IT employees or for those times when you may need assistance from an outside source. Create a document that includes

✦ The server name, network operating system (NOS), and services

✦ All network information including Internet Protocol (IP) address, gateway, Windows Internet Naming Service (WINS), Domain Name System (DNS), and so forth

✦ The model number and driver version of hardware components, such as memory, hard drives, network interface cards (NICs), modems, SCSI cards, and so forth

✦ The BIOS version and last flash update

✦ The BIOS set-up program settings

+ A list of all installed applications and their purposes

+ The location of the server in the server room, including where it is racked or what shelf it sits on

+ Which KVM switch the server is connected to, and what number it is

+ The date that the server was brought online

+ The date of the last shutdown or reboot, and why

+ The data stored on the server

+ Any important information about any services running on the server

  For example, if the server is a DHCP server, you need to document any scopes, exclusions, lease times, and so forth

+ A note detailing whether the server was included in the backup rotation

+ Information concerning the last hardware upgrades or repair

+ The date of last and next scheduled maintenance

You should also put a sticky label showing the server's name and IP address on the server in a place where it is easily seen.

Build on this list; add anything you feel might be important to the next person who takes over the network. When documenting the server configuration, you should also include any model numbers, part numbers, and other information about internal components just in case you need to order replacement components. Not having to unnecessarily open the chassis in the middle of a server crisis — or anytime, for that matter — is a great luxury.

Prep Test

1 Which of the following is the most important factor to consider when planning a server's configuration?

- **A** ○ Storage space required
- **B** ○ Network speed
- **C** ○ Role of the server
- **D** ○ Network size

2 What reference tool can be used to verify that a server's components are compatible with the NOS?

- **A** ○ HCL
- **B** ○ Motherboard manual
- **C** ○ NOS Readme file
- **D** ○ Component documentation

3 Which of the following environmental conditions can produce static electricity and increase the risk of ESD in the server room?

- **A** ○ High humidity
- **B** ○ Dust
- **C** ○ Dry air
- **D** ○ Bare floors

4 The type of UPS that constantly provides power from its battery to the devices connected to it is a(n) _____.

- **A** ○ Standby
- **B** ○ Failover
- **C** ○ Online
- **D** ○ Battery backup

5 Using the following figure showing the components of a PC motherboard, identify the component type located in area B.

- **A** ○ Chipset
- **B** ○ PCI slots
- **C** ○ AGP slot
- **D** ○ CMOS battery

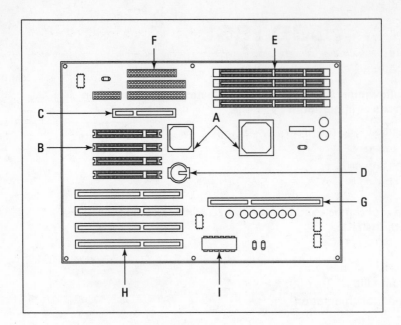

6 Which of the following should be included in a practical procedure for securing a server? (Choose two.)

   A ❏ Locking the server's cabinet

   B ❏ Motion detectors in the server room

   C ❏ Safety glass on all server cabinet doors

   D ❏ Locking the server room

7 Connecting four servers to a single-access control device requires what combination of hardware?

   A ○ Four sets of cables and a UPS

   B ○ Four sets of cables and a KVM

   C ○ Five sets of cables, a video cable, and a KVM

   D ○ Five sets of cables and a smart modem

8 What should you check if the server fails to recognize a SCSI device or a SCSI device that is acting abnormally?

   A ○ SCSI ID

   B ○ Termination

   C ○ Connection

   D ○ Power

9 A wide SCSI host adapter is typically assigned one of which two SCSI IDs?

A ❑ 0

B ❑ 8

C ❑ 15

D ❑ 7

10 What period should baseline data be collected to create an accurate baseline?

A ○ At least a week

B ○ 24 hours

C ○ Hours

D ○ Months

Answers

1 **C.** The role of the server is the determining factor when planning the configuration of a server. *Review "Planning the Server Installation."*

2 **A.** The HCL of an NOS is typically included on the distribution disks for the NOS. However, an up-to-date HCL can usually be found on the NOS manufacturer's Web site. *Review "Checking the list."*

3 **C.** Where there is dry air, there is ESD. But be careful when you're drying out the humidity in a room so that you don't go overboard. *Review "Avoiding ESD."*

4 **C.** An online UPS provides power to the server regardless of whether the AC power is available, at least as long as the battery holds out. *Review "Planning the UPS."*

5 **B.** Spend the time to get to know several motherboard layouts, especially the Baby AT and the ATX form factors. *Review "Form factors."*

6 **A** and **D.** Security is a big topic on the Server+ exam. Be sure you know how to protect your servers from evildoers and other intruders. *Review "Putting the Server on the Rack."*

7 **B.** You will need four sets of cables that connect to a KVM switch and the four servers. Remember that the mouse, keyboard, and monitor connect to the KVM switch via their built-in cables. *Review "Switching between Servers."*

8 **A.** Each device must have its own SCSI ID, or the devices will conflict with one another when trying to communicate. *Check out "Connecting to the SCSI bus."*

9 **A** and **C.** Wide SCSI supports up to 16 devices including the host adapter. *Review "Terminating the chain, gang."*

10 **A.** The longer you gather data, the more accurate your baseline is going to be, but normally a week is enough time to gather the necessary data. Review "Running the baseline."

Chapter 6: Configuring a Server

Exam Objectives

✔ **Listing the process used to install and configure a network operating system**

✔ **Defining network operating system functions and processes**

✔ **Detailing the procedure used to verify network connectivity**

✔ **Configuring external devices**

✔ **Creating server baselines and documentation**

The network operating system (NOS) provides services to other computers on the network. A server can be configured to provide many different services or play many different roles and the server's operating system must be configured to support whatever role the server is to play.

The Server+ exam focuses primarily on Windows NT and Windows 2000 Server with only a few questions on Novell NetWare or the UNIX operating system. Most of the really detailed questions relate to Windows NT. When necessary to know a factoid about Windows 2000, Netware, or UNIX, we'll point that out.

This chapter also includes information on dealing with Small Computer System Interface (SCSI) devices, especially configuring and troubleshooting SCSI storage devices and external SCSI devices. You need to know SCSI very well for the exam — it wouldn't be that much of a stretch if this exam were renamed the SCSI+ exam. You need to understand how external SCSI devices are connected to the SCSI bus and pretty much everything else you've always wanted to know about SCSI.

Another important topic grouped into this chapter is the creation of a server baseline. If you don't know what the normal or nominal operating levels are for a server, how can you know whether it's malfunctioning? Establishing a server baseline enables you to create a performance standard for a server so that you know when a server begins performing better than it should (which could happen, we suppose) — or, as is usually the case, worse than it should. The Server+ exam includes a question or two regarding system performance issues and how and when you should create a baseline.

Installing the NOS

The Server+ exam doesn't get into the nitty-gritty details of the processes used to install a network operating system (NOS). However, you really need to know the steps used to install a NOS in order to understand many of its key concepts. Several important configuration settings are made during the NOS installation, and these decisions directly impact the role, function, and features the server is able to provide. Understanding the installation processes and the choices that must be made during the installation will also help you to understand the NOS big picture, which is vital background information for the exam.

Checking for compatibility

Before beginning a NOS installation, you should probably take a minute to plan a few of the decisions you have to make, such as the file system, the server's role, the configuration of the network, and the optional NOS components to be installed.

To ensure that the server hardware and any applications you plan to run on it are compatible with the NOS you're preparing to install or upgrade, always refer to the Hardware Compatibility List (HCL) of your NOS. You can download a text file of the latest version of the Windows 2000 HCL from `ftp://ftp.microsoft.com/services/whql/hcl/win2000hcl.txt` or get HCL lists for all Microsoft operating systems (including the new Windows XP) at `www.microsoft.com/hcl`.

Starting the installation

You must have two essential elements to begin the installation: the distribution media and the product key (the very long and undecipherable code usually attached to the distribution disk) for your NOS. You place the distribution media (typically a CD-ROM these days) in the appropriate drive and boot the system to the installation screen. If you want to boot to the CD-ROM drive, you may need to adjust the boot sequences in the CMOS (complimentary metal-oxide semiconductor) settings of the BIOS (Basic Input/Output System). If the computer won't boot to a CD-ROM, you need to create bootable floppies by using a utility on the NOS distribution disk.

On a Windows NT or Windows 2000 system, use the following command to create a set of installation floppy disks:

```
Winnt32.exe /OX
```

Setting up a file system

At the beginning of the installation process, with the SETUP command or the autorun on the CD-ROM, you're prompted for the partition on which you want to install the NOS. You also have the option of creating a new partition and designating the type of file system to be used. Table 6-1 lists the most common file systems for each of the operating systems you should expect to see on the test. See Book V, Chapter 3 for more information on file systems.

Table 6-1	Operating Systems and Their File Systems
File System	*Operating System*
FAT (file allocation table)	DOS, Windows 3.*x*, Windows 9*x*, Windows NT/2000
VFAT (Virtual FAT)	Windows 3.*x*, Windows 9*x*, Windows NT/2000
FAT32 (FAT 32-bit)	Windows 95b and greater, Windows 2000
NTFS (NT File System)	Windows NT/2000
CDFS (CD File System)	The Windows NT/2000 file system for CD-ROM
UNIX File System	UNIX/Linux
HPFS (High Performance File System)	OS/2
NSS/NFS (Network Storage Services/ NetWare File System)	Novell NetWare

After choosing a file system, the Setup program performs a high-level format of the partition and makes it the active drive to prepare it for the operating system. After the partition is formatted, the install process proceeds. Remember that the operating system must be installed in a primary partition.

Licensing the server

During the installation, you must enter the number of client licenses that are associated with the operating system. Windows uses two licensing modes:

✦ **Per-server licensing:** Under this licensing scheme, the server sets up a Client Access License (CAL) for each license you have purchased. A CAL allows client workstations to connect to the server for network services. You should have one CAL for each concurrent user or the number of client workstations that connect to the server. For example, a network with 80 clients that has no more than 40 clients accessing the server at any one time should have only around 40, or a few more, CALs.

Per-server licensing is common with small businesses with only one server running Windows NT/2000 Server. Per-server licensing enables you to enter the maximum amount of concurrent connections to the server. If you set this to 50, only 50 concurrent connections can be made, and all additional attempts to connect to the server will be refused. If you aren't sure which mode to choose, your safest bet is to go with Per-server mode because you can change from Per-server to Per-seat mode later, but you can only make this change once.

✦ **Per-seat licensing:** This mode is less popular than the Per-server scheme, primarily because it is more expensive and licenses can go unused. However, in an environment where every client is likely to be connected or on larger networks in which the clients access multiple servers, this can be the way to go. Per-seat licensing requires a separate CAL for every client computer that accesses the server for network services.

Joining the network

A server must be assigned a computer name before it can join a domain or workgroup. A server cannot have just any old name either. The computer name must be completely unique on the domain or workgroup. The name can be anything that you want it to be, but it must be unique and it should be something you'll remember and recognize.

Naming the server

On a network located behind a firewall, servers are openly named by their function on the network. For example, a mail server in your Washington state headquarters may be called MAILWA and a sequel server on that same network might be SQLWA. Multiple or redundant servers may be indicated with a numeric value with the primary server named MAILWA1 and a secondary server named MAILWA2.

The naming convention used with servers available outside a firewall should yield names that are much more discreet about their functions. You really don't want to draw attention to a server by naming it MAILWA — you may as well name it PLZHACKME.

Welcome to my domain

During the Windows NT Server installation, you must indicate the domain or workgroup to which your newly named new server will belong. Normally, a server is added as a member of a domain because workgroups are more autonomous and don't provide the centralized administrative services available on a domain controller. To add an NT server to a domain, you must provide a domain name and your domain administrator username and password. After the domain administrator account is verified, the server is added to the domain.

When installing Windows NT Server, you're given the choice of designating the new server as a domain controller or a member server. The following is what you need to remember about these two server designations:

✦ **Domain Controller:** Windows NT Server supports users through two server configurations: Primary Domain Controller (PDC) and Backup Domain Controller (BDC). A PDC stores the master copy of the user and group security account database for a domain, which is regularly copied and synchronized to the Backup Domain Controllers (BDC) as a part of the Windows NT centralized security. Each type of domain controller has a Security Accounts Manager (SAM) that manages the domain user database that contains usernames, passwords, and the file access and share permissions of each network user.

✦ **Member Server:** A *member server* is a computer that runs Windows NT Server but is not a domain controller. A member server can serve any purpose on the network, such as application server, file server, Exchange mail server, and so on. Only servers on which you do not need to perform domain authentication services should be configured as a member server. Member servers do not receive copies of the SAM database. Member servers are also called *standalone servers*.

Unfortunately, after you choose a role — domain controller or member server — there's no going back. A member server cannot become a domain controller, and a domain controller cannot become a member server without reinstalling the operating system. You can promote a Backup Domain Controller to the lofty status of Primary Domain Controller by using the Windows NT Server Manager. A BDC is promoted to a PDC for several reasons, but the most common are that you need to perform maintenance on the PDC, or that you are experiencing problems on the PDC and need to shut it down. A PDC can also be demoted to a BDC, but only when another BDC is available to take its place.

Continuing with the installation

If you configure the server as a member server, the installation proceeds immediately; if you've chosen to configure it as a domain controller, it may take some time for the server to be synchronized to the PDC.

Windows 2000 has a great utility, DCPROMO, that is used to designate a server as a domain controller or a member server any time after the server is up and running. However, Windows NT servers can only be changed from domain controller or to member server with a reinstallation of the operating system. The Windows 2000 DCPROMO eliminates the headache of having to choose the server role during installation as described in the previous section "Welcome to my domain."

Getting the server ready to serve

Eventually in the installation process, you're prompted for the information that defines the network settings of the server. A server's network settings allow the server to address the network and to be addressed by other network elements. Included in the network settings of a server are

+ **IP addressing:** A server must be assigned a static IP address and a subnet mask. These are the addressing elements used to communicate with the rest of the network. Many organizations use designated IP address blocks to designate the type of network device, such as member servers, domain controllers, or networking devices. For example, the address 172.16.100.1 may be assigned as a network's gateway and 172.16.100.2 through .10 may be assigned to designate the switches and routers on the network. Continuing, the block 172.16.100.11 through .30 would then be used for servers, .40 to .50 is assigned to designate printers, and other blocks are reserved for other network elements.

+ **Gateway:** The gateway IP address designates the router that controls access to and from the network from other networks. Any IP address with a destination address not located on the local network is sent to the gateway. Generally, a gateway connects a local network to the Internet, but a gateway can also be used to send traffic to another network, such as the network of a remote office. In most networks that connect to the Internet or the outside world, the router's Ethernet port is typically the default gateway for the network.

+ **Windows Internet Naming Service (WINS):** The WINS utility *resolves* (which is network-speak for *translates*) IP addresses to their computer name (NetBIOS) equivalents. The address of the WINS server on a network is a required part of the network configuration of a server, provided that WINS is in use on the network. Beginning with Windows 2000, Microsoft has finally jumped on the DNS bandwagon. Windows 2000 networks use DNS instead of WINS (although WINS is still available and supported in Windows 2000).

+ **Domain Name System (DNS):** Each server is also configured with the IP address of the network server that's running the DNS service. DNS, which is the most widely used name resolution method, is the name/address resolution protocol used on the Internet. DNS resolves a hostname (such as gohighspeed.com) into its correlating TCP/IP address (204.200.106.1). The domain names used in DNS are actually Fully Qualified Domain Names (FQDNs), which means that the name includes all of the addressing elements needed to identify the server or host.

Other options that can be configured on the server during the installation process are Dynamic Host Configuration Protocol (DHCP); the Internet Information Server (IIS), Terminal Services; and several others (none of which you need to worry about for the exam).

Testing Connectivity

After you configure the operating system and the server reboots (what always seems like a couple of dozen times), the NOS installation is finally complete. At this point, you need to test whether or not the server is able to "see" the network clients, other servers, and the resources on the network — and conversely, whether these network resources are able to see the new server. You really need to know when and why each of the TCP/IP test utilities included in this section are used. The context here is that they're used to test the connectivity of the new server, but they can also be used for troubleshooting network problems.

Pinging across the network

A quick way to test whether a server, node, or workstation is connected to the network and able to communicate over it is to *ping* another network node. This is done through the PING utility that is included in the TCP/IP protocols that accompany virtually every operating system, especially network operating systems. The PING command sends an ICMP (Internet Control Message Protocol) ECHO_REQUEST datagram over the network requesting another network node to respond with an ICMP ECHO_RESPONSE datagram.

The bad news is that for the exam, you must know how to execute the PING command on Windows, Novell, and UNIX systems. The good news is that the PING command is universal (it's a TCP/IP protocol) and is executed the same on all these systems.

To ping a network host using the PING utility, type one of the following commands at a command line prompt:

```
PING yahoo.com
PING 216.115.108.243
```

If any echoes are received, they're displayed on-screen, as shown in Figure 6-1. The fact that echoes were received indicates that you're able to communicate over the network with another side. In the command example shown previously, we're pinging a node that is accessed over the Internet WAN, but the PING command can also be used to ping local nodes by using its computer name or IP address. However, if the PING request goes unanswered and times out, you need to double-check the IP configuration of the server or troubleshoot the network connection.

Checking the configuration

To verify the IP configuration of a server, use the IPCONFIG command on Windows NT/2000/XP systems, IFCONFIG on UNIX/Linux systems, or the

CONFIG command on a NetWare system. Expect to see these commands (relative to their operating systems) on the exam.

Using the IPCONFIG command displays the network settings for each network interface card (NIC) installed in a server, whether active or not. In Figure 6-2, you can see the last part of an IPCONFIG display for a system with two NICs. To display the details of the IP configuration of a server or workstation, enter the following command:

```
IPCONFIG /ALL
```

This command displays all IP configuration settings on a networked computer, including DNS, WINS, hostname, DHCP address and lease information, IP address, subnet, gateway, and more.

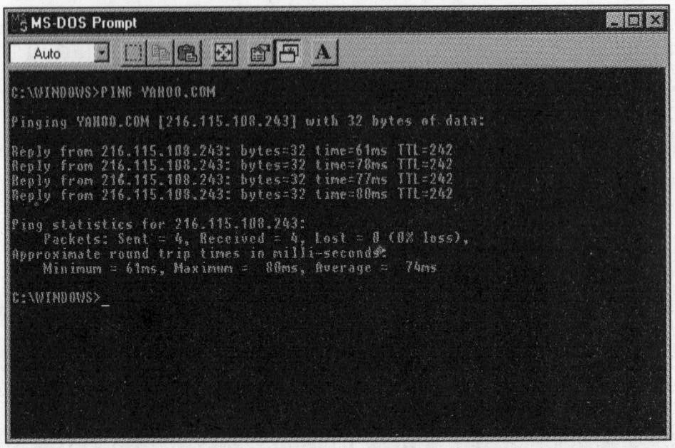

Figure 6-1: Use the PING command to verify the connection between two network nodes.

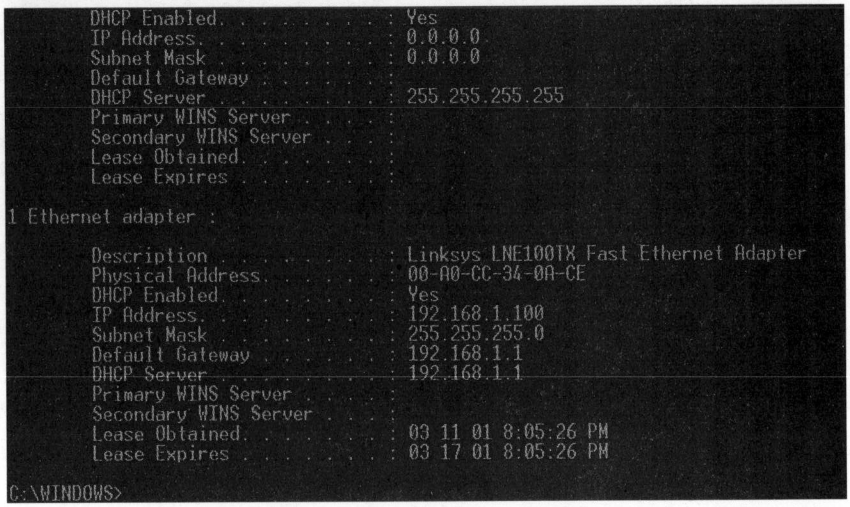

Figure 6-2: Use the IPCONFIG/ ALL command to view a Windows server's IP configuration.

Novell NetWare uses the CONFIG command, Windows uses the IPCONFIG command, and UNIX uses the IFCONFIG command to display the IP configuration of a networked computer.

Tracing a route

If, for some reason, you can't connect with a remote site over the network, you can use the TRACERT (Trace Route) command to display the network path used to send data from your computer to a destination computer. A TRACERT display pinpoints any bottlenecks being caused by a slow or inoperative server or router on the network. For example, if data packets are unable to pass through a particular router because of a configuration, connectivity, or other problem, the ICMP ECHO_REQUEST commands (much like a PING) will time out and isolate the problem point. A TRACERT command sends three PING requests to each router or gateway on the path between your computer and a destination computer. The time in milliseconds (ms) that it takes the three responses to reach your computer from each succeeding router then appears on-screen (see Figure 6-3). If a request goes unacknowledged, an asterisk appears.

```
C:\WINDOWS>tracert yahoo.com

Tracing route to yahoo.com [216.115.108.245]
over a maximum of 30 hops:

  1    12 ms    10 ms    23 ms  12.17.167.1
  2    39 ms    30 ms    28 ms  12.124.171.29
  3   129 ms   119 ms    50 ms  gbr1-p51.st6wa.ip.att.net [12.123.203.66]
  4   215 ms   167 ms   150 ms  gbr3-p70.st6wa.ip.att.net [12.122.5.157]
  5    68 ms   113 ms    70 ms  gbr4-p40.sffca.ip.att.net [12.122.2.197]
  6   237 ms    54 ms    70 ms  gbr2-p100.sffca.ip.att.net [12.122.1.190]
  7   182 ms    72 ms   184 ms  gr2-p3100.sffca.ip.att.net [12.123.12.241]
  8   177 ms    58 ms   146 ms  att-gw.sf.gblx.net [192.205.31.70]
  9   277 ms     *       52 ms  pos2-0-155M.br2.NUQ2.gblx.net [208.178.255.74]
 10   122 ms    75 ms    63 ms  208.178.255.94
 11   117 ms     *       92 ms  so4-0-0-2488M.wr1.SNV2.gblx.net [208.48.118.118

 12    84 ms    56 ms    65 ms  pos6-0-2488M.cr1.SNV.gblx.net [208.50.169.62]
 13    78 ms    70 ms    80 ms  ge0-0-1000M.hr8.SNV.gblx.net [206.132.254.37]
 14   203 ms   168 ms    99 ms  bas1r-ge3-0-hr8.snv.yahoo.com [208.178.103.62]
 15   263 ms    63 ms    66 ms  yahoo.com [216.115.108.245]

Trace complete.

C:\WINDOWS>
```

Figure 6-3:
The results
of a
TRACERT
command.

To run a TRACERT request on a location, enter the command in one of the following formats:

```
TRACERT yahoo.com
TRACERT 216.115.108.243
```

If you don't receive any indications of problems (other than slow routes) on the network and no hops are timing out, you know that your new server is good to go for communications over the network. Just for clarification, each router on the path between two points on the network is counted as a hop.

UNIX/Linux uses the traceroute command, which performs the same actions as the TRACERT command used in Windows.

Keeping the NOS Up to Date

You should make it a part of your regular maintenance program to check for updates for the NOS. Look for a question on the Server+ exam regarding the best places to find updates for your server's NOS and its device drivers.

Updating the NOS

The NOS publisher's Web site is the best place to check for the latest and greatest patches, fixes, and updates. For Microsoft products, go to www. microsoft.com; for Novell, see www.novell.com; or check out the publisher's site for the UNIX or Linux version in use. Windows NT is famous for its service packs that provide bug fixes, features, and additional security.

A new NOS version, and even some hardware device drivers, commonly require a certain service pack. For example, after installing the very latest video adapter device drivers, you find that the system will only boot into 640 x 480 256-color mode. Had you read the readme file or visited the video card manufacturer's Web site, you would've known upfront that the new device driver requires the next highest service pack than the one you installed.

Looking for new drivers

Along with keeping the NOS up to date, you need to check that your device drivers are up to date as well. Knowing which drivers are installed for which adapters can save you a lot of time when you encounter problems.

At least once a month you should use this inventory to surf the Web looking for updated drivers. This will ensure that your system is maintained in its best operating form. Avoid using generic drivers for the adapters and peripherals in components in your server and download new or updated drivers only from the NOS publisher or the hardware manufacturer. Many installation headaches result from loading the generic device drivers that came with the NOS. Your server will be better for the time you spent downloading and installing the specific drivers developed by the manufacturer for your specific devices.

Monitoring the Server's Performance

Several performance-monitoring tools are provided with virtually any NOS. Most of the performance-monitoring tools can be used for real-time observation and periodic logging of events on the system. These tools can acquire important information about the health of your system. For the test, you need to know how data is collected, what types of data are collected, and how to use the data to keep your system at its best.

Looking at the logs

Each time that Windows NT or Windows 2000 is started, event logging is also started. The event log records the activities, errors, and security events occurring on the server. The Event Viewer tool enables you to peruse the event log to troubleshoot various hardware and software problems and to monitor Windows NT Workstation and Windows 2000 Professional security events.

Virtually all network, workstation, or server problems are recorded as logical indicators in a log file. Most network operating systems, including Windows and NetWare, create and constantly update system actions, events, alerts, and errors to log files. The three general log file types are

+ **Application log files:** These log files contain events, messages, and errors posted by network applications and services. For example, when a program, such as a virus program, fails to load or is unexpectedly stopped or fails, an error will be recorded to the application log files.

+ **Security log files:** Security logs are security-related events and alerts generated by administrator-enabled auditing services of the NOS. A good example of this is the user who has the keyboard Caps Lock key enabled when typing in a log-on password. When this authentication fails, it's recorded in the security log files.

+ **System log files:** The system log contains messages, events, and errors posted by internal services and drivers. For instance, if the DHCP or WINS service fails to load during startup, you get an error stating that a service has failed to load during startup. If you check the system log files, you'll find exactly what service is having trouble.

Many log files (those with a .LOG file extension) are stored in text format and can be viewed with any text editor. However, those that have an .EVT file extension are event log files, which are stored in binary form, and can only be viewed with the Windows Event Viewer.

If you don't actually use these logs, generating endless log files wastes both system resources and very useful information about the network's performance. So, if you don't want to see the logs, either disable them or clear them on a regular basis.

Monitoring tools

You have several monitoring tools at your disposal to help you track system performance, network performance, security issues, and much more. For the exam, you need to be familiar with Windows Performance Monitor, Windows Task Manager, and Windows Network Analyzer.

Windows Performance Monitor

Windows Performance Monitor can be used to . . . well . . . monitor the system performance. You can gather critical information about system statistics, and then analyze and graphically display the information. Performance Monitor can also be configured to alert systems administrators when particular events occur. *Alerts* are critical security controls that help perform real-time monitoring, which helps notify the administrator about a violation when it happens. Reviewing the report a week later and finding a security breach after it's too late is pretty pointless. This utility is also used to track objects, such as processors, memory, cache, threads, processes, and services running on the server. Every object has counters that keep track of specific activities or events. These events or activities can be viewed by using any of four different types of viewing options: Chart, Alert, Log, and Report.

To start the Performance Monitor control, choose Start⇨Programs⇨ Administrative Tools⇨Performance Monitor. Or if you're into command lines, you can use the command PERFMON –y.

If the system performance drops suddenly, you may want to increase the size of the swap file or (ideally) increase the amount of physical memory (RAM) in the server.

Windows Task Manager

Windows Task Manager gives you a quick view of CPU and memory utilization. You can watch in real time how each application, application component, or system process is affecting system resources.

To run Task Manager, right-click the Windows toolbar to display the Toolbar menu and then select Task Manager. You can also press Ctrl+Shift+Esc or Ctrl+Alt+Del.

The Task Manager is the fastest way to determine whether a multiprocessor upgrade was successful.

Windows Network Analyzer

The Windows Network Analyzer tool is used to capture network traffic for display and analysis. You can use this utility to analyze captured network data in user-defined methods, extract data from defined protocol parsers, and review real-time traffic on your network. Network Monitor is great for capturing packets between Web servers, browsers, and SQL Servers. You can view packet size, network utilization, and many other statistics that can be helpful for managing system performance.

Several other tools can be used to check that the NOS install went well, but you don't need to worry a whole lot about picking them out of a lineup on the exam. The important detail to remember is that you need to verify whether the installation was successful by checking network connectivity and system performance. Read through Book V, Chapter 5 for more information on monitoring and creating a baseline.

Managing the network

Simple Network Management Protocol (SNMP) provides monitoring and managing of a network from one or more workstations, called SNMP managers. This protocol is a family of specifications that provides a way to collect network management data from the devices residing in a network. SNMP agents send information to one or many SNMP management systems. The management system requests information from an SNMP agent (usually a server or router).

Management Information Base (MIB) is a container object that stores all the information that the management system may request from the agent. The SNMP agent provides the management system with requested status information and also reports any unexpected events in the form of a trap. A *trap* is an alarm-triggering event on an agent. An alarm could be caused by a number of events, such as illegal access, RAID array failure, reboot, or many other events defined by the administrator.

The contents of an agent's MIB are descriptors that are encoded in Abstract Syntax Notation (ASN.1) format, which is a standard form used to create MIB entries. SNMP systems that use the ASN.1 standard are interoperable. Some vendors add their own proprietary wrinkle to their versions of SNMP, which can cause some problems between devices from different manufacturers. However, even newer versions of the SNMP manager (as long as they're ASN.1 compatible) are backward compatible with existing agents. If SNMP is being used on a network that's exposed to the Internet, a firewall should be placed between the Internet and the network to prevent intrusion of outside SNMP management consoles.

An SNMP community needs to be defined before installing SNMP. A *community* is a group to which systems running the SNMP service belong. The *community parameter* is just the name of the communities you want to monitor. An SNMP agent can belong to multiple communities but will not respond to any management system that's not a member of one of those groups. Defining community names provides some security and context for agents receiving requests and initiating traps. This is also true for management systems and their tasks.

Expect to see a question on the exam that asks about upgrading an SNMP manager to a newer version. You need to know whether the SNMP agents (on the network devices) need to be upgraded as well. Because SNMP is defined through the RFC (Request for Change) process, which defines a universal standard for TCP/IP protocols and their modifications, new versions are backward compatible. So, a new manager should work with existing agents, and new agents should work with an existing manager.

Wrapping Up the Configuration

After you've completed the internal configuration of the server, you have two (and possibly three) major steps left to perform: creating a baseline and fully documenting the system. The optional third step, which would actually precede the other two major steps, is configuring any external devices.

Configuring external devices

The time to add external devices that are supported by an internal interface bus is after the server is online with all its BIOSes, service packs, and programming updated to current and compatible levels. The server's configuration is now stable and ready to support whatever else you want to throw on or at it.

For the Server+ exam, you should know about adding and configuring external Small Computer System Interface (SCSI) devices. The SCSI bus and SCSI devices can be finicky and a real pain to troubleshoot. You definitely want the server to be in its tip-top shape so that when you're faced with a SCSI challenge — and you will be — you can concentrate on solving SCSI problems and not other system issues.

See Book V, Chapter 5 for more information on configuring external SCSI devices.

Establishing a server baseline

After the server has been configured completely, your next step should be to create a server baseline. By collecting information for a baseline of the network servers and network devices, such as routers and switches, you will have an accurate picture of network traffic flow to the servers and network devices. A network and server baseline provides you with the data needed to evaluate the growth of the network and to pinpoint network or server bottlenecks. See the discussion on running a server baseline in Book V, Chapter 5.

Documenting the system

The third and final major task that must be performed when configuring or re-configuring a network server is to create the system documentation. Your documentation and how complete it is falls under the Networking Golden Rule: "Do unto other networking technicians as you would have them do unto you."

We can't overly emphasize the importance of the server's (or the network's) documentation. Documentation and its creation and maintenance is an important part of the Server+ exam.

See Book V, Chapter 5 for a more detailed discussion on what should be included in a server's documentation and when it should be created and updated.

Prep Test

1 The _____ command displays the path a packet takes to get to a destination host.

A ○ NETSTAT

B ○ IPCONFIG

C ○ PING

D ○ TRACERT

2 The command used to verify connectivity using Novell is _____.

A ○ PCONSOLE

B ○ NDPS

C ○ ConsoleOne

D ○ CONFIG

3 Name the log in which security-related events and alerts generated by administrator-enabled auditing services are recorded.

A ○ System logs

B ○ Security logs

C ○ Application logs

D ○ Authentication logs

4 Name the container object that stores all the information that the management system might request from the agent.

A ○ MIB

B ○ SAM

C ○ User

D ○ NTUSER.DAT

5 Which network-management tool can be used to get a quick view of CPU and memory utilization?

A ○ Task Manager

B ○ Network Analyzer

C ○ Processor Manager

D ○ Performance Monitor

6 The FAT32 file system is supported by which of the following operating systems? (Choose all that apply.)

A ❑ Windows 95a

B ❑ Windows 98

C ❑ Windows 2000

D ❑ Windows 3.1

7 What are the options available for licensing a Windows operating system on a sever or network clients?

A ○ Open licensing

B ○ Per-server licensing

C ○ Per-user licensing

D ○ Per-seat licensing

8 What is the type of network server that runs Windows NT Server but is not a domain controller?

A ○ PDC

B ○ Member

C ○ Application

D ○ BDC

9 Which Windows networking utility resolves IP addresses into their NetBIOS equivalents on Windows 9x and NT systems?

A ○ DNS

B ○ ARP

C ○ RARP

D ○ WINS

10 What utility can be used to verify the IP configuration of a UNIX/Linux system?

A ○ IPCONFIG

B ○ CONFIG

C ○ IFCONFIG

D ○ WINIPCFG

Answers

1 **D.** TRACERT is handy for finding the source of network problems. *Take a look at "Tracing a route."*

2 **D.** All versions of NetWare use the CONFIG command to display the configuration settings of the network adapters. *See "Checking the Configuration."*

3 **B.** Security logs are only concerned with events and alerts concerning security. *Check out "Looking at the logs."*

4 **A.** Management Information Base (MIB) is used to store everything the management system requires the agent to trap. *Review "Managing the network."*

5 **A.** Task Manager is a fast, easy way to check the CPU and memory utilization. *Look at "Windows Task Manager."*

6 **B** and **C.** FAT32 was introduced by Windows 95b and is supported by Windows 98 and Windows 2000. *Review "Setting up a file system."*

7 **B** and **D.** Microsoft offers two primary programs for licensing its operating systems: per-seat and per-server. *See "Licensing the server."*

8 **B.** A Windows NT server can be configured as either a domain controller (PDC or BDC) or a member server. *Look over "Welcome to my domain."*

9 **D.** WINS is supported on Windows 9*x* and NT systems, but Windows 2000 uses DNS to resolve network addresses. *Check out "Getting the server ready to serve."*

10 **C.** Be sure you know the utility used by each operating system for the exam. *Study "Checking the configuration."*

Chapter 7: Interfacing with a Network

Exam Objectives

✔ Identifying common network interfaces and protocols

✔ Naming common network cable types

✔ Explaining network adapter principles

✔ Listing common TCP/IP protocols

✔ Detailing IP addressing

✔ Defining DHCP

✔ Identifying TCP/IP well-known ports

A significant part of a network technician's job deals with the physical components of a network, including the cabling, network adapters, and the physical layout of the network and its nodes.

You should expect to see questions on the Server+ exam dealing with network connectivity issues and how to troubleshoot them when things stop working. You can expect to be asked about what to do when there is no link light, or you can't ping a computer by its name, or whether you use a crossover cable or a straight-through cable when you directly connect two devices, and the like. Or, in other words, you need to know a bit more than just the server and its software to pass this test. This is the on-the-job knowledge the exam assumes that you have.

If you haven't read Book IV (especially Chapter 2), now would be an excellent time. You need to know and understand the basics of networking concepts, and its hardware, software, and terminology. If you're new to networking, read Book IV before diving into this chapter.

Getting Down to Networking Basics

To understand networks and networking, you really should start at the beginning. If you are a networking expert — which means you've worked on a network for more than a day or two — you may want to skip this first section because most of it is background material intended to help you understand questions and answers that include networking terms and concepts. For example, if an exam question poses a scenario such as

You are connecting your server to an Ethernet network. You plan to use thinnet cabling, but one of the workstations is 300 meters from the next closest network node.

then you must be able to understand the ramifications implied in these statements. Even if you're a seasoned network expert with weeks of experience, you may want to review this section, just to familiarize yourself with the language.

A *network* is two or more computers that are connected with a communications link for sharing resources.

Serving peers and clients

A network can be one of two fundamental types. A network can be constructed by directly connecting computers together to form a peer-to-peer network, or it can be a more elaborate affair that includes servers and clients. Here are definitions of each of these two types of networks:

✦ **Peer-to-peer:** Also known as a *peer-based* network, a *peer-to peer* network is simply a client-based network with computers connected to one another to share resources. Peer-to-peer networks are voluntary, you-trust-me-and-I'll-trust-you affairs. No servers are on a peer-to-peer network, only clients.

✦ **Client/server:** A *client/server* network has a centralized server or host computer that provides the resources to the workstations attached to the network: the *clients*. These networks can be complicated, and it's common for IT professionals to lose some sleep over these complicated networks. Client/server networks are the subjects of nearly all the questions on the Server+ exam.

In Table 7-1, we list a few of the important factors that differentiate peer-based and client/server networks.

Table 7-1	Peer-to-Peer Compared to Client/Server Networks	
Factor	*Peer-to-Peer*	*Client/Server*
Number of nodes	2–10	Limited only by the network hardware and software in use
Relative cost	Inexpensive	Can be very expensive, depending on network size
Security	User-managed	Centrally administered
Administration	User-managed	Centrally administered
Data backups	User-managed	Centrally administered

Controlling access and security

One of the most important differences between client/server and peer-based networks is security. In a peer-based network, security — that is, who and when can others access a computer and its resources — is controlled by the owner/operator of each particular workstation. Security is granted to individual users on the peer network one at a time and one folder at a time, completely under the control of the workstation owner.

Share-level security

Access granted by the owner (user) of a workstation to the files and hardware resources on a particular workstation is called *share-level security*. In a peer-to-peer network, each peer (that is to say, each user) is in charge of his or her own workstation, playing gatekeeper to the other users on the network.

User-level security

The access granted by the network administrator to network resources — such as data, software, or hardware — using the rights of individual users or groups is called *user-level security*. In other words, permission to access a resource is granted directly to an individual user (or group of users). One or more network administrators, who are responsible for the function, security, and integrity of the entire network, including the workstations, centrally administer client/server networks.

The full responsibility for security falls directly on the network administrator, who is responsible for assigning and managing the permissions and rights of network users and groups of users so that they have access to network resources, such as software, data, and hardware. This task is very much like herding cats.

Although most of this information is to provide you with background, you really do need to know the difference between user-level and share-level security for the exam.

Taking on topologies

You won't see questions specifically about network topologies, but you should know how a particular network topology impacts the configuration of the network and server. You are more likely to see references to Ethernet networks than you are to see Token Ring or any other.

You can choose from quite a few different ways to connect your workstations, servers, and network devices. The pattern of connections that tie the network devices to the network is its *topology*. Here are the most common network topologies:

✦ **Bus:** Nodes are connected to a central cable, called a *backbone,* that runs the length of the network. The bus topology is commonly used for the backbone of an Ethernet network. However, at the workstation end of an Ethernet network, the topology is more likely to be a form of a star network.

✦ **Ring:** The primary network cable is installed as a *loop* (or *ring*), and the workstations are attached to the primary cable at points on the ring. The ring topology is the basis for Token Ring networks.

✦ **Star:** In its purest form, each workstation on a star topology is connected directly to the central server, hub, or switch with its own cable, which creates a starburst-like pattern. The star topology, which is common to ARCNet networks, connects workstations directly to a server. The star topology is more commonly used today with Ethernet and Token Ring networks to cluster workstations to hubs or MSAUs (multistation access units), which are then attached to the primary network cable.

✦ **Mesh:** Each workstation is directly connected to the server and all other workstations, creating a mesh of network connections. This topology is not very common because it's pretty expensive to have all those cables going everywhere.

Riding the bus

The Server+ exam deals a lot with Windows NT Server Ethernet networks, which commonly use a hybrid form of the bus and star topologies. In this arrangement, the nodes are clustered to hubs, which are in turn connected to the network backbone. The network *backbone* is the primary network cabling that interconnects the primary devices (switches, routers, and servers) of the network. In its simplest form (a thinnet network), a bus network backbone runs from one computer to the next in a daisy-chain pattern. In this arrangement, the backbone runs from the first computer in the network to the last computer in the network.

Bus topologies have three primary characteristics: signal transmission, cable termination, and continuity.

Signal transmission

To avoid problems, only one computer at a time can transmit on a bus network. Like good little nodes, when one node is "talking," the other nodes are "listening." As a signal travels down the cable, each node examines the signal to see whether it was sent to them. If not, the signal passes on down the cable uninterrupted.

Because bus network nodes only listen for messages sent to them and do not actually pass signals along by regenerating the signal, the bus topology is considered to be a *passive* network structure. Also remember that the bus topology is the underlying topology of Ethernet networks; therefore, Ethernet networks are passive networks.

Cable termination

Without something to stop it from bouncing back and forth on the network backbone, a signal would ricochet indefinitely, preventing any other signals from being sent. By definition, only one signal should be on the network at a time. Terminating the cable at each end helps prevent a message from riding the bus indefinitely. The terminator is a resistor that is placed on each end of the backbone to absorb errant signals and clear the cable (see Figure 7-1). If the backbone becomes broken or has an open end (an open connection, for example), the network is sure to malfunction because signals are too busy bouncing about to reach the terminators.

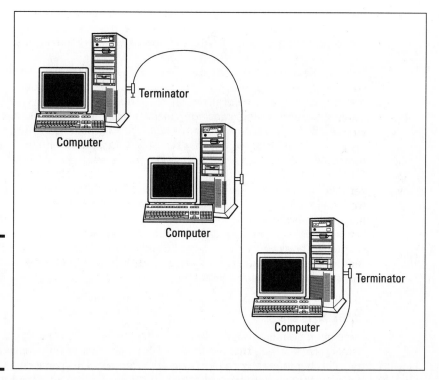

Figure 7-1:
A bus topology with backbone cable terminators installed.

If the network is connected to another network through a bridge, router, or other connectivity device, the terminated cable is also known as a *segment*. Two computers on the same wire are on the same segment. Two computers on two different wires may be on the same network, but they are on separate segments of the network.

Continuity

As long as a bus network's cable has no open ends and is properly terminated, the network continues to function. However, if one of the nodes on the network fails, the network cable is operable as long as its cable connections are intact. This doesn't mean that any problems that the failed node is causing magically disappear — it only means the network cable is still okay.

Won't you wear my ring around your net?

In a ring topology, the backbone cable loops around and connects the beginning of the cable to its end, forming a ring. The network backbone cable forms a loop that, in effect, has no beginning or end, thus eliminating the termination requirement of a bus network. A signal travels around the ring from node to node until it reaches its destination.

In contrast to the bus topology, the ring topology is an *active topology*. Each node (computer or MSAU) on the ring network receives the signal, examines it, and then regenerates it onto the network. If a node fails and is unable to regenerate the signal, the entire network is affected, and continuity is lost.

You may have had the pleasure of attending one of those meetings where some object is used to control who can talk. We once attended a meeting at which a small pine tree branch was passed around a circle. The person holding the pine branch was supposed to share his thoughts on a particular subject. Well, as lame as this may sound, this is essentially the concept used on the ring topology, except that the object passed around is called a *token*. Strangely enough, this process is called *token passing*.

Like the bus network, only one ring network node can transmit at a time — the node holding the token. The node proves it has the token by embedding it in the message it sends — kind of like a hall pass, in a way. None of the other nodes can send messages to the network because they cannot access the token. The destination node of the message includes the token in its response to the sender. The sending node releases the token when its message session is completed.

Seeing stars

Once upon a time, terminals were directly connected to mainframes by individual pieces of wire that resulted in a configuration of wires emanating from the central unit creating a starburst arrangement. This same configuration is the basis for the star topology in which network nodes are directly connected to a central server or, as is much more common today, a hub or switch.

The star topology is more commonly used in conjunction with another topology. You can use the star topology to improve the configuration and performance of the bus and ring topologies by creating clusters of workstations that attach to the bus or ring backbones. The result is hybrid or mixed topologies, such as the star-bus and the star-ring (which is also called a ringed-star).

Cabling the Network

Networks use cables made of essentially three materials, copper, glass, or plastic — yes, the same stuff you find in pennies, windows, and milk jugs. These substances are relatively inexpensive and abundant; but more importantly, they're excellent conductors of electricity or light. Copper is a great conductor of electricity, and glass and plastic are conductors for light, which brings us to the reason for cable media in the first place.

In order for one computer to carry on a conversation with another computer, the computers must be able to transmit and receive electrical or light impulses representing commands or data. In a networked environment, the computers and peripherals of the network are interconnected with a transmission medium to enable data exchange and resource sharing. Cable media has laid the foundation on which networks grew — literally.

The big three of cabling

Three major cable types are used in today's networks. When dealing with servers and networks, you need to know what type of cable is best for different situations. Following is a description of the three cable types:

✦ **Coaxial (coax) cable:** This type of cable is a little like the cable used to connect your television set to the cable outlet. Actually, networks use two types of coax cable: thick coaxial cable and thin coaxial cable.

✦ **Twisted pair (no, not the upstairs neighbors):** Twisted pair (TP) cable is made from one or more (usually four) pairs of copper wires that are twisted around each other to minimize the impact of outside electrical noise and interference. TP cable is available in two types: unshielded twisted pair (UTP) and shielded twisted pair (STP). UTP is similar to the wiring used to connect your telephone. We explain each of these cable types in the section "Terminating the twisted pair" later in this chapter.

✦ **Fiber-optic:** Glass or plastic fibers carry modulated pulses of light to represent digital data signals. Because it uses light and not electrical signals, fiber-optic cabling is not susceptible to EMI or RF interference, which accounts for its incredibly long attenuation and segment lengths, which can stretch up to 2 kilometers or a little over a mile. See "Technical cable stuff" later in the chapter for information on attenuation and cable length limitations.

Of course, these cables all have advantages and disadvantages, but for the Server+ exam, you really don't need to know that. However, if you are really into that sort of thing, you may want to check out Book IV.

Technical cable stuff

All network cabling has a set of general characteristics that guides you in picking the most appropriate cable for a given situation. Here are definitions of the characteristics you should know for the exam:

✦ **Bandwidth (speed):** The amount of data a cable can carry in a certain period, typically one second. Bandwidth is often expressed as the number of bits (either kilobits or megabits) that can be transmitted in a second. For example, UTP cable is nominally rated at 10 Mbps, or 10 million bits per second.

✦ **Cost:** This is always a major consideration when choosing a cable type. The Network+ exam deals with this characteristic on a comparative basis. The relative cost comparisons for the major cable media are

  • Twisted pair cable is the least expensive, but has limitations that require other hardware to be installed.

  • Coaxial cable is a little more expensive than TP, but it doesn't require additional equipment, and it's inexpensive to maintain.

  • Fiber-optic cabling is the most expensive, requires skilled installation labor, and is expensive to install and maintain, but if you need long runs with lots of bandwidth, fiber-optic is the cable to use.

✦ **Maximum segment length:** Every cable is subject to a condition called *attenuation,* which means that the signal weakens and can no longer be recognized. Attenuation occurs at a distance specific to every type of cable. This distance (measured in meters) also represents the maximum segment length for a cable medium, or the distance at which signals on the cable must be regenerated.

✦ **Maximum number of nodes per segments:** Each time that a device is added to a network, the effect is like another hole being put in the cable. Like leaks from pinholes in a balloon, having too many devices attached to a network cable reduces the distance at which attenuation begins. Therefore, each type of cable must limit the number of nodes that can be attached to a cable segment.

✦ **Resistance to interference:** The different cable media have varying vulnerability to electromagnetic interference (EMI) or radio-frequency interference (RFI) caused by electric motors, fluorescent light fixtures, your magnet collection, the radio station on the next floor of your home or office, and so on. As the construction of the cable and its cladding (coverings) varies, so does its resistance to EMI and RFI signals.

Just for clarification, a network segment is created each time you add a bridge, switch, or router, which are devices that regenerate and redirect signals.

You don't have to memorize the characteristics of thin and thick coaxial cable, unshielded twisted pair cable, and fiber-optic cable. You do need to know that they are used in an Ethernet network. Table 7-2 lists the characteristics of the different cabling used for Ethernet networks.

Table 7-2	Ethernet Cable Types and Their Characteristics		
Cable	Bandwidth	Maximum Segment Length	Maximum Nodes per Segment
Thin coax	10 Mbps	185 meters	30
Thick coax	10 Mbps	500 meters	100
UTP	10–1,000 Mbps	100 meters	1,024
STP	4–1,000 Mbps	100 meters	1,024
Fiber-optic	100–10,000 Mbps	2,000 meters	No limit

What's this 10Base stuff?

In the Ethernet world, the designation of cable is also descriptive of its characteristics. Thick coax cable is designated as *10Base5*, thin coaxial cable is *10Base2*, and UTP is generally *10BaseT*. The *10Base* part indicates that these cables carry 10 Mbps bandwidth and that they carry baseband signals. For coax cable, the *5* and *2* mean 500 meters and 200 meters respectively, which is the approximate maximum segment length of each cable. Actually, the maximum segment length of thin coax is 185 meters, but 200 works better in this case — besides, it's easier to remember. The *T* in *10BaseT* refers to twisted pair cable.

Using twisted pair cable

The most popular cabling in use for Ethernet and Token Ring networks is twisted pair copper wire. Copper wire is the lightest, most flexible, least expensive, and easiest to install of the popular network media. The bad news is that it's quite vulnerable to interference and has attenuation problems as well. But, given the right network design and implementation, these problems can be largely avoided.

As mentioned earlier in the section "Technical cable stuff," there are two types of twisted pair wire in networks: unshielded (UTP) and shielded (STP). Of the two, the more common choice is UTP, which is particularly popular for Ethernet networks. UTP wire is just about what its name implies — two unshielded wires twisted together.

Unshielded twisted-pair cable

For use in networks, UTP is clearly the most common pick among cabling types. For all the reasons we present in the introductory paragraph of this section, unshielded provides the most installation flexibility and ease of maintenance of the big three cabling media. The Ethernet specifications refer to UTP as 10BaseT.

The Electronics Industries Association and the Telecommunications Industries Association (EIA/TIA) define UTP cable in five (actually, it is now up to around seven) categories, or "cats" as the real techies call them (as in Cat 3 or Cat 5):

+ **Category 1 and 2:** These two categories aren't used in networking. Just pretend that this isn't here and that you didn't see it . . . just read on and you won't get hurt on the exam.

+ **Category 3:** This is a 4-pair cable supporting bandwidth up to 10 Mbps — the minimum standard for 10BaseT networks.

+ **Category 4:** This is a 4-pair cable commonly used in 16 Mbps-Token Ring networks.

+ **Category 5:** This is a 4-pair cable with bandwidth up to 1,000 Mbps, used for 100BaseTX and ATM (asynchronous transfer mode) networking.

Terminating the twisted pair

Different connectors and termination methods are used with twisted pair cabling. For example, connecting a hub to another hub requires that an Ethernet cable be terminated with what's known as *crossover* (rather than your run-of-the-mill straight-through) cable. However, some hubs also have an uplink, or *X* port, that implements the crossover function internally. The *X* refers to the crossover function. *Straight-through cables* are used between workstations and network devices, such as hubs and switches.

Beware! The Server+ exam uses the term *MDI* (Media Dependent Interface) when asking about connecting with a crossover or straight-through cable. MDI is the IEEE standard for UTP interfaces; in most cases, it's the same thing as a hub. If you're asked a question about what type of cable to use when connecting an MDI port to a MDI-X port, the answer is a straight-through cable because the MDI-X device provides the crossover. Study Table 7-3 to discover what type of cable should be used in each particular connection situation.

Table 7-3	Matching Cables to Connections
For This Type of Connection	*Use This Type of Cable*
Workstation to workstation	Crossover
Workstation to server	Crossover
Hub to hub	Crossover
Hub to switch	Crossover

For This Type of Connection	Use This Type of Cable
Switch to switch	Crossover
Workstation to hub	Straight-through
Workstation to switch	Straight-through
Server to hub	Straight-through
Server to switch	Straight-through

Pinning your hopes on the cable

Expect to see a question that asks you to identify a cable connector by its pinouts, which is the pattern used to assign cable wires to the pins in the connector. Check out Tables 7-4 and 7-5 to see the pin and wire arrangements used on Ethernet crossover cables and straight-through cables, respectively. Ethernet cables are terminated with an RJ-45 connector (see Figure 7-2). The wires in a UTP cable are color-coded for easy reference. Each wire has two colors. The first color is the solid color of the wire's sheathing, and the second color is the color of the stripes on the sheath.

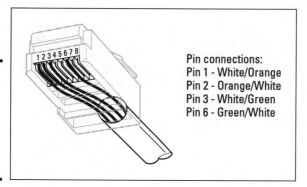

Figure 7-2:
An RJ-45
connector
with its
twisted pair
cable
pinouts.

Pin connections:
Pin 1 - White/Orange
Pin 2 - Orange/White
Pin 3 - White/Green
Pin 6 - Green/White

Table 7-4	Ethernet Crossover Cable Pinouts	
End 1	*End 2*	*Wire*
Pin 1	Pin 3	White/Orange
Pin 2	Pin 6	Orange/White
Pin 3	Pin 1	White/Green
Pin 4	Pin 7	Blue/White
Pin 5	Pin 8	White/Blue
Pin 6	Pin 2	Green/White
Pin 7	Pin 4	White/Brown
Pin 8	Pin 5	Brown/White

On the Server+ exam, you may encounter a question that includes a diagram of a crossover cable. Look for the 1-3, 2-6, 3-1, and 6-2 connections for the correct configuration.

Table 7-5		Ethernet Straight-Through Cable Pinouts
End 1	*End 2*	*Wire*
Pin 1	Pin 1	White/Orange
Pin 2	Pin 2	Orange/White
Pin 3	Pin 3	White/Green
Pin 4	Pin 4	Blue/White
Pin 5	Pin 5	White/Blue
Pin 6	Pin 6	Green/White
Pin 7	Pin 7	White/Brown
Pin 8	Pin 8	Brown/White

Teaming Up with NIC

A network interface card (NIC) or network adapter provides network connectivity to workstations, printers, and servers. However, on the exam you may encounter a few NIC-specific terms, including Wake-on-LAN, adapter teaming, and multihoming. Familiarizing yourself with these terms is probably a good idea, but you don't need to know the dirty details.

Waking up across the network

Wake-on-LAN (WOL) is a remote wake-up technology that enables you to remotely power on a server. This technology is a great timesaver, allowing remote access for automated software installations, upgrades, disk backups, and virus scans. Wake-on-LAN uses what's referred to as the "magic packet." The magic packet tells the system to power on, thus allowing the system administrators to access the computer remotely. This reduces system management workload and provides flexibility.

Wake-on-LAN is, for the most part, a hardware function. You may see a question on the exam asking just that. Remember that WOL requires

✦ An ATX motherboard with the 3-pin WOL connector.

✦ An ATX-only power supply that meets ATX 2.01 specifications. It's important that the power supply provide the 5-volt (V) stand-by current.

✦ A network card that supports WOL.

✦ A cable connected to the NIC and motherboard is required.

✦ The BIOS Power Management must have the LAN (local area network) Wakeup option.

✦ Your system must be in a Soft-Off power state.

Remember that the system is powered off, so software is not loaded for this process.

Multihoming a server

Multihoming is a term used to refer to a server being connected to two or more networks or having two or more network addresses. A good example is a network server that is connected to both a serial line and an Ethernet LAN cable.

Teaming up the adapters

Adapter teaming, also referred to as *adapter fault tolerance,* is the addition of a second NIC as a redundant link providing extra bandwidth and redundancy to the primary network link. Adapter teaming allows the server to be accessed by either NIC, thus improving network throughput as well as keeping network traffic flowing in case the other NIC fails. This is where PCI (Peripheral Component Interconnect) hot-plug NICs come into play — when a NIC dies, you can swap it out without having to power down the server.

Working with TCP/IP

The *Transmission Control Protocol/Internet Protocol (TCP/IP)* protocol suite, also known as simply the Internet Protocol suite, serves communications at both the global and local levels. From its conception, TCP/IP evolved with a definite emphasis on portability and universal support. Its adaptability and open structure are important reasons for its rapid and widespread growth. TCP/IP is the protocol of choice on most LANs and virtually all WANs (wide area networks) because it's the primary protocol of the Internet.

The protocols that make up the TCP/IP protocol suite also provide a wide range of functionality, versatility, and interoperatability options to networked users. It's now the default protocol for all the most popular network operating systems.

Prior to NetWare 5.0, Novell networks used IPX/SPX as their default protocol suite. NetWare 5.0 uses TCP/IP, but it still will support IPX/SPX for backward compatibility.

Listing the TCP/IP protocols

TCP/IP refers to a suite of protocols rather than an individual protocol. These protocols work together to provide reliable and efficient data communications across an internetwork.

You do need to know the following protocols included in this section. Don't waste time memorizing the characteristics of each protocol, but you should know the purpose of each. Knowing the individual functions of these protocols is more important than memorizing this list.

Transmission Control Protocol (TCP)

Transmission Control Protocol (TCP) is the primary transport protocol of the TCP/IP protocol suite. TCP is a connection-oriented, reliable delivery protocol that ensures internetwork packets arrive at their destinations error free. TCP accepts variable-length messages, fragments them into packets for transmission, and then directs the transport of the packets to the TCP protocol on the destination network.

User Datagram Protocol (UDP)

User Datagram Protocol (UDP) is TCP's evil twin. UDP is a connectionless, unreliable message delivery protocol that makes no guarantees about whether packets will arrive at all — and if they do, that they will be in the correct sequence. It even uses a different name — *datagrams* — for the packets it sends.

UDP is generally used in situations where the message packet does not need to be fragmented and where the speed of the delivery is more important than the overhead required to ensure the delivery. UDP is often used with SNMP (Simple Network Management Protocol).

Domain Name System (DNS)

The *Domain Name System* (DNS) uses a distributed database of system names and their related IP addresses to enable Internet users to work with the human-friendly system names, such as www.wiley.com, rather than their less-friendly IP addresses, such as 206.175.162.18.

Internet Protocol (IP)

Internet Protocol (IP) provides for source and destination addressing and the routing of the packets across the internetwork. In contrast to TCP, IP is connectionless and unreliable, but it is fast. IP, like all connectionless protocols, is called a *best effort protocol* and relies on other protocols to handle reliability and other delivery issues.

Address Resolution Protocol (ARP)

When delivering an IP packet on a network, the *Address Resolution Protocol* (ARP) picks up where DNS leaves off. DNS resolves the text domain name of a destination to its numeric IP address. ARP then resolves the IP address to the physical MAC (media access control) address of the destination.

ARP broadcasts a request packet to the network with the destination's IP address. The workstation or device that matches the IP address is expected to identify itself by sending back an ARP reply packet that contains its MAC address. The reply is stored in the ARP cache table, which is completely refreshed every two minutes.

File Transfer Protocol (FTP)

File Transfer Protocol (FTP) is used to transfer files from one Internet computer to another, which you've probably done sometime in your networking life. It's now commonly supported in virtually every network operating system, and as a built-in part of most World Wide Web browsers. If you want to transfer files independent of your Web browser, a variety of FTP shareware and freeware clients are available.

When you transfer a file from your computer to a remote computer by using FTP, you're uploading the file. Downloading a file is the reverse action — the file originates at the remote computer and copies to your computer. FTP clients (that is, the software running on your computer) communicate with the FTP server (the software running on the remote host) to perform a variety of file-management actions in addition to file transfers.

Simple Mail Transport Protocol (SMTP)

Simple Mail Transport Protocol (SMTP) is the protocol that provides the foundation services for e-mail transfer across the Internet. SMTP makes sure that e-mail messages are delivered from the sender's server to the addressee's server. It does not deal with delivery to the addressee's mailbox, leaving that task to other protocols. SMTP is more like the postal service's trucks and airplanes that move mail from post office to post office, where those letters from Aunt Sally can then be sorted and delivered to the addressee by other services.

SMTP transfers e-mail across the Internet, and your mail server holds the mail for you in your mailbox. What happens to your e-mail from this point on depends on the type of mail client you're using.

Post Office Protocol (POP3)

If you're using the *Post Office Protocol* (POP3) e-mail protocol, POP3 uploads your mail to your PC when you log into your mailbox. The number *3* in POP3 refers to the latest version of this popular e-mail protocol. POP mail stores your e-mail until you log on, at which time your mail moves to your client computer and off the server. POP works well in situations where users log on from the same permanently assigned workstation.

Internet Message Access Protocol (IMAP)

If you're using the *Internet Message Access Protocol (IMAP)*, which used to be called the *Interactive Mail Access Protocol*, your e-mail remains on the server regardless of what you do with it on your client computer. Your e-mail is stored on the server indefinitely until you decide to remove it. IMAP e-mail works very well in situations in which clients regularly access their mail from different locations on the network.

Internet Control Message Protocol (ICMP)

The *Internet Control Message Protocol* (ICMP) acts as a sort of intercom system for the TCP/IP protocol suite. ICMP carries control, status, and error messages between systems. ICMP messages are encapsulated inside of IP datagrams for transport over the network. For example, gateways and Internet hosts use the ICMP to transmit datagram problem reports back to the message source. Internet utilities, such as PING and TRACERT (see Book V, Chapter 6 for more on server connectivity), send echo request messages and wait for echo responses to time and trace the route to a remote location.

Routing Information Protocol (RIP) and Open Shortest Path First (OSPF) Protocol

Routers work at maintaining the more efficient route to a remote destination at any given moment. To do this, they must communicate with one another and manage statistics (called *metrics*) about the number of hops and other route information that is used to calculate the best path for a packet to take. The Routing Information Protocol and the Open Shortest Path First protocols perform this job.

✦ **Routing Information Protocol (RIP):** The *Routing Information Protocol* (RIP) counts the number of routers and network devices (called *hops*) a packet must pass through to reach its destination. The number of hops is then used to calculate the best and most efficient path available to a packet. The least number of hops is considered the best path.

✦ **Open Shortest Path First (OSPF):** The *Open Shortest Path First* (OSPF) protocol uses other factors in addition to the number of hops to determine the best path, including the speed of the network between hops and the amount of network traffic on each segment.

Identifying the TCP/IP utilities

The TCP/IP utilities are used to access, troubleshoot, and analyze TCP/IP operations. The most common of these utilities and their uses are as follows:

✦ **ARP (Address Resolution Protocol):** Serves to display and edit the ARP cache on a computer.

✦ **IPCONFIG (IP Configuration):** Displays the entire TCP/IP configuration of a computer and renews DHCP (Dynamic Host Control Protocol) IP address leases (more information on DHCP is coming up later in this chapter). Windows 9*x* has a unique version of this protocol named WINIPCFG. UNIX/Linux systems use ifconfig, and NetWare systems use CONFIG.

✦ **NBTSTAT (NetBIOS over TCP/IP Statistics):** Actually a Windows utility, but it performs a function very much like other TCP/IP utilities. NBTSTAT displays the contents of the NetBIOS over TCP/IP to name cache on a computer and to repair the contents of the hosts file.

✦ **NETSTAT (Network Statistics):** Displays information on current TCP/IP connections.

✦ **NSLOOKUP (Name System Lookup):** Troubleshoots DNS problems and displays the DNS entry for a certain IP address or DNS name.

✦ **PING (Packet Internet Gopher):** Checks validity of a remote IP address.

✦ **ROUTE:** A Windows NT/2000 command that displays, configures, and maintains network routing tables.

✦ **TRACERT (Trace Route):** Traces the route a packet uses to reach a destination on the internetwork and can be used to find disconnects or bottlenecks on the path used between two points. UNIX/Linux systems use the command traceroute.

Looking up names and addresses

Networked computers, like people, must have some identity by which other computers can refer to them. "Hey, you," doesn't work any better on a network than it does in a group of people. Each computer must have a unique identifier assigned to it. Depending on the protocol or process communicating with a computer, the ID may have a number, a "friendly" name, or an address. Just like a person has a government-assigned Social Security number, given name, and a home address, a computer has a MAC address, an IP address, and perhaps a share name.

What's your address, MAC?

Media access control (MAC) addresses are used to physically address network devices, usually NICs on a network. MAC addresses, also called

Ethernet addresses, are assigned by manufacturers and then burned into the electronics during manufacturing. A MAC address is a 6-byte (48-bit) hexadecimal number in the form of six 2-digit numbers separated by colons or dashes: for example, 00-11-22-33-44-55. Each digit of the MAC address can be in the range of the hexadecimal values 0-F.

Naming names

The Universal Naming Convention (UNC) is the generally accepted network-naming syntax used to reference network resources. UNC names take the form of

```
\\SERVER_NAME\SHARE_NAME or PATH
```

where the computer name and the share name are names that have been assigned by the network administrator or the users who own a shared resource. For example, in the Windows UNC name

```
\\Server1\yourfiles
```

`Server1` is the network (or "friendly") name for the computer — this is the name used by the network to refer to that device. The second part of this code — `yourfiles` — is a shared folder name on that computer. Users on other computers can request access to both the computer and its resources by using the UNC name format.

Remember which way the slashes face — Windows uses backward slashes, and UNIX uses forward slashes — and that two of them appear at the beginning of the name.

Comparing names and addresses

The examples in Table 7-6 summarize and contrast UNC names (made up of server names and share names), MAC addresses (device physical addresses), and IP (Internet Protocol) addresses.

Table 7-6	UNC Names, and MAC and IP Addresses		
Actual Name	*UNC Name*	*MAC Address*	*IP Address*
Primary network server	\\SERVER1	00.00.0C.33.56.01	10.0.100.1
Susan's PC in Accounting	\\SERVER1\ACCTG_SUSAN	00.00.1D.78.21.09	10.0.100.22
The Documents folder on Susan's computer	\\SERVER1\ACCTG_SUSAN\DOCUMENTS	00.00.1D.78.21.09	10.0.100.22

Note the following three principles of network naming and addressing in Table 7-6:

✦ The UNC format is used to designate servers and network-shared resources.

✦ No direct relationship exists between MAC and IP addresses. The relationship is logical and strictly platonic.

✦ MAC and IP addresses are assigned to devices.

Assigning NetBIOS and NDS names

Every computer in a Microsoft network has a NetBIOS (Network Basic Input/ Output System) name assigned to it. NetBIOS is the standard network BIOS used by Windows NT and Windows 9*x*.

Likewise, every resource you want to reference on a NetWare 4.*x* and NetWare 5.*x* network must have an NDS name. NDS (Novell Directory Services) is a database that contains all the users, devices, and computers of the network and the NDS name for each.

NetBIOS names follow the UNC format that we describe in the previous section, but NetWare names are slightly different. For example, the format that Windows uses is

```
\\SERVER\FOLDER
```

Under the Novell NDS, this name is

```
\\SERVER\VOLUME\DIRECTORY\SUB-DIRECTORY
```

Remember that data resources are referenced by server/folder on a Windows system and server/volume on a Novell NetWare file system.

Dealing with domain names

Every device on a TCP/IP network has two pieces of identification: an IP address and a domain name, which consists of a hostname and a domain name. The network administrator assigns a hostname to uniquely identify the device, usually a computer, on the network. Domain names are registered with a registry authority, such as Network Solutions, Inc., InterNIC, and others.

For example, for the domain name `www.dummies.com`

✦ The network administrator assigned the clever and unique name `www` to the network host.

and

✦ Network Solutions blessed, ordained, and registered the domain name `dummies.com` to the network server's assigned IP address.

Together, www.dummies.com, the hostname, and the domain name create the Fully Qualified Domain Name for this Internet site.

Domain names are registered in the DNS database that is distributed around the Internet and used to look up a domain name and convert it into its IP address. The collective DNS database literally contains all the domain names and their IP addresses for the entire Internet, a collection of information that requires frequent updating. You can use the DNS database to look up names on any TCP/IP network, including a LAN using TCP/IP, but DNS comes into play mostly for finding names on a WAN.

Using the DNS database

If you want to connect to a host on a remote network, you must use the host's IP address to connect over the Internet. If all you know is the host's domain name, DNS can search through its database to find the domain you're looking to reach and supply its IP address to your system.

The following example shows the effect of name resolution before and after the command is entered. If you enter the command

```
telnet www.dummies.com
```

the name changes to

```
telnet 206.175.162.18
```

In this example, www.dummies.com is resolved (converted) to its IP address.

DNS database architecture

The DNS database is actually a series of interconnected files, each representing a group of what are called Fully Qualified Domain Names (FQDNs) and their associated IP addresses. An FQDN includes all of the logical elements needed to address a server or host on the Internet. For example, www.dummies.com is an FQDN. Each of the local host databases is connected to parent — or root — servers above them in the DNS hierarchy.

Resolving a domain name

When a host at husky.uwashington.edu needs to access www.lotus.com, a number of small requests are generated. The first request goes to uwashington.edu, an address that husky.uwashington.edu already has. The primary DNS server at uwashington.edu tries to solve the request locally from its own database, but failing that, the request is passed up the hierarchy to the .edu server, which looks in its local databases. If the .edu server cannot find an entry for `www.lotus.com`, it passes the request to the `.com` server, which then searches down its hierarchy until the IP address shows up (or is found to not exist).

If the FQDN cannot be resolved — you may have entered it incompletely or misspelled it — you get an error message that says the domain name cannot be found. Try searching for your name as `www.your_name_here.com`, and you'll see this same error message. That is, of course, assuming you haven't already generated your own commercial site using your name.

You don't need to memorize the inner workings of the DNS for the test, but you do need to know that if you can ping a host by its IP but not its name, most likely a problem is with the name server or the DNS settings or data.

Using host names and WINS

Some systems use local files and services in place of the DNS database. These local files provide an abridged and more relevant database of names-to-IP-address and names-to-MAC-address conversions. Generically, these files are called *hosts files* because they contain a list of network hosts and their corresponding addresses. The most commonly used local name resolution service is WINS.

The *Windows Internet Name Service (WINS)* is a dynamic service used to resolve NetBIOS computer names to their IP addresses on Windows-based networks. Whenever a network client computer boots up, it registers its name, IP address, the account name of its user, and whatever network services it's using with the WINS server. Notice that the word *Windows* is part of the name of this service. That tells you that this is a Microsoft product, and that other network operating systems (UNIX, NetWare, and so forth) are not going to support its use.

A *WINS server* is any Windows server on a TCP/IP network running the WINS service. It processes requests from client computers to register or to look up IP addresses.

Another hosts file associated with NetBIOS name lookup is the LMHOSTS file. This static file, which requires manual maintenance, was essentially replaced by the WINS service, but many administrators use LMHOSTS as a backup name resolution technique. The LM in its name stands for *LAN Manager*, which is a good indicator of its age. The LMHOSTS file is also used to map NetBIOS names to their IP addresses.

For the Server+ exam, be sure that you understand the NetBIOS, UNC, NDS, FQDN, domain, host, and WINS naming conventions.

Troubleshooting Network Connections

You'll find many questions on the exam that concern troubleshooting network connections. Much of this knowledge comes from hands-on experience and knowing what tools to use in different situations. This section contains the scenarios you may see on the test, including server inaccessibility, pings that pong and those that don't, network name problems, and cabling issues.

You'll likely see questions stating that the clients can't reach the server. As with any troubleshooting situation, you should always start with the simple things, such as checking settings before you open the case. Reread the question and determine exactly what the problem is.

Using PING

If an exam question poses that the problem is occurring with just one workstation, it's a safe bet that the workstation is the problem and not the server. First try to ping the server and a few other computers by IP and name. If you can successfully ping with the IP address but not with the domain or computer name, double-check the DNS and WINS settings on the workstation. If these settings are correct, try reinstalling the TCP/IP protocol stack. This works in reverse as well, so if your clients can't access the server, troubleshoot the server by using the same process.

If you can ping other computers by both name and IP, but only one computer is having trouble pinging the server by name (which means it can ping the server by IP and it can ping other computers by name), try adding the server to the LMHOST file on the problem computer. If that doesn't work, reinstall the TCP/IP stack.

Another thing to check when experiencing connectivity issues is the subnet of the problem computer. Make sure that it's on the proper subnet or else you're going to experience unnecessary headaches.

Using network names

If you're working on a workstation or server that can't ping any other computers, try pinging the loopback address. If you don't get a reply from the loopback, you need to reinstall the NIC drivers and possibly move the NIC to another slot on the motherboard. If the loopback ping does provide a reply, the problem is probably a network hardware issue.

Troubleshooting cabling issues

When troubleshooting cabling issues, you can use a LAN analyzer to help you defeat the gremlins. A LAN analyzer or network analyzer is used to troubleshoot and monitor cabling, protocols, and network devices. These handy (and expensive) little doohickeys can save hours of tracking down the source of a network problem. Unfortunately, not everyone can afford to have one of the wonderful devices, so you have to rely on experience and troubleshooting skills.

Cabling issues can be the result of a bad network device, cabling, or even a security issue. When troubleshooting a bad network connection, try the following:

✦ Look for link lights on the NIC and the hub.

✦ Check that the cable is plugged in securely.

✦ Check that the cable is not run in a way that it might be accidentally unplugged.

✦ If the machine is a server, be sure that the server room is locked and that the rack the server is located in is locked.

✦ If the cable is plugged in and you have link light, try replacing the cable with a known good cable.

✦ Make sure that you're using the correct cable for the job.

If the network cable is repeatedly disconnected from a server mysteriously, be sure that the server cabinet and the server room are kept locked and that unauthorized people are being kept out.

Troubleshooting knowledge usually comes from experience, but most of it is just common sense. If you get stumped on a question, reread it and remember to keep it simple. Remember that you don't break open a computer's case until you check the small and "obvious" stuff.

Addressing with the IP Class System

Two versions of Internet Protocol addresses are presently in use on the Internet: IP version 4 (IPv4) and IP version 6 (IPv6). We mention this only to clarify that when the Server+ exam mentions IP addresses, only the IPv4 addresses are being discussed or asked about. Don't waste your time learning IPv6 for the Server+ exam.

For a refresher on IP addressing, read Book IV, Chapter 5.

Putting IP into its classes

IP address classes are used primarily to group IP addresses for purposes of assigning them to issuing authorities, such as telephone companies and Internet service providers (ISPs). Typically, the larger the organization, the more IP addresses it can justify the use of and afford. You may get your IP address free from your ISP, but somewhere along the line, somebody paid a fee for a block of IP addresses. The fees are paid to a registering agency. In the United States, the agency is the Internet Corporation for Assigned Numbers and Names (ICANN).

Table 7-7 summarizes the breakdown of IP address classes. Each IP address class provides a range of numbers that can be translated into a certain number of networks that have a certain number of hosts (individually addressed nodes) each. For example, a Class C IP address block, which is typically assigned to a relatively small network, uses 24 bits (three octets) to networks (allowing for more than 2 million networks) and 8 bits (one octet) to identify host computers (allowing for 254 hosts on each of the 2 million plus networks).

Don't bother to memorize the information in Table 7-7, but do look it over to familiarize yourself with IP address structures.

Table 7-7		Characteristics of the IP Address Classes			
Class	Bits in Network ID	Number of Networks	Bits in Host ID	Number of Hosts/Network	Address Range
A	8	126	24	16,777,214	1.0.0.0–126.255.255.255
B	16	16,382	16	65,534	128.0.0.0–191.255.255.255
C	24	2,097,150	8	254	192.0.0.0–223.255.255.255

Classes D and E addresses

Class D IP addresses are set aside for network *multicasting*, which sends datagrams to a group of hosts typically located on many remote networks. Class E addresses are reserved for future use.

Special network addresses

Network addresses that are all binary zeros, all binary ones, or IP addresses that begin with 127, are special network addresses. These IP addresses are reserved for use by networks as shortcut addresses to specific locations, such as the current host or a nearby host computer, to broadcast to a LAN or WAN, or to perform testing. Table 7-8 lists the special addresses you should be familiar with for the Server+ exam.

Table 7-8		Special Purpose IP Addresses	
Network ID	Host ID	Sample	Description
All 0s	All 0s	0.0.0.0	This host
All 0s	Host address	0.0.0.34	Host on this network
All 1s	All 1s	255.255.255.255	Broadcast to local network

Network ID	Host ID	Sample	Description
Network address	All 1s	197.21.12.255	Broadcast to network
127	1s or 0s	127.0.0.1	Loopback testing

The binary equivalent of an octet with all zeroes (000) is zero, and the binary equivalent for an octet with all ones (111) is 255.

Addressing private networks

Within each IP address class, a range of addresses is set aside for network administrators to use on internal networks, intranets not connected to the Internet, or networks that connect to the Internet through a firewall. These addresses are in three ranges:

> 10.0.0.0 through 10.255.255.255
>
> 172.16.0.0 through 172.31.255.255
>
> 192.168.0.0 through 192.168.255.255

Subnet addressing

IP addresses contain information on both the network ID and the host ID. To pull this information out of an IP address, a filter mechanism is applied that masks the unneeded bits and highlights the address portion needed. This mechanism is the subnet mask, which you can also call the subnetwork address mask.

The basic function of a subnet mask is to determine whether an IP address exists on the local network or outside on a remote network. The subnet mask is used to extract the network ID from a message's destination address. It is then compared with the local network ID. If they match, the host ID must be on the local network. Otherwise, the message requires routing outside of the local network. The process used to apply the subnet mask uses the properties of Boolean algebra to filter out nonmatching bits to identify the network ID.

The *subnet mask* is the mechanism applied to either a network message's source or destination IP address to determine whether its network ID is the same as the local network — and, if it is, to extract the host ID. Table 7-9 lists the commonly used default subnet masks for each IP address class. Take the time to memorize these subnet masks.

Table 7-9	Default Subnet Masks
IP Address Class	*Subnet Mask*
Class A	255.0.0.0
Class B	255.255.0.0
Class C	255.255.255.0

Subnet masks apply only to Class A, B, or C IP addresses.

Assigning IP Addresses Dynamically

Every client workstation on a TCP/IP network must be assigned an IP address in order for it to send and receive Internet packets during an Internet session. IP addresses can be assigned to a client computer in one of two ways:

+ **Manually,** by the network administrator: A manually assigned IP address is also called a *static address*.

+ **Automatically,** by a server: An automatically assigned IP address is more commonly called a *dynamic address*.

In this section, we focus on the dynamic addresses, namely those used in the DHCP protocol.

Deciding to use DHCP

The administrator of a fairly small network has an ample number of IP addresses for the network workstations and devices, and may not have a hard time assigning each node its own static IP address. However, if you must configure a network with 50, 100, 200, or more workstations, or you don't have quite enough IP addresses available to permanently assign the IP addresses to each node, then you should consider using the Dynamic Host Configuration Protocol (DHCP).

The use of DHCP is fairly common for just about any network, large or small. DHCP provides you, the network administrator, with a number of benefits, including

+ **Automatic configuration:** At a minimum, a DHCP server provides a client with its IP address, subnet mask, and normally the default gateway option when the client identifies itself during logon.

+ **Configuration control:** DHCP assignments are defined by a DHCP scope, which is an administrative tool that enables you to set the range, value, and exceptions for client configurations. The DHCP scope usually defines a range of available IP addresses, the subnet mask, and gives the option to configure the default gateway (router) for a range of addresses, and any IP addresses that have been set aside or reserved for other devices. Other values that can be configured into a scope for its IP addresses are

- DNS server
- WINS server
- Lease time
- Renewal time
- Length of use

DHCP IP address assignments are called *leases*. When a client receives assignment of an IP address, the length of time that the client can use that particular address is also set. A three-day period is a common default lease period. The length of the lease is a configurable value controlled by the network administrator.

Working with DHCP

Don't worry about the details, but do review the sequence of events that the DHCP uses to control IP address assignments on its clients. The DHCP process is divided into four phases: initializing, selecting, requesting, and binding. The following describes the actions of each phase:

✦ **Initializing:** The DHCP client boots up with a null IP address and broadcasts a discover message, containing its MAC address and computer name, to its server. The source address of the discover message is 0.0.0.0 and its destination is 255.255.255.255, which are reserved IP addresses (see the section "Special network addresses" earlier in this chapter).

✦ **Selecting:** The DHCP server receives the discover message and, if it has a valid configuration available for the client, responds with an offer message that contains the client's MAC address (for delivery purposes) and the offered IP address, subnet mask, gateway, the address of the DHCP server, and the length of the lease. If the server doesn't have an IP address available to the client, the client nags the server four times in the next five minutes. If the server still doesn't have an available IP address, it waits five minutes, and then repeats the discover cycle.

✦ **Requesting:** To accept the IP address offered to it, the client responds with a request message. Some networks can have multiple DHCP servers, all of which may have made offers to the client. The request message is a broadcast message so that all DHCP servers know to withdraw their offers.

✦ **Binding:** This phase is also called the *bound phase*. The DHCP server that had its offer accepted politely sends a request message that includes an acknowledgement of the client's acceptance. When the client receives this acknowledgement, it proceeds with its initialization of TCP/IP and becomes a bound DHCP client.

Windows 2000 Server requires you to authorize the DHCP server and activate the DHCP scope to allow clients to obtain DHCP configuration information. Remember the usage of the words *authorize* and *activate* in this statement.

Getting to Know TCP/IP Ports

The Internet Assigned Numbers Authority (IANA) registers service ports for use by the various TCP/IP protocols. Ports are used for interprocess communications between two connection points. Port numbers and keywords are used to designate the ends of the logical connections created when protocols, such as TCP (remember that TCP is a connection-oriented protocol), connect over the Internet for long-term interaction. Ports are especially handy for providing services to unknown callers, such as during an anonymous FTP session.

Ports are numbered and assigned keywords for easy reference. Some of the more common TCP/IP ports are port 80 (HTTP), ports 20 and 21 (FTP), and port 25 (SMTP). The port number assigned to a service by IANA is usually the server-side contact port, also called the *well-known port*.

IANA divides port numbers into three groups:

✦ **Well-known ports:** These are the most commonly used TCP/IP ports. These ports are in the range of 0 through 1023. Only system processes or privileged programs can use these ports. Well-known ports are TCP ports, but are usually registered to UDP services as well.

✦ **Registered ports:** These are the ports in the range of 1024 through 49151. On most systems, user programs use registered ports to create and control logical connections between proprietary programs.

✦ **Dynamic (private) ports:** These are the ports in the range of 49152 through 65535. These ports are unregistered and can be used dynamically for private connections.

A network operating system uses the port number to identify the service to which an incoming or outgoing packet should be passed. You may have noticed ports in use in the location bar (navigation bar) of your World Wide Web (WWW) browser. Check out this URL:

```
http://www.dummies.com:80
```

The port may appear as you are navigating forward or backward on some sites. The :80 in the above address indicates a port that is used to track the connection to a remote site.

On the exam, be expected to identify the port assignment of some of the more common TCP/IP protocols. If you know the ports listed in Table 7-10, you'll definitely know more than you need for the test.

Table 7-10	TCP/IP Well-Known Port Assignments
Port Number	*Assignment*
20	FTP (File Transfer Protocol) data transfer
21	FTP control
23	Telnet
25	SMTP (Simple Mail Transport Protocol)
53	DNS (Domain Name System)
70	Gopher
80	HTTP (Hypertext Transfer Protocol)
110	POP3 (Post Office Protocol)
119	NNTP (Network News Transport Protocol)
137	NetBIOS name service

Prep Test

1 What type of cable is used to connect an MDI port to a MDI-X port?

A ○ Rolled cable

B ○ Crossover cable

C ○ Straight-through cable

D ○ It depends on the manufacturer of the device.

2 A(n) _____ cable carries data in the form of modulated pulses of light.

A ○ UTP

B ○ Coax

C ○ Fiber-optic

D ○ STP

3 Which of the following cable types can be used on an Ethernet network? (Choose three.)

A ❑ UTP cable

B ❑ Thin coaxial cable

C ❑ Fiber-optic cable

D ❑ Telephone cable

4 WOL (Wake-on-LAN) is a _____ function.

A ○ Software

B ○ Hardware

C ○ Driver

D ○ Network

5 Rather than using the TCP/IP protocol suite, some Novell NetWare networks use _____.

A ○ SMTP

B ○ POP3

C ○ NetBEUI

D ○ IPX/SPX

6 ARP resolves an IP address to what other form of network address?

A ○ MAC

B ○ NetBIOS

C ○ DNS

D ○ LMHOST

7 Which TCP/IP utility is used to check the validity of a remote IP address?

A ○ TRACERT

B ○ IPCONFIG/IFCONFIG

C ○ PING

D ○ NETSTAT

8 If you can ping a network node by using its IP address but cannot ping it by using its network name, the problem is probably with what network function?

A ○ PING

B ○ SNMP

C ○ ICND

D ○ DNS

9 What action must be taken to enable a DHCP server on a Windows 2000 network to allow clients to obtain DHCP information?

A ○ Install

B ○ Authorize

C ○ Initiate

D ○ Activate

10 The Hypertext Transfer Protocol (HTTP) uses which TCP/IP well-known port?

A ○ 20

B ○ 70

C ○ 80

D ○ 110

Answers

1 **C.** The -*X* port does the crossover internally on the MDI. *See "Terminating the twisted pair."*

2 **C.** The core of a fiber-optic cable consists of two (or more) very thin strands of glass (or plastic) used to transmit data that is converted to pulses of light. *Review "The big three of cabling."*

3 **A, B,** and **C.** Standard telephone wire cannot provide the bandwidth and distance capabilities required for high-speed networks. UTP, coaxial, and fiber-optic cable are designed for this purpose. *Look over "The big three of cabling."*

4 **B.** WOL requires a compatible BIOS, motherboard, and NIC, all of which are hardware components. *Check out "Waking up across the network."*

5 **D.** IPX/SPX is still prominent in NetWare networks, but they too are beginning to switch to TCP/IP as their default network protocol. *Look at "Working with TCP/IP."*

6 **A.** MAC addresses are stored in the ARP table. If you need to reverse the lookup — that is, look up an IP address by using a MAC address — you would use another TCP/IP protocol, the Reverse ARP (RARP) protocol. *See "Address Resolution Protocol (ARP)."*

7 **C.** PING sends out a request to a remote node to echo its message. If no echo returns, either the station is down or there is a connectivity problem on the network between the two stations. *Review "Identifying the TCP/IP utilities."*

8 **D.** Check your DNS settings because your computer is not able to perform name resolution. *Check out "Resolving a domain name."*

9 **B.** You have to authorize the DHCP server and then activate the DHCP scope before the DHCP server will begin issuing DHCP information to clients. *Take a look at "Working with DHCP."*

10 **C.** Port 80 identifies the default browser to which all incoming HTTP traffic is assigned for processing. *Study "Getting to Know TCP/IP Ports."*

Chapter 8: Flirting with Disaster

Exam Objectives

✓ Detailing disaster recovery planning

✓ Defining data backup procedures

✓ Listing backup media

✓ Explaining proper storage and safekeeping of backup media

You've probably heard this a thousand times: *Back up your data before you do any type of upgrade or service on your systems.* Don't ever assume that an upgrade is going to go smoothly. Even a simple software patch can be the beginning of the end for your system because of the many aspects of proper data storage and safekeeping practices. Even if your data is being backed up to tape, are you sure it's reliable? A wise man once said, "Life is the part that you don't plan on." You need to plan for the worst and know how to respond when it does happen.

Maintaining a well-thought-out backup plan is the key to not only your survival as an IT professional but to the survival and success of your company, as well. The exam expects you to know the different backup methods, media types, storage practices, integrity verification, and other variables involved in protecting yourself and your company from disaster.

The Disaster Recovery domain of the Server+ exam covers the concepts, procedures, and processes you should use to prepare and perform daily and periodic data backups, as well as actions you would use in the event of a disaster to restore a server. You can expect 10 to 12 questions on the exam from this area.

Planning to Avoid Disaster

Disaster recovery planning is a serious enough topic that an entire domain is dedicated to it, along with 12 percent of the questions on the Server+ exam. Although the emphasis in the Server+ blueprint is seemingly on disaster recovery, you should be prepared to answer questions dealing with disaster preparedness and how to guard against data loss, as well.

A disaster recovery plan details how you restore the computing, application, and data resources of your network should any of these resources be lost, stolen, or destroyed. The disaster recovery plan should detail — for any conceivable event — what steps should be taken to restore the server or its resources. The events covered should comprise all levels of severity, from minor events (such as a single corrupted file) all the way to agreements with other companies or agencies for the use of their computers should your facilities be totally destroyed.

Arguably, the most important parts of a disaster recovery plan deal with how the data resource is to be protected against loss and, if lost, and how it will be restored. If your disaster recovery plan includes agreements that allow you to use another company's computers in the event of an emergency, your recovery plan is pointless if you don't have a copy of the current data resources. The Server+ exam and this chapter focus on the ways you can protect your data resource.

Dealing with accidental data loss

Most data crises and disasters are the direct result of plain old human error, such as a user who deleted the report he worked on all night, or the rookie in the IT department restoring the wrong backup or accidentally removing the Accounting department's folder. The most common data loss is the mysterious missing file — a network user is suddenly missing a file. How many times have you heard, "I *swear* that file was there yesterday, but now all of a sudden, it's just *gone!*" Hmmm, where could it have gone? You probably have a pretty good idea why it's missing and who the culprit is. But because you're prepared, you're able to recover the file and become someone's hero, at least for a while.

Of course, not all data problems result from human error; some are caused by hardware problems. In many ways, hardware problems are less predictable than those caused by network users. Don't rule out network technicians and administrators as contributors to data loss errors either because they can contribute equally to a disaster.

Backing up to be safe

The most common disaster preparedness procedure is a data backup. Users and network technicians alike are only human, and you know how notorious we humans are for making mistakes. To paraphrase the familiar saying, "To err is human, but to back up the server, divine." A well-defined and executed backup procedure can provide you with the ability to replace lost or corrupted data.

The first step when developing a data backup procedure is to decide your overall data strategy. Gilster's Law on Data Backup Procedure Effectiveness is "You never can tell, and it all depends." The best procedure is one that fits your particular situation. If the network server is used only as an application server and no data files are stored there, your backup procedure will need to address how each user workstation will be backed up and which files on each workstation will be included. If a network server is used to hold user files (the very best way to go), the data backup procedure for user data files can focus on backing up the server.

Committing data to a file server

The best way to avoid the territorial angst of users when you force them to save their files to a central file server is to make this action as transparent as possible. A very good way to do this is to use one or all of the following:

✦ **Log-on script:** When the users log on to the network, their home directories on the server can be mapped to logical drives on their PCs.

✦ **Desktop icon:** Placing a shortcut icon on the user's Desktop display provides an easy and hassle-free way for users to back up their data. The trick, of course, is getting them to remember to use it.

✦ **Redirect:** The users' My Documents folders (assuming that they're Windows clients) can be mapped to a home directory on the file server.

Data disasters of the hardware kind

For the most part, hardware is very reliable these days, especially hard disk drives. But hard disks can and do fail, and the thought of losing everything — the operating system, application programs, and system and user data — from one fatal failure is the network technician's nightmare.

Here are some ways to prevent data loss from hard drive failure. The most commonly used (and something you'll see many questions about on the exam) is RAID (redundant array of independent disks). See Book V, Chapter 4 for more information on RAID systems. However, putting all your disaster preparedness eggs in one basket is generally not a good idea. You also need to protect against the failure of several other hardware components. Here are the ones you're likely to encounter in the situations posed in the questions on disaster planning:

✦ **Memory errors:** Book V, Chapter 3 discusses ECC (error checking and correcting) memories that use error correction code to protect the integrity of their data. Most user workstations do not include this type of memory because of its cost. Memory errors are another reason why users should save to a file server (see the section "Committing data to a file server" earlier in this chapter). A properly built server uses ECC RAM to help prevent memory errors.

✦ **Power loss:** A loss of power at the wrong time can be devastating. The data in RAM and even cache memory is lost when the power source is lost. An appropriately sized UPS (uninterruptible power supply) and, of course, a data backup are the best ways to protect against a power failure. (See Book V, Chapter 5 for more information about installing a UPS.)

✦ **Resource conflicts:** If two peripheral devices are set up with conflicting system resources, which include IRQs (interrupt requests), I/O (input/output) addresses, and DMA (direct memory access) channels, the conflicts can cause data to become corrupted.

✦ **System timing problems:** The BIOS timing settings for memory and cache access should be set appropriately. Don't get overzealous when it comes to setting hard drive transfer modes and memory speeds and overclocking processors (running the processor above its rated speed). The benefits you gain by squeezing out a little more speed are not worth risking the stability of the file server.

Data disasters of the software kind

You should expect to see a question or two about software-related data disasters on the Server+ exam. Software-related data disasters are those caused by buggy software, viruses, and file system failures. Remember that data backups are your best defense against the loss of data from software.

Rushing to disaster

Unfortunately, many software developers believe they are forced to push out their programs as fast as possible to stay ahead of the competition. The result is software that is buggy and unpredictable. These days buggy software is almost the norm. New software releases is definitely one of the top two reasons to have a solid data backup program (the other is hardware, if you couldn't guess).

One of the biggest problems with new software releases is that some over-write older files with the same names, which is the safe way to go. However, some software deletes the old file version before installing the new one. If the software installation crashes or a power failure happens at just the right time, you can be left without either the old file or the new one.

If you've ever come up missing a DLL (Dynamic Link Libraries) file after an aborted install, this is likely the reason. Even when the new version is installed without problems, new file versions (and especially DLLs) may not be compatible with every piece of software that uses it. Several applications share many files, and updating a file for one application may cause problems in another.

Taking steps against a virus infection

Obviously software viruses can cause a loss of data. Because of this potential damage, you should definitely install a reputable antivirus program on your server. Don't be lulled into a false sense of security, however, just because you've taken this precaution: You must also keep the antivirus software up to date. New viruses hatch almost daily, and even the best antivirus software is useless if you're not maintaining and updating it regularly.

Most of the antivirus software programs you would use on your server include utilities to keep itself current over the Internet and all user workstations over the network. Virus attacks can be very malicious and result in severe data loss. Remember that even the best antivirus software is no guarantee that your server is safe.

Be prepared to answer at least one or two questions on the Server+ exam about antivirus software. See the section "Protecting data from disease" later in this chapter for more information on viruses and antivirus software.

Protecting against corruption

Keep the server hard disk in tip-top shape by performing regular maintenance and having the file system scanned on a regular basis. Keep an eye on the server's file system because the file structures that contain programs and data can become damaged; in some cases, this corruption can result in data loss.

Data disasters of the other kind

The loss of data does not have to be electronic, caused by faulty hardware, or bad or malicious software. Data can be stolen or destroyed by network users or outside evil-doers. Many studies have shown that the largest threat to a network is from within — meaning from a logged-on network user. The safeguards against data catastrophes caused by people are a well-defined and administered password security program and an active data backup program.

Locking out thieves

Theft is one area many administrators overlook. You don't have much risk of a server walking away . . . but a workstation, laptop, or storage media can easily be "liberated" by sticky fingers. This is another good reason for users to save data on the file server. Any stolen equipment can be replaced, but replacing any data taken along with the equipment, especially user data that is not backed up, may be virtually impossible to replace.

The best way to protect a server against outside intrusion is to secure it in a locked cabinet inside a locked room to which there is limited access.

Securing against sabotage

A disgruntled employee, a hacker, or maybe a competing company can also cause data loss by intentionally deleting or infecting the data files on your network file server. Backups are the only protection you have against an individual determined enough to cause data loss; even then, sometimes the backups aren't enough.

Living with Mother Nature

An essential element in any disaster plan must be your plans for dealing with natural disasters, such as a lightning strike, fire, flood, earthquake, mud slide, hurricane, or a locust swarm. Each of these natural disasters is capable of destroying your office, including its network servers and the data they contain.

Our point: The network technician must prepare for human error, theft, and sabotage as well as natural disasters. As a network technician, your responsibility (and that of the data recovery plan) is to ensure that the business or organization can be operational with as much of its data as possible, as soon as possible.

Backing It Up

You will encounter several different types and levels of data backups on the Server+ exam. You need to understand when each particular type of backup is best used as a part of your backup program and the type of data that should be included.

Capturing the good data

A server stores three types of data that should be included in a backup strategy. We assume that the network users are storing their important data on a file server so that the data is centrally located. The three types of data that should be included in your backup program are

✦ **Application data:** An *application* is any software program running on the server or a network workstation. The software on an application server has two levels: the applications used by network users and system-level software used to maintain the system, such as disk defragmenter programs and backup programs. Should the application server crash, the programs can easily be restored from the release disks. However, any software parameters or special configurations used to set up the software environment would have to be re-created or re-entered manually if they are not backed up.

✦ **Operating system files:** From the "duh" files — every network server has an operating system (OS) installed. Without an OS, none of the other server stuff matters too much. Backing up the OS files matters because if a server crashes, the operating system can be restored from the original disks. All the tweaking, special settings, and custom configuration changes must be re-created manually, however, if the OS system files are not backed up.

✦ **User data:** Depending on whom you ask, the most important data on the network is the data network that users save to the network server.

Users trust that their data is safe. Should a disaster strike, all eyes are on you to save the day, along with the data. Remember — you wanted this job!

Files not worth backing up

Some data files have no real significant impact on disaster recovery. For the most part, everything on the server can be backed up, but to save time and media space, the following files can normally be excluded from the backup program:

✦ **Compressed volume files:** In volume-based disk compression, the *compressed volume* is mounted as a drive letter that is actually stored as one large CVF (compressed volume file). Every file stored on the compressed disk is located in this file. The *CVF file* is a very large file that doesn't need to be included in the regular backup process. Compressed volumes should be backed up separately from the uncompressed volumes.

✦ **Downloaded program files:** *Downloaded program files* are used to install downloaded updates and upgrades to Windows, Internet Explorer, antivirus software, and other software updated over the Internet.

✦ **Recycle Bin files:** *Recycle Bin files* have been already deleted and are being held in a "Are you sure you want to delete this?" mode. If you really aren't sure, you should keep these files in their original folders and keep the Recycle Bin empty.

✦ **Swap files:** *Swap files*, used for a system's virtual memory, are large files that are used by the operating system as an alternate to main memory when more memory is needed to keep up with the tasks being performed. This dynamic file is constantly being re-created.

✦ **Temporary Internet files:** Internet browsers cache downloaded HTML (HyperText Markup Language) files and graphic objects to save time when they are requested again in the near future. You don't really gain much from backing up these files.

✦ **Temporary files:** *Temporary files* are stored in the Windows TEMP folder, which is a catch-all of miscellaneous and transitory files, including e-mail attachments, and self-extracting set up and install programs.

Newer backup software automatically deselects the file types listed in the preceding bullets. If you want to include them in the backup, you must override the default settings. Virtually all backup software enables you to select the file types that you want to include or exclude. In Figure 8-1, you can see the Microsoft Windows Backup utility's Backup Wizard that enables you to choose an entire drive, a folder, or just the specific files that you want to include in the backup.

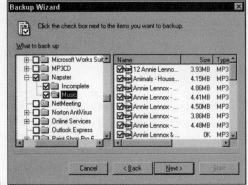

Figure 8-1:
The
Windows
Backup
utility allows
you to
choose the
files to be
included in
a backup.

The newer Windows versions (everything after Windows 95) include the
Disk Cleanup system tool that can be used to remove or minimize unnecessary files on a system. Figure 8-2 shows the file choices that this utility will
remove.

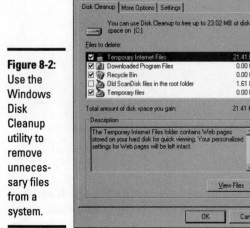

Figure 8-2:
Use the
Windows
Disk
Cleanup
utility to
remove
unneces-
sary files
from a
system.

Designing the Backup Strategy

It is very difficult to pose a data recovery scenario question without involving some type of hardware. The Server+ exam expects you to be familiar
with the various backup hardware and their associated media, and its
questions assume that you are.

The media and hardware used to capture system files on your server should be matched to the data that you want to back up. A network's data storage requirements commonly double over a two-year period. Therefore, the media and hardware used in the backup program should provide some room for growth.

Choosing the right backup technology

When designing a backup system, the media is usually chosen first. The media must have sufficient capacity to hold the data to be backed up. It must also be easily purchased at a reasonable price and be supported by hardware and technology that's likely to be around for a while. After the media is chosen, the hardware choice is narrowed down a bit. If the media of choice is a 40GB (gigabyte) tape cartridge, the choice is between the different types of tape drives that support tape cartridges with at least that capacity.

The capacity of the media should always exceed the amount of data to be backed up. Otherwise, you might be forced to manually insert additional media units after the first one is filled to capacity. That is, unless you want to invest the money in a multiple-unit media drive.

The Server+ exam focuses mostly on tape backup because it's the most common form in use, but the exam does cover other backup technology as well. Here are the ones you that should know for the exam:

✦ **Removable disk drives:** *Removable disk* storage includes floppy and Zip disks; SuperDisks; CD-R (compact disc recordable); CD-RW (compact disc readable/writeable); and a few others. Data is stored to the media, and then the disk can be removed from its drive to be stored outside the server. Although some type of removable media have fair capacities (as much as 650MB), these devices are more appropriate for workstations.

✦ **Storage area network (SAN):** A *storage area network* is a collection of storage devices linked to a common backplane structure that's connected to the network over a very high-speed connection, typically fiber-optic or gigabit Ethernet. A SAN provides centrally managed redundant storage devices that share common speed and reliability. This approach to network storage is mostly limited to larger enterprise networks because of its high initial costs.

✦ **Tape drives:** Several types of tape drives are on the market, but the most common is Digital Data Service (DDS). Compared with faster storage technology, such as a disk drive or a SAN, a tape drive is not fast, but its cost per megabyte of stored data is among the best. Tape storage is the most common backup media and hardware used today.

Picking the right tape

The tape media used to back up servers is either four or eight millimeters (mm) in width. These tape drives operate just like an everyday cassette recorder. The data reads or writes to the tape in a physically sequential pattern. In other words, data is written one bit after the other on the tape; the first data written to the tape is at the beginning of the tape and the last file is toward the end. To selectively restore a file that was written to the tape toward the end of the backup requires that the tape drive bypass all the tape and data that precedes the desired file.

You definitely see different types of tape drives and media on the test. Study the following tape types so that you recognize them on the exam. Don't worry about capacity or compatibility issues — the different types are used to describe a situation rather than to see if you're an expert on tape media. Here are the ones you should know for the exam:

+ **Digital Audio Tape drives (DAT):** DAT drives have become the standard backup drive for companies that require a high-speed, reliable, and simple storage device. The DAT drive uses the same technology found in a VCR (video cassette recorder). DAT drives come in two formats, DDS and DLT:

  • **Digital Data Service drives (DDS):** The current DDS standard is DDS-4 that uses a 120-meter cartridge tape to store up to 40GB.

  • **Digital Linear Tape (DLT):** DLT is a high-capacity tape storage format that stores as much as 80GB on a single tape cartridge. DAT and DLT — a DLT is shown in Figure 8-3 — are often confused as competing storage formats.

+ **Quarter Inch Cartridge (QIC):** QIC was one of the original cartridge tape media used for data backup. In fact, QIC tape was developed specifically for this purpose. Its name — *quarter inch* — refers to the width of the original tape. QIC comes in two cartridge sizes: a 3.5-inch mini-cartridge that stores up to 20GB and a 5.25-inch data cartridge that stores up to 50GB. Figure 8-4 shows the standard DC-2000 (40MB) mini-cartridge and the DC-6000 (2.5GB) data cartridge sizes of QIC.

+ **Travan drives:** Travan tape is an enhancement of the QIC mini-cartridge format. Until recently, Travan tape drives, which hold up to 8GB of data, have been better for desktop PCs than servers. However, the newer Network Series models have improved data compression to hold up to 10GB.

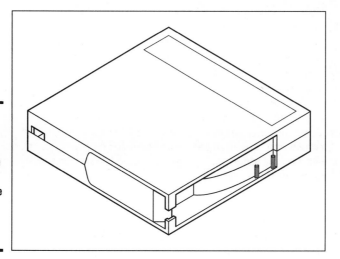

Figure 8-3:
A DLT cartridge, which is the most popular type of DAT backup media.

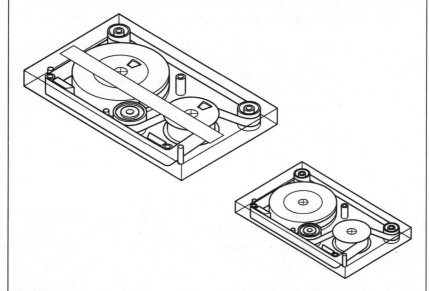

Figure 8-4:
Two popular QIC tape cartridges: the DC-6000 (left) and the DC-2000 (right).

Deciding on a backup method

The Server+ exam includes one or two questions on the strategies included in a disaster recovery plan, including the part played by a backup strategy. The design of an effective backup strategy should consider such details as how often the data needs to be backed up and the accessibility of the data should a disaster occur. Each of the different backup methods, which are largely based on how frequently they are performed, has its advantages and disadvantages.

Before delving into a review of the different backup types, you need to understand the use of the archive bit. An *archive bit* is a file property that indicates whether a file has been changed since the last time it was archived (backed up). When a modified file is written back to the disk, the archive bit is set on (which means it is set to a value of one). The archive bit works much like the flag on a mailbox to indicate to the postal carrier that outgoing mail sits in the mailbox. With the archive bit on, backup software sees that the file should be backed up.

Picking the right backup for the right time

Designing a backup strategy involves a combination of the right backup type and the right frequency or timing. The characteristics of the data should drive the design more than any other factor. Data that changes rarely may not need to be backed up as frequently as data that changes hourly.

For the exam, you most definitely want to know exactly what each of the following backup types do and when they are best applied:

✦ **Full backup:** A *full backup* is also referred to as a normal backup or an archive backup. Full backups do not pay attention to the archive bit. As its name implies, a full backup copies all the files selected for inclusion to the backup media without regard as to when it was or wasn't last backed up. By definition, a full backup should copy all the active files on the hard drive, including the Registry (or Bindery, for the NetWare people), system files, application data, and user data. A full backup should be taken according to a regular schedule that reflects how often a majority of the data on the system is changed. In most situations (and in most of the questions on the exam), a full backup is taken weekly or monthly.

✦ **Differential backup:** Be certain that you understand the difference between a differential and an incremental backup. A *differential backup* copies all new or modified files (those with their archive bit set on) created or changed since the last full or incremental backup. The differential backup does not reset the archive bit, which is the primary difference between it and an incremental backup. Typically, a differential backup is used to capture new or changed data between full backups. A commonly used program is to take a full backup on Sunday and a differential backup each night from Monday through Saturday. In this program, if the server were to crash on Wednesday morning, only the Sunday night full backup and the Tuesday night differential backups are needed to restore the system to where it was on Tuesday night.

✦ **Incremental backup:** An *incremental backup* is one that backs up only those files created or changed since the last full or differential backup. It differs from a differential backup in that an incremental backup clears the archive bit of each file backed up. A common backup program is to take a full backup every Sunday night and an incremental backup on each night Monday through Saturday. Should the server crash on Friday morning, the full backup and each of the daily incremental backups need to be restored, and very importantly, in sequence. An incremental backup uses much less tape space than a differential backup, which continues to grow larger each day until the next full backup clears the archive bits.

✦ **Copy backup:** This method is not a particularly useful backup method for a server. In effect, data files are copied to a storage media by using the DOS COPY or XCOPY commands or the drag-and-drop function of a file manager, such as Windows Explorer. The archive bit is not affected at all. A common use of a copy backup is to capture files without altering the normal backup program, such as before installing new hardware.

Compare the different backup methods — and the advantages and disadvantages of each — in Table 8-1.

Table 8-1	A Comparison of Backup Methods	
Method	*Backs Up*	*Archive Bit*
Full	All files on the server	Cleared on all backed-up files
Differential	New files and files modified since last full or incremental backup	Not cleared
Incremental	New files and files that have changed since last full or incremental backup	Cleared on all backed up files
Copy	Selected files	Not affected

The heartbreak of the open file

Many backup utilities will not include an open file or a file that is in use. If this type of backup software is in use, a truly reliable backup should only be made when all users are logged off the network. However, most newer enterprise-level backup software has the ability to include open files. Too many network technicians have learned the hard way about backing up network service files from an active network. When disaster strikes, none of the files are on the backup media. Not to worry! — explaining to the CEO of your company why all her e-mail files are gone forever is a very good career opportunity.

Using the XCOPY command

The Server+ exam refers to the DOS XCOPY command in the Disaster Recovery domain questions. Here is a brief overview of its syntax and usage.

The XCOPY command is used to copy files and subdirectories from one directory or disk to another. Its basic syntax is very much the same as the DOS COPY command. For example, the following command is used to copy all files from the root directory to the H: drive:

```
C:\>XCOPY *.* H:
```

However, its ability to copy subdirectories makes it special. The following command copies all the files and all subdirectories (and all of their files) from the C: drive root directory to the H: drive (the /s option copies any subdirectories as well).

```
C:\>XCOPY *.* H: /S
```

The XCOPY command also compares the new copy of the file with the old copy of the file to make sure the copy went well. To do so, add a /v option to the command:

```
C:\>XCOPY *.* H: /S /V
```

However, the way the Server+ exam deals with the XCOPY command is in its ability to create backup files. The /m option of the XCOPY command creates an incremental backup, copies only those files with an active archive bit, and then clears the archive bit. The following command creates what, in effect, is a full backup to the H: drive:

```
C:\>XCOPY *.* H: /S /M
```

A final word on the archive bit

The archive bit is actually one of four file properties called *attributes* that Windows uses to indicate how a file may be used. The four attributes are

+ **Archive:** The *archive attribute* (or *archive bit*) indicates that a file has changed or was created since the last full or incremental backup.

+ **Hidden:** Files with a *hidden attribute* activated are not included in file lists, such as the DOS DIR command or Windows Explorer.

+ **Read-only:** Files with a *read-only attribute* activated cannot be saved to the disk after being modified (without being renamed). This protects a file from being changed or deleted.

+ **System:** Files with a *system attribute* activated are special files reserved for use by the operating system.

A file's attributes can be modified through the DOS ATTRIB command. This command is used to add or remove (activate or deactivate) the file attributes. For example, the following command removes the read-only (indicated by the r) protection of a text file.

```
ATTRIB myfile.txt -r
```

To display the attributes of the files in a directory, the following command is used (the standard wildcard * is used to represent any filename and any file extension is to be displayed):

```
ATTRIB *.*
```

Another way to change or view the attributes of a file is to right-click the file in Windows Explorer and choose Properties from the menu that appears. The General tab of a file's Properties window (see Figure 8-5) includes check boxes at the bottom of the window that you can select or deselect to alter the file's attributes.

Figure 8-5:
A file's
Properties
window
displays the
file's
attribute
values on a
Windows
system.

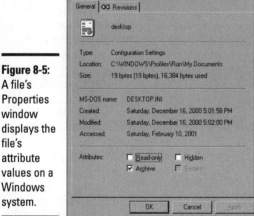

Doing the Media Shuffle

The Server+ exam asks you at least once about setting up a backup media rotation schedule. Be sure that you understand why and when each of the standard methods would be used.

A successful backup program must also define the rotation of the backup media. Because the most popular media used for backups is tape, we use tape as the media of choice in this discussion. Nobody wants to keep or can afford to maintain, manage, and purchase an unlimited amount of tape cartridges.

Besides, with the right tape rotation scheme, it shouldn't be necessary anyway.

The most popular tape rotation schedule is known as the Grandfather-Father-Son (GFS) method that maintains backups on a daily, weekly, and monthly schedule. The GFS uses a series of repeating rotations to provide a fallback point in the data at all times. To begin the GFS rotation, a full backup is created and set aside. The daily differential or incremental tapes create the sons to this father. At the end of the week, a new full backup is taken and the seven daily tapes are recycled. Each week, a new weekly archive is created that replaces the previous father tape. At the end of the month, another full backup is taken, creating the grandfather. The grandfather backup tape resets the process to repeat for the next month. By the end of a year, you have 12 grandfather tapes that you should safeguard by storing them offsite.

Some processes also add great-grandfathers (quarterly backups) and great-great-grandfathers (an annual backup) to the rotation. Each monthly, quarterly, or annual backup establishes a fallback point on which recovery during any week can be based.

The most common GFS rotation includes daily differential backups and a full weekly backup. Some businesses add accounting control backups over and above the disaster recovery backups at the end of a month or the end of a quarter. These are strictly for accounting purposes and do not figure into the disaster recovery program.

You'd be wise to clean the backup drives regularly because so much is riding on them. You should also remove tapes from the rotation after a year because the tapes will eventually stretch and wear out. If you continue using old tapes, you run the risk of not being able to recover lost data that you thought was backed up.

Storing your backups in a safe place

After carefully planning and executing your data recovery plan, you should consider where you will store your backups. Much of what you read on the subject usually recommends that the safest place for your data backups is an offsite storage location that is built like Fort Knox, only with more security. However, the safety of the data must be balanced against its availability in the event of a problem. What's the advantage of a secure offsite location for your backup tapes if the time required to access them is longer than the downtime window specified in your disaster recovery plan?

Backup tapes should be stored according to their GFS levels. Daily backups (sons) should be in a fireproof safe somewhere in the building, but outside of the server area. The current father backup should also be kept on premise or at least in a location that is readily accessible. Grandfather backups can be stored offsite in secure locations that may require more time to access.

Expect to see a question on backup media storage. Remember to read the question and then look for the most common sense answer available. If you understand the GFS rotation, you should do just fine.

Maintaining your integrity

Another important part of a good data recovery plan is to regularly verify the integrity of the data being saved to tape. Don't fool yourself going along for months, or even years, thinking that you're safe because you have a solid backup plan working on a set rotation. Even if you replace tapes after six months for added insurance, what if the tape drive has not been recording properly or the tapes were bad out of the box? Without some means of verifying the backups, you wouldn't even know that you had a problem until you needed to restore the data in the event of a data disaster. Trust us — by then, it's too late, and you are so in trouble.

The Server+ exam has a question or two about the ways you can test the integrity of your data backup program. The best way is to set up a test server or designate some free space on a server and then regularly restore randomly selected files from the backup tapes. At a minimum, do this once a month, although more frequently is certainly better. Consider this preventive maintenance — you're preventing yourself from having to do maintenance to your resume.

Safeguarding against upgrade disasters

When you prepare to do an upgrade, software or hardware, you need to create an upgrade check list that documents your game plan. You also need to gather everything needed for the upgrade and, if necessary, inform the network users of the upgrade and when it will take place.

After you have your check list and you're absolutely sure that you covered everything that could possibly happen, develop your contingency plan. What are you going to do if the upgrade goes sour? This scenario is where your backup files are normally going to save the day. Even if your system becomes totally unrecoverable, you should be able to rebuild it from scratch, if needed — that is, IF you have your data backed up.

Protecting data from disease

Viruses are nasty pieces of software that have taken on the characteristics of an infectious disease, spreading themselves to infect unsuspecting and unprotected PCs. You can expect at least one question on the exam about what a virus is and the software used to detect and remove it.

The following characteristics define a computer virus. A virus

✦ Attaches itself to another piece of programming code in memory, on a floppy disk, or on a downloaded file

✦ Bears the form of an executable file and runs when opened on the target system

✦ Replicates itself and infects other systems, propagating itself from one computer to another

Viruses and how they spread

Computer viruses are a form of electronic warfare developed solely to cause human misery. The evil, sick, and quite talented minds that develop computer viruses would like nothing better than to have your boot sectors catch cold or have your disk drives develop dysentery. Five major virus classes exist, each with many subclasses:

✦ **BIOS program viruses:** *BIOS program viruses* attack flash BIOS programs by overwriting the system BIOS program and leaving the PC unbootable.

✦ **Boot sector viruses** (system viruses): *Boot sector viruses* target the boot program on every bootable floppy disk or hard disk. By attaching itself to the boot sector program, the virus is guaranteed to run whenever the computer starts up. Boot sector viruses spread mostly by jumping from disk to disk.

✦ **E-mail viruses:** *E-mail viruses* comprise the latest trend in viruses and get most of the press these days. The Melissa virus was an e-mail virus that spread by e-mailing itself from one computer to another by using e-mail address books.

✦ **File viruses:** *File viruses* modify program files, such as `.EXE` or `.COM` files. Whenever the infected program executes, the virus also executes and does its nastiness. File viruses spread by infected floppy disks, networks, and the Internet.

✦ **Macro viruses:** The newest general class of virus, *macro viruses* take advantage of the built-in macro programming languages of application programs, such as Microsoft Word and Microsoft Excel. Macro languages enable users to create macros, which are script-like programs that automate formatting, data-entry, or frequently repeated tasks. A macro virus, most commonly found in Microsoft Word documents, can cause as much damage as other viruses and can spread by jumping from an opened document to other documents.

Because a virus is a program, it can only infect programs. A virus can't hide anywhere that it doesn't blend into the scenery. Viruses that infect graphic files, e-mail, or text files are just myths. It would be like trying to hide a bright red ball among bright white balls. However, viruses can be attached to text files or e-mail and transmitted or copied to a new host system.

Combating viruses

Viruses manifest themselves on a PC in a wide variety of ways, including spontaneous system reboots; system crashes; application crashes; sound card or speaker problems; distorted, misshapen, or missing video on the monitor; corrupted or missing data from disk files; disappearing disk partitions; or boot disks that won't boot.

In spite of the efforts of the virus developers, the best defense against virus infection is antivirus software, also called *scanners* or *inoculators*. Don't you just love all this medical talk?

Here are the general types of antivirus software in use today:

+ **Virus scanner software:** This run-on-demand software scans the contents of memory and the disk drive, directories, and files that the user wants to check. This type of software is the most common form of antivirus program.

+ **Memory-resident scanner software:** This kind of scanner stays in memory, automatically checking the environment, including incoming e-mail and browser documents for viruses.

+ **Behavior-based detectors:** A more sophisticated form of memory-resident scanner, a behavior-based detector looks for suspicious behavior typical to virus programs. Some stereotyping is involved, and some good processes may be interrupted, but being safe is better than being sorry.

+ **Start-up scan antivirus software:** This software runs when the PC boots and does a quick scan of boot sectors and essential files to detect boot sector viruses before the PC boots up.

Most antivirus software uses a database of virus profiles and signatures for reference, commonly referred to as *DAT* (short for data, or database) files. This database should be updated frequently; most antivirus packages include a provision for a set number or an unlimited number of updates.

Before installing new software or updating the operating system or any other hardware or software that will change or add to the Windows Registry, disable your antivirus software. Nearly all antivirus programs place an icon in the Task Bar tray and can be disabled (exited) by right-clicking the icon and choosing Close or Exit or the equivalent choice. The antivirus program — if it is running — may attempt to block changes to certain binary-formatted files.

Prep Test

1 What elements should a disaster recover plan include? (Choose three.)

    A ❑ Provisions for emergency power

    B ❑ Provisions for emergency medical care

    C ❑ Provisions for the safe storage of backup media

    D ❑ Provisions for emergency computer equipment

2 Which of the following is true about an incremental backup?

    A ○ Backs up all files on the network

    B ○ Backs up all files on the server

    C ○ Backs up all files with the archive bit set

    D ○ Backs up all files with the archive bit cleared

3 Which type of backup copies only files that have been changed since the last full backup and does not clear archive bits?

    A ○ Differential

    B ○ Incremental

    C ○ Copy

    D ○ Discretional

4 In a GFS rotation schedule, which tape is rotated after five weeks?

    A ○ Son

    B ○ Grandfather

    C ○ Father

    D ○ Great-Grandfather

5 In a GFS rotation schedule, which tape is the grandfather?

    A ○ Weekly

    B ○ Daily

    C ○ Monthly

    D ○ Yearly

6 What is the most common type of backup hardware and media in use today?

    A ○ SAN

    B ○ CD-R

    C ○ Tape

    D ○ RAID

7 Which of the following safeguards are recommended for physically securing a server? (Choose two.)

A ❑ Biotechnical scanners
B ❑ Locked room with limited access
C ❑ Locked cabinets with limited access
D ❑ Secret hand signs

8 DLT and DDS tape formats are types of what tape format standard?

A ○ QIC
B ○ Travan
C ○ DAT
D ○ DVD

9 A thorough data recovery program includes which of the following? (Choose two.)

A ❑ Random testing of the backup media
B ❑ Disposal of backup media after one use
C ❑ Secure offsite storage for grandfather tapes
D ❑ Cleaning of tape drive read-write heads

10 Which XCOPY option creates the equivalent of an incremental backup?

A ○ /S
B ○ /X
C ○ /I
D ○ /M

Answers

1 **A, C,** and **D.** A thorough disaster recovery plan includes provisions to address any conceivable event that may require hardware, software, or data to be restored. *See "Planning to Avoid Disaster."*

2 **C.** Incremental backups are used to back up all files with the archive bit set. An incremental backup also clears the archive bit, which is what differentiates it from a differential backup. *Review "Picking the right backup for the right time."*

3 **A.** Take a differential backup to back up those files that have been created or modified since the last full or incremental backup. Be sure that you understand that both the full and incremental backups clear the archive bit. *Check out "Picking the right backup for the right time."*

4 **C.** Father tapes are created each week; on the fourth week, a grandfather tape is created, which frees up the oldest father tape to be reused. *Look at "Doing the Media Shuffle."*

5 **C.** Son tapes are dailies; fathers are weeklies; and grandfathers are monthlies. *Study "Doing the Media Shuffle."*

6 **C.** Tape backup is the most common backup hardware and media because it's affordable, reliable, and relatively fast. *See "Choosing the right backup technology."*

7 **B** and **C.** The other choices are not all that bad, but locking the server room and placing the server inside a locked cabinet are very practical and cost-effective ways of physically securing the server. Of course, if you really want to be truly safe. . . . *Review "Locking out thieves."*

8 **C.** DAT (Digital Audio Tape) is a standard tape recording format. Both DDS and DLT, the two most popular types of backup tape-recording formats, are DAT formats. *Check out "Picking the right tape."*

9 **A** and **C.** Backup tapes should be randomly tested by restoring one or more folders or files from them routinely. Storing all tapes in secure and environmentally safe locations is another element of a good data recovery program. *Look at "Maintaining your integrity."*

10 **D.** The /M option of the XCOPY command copies only those files with active archive bits and then clears the archive bit, creating the equivalent of an incremental backup. *Look over "Using the XCOPY command."*

Chapter 9: Securing and Monitoring the Server

Exam Objectives

✔ Detailing network security concepts

✔ Defining the attributes, function, and purpose of SNMP and RMON

✔ Using maintenance, service, and security logs to monitor network activities

✔ Understanding the need for antivirus software

Security is a big concern for all systems administrators and is an area of emphasis on the Server+ exam. In today's world of happy hackers and mischievous users, systems administrators must batten down the hatches as best as possible. Unfortunately, networks are prone to hack attacks much more than most people realize. This is especially true for networks connected to the Internet. In this chapter, we discuss the network management protocols and tools used to maintain the network and fend off evildoers and unfriendly sorts.

Most security risks come from insiders — which is to say, users on your network, authorized or not. Although most of the press attention goes to outside hackers — and you should certainly do everything you can to keep them out of your system — you also need to protect the network from those you would think you could trust (your network users). Just how you go about doing so is a major topic on the Server+ exam.

Along with protecting the network from outsiders, we also discuss keeping the server physically secure. You need to know the procedures used to keep the server room safe from people who could and would intentionally or unintentionally cause harm to the network server or the other equipment located in the server room. You'll find several questions on the exam regarding server security. Security is very important (and often overlooked) for real-world application, so this review is a good reminder for both the exam and your everyday working life.

Locking Down the Server Room

Server security starts with physical security. It's critical that your server be located in a safe location out of the reach of children, evildoers, and other potentially disruptive and bad people. Book V, Chapter 5 discusses the key issues that must be considered when planning a server room, but there is more to it than just planning the layout of the server room. Security is a very important server room issue of that planning. Server room security is too often an afterthought, but you should rank it as important as protecting the server from network attacks. The Server+ exam expects you to understand how to apply server security. In the following sections, we discuss a few of the server room security issues you'll most likely see on the exam.

Accessing the server room

The purpose of a server room is to provide a cool, clean, and secure location for your servers and any associated equipment. No ordinary network user, nor even a not-so-ordinary network user, should need access to the server room. Very few people other than the server technicians and perhaps a few other IT (information technology) department people ever need access to the server room.

The server room contains servers, right? So why would anyone other than the systems administrators or server technicians need access? Simple: No one does. The server room is not a safe place to store human resource documents, or the paper shredder (please don't use a paper shredder in the server room!), or anything other than the equipment that makes the IT world go 'round. The point here (and on the test) is that in order to control access, the server room should have a door on it, and that door should be closed and locked at all times.

Key card systems are great for this purpose because they provide excellent security. Key card systems are typically server-based (server security is also excellent for providing job security) systems, and each key card is assigned to a specific person for whom only a specified set of doors will unlock. If someone uses a key card to enter a room, including the server room, the security server logs the request. The logs can then be used to determine who is coming from and going into particular rooms, as well as those who are trying to access rooms they shouldn't be. We repeat: Very few people should have access to the server room.

For security reasons, only authorized personnel (and not many of them) should have access to the server room.

Key cards are convenient, too — you don't fumble for yet another key to open the door. Just wave your badge at the reader to activate it, and you're allowed entry.

Locking the server cabinet

Server racks (in the form of lockable rackmount cabinets) are designed to store the network servers, network devices, such as routers, switches, and other equipment, including tape drives and UPSs. We guarantee that the test asks you how to keep unauthorized people away from your network server; the answer is painfully obvious — *lock the server cabinet door*. As obvious as this may seem, this is seldom done. Whether IT people are inherently lazy or lulled into a false sense of security, many simply don't lock the server cabinet doors. In most cases, you don't even need to open the cabinet to gain access to the server because the servers are connected to a KVM (keyboard, video, and mouse) switch, anyway. Thus you have no reason to leave the server cabinet doors unlocked. Remember this for the test and for improving your own peace of mind: Lock server cabinet doors.

To increase server security, you should keep the server cabinet locked at all times.

If your servers are in a locked room (and they should be) and are located in a locked server rack (as they should be), you are definitely headed in the right security direction. However, you do need to prepare for the unexpected. What if someone did gain access to the server room? Could they then gain access to the servers? In the next section, we discuss how to prevent unauthorized users from accessing the servers.

Locking the server

Even if the server room door and the server cabinets are locked, you can never be too safe. When it comes to security, you should remember to always secure the server before you walk away from it. With Windows NT/ 2000/XP, you should either log out entirely or lock the server by pressing Ctrl+Alt+Del keys and choosing Lock Computer. On NetWare servers, load MONITOR.NLM, select Lock File Server Console, and enter the password. In either case, the server won't be accessible until the administrator or supervisor password is entered.

Locking the server through the operating system prevents intruders from gaining access to the server even if they gain access to the server room and the cabinet. If they try to guess at the username and password required to unlock the server, it is recorded in the security logs for later investigation, but they won't be able to access the server without the correct username and password, which of course, only you and other authorized users know.

The exam expects you to know how to keep an eye on server activity. Even if the server room doors are locked and the server console is locked as well, you always face the chance that someone may still gain access to the server. You should keep audit trails of events on the network so that you can determine whether marauders have tried to break in or if they've actually succeeded.

Monitoring server security

An administrator has a few ways to monitor a server's activity. For the exam, you need to know that the administrator can use the security log to obtain information about events such as failed and successful logon attempts or file accesses.

The security log can be viewed by using the Event Viewer on a Windows system. Successful logon attempts are displayed as a key icon, and failed logon attempts are displayed as a lock icon. The Event Viewer also provides information about events, such as the type of event, the date and time the event occurred, and which user generated the event. See Book V, Chapter 5 for more information on log files. The test doesn't get into specifics with log file auditing or the processes involved in monitoring the system logs, but you do need to know what the security logs are and that they can be viewed by using the Event Viewer. Figure 9-1 shows the system log as viewed in the Event Viewer.

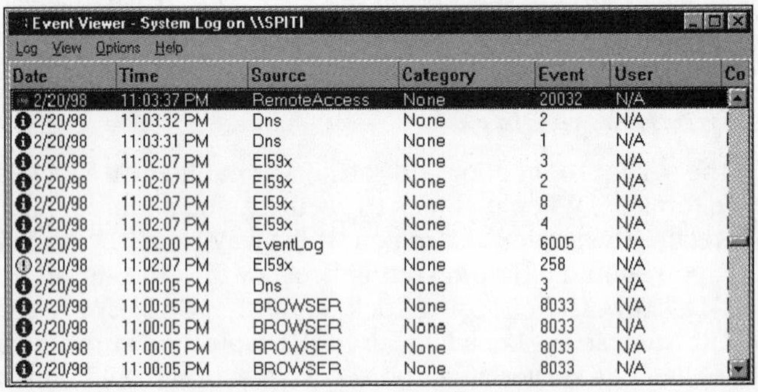

Figure 9-1:
A system log
file viewed
in the
Windows
Event
Viewer.

Date	Time	Source	Category	Event	User	Co
2/20/98	11:03:37 PM	RemoteAccess	None	20032	N/A	
2/20/98	11:03:32 PM	Dns	None	2	N/A	
2/20/98	11:03:31 PM	Dns	None	1	N/A	
2/20/98	11:02:07 PM	EI59x	None	3	N/A	
2/20/98	11:02:07 PM	EI59x	None	2	N/A	
2/20/98	11:02:07 PM	EI59x	None	8	N/A	
2/20/98	11:02:07 PM	EI59x	None	4	N/A	
2/20/98	11:02:00 PM	EventLog	None	6005	N/A	
2/20/98	11:02:07 PM	EI59x	None	258	N/A	
2/20/98	11:00:05 PM	Dns	None	3	N/A	
2/20/98	11:00:05 PM	BROWSER	None	8033	N/A	
2/20/98	11:00:05 PM	BROWSER	None	8033	N/A	
2/20/98	11:00:05 PM	BROWSER	None	8033	N/A	
2/20/98	11:00:05 PM	BROWSER	None	8033	N/A	

Event Viewer - System Log on \\SPITI
Log View Options Help

The server is not the only network device that can be monitored. Using a protocol known as the Simple Network Management Protocol (SNMP), you can monitor most network devices. The exam asks a couple of questions regarding this protocol. Check out the following section for a review of SNMP.

Using the Simple Approach

The Server+ exam also asks questions concerning monitoring and securing the network by using SNMP.

The two main pieces to the SNMP concept are the manager and the agent. The *manager* is a software application that runs on a server or large workstation. It communicates with an agent process running on an individual device that is being monitored. An *agent* is any device running the SNMP agent application. A hub, bridge, router, workstation, and even a server can all be configured as agents. The SNMP manager polls the agent, and the agent responds with the data requested.

Gathering device data

The specific data that a SNMP manager requests depends on the SNMP manager software application in use. These applications vary in price and functionality, but generally SNMP manager applications are used to perform tasks such as the following:

✦ Trapping specified events and alarming the manager when an event occurs

✦ Monitoring network traffic

✦ Mapping the topology of the network

✦ Reporting specific variables

The data collected from the SNMP agents can be used to troubleshoot network problems. Some more advanced SNMP management applications can produce trend analysis reports that are used for capacity planning to help you determine long-term goals. The information that the agent returns to the manager is contained in a Management Information Base (MIB). A *MIB* is a data structure that defines what is obtainable from the device and what can be controlled (turned on, off, or otherwise manipulated).

Using the simple and primitive SNMP

Not a lot of complicated commands are involved with SNMP, which was designed to be simple enough that it could be used with not-so-smart devices, such as hubs (hence, *Simple* Network Management Protocol).

SNMP agents and devices communicate by using only a few basic commands known as primitives. A *primitive command* is one that performs a simple function, such as those you enter on the command line of an operating system. The following primitives are the commands used by the SNMP manager to initiate communication with the agents.

✦ **get:** This primitive command is used to request a single piece of information from an agent.

✦ **get-next:** This command is used when the manager is requesting more than one piece of information. The get-next command is used to sequentially receive data, such as values from a database.

✦ **set:** This command is used to tell an agent to set a specific variable to a particular value.

The agent replies to the SNMP manager by using primitives as well:

✦ **get-response:** This primitive command is used to respond to the SNMP manager's get or get-next request.

✦ **trap:** In many cases, you want the agent to send data to the manager when certain events happen. An example of this would be when a specified event triggers an agent alarm. The agent notifies the manager that a specified event has occurred.

Through the years, SNMP has been built on to attempt to improve its functionality and security. However, because the original SNMP was only capable of certain simple tasks, the newer versions were developed with little concern for compatibility. The result is that you can mix and match devices with SNMP versions, but what you are requesting from one device may not be achievable from another. Keeping all SNMP agents updated to the same version of SNMP is recommended, although not necessarily the most recent SNMP — just try to keep them all on the same version. With SNMP, newer is not better.

The first version of SNMP, version 1 (duh!), was simple, required minimal resources to operate, and was also easily extensible, meaning that vendors could tailor some aspects of the way their products were managed and address new and unique attributes. The biggest bummer with SNMP version 1 was security, or the lack thereof. SNMP version 2, for the most part, consisted of some minor tweaks to the original, but SNMP version 3 has made some considerable changes to the protocol and its implementation. Despite its strengthened security, version 3 lacks backward compatibility to the previous SNMP versions and is much more complex (less simple) than its predecessors. This complexity has resulted in many companies sticking with earlier versions of SNMP.

Remember that you should run the same version of SNMP on all SNMP agents and managers on the network.

Overall SNMP is a great tool, but this protocol does have several shortcomings. One concern is that it uses User Datagram Protocol (UDP), which has a packet plenty large enough to hold more than one piece of data, yet doesn't. Another concern is security because SNMP has no real means of data encryption or user authentication. Another monitoring tool, Remote Monitoring, was developed to overcome the limitations of SNMP.

Monitoring a network remotely

Remote Monitoring (RMON) is similar to SNMP in that agents and managers communicate with one another to track important network events. RMON uses MIBs just like the SNMP, but the way the data is communicated is quite different. The agents, also called probes, are the active devices where the manager just sits and waits for updates from the agents. Rather than waiting to be polled by the manager, agents send SNMP traps to the manager as soon as an important event occurs. The test doesn't get into specifics concerning RMON, but you need to know that it works similarly to the SNMP and how it is more efficient.

Fighting off a Virus

Virus protection is another must-know for the real world, and you probably see a question or two on the exam about this, as well. A *virus* is simply a software program, just like the other programs installed on your computer. The only problem is that unlike the programs you install on your computer, a virus is a nasty program that is intended to cause your system pain. Some viruses are extremely destructive, capable of completely wiping out data on the hard disk, and some viruses are simply a nuisance, such as the annoying pop-up window or the ejecting CD-ROM tray/cup holder.

The first step to protecting your network from viruses is educating your network users. Teach your users what a virus is and how viruses infect computers. Explain to them why they should not open unnecessary (such as jokes and non-work related) e-mail attachments. Simply avoiding attachments from unknown sources isn't enough nowadays because viruses today are often sent from your friends and co-workers. Encourage your users to ask someone in the IT department to check out jokes or suspicious-sounding attachments before they're opened. When in doubt, don't open it. Common sense is a great weapon in the war on viruses.

An absolute must-have weapon in today's war on bugs is antivirus software. This is a crucial tool when it comes to protecting your network, but it is also the most misused tool, as well. You've probably seen the following scenario many times. Joe User has an antivirus program installed on his computer. He's so proud of himself, but to his dismay (and yours), his computer is infected with the latest, greatest virus. Of course, the reason why his computer was infected is because his antivirus program was last updated 14 months ago. Users and administrators alike commonly install antivirus software and then forget about updating it. You absolutely must configure the antivirus program to update the virus signature files, or *DAT* files, on a very regular basis. Hundreds of new viruses are released every month, and if you're not updating your antivirus software, it's not protecting you against these new viruses.

Signature files, also known as DAT files, need to be updated on a regular basis to keep your antivirus software up to date.

Prep Test

1 Who are the only employees who should require access to the server room?

A ○ Owners of the company

B ○ Human Resource personnel

C ○ IT personnel

D ○ Software developers

2 The use of a KVM switch allows you to keep a server _____ locked at all times.

A ○ Cabinet

B ○ Chassis

C ○ Keyboard

D ○ Console

3 What should you always secure when you walk away from the keyboard and monitor?

A ○ Cabinet

B ○ Chassis

C ○ Keyboard

D ○ Console

4 Which of the following can a server technician view with the Event Viewer to obtain information about events. such as failed and successful logon attempts or file accesses?

A ○ Application log

B ○ System log

C ○ Server log

D ○ Security log

5 Which of the following protocols can you use to monitor and manage a network from one workstation or server?

A ○ SMTP

B ○ SNMP

C ○ UDP

D ○ NetBEUI

6 A hub, bridge, router, workstation, or even a server can all be configured as an SNMP _____.

A ○ Manager

B ○ Probe

C ○ Primitive

D ○ Agent

7 The basic commands used by SNMP agents and devices to communicate with one another are called _____.

A ○ Managers

B ○ Probes

C ○ Primitives

D ○ Agents

8 What should you do if different versions of SNMP are running on the agents and managers of a network? (Choose two.)

A ❑ Do nothing; they are all compatible.

B ❑ Downgrade them all to the same SNMP version.

C ❑ Upgrade them all to the same SNMP version.

D ❑ Use RMON on devices using an older SNMP version.

9 What does RMON use to send information between the devices?

A ○ Agents

B ○ Managers

C ○ MIBS

D ○ Alerts

10 Which files should be updated on a regular basis to keep an antivirus program up to date?

A ○ DAT

B ○ Virus update

C ○ VAT

D ○ Antivirus

Answers

1 **C.** IT personnel are the only employees that have any real need to be in the server room. *See "Accessing the server room."*

2 **A.** The doors of the server cabinet (rack) should always be locked. Use a KVM switch to provide access to the servers without having to open the cabinet. *Review "Locking the server cabinet."*

3 **D.** To prevent unauthorized users from accessing the server, you should always lock the server console anytime you leave it. *Check out "Locking the server."*

4 **D.** The security logs record any authorized and unauthorized attempts to gain access to the server. *Take a look at "Monitoring server security."*

5 **B.** The Simple Network Management Protocol (SNMP) is used to monitor and manage network devices. *Study "Using the Simple Approach."*

6 **D.** Virtually any network device can be configured as an SNMP agent. SNMP was designed to work with the simplest, as well as the most complex, network devices. *See "Using the Simple Approach."*

7 **C.** The commands used with SNMP are referred to as *primitives. Review "Using the simple and primitive SNMP."*

8 **C and D.** The agents and managers on the network should be using the same SNMP version to ensure compatibility. RMON overcomes SNMP compatibility problems. *Look over "Monitoring a network remotely."*

9 **C.** A *Management Information Base* (MIB) contains the information sent between SNMP devices. *Check out "Monitoring a network remotely."*

10 **A.** The files that hold the signatures (profiles) of the various viruses have the file extension of DAT. You should configure your antivirus software to autoupdate the DAT files on a regular basis. *Study "Fighting Off a Virus."*

Chapter 10: Updating the BIOS

The BIOS is another component you need to be very familiar with, not only for the exam, but for real-world application as well. The BIOS is very delicate, and without proper handling and maintenance, you can find yourself in big trouble. Some of the larger BIOS manufacturers are AMI and Award, now that Phoenix has merged with Award. Each of these manufacturers licenses its BIOS ROM to motherboard manufacturers, leaving the motherboard manufacturers to support the ROM.

American Megatrends (AMI) was the sole provider of BIOS ROM chips to Intel, the market leader of motherboards. Phoenix recently landed a contract with Intel (meaning that more than 80 percent of the motherboards on the market are Intel boards with Phoenix BIOS programs). The other of the big three BIOS manufacturers is, or should we say was, Award. Phoenix bought Award in 1998, and Phoenix now markets the Award brand with the Phoenix name. Award targets OEMs by selling them what is essentially a highly customizable BIOS along with the source code that enables the OEMs to do whatever they please without having to write the code from scratch.

BIOS Chips and Other Party Fare

BIOS, which stands for Basic Input/Output System, provides the basic interface between the operating system and the software device drivers of the peripheral devices on a server. The BIOS also contains the instructions used to boot the server, verify its hardware, and start the operating system and device drivers.

The BIOS in nearly all server-class PCs is stored on an EEPROM (Electronically Erasable Programmable Read-Only Memory). However, over the years, the BIOS has been stored on a variety of ROM (Read-Only Memory) types. They are the following:

+ **Read-Only Memory (ROM):** A ROM permanently stores data or instructions that are loaded to it during manufacturing. The instructions stored on a ROM are called *firmware*. ROM is nonvolatile, which means that its data is held even after the power has been turned off. This factor makes ROM ideal for storing system startup instructions.

+ **Programmable ROM (PROM):** This type of ROM can be programmed after manufacturing with a PROM burner. The programming can be stored, or burned, onto the PROM chip one time.

+ **Erasable PROM (EPROM):** This variation of the PROM, EPROM can be erased and the chip reused. The EPROM chip has a quartz-crystal window on the top of the chip through which it can be erased with ultraviolet light.

+ **Electronically Erasable PROM (EEPROM):** When used on a server, this type of ROM is more commonly referred to as *Flash ROM,* which can be reprogrammed without removing the chip from the motherboard — a big improvement over previous ROM BIOS chips.

+ **Complimentary Metal-Oxide Semiconductor (CMOS):** CMOS is not a type of ROM, and the BIOS is not stored in CMOS, but CMOS memory is where the system configuration data is stored. Virtually all integrated circuits (ICs) in the server use CMOS technology; originally this technology was too expensive for anything other than holding the BIOS setup configuration data, and the name stuck. The CMOS memory is powered by about one-millionth of an amp of electrical current and can store data for many years with the power from a lithium battery. When the computer is first powered on, the CMOS memory is accessed, and the information stored on it is used to determine how the system is configured.

Keeping the BIOS up to date

On virtually all Pentium-class servers, no special equipment is needed to update the BIOS stored on the Flash ROM. An EEPROM is updated through a process called *flashing,* which involves the use of a specialized (and often proprietary) software utility that either the BIOS manufacturer or the motherboard manufacturer usually supplies. No trench coat is required for this operation.

The flashing operation implements bug fixes or adds new features to the BIOS — features that may not have been available at the time your system was manufactured, such as booting to CD-ROM drive. In most cases, the flashing upgrade adds new features to the BIOS that improve the server's system performance.

For the exam, you need to know what the system BIOS is and does and when you would use a flashing operation to update the BIOS. It can't hurt to also know what could possibly go wrong when flashing your BIOS and what you should do to recover. Know the sources for the BIOS update file as well. The best source for a BIOS update (flashing file) is the BIOS manufacturer or the motherboard manufacturer, which on some BIOS programs will be the same.

Flashing or not flashing

The first step involved in the flashing process is to decide whether or not you need to upgrade the BIOS at all. Many reasons to upgrade the BIOS are valid, the least of which is simply because a new version is available. Other reasons are

✦ **Operating system support:** New releases of operating systems often include features not previously supported by the BIOS, such as Plug and Play (PnP). Adding support to the BIOS for features in the operating system is a very good reason to upgrade the BIOS.

✦ **New CMOS settings:** A newer release of the BIOS may add features to the BIOS setup configuration data, such as Wake-on-LAN (WOL) or booting from a CD-ROM or a SCSI drive.

✦ **Enhanced hardware support:** Updating the BIOS may add support for new hardware devices or hardware accessibility features, such as LBA (Logical Block Addressing) and the like.

✦ **Bug fixes:** Of course, bug fixes are a very important reason to upgrade the BIOS, especially if the bugs are affecting your server's performance. However, follow the adage: "If it isn't broke, don't fix it." If you aren't experiencing problems, you may want to avoid any potential disasters and just leave things as they are.

Preparing to flash

Using a check list of the actions required to upgrade the BIOS on a server is a very good idea. The check list could be one prepared by the manufacturer or one of your own making. The important factor is that you do not forget a vital step that could damage the server or worse.

A BIOS upgrade check list should include the following:

✦ **Manufacturer:** Include in your check list the name of the BIOS manufacturer and, if different, the manufacturer and model number of the motherboard. Include the URL for each manufacturer's Web site.

✦ **Processor:** Also identify the processor or processors in the server, which should automatically also identify the manufacturer.

✦ **Current BIOS version and ID:** This information appears on the monitor after the video BIOS is loaded and the POST displays the system messages. At this point of the boot, pressing the Pause key on the keyboard should cause this information to display. If not, reboot until you have the version number. You can also use a software product, such as the BIOS Wizard from eSupport.com from Unicore Software (`www.uni-core.com/bioswiz`) to display your BIOS ID and other facts.

✦ **New version of BIOS:** Using the information already gathered for your check list, you should be able to get the information on the new BIOS version number from the manufacturer's Web site or by calling the manufacturer directly.

✦ **A list of the features or bug fixes the upgrade will provide:** This part of the check list should be transferred to the server maintenance logbook when the upgrade is completed.

✦ **A list of the actions of the flashing process:** This part of the check list is actually a check list itself. It should list the steps to be performed to update the BIOS. The steps should include the following:

- Decompressing software, such as WinZip or the like, that's available. BIOS files are often compressed for downloading purposes.

- The flash utility that you can download from the motherboard, computer, or BIOS manufacturer.

- The upgrade BIOS file that you can download from the motherboard, computer, or BIOS manufacturer.

- The key or keys used to access the BIOS Setup.

- A boot disk that you create to boot the server to a real-mode DOS prompt that excludes memory drivers, such as `HIMEM.SYS` and `EMM386.EXE`.

Never flash the BIOS from a Windows DOS prompt command box. Remember that if the system locks up, your BIOS may be only partially upgraded and virtually useless.

- Verification that the server is connected to power through a UPS (uninterruptible power supply) of sufficient size to keep the server powered up until the flashing process completes. The flashing process usually takes much less than a minute.

- A paper backup that you create of the BIOS configuration settings. Enter the BIOS Setup and copy down all settings, including all advanced menu functions. Flashing the BIOS resets all settings to their default values.

- A list of the steps performed in the BIOS upgrade operation (see the following section).

Creating a Windows 9x boot disk

Upgrading the BIOS with the absolute minimum of software running on the server is very important. To ensure this, you should create a boot disk that has only the essential files required to boot the system to a command prompt. For example, to do this on a Windows 9*x* system, follow the steps in Lab 10-1. Windows NT/2000/XP systems also have similar processes available. Having a boot disk ready in case of problems is a great idea.

Lab 10-1   Creating a DOS Boot Disk on a Windows Server

1. **Insert a blank formatted 3.5-inch disk in the floppy disk drive, assuming that it is a 3.5-inch disk drive.**

2. **Open the Start Run box, enter the command SYS A: in the Open box, and click OK.**

    A DOS prompt box appears. The command is complete after the `System Transferred` message appears, and you can then close the box.

3. **Use Windows Explorer to list the contents of the disk by choosing View➪View All Files option. Then remove all files except the COM-MAND.COM file, the IO.SYS file, and the MSDOS.SYS files.**

    These files are the only ones needed to boot to a DOS command prompt.

Flashing the BIOS

Before you can actually begin the BIOS upgrade operation that involves flashing the BIOS ROM, you should already have downloaded the two files that you need to carry out this procedure: a BIOS ROM file that contains the new BIOS code, and the flashing utility software. These two files may be bundled together in a single compressed downloadable file. The BIOS ROM file typically has a file extension of either `.bin` or `.awd` (for Award BIOS files), and the flashing software usually has an `.exe` extension. If any readme or text files are included with the ROM file and flashing utility, be sure to print and read them.

Running the flashing software

After downloading the ROM file and the flashing utility, you are ready to begin the flashing process. The steps in Lab 10-2 show the general steps used to upgrade a BIOS. However, your particular BIOS may use a slightly different approach.

Lab 10-2   Upgrading the BIOS

1. **Reboot the server and enter the BIOS Setup.**

2. **Disable the video and system BIOS caching if necessary. (This assumes that you have already created a paper backup of the BIOS settings.)**

   These settings should be listed as Video BIOS cacheable and System BIOS cacheable.

3. **Save and exit the BIOS Setup.**

4. **Reboot the server by using the DOS boot disk that you created for this purpose.**

5. **At the command line prompt, type the command that begins the flashing operation.**

   The readme file or the manufacturer's Web site should prescribe this command; but in general, the command should be something like the following:

   ```
   BIOSFLSH NEWBIOS.BIN OLDBIOS.BIN /opt /opt ...
   ```

   The options (/opt) in the command vary by manufacturer, but they are commonly used to disable DMI (Desktop Management Interface), PnP ESCD (Extended System Configuration Data), and CMOS data while the BIOS is being programmed.

6. **When the flashing operation completes, reboot the server normally (without the DOS boot disk) and enter the BIOS Setup. Choose the option that resets the CMOS to its default settings, save this change, and exit the Setup.**

7. **If you need to manually change any settings recorded before the upgrade, reboot, enter the BIOS Setup, and make the modifications.**

After the flashing operation begins, absolutely — under no circumstances — disturb the server. This operation doesn't take long, and as long as you don't have a major power failure, have lightning strike the building, or have an intern trip over the UPS power cord (again), you should have no worries.

Other flashing considerations

Another BIOS setting that you should disable before flashing the ROM is ROM Shadowing (or *Shadow RAM*, as it is also called). RAM is much faster than ROM, and many systems copy the BIOS into RAM when the server is booted to gain some speed during the boot process.

You can also use the DOS DEBUG command to reset the BIOS Setup configuration to its default settings. The command varies by manufacturer, but for the majority of BIOS programs (meaning AMI and Award), you can enter the following command on a DOS command line prompt (not in a Windows DOS box):

```
C:\DEBUG
-O 70 17
-O 71 17
Q
```

Entering the BIOS setup

To enter the BIOS CMOS setup program, you must press the predefined key or keys. Some of the more common keystrokes appear in Table 10-1. As shown in Table 10-1, these keys can vary by manufacturer. Check the motherboard's documentation or watch the monitor very closely during a boot sequence to get the key or keys for your system.

Table 10-1	Keys Used to Access BIOS Setup
Manufacturer	*Keys*
AMI BIOS	Delete
Award BIOS	Delete or Ctrl+Alt+Esc
IBM Aptiva	F1
Phoenix BIOS	F2
Compaq	F10

Reacting when things go wrong

You should be very cautious and be sure that you have the exact software version for your specific BIOS. Installing the wrong BIOS software is a great way to corrupt your BIOS. The BIOS program that you are most likely to be using, such as Award and AMI, includes features to double-check the flash file's version against the motherboard model, processor, and chipset and to warn you of any mismatches. Be very careful because not all manufacturers include this type of safety feature to prevent the wrong BIOS version from being flashed to the wrong BIOS ROM.

Should any of the possible disasters that could happen when you are flashing your BIOS actually happen, you can make a few recoveries:

✦ **Boot-block:** Virtually all server motherboards have a boot-block BIOS, which is a small part of the BIOS that is not overwritten when you flash the ROM. Although boot-block sounds as if it would stop the boot, it's actually a block of the BIOS programming that provides support for the floppy disk drive and ISA video cards should it be necessary to reboot the system from the boot disk created for use in the flashing process. You can then reflash the BIOS. The boot-block's capabilities vary by manufacturer, so check the documentation or the manufacturer's Web site for information.

✦ **Flash-recovery jumper:** Intel motherboards include a jumper that can be used to enable and disable access to the boot-block BIOS. After moving the jumper to the enable position, boot the system to the DOS boot disk. No video will be available, so you must wait for a single beep code and the drive LED to go out, which indicates that the recovery has been completed; then you can reboot to the disk and reattempt the flashing operation.

✦ **New BIOS chip:** Most manufacturers will either sell or give you a new BIOS chip. In fact, you can purchase chip replacement kits from companies such as Unicore Software (www.unicore.com) or Micro Firmware (www.firmware.com). This option is not available for all systems, however.

Visiting a couple of very good BIOS sites

For more information on BIOS, flashing, and tons of tips and links to other information sites, visit the following URLs:

✦ Wim Bervoets BIOS Web site: www.wimsbios.com

✦ The PC Guide's BIOS pages: www.pcguide.com/ref/mbsys/bios

Booting the Server

When you power-on your system, the BIOS initiates the Power-On Self-Test (POST). If your system beeps at you when booting, you need to know how to understand its cry for help, or you are going to be shooting in the dark while trying to troubleshoot the problem. The POST and beep codes are provided to help you troubleshoot problems that occur during the initial boot sequence.

Remember that the Server+ exam is not the A+ exam (but, it could be called the A++ exam), and you don't need to remember the beep codes for any manufacturer. (These codes vary by manufacturer, anyway.) Just understand that before the video BIOS is loaded, the system has no way to communicate its displeasure and must resort to beeping at you.

Running the POST

The POST is actually run by the BIOS every time you start your PC. POST is often the best indicator of system problems. Pay close attention to the POST audio and video messages. If the POST executes successfully, you can assume that the necessary hardware was detected and is operating properly. If the POST runs into a problem, such as if a hardware component is not detected or is found not to be operating properly, the BIOS issues an error message, which is a text message and/or a series of coded beeps, depending on the source of the problem.

Because the POST is executed before the computer's video card is activated, it may not be possible to progress to the display screen. The pattern of beeps may be a variable number of short beeps or a mixture of long and short beeps, depending on what type of BIOS is installed.

When you power up the server, a sequence of events takes place under the control of the BIOS:

1. The power supply builds up its power, and when it is ready, it sends a Power_Good signal to the motherboard that wakes up the CPU. The CPU reads the x86 code from the BIOS chip and starts the POST process.

2. During the POST process, the BIOS performs the following tasks:

   - Initializes the system hardware and chipset registers

   - Starts the power management

   - Tests the main memory (RAM)

   - Enables the keyboard

   - Tests the serial and parallel ports

   - Initializes the floppy disk controller and the hard drive controllers

   - Displays the system summary on the monitor

   If the information about the hardware environment that is collected during the POST differs from that stored in the CMOS, a boot error is generated. If the error is detected prior to the video BIOS being loaded, beep codes are used; otherwise, an error message appears, and the boot sequence halts.

3. After the POST completes the preceding tasks, the BIOS loads the boot program that will, in turn, load the operating system. The boot program loads the system configuration information (contained in the Windows Registry) and the device drivers.

4. The final step of the boot sequence loads the operating system.

Setting up BIOS security

Virtually all BIOS settings include options for a user password and a supervisor password. With the user password set, the computer will not be allowed to boot until the proper password is entered. The supervisor password is used when accessing the BIOS settings. Without the supervisor password, users can't access the BIOS settings; however, the system is allowed to boot.

By setting either of these passwords, you are committing yourself to always remembering the passwords. If you forget the user password but know what the supervisor password is, you can enter the BIOS and clear the password by pressing the Enter key when prompted to do so.

If you forget a password, you will be unable to boot the server (without the user password) or to gain access to the BIOS (without the supervisor password). To clear the passwords and reset the CMOS settings to their default values, you can adjust the password-clear jumper. Typically, this jumper is located very near the ROM. Check the motherboard's documentation for the appropriate settings to use.

On many motherboards, this jumper is located near the lithium battery or the BIOS ROM chip. Another way to clear the password is by removing the CMOS battery and allowing the CMOS memory to clear. By doing either of these procedures, you should be aware that any existing BIOS settings will be lost. Be sure to have this information documented in case the situation arises. Another way of resetting the CMOS is to remove the CMOS battery for five minutes or so. It takes about that long for the CMOS to drain away any power it holds.

The Other BIOS

Many of the system components contain their own BIOS programs. A good example is the video card. Without a set of drivers in a ROM on the video card, you wouldn't be able to see the video display until the drivers were loaded from the hard drive. Many devices have a ROM onboard, and keeping the BIOS in each ROM up to date is a very good idea. The most common devices with onboard ROM are the following:

✦ **SCSI adapters:** In general, the SCSI adapter with onboard ROM is going to be for the system's hard drives. If your system has SCSI CD-ROM, Zip, tape drive adapter, and the like, those devices can wait until the OS loads the necessary drivers from the hard drive.

✦ **Network adapters:** Those network adapters that allow a PC to be started up from a server have a boot ROM or IPL (Initial Program Load) ROM on the adapter. For example, with Windows 2000 server or the many disk-imaging programs on the market, you can boot from the system's network card and obtain an IP address from a DHCP server. After the system has IP connectivity, the system can download and install a disk image from a server on the network. Smart terminals act in the same manner; they boot directly from the network server.

✦ **IDE and floppy upgrade boards:** In order for the system to boot from CD or floppy disk, the drives must be connected to an adapter that has its own ROM. On most newer systems, the motherboard supplies the ROM and the BIOS, which includes the drivers needed to boot the PC from the IDE or floppy devices. If you add an adapter to support additional floppies and IDE devices, the onboard ROM is needed to allow the devices to be active during startup; otherwise, the devices connected to that adapter will not be available until the OS loads the adapter drivers from the hard drive.

Prep Test

1 **How do you clear the CMOS settings and any unwanted or forgotten BIOS passwords?**

A ○ Format the hard drive.

B ○ Run FDISK utility.

C ○ Edit the `AUTOEXEC.BAT`.

D ○ Adjust the CMOS/password-clear jumper.

2 **The BIOS ROM performs which of the following? (Choose two.)**

A ❑ Gathering system configuration information and initializing the computer when powered on

B ❑ Storing configuration data for use by the CMOS

C ❑ Providing software needed to communicate with the hardware components when the OS is running

D ❑ Collecting statistics on CPU utilization

3 **Which of the following information should be gathered prior to beginning to upgrade the BIOS ROM? (Choose two.)**

A ❑ BIOS ID number

B ❑ Amount of RAM on the server

C ❑ Processor type

D ❑ Amount of hard drive free space

4 **How is the BIOS setup menu accessed?**

A ○ Type **setup** at the DOS prompt.

B ○ Press the key specified on the display during the POST.

C ○ Remove the CMOS jumper on the motherboard.

D ○ Hold Shift during the POST.

5 **What does CMOS stand for?**

A ○ Ceramic Metal-Oxide Semiconductor

B ○ Complimentary Metal-Oxide Semiconductor

C ○ Compatible Metal Overdrive Semiconductor

D ○ Costly Metal-Oxide Semiconductor

6 **What is the name of the process used to upgrade a BIOS on an EEPROM chip called?**

   A ○ Booting
   B ○ Firming
   C ○ Flashing
   D ○ Pipelining

7 **BIOS stands for which of the following?**

   A ○ Basic Input/Output System
   B ○ Ballistic Input Override Semiconductor
   C ○ Basic Instructions On Startup
   D ○ Boot Instructions On Startup

8 **The series of hardware tests that is run each time the server is powered on is called _____.**

   A ○ BIOS
   B ○ CMOS
   C ○ WIN.INI
   D ○ POST

9 **Beep codes are used to indicate that _____.**

   A ○ The system battery is low.
   B ○ The processor is running at optimal performance.
   C ○ The keyboard and mouse are present.
   D ○ A hardware problem was discovered during the POST process.

10 **During a flashing operation, the power fails on a Pentium-class server that is not attached to a UPS. The server has a PCI video card. Attempts to reboot the server end with no video display and no beep codes sounding. What is likely to be the problem and what is the best course of action?**

   A ○ The power supply was damaged by the power failure and must be replaced.
   B ○ The BIOS ROM is physically damaged and must be replaced.
   C ○ Reboot the system by using a DOS boot disk to activate the boot-block BIOS and redo the flashing operation on the BIOS ROM.
   D ○ The video card is damaged and must be replaced.

Answers

1 **D.** Resetting the CMOS jumper on the motherboard causes CMOS values, including password settings, to be reset to their default values. *See "Setting up BIOS security."*

2 **A** and **C.** Remember that the function of the BIOS is to store the information the server needs to determine the devices connected to it. *Review "BIOS Chips and Other Party Fare."*

3 **A** and **C.** In order to find out whether any upgrades are available, you need to know these bits of information plus the manufacturer of the BIOS or motherboard. *Check out "Preparing to flash."*

4 **B.** Although the key used to access the BIOS setup varies, it always appears on the monitor at the end of the POST process. *Take a look at "Entering the BIOS setup."*

5 **B.** CMOS is actually an integrated circuit technology used on virtually all ICs. However, it is synonymous with the BIOS setup configuration data. *Review "BIOS Chips and Other Party Fare."*

6 **C.** Flashing is used to upgrade the BIOS ROM (also known as Flash ROM) under software control. *Look over "Running the flashing software."*

7 **A.** This is something you should always remember. *See "BIOS Chips and Other Party Fare."*

8 **D.** The POST processing verifies that the devices listed in the CMOS are actually available for use by the system. *Check out "Running the POST."*

9 **D.** Until the video BIOS is loaded to the system, the only means of notifying you of an error is the system speaker. *Study "Running the POST."*

10 **C.** The boot-block BIOS is never overwritten and allows the system to boot to the floppy disk and an ISA video. Don't think that just because Answer C was the longest answer that this is a trend on the Server+ exam. *Take a look at "Reacting when things go wrong."*

Book VI

Appendix

Contents at a Glance

Appendix: About the CD

In This Appendix
- System requirements
- Using the CD with Windows
- What you'll find on the CD
- Troubleshooting

*M*ake sure that your computer meets the minimum system requirements shown in the following list. If your computer doesn't match up to most of these requirements, you may have problems using the software and files on the CD. For the latest and greatest information, please refer to the ReadMe file located at the root of the CD-ROM.

- ✦ A PC with a Pentium or faster processor; or a Mac OS computer with a 68040 or faster processor

- ✦ Microsoft Windows 98 or later; or Mac OS system software 7.6.1 or later

- ✦ At least 32MB of total RAM installed on your computer; for best performance, we recommend at least 64MB.

- ✦ A CD-ROM drive

- ✦ A sound card for PCs; Mac OS computers have built-in sound support.

- ✦ A monitor capable of displaying at least 256 colors or grayscale

- ✦ A modem with a speed of at least 14,400 bps

If you need more information on the basics, check out these books published by Wiley Publishing, Inc.: *PCs For Dummies,* by Dan Gookin; *Macs For Dummies,* by David Pogue; *iMacs For Dummies* by David Pogue; *Windows 95 For Dummies, Windows 98 For Dummies, Windows 2000 Professional For Dummies, Microsoft Windows ME Millennium Edition For Dummies,* all by Andy Rathbone.

Using the CD with Microsoft Windows

To install the items from the CD to your hard drive, follow these steps.

1. **Insert the CD into your computer's CD-ROM drive.**

2. **Choose Start⇨Run.**

3. **In the dialog box that appears, type** D:\Start.EXE.

   Replace *D* with the proper drive letter if your CD-ROM drive uses a different letter. (If you don't know the letter, see how your CD-ROM drive is listed under My Computer.)

4. **Click OK.**

   A license agreement window appears.

5. **Read through the license agreement, nod your head, and then click the Accept button if you want to use the CD — after you click Accept, you'll never be bothered by the License Agreement window again.**

   The CD interface Welcome screen appears. The interface is a little program that shows you what's on the CD and coordinates installing the programs and running the demos. The interface basically enables you to click a button or two to make things happen.

6. **Click anywhere on the Welcome screen to enter the interface.**

   Now you are getting to the action. This next screen lists categories for the software on the CD.

7. **To view the items within a category, just click the category's name.**

   A list of programs in the category appears.

8. **For more information about a program, click the program's name.**

   Be sure to read the information that appears. Sometimes a program has its own system requirements or requires you to do a few tricks on your computer before you can install or run the program, and this screen tells you what you may need to do, if necessary.

9. **If you don't want to install the program, click the Back button to return to the previous screen.**

   You can always return to the previous screen by clicking the Back button. This feature allows you to browse the different categories and products and decide what you want to install.

10. **To install a program, click the appropriate Install button.**

    The CD interface drops to the background while the CD installs the program that you chose.

11. **To install other items, repeat Steps 7–10.**

12. **After you finish installing programs, click the Quit button to close the interface.**

You can eject the CD now. Carefully place it back in the plastic jacket of the book for safekeeping.

What You'll Find on the CD

The following sections are arranged by category and provide a summary of the software and other goodies you'll find on the CD. If you need help with installing the items provided on the CD, refer back to the installation instructions in the preceding section.

Shareware programs are fully functional, free, trial versions of copyrighted programs. If you like particular programs, register with their authors for a nominal fee and receive licenses, enhanced versions, and technical support. *Freeware programs* are free, copyrighted games, applications, and utilities. You can copy them to as many PCs as you like — for free — but they offer no technical support. *GNU software* is governed by its own license, which is included inside the folder of the GNU software. Distribution of GNU software has no restrictions. See the GNU license at the root of the CD for more details. *Trial, demo,* or *evaluation* versions of software are usually limited either by time or functionality (such as not letting you save a project after you create it).

Dummies test prep tools

This CD contains questions related to MCSA certification. The questions are similar to those you can expect to find on the exams.

Dummies test engine

The test engine offers hundreds of questions on all five of the MCSA exams: the Microsoft exams (70-210, 70-215, and 70-218), Network+, and Server+.

Practice Exams

This CD-ROM contains five Practice Exams in PDF (Portable Document Format): one for each certification exam. To view the PDFs, we have provided a copy of Adobe Acrobat Reader, free software that lets you view and print Adobe Portable Document Format (PDF) files on all major computer platforms.

Troubleshooting

This CD should be accessible on most computers with the minimum system requirements. Alas, your computer may differ, and some programs may not work properly for some reason.

The two likeliest problems are that you don't have enough memory (RAM) for the programs you want to use, or you have other programs running that are affecting installation or running of a program. If you get an error message, such as Not enough memory or Setup cannot continue, try one or more of the following suggestions and then try using the software again:

✦ **Turn off any antivirus software running on your computer.** Installation programs sometimes mimic virus activity and may make your computer incorrectly believe that it's being infected by a virus.

✦ **Close all running programs.** The more programs you have running, the less memory is available to other programs. Installation programs typically update files and programs; so if you keep other programs running, installation may not work properly.

✦ **Have your local computer store add more RAM to your computer.** This is, admittedly, a drastic and somewhat expensive step. However, if you have a Windows 95 PC or a Mac OS computer with a PowerPC chip, adding more memory can really help the speed of your computer and allow more programs to run at the same time. This may include closing the CD interface and running a product's installation program from Windows Explorer.

If you still have trouble with the CD, please call the Customer Care phone number: (800) 762-2974. Outside the United States, call (317) 572-3994. You can also contact Customer Service by e-mail at techsupdum@wiley.com. Wiley Publishing Inc. provides technical support only for installation and other general quality control items; for technical support on the applications themselves, consult the program's vendor or author.

Index

• T •

• U •

• V •

• *W* •

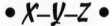

Wiley Publishing, Inc.
End-User License Agreement

5. **Limited Warranty.**

    (a) WPI warrants that the Software and Software Media are free from defects in materials and workmanship under normal use for a period of sixty (60) days from the date of purchase of this Book. If WPI receives notification within the warranty period of defects in materials or workmanship, WPI will replace the defective Software Media.

    (b) WPI AND THE AUTHOR OF THE BOOK DISCLAIM ALL OTHER WARRANTIES, EXPRESS OR IMPLIED, INCLUDING WITHOUT LIMITATION IMPLIED WARRANTIES OF MERCHANTABILITY AND FITNESS FOR A PARTICULAR PURPOSE, WITH RESPECT TO THE SOFTWARE, THE PROGRAMS, THE SOURCE CODE CONTAINED THEREIN, AND/OR THE TECHNIQUES DESCRIBED IN THIS BOOK. WPI DOES NOT WARRANT THAT THE FUNCTIONS CONTAINED IN THE SOFTWARE WILL MEET YOUR REQUIREMENTS OR THAT THE OPERATION OF THE SOFTWARE WILL BE ERROR FREE.

    (c) This limited warranty gives you specific legal rights, and you may have other rights that vary from jurisdiction to jurisdiction.

6. **Remedies.**

    (a) WPI's entire liability and your exclusive remedy for defects in materials and workmanship shall be limited to replacement of the Software Media, which may be returned to WPI with a copy of your receipt at the following address: Software Media Fulfillment Department, Attn.: MCSA All-in-One Desk Reference For Dummies, Wiley Publishing, Inc., 10475 Crosspoint Blvd., Indianapolis, IN 46256, or call 1-800-762-2974. Please allow four to six weeks for delivery. This Limited Warranty is void if failure of the Software Media has resulted from accident, abuse, or misapplication. Any replacement Software Media will be warranted for the remainder of the original warranty period or thirty (30) days, whichever is longer.

    (b) In no event shall WPI or the author be liable for any damages whatsoever (including without limitation damages for loss of business profits, business interruption, loss of business information, or any other pecuniary loss) arising from the use of or inability to use the Book or the Software, even if WPI has been advised of the possibility of such damages.

    (c) Because some jurisdictions do not allow the exclusion or limitation of liability for consequential or incidental damages, the above limitation or exclusion may not apply to you.

7. **U.S. Government Restricted Rights.** Use, duplication, or disclosure of the Software for or on behalf of the United States of America, its agencies and/or instrumentalities "U.S. Government" is subject to restrictions as stated in paragraph (c)(1)(ii) of the Rights in Technical Data and Computer Software clause of DFARS 252.227-7013, or subparagraphs (c) (1) and (2) of the Commercial Computer Software - Restricted Rights clause at FAR 52.227-19, and in similar clauses in the NASA FAR supplement, as applicable.

8. **General.** This Agreement constitutes the entire understanding of the parties and revokes and supersedes all prior agreements, oral or written, between them and may not be modified or amended except in a writing signed by both parties hereto that specifically refers to this Agreement. This Agreement shall take precedence over any other documents that may be in conflict herewith. If any one or more provisions contained in this Agreement are held by any court or tribunal to be invalid, illegal, or otherwise unenforceable, each and every other provision shall remain in full force and effect.